Multiple-Lines Insurance Production

Multiple-Lines Insurance Production

RICHARD D. TURNER, CPCU
Regional Director
Cincinnati Insurance Company

STEPHEN HORN II, CPCU
Executive Vice President
Jones Horn Insurance Brokers

SEEMAN WARANCH, CPCU
President
Insurance Agency of Norfolk, Inc.

PETER R. KENSICKI, D.B.A., CPCU, CLU, FLMI
Director of Producer Education
Insurance Institute of America

First Edition • 1981

INSURANCE INSTITUTE OF AMERICA
Providence and Sugartown Roads, Malvern, Pennsylvania 19355

First Printing • December 1981

Library of Congress Catalog Number 81-80772
International Standard Book Number 0-89462-007-X

Printed in the United States of America

The Accredited Adviser in Insurance
designation (AAI) is
the result of a joint effort
of the
Insurance Institute of America, Inc.
and the
Independent Insurance Agents
of America, Inc.

Foreword

Over the years, the American Institute for Property and Liability Underwriters and the Insurance Institute of America have responded to the educational needs of the property-liability insurance industry by developing new programs.

The American Institute maintains and administers the program leading to the Chartered Property Casualty Underwriter (CPCU) professional designation.

The Insurance Institute of America offers programs leading to the Certificate in General Insurance, the Associate in Claims (AIC) designation, the Associate in Management (AIM) designation, the Associate in Risk Management (ARM) designation, the Associate in Underwriting (AIU) designation, the Associate in Loss Control Management (ALCM) designation, and the Associate in Premium Auditing (APA) designation. This volume represents the second of three texts to be issued by the Institute in a newly developed program leading to the Accredited Adviser in Insurance (AAI) designation, a program especially designed for producers.

Throughout the development of this series of texts it has been—and will continue to be—necessary to draw on the knowledge and skills of Institute staff members. These individuals will receive no royalties on texts sold, and their writing responsibilities are seen as an integral part of their professional duties. We have proceeded in this way to avoid any possibility of conflicts of interests.

We invite and welcome any and all criticisms of our publications. It is only with such comments that we can hope to provide high quality texts, materials, and programs. Comments should be directed to the curriculum department of the Institutes.

Edwin S. Overman, Ph.D., CPCU
President

Preface

This text represents a continuation of and a conclusion for the material in *Principles of Insurance Production* (PRO 81). The application of technical information in insurance policies to the needs of prospects and clients is still stressed. According to sales theory, the technical characteristics of an insurance policy are known as the *features* of the product. The exposures of the client represent the client's *needs*. The major goal of this and the PRO 81 text is to bring the producer to the point of recognizing the prospect's or client's needs and to match those needs with the appropriate features of insurance policies. This is known in sales theory as *need* satisfaction selling.

The stress is not on price for two principal reasons. First, price is an ever changing factor. As this is written, the insurance business is in a period of "soft pricing." Soft prices mean lower prices or premiums charged to insureds. In a couple of years prices will rise, making an emphasis on price almost impossible. The second reason price is not stressed is that price is only one part of the product the producer delivers to an insured. The other two ingredients are the insurance policies and the service producers and their firms give clients. Because the producer can control policy selection and level of service, these two ingredients are stressed.

The text continues to emphasize service. Hints are given on selling the underwriter—because having the underwriter on the producer's side helps the client. Examples of how other insurance production firms sell and service insurance are also given.

In a sense, these books are both texts and reference volumes. Technical information was up-to-date when the texts went to press. More current material is published in the Course Guides for these courses, which are revised annually.

As a text, this book serves to educate the inexperienced producer. It serves as a source of background information on the important technical and sales needs of producers. As a reference work, the text serves all producers and those associated with insurance production by giving them a "one-stop" source of valuable technical and sales information.

One significant difference between this text and the PRO 81 book is the greater number of producers involved in writing this text. Richard D. Turner, CPCU, is the Regional Director in South Carolina for the Cincinnati Insurance Company. In his "fieldman" role, Rick actively helps producers write and place business. He joins them in physical inspections and offers concrete assistance as to how to properly submit an application. Stephen Horn II, CPCU, is a principal in a successful commercial lines-oriented brokerage firm in the highly competitive San Francisco area. Steve is the son of a now retired principal of the firm and has grown up on the production side of commercial lines. Seeman Waranch, CPCU, is another successful producer in the profitable state of Virginia. Seeman not only is a highly successful producer and principal of his firm but, at this writing, is also president of The Society of CPCU. He therefore brings not only his sales success to this text but also a high degree of professionalism, necessary to the growth of all serious producers. Peter R. Kensicki, D.B.A., CPCU, CLU, FLMI, is the only major author not involved in day-to-day production of insurance. Pete is Director of Producer Education for the Insurance Institute of America and The American Institute for Property and Liability Underwriters. He did, in a former life, sell life insurance and organized sales schools for property and liability producers with a successful regional insurance company.

Rick Turner's contributions can be seen in Chapters 4, 6, 9, 10 and 13. Steve's efforts are recorded in Chapters 5 and 12. Seeman was responsible for Chapters 2 and 3. Pete wrote Chapter 7 and served as general editor of the entire text in an attempt to merge different authors' styles into an even flow. Many other authors contributed to entire chapters and portions of chapters. Those Contributing Authors are acknowledged elsewhere on a special page.

No work of this nature can be written and edited in an ivory tower. Many producers read and offered comments on the original manuscripts. For example, in addition to his authoring activities, Steve Horn read and offered excellent comments on all chapters in this text. Ronald T. Anderson, J.D., CPCU, CLU, also offered critical reviews of each chapter. Kenneth W. Morrison, J.D., CIC, was the final producer to critically review each chapter. Ken's services were arranged through the efforts of the Professional Insurance Agents and, specifically, by The Professional Insurance Agents Association of Virginia and the District of Columbia, thanks to the continuing interest and support of its Executive Vice President, Ms. Elsie Reamy.

Many other producers read individual manuscripts for specific chapters. The Independent Insurance Agents of America, Inc. again provided two reviewers for each chapter in this text. Those valuable reviewers were Edwin Lucie, CPCU, Sullivan, Shugrue, and Lucie; John F. Reilly of Miller, Schwartzman & Reilly, Inc.; Richard N. Schafer, CIC, Schafer's "House of Security"; James Lane, CPCU, Klipstein Lane & Associates; Charles T. Bidek, INSURORS of Tennessee; Carl T. Ernstrom, CPCU, CLU, Ernstrom Associates, Inc.; William Schramm, Blackmore-Rowe Agency, Inc.; and Joe Fowler, Walden Insuring Agency. Reviewers not specifically provided by the IIAA were Ralph C. Hamm, Jr., CPCU, Ralph Hamm Insurance; Eric A. Wiening, CPCU, ARM, Assistant Director of Curriculum, The American Institute for Property and Liability Underwriters; Frank D. Love, CPCU, Vice President, The Cincinnati Insurance Company; James A. Robertson, CPCU, Editor, *The Umbrella Book*, Warren, McVeigh and Griffin; Jonathon K. Fish, Associate Editor, *The Umbrella Book*, Warren, McVeigh and Griffin; and Keith Sears, Director, CP Field Division-Crime Unit, The Travelers Insurance Companies.

There is always a group of "unsung" heroes in the production of any book. This group reads, types, edits, proofs, and does a hundred other vital activities to bring a project to conclusion. Our thanks to those members of the Institute staff who performed those functions.

The authors accept full responsibility for all errors and omissions. Readers detecting errors or wishing to add to the content of future editions are encouraged to send their contributions and criticisms to the curriculum department of the Institute.

Richard D.Turner
Stephen Horn II
Seeman Waranch
Peter R. Kensicki

Contributing Authors

The Insurance Institute of America and the authors acknowledge, with deep appreciation, the help of the following contributing authors:

Walter J. Dabrow
Regional Director
The Cincinnati Insurance Company
Valley View, Ohio

Edward M. Glenn, Ph.D., CPCU, CLU
Vice President
Marsh and McLennan
Birmingham, Alabama

John C. Hawley, CPCU
William L. Hawley Agency
Montrose, Pennsylvania

Frank D. Love, CPCU
Vice President
The Cincinnati Insurance Company
Cincinnati, Ohio

Donald S. Malecki, CPCU
Editor, Property and Casualty Publications
The National Underwriter Company
Cincinnati, Ohio

James J. Ross
Director of Education
Independent Insurance Agents of Kentucky, Inc.
Louisville, Kentucky

Eric A. Wiening, CPCU, ARM
Assistant Director of Curriculum
The American Institute for Property and
    Liability Underwriters, Inc.
Malvern, Pennsylvania

Table of Contents

Chapter 1—Garage and Truckers Insurance.................... 1

Garage Policy ~ *Markets—Eligibility; Coverage Characteristics; Garage Operations Exposures Covered; Garage Auto Liability Exposures Covered; Garage Liability Insurance; Garage Policy Options and Endorsements; Garage Physical Damage Exposures Covered; Garage Physical Damage Insurance; Garagekeepers Insurance; Rating—Basic Concepts; Underwriting Information*

Truckers Policy ~ *Markets—Eligibility; Coverage Characteristics; Truckers Liability Insurance; Truckers Physical Damage Insurance; Trailer Interchange Insurance; Product Targeting; Rating—Basic Concepts; Underwriting Information*

Marketing Garage and Truckers Insurance ~ *Specialized Needs of Markets; Matching Markets with Insurers; Working Knowledge of Products*

Summary

Chapter 2—General Liability Insurance........................ 65

Introduction

Commercial Liability Exposures ~ *Premises Liability Exposures; Operations Liability Exposures; Products and Completed Operations Hazards; Contractual and Protective Liability Exposures; Professional Liability Exposures*

Commercial Liability Insurance ~ *Introduction; Policy Jacket*

Commercial Liability Insurance Coverage~*Comprehensive General Liability Coverage Part; Owners, Landlords, and Tenants Coverage Part; Manufacturers and Contractors Coverage Part; Storekeepers Liability Form; Owners and Contractors Protective Liability Coverage Part*

Summary

Chapter 3—General Liability Insurance (Continued) 121

Introduction

Broad Form CGL Endorsement~*Coverages; Value of Broad Form Endorsement*

Underwriting Information~*Underwriting the Commercial Liability Risk; Typical Loss Exposures; Safety; The Application for Comprehensive General Liability Insurance; Underwriter Relations*

Products and Completed Operations and Professional Liability Insurance~*Products and Completed Operations; Professional Liability, Professional Liability Summary*

Summary

Chapter 4—Workers' Compensation and Employers' Liability 169

Introduction

Basic Concepts~*Right of Recovery; Covered Injuries; Assault by Employer; Accident; Third Party Claims*

Workers' Compensation Laws~*Compulsory Versus Elective; Who Is Covered; Methods of Providing Workers' Compensation Benefits*

The Workers' Compensation Policy~*The Declarations Page; The Insuring Agreements; Agreement II—Defense, Settlement, Supplementary Payments; Agreement III—Definitions; Agreement IV—Application of the Policy; Exclusions; Policy Conditions; Endorsements*

Other Aspects of Workers' Compensation ~ *Occupational Safety and Health Act of 1970 (OSHA); Assigned Risk Plans; Second Injury Funds; What the Underwriter Needs to Know*

Rating Procedures ~ *Classification; Experience Modification; Rating Sample; Retrospective Rating; Sales Tips*

Case Studies ~ *J&T Appliances; Premier Door and Window Company, Inc.*

Summary

Chapter 5—Commercial Inland Marine Insurance......... 223

Introduction

Origins of Inland Marine Insurance

The Nation-Wide Marine Definition

Types of Inland Marine Insurance Policies ~ *Transportation Insurance on Domestic Shipments; Bailees' Customers Insurance; Insurance on Movable Equipment and Other Property; Insurance on the Property of Certain Dealers; Insurance on Instrumentalities of Transportation and Communications; Examples; Filed and Nonfiled Lines*

Common Characteristics of Commercial Inland Marine Insurance Policies ~ *Policy Format; Declarations; Insuring Agreements; Conditions; Exclusions; Miscellaneous Policy Provisions; Collateral Documents*

Selling Commercial Inland Marine Insurance ~ *Transportation Insurance; Bailees' Customers Insurance; Floaters; Dealers Policies; Instrumentalities of Transportation and Communication; Writing Manuscript Policies; Inland Marine Forms in Package Policies*

Case Studies ~ *J&T Appliances; John Gale, M.D.; R.P.Davis, Contractor; Premier Door and Window, Inc.*

Appendix

Chapter 6—Ocean Marine and Aviation Insurance........ 287

Introduction

Whom to Insure~ *Insurable Interests of Owners; Bills of Lading; Nonownership Insurable Interests; A Typical Transaction; Identifying Prospects*

How to Insure ~ *Voyage Policies; Open Cargo Policies*

How Much to Insure ~ *Valuation of Cargo; Exposure Limits; Percentage of Value Lost; Loss of Profit, Expense, or Income; Factors to Consider in Determining How Much to Insure*

Open Cargo Policy Coverage~ *Duration of Cargo Coverage; Perils Covered and Excluded; Losses Covered; Franchise and Deductible Clauses; Warranties*

Handling a Submission~ *Ocean Marine Insurance Rates; What the Underwriter Needs to Know*

Ocean Marine Insurance for Other Exposures

Case Study 1—Premier Door and Window Co., Inc.

Case Study 2—Wingate Equipment Co.

Case Study 3—Exports International

Commercial Aviation Insurance~ *Shipments by Air; Other Commercial Aviation Exposures and Insurance*

Summary

Appendix

Chapter 7—Commercial Crime Insurance..................... 339

Introduction~ *Types of Crimes; Crime Insurance Categories; Format for Analysis of Crime Policies*

Comprehensive Dishonesty, Disappearance, and Destruction Policy (3-D)~ *Introduction; Combinations of Coverage Forms; 3-D Coverages*

Endorsements of Crime Policies~ *Introduction; Specific Endorsements to the 3-D Policy; Mercantile Open Stock*

Marketing Crime Insurance~*Introduction; Rating Crime Insurance; Underwriting Information*

Cases~*J&T Appliances; John Gale, M.D.; R.P. Davis, Contractor; Premier Door and Window Company, Inc.*

Financial Institution Coverage~*Introduction; Bankers Blanket Bond; Excess and Catastrophe Coverages for Banks; Bonds for Other Financial Institutions; Kidnap-Ransom-Extortion Coverage*

Summary

Chapter 8—Surety Bonds **383**

Introduction~*How Suretyship Operates; Characteristics of Surety Bonds; General Types of Surety Bonds*

Contract Bonds~*Types of Contract Bonds; Contract Bond Study Case—R.P. Davis; Additional Case Studies; Kinds of Contract Bonds for Underwriting Purposes; Selling Contract Bonds; What the Bond Underwriter Needs to Know; Surety Bond Guarantee Program for Small Contractors*

License and Permit Bonds~*Purposes of License and Permit Bonds; Types of Guarantees—Examples; Selling License and Permit Bonds*

Public Official Bonds~*Public Official Bonds Versus Fidelity Bonds; Those Who Must Be Bonded*

Judicial Bonds~*Types of Judicial Bonds; Selling Judicial Bonds and Developing Leads; Qualifying as a Bond Representative*

Summary

Chapter 9—Excess and Property Liability Coverage **443**

Introduction

Difference in Conditions~*Introduction; The DIC Policy; Rating and Underwriting Information*

Excess Liability Coverage ~ *Introduction; Straight Excess Liability Policy; Rating and Underwriting Information*

The Commercial Umbrella ~ *Introduction; Purpose; Umbrella Requisites; Policy Structure; Umbrella Policy Analysis; Underwriting; Professional Umbrella Coverage; Producers' Errors and Omissions Exposure from Umbrellas; Case Studies; In Conclusion*

Marketing Excess Coverages

Summary

Chapter 10—Other Commercial Coverages.................... 495

Introduction

Comprehensive Glass Policy ~ *Declarations Page; Insuring Agreement; Exclusions; Conditions; Rating; Underwriting; Sales Tips*

Boiler and Machinery Insurance ~ *Declarations Page; Policy Jacket; Schedules; Indirect Damage; Underwriting; Sales Tips; Insurers*

Credit Insurance ~ *Introduction; Type of Policy; Policy Analysis; Rating and Underwriting*

Government Programs ~ *Introduction; FAIR Plans; Federal Crime Insurance; National Flood Insurance Program; Windstorm and Hail Pools*

Business Life Insurance ~ *Introduction; Taxation and Business Life Insurance; Business Continuation Life Insurance; Special Uses of Business Life Insurance; General Employee Benefits*

Summary

Chapter 11—Businessowners Policy........................... 549

Introduction

Eligibility

Property Coverages ~ *Standard Form BOP; Special Form BOP*

Liability Coverages~*Business Liability; Medical Payments; Named Insured*

General Conditions and Other Provisions~*War Risk, Governmental Action, and Nuclear Exclusions; General Conditions; Conditions Applicable to Section I; Conditions Applicable to Section II*

Rating and Underwriting~*Rating; Underwriting*

Case Studies~*John Gale, M.D.; J&T Appliances*

Summary

Chapter 12—Special Multi-Peril Policies 585

Introduction~*General Requirements; SMP Conditions and Definitions*

Section I—Property~*Property Conditions; Property Forms*

Section II—Liability Coverage Forms~*SMP Liability Conditions and Definitions; SMP Condominium Additional Policy Provisions; SMP Liability Insurance Form; Other Liability Endorsements*

Section III—Crime Coverage Forms~*SMP Comprehensive Crime Coverage; SMP Blanket Crime Coverage; SMP Public Employees Blanket Coverage; Additional Crime Forms and Endorsements*

Section IV—Boiler and Machinery Coverage~*SMP Boiler and Machinery Coverage Endorsement*

Independent Forms

Identifying and Qualifying SMP Prospects

Case Studies~*J&T Appliances; John Gale, M.D.; R.P. Davis, Contractor; Premier Door and Window Company, Inc.*

Summary

Chapter 13—Case Studies.. **639**

Introduction~*Ben's TV Sales; Joseph R. Richards, D.D.S.; The Shopper; Ellenburg Furniture Store; J-R Mechanical, Inc.; Casey Fishing Equipment Company; Exposure Identification*

Summary

Index.. **671**

CHAPTER 1

Garage and Truckers Insurance

GARAGE POLICY

With most types of organizations, it is possible to classify a given loss exposure as a *general liability exposure* or as an *auto exposure.* General liability insurance, such as the comprehensive general liability (CGL) policy, is used to cover the former exposure, and the business auto policy (BAP) is used to cover the latter. These insurance policies attempt to define precisely where auto liability stops and general liability begins in areas where there might be some coverage overlaps—such as loading or unloading, or mobile equipment.

With *some* auto-related types of businesses, auto exposures cannot be separated from the general liability exposures. For example, an auto service station has premises and products liability exposures similar to those of many other businesses, and typically has one or more pickups or private passenger vehicles. The service station business also directly involves such activities as towing, test-driving, and performing repairs on customer-owned autos in its custody.

An auto dealer generally performs many of the activities of a service station. In addition, a dealer owns an ever-changing number of new and used cars for which liability and physical damage coverage is needed. Most autos in a dealer's inventory may be driven at any time by an employee or prospective customer. Other autos are constantly in use as "executive" autos, service vehicles, customer loaners, or even driver-training autos loaned to the local high school. "Demonstrators" may be regularly furnished for sales representatives, but which vehicles are "demonstrators" is subject to change at any time. Parking lots with or

1

without attendants face liability and physical damage exposures that do not fit well with CGL and BAP coverages.

The garage policy was developed for auto-related businesses like these to provide three basic coverages:

1. *Liability insurance*—general and auto liability coverage in a single insuring agreement.
2. *Physical damage insurance*—coverage for damage to those covered autos specified in the policy (the insured's own autos and others).
3. *Garagekeepers insurance*—coverage when the insured is legally responsible for damage to nonowned vehicles, such as those belonging to customers.

Markets—Eligibility

The two principal classes of markets eligible for the garage policy are dealers and nondealers. Because the application of some coverages differs between these two markets, it is important to understand what each encompasses.

Dealers A *dealer* is one who sells new or used private passenger autos, trucks, motorcycles, recreational vehicles other than mobile homes, mobile equipment, or farm implements. A dealer may be either franchised or nonfranchised. A *franchised dealer* has an arrangement with the manufacturer to sell a certain make of vehicle. A *nonfranchised dealer* does not represent a particular manufacturer. The typical new car dealer is franchised; the typical used-car-only dealer is nonfranchised.

Nondealer A *nondealer* is categorized as a repair shop, service station, storage garage, or public parking place, franchised or nonfranchised dealer of mobile homes or commercial trailers, or a tow truck operator. Although there is no rate differential among these classes, producers are required to designate the proper type of operation on the application for underwriting and coding purposes.

Repair shops engage in major auto repairs, provide towing services, and, as an incidental part of their businesses, sell gasoline and oil.

Service stations engage in servicing autos (exclusive of major engine or body work), sell gasoline and oil, and install various accessories, such as tires and batteries.

Storage garages and public parking places principally store or park autos of others.

Franchised and nonfranchised residential mobile-home dealers sell new or reconditioned mobile homes. The franchised dealer is likely to handle one make of mobile home, while the nonfranchised dealer will handle various makes. Some dealers may have the equipment to transport the mobile homes to sites of owners, while others will hire independent contractors. These dealers may also sell accessories, such as cabanas, awnings, and carports.

Franchised and nonfranchised commercial trailer dealers engage in the sale and repair of new and used vans, petroleum and other tanks, platforms, low-bed heavy haulers, dump trailers, and other commercial-type trailers. They may also sell and install various types of equipment, perform body work and painting, and offer towing services.

Tow truck operators *exclusively* engage in operating tow trucks. As independent contractors, tow truck operators may perform their services directly for the public, as well as for dealers and nondealers.

Coverage Characteristics

The ISO garage policy contains "readable" language like the BAP, and, in many ways, has a similar format.

Policy Sections The garage policy contains seven parts (instead of the six parts of the BAP):

1. Part I—Words and Phrases with Special Meaning
   All words and terms in bold-face type are defined. With the exception of the terms "garage operations," "products," and "work you performed," explained as they are introduced, all other terms correspond to those of the BAP.

2. Part II—Which Autos Are Covered Autos
   This section, like that of the BAP, describes which of the covered autos, by symbol, are granted blanket automatic coverage. Also explained are the conditions under which coverage may be maintained other than with the blanket automatic coverage. Trailers with a load capacity of 2,000 pounds or less are considered to be covered automatically.

3. Part III—Where and When This Policy Covers
   This section defines the territorial scope of coverage, similar to the CGL. Bodily injury or property damage caused by one of the named insured's products anywhere in the world is covered, so long as the product was sold for use within the United States, its territories, possessions, Puerto Rico, or Canada, and the original suit is brought in one of these places.

4. Part IV—Liability Insurance
   This section contains the liability insuring agreement, supple-

mentary payments, exclusions, persons insured and other pertinent provisions. It explains the scope of "garage operations."

5. Part V—Garagekeepers Insurance
This section explains the coverages provided when the insured is legally responsible for damage to vehicles of others, such as a customer's car.

6. Part VI—Physical Damage Insurance
This section deals with physical damage to those covered autos specified in the policy. This coverage may apply to the insured's own autos and also some others.

7. Part VII—Conditions
The conditions section establishes some boundaries on coverage.

Description of the Insured's Operations   Whether a garage policy is written for a dealer or nondealer, two important components of the policy are (1) the declarations and (2) the supplementary schedules.

Declarations.   The declarations indentify the insured, the policy period, policy number, and list applicable forms and endorsements. There is a provision that the estimated premium is based "on exposures you told us you would have when this policy began." Thus the initial premium is an estimate with the final premium subject to an audit at the end of each policy term. However, the insurer reserves the right to examine the named insured's records any time during the coverage period and up to three years thereafter.

"Item Two" of the declarations, reproduced as Exhibit 1-1, lists the garage policy coverages and limits. The coverages listed are the same as for the BAP, except for the addition of garagekeepers insurance.

The second column, Covered Autos, calls for entry of one or more numerical symbols, the key to proper tailoring of coverages.

The third column lists limits and deductibles applicable and the final column shows the estimated premium for each coverage.

Supplemental Schedules.   In addition to the basic policy form and declarations, the garage policy also requires the attachment of a supplementary schedule. Although different schedules are used for dealers and nondealers, both generally show the locations where operations are conducted, along with the rate and premium information for all coverages. The nondealer supplementary schedule lists all covered autos. For dealers, the schedule is used to show dollar amounts of physical damage exposures at each location.

Exhibit 1-1
Garage Policy Schedule of Coverages and Covered Autos

Item Two SCHEDULE OF COVERAGES AND COVERED AUTOS
This policy provides only those coverages where a charge is shown in the premium column below. Each of these coverages will apply only to those autos shown as covered autos. Autos are shown as covered autos for a particular coverage by the entry of one or more of the symbols from Item Three next to the name of the coverage. Entry of a symbol next to LIABILITY provides coverage for garage operations.

COVERAGES		COVERED AUTOS Entry of one or more of the symbols from Item Three shows which autos are covered autos	LIMIT THE MOST WE WILL PAY FOR ANY ONE ACCIDENT OR LOSS	PREMIUM
LIABILITY INSURANCE			$	
PERSONAL INJURY PROTECTION (or equivalent No-fualt coverage)			SEPARATELY STATED IN EACH P.I.P. ENDORSEMENT MINUS $ Ded. APPLICABLE TO THE NAMED INSURED AND RELATIVES ONLY	
ADDED P.I.P. (or equivalent added No-fault coverage)			SEPARATELY STATED IN EACH ADDED P.I.P. ENDORSEMENT	
PROPERTY PROTECTION INSURANCE (Michigan only)			SEPARATELY STATED IN THE P.P.I, ENDORSEMENT MINUS $ Ded. FOR EACH ACCIDENT	
MEDICAL PAYMENTS INSURANCE			$	
UNINSURED MOTORISTS INSURANCE			$	
GARAGEKEEPERS INSURANCE	COMPREHENSIVE COVERAGE		$ EACH LOCATION MINUS Ded. FOR EACH COVERED AUTO FOR LOSS CAUSED BY THEFT OR MISCHIEF OR VANDALISM SUBJECT TO $ MAXIMUM DEDUCTIBLE FOR ALL LOSS IN ANY ONE EVENT	
	SPECIFIED PERILS COVERAGE			
	COLLISION COVERAGE		$ EACH LOCATION MINUS $ FOR EACH COVERED AUTO	
PHYSICAL DAMAGE INSURANCE	COMPREHENSIVE COVERAGE		ACTUAL CASH VALUE OR COST OF REPAIR, WHICHEVER IS LESS MINUS	$ Ded. FOR EACH COVERED AUTO FOR ALL LOSS EXCEPT FIRE OR LIGHTING - Non-dealers only. For dealers see ITEM EIGHT
	SPECIFIED PERILS COVERAGE			$25 Ded. FOR EACH COVERED AUTO FOR ALL LOSS BY MISCHIEF OR VANDALISM - Non-dealers only. For dealers see ITEM EIGHT.
	COLLISION COVERAGE			$ Ded. FOR EACH COVERED AUTO - Non-dealers only. For dealers see ITEM EIGHT.
FORMS AND ENDORSEMENTS CONTAINED IN THIS POLICY AT ITS INCEPTION				
			PREMIUM FOR ENDORSEMENTS	
			ESTIMATED TOTAL PREMIUM	

The estimated total premium for this policy is based on the exposures you told us you would have when this policy began.
We will compute your final premium due when we determine your actual exposures. The estimated total premium will be credited against the final premium due and you will be billed for the balance, if any. If the estimated total premium exceeds the final premium due you will get a refund. To determine your final premium due we may examine your records at any time during the period of coverage and up to three years afterward. If this policy is issued for more than one year, the premium shall be computed annually based on our rates or premiums in effect at the beginning of each year of the policy.

Garage Operations Exposures Covered

The insuring agreement of Part IV—Liability Insurance applies to bodily injury or property damage, resulting from "garage operations," caused by accident, during the period of coverage.

"Garage operations" encompass three principal exposures:

1. the ownership, maintenance, or use of locations for the garage business, including roads and accesses that adjoin these locations;
2. all operations necessary or incidental to a garage business; and
3. the ownership, maintenance, or use of covered autos indicated by the symbols in the declarations.

The general liability exposures covered within (1) and (2) above—because they are not excluded—are premises and operations liability, incidental contractual liability, owners' protective liability, products liability, and completed operations liability.

Premises and Operations Coverage is provided for liability arising from the premises listed in the supplementary schedule. Any other similar premises acquired during the policy period are covered without declaring them until policy expiration.

Coverage would also apply for liability arising out of the existence and use of auto hoists, elevators, and escalators. However, damage to property in the insured's care, custody, or control, such as customers' autos, is excluded under the liability insurance part. (To obtain protection for the damage to customers' autos, producers should recommend the purchase of garagekeepers' insurance.)

Business operations conducted by a dealer or nondealer are covered only when they are "necessary or incidental" to the garage business. For example, an owner of a service station may have protection for a claim stemming from a car wash operation on the premises. Producers therefore have to be especially careful to question garage owners about all operations, to inform them of the importance of exposure identification, and to discuss all operations with the insurer, preferably in writing. Many underwriters will provide comprehensive general liability (CGL) coverage for a nominal premium (like $25) so any other new operations will be automatically covered when they are added. Other operations may be scheduled as well to obtain the necessary coverage.

Incidental Contractual Liability The garage policy excludes liability assumed by the insured under any contract or agreement except *incidental contracts* such as lease of premises agreements, easement agreements, sidetrack agreements, and elevator maintenance agreements.

The garage policy does not automatically cover as "incidental contracts" liability assumed under agreements to indemnify a municipality as required by law. A garage owner or operator may be required to obtain a permit before using adjoining public property to park customers' autos, to place signs, or to use dumpsters. Sometimes these permits are not issued until the business furnishes the municipality with a license and permit bond (Chapter 8). If a dealer or nondealer is required to hold harmless a public body, as a condition of a permit, it is the producers' obligation to obtain contractual liability insurance for the insured, as well as a license and permit bond, if required.

Owners' Protective Liability Covered under the garage policy is the vicarious liability of an insured stemming from work performed at garage locations by independent contractors, such as ordinary premises repairs, structural alterations, new construction, and demolition work.

Products Liability Bodily injury or property damage resulting from products, i.e., "goods or products you (the named insured) made or sold in the garage business," are automatically covered as part of the garage policy. The goods or products must be of the kind necessary or incidental to garage operations. The sale of candy and soft drinks, a common activity among dealers and nondealers, should be checked with the insurer as it may not be considered "incidental." However, dealers and nondealers who decide to also sell appliances, towels, linens, rugs, or who operate restaurants clearly would not have products liability coverage without a CGL. Liability for damages is covered, subject to three important exclusions common to most products liability policies. There are two important points about products liability which producers must keep in mind when explaining the coverage. Coverage does not apply to damage *to* a product of an insured nor loss of use of the product.

Damage to the Named Insured's Products. No coverage applies for damage to the products or any part caused by defect at the time the product was sold or transferred to another person. For example, suppose a service station sells a tire which blows out because of a defect. There is no coverage for damage to the tire, but bodily injury or damage to other property from a resulting accident would be covered, as well as any loss of use of other tangible property. This exclusion can be deleted by endorsement.

Failure to Perform. No coverage applies for loss of use of other property not physically damaged if caused by:

1. The named insured's delay or failure to perform any agreement or contract. (An auto dealer who promises to repair a customer's trailer will have no coverage for loss of use of the trailer by its owner because the dealer fails to fulfill that promise.)
2. The failure of the named insured's products to meet the quality warranted or the level of performance represented. If a customer loses the use of an auto because a recently purchased battery does not work, the loss is not covered. Loss of use of other property is covered if caused by sudden and accidental damage or destruction of the named insured's products. Thus, if the battery explodes, damages the auto engine, and the owner loses the use of the auto, the loss of use is covered.

Products Recall. No coverage applies for costs and expenses incurred by the insured in recalling products because of a known or suspected defect.

Completed Operations Liability arising from work performed by or on behalf of the insured is covered, subject to a deductible of $100. (This may be deleted for an additional charge.) The same three exclusions applying to "products" apply to completed operations.

Thus, if a service station subcontracts the rebuilding of an auto generator, and a faulty part in the generator causes an electrical malfunction, the service station has no coverage for damage to the generator or for loss of use of the auto. The service station's only recourse is against the subcontractor who, in turn, may have recourse against the manufacturer of the part. However, if the generator were to cause an electrical fire that damages the auto, the service station would have coverage for damage to the auto, including its loss of use, except for damage to the generator.

Checkpoints

1. Distinguish between a dealer and nondealer.
2. Identify the three principal exposures encompassed by the term "garage operations."
3. Identify and describe briefly the five general liability coverages of the garage policy.
4. List the exposures of products liability and completed operations which are not covered.

Garage Auto Liability Exposures Covered

The garage policy provides flexible coverages tailored to almost any kind of auto exposure. This flexibility is accomplished through the use of twelve "covered auto symbols," discussed later. (Except for the series "20" and "30" symbols, which are used with the garage policy to avoid complications with the numerical symbols of the BAP and truckers policies, the first eight symbols of the garage policy are similar to the first eight symbols of the BAP.) Each of the twelve symbols represents a combination of four elements of coverage on garage autos or exposures: (1) the type of auto and its exposure; (2) the insured's legal relationship to the auto; (3) the insurance applicable; and (4) scope of coverage after policy inception.

The first element identifies the type or class of covered auto or exposure. Any auto, owned autos only, and specifically described autos are examples of covered autos by type or class. Hired autos only, nonowned autos used in the garage business, and autos left for service, repair, storage or safekeeping, are examples of covered auto exposures.

The second element of coverage defines the insured's legal relationship to the covered auto. The insured may be the owner or nonowner of the auto (lessee, renter, user, bailee, or borrower).

The third element relates to the insurance coverage purchased for the covered auto exposure. From Exhibit 1-1, the coverage possibilities of the garage policy can be seen. Each symbol used in the "covered autos" column 2 of the declarations indicates the appropriate coverage.

The fourth element defines the scope of coverage on covered autos acquired after the inception of the policy. Symbols 21 to 26, as entered under the "covered autos" column of the declarations, grant blanket and automatic coverage for all autos of the type designated which may be acquired after policy inception. This means that an audit will be necessary at the end of the policy period to determine the actual exposure and the final premium. When symbol 27 (specifically described autos) is designated next to a coverage in the declarations, an auto the insured acquires during the policy period will be a covered auto if:

a. **We** already insure all **autos** that **you** own for that coverage or it replaces an **auto you** previously owned that had that coverage; and

b. **You** tell **us** within thirty days after **you** acquire it that **you** want **us** to insure it for that coverage.

The provision is identical to that of the BAP for symbol 7 covered autos. The thirty-day automatic coverage provision would *not* apply, when all owned autos are not insured under the policy, or when a newly acquired auto replaces one that is not insured by the policy. Changes on autos may not be too frequent under this symbol, but it is nevertheless important to establish good communications between the client and the producer.

None of the other symbols, i.e., 28 to 32, is subject to blanket and automatic or limited automatic coverage of the policy, in the same sense as the previously mentioned symbols, because they have nothing to do with ownership. There nonetheless is automatic coverage on all autos within a given exposure. For example, the insured who selects *hired autos only* will have automatic coverage on any auto the insured rents.

Application of Symbols—Liability Coverages It is very important for producers to understand when a particular symbol may be used, and what it does when used. Designating an improper symbol, failing to designate a symbol, or designating the proper symbol for the wrong coverage could place the burden of loss on the producer. Since several of the symbols can be used for a combination of coverages, the discussion of symbols and their application will be based upon liability and liability-related coverages first. The application of symbols for physical damage coverages will be addressed when those coverages are discussed later.

Any Auto. Symbol 21 is defined: ANY AUTO. This symbol is reserved solely for dealers, and, in fact, *must always be used* when a dealer is written under the garage policy. The only two coverages available with this symbol are liability and auto medical payments. When this symbol is designated opposite either or both of those coverages, such protection applies to all owned autos at policy inception, any newly acquired and replacement autos on a blanket and automatic basis, all nonowned autos, and all hired autos. Since the term "auto" is defined in the policy to mean "a land motor vehicle, trailer or semitrailer," *any auto* can include private passenger autos, trucks, truck-tractors, buses, taxis, motorcycles, and trailers of any type.

Although this symbol is the broadest of any available, it *does not* extend to such coverages as no-fault, uninsured motorists, or for damage to customers' autos. If any of these latter coverages is desired, other symbols are required. Furthermore, when symbol 21 is designated opposite medical payments insurance, an auto medical payments coverage endorsement is necessary because that coverage is not automatically included within the basic policy provisions.

Owned Autos. The policy definition for symbol 22 reads:

> Only those autos you own (and for liability coverage any trailers you don't own while attached to power units you own). This includes those autos you acquire ownership of after the policy begins.

Symbol 22 is the broadest coverage available to nondealers from the standpoint of autos covered, because it applies to any type of land motor vehicle, trailer, or semitrailer, so long as it is owned, with one exception. When this symbol is designated opposite liability insurance, such coverage also applies on a primary basis to any type of nonowned trailer which is attached to any type of owned auto.

In addition to liability insurance, symbol 22 also may be used by dealers and nondealers to obtain noncompulsory uninsured motorists insurance, and for nondealers who desire medical payments.

Owned Private Passenger Autos. Symbol 23 provides blanket and automatic coverage on all private passenger autos including those newly acquired. In addition to liability insurance, this symbol can be used to obtain noncompulsory uninsured motorists insurance. When a dealer desires to limit its noncompulsory uninsured motorists insurance to owned private passenger autos only, symbol 23 is the appropriate one to use.

Symbol 23 also includes coverage for trailers with a load capacity of 2,000 pounds or less.

Owned Nonprivate Passenger Autos. Symbol 24 serves the same purpose as symbol 23, except any "auto," as defined, which is not a private passenger auto, will be covered on a blanket and automatic basis. Symbol 24 applies to liability, medical payments, and noncompulsory uninsured motorists coverages. Dealers who may desire noncompulsory uninsured motorists coverage on this class of autos may also use symbol 24.

No-Fault Coverage for Owned Autos. Symbol 25 may not be used for any coverage other than mandatory no-fault.

> Only those autos you own which are required to have No-Fault benefits in the state where they are licensed or principally garaged. This includes those autos you acquire ownership of after the policy begins provided they are required to have No-Fault benefits in the state where they are licensed or principally garaged.

Symbol 25 is designed to provide blanket and automatic coverage on all owned autos of the named insured subject to no-fault laws. While it is permissible to apply symbol 27 (below) to no-fault, symbol 25 is preferred to assure that needed coverage is always in place and the insured is in compliance with the law.

Compulsory Uninsured Motorists (UM) Coverage for Owned Autos. Symbol 26 may be used only in states that have compulsory uninsured motorists insurance laws, with no right to reject the coverage.

Specific Autos Only. Symbols 21 through 26 provide a form of blanket and automatic coverage. Symbol 27, however, may be used to confine such coverage to specifically described autos:

> Only those autos described in ITEM EIGHT of the Non Dealers' and Trailer Dealers' Supplementary Schedule or ITEM ELEVEN of the Dealers' Supplementary Schedule for which a premium charge is

shown (and for liability coverage any trailers you don't own while attached to a power unit described in ITEM EIGHT OR ITEM ELEVEN).

When symbol 27 is selected, all autos must be specifically described. If nondealers or dealers of mobile homes or commercial trailers acquire any new autos during the policy period, each *must be reported* to the insurer within thirty days, if coverage is to continue.

When used for liability insurance, any nonowned trailer is covered if it is attached to a specifically described auto. An additional premium will be required for such nonowned trailer, unless it has a load capacity of 2,000 pounds or less.

For nondealers, symbol 27 may be used for any policy coverage. Because symbol 21 will always be used by dealers, but is restricted to liability and medical payments, dealers may use symbol 27 to also obtain noncompulsory UM, compulsory UM, if the law permits the latter coverage on selected autos, or no-fault insurance. Despite the flexibility of symbol 27, especially for nondealers, it is advisable to use some other symbol whenever possible, because this symbol will not encompass exposures for which coverage should be provided if the need exists at policy inception or develops during the policy term.

Hired Autos.   Symbol 28 is defined as:

Only those autos you lease, hire, rent or borrow. This does not include any auto you lease, hire, rent or borrow from any of your employees or members of their families.

This symbol may be used alone or in combination with symbols 22, 23, 24, or 29 to complement the liability insurance of nondealers. Even if a firm never leases, hires, or rents an auto, symbol 28 still is useful to cover a borrowed auto exposure, which could be common among some nondealers, and therefore is recommended. Since symbol 21 for dealers already includes the hired auto liability exposure, symbol 28 is not necessary.

Nonowned Autos—Garages.   Symbol 29 is defined:

Any auto you do not own, lease, hire or borrow used in connection with your garage business described in these declarations. This includes autos owned by your employees or members of their households while used in your garage business.

This symbol, designed solely for liability insurance, can be used alone, or in combination with symbols 22, 23, 24, or 28. However, it is *always* recommended. This symbol is not to be used with dealers, since symbol 21 automatically includes it.

The coverage provided by symbol 29 is commonly referred to as "employers nonownership liability." Because employers commonly obtain primary protection under the personal auto policies of their employees, employer's nonownership is meant to apply as excess insurance, for example when the auto liability limits of an employee are inadequate following an accident. However, if an employee does not have auto liability insurance, employer's nonownership will then apply as primary insurance, but only for the employer.

If employers permit employees to use their personal autos on garage business, the producer should make sure that employers establish a company guideline on this exposure, such as a stipulation that part of the mileage reimbursement is allocated toward carrying auto liability insurance.

Unusual Auto Exposures. Symbol 32 is purposely left blank for a dealer or nondealer with an unusual exposure that may require coverage not available under any of the other symbols. For example, when a dealer furnishes autos to other than its proprietors, partners, managers, or employees, such as to school driver training programs, or for use as "welcome wagons," symbol 32 may be used to designate those exposures.

Symbol 32 is like symbol 27 in three ways: (1) it is used for any policy coverage, (2) all such furnished autos of a dealer must be specifically described in Item Eleven of the dealers' supplementary schedule, and (3) newly acquired autos are subject to the thirty-day reporting requirements.

Remaining Symbols. The remaining symbols for use with the garage policy deal strictly with physical damage exposures. These symbols and the physical damage coverages as included with the aforementioned symbols will be discussed later with the physical damage and garagekeepers coverages.

Symbol Summary. Exhibit 1-2 summarizes how covered auto symbols may be used to cover differently defined auto exposures for each of the policy coverages discussed thus far. Exhibit 1-3 gives a complete summary of permissible application of symbols to each of those coverages.

Producers must be careful in selecting the covered auto symbols. Nondealers are not allowed comprehensive auto liability coverage with the use of one symbol (21), so care must be exercised to obtain coverage commensurate with the exposures. Thus, as a rule, always suggest symbols 28 and 29 for nondealers, because there is no way to determine when the hired and nonowned auto liability exposures might arise.

Checkpoints

1. Describe the coverages (other than physical damage and garagekeepers) that may be included in the garage policy.

Exhibit 1-2
How Symbols May Be Used

If the intent is to cover:	The Covered Auto Symbol				
	Liability	PIP	Med. Pay	Noncomp. UM	Compul. UM
Any auto (dealers only)	21	N/A	21	N/A	N/A
Owned autos only	22	N/A	22	22*	22*
Owned private passenger autos only	23	N/A	23	23*	23*
Owned autos other than private passenger	24	N/A	24	24*	24*
PIP on all owned autos subject to no-fault	N/A	25* 27*	N/A	N/A	N/A
Compulsory UM on all owned autos	N/A	N/A	N/A	N/A	22* 23* 26* 27*
Specified autos only	27	27	27	27*	27*
Hired or borrowed autos	28	N/A	N/A	N/A	N/A
Nonowned autos only	29	N/A	29	N/A	N/A

*Dealers and Nondealers

Exhibit 1-3
Permissible Use of Symbols

Coverages	Covered Auto Symbols									
	21	22	23	24	25	26	27	28	29	32
Liability	X	X	X	X				X	X	X
Medical Payments	X	X	X	X			X		X	X
PIP					X		X			X
UM (noncompulsory)		X	X	X			X			X
UM (compulsory)		X	X			X	X			X

2. List the covered auto symbols 21-29 and 32 and describe the exposures each includes for other than physical damage and garagekeepers.

Garage Liability Insurance

The insuring agreement for liability insurance on covered autos and operations of the garage policy reads:

> **We** will pay all sums the **insured** legally must pay as damages because of **bodily injury** or **property damage** to which this insurance applies caused by an **accident** and resulting from **garage operations.**

The agreement contains several defined terms (words in bold-face type). With the exception of the previously defined term garage operations and temporarily deferring the definition of insured, the other policy definitions are:

> **"Bodily injury"** means bodily injury, sickness or disease including death resulting from any of these.
>
> **"Property damage"** means damage to or loss of use of tangible property.
>
> **"Accident"** includes continuous or repeated exposure to the same conditions resulting in **bodily injury** or **property damage** the **insured** neither expected nor intended.

In addition to the protection provided to insureds for defense and/or payment of damages, the garage policy, like other liability policies, includes a number of additional benefits under a provision entitled, "We Will Also Pay." The insurer agrees to pay (1) up to $250 for the cost of bail bonds required because of covered accident, but with no obligation to furnish such bonds, (2) reimbursement for loss of earnings up to $50 per day to an insured for attendance at trials or hearings at the insurer's request, (3) other reasonable expenses incurred at the insurer's request, and (4) premiums on appeal and release of attachment bonds, as well as all costs and interest related to claims litigation.

Insured All benefits, including defense and/or the payment of damages will be paid only if the person against whom claim is made or suit is brought is an insured. The general definition of insured reads:

> "Insured" means any person or organization qualifying as an insured in the WHO IS INSURED section of the applicable insurance. Except with respect to **our** limit of liability, the insurance afforded applies separately to each insured who is seeking coverage or against whom a claim is made or suit is brought.

The first sentence leads to the definitions below. The second sentence is a "severability of interests" condition which treats each person or organization seeking protection as if each of them has separate coverage by that policy. So, if one insured is determined to be without coverage, this has no effect on other insureds seeking coverage. However, the limits of liability are not cumulative regardless of how many claims or suits are brought.

Because the garage policy deals with covered auto as well as nonauto exposures, there are separate definitions of insureds for each. The first provision concerns insureds of covered autos, and the second deals with insureds for garage operations other than covered autos.

Insureds of Covered Autos. Who is an insured under the garage policy is similar in some ways to who is a covered person with the BAP. The policy protects the insured named in the declarations (**"you"**), for any covered auto. For a dealership, the named insured is covered for any owned, nonowned, or hired auto (symbol 21). For any nondealer, coverage of the named insured hinges on the symbols that apply.

Permissive users, such as officers, partners, employees, and even high schools which are furnished autos for driving training programs, are likewise protected when using a covered auto, subject to the following limitations.

There is no coverage for any employee or member of his or her household whose auto is used in the employer's business. However, the permissive user would have protection when either symbol 21 or 29 applies. Thus, if employee A borrows an auto of employee B for business purposes with the employer's permission, both A and the employer would be protected under B's policy on a primary basis and under the garage policy for any excess. B, however, would not be protected under the garage policy. B may be insured under a personal auto policy which covers B and family members while employed or otherwise engaged in the garage business.

There is no coverage for anyone who is using a covered auto in the garage business, other than the garage business of the named insured. Suppose the Witek Repair Shop performs some repairs on a customer's auto, but requires the specialized assistance of MacIntire's Garage to perform certain other repairs. While an employee of MacIntire is using the customer's auto, it is involved in an accident. Witek would have protection under its garage policy for any vicarious liability, but MacIntire would not be protected under Witek's policy. MacIntire's only recourse for protection is under its own garage policy. (Neither of the two garage owners would have protection for physical damage to the customer's auto unless each had garagekeepers insurance.)

A final restriction limits the extent to which customers, as permissive users of auto dealerships, have protection. The effect of this provision is to treat customers who use loaners or new autos as permissive users only when the customers do not have their own auto liability insurance, or when the limits of their own auto insurance are less than the compulsory or financial responsibility limits that apply to the covered auto.

Another section of "who is insured for covered auto" serves two purposes. The first part provides protection to any person or organization which may be vicariously liable for the conduct of any insured. Thus a high school to whom a dealer-owned auto has been furnished for driver education would have protection if one of the instructors or students were to become involved in a suit. However, specifically ruled out for vicarious liability protection, under the second provision, is the owner or anyone else from whom the named insured hires or borrows a covered auto, unless the covered auto is a trailer. In this latter instance, the owner of a trailer has protection under the garage policy for any vicarious liability when such trailer is connected to a covered auto which the named insured owns.

Insureds Other Than Covered Autos.   The second part of the WHO IS INSURED provision reads:

For Garage Operations Other than Covered Autos.

a. You are an insured.

b. Your employees, directors or shareholders are insureds but only while acting within the scope of their duties.

Except for the addition of employees, these persons are commonly covered under most liability policies.

Exposure Excluded   Of the fourteen exclusions that apply to the basic policy provisions, five have been discussed (contractual liability other than incidental contracts, damage to "your products," damage to "work you performed," loss of use of other property stemming from failure of "your products" or "work you performed," and products recall). The remaining exclusions are:

1. The insured's liability under a workers' compensation or similar law.

2. Any obligation imposed on the insured to indemnify someone else because of injury to an employee of the insured. Suppose a garage employee is using an electrical tool which is not properly grounded. As a result, the employee suffers injuries from electrical shock. After collecting workers' compensation benefits, the employee decides to sue the manufacturer of the tool, because he is barred from suing his employer. The manufacturer either may pay the damages and then seek retribution from the employer for being contributorily negligent, or the manufacturer may implead the employer in the suit. In either instance, the employer is not protected under the garage policy for defense or payment of damages. The employer's only recourse for protection is under employer's liability insurance, except in cases when an employer agrees under contract to be held accountable for employee injuries. In this latter event, contractual liability insurance is necessary.

3. There is no coverage for injury to any employee of the insured arising out of his or her employment. Some employers, depending upon jurisdiction, may not be subject to the workers' compensation law, or the employee may sustain an injury which is not otherwise compensable. If an employer-insured is confronted with a suit for damages in either of the two instances, employers' liability insurance is required.

4. Liability of an insured to a fellow employee injured in the course of employement is excluded. This is another workers' compensation-related exclusion. Its rationale is to make workers' compensation the exclusive remedy to the injured employee.

   Fellow employee suits arising from auto accidents can be covered in one of three ways depending upon the exposure. First, an employee has automatic protection against fellow employee suits under the PAP, if such suit involves a covered auto of that policy. Second, if the vehicle being used by the employee is a commercial auto or a private passenger auto furnished or available for that employee's regular use, the exposure may be covered by adding the extended nonowned liability coverage endorsement to the personal auto policy. The third alternative, which applies similarly to the second method, is when the employee is added to the drive other car coverage endorsement of the garage policy.

5. There is no coverage for damage to property owned or transported by the insured or in the insured's care, custody, or control. Fire legal liability can be purchased with regard to the real property exposure. Exposures involving personal property, other than autos, are commonly handled by inland marine insurance (Chapter 5), while autos of others such as customers can be covered under garagekeepers insurance.

6. No coverage applies to any covered auto while leased or rented to others. Coverage can be added by endorsement for an additional premium. This exclusion does not apply when a covered auto of the named insured is rented to one of its customers while the latter's auto is left with the named insured for service or repair. Dealers refer to such vehicles as "daily rentals." Such coverage applies whether the covered auto is rented or simply loaned to the customer.

7. This policy, like all other liability policies, is subject to the common exclusion of pollution or contamination, unless the discharge is sudden and accidental.

8. Covered autos *while used* in any professional or organized racing, demolition contest or stunting activity are not covered against liability claims or suits. But there is coverage while these covered autos are being prepared for such contest or activity. Those who sponsor autos in these activities will require special insurance.

9. There is no coverage under the garage policy for any watercraft or aircraft.

Although not a part of the basic policy provisions, the broad form nuclear energy liability exclusion is also mandatory.

Limit of Liability Given that a person or organization is an insured under the garage policy, and is legally responsible for damages in an otherwise covered claim or suit, the amount ultimately payable hinges on the limit of liability and the conditions pertaining to it:

OUR LIMIT OF LIABILITY

Regardless of the number of covered autos, insureds, claims made or vehicles involved in the accident, the most we will pay for all damages resulting from any one accident is the limit of LIABILITY INSURANCE shown in the declarations. However, we will deduct $100 from the damages in any accident resulting from property damage to an auto as a result of work you performed.

The applicable limit is not increased because more than one insured may be involved in a claim or suit. Nor does the limit apply separately to more than one claimant. Further, a $100 deductible applies to damages resulting from work an insured did to an auto if such work resulted in a loss. The deductible may be modified by endorsement. Bodily injury and property damage resulting from continuous or repeated exposure to substantially the same conditions are considered one accident. The intent is to prevent pyramiding of limits when injury or damage losses are of a prolonged nature.

The policy provides liability coverage on a single limit basis. One limit, such as $300,000 per accident, applies for all damages to one or more persons for bodily injury liability and for property damage liability. However, split limits can be substituted by endorsement. Since both products and completed operations coverages are built into this policy, no separate aggregate limit applies to these hazards.

Auto and premises medical payments coverages also are written on a single limit basis with a range from $500 to $2,000.

Out of State Coverage If a covered auto is away from the state in which it is licensed where (1) specified compulsory or financial responsibility limits, or (2) other coverages, such as no-fault, are required of all drivers, including nonresidents who may operate vehicles in that state, the garage policy automatically provides the minimum limits or coverages required.

Garage Policy Options and Endorsements

Many different endorsements are available for tailoring coverages to the particular needs of dealers and nondealers. Attention here will be focused on endorsements with which the producer should be familiar in a sales context.

Broad Form Products Coverage By attaching the broad form products coverage endorsement, for an additional premium, the exclusion relating to property damage to "your products" is deleted. However, subject to the policy limit, coverage only applies to that amount of property damage to the named insured's products which exceeds $250 for any one accident.

Deletion of $100 Deductible for Completed Operations The $100 deductible applying to property damage to autos which results from work completed by or for the named insured as part of the latter's garage operations may be deleted.

Individual Named Insured Endorsement When the named insured under a garage policy is an individual, the individual named insured endorsement should be attached. This provides the named insured, spouse, and family members with coverage equivalent to that of a personal auto policy (PAP), if the named insured owns a private passenger auto and/or a pickup, panel truck, or van not customarily used in the business. The only advantage of this endorsement, over the PAP, is that there is an absence of any exclusion to any person using a vehicle "without a reasonable belief that the person is entitled to do so."

Medical Payments Medical payments may be added either for the garage operation or autos covered or both.

Garage Locations and Operations Medical Payments Insurance. Medical payments insurance for garage premises and operations can be designated by symbol in the policy declarations. However, the coverage provisions themselves must be added by endorsement. When the garage locations and operations medical payments insurance endorsement is attached to the policy, the coverage provided is similar to what normally applies when premises medical payments insurance is added to other commercial liability policies. Medical payments are made if there is reason to believe that the resulting injury or death would not have occurred but for some condition on the premises or operations conducted by the insured. However, no coverage applies for bodily injury (1) resulting from the maintenance or use of any auto (auto medical payments insurance is necessary); (2) to the named insured or to anyone else arising out of and during the course of employment in the named insured's business (workers' compensation insurance will likely apply); and (3) caused by declared or undeclared war, insurrection, or any of their consequences (these exposures are uninsurable).

The rationale for selling this insurance is to maintain a business's goodwill, i.e., paying those expenses incurred by others without having to prove the insured legally liable. However, the coverage can be quite expensive, and liability insurance would pay many of the same claims.

Auto Medical Payments Insurance. Auto medical payments coverage must be added to the garage policy by endorsement when such coverage is designated by symbol in the policy declarations. Although auto medical payments insurance may not be widely used with commercial autos because a large part of the exposure concerns employees covered by workers' compensation insurance, there may still be some circumstances when the coverage is desirable. Dealers and nondealers, for example, may desire medical payments coverage on certain autos that will be used by customers, as well as other permissive users, not to mention the members of their own families who ride in company-owned cars.

In some ways, auto medical payments is similar to medical payments written in connection with garage locations and operations.

Coverage is restricted by the limits applying to each person, and only a few exclusions apply. For the most part, these are meant to prevent overlapping coverage that may be available under workers' compensation insurance, and to prevent losses stemming from war and insurrection. There are distinct differences, however, in that medical payments for garage locations and operations is not intended to provide coverage for injuries to the insured. Auto medical payments covers the reasonable expenses necessarily incurred within three years of the accident, whereas garage locations and operations medical payments is silent on the period of coverage.

Personal Injury Liability Insurance Not all businesses which come within the scope of the garage policy are necessarily candidates for personal injury liability coverage. However, many businesses such as auto dealers, or equipment and implement dealers, may desire the coverage, particularly personal injury to any person resulting from an offense related to the named insured's employment of such person. It will be recalled that personal injury includes:

1. false arrest, detention or imprisonment, or malicious prosecution;
2. libel, slander, defamation, disparagement or violation of the right of privacy; and
3. wrongful entry or eviction, or other invasion of the right of private occupancy.

Fire Legal Liability Insurance Fire legal liability, as provided by endorsement for garages, is intended for the tenant or lessee of a commercial building who agrees under contract to be responsible for the building, or that part of the building which is in its care, custody, or control. The coverage is for property damage liability caused by one peril, fire, when fire is the result of an insured's negligence.

Only one exclusion applies to fire legal liability coverage, and it concerns any liability assumed by the insured under any other type of contract or agreement. The exclusion precludes coverage for claims which arise solely from a contractual obligation that is not also grounded in real or alleged negligence on the part of the insured.

Checkpoints

1. List the criteria necessary for liability insurance to apply, in general, under the garage policy.
2. List those persons or organizations (a) who are and (b) who are not insureds for covered autos.
3. Explain how the exposures excluded in the garage policy may be insured.

Exhibit 1-4
Covered Auto Symbols—Physical Damage Insurance

Class of Covered Auto Exposures	Dealer	Nondealer
Owned autos only	22	22
Owned private passenger autos only	23	23
Owned autos other than private passenger autos	24	24
Specifically described autos	27	27
Hired autos	—[1]	28[2]
Consigned autos	31	—[3]
Special auto exposures	32	32

[1] Special accommodations are required for this exposure.
[2] Unless otherwise specified, coverage applies as excess.
[3] Incidental coverage is provided by indicating such interest under Item Eleven of the supplementary schedule.

Garage Physical Damage Exposures Covered

Producers familiar with the covered auto symbols that apply to liability insurance, particularly from the standpoint of the class of autos covered by symbol and the insured's legal relationship to such autos, should find the auto physical damage coverage symbols easy to comprehend and use. In addition to the designation of symbols in the policy declarations, the coverage process requires completion of the appropriate physical damage coverage items in the dealers' and nondealers' supplementary schedules.

Seven symbols (22, 23, 24, 27, 28, 31, and 32) are available for use with three physical damage coverages: (1) comprehensive, (2) specified perils, and (3) collision. Of these symbols, five can be used by dealers and nondealers. One symbol is reserved for the hired auto exposures of nondealers, and the final one is earmarked solely for use by dealers for consigned auto exposures. Since five of the symbols have been previously defined, it is only necessary here to identify and briefly describe what each entails. Exhibit 1-4 provides a composite of these symbols and their application.

Owned Autos Only Symbol 22 may be used by dealers and nondealers. When designated opposite one or more of the physical damage coverages, insurance applies to those autos the named insured owns, i.e., any land motor vehicle, trailer, or semitrailer. It also includes blanket and automatic coverage on newly acquired autos.

Owned Private Passenger Autos Only Symbol 23 may be used by dealers and nondealers. When designated opposite one or more of the physical damage coverages, insurance applies only to those private passenger autos the named insured owns, including owned trailers and semitrailers for use with those owned private passenger autos. It also includes blanket and automatic coverage on newly acquired private passenger autos, as well as trailers and semitrailers for use with those autos.

Owned Autos Other Than Private Passenger Autos Symbol 24 may be used by dealers and nondealers. When designated opposite one or more of the physical damage coverages, insurance applies only on those autos, i.e., any land motor vehicle, trailer, or semitrailer the named insured owns that is not of the private passenger type. It also includes blanket and automatic coverage on newly acquired autos of other than the private passenger type.

Specifically Described Autos Symbol 27 may be used by dealers and nondealers, but is more likely to be used by the latter. When designated opposite one or more of the physical damage coverages, insurance applies only to those autos, i.e., any land motor vehicle, trailer, or semitrailer, described in Item Eight of the nondealers' supplementary schedule, or Item Eleven of the dealers' supplementary schedule. Because of the foregoing requirements, no blanket and automatic coverage applies on newly acquired autos. Each must be reported to the company within thirty days.

Even when symbol 27 is not used by a nondealer, all covered autos owned by the nondealer at policy inception must still be specifically described in the nondealers' supplementary schedule for physical damage and other coverages. However, the essential difference between symbol 27 and symbols 22, 23, and 24 is that no physical damage coverage will apply to a newly acquired auto under symbol 27, unless that auto is specifically described by endorsement, whereas any newly acquired auto under the other symbols is automatically covered. On the other hand, a dealer is not normally required to specifically describe its owned autos at policy inception under the dealers' supplementary schedule. The only exceptions are when symbol 27 is designated for physical damage, uninsured motorists, or no-fault coverages, or when autos are furnished to certain persons.

Hired Autos Only Symbol 28 may be used by dealers and nondealers. When designated opposite one of more of the physical damage coverages, insurance applies only to those autos the named insured leases, hires, rents, or borrows, exclusive of those autos of the named insured's employees or members of their families.

As written for nondealers, physical damage insurance on hired or borrowed autos applies as excess over any other collectible insurance. However, to effect primary coverage, a check mark may be designated in the appropriate section under Item Seven of the nondealers' supplementary schedule. When specifically designated by a check mark, the policy condition entitled "Other Insurance" automatically treats a covered auto the named insured hires or borrows as a "covered auto you own."

Consigned Autos   Symbol 31, used solely by dealers, is defined:

> Any auto not owned by you or any creditor while in your possession on consignment for sale.

A consignment concerns an exposure when a dealer has possession of an auto belonging to someone else, such as another dealer or an auto manufacturer, for purposes of sale. Although responsibility for such auto may be subject to contract, a consignment is commonly viewed as a bailment. As such, the dealer may wish to protect its interests in such auto while in its possession against direct and accidental physical loss. When a dealer has autos on consignment for which coverage is desired, Item Eight of the dealers' supplementary schedule must be completed, by indicating whether the autos are new and/or used, the interests covered, and the coverages desired.

Symbol 31 must be designated opposite the physical damage coverages desired in the policy declarations. The consigned autos do not have to be specifically described in the schedule. The value of these autos will be taken into consideration at expiration of the policy upon audit, or during the policy period if coverage is written on an interim or reporting basis.

When autos are financed for a dealer, the autos are encumbered and no longer qualify for coverage under symbol 31. Coverage on encumbered autos is handled just as if the autos were fully owned by the dealer. Thus, symbol 22, 23, 24, or 27 will be designated opposite the physical damage coverages in the policy declarations, but with the additional requirement that the interests of the dealer and creditor be designated in Item Eight of the schedule.

Since the consigned auto exposure of a nondealer is likely to be the exception rather than the rule, coverage for this incidental exposure of a nondealer is handled differently. In lieu of symbol 31, a nondealer need only signify an auto consignment interest under Item Eleven of the nondealers' schedule, and the coverages desired, the same procedure required of a nondealer on encumbered autos.

Unique Exposures   When an unusual exposure develops which requires physical damage coverage, symbol 32 may be used, just as it may be used for liability and other insurance coverages.

Checkpoints

1. Briefly describe the physical damage exposures of garages.
2. Which of the auto physical damage symbols provides blanket and automatic coverage on newly acquired autos?
3. Explain the most important point to remember when a non-dealer desires physical damage insurance on a hired auto exposure.

Garage Physical Damage Insurance

The insuring agreement of garage physical damage insurance applies to direct and accidental loss or damage, to a covered auto or its equipment, if not otherwise excluded, under one or more of the following three basic coverages:

1. comprehensive,
2. specified perils, and/or
3. collision.

Comprehensive applies to loss from any cause not excluded, except collision or overturn. The specified perils are fire, explosion, theft, windstorm, hail, earthquake, flood, mischief or vandalism, or the sinking, burning, collision, or derailment of a conveyance transporting the covered auto.

The decision of whether to select comprehensive or specified perils involves the usual issues of comparing "all-risks" to named perils coverage. Comprehensive coverage will be higher in cost. Where glass breakage is a prevalent exposure, such as with private passenger autos, it is well to recommend comprehensive coverage.

However, one of the additional features of comprehensive coverage, on the subject of glass breakage and certain other losses, is the provision entitled:

GLASS BREAKAGE—HITTING A BIRD OR ANIMAL—FALLING OBJECTS OR MISSILES.

We will pay for glass breakage, loss caused by hitting a bird or animal or by falling objects or missiles under Comprehensive Coverage if you carry Comprehensive Coverage for the damaged covered auto. However, you have the option of having the glass breakage caused by a covered auto's collision or overturn considered a loss under Collision Coverage.

Two purposes are served by the provision. The first one is to make clear that loss resulting in breakage of glass or other damage to a covered auto by any of the foregoing perils is to be paid as a comprehensive loss. The second is to avoid the application of two deductibles, if collision coverage also applies.

Supplementary Payments The supplementary payments provision, which provides additional sums over the amount of any loss or damage to covered autos, only applies to nonauto dealer garage businesses. In addition to that limitation, this provision applies only to covered autos of the private passenger type covered for comprehensive or specified perils. It provides that in the event of *total* theft of a covered auto, the insurer will pay for transportation expenses incurred because of the loss of use of such auto. Payment commences forty-eight hours after the theft and ends, regardless of the policy's expiration period, when the covered auto is returned to *use* or when the insurer pays for the loss. The most the insurer will pay in any event during that period is $10 per day up to a maximum of $300.

Specified Car Versus Blanket Coverage Dealers and nondealers have the same physical damage coverage options, but the insurance is generally handled differently for each.

Coverage for Nondealers. Physical damage insurance on covered autos of nondealers is written on a *specified car basis* (which may be used by dealers who have a limited number of autos). The rating for specified cars is handled in the same way as autos covered under the BAP, and the limit of coverage on each is described in the declarations as the actual cash value or cost to repair, whichever is less, minus the applicable deductible.

Trailer dealers and nondealers who desire physical damage on autos held for sale may obtain blanket coverage comparable to what is available to dealers by completing Item Eleven of the schedule.

Coverage for Dealers. Physical damage insurance on covered autos of dealers is on a blanket basis. However, for limited operations, dealers may elect coverage on a specified car basis, as well. The dealers' supplementary schedule under Item Eight states one amount as applicable to all covered autos at each of the described locations, less the deductible which is to apply to each covered auto, as well as the maximum deductible which is to apply to all losses in any one event, for example, when two or more autos are damaged or destroyed. If a dealer acquires additional locations during the policy period for purposes of auto storage or display, a separate amount of insurance designated in the schedule will apply to those autos for forty-five days. The supplementary schedule for auto dealers makes provision for coverage while covered autos are in transit.

Regardless of the number of covered autos involved in a loss, the most the insurer will pay is the amount stated in the supplementary schedule for the location involving the loss. Likewise, the most the insurer will pay for loss to covered autos in transit is the amount shown in the schedule for transit coverage. These limits are maximums. But whether these amounts are paid depends, in part, on whether the dealer is in compliance with the other special limit of liability provisions. Which of these provisions applies depends on whether a dealer's reporting form or nonreporting form is used.

A reporting form is often used when the value of autos in stock fluctuates. The nonreporting form is used when values are relatively stable or to avoid the need to file periodic reports.

NONREPORTING FORM. When coverage is written on a nonreporting basis, the premium is based on total value of the covered autos stated in the declarations. Insurance to value is enforced by what is comparable to a 100 percent coinsurance clause. The most the dealer can recover is the policy limit for physical damage insurance. If the value of covered autos, at the time of loss, is higher than the policy limit, the dealer will suffer a penalty for underinsurance, because the insurer will pay less than the policy limit. What percentage will be paid is determined by dividing the policy limit by the total value of covered autos at the time of loss.

REPORTING FORM. The dealers' reporting form is similar in concept to the reporting forms used with fire insurance. Because of fluctuating values at one or more locations, coverage is written initially for a provisional amount. Premiums are then based on a monthly or quarterly basis with reports of values submitted to the insurer for those periods with a so-called "honesty clause" which encourages the reporting of proper values. If the value of covered autos at the location in question exceeded what was actually reported in the last monthly or quarterly report, the insurer will determine what percentage the total reported value was of the actual value on the date of the last report and pay that percentage of the loss.

If the report is delinquent on the date of the loss, the most the insurer will pay is 75 percent of the amount of insurance applying to the scheduled location.

Exclusions All of the physical damage insurance exclusions in the BAP are also found in the garage policy. Briefly, these exclusions are wear and tear, freezing, and mechanical or electrical breakdown; blowouts, punctures, or other road damage to tires, unless any one of the foregoing is caused by an otherwise covered loss; loss caused by declared or undeclared war, explosion of a nuclear weapon, or by radioactive contamination; and loss to sound reproducing equipment and accessories (with some exceptions when permanently installed).

In addition, for dealers and nondealers alike, no coverage applies for:

- Covered autos leased or rented to others, except covered autos rented to customers while their autos are left for service or repair. This is a potentially serious exposure because the driving skills and other habits of renters or lessees cannot be determined. For this reason, coverage may be available only from specialty insurers.
- Any covered auto while being prepared for or used in any professional or organized racing contest or demolition or stunting activity. Obtaining coverage on this exposure is often very difficult.
- Loss to any covered auto which is voluntarily parted with by trick or scheme under false pretenses. This exposure may be covered by purchasing false pretense coverage by endorsement.

When an insured is an auto dealership, the following additional exclusions apply:

- The dealer's expected profit on the loss of covered autos.
- Loss to any covered auto at a nonscheduled location that is not reported to the insurer within forty-five days after the dealer's use of the location begins.
- Loss to any covered auto caused by collision or upset of any vehicle transporting it, if the covered auto is insured for specified perils only. Comprehensive or collision insurance is necessary for such losses.

Valuation Physical damage insurance under the basic provisions of the garage policy applies on an actual cash value basis. Thus, aside from any limit that may be designated for this coverage at a particular location, such as when blanket physical damage insurance applies to dealers, payment of loss is limited to the lesser of one of two amounts, over any deductible. The first is the replacement cost of the covered auto and/or its equipment, less any depreciation. The second is the sum required to repair or replace the covered auto and/or its equipment with materials of like kind or quality.

Sometimes a dealer or nondealer may have a vehicle, such as a tow truck, which has expensive specialized equipment that reflects higher than normal values. When this is the case, the vehicle may be written on a stated amount basis by endorsement. When physical damage insurance is written on a stated amount basis, a dollar amount is designated in the endorsement opposite the described auto to be covered in that manner. However, the fact that an auto is written on a stated amount basis does not mean losses are paid at that stated value. In the event of loss to such vehicle, the most the insurer will pay is the *smallest* of the following: (1) the stated amount, (2) the actual cash value at the time of loss, or (3) the cost to repair or replace with like kind or quality.

Deductibles Physical damage insurance is subject to deductibles. When covering an auto dealership, the comprehensive or specified perils deductible applies only to loss by theft, vandalism or mischief. The applicable deductible applies to each covered auto, subject to a maximum per loss deductible, applying to all damaged autos per location. For example, assume nine of a dealer's covered autos are vandalized. Comprehensive coverage is subject to a $100 deductible per auto and a $500 per loss deductible. The most the dealer will have to retain is $500, since that is the maximum per loss deductible.

For all businesses other than auto dealers, the deductible per covered auto applies to all loss under specified perils and under comprehensive to all loss other than fire and lightning.

When dealers and nondealers elect deductibles higher than minimums, credits are applied to the rates. For autos of nondealers, the credits must be computed for each vehicle because the rates are based on such variables as original cost new of the vehicle, its age and territory. For dealers, both comprehensive and specified perils coverage are subject to minimum deductibles of $100 per auto and $500 per occurrence or loss. When the deductible is increased, on either of the two coverages, to $250/$1,000, the rates are reduced by 10 percent, whereas they are reduced by 25 percent when the deductible is raised to $500/$2,500.

Optional Coverages Two types of protection not provided under the basic provisions of the garage policy available for dealers by endorsement at an additional cost are (1) dealers' driveaway collision coverage and (2) false pretense coverage.

Dealers' Driveaway Collision Coverage. Under collision insurance, no coverage applies to any auto while being driven or transported from point of purchase to point of destination if the distance is more than fifty miles apart. Since interdealership transfers of autos are common, the exclusion can create an important gap in coverage. If coverage is desired, driveaway collision coverage may be purchased.

False Pretense Coverage. The physical damage coverage of the garage policy does not apply to loss of any auto which is voluntarily parted with by trick, scheme, or false pretenses of any person entrusted with the possession of a covered auto. For example, if a prospective customer were to test-drive an auto and steal it, the dealer would be without coverage for the loss of the auto (unless endorsed).

When false pretense coverage is purchased by endorsement, it applies to any auto the named insured owns against loss that results from:

    a. Someone causing you to voluntarily part with the covered auto by trick, scheme or under false pretenses.

    b. Your acquiring an auto from a seller who did not have legal title.

Conditions of false pretense coverage are that the named insured (1) must have had legal title to the covered auto prior to loss, (2) must obtain a warrant for the arrest of the person who took wrongful title or possession of the covered auto, as soon as practicable after the loss, and (3) must make every effort to recover the auto when it is located.

The false pretense coverage endorsement requires the location number taken from ITEM FOUR of the dealers' supplementary schedule where coverage is to apply, along with the limit that is to apply to each such location. Regardless of the limits that apply, the most the insurer will pay in the *aggregate* for all loss within a period of one year is $25,000. After that limit is exhausted, the named insured must again purchase the coverage, just as if it were newly purchased. If losses are too frequent, the dealer may have to implement more stringent loss control measures in order to repurchase the coverage.

General Conditions Part VII of the garage policy contains all the conditions applicable to the basic provisions of the policy. All of the conditions of this policy are identical in kind and number to the BAP.

Checkpoints

    1. Compare physical damage insurance written on a specified car versus blanket basis from the standpoint of coverage, limits, and mechanics of coverage.

    2. On what basis is the limit for physical damage insurance on a nonreporting form determined?

    3. List the advantages and disadvantages of physical damage insurance written on a reporting form basis.

    4. Describe the physical damage exclusions and how they may be eliminated for:

        (a) dealers

        (b) nondealers

    5. Explain the conditions under which both driveaway and false pretense coverages may be desirable.

Garagekeepers Insurance

Markets When auto dealers, repair shops, service stations, auto storage garages, public parking facilities, and tow truck operators have the care, custody, or control of customers' autos, they are *bailees for hire.* As such, they may be legally liable for loss to nonowned autos in their possession. If nonowned autos are insured by their owners for physical damage, insurers of the autos may exercise their right of subrogation against the garage. Suits by customers may be brought for the entire amount of loss in absence of physical damage insurance, or for the amount of the deductible when insurance applies.

Garagekeepers insurance is essential to cover these exposures, since the liability coverage of the garage policy excludes damage to property of others in the insured's care, custody, or control.

Nature and Scope of Coverage The garagekeepers insurance included within the basic provisions of the garage policy provides protection on the basis of the garage business's *legal liability.* Thus, for coverage to apply the claimant must prove the garagekeeper failed to exercise the proper degree of care required by the circumstances.

To obtain garagekeeper's insurance, which can be written with or without the liability coverage, symbol 30 must be designated in the policy declarations opposite those of the three groups of perils desired: (1) comprehensive, (2) specified perils, or (3) collision.

Symbol 30 is defined as:

AUTOS LEFT WITH YOU FOR SERVICE, REPAIR, STORAGE OR SAFEKEEPING.

Any auto not owned by you or any of your employees while left with your garage operations for service, repair, storage or safekeeping.

In addition to the symbol designation, the amount of insurance that is to apply at each location is designated in the declarations. The declarations also show the deductible per vehicle, and for dealers, the maximum deductible applicable for all loss involving comprehensive or specified perils in any one event.

When symbol 30 is designated in the policy declarations, the insurer agrees to pay those sums for which the insured legally must pay, subject to three provisos. One is that the insured was attending, servicing, repairing, parking, or storing the covered auto(s) in its garage operations. The second condition is that loss be caused by a peril insured against, and the third condition limits liability for loss at each location to the amount shown in the declarations (or supplementary schedule) for that location, less the applicable deductible.

The insurer also promises to provide defense and to pay all defense costs in any suit involving an otherwise covered auto. However, the insurer's duty to defend or settle any claim or suit ends when the limit of liability is exhausted. In addition to the limit of liability, the insurer agrees to pay a number of other expenses and costs (or supplementary payments) of the same kind and extent as are covered under the BAP and garage liability section.

Persons Insured The persons to whom garagekeepers insurance applies against loss to covered autos are:

1. You are an insured.
2. Your employees, directors or shareholders are insureds but only while acting within the scope of their duties as such.

Presumably "shareholders" is a broad enough term to encompass partners of a partnership, since each partner technically owns a part of such business.

Exposures Excluded Of the seven exclusions that apply to garagekeepers insurance, three are identical to garage policy provisions (loss to sound reproducing equipment, tapes and records, and citizens band radios and similar devices). The fact that coverage against loss to this type of equipment is not covered, and they are especially vulnerable to loss by theft, means that garage businesses must exercise special precautions, such as locking the vehicles when unattended.

In addition, no insurance applies to:

1. Liability which results from any agreement by the insured to accept responsibility for loss (a contractual liability exposure).
2. Loss by theft or conversion caused by the named insured, its employees, or shareholders. It would be against public policy to pay for theft caused by the named insured. Loss by theft or conversion caused by the named insured's employees can be covered with a fidelity bond.
3. Defective parts or materials and faulty work. These two exclusions merely reinforce the intent that defective products or faulty work is a "business risk." To provide coverage against such losses would make the insurer a guarantor of products or workmanship, rather than a provider of insurance.

Garagekeepers Direct Coverage If desired, one of two other forms of garagekeepers insurance may be substituted for coverage on a legal liability basis. One provides direct coverage without regard to liability, on a *primary* basis, and the other provides the same such coverage on an *excess* basis, subject to the same minimum deductibles applicable to legal liability coverage.

Direct Coverage—Primary Basis. With this form losses are paid without regard to the named insured's legal liability. There is no requirement that the vehicle owner first try to collect under the owner's insurance.

Direct Coverage—Excess Basis. With this form losses are paid without regard to the named insured's liability, but coverage only applies as excess over any other collectible insurance.

Rating—Basic Concepts

Rating differs for dealers and nondealers (auto service or trailer sales).

Dealers' Class Plan All persons are first classified into two broad categories: (1) Class I (employees) and (2) Class II (nonemployees). Since the dealers class plan takes into consideration all persons whether or not they are employees, it is very important for producers to cover all ground in determining the operators, the extent to which they will operate a dealer's autos, and their ages.

Class I (Employees). Class I employees are (1) those employees whose duties normally involve the *regular* use of a dealer's autos, such as owners, managers, salespersons, and (2) all other employees who do *not* regularly operate a dealer's autos, such as clerical office and other employees.

Class II (Nonemployees). Those within the Class II nonemployee group could include inactive proprietors, partners, or officers, and family members of active and inactive proprietors, partners, or officers who are furnished or who have regular use of a dealership's autos. This class is also divided into two groups: nonemployees age twenty-five or older and nonemployees under age twenty-five.

Rating Factors. The rating factors, subject to change, are:

- 1.00 for all Class I employees who regularly operate a dealer's auto
- 0.40 for all other employees
- 1.15 for all nonemployees under age twenty-five
- 0.50 for all nonemployees over age twenty-five

DETERMINING THE LIABILITY INSURANCE PREMIUM. First, the number of persons in each class is multiplied by the rating factor to obtain the rating unit. Second, rating units are added together. The resulting sum is multiplied by the liability base premium to obtain the liability premium at basic rates.

MEDICAL PAYMENTS PREMIUM. Medical payments coverage is available for autos only, garage operations only, or for a combination of auto and garage operations. Each of these three options is assigned a factor which varies additionally by the choice of limits desired, ranging from $500 per person to $2,000 per person. Medical payments premium is determined by multiplying the liability premium, at basic limits, by the appropriate factor.

PHYSICAL DAMAGE PREMIUMS. The method of determining the premium for collision coverage is different from that of comprehensive and specified perils coverages.

Insurable values of autos and the "over-the-road" exposure are the two major factors in collision insurance for dealers. For collision rating the following information is necessary:

1. Rating units as for liability insurance.
2. Total values of all owned autos divided by the rating units to determine the "value per rating unit."
3. The adjustment factor, from the table in the garage section of the commercial auto manual, which varies on a graduated scale according to the value per rating unit (the higher such value per rating unit, the lower the adjustment factor).
4. The blanket collision premium (rates per $100 of value) multiplied by the adjustment factor.

The premiums for both comprehensive and specified perils coverages are based on (1) the territory of principal garaging, and (2) whether the autos are garaged in buildings, standard open lots, or nonstandard open lots.

The rates as quoted for types of lots are applied to each $100 value of the covered auto.

GARAGEKEEPERS PREMIUMS. The method of determining garagekeepers premiums is the same for dealers and nondealers. For specified perils and comprehensive coverages, the *premiums*, not the *rates*, vary with (1) the maximum limit of liability (minimum of $6,000), and (2) legal liability or direct primary coverages. Direct coverage excess is determined by multiplying a given factor by the legal liability premium for either specified perils or comprehensive coverage.

Garagekeepers collision coverage is also quoted on the basis of premiums based on the maximum limit of liability and whether legal liability or direct primary coverage is to apply. However, the premiums are further subdivided by the appropriate deductible that is to apply, i.e., $100, $250, or $500. The collision premium for direct excess coverage is determined by multiplying the legal liability premium for the appropriate deductible by a given factor.

Producers should note that the pricing of insurance for new car dealers in many jurisdictions is very competitive and that larger accounts are often written at rates well below publishers manual rates.

Nondealers' Premiums The premiums for repair shops, service stations, storage garages, public parking places, and franchised and nonfranchised trailer dealers are calculated similarly to, and differently from, the approach taken with auto dealers, depending on the coverage.

Liability Premiums. Both auto service operations and trailer sales businesses have less owned auto exposures than do auto dealers. Because of this, the liability premiums of auto service operations and trailer sales do not take into consideration the "over-the-road" exposure. Instead, the basis of premium is $100 of payroll. The rates per $100 of payroll by territory and limit of liability are multiplied by the estimated annual payroll to determine the premium. Annual payroll is determined by using the actual salary of each employee subject to an average maximum of $100 per week. All active proprietors or officers must likewise be included at the fixed amount of $100 per week. Inactive proprietors and officers are not taken into consideration.

Medical Payments Premium. The premium for medical payments is calculated in the same way as for auto dealers.

Physical Damage Premiums. The physical damage premium on trailers held for sale is developed by using the rules and rates applicable to auto dealers. The physical damage premium on autos of both auto service operations and trailer sales is the same as if the autos, trailers, or trucks were to be rated under the BAP.

Garagekeepers Premium. The premium calculation for garage-keepers insurance of auto service operations and trailer dealers is the same as for auto dealers.

Underwriting Information

Insuring garages is a complicated and detailed process. The most important need of the underwriter is a detailed, completed application with all appropriate schedules attached. Pictures of operations and locations are helpful, as are special comments on potentially adverse underwriting information. The producer's goal is to have the insurance written with coverages and a premium appropriate to the exposure. Total honesty is essential.

Checkpoints

1. Explain the exposures covered by garagekeepers insurance.

2. List the garagekeepers exclusions and explain how they might be eliminated.
3. Compare garagekeepers written on a (a) legal liability, (b) direct primary, and (c) direct excess basis.

TRUCKERS POLICY

Because truckers are subject to complex exposures that require special treatment, a special truckers policy was developed. In addition to the standard truckers policy, coverage is also available through specialty insurance companies that draft their own policies.

Because space limitations would make it impractical to discuss the features of all policies presently available to the trucking industry, the remainder of this chapter is devoted to the standard truckers policy of the ISO.

Markets—Eligibility

The commercial auto manual defines "trucker" as "a person, firm or corporation in the business of transporting goods, materials or commodities for another." This definition is broad enough to encompass public, contract, and "exempt commodity" carriers, furniture movers, and even contractors and building supply dealers who haul sand, gravel, and materials for others.

Not eligible by implication are private carriers, i.e., those who haul their own goods, materials, or commodities, and public or private passenger liveries. The truckers policy also is not required by owner-operators of trucks or truck-tractors who hire out their services to other truckers, even though these owner-operators come within the definition of a "trucker." This exception exists because these owner-operators are covered as insureds under the truckers policy of the trucking firm that engages them. However, when these truckers are not engaged in transporting goods for another (such as when the truck-tractor is unhooked from the semi-trailer at its destination), the trucker could be without insurance. This exposure may be covered by using the "truckers—insurance for nontrucking use" endorsement to the BAP, discussed later.

Coverage Characteristics

The ISO truckers policy is patterned after the BAP, and the same readable language approach and coverage mechanics are used. Ten numerical symbols are used to activate coverage using the "40" series of digits. Each of the symbols selected must be designated under the "covered autos" column of the declarations opposite the appropriate coverages in the same fashion as required with the BAP.

With the exception of a few specialized coverages, the addition of two definitions, the modification of another, and a modified persons insured provision, most of the protection offered by the truckers policy corresponds to the BAP. Identical to the BAP are:

Part II—Which Autos Are Covered
Part III—Where And When This Policy Covers
Part IV—Liability Insurance
Part VI—Physical Damage Insurance, except for loss to an auto in the possession of anyone under a trailer interchange agreement
Part VII—Conditions, except for the other insurance provision

Definitions Those definitions of the truckers policy, under Part I—Words and Phrases With Special Meaning, identical to the BAP are: "you" and "your"; "we," "us," and "our"; "accident"; "auto"; "bodily injury"; "insured"; "mobile equipment"; and "property damage."

A definition of the BAP modified under the truckers policy is "trailer." Under the BAP, "trailer" is defined as a semitrailer. Under the truckers policy, "trailer" is extended to include "a dollie used to convert a semitrailer into a trailer."

Two terms found in the truckers policy which do not apply to the BAP are "private passenger type" and "trucker." "Private passenger type" is defined to mean "a private passenger or stationwagon type auto and includes an auto of the pickup or van type if not used for business purposes." The term "trucker" means "any person or organization engaged in the business of transporting property by auto for hire."

Covered Autos and Symbols The truckers policy provides flexible application of policy coverages to exposures through the use of ten "covered auto" symbols. (Actually, there are twelve symbols. However, the last two, 51 and 52, are left blank so they can be used for special covered auto classes when the need arises.) Each of the ten symbols represents a combination of four coverage elements, just as with the other auto-related ISO readable policies.

The first element identifies the type or class of covered auto, such as any auto, owned autos only, or hired autos. The second element defines the insured's legal relationship to the covered auto. Thus, the insured may be the owner or nonowner of the auto. Autos an insured does not own may be further subdivided by (1) hired autos, and (2) nonowned autos, with each having comparable meaning to what applies to the BAP. The third element concerns insurance coverage purchased for the covered auto exposure, as shown in Exhibit 1-5. The fourth element defines the scope of coverage on covered autos acquired after inception of the policy. Symbols 41, 42, 43, 44, and 45, as entered next to a coverage under the "covered autos" column of the declarations, signify blanket and automatic coverage for all autos of the type designated when acquired after the policy inception. On the other hand, symbol 46, which deals with specifically described autos, is subject to the same reporting requirements for newly acquired autos as symbol 7 of the BAP.

Application of Symbols Producers must fully understand when a particular symbol, or combination of symbols, may be used, and what each such symbol does when used. Designating an improper symbol, failing to designate a symbol, or designating the proper symbol for the wrong coverage on the declarations could possibly create problems for the producer.

As shown in Exhibit 1-6, several of the symbols may be used for a combination of coverages, e.g., liability, medical payments, and physical damage. The discussion of symbols and their application will be based on all of the coverages, except trailer interchange agreements. These interchange agreements, peculiar to the trucking industry, are described in detail later.

Any Auto Liability. Symbol 41 is defined as "any auto." The word "auto" appears in bold face type, so the definitions section of the policy determines what that term encompasses. "Auto" includes any land motor vehicle, trailer or semitrailer designed for use on public roads, except "mobile equipment." The term mobile equipment also appears in boldface type, and refers to a variety of land vehicles that generally have little, if any, road use exposure, except for specialized purposes. The reason mobile equipment is not covered by the truckers policy is that the liability exposure for such equipment is normally covered by general liability insurance (Chapter 2). When physical damage insurance is desired on that kind of equipment, it can be handled by inland marine insurance (Chapter 5), or by endorsement to the BAP.

Symbol 41, like symbol 1 of the BAP, is restricted solely to liability insurance. When symbol 41 is used, however, the coverage is referred to as "comprehensive automobile liability insurance," because it provides liability protection on any auto whether owned, nonowned, or hired. The coverage is blanket and automatic, and all auto changes throughout the policy period are accommodated without requiring the insured to report such change or make the change by endorsement. All of these are taken into account at policy expiration or on audit.

Although symbol 41 provides the most desirable liability coverage

Exhibit 1-5
Application of Symbols for Truckers

If the intent is to cover:	The Covered Auto Symbol is:							
	Liability	PIP	Med. Pay	UM	Trailer Interchange	Physical Damage	(Pvt. Pass.) Towing	
Any auto	41	N/A	N/A	N/A	N/A	N/A	N/A	
All owned autos only	42	N/A	42	42	N/A	42	42	
All owned commercial autos only	43	N/A	43	43	N/A	43	N/A	
PIP on all owned autos subject to the law	N/A	44	N/A	N/A	N/A	N/A	N/A	
UM on all owned autos subject to a compulsory UM law	N/A	N/A	N/A	45	N/A	N/A	N/A	
Specifically described autos only	46	N/A	46	46	N/A	46	46	
Hired autos only	47	N/A	N/A	N/A	N/A	47	N/A	
Trailers under interchange agreement (nonowned trailers)	N/A	N/A	N/A	N/A	48	N/A	N/A	
Trailers under interchange agreement (owned trailers)	N/A	N/A	N/A	N/A	49	N/A	N/A	
Autos not owned, hired, or borrowed	50	N/A	N/A	N/A	N/A	N/A	N/A	

Exhibit 1-6
Which Covered Autos Symbols May Be Used
with Each Policy Coverage

Coverage	Covered Auto Symbols									
	41	42	43	44	45	46	47	48	49	50
Liability	X	X	X			X	X			X
Personal Injury Protection				X		X				
Medical Payments		X	X			X				
Uninsured Motorists		X	X		X	X				
Interchange Agreements								X	X	
Physical Damage		X	X			X	X			
Towing and Labor		X				X				

for truckers, and is always recommended, it may not always be possible to obtain it, such as when a trucker's business is split among two or more producers. When a trucking firm is small or is not especially attuned to the loss control programs desired by insurers, underwriters may be reluctant to grant coverage under this symbol. Whatever the reason, producers must keep in mind that it will take three symbols to accomplish what is provided by symbol 41.

Owned Auto Coverage. Symbol 42 may be applied to all policy coverages, subject to one limitation and two exceptions. The limitation is that towing and labor coverage is available only to owned autos of the private passenger type. The exceptions are that symbol 42 cannot be used to obtain no-fault or compulsory uninsured motorists coverages because special symbols apply. Like symbol 2 of the BAP, it nonetheless gives the broadest available protection for all permissible coverages, other than liability, and provides blanket and automatic coverage on all owned autos, trailers, and semitrailers acquired during the policy period. Because liability insurance under symbol 42 applies only to owned autos (trailers the insured does not own while connected to an owned power unit are covered, however), it is essential for producers to designate symbol 47 (hired autos), to obtain insurance on nonowned trailers in an insured's possession which are not connected to an owned power unit, as well as any on other autos of others in the insured's possession. Symbol 50 likewise is recommended for coverage on any nonowned auto exposures which apply at policy inception or arise during the policy period.

Owned Commercial Autos. Symbol 43 is defined as:

OWNED COMMERCIAL AUTOS ONLY

Only those trucks, tractors and trailers you own (and for liability coverage any trailers you don't own while connected to a power unit you own). This includes those trucks, tractors and trailers you acquire ownership of after the policy begins.

This symbol, which has no direct counterpart to the BAP, applies to the same coverages as symbol 42, including blanket and automatic coverage on newly acquired vehicles. This symbol would not be recommended for liability insurance if an insured owns other kinds of autos. But it has advantages when delineating nonliability coverages. For example, if an insured desires specified perils physical damage coverage on trucks and tractors, and comprehensive physical damage coverage on private passenger autos, symbol 42 can be designated for the former coverage and symbol 43 for the latter coverage. If symbol 43 is ever selected for liability insurance, symbols 47 and 50 should be designated.

No-Fault Coverage. Symbol 44 provides blanket and automatic coverage on owned autos subject to no-fault. This symbol is identical in scope and application to symbol 5 of the BAP. When an insured owns any auto subject to a no-fault law in any state, symbol 44 should be designated opposite no-fault coverage in the policy declarations. While it is permissible to use symbol 46 (specifically described autos) instead, symbol 44 is the better of the two approaches to take. It applies to all owned autos subject to the law on a blanket and automatic basis, whereas symbol 46 requires the insured to report each such newly acquired auto for the coverage. Symbol 44 may not be used for any coverage other than no-fault.

Compulsory Uninsured Motorist (UM) Coverage. Symbol 45 may be used only in states with a compulsory uninsured motorists law. This symbol is identical to symbol 6 of the BAP and may be used only for compulsory uninsured motorists insurance. When used, coverage is on a blanket and automatic coverage basis. In states where uninsured motorists coverage is not compulsory, symbols 42, 43, or 46 may be used.

Specific Autos. Symbols 41 through 45 all provide a form of blanket and automatic coverage. Symbol 46, however, confines coverage to specifically described autos, like symbol 7 of the BAP.

Symbol 46 may be used for any policy coverage except interchange agreements. However, it is the least desirable of the symbols because it does not provide blanket and automatic protection and this could present a problem for exposures that arise during the policy period.

Hired Autos. Symbol 47 is defined:

HIRED AUTOS ONLY

Only those autos you lease, hire, rent or borrow. This does not include any private passenger type auto you lease, hire, rent or borrow from any member of your household, any of your employees or agents or members of their households.

Except for two differences, this symbol is the equivalent of symbol 8 of the BAP.

First, hired auto coverage of the truckers policy *does not apply* to any private passenger auto owned by any member of the named insured's household. Without this restriction, the truckers policy could conceivably be used to provide liability or physical damage insurance on a primary basis, if a family member's uninsured auto were to be used in the business. Generally, hired auto coverage applies on an excess basis, if there is other collectible insurance. But if no other insurance applies, hired auto coverage applies on a primary basis.

The second difference is hired auto coverage *may apply* to commercial autos hired from the named insured's employees. The rationale for this provision is to allow coverage in those situations when employees use their own trucks to further the business purposes of their employers. Although a trucking firm does not always have control over the insurance limits that may apply to, say, a hired auto, it would have such control when its own employees are operating personally owned trucks. Producers therefore should recommend that the named insured require liability insurance on employees' trucks at limits comparable to those carried by the named insured in order to maintain hired auto coverage on a true excess basis. A frequency of losses that activates hired auto coverage could present some future availability problems to the trucking firm.

Except when symbol 41 applies, symbol 47 should be used as follows:

1. Liability—alone or in combination with symbols 42, 43, 46, and 50.
2. Physical damage—alone or in combination with symbols 42, 43, or 46. When physical damage insurance is desired on hired autos, the named insured also must decide whether coverage is to apply on an excess or primary basis. If the latter, a section under the supplementary schedule of the policy must be designated as such. In this event, any hired auto will be treated as though it is an owned auto. If this section is not designated, coverage automatically applies on an excess basis.

Nonowned Autos. Other than symbols 48 and 49, which apply to trailer interchange agreements and are discussed later, symbol 50 is the final specific definition:

NONOWNED AUTOS ONLY

Only those autos you do not own, lease, hire, rent or borrow which are used in connection with your business. This includes private passenger type autos owned by your employees or members of their households but only while used in your business or your personal affairs.

This coverage is commonly referred to as "employers' nonownership liability." As such, it generally applies only as excess protection for the named insured, because primary coverage would be afforded to the employer, as any person or organization legally responsible for the use of the owner's auto, under the latter's personal insurance. If no other insurance applies, this coverage under symbol 50 applies on a primary basis to the employer only. Because nonowned autos may be uninsured or insured for inadequate liability limits, symbol 50 is always recommended if symbol 41 is not used for truckers liability exposures.

Trailer Interchange Agreement—Insurance. A trailer interchange agreement among common carriers is an arrangement whereby one trucker will transfer a trailer containing a shipment to a second trucker to transport the trailer to its destination, or to a point of interchange with yet another trucker. This arrangement continues until the cargo reaches its destination. The effect of such an arrangement, which must be in writing, is that truckers will be hauling trailers of others.

Although this arrangement facilitates the movement of property, it creates a loss exposure, because truckers who have possession of nonowned trailers may be held accountable for any damage to such nonowned equipment. Further complicating this situation is that standard and nonstandard truckers policies, alike, exclude loss under (1) liability for property of others in the insured's care, custody, or control, and under (2) physical damage for loss to any covered auto while in anyone else's possession under a written trailer interchange agreement. To overcome these exclusions and obtain protection in these circumstances, truckers must obtain trailer interchange insurance. Under the standard truckers policy, such insurance may be obtained by designating symbol 48 opposite the trailer interchange agreement physical damage perils desired in the declarations of the policy.

POSSESSION COVERAGE. This symbol reads:

TRAILERS IN YOUR POSSESSION UNDER A WRITTEN
TRAILER INTERCHANGE AGREEMENT.

Only those trailers you do not own while in your possession under a written trailer interchange agreement in which you assume liability for loss to the trailers while in your possession.

If there is an even interchange of owned and nonowned trailers, and the insurance ceases when owned trailers of a trucker are in the possession of others, there is no additional premium for this exposure. Of importance, obviously, in understanding precisely when this circumstance applies is the meaning of an *even* interchange.

Assume Alpha, Beta, and Charlie are three truckers who have agreed in writing to interchange each of their five trailers. These truckers agree (1) to insure owned trailers for physical damage from specified perils, and collision with deductibles of $500 applying to both coverages, and (2) to provide the same coverage on each other's trailers while in their care, custody, or control. Thus, when each trucker designates symbol 48 opposite the appropriate coverages in the policy declarations, trailer interchange insurance offsets the two aforementioned exclusions with the following result:

- Alpha's truck policy will cover loss to the trailers in its possession and owned by Beta and Charlie.
- Beta's truck policy will cover loss to the trailers in its possession and owned by Alpha and Charlie.
- Charlie's truck policy will cover loss to the trailers in its possession and owned by Alpha and Beta.

The reason there is no additional premium for this arrangement is that each insurance company is charging a premium for the same exposures, i.e., five trailers for like coverages. It therefore does not make any difference, technically, which trailers they are. But because symbol 48 concerns only those trailers an insured does not own, the insurer of Alpha, in effect, will be insuring the trailers of Beta and Charlie, the insurer of Beta will be covering the trailers of Alpha and Charlie, and the insurer of Charlie will be covering the trailers of Alpha and Beta. The exposures among the three insurance companies will balance in the long run.

TRAILERS IN ANOTHER'S POSSESSION. The occasion could arise when it is impractical to have an even interchange of trailers. Alpha, for example, may have eight owned trailers in the possession of Beta and Charlie, whereas the latter two truckers have only five owned trailers available under the agreement. In a situation such as this one, if coverage is desired, Alpha will be required to purchase additional physical damage insurance on three of its owned trailers because neither Beta's nor Charlie's insurer would be willing to assume liability for more trailers than Alpha and its insurer are required to assume. To obtain physical damage insurance on the additionally owned trailers, symbol 49 must be designated in the declarations of the truckers policy opposite the desired coverage(s).

This symbol reads:

YOUR TRAILERS IN THE POSSESSION OF ANOTHER TRUCK-ER UNDER A WRITTEN TRAILER INTERCHANGE AGREE-MENT.

Only those trailers you own or hire while in the possession of another trucker under a written interchange agreement. When symbol "49" is entered next to a PHYSICAL DAMAGE INSURANCE coverage in ITEM TWO the PHYSICAL DAMAGE INSURANCE exclusion relating to loss to a trailer in the possession of another trucker does not apply to that coverage.

Symbol 49 provides primary insurance on an owned trailer while in the possession of others under an interchange agreement.

Checkpoints

1. Who is eligible for coverage under the truckers policy?
2. Explain the one unique feature of the truckers policy that distinguishes it from the BAP.
3. List the covered auto symbols of the truckers policy which are identical in scope and application to the BAP.
4. Describe a trailer interchange agreement insurable by symbols 48 and 49.

Truckers Liability Insurance

Coverage as provided by the truckers policy is similar in many respects to the BAP. For that reason, the similarities of the truckers policy will be highlighted, while areas of departure from the BAP will be discussed in more detail.

Insuring Agreement The basic provisions of the truckers policy are few, but additional provisions may be required by law and/or may be needed in targeting coverages to the needs of insureds. The basic liability coverage of this policy, like that of the BAP, includes only one peril—the legal liability of an *insured* under common law, statute, or contract—for two coverages, bodily injury liability and property damage liability, caused by an accident and resulting from the ownership, maintenance, or use of a covered auto. The boldface terms which appear in the insuring agreement are all defined under Part I of the policy.

In addition to its promise to pay sums on behalf of the insureds, the insurer agrees to defend any suit for damages, provided bodily injury or property damage is covered. While the defense costs are in addition to the limit of liability, the insurer's duty to defend or settle any claim or suit ends when the limit of liability for any one accident has been paid as damages.

Supplementary Payments Complementing the protection provided to an insured for the payment of defense and/or damages, the truckers policy, like the BAP, includes a number of other benefits under the provision entitled, "We Will Also Pay." These other benefits are exactly the same as discussed earlier for the garage policy.

Exclusions The same nine exclusions that apply to the BAP apply to the truckers policy. Because of the importance of exclusions, particularly in restricting the scope of coverage granted by the broad insuring clause, each will briefly be explained including how the exposures may be covered, if possible.

Insurance does not apply under this policy to:

1. Liability assumed under any contract or agreement. The purpose of this exclusion is to preclude coverage on exposures that can best be handled under other policies or coverages. This is an important exclusion, particularly to truckers who hire vehicles. Generally, when a trucker hires a vehicle and agrees to be responsible for any bodily injury or property damage stemming from the use of such hired vehicle, this exclusion will not preclude coverage, if the trucker would have been liable for the vehicle's use even in absence of such contractual agreement. On the other hand, if the trucker agrees to be responsible for any damage to a hired vehicle, it will be necessary for the trucker to purchase physical damage insurance, most likely on a primary basis. But, as noted later, limitations subject to this latter insurance, such as wear and tear, road damage to tires, and mechanical failure, along with mandatory deductibles, are exposures that will have to be retained by the hirer of such vehicle. As noted, when a trucker agrees to be responsible for damage to any nonowned trailer under a *written* trailer interchange agreement, coverage is available. If a trucker assumes other forms of liability, such as damage to leased premises for truck garaging, fire legal liability insurance may be necessary, as well as, perhaps, other forms of general or contractual liability insurance to handle exposures concerning premises and operations.

2. Any obligation for which the insured or insurer may be held liable under any workers' compensation or disability benefits law or any similar law. Workers' compensation insurance is necessary.

3. Any obligation of the insured to indemnify another for damages resulting from bodily injury to the insured's employee. The purpose of this exclusion is to uphold workers' compensation insurance as the exclusive remedy against the employer, and to

make any such claims or suits against the insured subject to employers' liability insurance.

4. Bodily injury to any fellow employee of the insured arising out of and in the course of employment. The purpose of this exclusion, like (3) above, is to uphold workers' compensation as the exclusive remedy of an injured employee. However, in some states, employees are considered to be third parties against whom injured employees may maintain actions of retribution for injuries caused. While most insurers will not delete this exclusion, they sometimes will agree to provide an employee with defense, when sued by a fellow employee.

5. Bodily injury to any employee of the insured arising out of and in the course of employment by the insured. However, this exclusion does not apply to bodily injury to domestic employees not entitled to workers' compensation benefits. The purpose of this exclusion is to require the employer to purchase workers' compensation insurance, if it is required by law, or employers' liability insurance, if the exposure is not subject to workers' compensation.

6. Property damage to property owned or transported by the insured or in the insured's care, custody, or control. This exclusion is directed at a number of exposures either more appropriately handled under other forms of insurance, or involving too much of a moral hazard to cover. Damage to owned property is excluded because insureds cannot be liable to themselves for damage to their own property. The exclusion of property transported by the insured may have limited application in the future. As a result of the Motor Carrier Act of 1980, truckers are now permitted to negotiate the extent of their liability by providing lower rates for this consideration. Where coverage is needed, cargo insurance (Chapter 5) is available.

7. Bodily injury or property damage resulting from the handling of property:
   a. before it is moved from the place where it is accepted by the insured for movement into or onto the covered auto, or
   b. after it is moved from the covered auto to the place where it is finally delivered by the insured.

This same "loading and unloading" exclusion applies to the BAP. Although this exclusion excepts (and therefore covers) injury or damage during the actual movement of property to and from the covered auto, the remainder of excluded exposure is covered under general liability insurance.

8. Bodily injury or property damage resulting from the movement of property by a mechanical device (other than a hand truck) not

attached to the covered auto. This exclusion, related to the loading and unloading process, is identical to the BAP. General liability insurance is necessary.

9. Bodily injury or property damage caused by the dumping, discharge, or escape of irritants, pollutants, or contaminants. This exclusion does not apply if the discharge is sudden and accidental.

Persons and Entities Insured The truckers policy version of the **WHO IS INSURED** provision is more extensive than the BAP because it coincides with various regulations of the Interstate Commerce Commission (ICC).

Who Is Insured. There are five sections defining who is insured.

YOU FOR ANY COVERED AUTO. The named insured of the truckers policy, like the BAP, is given the broadest coverage of any insured. Such coverage applies to the direct and vicarious liability of the named insured. And, unlike other insureds whose protection is limited to *use* of a covered auto, the named insured also has protection stemming from the ownership and maintenance of covered autos.

PERMISSIVE USERS. Section 2 deals with who is a permissive user of a covered auto. Thus, anyone who has permission of the named insured to use a covered auto, as designated by the symbol(s) in the policy declarations, is an insured with three exceptions.

First, the employee whose owned private passenger type auto is used in the business of the employer (named insured) is not an insured. But anyone else who uses another employee's owned private passenger type auto in the named insured's business, with the latter's permission, is covered—if the auto is an otherwise covered auto. Thus, as to other persons, symbol 41 or 50 is necessary. Because this exception applies only to a private passenger type auto, coverage would apply to an employee who furnishes a commercial vehicle to the named insured employer for trucking use. This provision therefore is unlike the provision of the BAP which precludes coverage to an employee-owned vehicle, regardless of type.

The second excepted permissive user is identical to the BAP. The intent is to prevent coverage on an exposure which is, or should be, covered by a garage policy.

The purpose of the third permissive user exception is to provide coverage for anyone other than the owner of an auto hired by the named insured, including the owner's employees or agents, because the latter should have their own insurance. However, when the named insured is a sublessee of a hired auto, the lessee is considered to be an insured, along with the lessee's employees, but only for the loading or unloading of the covered auto.

BORROWED TRAILERS. A third group of insureds encompasses the owner of a trailer or anyone else from whom the named insured hires or borrows a trailer, when it is connected to another covered auto which is a power unit, such as a truck-tractor. (Aside from symbol 41 which is all-encompassing from the standpoint of covered autos, recall that symbols 42, 43, and 46 include liability coverage on any trailers the named insured does *not* own while connected to a power unit the named insured owns.) However, if the trailer is not connected to a power unit that is a covered auto, coverage will be provided for the owner of such trailer, only while the trailer is (1) being used *exclusively* in the named insured's business, *and* (2) over a route the named insured is authorized to serve. (Since a trailer must be a covered auto, it is important that symbol 41 or 47 apply.) Thus, if an accident should occur while a trucker is carrying part of another's load on the trailer, or the trucker is using the trailer in a deviated route, such owner or lessee of the hired trailer cannot qualify as an insured. However, the qualified route reference is likely to have less significance than when this policy was devised. The reason is the Motor Carrier Act of 1980, which deregulated the trucking industry, also reduced or eliminated some of the restrictions on routes as a fuel conservation measure.

HIRED OR BORROWED AUTOS. The fourth who is insured provision provides the same coverage (or makes the same restriction) on an owner of a hired auto as for an owner of a hired trailer.

OTHER INSURED. The fifth who is insured provision is common throughout all forms of commercial and personal auto insurance. Its purpose is to provide protection to any person or organization which may be vicariously liable for the conduct of any insured. For example, if the named insured were to hire or borrow a commercial vehicle from another trucking firm, and the vehicle furnished is owned by an employee of that firm, the latter would have protection in the event it were brought into a claim or suit, along with the owner of the vehicle and the named insured.

Who Is Not an Insured. The last section of the who is insured provision deals with two groups of persons who are *not* insureds. Under the first "who is not an insured" group, a trucker (other than the named insured and its employees) is not an insured if such trucker either retains losses or does not protect owners of borrowed autos with primary insurance.

For example, a trucker is engaged in transporting property of the named insured on an exclusive basis over an authorized route but uses retention rather than insurance to meet the security requirements of any motor carrier law, such trucker is not considered to be an insured. Such trucker must have auto liability insurance in order to qualify as an insured. This restriction is viewed as a protective measure from the named insured's standpoint, because trucking firms that retain their losses are thought of as being less cooperative in claim situations than insurance companies.

Also, a trucker is engaged in the exclusive transportation of property for the named insured over an authorized route and uses a hired auto, such trucker is not considered to be an insured if the trucker's policy does not cover the owner or lessee of the hired auto on a primary basis. The purpose of this provision is to place the obligation of protecting an owner or lessee of a hired auto—on a primary basis at least—on the hirer of such auto. This is as it should be since motor carrier regulations make truckers responsible to the public for the use of all autos operated by them under their permits whether such autos are owned, hired, leased, or borrowed. On the other hand, if the trucker hired by the named insured does carry insurance covering the owner or lessee of such auto on a primary basis, the trucker is considered to be an insured under the named insured's truckers policy.

The second group in "who is not an insured" includes any rail, water, or air carrier if bodily injury or property damage occurs while the trailer, being transported, loaded, or unloaded by any such carrier is detached from the named insured's covered auto. Although such trailer may be instrumental in injury or damage, coverage is precluded while such trailer is in the care, custody, or control of the designated carriers. Without this restriction, one employee of such carrier would obtain insured status, and, hence, protection under the named insured's truckers policy in the event claim is made against that employee by an injured fellow employee.

Other Liability Provisions Two other provisions under the liability section of the policy concern the application of limits and out-of-state extensions of coverage.

Limit of Liability.   The way in which the policy limit applies when written on a single or split limit basis is identical to the BAP.

Stacking of limits is not allowed in a situation where damages sought are higher than the limits provided. The fact that there may be two (or more) covered autos does not mean that the limits of liability are doubled (or tripled, and so forth). Complementing this provision is the so-called "severability of interests" clause under the definition of "insured," which reads in part, that, except for the limit of liability, the insurance applies separately to each insured who seeks coverage or against whom a claim is made or suit is brought. Thus, if one of the insureds against whom claim is made is found to be without coverage, the policy will still protect others who are covered, up to the limit of liability.

Further, the limit of liability is restricted in a situation where multiple bodily injury or property damage claims or suits are related to one accident. Thus, if a trucker were to be involved in an accident in a tunnel whereby chemicals spill from the tanker, all bodily injury and property damage sustained by motorists, and property damage to the tunnel and its loss of use, including cleanup costs, would be considered as one accident.

The minimum liability limits for common and contract truckers subject to the Motor Carrier Act of 1980 and to the control of the ICC appear in the PRO 82 Course Guide. Whether these *minimum* limits are adequate depends on the exposure. If a trucker desires umbrella liability insurance, chances are that an insurer will require underlying limits of at least $500,000. When truckers are not subject to ICC control, the minimum limits are prescribed by the financial responsibility laws of states. Whether the limits are single or split, there is no issue more crucial to proper coverage than an adequate limit for the insured's needs. The determination of adequate limits for a particular insured is necessarily subjective, but many experienced producers view $100/300/50, or $300,000, as a minimum for any business.

Out-of-State Extensions of Coverage. This provision of the truckers policy is related in scope to that of the BAP. Its purpose is to automatically adjust the auto liability limits of an insured's covered auto, while out of state, where the limits of liability prescribed by public authority or by the financial responsibility law are higher. Also included, when necessary, are minimum amounts and types of other insurance, such as no-fault, while a vehicle is being used in a jurisdiction where such coverage is required. With the possible exception of no-fault insurance as may be required by other states where truckers operate, this provision is likely to have only limited application as to limits, especially if truckers maintain at least $100/300/50 or $300,000 liability limits. The reason is that the financial responsibility limits prescribed by most states are considerably lower. Nonetheless, if a trucker should have lower limits than may be required in another state, the truckers policy will automatically adjust to that higher, minimum amount.

Checkpoints

1. (a) List the exclusions that appear in the truckers policy.
   (b) Where applicable, explain how the exposure excluded can be insured.

2. Define (a) who is and (b) who is not an insured for truckers liability insurance.

Truckers Physical Damage Insurance

All physical damage insurance provisions of the truckers policy are identical to the BAP except for one additional exclusion.

Physical Damage Coverages There are four basic physical damage coverages in the truckers policy:

1. comprehensive,
2. specified perils,
3. collision, and
4. towing (available only for private passenger type autos).

The only supplementary coverage available concerns total theft of a private passenger auto. If a private passenger type auto is a covered auto under this policy for either comprehensive or specified perils, the insurer agrees to pay transportation expenses incurred by the insured of up to $10 per day to a maximum of $300 because of loss of use of such stolen auto beginning forty-eight hours after the theft and ending when the auto is returned or the insurer pays for the loss.

Exclusions The first eight exclusions in the truckers policy are identical to the eight exclusions of the BAP. Briefly, no coverage applies to:

- Wear and tear, freezing, mechanical or electrical breakdown; blowouts, punctures, or other road damage to tires—unless these are caused by other loss covered by the policy.
- Loss caused by declared or undeclared war or insurrection; by the explosion of nuclear weapon; or by radioactive contamination.
- Loss to tape decks or other sound reproducing equipment not permanently attached or installed in the covered auto; tapes, records or other sound reproducing devices; any sound receiving equipment, such as CB radios, two-way mobile telephones, scanning monitor receivers and accessories, unless permanently installed in the covered auto. If coverage is desired for such equipment not permanently attached, it can be purchased by endorsement to the truckers policy, just as it can with the BAP.

The one exclusion unique to physical damage insurance of the truckers policy reads:

Loss to any covered auto while in anyone else's possession under a written trailer interchange agreement. This exclusion does not apply to a loss payee; however, if we pay the loss payee, you must reimburse us for our payment.

Physical damage insurance on an owned covered trailer in the possession of another trucker under a written trailer interchange agreement will be handled by the trucker who has possession of such covered trailer, and symbol 48 is designated in the policy declarations. The exclusion assumes an even interchange of trailers. If a trucker has more of its trailers in the possession of other truckers than the trucker is likely to have in its possession belonging to others, the trucker will require physical damage insurance on those extra trailers, since they will not be covered under the even exchange agreement. To obtain physical damage insurance on those additional owned trailers, it is necessary that symbol 49 be designated in the policy declarations or by endorsement and an additional premium paid. When those requirements are met, the exclusion in question no longer applies.

The fact that this exclusion of physical damage insurance only applies to written trailer interchange agreements means the exclusion does not apply to a covered auto of an insured while in the possession of anyone else, if the possession does not concern an interchange agreement. Thus, a covered auto or trailer in someone else's possession would be covered on a primary basis under the owner's policy, and on an excess basis under the borrower's policy, unless the latter is required to provide physical damage insurance on a primary basis.

Other Physical Damage Coverage Provisions   The two other provisions of the physical damage insurance section of the truckers policy concern (1) the insurer's options for paying losses, and (2) the insured's options for handling glass losses caused by hitting a bird or an animal, or by falling objects or missiles. Both of these provisions are identical to those of the BAP.

Trailer Interchange Insurance

Knowing the purposes for which written trailer interchange agreements are used, and the application of symbols 48 and 49, it is important for producers to become familiar with the protection offered by trailer interchange insurance.

Although an insured under trailer interchange insurance has the option of selecting from among the same coverages (other than towing and labor) as are available with truckers physical damage insurance, there are some important differences between the two coverages.

Nature of Coverage   First, trailer interchange insurance is a "third party" liability rather than a "first party" physical damage coverage.

Coverage is restricted to nonowned trailers, i.e., a trailer, semitrailer, or a dollie used to convert a semitrailer into a trailer, including the trailer's equipment, such as mats, blankets, two-wheeled carts, and permanently attached cranes or refrigeration units. While the perils included under the coverage usually stem from fortuitous and accidental means, coverage is contingent on the named insured's legal liability—meaning the named insured's assumption of liability for loss to a trailer, however a covered loss occurs.

Because trailer interchange insurance hinges on the legal liability of an insured, defense coverage also is provided to the same extent as is available with the liability sections of the truckers policy and BAP.

Exclusions Only six exclusions apply to this coverage. Five of these also apply to physical damage insurance: (1) wear and tear, (2) freezing, (3) mechanical or electrical breakdown, (4) blowouts or punctures to tires, or (5) other road damage—unless these losses are covered under trailer interchange insurance. Also excluded are the catastrophic nuclear and war perils.

Other Insurance Any vehicle of an independent trucker or employee of the named insured which is hired or borrowed *exclusively* for the named insured's business is covered on a primary basis for liability insurance. Also, if someone else hires or borrows a covered auto of the named insured, the latter's policy applies as excess, since primary liability coverage will be provided by the policy of such borrower. Finally, primary coverage on a trailer will at all times be provided by the policy covering the power unit. Thus, if a trailer is connected to a power unit, coverage applies as (1) primary when the power unit is owned, hired, or borrowed by the named insured and used in the named insured's business, (2) excess if the trailer is attached to a power unit that is hired or borrowed by someone else, or (3) excess if the trailer is attached to a nonowned power unit. When a nonowned trailer is not connected to a power unit, coverage is on a primary basis only while used in the named insured's business.

As noted earlier, any nonowned trailer in the named insured's possession under a written trailer interchange agreement is covered on a primary basis. Trailers that an insured owns which are in the possession of another trucker under a written interchange agreement likewise are covered on a primary basis of that other trucker's policy.

For a covered auto the named insured owns, both liability and physical damage coverages are on a primary basis. But when the named insured hires or borrows a covered auto, both liability and physical damage coverages are on an excess basis, except as otherwise provided.

Should the situation arise when this policy of a trucker applies on the same basis of another trucker's policy, this policy will adjust the loss on a pro rata limits basis. However, the situation could even apply when the named insured has two policies in force applying in different jurisdictions. To prevent the stacking of limits, the "other insurance" provision will operate in such a way as to pay the named insured for loss without any possible gain.

Checkpoint

1. Designate whether insurance on the truckers policy is primary or excess in the following circumstances:
   (a) Owned covered autos of the named insured.
   (b) Hired or borrowed autos not used exclusively in the named insured's business.
   (c) A truck-tractor of an independent trucker which is hired for use exclusively in the named insured's business.
   (d) A nonowned trailer attached to the named insured's covered auto.
   (e) A nonowned trailer attached to a hired covered auto of the named insured.
   (f) A nonowned trailer in the named insured's possession under a written interchange agreement.
   (g) An owned trailer of the named insured in the possession of another trucker under an interchange agreement whereby the latter trucker has not agreed to be legally liable for loss.

Product Targeting

The basic coverage provisions of the truckers policy are intended to provide minimum required coverage for the average trucker. If other coverages are needed to target the insurance to the particular needs of truckers, a variety of endorsements are available. Since there are many endorsements, attention here will be focused on those additional coverages with which the producer should be familiar in a sales context.

No-Fault Coverages The truckers policy contains no provisions for no-fault coverages, except reference in the policy declarations. In those states that have no-fault auto insurance laws, a state endorsement is available to meet the requirements. The basic form is usually entitled "personal injury protection endorsement." When this coverage is desired, symbol 44 must be designated opposite those owned autos to be covered and the endorsement must be attached.

Auto Medical Payments Medical payments coverage is not as widely used in commercial auto insurance because workers' compensation is the leading method for handling work-related injuries in autos. However, the occasion may arise when a trucking firm may have company-owned private passenger type autos which may be used for the personal use of the sole proprietor, partners, company executives, or employees, and sometimes to provide transportation for customer-clients or guests. In these circumstances, auto medical payments insurance may be purchased by endorsement. When this coverage is desired, the appropriate owned auto symbol must also be designated opposite this coverage in the policy declarations.

Uninsured Motorists (UM) Insurance Some states require the purchase of uninsured motorists insurance without right of rejection, while other states require it except when rejected in writing by the insured. Although there are significant differences in the uninsured motorists insurance laws of states, most specify that the benefits payable under uninsured motorists insurance will be reduced by any benefits payable under workers' compensation, disability benefits, and other similar laws. If coverage is desired, symbol 45 must be designated if such insurance is compulsory without right of rejection, whereas symbols 42, 43, or 46 are used when such insurance is not compulsory.

Trailer Interchange—Fire and Theft In the event truckers using a written trailer interchange agreement want less expensive insurance on their trailers, coverage can be purchased solely for fire, or for fire and theft. When coverage is purchased for fire only, loss to a trailer the named insured does not own will be covered for fire or explosion, as well as the sinking, burning, collision, or derailment of any conveyance transporting the trailer. When theft coverage is desired, it can be purchased along with the foregoing perils. Theft coverage cannot be purchased alone.

Truckers—Insurance for Nontrucking Use It is common for an owner or lessee of a truck-tractor to haul goods of another firm using that firm's semitrailer for a one-way trip. The trucker carrying the goods of another exclusively and over an authorized route of such other firm is covered under the truckers policy of the firm that hires the trucker. However, once the truck-tractor is unhooked from the semitrailer at its destination, the trucker is without insurance. What the trucker needs for protection while the truck-tractor is unhooked is the "truckers—insurance for nontrucking use endorsement" on its BAP. A trucker is given protection only during the time the truck-tractor is being used for nontrucking purposes. This endorsement is commonly referred to as *bobtail* liability insurance. A truck-tractor is said to be bobtailed when the semitrailer is disconnected from the truck-tractor and is being used by the trucker in circumstances not covered in any lease agreement.

It is common for a trucking firm to lease out its combined truck-tractor and trailer to haul goods exclusively for another concern. When the complete unit is thus used, the truckers policy of the concern whose goods are being transported will protect the trucker to the point of destination or for a round trip if the hirer requires such services and so agrees in writing. However, when the lease agreement between the trucker and the hirer ends with the unloading of the trailer at point of destination, and the trucker must return without a load, the return trip is referred to as *deadheading*.

The essential difference between bobtailing and deadheading is that in bobtailing the trucker is returning only with the truck-tractor while in deadheading the trucker is returning an unloaded trailer. A trucker who is deadheading is in need of the same protection following the completion of a hauling contract as the trucker who is bobtailing.

To avoid any overlap in coverage, as well as any coverage gap, the truckers—insurance for nontrucking use endorsement, when attached to a truckers BAP, does not apply to (1) a covered auto while used to carry any property in any business, or (2) a covered auto while used in the business of anyone to whom the auto is rented. Both of the exposures in (1) and (2) are covered on a primary basis for the trucker engaged to haul for others. This is one of the unique features of the truckers policy. This endorsement provides the trucker with protection when the truck-tractor is not being used for trucking purposes.

Rating—Basic Concepts

In addition to knowing what each symbol of the truckers policy represents, along with the coverages provided in the basic contract and any endorsements, producers must also be familiar with the elements that determine the premiums.

Rating Elements of Liability Insurance In order to determine liability insurance premiums of the truckers policy, producers must first classify the covered autos according to the following categories:

1. *Fleet or nonfleet.* A fleet comprises five or more self-propelled autos of any type which are under one ownership. Not to be included in calculating a fleet are (a) autos of a subsidiary, unless the insured owns majority interest, (b) mobile equipment insured under a general liability policy, or (c) trailers.
2. *Size.* There are six different size classifications of autos, and three classes of trailers. The determinate factor for autos is

gross vehicle weight or gross combination weight. *Gross vehicle weight* (GVW) is defined as the maximum load weight for which a single automobile is designed, as specified by the manufacturer. *Gross combination weight* (GCW) is defined as the maximum loaded weight for a combination truck-tractor and semitrailer or trailer for which the truck-tractor is designed, as specified by the manufacturer.

Trailers are classified according to their load capacity. The various size classes of autos are:

(a) Light trucks—those that have a GVW of 10,000 pounds or less.
(b) Medium trucks—those that have a GVW of 10,001 to 20,000 pounds, including crawler type trucks.
(c) Heavy trucks—those that have a GVW of 20,001 to 45,000 pounds.
(d) Extra-heavy trucks—those that have a GVW of over 45,000 pounds.
(e) Truck-tractors—motorized autos with or without body for carrying commodities or materials, equipped with fifth wheel coupling device for semitrailers. Truck-tractors are of two sizes:
    (1) Heavy truck-tractors—those that have a GCW of 45,000 or less.
    (2) Extra-heavy truck-tractors—those that have a GCW of over 45,000 pounds.

The various size classes of trailers are:

(f) Semitrailers—those that are equipped with fifth wheel coupling devices for use with truck-tractors, with a load capacity over 2,000 pounds. This includes "bogies" used to convert containers into semitrailers.
(g) Trailers—those with a load capacity over 2,000 pounds, other than a semitrailer.
(h) Service or utility trailer—any trailer or semitrailer with a load capacity of 2,000 pounds or less.
  3. *Business Use.* If a truck, tractor, or trailer has more than one of the following uses, the highest rated classification is to be used, unless 80 percent of the use is in a lower rated activity. In that event, the lower rated classification is to be used.
    (a) Service use—for transporting the insured's personnel, tools, equipment, and incidental supplies to and from job locations. This classification is confined to autos principally parked at job locations for the majority of the working day or used to transport personnel between jobs.

(b) Retail use—autos used to pick up property form, or deliver property to, individual households.

(c) Commercial use—autos used for transporting property other than autos defined as service or retail.

4. *Radius.* Radius is determined on a straight line from the street address of principal garaging. The three classes are:

(a) Local—up to 50 miles. The auto is not regularly operated beyond a radius of 50 miles from the street address where such auto is principally garaged.

(b) Intermediate—51 to 200 miles. The auto is operated beyond a radius of 50 miles but not regularly beyond a radius of 200 miles from the street address where such auto is principally garaged.

(c) Long distance—over 200 miles. The auto is operated regularly beyond a 200 mile radius from the street address where such auto is principally garaged.

5. *Zone Rated.* Trucks, tractors and trailers, other than light trucks and trailers, regularly operated at a distance of over 200 miles from the street address where such auto is principally garaged is subject to zone rating, under a separate rating section.

In addition to the foregoing primary rating factors, trucks, tractors, and trailers used in special industry classifications are subject to secondary classifications where rates are either increased or decreased, from the primary rating factor. These secondary rating classifications concern "exempt carriers" (an Interstate Commerce Commission classification) of livestock, other than livestock, all other "exempt carriers"; food delivery; specialized delivery; waste disposal; farmers; dump and transit mix trucks and trailers; contractors; and not otherwise specified classes.

Physical Damage Rating Elements All autos, other than those that are zone rated, are rated for physical damage insurance based upon the primary and secondary rating factors, as used with liability insurance. The combination of the two factors is then applied to a base rate which depends on the appropriate territory of garaging, size of vehicle, age group, original cost new, the coverages desired, and applicable deductible.

Premiums for zone rated autos are calculated by using the zone rating table, based on the original cost new and age group of the auto, along with the long distance rating factor taken from the primary classification table.

Trailer Interchange Factors When there is an even interchange of nonowned trailers and owned trailers with insurance on owned trailers ceasing when in the possession of others, there is no additional premium because the insurer's total liability remains the same.

When insurance on owned trailers is to remain in force while the trailers are in possession of others, coverage is determined by taking into consideration the trailer's radius class while used in the insured's business, a daily per-trailer base rate depending on the radius of use, the coverages desired, the deductible, and the limit of liability per accident.

Underwriting Information

Space limitations do not allow for reproduction of the ACORD application and all relevant truckers policy schedules. However, as with any line of insurance, a complete and honest application is the minimum an underwriter deserves to receive from a producer. A multitude of supporting information can and should be submitted when application information appears detrimental to the producer's client. For instance, if loss history indicates high loss frequencies or severities, these should be explained and corrective actions noted. Pictures of new twelve-foot, chain link fencing to minimize vandalism losses and copies of new maintenance schedules or mechanic training requirements are just a few examples of supporting evidence. In some cases, even a visit by the underwriter with the trucker's management may be helpful. Truckers insurance is a difficult line to place, and extra work on the application and supporting information is essential for the producer of this business.

Checkpoints

1. For whom is the "truckers—insurance for nontrucking use endorsement" intended and to what policy is the endorsement attached?
2. List the five rating factors for truckers liability insurance.
3. List the information required to rate a trucker for physical damage insurance.

MARKETING GARAGE AND TRUCKERS INSURANCE

Producers who wish to sell insurance to garage and trucker businesses meet three prerequisites before they can begin to prospect. They will have to: (1) learn as much as they can about the special needs of the markets, (2) match the prospective markets with insurers willing to accommodate those markets, and (3) have a working knowledge of the products, including rating techniques.

Specialized Needs of Markets

With the possible exception of the larger franchised auto dealerships, the needs of most garage businesses are not any more complex than any other commercial account. A tool for the producer who desires to handle the more complex garage businesses is a survey and/or questionnaire form which will alert the producer to the kinds of coverages that should be considered.

The trucking business, on the other hand, is a highly specialized business, particularly with respect to common (public) and contract carriers. Generally, specialty insurers offer expert coverage assistance, with the proper information about a prospective insured, so the producer does not have to be well-versed on the subject. Nonetheless, the more producers know about the trucking industry, the better off they will be. Unfortunately, there is no single source of information available to assist producers with the complexities of this business. To learn about the various aspects of the trucking industry, producers may have to subscribe to trucking association magazines, attend trucking association meetings, if possible, and attend risk management and insurance seminars on this specialty which are occasionally offered by various professional organizations. Producers may find trade publications that feature articles on these markets worthwhile reading.

Matching Markets with Insurers

Producers who arrange coverage for auto dealers and/or nondealers may sometimes find the standard insurers highly selective about this class of business. For example, not all insurers are willing to write franchised dealers, while other insurers are not interested in nonfranchised auto dealers, dealers with nonstandard open lots, or auto repair shops that perform diagnostic or other specialty work. In the final analysis, much of the producers' success in placing the business with standard insurers will depend on the individual characteristics of the prospective insured, the loss history, particularly with respect to the auto exposure, the potential premium volume in relation to the exposure, and the need to provide accommodation lines.

If producers are going to prospect, they should have a general understanding with the insurers on what markets are acceptable. Since not all such markets will be acceptable, producers should also develop a secondary source in which to place the business. An alternate source is with specialty or excess and surplus line insurers. Because some excess and surplus lines insurers offer packaged programs for certain garage businesses, one or two of these insurers may very well turn out to be the primary insurers for producers.

Most standard insurers will handle some smaller truck accounts, including building and supply dealers and dump truck contractors. However, with the exception of a few standard insurers that have the expertise and willingness to write long-haul truckers, most such firms are handled either by specialty insurers or excess and surplus lines insurers.

There are many stable specialty insurance companies that make a market for truckers. The policies are generally designed by the insurers and therefore will be nonstandard in nature.

Specialty insurers or their brokers advertise in insurance trade publications, and producers should have no problem contacting one or more of them. Even if the producer knows little about the coverage needs of trucker markets, there are certain factors which the producer must first consider before selecting a specialty insurance company. First, and perhaps most important, is the stability of the insurer, i.e., its willingness to remain in that business despite losses or cyclical downturns. Other factors to consider are the insurer's willingness to provide high limits, coverage for unusual or difficult exposures that may arise, and prompt coverage, loss control, claims, and underwriting services. Once the producer is satisfied with a specialty insurer, the producer may have to be licensed with that insurer, although in some cases the business can be placed on a brokerage basis.

Not all truckers necessarily will meet the qualifications of specialty insurers, especially those with high loss frequency or severity, or those without suitable loss control programs. To continue servicing such accounts, producers again will have to establish a secondary source for placing such business. The only alternative might be an insurer that specializes in substandard business.

Working Knowledge of Products

Whether producers deal with standard, specialty, or excess and surplus line insurers, producers must understand the coverage provisions of the policies for no other reason than to explain them to clients. To this end, the policies of standard insurers will be the easiest to understand, since, with the possible differences in format, most of the provisions will be the same among the insurers. On the other hand, the policies of specialty insurers, including excess and surplus lines insurance companies, do not use the simplified language approach. In fact, some of the terms and conditions may be completely foreign to the usual insurance terminology.

SUMMARY

Garage and trucking businesses present auto exposures similar to other businesses. In response to these similar exposures, garage and trucker's auto insurance policies resemble the BAP. However, because garage and trucking businesses have unique auto exposures (care, custody, and control, and trailer interchange agreements), the commercial policies for the complete auto exposures are necessarily different. Because the general liability exposures of garages and trucking businesses are relatively minor compared to the auto exposures, many insurers will include general liability insurance at little or no extra premium.

Of the commercial insurance coverages discussed to this point in the Producer's Program, this chapter offers producers the clearest opportunity to segment markets and target products. There are many types of potential clients for "garage" coverages, and truckers are reasonably easy to identify. Yet within each of these segments of the commercial auto insurance market are groups that can be further segmented. For instance, the garage segment contains the "auto body shop" segment and the trucker's segment contains the contract trucker segment. Each prospect within these subsegments has exposures unique to its business. Understanding the basic nature of the garage or trucking business and the uniqueness of the subsegments offers the producer the opportunity to target the garage or trucker's policy to the needs of these markets.

As the producer further segments a market like garages, it is possible and probable that a specialty insurer will have to be found. The specialty insurer could be a division or department of a so-called "standard" insurer or could be an excess and surplus lines insurer. In any event, a producer who understands the needs of either the garage or trucker's markets (the exposures to loss of those markets), who can target a product to those needs (suggest and use appropriate endorsements), and can locate an insurer willing to write the business has found one area of specialization in the insurance production business. Coupled with learning the general liability exposures and available insurance products for those exposed presented in the next two chapters, producers can become expert in selling a specialized product to a market segment.

CHAPTER 2

General Liability Insurance

INTRODUCTION

Liability insurance has been readily available except for coverage of the most hazardous operations. Even the availability crisis in products liability insurance during the early and mid-seventies never quite reached its expected or fabled proportion. The so-called "products liability crunch" did have serious implications, but only in selected areas—not for liability insurance generally. Where problems did exist, they were problems of cost rather than problems of availability.

Since the mid-seventies, premiums for liability insurance have been lowered in many states and in almost every state it can be said that premium increases, if any, have not kept pace with the rate of inflation. In those states having open competition rating laws, liability insurance often is the line of insurance sought most zealously by insurers and thereby receiving the largest premium discounts.

Producers face an ideal situation regarding liability insurance. Most insurance companies that write liability insurance willingly accept, even encourage, placement of the liability policy. Premiums are generally reasonable. There is a sizable market of buyers: every organization needs liability insurance.

Owners and operators of every kind of organization—business, nonprofit, and governmental—need liability insurance, and they need it even before opening the doors. In fact, it could be ruinous to operate an organization without this protection unless all liability exposures have been effectively transferred (an impossibility) or proper retention techniques have been utilized.

The firm's premises and, usually to a greater extent, operations, provide the potential for claims for bodily injury or property damage arising out of negligence. Since negligence is decided by law, often in the courts, the producers' job should be relatively simple. That is, the producer's job would appear to be to sell a policy that insures against the results of negligent acts with high enough limits of liability protection. Unfortunately, it is not that simple.

The operations of any organization present a variety of liability possibilities. Liability insurance, like all kinds of insurance, contains exclusions. Some excluded exposures can be added by endorsement. Other exposures cannot be endorsed, creating gaps in coverage that must be explained. Finally, there is the question of how much liability insurance is enough. There is no reliable formula for determining how much liability insurance is needed. This problem may be solved when an umbrella liability policy is sold, if the producer sells enough insurance to satisfy the underlying insurance requirement of the umbrella liability policy. Otherwise producers should always recommend very high limits of liability coverage, insist the insured buy enough, and let clients know in writing when they purchase less than the amount recommended. This may not help the producer retain the business if a loss exceeds policy limits, but it may help mitigate an errors and omissions claim.

COMMERCIAL LIABILITY EXPOSURES

Commercial liability exposures vary based on the type of organization under consideration. For instance, the preceding chapter discussed the auto related liability exposures of garages and trucking firms. The discussion here relates to liability exposures arising from the possession of land and the activities of the organization. For instance, J&T Appliances has certain exposures because it leases a building. It has some additional exposures because of the particular type of business it operates. Similarly, Dr. Gale has a "professional liability exposure" because of his medical practice.

Exposures arising out of the possession of land are called *premises* exposures. Exposures arising out of the activities of the organization are called *operations* exposures. Each of these exposures and exposures arising from contractual agreements, the use of subcontractors, and professional operations will be reviewed in this section. The forms of liability insurance available to cover these exposures will be treated in the concluding section of this chapter and in the next chapter.

Premises Liability Exposures

Premises liability exposures arise from the nature of our legal system (torts) and the possession of land.

Legal Requirements Most organizations are exposed to tort liability from the concept of negligence. On occasion they are exposed to liability for intentional interference. Some are further exposed because the law imposes strict liability. In all three cases, the producer should be aware of potential liability to be able to recommend the most appropriate liability insurance coverage for a client.

Negligence. Negligence is the failure to use that degree of care which a reasonable person in the same situation would use in order to avoid injury to another. Negligence can be an act or the failure to act to correct a situation. For example, a store owner, in an attempt to have an attractive store, may have plants and hanging baskets throughout the store. An employee may be charged with the care of the plants. If the employee excessively waters the plants and water overflows the containers, the act of watering the plants (an overt act) could make the floor slippery and result in an injury to a customer. In the same situation, if the employee knew that the floor was slippery and made no attempt to mop up the spilled water, the failure to act could create the negligence.

Intentional Interference. The torts associated with intentional interference are trespass and nuisance. In either case, the possessor of land takes some action that either interferes with others' rights (trespass) or creates a condition which is dangerous to health, is indecent, offensive to the senses or creates an obstruction (nuisance).

Assume J&T Appliances begins construction on a new facade for its building. During the construction, the front entrance to an upstairs office is blocked. Blocking the entrance deprives the organization operating out of the second floor of some rights to their property and may be classified as trespass on the part of J&T. Similarly, if J&T made a practice of burning the shipping crates of appliances they received for sale, the resulting smoke could create a nuisance to others in the area.

Strict Liability. Strict liability may be imposed when a condition or activity exposes others to an unreasonable potential for harm. The degree of care used to protect others usually is not considered. The condition or activity is so dangerous, the possessor is held strictly liable. Strict liability is most likely to be imposed when a dangerous instrumentality is used or an ultra hazardous operation is conducted.

DANGEROUS INSTRUMENTALITIES. Dangerous instrumentalities include dynamite, gasoline, explosives, firearms, animals, and others. For example, a jewelry store may use tarantulas in their display cases to discourage theft. If an individual establishes that he was bitten by one of these tarantulas while "peaceably conducting himself in a place where he may lawfully be," the owner of the store could be held strictly liable.

ULTRA HAZARDOUS OPERATIONS. The classic example of an ultra hazardous operation is blasting activities. Blasting is considered so inherently dangerous that, regardless of negligence, the blaster is strictly liable for injury or damage.

Legal Requirements and Duties. An important link proving a tort is the existence of a duty to the injured person (see Chapter 3, *Principles of Insurance Production).* The liability exposures arising out of negligence, intentional interference and strict liability can be more clearly seen in conjunction with the duties possessors of land owe to others.

Duties of Possessors of Land The possessor of land owes different duties to those outside the premises and to those on the premises.

Duties to Those Outside the Premises. Premises must be maintained in a manner which will protect persons from all chance of harm arising from the use of the premises. An owner or possessor of land has a duty for hazards of use from such things as signs, sidewalks, snow and ice, parking lots, pollution and conditions of the land. A sign, for instance, must be erected with care for the safety of others and must be maintained safely. Similarly, a mercantile operation holding a "sidewalk sale" will be responsible for any unsafe conditions created by the sale. With a snowfall, the usual rule is once possessors have voluntarily undertaken snow or ice removal, they are under duty to exercise care in the removal. Parking lots for customers must be maintained in a safe condition. Pollution, voluntary (as in the J&T burning example) or involuntary (an oil leak), may create a nuisance. Finally, natural conditions on the land usually do not create a duty. However, if a natural condition, such as a lake, is used by the organization for business purposes (swimming), the possessor of that lake must take care for the safety of the customers.

Duties to Those on the Premises. Persons entering premises of another would usually fall into three categories recognized by the majority of courts: business invitees, licensees, or trespassers.

BUSINESS INVITEES. A business invitee usually is an individual invited onto the land for the mutual benefits of the occupier and invitee. Commonly included as business invitees are such persons as customers, those accompanying customers, people making deliveries, meter readers, garbage collectors, and even tax appraisers and collectors. The slightest business advantage to the possessor places the person in the business invitee category.

The duties owed to business invitees are:

- Exercise reasonable care for their safety
- Warn them of any dangerous conditions which are not obvious and are known to the possessor
- Make inspections at reasonable intervals to discover and correct dangerous conditions

The failure to do any of these duties may result in negligence.

DUTIES TO LICENSEES   A licensee usually has the consent of the possessor of land but is on the land for the licensee's personal benefit. Persons normally included in this category are door-to-door salespersons, solicitors, people borrowing tools, visitors on land at the visitor's request, and social guests (in most states).

The duties to invitees are to exercise reasonable care for the safety of the invitee and to warn them of any dangerous conditions known to the possessor of the land. There is no duty to inspect the land. The invitee accepts the land in the same condition and circumstances as the occupier.

TRESPASSERS.   A trespasser is a person who is making illegal use of another's real property. The possessor of land owes no duties to a trespasser but may not create any dangerous conditions expressly for the trespasser. A business could not, for instance, set a shotgun aimed at the back door that will automatically fire at a burglar on entry.

EXCEPTIONS.   As with any common law rule, the exact interpretation of invitee, licensee, and trespasser will vary from jurisdiction to jurisdiction. The producer should be aware of local law. Similarly, children may or may not be exempted from the trespasser category depending on a number of factors, including the child's age and the relative attractiveness of the property to the child. Landlords and tenants may also have certain contractual relationships that modify the extent of liability between themselves and among the general public. The producer should always examine any leases or other contracts that may modify existing law in the state of residence.

Operations Liability Exposures

Any organization is under a duty to conduct its operation with reasonable care to avoid injury or property damage to others. The duty of care will vary depending on the type of operations conducted. An explosives manufacturer might be required to exercise extreme care to prevent explosion and fire and to have fire-fighting equipment readily accessible. A manufacturer of screws, nuts, and bolts would probably not have the same requirements.

Operations liability exposures can exist on or off the premises.

On Premises Operations Liability Exposures On premises liability exposures from operations are similar to those of the explosives and bolt manufacturers. Also included would be such items as operations of elevators, safe operations for employees (covered by workers' compensation insurance) and any other liability exposures from the use of premises.

Off Premises Operations Liability Exposures Three general categories of off premises operations exposures are business operations, use of autos (covered by business auto insurance), and products. An example of business operations would be J&T Appliances installing a dishwasher or repairing an appliance in the home. R. P. Davis's construction activities would most likely take place off premises. Dr. Gale's activities in a hospital or on a house call could be considered off premises. The products exposure, discussed next, occurs when a firm places a product in the "stream of commerce." The firm may be subject to liability if a defective product causes bodily injury or property damage to others.

Products and Completed Operations Hazards

A second identifiable set of exposures to liability arise from the products manufactured or sold by a firm (products liability) and the use of property after construction or installation by the firm (completed operations liability). In products liability, an article or personal property reaches the user or consumer through a chain of distribution beginning with the manufacturer. Completed operations refers to erection, repair, or alteration, usually of real property. The products hazard involves losses resulting from goods or products manufactured, sold, handled, or distributed by an organization. The completed operations hazard includes situations in which the organization is engaged in rendering services rather than in the business of handling goods or products.

Products Liability Exposures If a user or consumer sustains an injury or property damage caused by a product that was unsafe, dangerous, or defective, or if the manufacturer, distributor, or retailer failed to meet the legal duties imposed with respect to a particular product, legal liability may be imposed. The liability may be imposed based on an alleged contractual relationship or based on tort liability.

Contractual Actions. Historically, courts reasoned that only contracting parties—the buyer and seller—were able to assert a cause of action against the other. This was known as privity of contract. One who was not a party to the contract of sale had no legal status and could not maintain an action. In 1916, privity was upset and few jurisdictions still adhere to it as an element to be established in a products action based on contract. In fact, in those states where the Uniform Commercial Code (UCC) has been enacted, the privity requirement is abolished. Instead, under the Code, actions are based on breaches of either express or implied warranties.

EXPRESS WARRANTIES. In the sale of personal property, a warranty may be described as a statement or representation as to the character or quality of goods sold made by the seller to induce the sale and relied on by the buyer. It usually arises as part of the sales contract. If the warranty is breached and the buyer sustains injury as a result of reliance on the warranty, the seller is liable in an action for damages.

Under the UCC, a "seller" is anyone who places the goods in the stream of commerce. The term includes not only the immediate retailer but the manufacturer as well. Both may make an express warranty, in which case either or both may be held liable. Advertising representations, particularly with regard to safety, have been found to be "material misrepresentations" which create express warranties.

IMPLIED WARRANTIES. There are three general types of implied warranties in the sale of a product:

- Warranty of title
- Warranty of merchantability
- Warranty of fitness for a particular purpose

When an article is sold, the seller warrants that the seller has title and ownership or that the seller has been authorized by the owner to pass title. The *warranty of title* rarely is a cause of products liability actions.

The *warranty of merchantability* means the seller warrants the goods are of such quality that they will be reasonably fit for the ordinary uses to which such products are put. For example, a football helmet should be designed and constructed in such a manner that it can safely be used to play football. Further, the helmet is warranted to be of medium quality (unless statements are made to the contrary) and will compare favorably with other helmets of like kind and description on the market.

A *warranty of fitness for a particular purpose* generally means the seller, if the seller knows the intended use of the product, has warranted the product as fit for that use. For example, if a customer wants a hammer to use with a cold chisel to break up concrete and the seller recommends the wrong type of hammer for that particular use and damage results, there may be a breach of warranty of fitness for a particular purpose.

BREACH OF WARRANTY DAMAGES.   The damages sought for a breach of warranty action could be for any or all of:

- Property damage—the measure of damages will be an amount which will reasonably compensate the user or consumer for the loss sustained.
- Bodily injury—the measure of damages might consist of an amount which will reasonably compensate the injured person for out-of-pocket expenses, loss of wages, pain and suffering, and permanent injury if any.
- Wrongful death—a statutory remedy sometimes not allowed in a products action.

Tort Actions.   The user or consumer of a product may bring a tort action against a seller including the retailer or manufacturer if it can be established that the seller failed in one of the duties owed to the user or consumer. The usual duties of the seller include avoiding intentional deceit, not being negligent, or incurring strict liability.

INTENTIONAL DECEIT, FRAUD, OR MISREPRESENTATION.   A seller who makes untrue statements to the buyer, either through general advertising or by direct statements is liable to the user or consumer if the product does not meet the standards claimed for it and the user or consumer has suffered injury. Sellers are considered to be experts when it comes to the ingredients and properties of the article which they sell. The consumer is not such an expert. Therefore, the burden of providing proper information lies with the seller.

NEGLIGENCE.   The allegation that a manufacturer was negligent may be raised with respect to the manufacturer's violation of a duty in (1) product design, (2) construction or assembly or packaging of the product, or (3) warnings, labels, and instructions which accompanied the product. Therefore, the manufacturer owes the buyer the following duties:

- Safe design
- Safe manufacture, construction, assembly, and packaging
- Test and inspect
- Warn and instruct

In some negligence actions, the plaintiff does not have to prove negligence or failure to perform a duty. Instead, the plaintiff would argue that injury could not have occurred had the manufacturer not been negligent. In other words, the occurrence "speaks for itself" *(res ipsa loquitur).* The classic example is the explosion of a soft drink container.

Completed Operations Exposures Completed operations exposures arise out of services performed by a firm, after the performance of such services has been completed. The work could consist of the erection of an entire building, an alteration, or minor repairs. The phrase "completed operations liability exposures" refers specifically to the liability, if any, of a contractor which remains *after all of the work has been completed and abandoned by the contractor.*

Criteria for Loss. The completed operations hazard has at least two criteria that must be met for a loss to have occurred. First, the bodily injury or property damage must arise from improper performance of a completed task; from the contractor's use of defective materials, parts, or equipment; or from an operation, which while not performed erroneously or with inappropriate materials, is not as warranted by the contractor. The second necessary element is that the performance giving rise to the injury be completed or abondoned by the contractor at premises other than those owned by or rented to the contractor.

Examples of Losses from Completed Operations. Losses from completed operations may fall into any or all of the following five categories:

- Bodily injury or property damage to the user caused by completed work—collapse of a finished building is an example.
- Loss of use of property because of failure of the completed work to serve its purpose or function—a defect such as a faulty gas installation causing a building to be declared untenable until repairs are made. The subsequent loss of rents could serve as a measure of damages.
- Damage to completed work arising out of the work or out of the materials or equipment furnished—an example would be engine damage because the wrong type of oil was put in the engine after an oil change.
- Expenses to withdraw, inspect, repair, or replace any work which has been completed—in the engine example, the cost to repair or replace the engine would be an example.
- Loading and unloading of vehicles—if a contract calls for delivery or pickup of an item, the contractor may be held liable for any loss or damage to the load which is transported, from the time of pickup until the load reaches its destination.

Two examples of firms with a completed operations exposure from the four cases are R. P. Davis's contracting firm and J&T Appliances.

Contractual and Protective Liability Exposures

A third set of liability exposures are contractual (liability assumed under contract) and protective (liability arising out of the use of independent contractors) liability exposures.

Contractual Liability Exposures Almost every commercial transaction in which a contract is involved exposes the parties to the contract to liability. These agreements sometimes determine who shall bear the cost of suit. Parties to a construction contract, for instance, may agree in advance on who will bear the liability should bodily injury or property damage losses occur because of the activities involved in the contract. Municipalities ordinarily require an indemnity agreement before they will issue a permit to build a vault under a sidewalk area—that is, the property owner bears the exposure to loss.

As a general rule, courts will enforce an agreement to transfer the exposure to liability loss, if it shifts the cost of ordinary negligence to a party that is voluntarily assuming the exposure. Usually, such provisions or agreements either indemnify the party or exempt a party from liability with respect to a certain matter.

Examples of Contracts with Tort Liability Assumption. Liability loss exposures are often transferred in connection with construction contracts, purchase order and sales agreements, incidental agreements, and surety agreements.

CONSTRUCTION CONTRACTS. Usually the contractor will agree to indemnify the owner against tort liability resulting from a class or classes of occurrences specified in the contract. Courts will uphold contractual assumptions of tort liability in construction contracts which are reasonable attempts to predict and allocate the costs of possible accidents associated with a construction project, especially where one party assumes liability for actions, negligence or omissions connected with its own activities.

Purchase Order and Sales Agreements. There is uncertainty as to whether, in a contract for the sale of goods, an attempt by one party to shift tort liability to the other party will be effective. Courts sometimes limit shifts of liability, discussed later. Sales agreements and purchase orders may contain terms intending to shift or transfer liability. Parties to such contracts must be made aware of the attempt to transfer liability in order to insure them, if possible.

Incidental Contracts. There are a number of contracts an organization enters into which contain transfers of liability. Almost universally, liability insurance contracts will assume the liability in certain so-called *incidental contracts:*

- Leases
- Easement agreements except in connection with construction or demolition operations on or adjacent to a railroad
- Indemnification of a municipality when required by municipal ordinance, except in connection with work for the municipality
- Railroad sidetrack agreements
- Elevator or escalator maintenance agreements

SURETY AGREEMENTS. Generally a surety is one who is primarily liable for the debt or obligation of another. A surety agreement involves three parties: (1) the *surety* who is liable for (2) the *principal* (debtor or obligor) who in turn is obligated to the (3) *obligee* or creditor. The liability of a surety is measured by and is limited to that assumed by the terms of the surety agreement or "bond." Surety agreements are not covered by general liability insurance and are discussed in Chapter 8.

Limitations on Liability Transfers. Three types of agreements transferring liability that courts usually will not uphold are (1) contracts of adhesion, (2) contracts with public carriers, and (3) employment contracts.

Where one party drafts the contract and the other party must either accept or reject it, courts fear the nondrafting party may have had to sign the contract and will hence not enforce its provisons against that party. These situations are common when any party is in an inferior bargaining position. A disclaimer of liability in small type on the reverse side of a job order is a good example of a contract of adhesion unlikely to be upheld by the courts.

It is generally held that those engaged in public service may not bargain against liability for harm caused by their negligence in the performance of their public duties. A common carrier, for example, may not attempt to exempt itself from liability for the negligence of itself or its servants. In some cases, common carriers may limit their liability, but a total exemption is not allowed.

In an employment contract, an employer may not attempt to exempt itself from liability for injury to its employees. This rule recognizes the courts' reluctance to lessen the employer's duty to keep the job area safe for its employees.

Protective Liability Exposures The principle of protective liability exposures is that one party may be held liable for the negligent acts of a second party—even though the first party is otherwise free from all fault, did nothing to aid or encourage the second party's negligence, played no part in it, or even possibly did everything possible to prevent it.

The following example will clarify the type of loss exposure involved. Contractor A employed subcontractor B to perform the plumbing work in A's construction project. A presumed that any negligence by B would result in a claim against B, and that A would not be implicated. Therefore, A did not recognize that a new exposure had developed, and made no preparation to treat the exposure. However, when a claim developed because one of B's plumbers negligently dropped a pipe on the head of a passerby, the claimant sued both A and B. (Although A was not actually doing the plumbing work, it was alleged that A was vicariously liable for the acts of B.) Because A had not recognized the exposure to loss arising out of the acts of independent contractors, and had not made plans to treat the exposure, A was faced with defense cost. If the courts found A responsible for any liability in this case, A would also have been responsible for paying the damages.

The term "protective liability" is derived from the name of the insurance policies that provide coverage against this exposure by "protecting" a building owner or contractor against third-party claims arising from hiring independent contractors.

Professional Liability Exposures

The final liability exposure treated here is professional liability. A professional is one who possesses the special knowledge and skill necessary to render a professional service. Typically, this knowledge and skill result from a combination of the person's education and experience in a particular branch of science or learning. Professionals include physicians, surgeons, dentists, attorneys, engineers, accountants, architects, insurance agents, and brokers.

Two types of actions—contract or tort—are possible in a professional liability claim. Contract actions are created to protect the interest of the parties in having promises performed. Tort actions protect a party's right to freedom from various kinds of harm. The underlying duties of conduct are imposed by the law for social reasons. A professional's violation of a duty owed a client can give rise to a contract cause of action, a tort cause of action, or both.

Contractual Obligations of a Professional When a client hires a professional to perform a particular service, a contractual arrangement is created. A contract is a promise or a set of promises which the law recognizes as a duty. The law also provides a remedy should this duty be breached. To have a valid, enforceable contract, there must be (1) an offer, (2) an acceptance of the offer, (3) some consideration, (4) parties having capacity to contract, and (5) a lawful objective. A contract can be either oral or written, unless specifically required by statute to be written.

The person making the offer to form a contract is usually the person seeking the services of the professional. Although written contracts may be entered into—for example, when attorneys agree to represent injured parties on a contingent fee basis—most professional contracts are undoubtedly oral and usually are created when the professional verbally agrees to perform certain services for the client. Acceptance of the contract usually occurs when the professional either affirmatively indicates willingness to perform the service or actually performs the specified act required.

A professional who agrees to perform services for a client is under a duty to perform as promised and at the specified time.

There are three recognized levels of performance: (1) complete or satisfactory performance, (2) substantial performance, and (3) material breach. Complete or satisfactory performance consists of performance which meets accepted standards; this level of performance entitles the professional to the contract price. Substantial performance falls short of complete performance only in minor respects; it entitles the professional to the contract price less any damages the client may have incurred from not getting complete performance. A material breach occurs when the professional's performance is defective in some major respect. In this case, the professional may not be able to recover the contract price and may be liable in money damages to the client for all injuries suffered by the client as a result.

When a professional has failed to perform contractual obligations as promised and the other party has suffered an injury or damage as a result, the injured party is entitled to be placed, as nearly as is practical, in the position he or she would have occupied had the contract been performed as promised. In most cases, especially where professionals are involved, money damages will substantially place the injured party in the position the client would have held had the contract been performed.

Tort Obligations of a Professional Each member of society is required to follow a course of conduct which does not fall below a recognized standard in the course of daily activities. Professionals are held to a *higher standard*. In either case, failure to maintain the accepted standard of conduct will expose the person to liability for any damage caused to another person.

Checkpoints

1. Is liability insurance generally an "easy" sale?
2. List the major commercial liability exposures.

3. List the duties of a possessor of land to:
   a. business invitees
   b. licensees
   c. trespassers
4. Briefly define:
   a. warranty of merchantability
   b. warranty of fitness for a particular purpose
5. Explain the protective liability exposure.

COMMERCIAL LIABILITY INSURANCE

Introduction

There are a variety of liability insurance policies available. The type of liability insurance policy a client buys is primarily determined by the client's liability loss exposures and by the recommendation of the producer. In some cases, the selection of a coverage by a producer is based on the nature of the rating procedure—indicating duplication of coverages among some liability insurance forms. The commercial liability policy consists of two major parts, a policy jacket and the coverage part appropriate for the client's exposures.

Policy Jacket   The policy jacket in essence attempts to define the scope of liability exposures. The jacket is geared to liability in general for any organization. The jacket is identical no matter what coverage part is selected.

Coverage Part   The coverage part matches the liability insurance with the client's liability exposures whether they are premises and operations, products and completed operations, contractual, protective, or professional liability exposures. With some insurers, it is even possible to insure the automobile liability hazard under a general liability coverage part.

The coverage parts discussed in this chapter are comprehensive general liability (CGL), manufacturers and contractors (M&C), owners, landlords, and tenants (OL&T), storekeepers (SKL), and owners and contractors protective (OCP). Endorsements to these coverage parts and the coverage parts for contractors, contractors protective, and professional liability are discussed in the following chapter.

Policy Jacket

The policy jacket contains a declarations page which describes pertinent information about the nature of the insured business. The jacket also contains provisions common to all liability coverages:

1. a supplementary payments section, which includes coverage agreements concerning defense costs and similar expenses incurred by an insured following loss;
2. definitions of the common terms; and
3. general conditions on such matters as other insurance, cancellation, and the duties of an insured in the event of loss.

Supplementary Payments   The insurer agrees, under the supplementary payments provision of the policy jacket, to pay the following expenses and other costs *in addition to* the applicable limits of liability of the policy:

1. All expenses incurred by the insurer and all costs assessed against the insured in any suit which is defended by the insurer. Also, all interest which accrues on the entire amount of any court award, after such an award is made but before the insurer pays, tenders, or deposits that part of the award which does not exceed the limit of the insurer's liability. In many respects, this could be the most valuable coverage in a liability policy. It is said, "You can sue for anything." Being a defendant in a groundless suit still may require expensive defense costs to hire an attorney. This provision pays such costs.
2. Premiums on appeal bonds which may be required in any suit, and premiums on bonds to release attachments, provided the bond penalty does not exceed the applicable limits of liability. Also, the costs of any bail bonds required of the insured following an accident or a traffic violation and arising out of the use of any vehicle to which the policy applies. However, compensable costs are limited to $250 per bail bond, and the insurer is under no obligation *to apply for or to furnish* the bail bonds or the appeal and release of attachment bonds.
3. Expenses incurred by the insured for first aid to others at the time of an accident for bodily injury which is covered by the policy. (If a restaurant is without products liability insurance and its owner incurs first aid expenses because a customer is taken ill following the consumption of food on premises, such expenses are not covered.)
4. Reasonable expenses incurred by the insured in assisting the insurer in the investigation or the defense of any claim or suit. Such expenses must be incurred at the insurer's request and they include actual loss of an insured's earnings up to a maximum of $25 per day.

While some of the supplementary payments provisions discussed involve expenses incurred in the defense of an insured, the basic obligation of an insurer to defend an insured appears within the insuring agreements of each coverage part. The purpose of this format is to relate the insurer's defense obligations more closely to the coverages in question.

Definitions The terms defined in the definitions section of the policy jacket appear in boldface type within the jacket and within appropriate provisions of the coverage parts. Thus, when a boldface term appears within the provisions of a coverage part, one need only refer to the definition of the term in the policy jacket to determine its meaning.

Automobile. The meaning of automobile is especially important to the provisions of the coverage parts, because almost all automobile liability exposures are excluded. The term automobile means "a land motor vehicle, trailer or semi trailer designed for travel on public roads (including any machinery or apparatus attached thereto) but does not include mobile equipment." An automobile, as a land motor vehicle designed for public road travel, does not include aircraft, watercraft, locomotives operated on rails, and self-propelled equipment not designed for road travel, such as contractors' cranes and bulldozers, even though the equipment travels on public roads. Also, the term "automobile" is not limited to four-wheel vehicles, as is the case under many personal automobile policies. Thus, an automobile, as defined in the policy jacket, can consist of vehicles with one or more wheels, as well as land vehicles operated on treads if they do not otherwise qualify as mobile equipment. Finally, machinery or apparatus attached (towed or carried) to a land motor vehicle is a part of the automobile liability exposure, as indicated in Chapter 13 of the PRO 81 text.

Mobile Equipment. The definition of mobile equipment is important, because the liability exposure of any mobile equipment is automatically covered under the various coverage parts. To qualify as mobile equipment, a land vehicle, self-propelled or not, must come within *one* of four categories:

- Not subject to motor vehicle registration;
- Maintained for use exclusively on owned or rented premises of the named insured, including the ways immediately adjoining such premises;
- Designed for use principally off public roads; or
- Designed or maintained for the sole purpose of conveying equipment which either forms an integral part of the land vehicle or is permanently attached to such vehicle.

Among the types of equipment specifically listed in the definition are power cranes, shovels, concrete mixers (other than the mix-in-transit type), road construction equipment, welding and building cleaning equipment, and well servicing equipment.

To illustrate the definition of mobile equipment, assume a firm is in the business of sandblasting buildings. It owns a truck used for transporting building cleaning equipment permanently attached to the truck. The truck is licensed and operated on public roads while going from one job site to another. If this vehicle is to qualify as mobile equipment, it must fall into one of the four categories. Because the truck is licensed and is operated on public roads, it does not meet the first three categories. However, as that truck is designed or maintained for the sole purpose of conveying building cleaning equipment, it qualifies as mobile equipment. Accordingly, the liability insurance for the truck, as mobile equipment, is provided under the various coverage parts, and automobile liability insurance on the truck is not necessary.

Bodily Injury. The term bodily injury is defined, in brief, to mean bodily injury, sickness, or disease sustained by any person during the policy period, including death which results at any time. Bodily injury must occur during the policy period. Death is covered whenever it occurs, even after expiration of the policy term, if the death resulted from an injury, sickness, or disease which *occurred* during the policy period. Damages resulting from personal injury, invasion of privacy, or slander, are not included in the definition of bodily injury liability. Coverage for the latter kinds of losses is obtainable by purchasing "personal injury" liability insurance, which may be added to almost any type of commercial liability policy.

Property Damage. Covered losses to others resulting from property damage, as defined in the policy jacket, include those involving (1) physical injury to or destruction of tangible property that occurs during the policy period, (2) any loss of use of tangible property resulting from property that is physically damaged, regardless of when it occurs, and (3) loss of use of tangible property which has not been physically damaged or destroyed, provided the loss of use is "caused by an occurrence" during the policy period.

An example of a property damage loss of the first type is the demolition contractor who physically damages an adjoining building. Following damage, it is discovered that the adjoining building was rendered structurally unsound and has to be repaired over a period of one year. Any loss of use resulting therefrom, such as the interruption of business sustained by occupants of that building, also is considered to be a property damage loss. An example of a loss involving the third type of covered loss is the demolition contractor whose crane topples onto a main thoroughfare. Although the accident does not physically damage any property, access to several businesses is prohibited or inhibited until the crane can be removed. Any interruption of business sustained by those affected by the incident is considered to be loss of use of tangible property (the business establishments) that has not been physically injured or destroyed. However, the covered loss in this third situation must be "sudden and accidental" and occur during the policy period.

Note that in all three examples the property was tangible in nature. To be covered, any physical injury or any loss of use giving rise to damages must first involve tangible property. Loss to intangible property, such as loss of goodwill or loss of profits, is not covered, unless tangible property somehow is involved in the loss.

Elevator. The definition of elevator is treated at length in the policy jacket. In brief, an elevator means any hoisting or lowering device to connect floors or landings, including its appliances, such as any car, platform, stairway, power equipment, or machinery. However, an elevator does not include (1) an automobile servicing hoist, (2) a hoist without mechanical power and without a platform which is used outside a building, (3) a material hoist which is used in alteration, construction, or demolition operations, (4) an inclined conveyor used exclusively for conveying property, and (5) a dumbwaiter which has a compartment height not exceeding four feet.

The meaning of "elevator" is not as important as it once was to insurers, especially since coverage on the liability exposures of elevators is now automatically provided under the premises and operations feature of most coverage parts. Nonetheless, its definition is pertinent for three reasons. First, the almost universal exclusion of liability for damage to property in the care, custody, or control of an insured does not apply to accidents occurring on elevators. Second, the definition is broad enough to include passenger escalators; however, passenger escalators are subject to an additional premium if coverage is desired. And third, state laws usually require the safety inspection of elevators at certain specified intervals. While state inspectors can perform that service, some insurers also will inspect them for an additional charge.

Incidental Contract. Generally, protection for liability contractually assumed by a firm must be separately covered for an additional premium. However, the so-called incidental contracts are automatically covered under most commercial liability policies.

Following are specific illustrations of the types of written agreements considered to be incidental contracts and therefore covered:

1. *Lease of premises.* For example, a firm, as a tenant or a lessee, may agree to hold the landlord harmless, under a written lease agreement, for any bodily injury or property damage arising

from any physical defects of the premises or from any negligent operations within that firm's control. The liability assumed by the tenant automatically would be covered under most commercial liability forms.

2. *Easements.* Easements involve a variety of legal complexities but can be simply defined as limited rights to use land belonging to others. An example is owners who contribute portions of their land to construct a common thoroughfare. Another example is the right-of-way on property owned by a township that gives the public access to a body of water. When an entity agrees, in writing, to hold an owner of property harmless for liability that may result from the user's negligence, such negligence resulting in loss is automatically covered under virtually any commercial liability policy. However, if the easement agreement is required in connection with any construction or demolition operations on or adjacent to any railroad, separate contractual liability coverage must be obtained.

3. *Agreements required by municipalities.* Municipalities often have ordinances requiring other entities to hold the municipalities harmless for any liability stemming from devices or obstructions which can cause bodily injury or property damage to members of the public. A store owner, for example, often will be required to enter into an agreement if the owner desires to erect a sign or a canopy which will hang over a public walkway. The owner agrees, in writing, to hold the city harmless for any claims that may arise because of that sign or canopy. Such assumed liability automatically is covered as long as the indemnification is required by a municipal ordinance. However, if work is to be performed for a municipality and a hold harmless agreement is required, separate contractual liability insurance must be purchased to cover the work exposure.

4. *Sidetrack agreements.* Railroads often require business firms, as a condition to installing sidetracks or spurs to facilitate private operations, to hold them harmless from losses arising from the use of such railroad property. Such agreements also may hold firms responsible for any damage to the property itself. A wholesale distribution firm, for example, that desires a railroad sidetrack to its premises in order to load or unload goods from boxcars is automatically covered against the assumption of such liability as it may have assumed under a written contract.

5. *Elevator maintenance agreements.* Building owners or lessees are frequently required to hold harmless firms which

install and/or service elevators, in the event of any claim stemming from an elevator. The resulting contractual liability of the owner or lessee is covered automatically, having been assumed under an incidental contract. Escalator maintenance agreements would also be considered incidental contracts because of the broad definition of "elevator."

Insured. As defined in the policy jacket, insured means any person or entity which qualifies as an insured within the "persons insured" provisions of the respective coverage parts. While each of the liability coverage parts has its own "persons insured" provisions, they are identical for the CGL, OL&T, and M&C coverage parts:

1. An individual, when such person is designated in the policy declarations as the named insured, but only to the extent of that person's business conducted as a sole proprietorship.
2. A partnership or joint venture, when such firm is designated in the policy declarations as the named insured, including any partner's or member's liability during the conduct of a partnership or joint venture.
3. Any organization other than a sole proprietorship, partnership, or joint venture, such as a corporation or unincorporated association, when such organization is designated in the policy declarations as the named insured, including the liability of any executive officer, director, or stockholder while such person is acting within the scope of his or her duties.
4. Any person or organization while acting as a real estate manager for the named insured, other than employees of the named insured.

The "persons insured" provision also contains a so-called "ominbus clause" which designates those who are and are not considered to be insureds while operating mobile equipment registered under any motor vehicle registration law for purposes of locomotion upon public highways.

Coverage does not apply to bodily injury or property damage which arises out of the conduct of any partnership or joint venture of which an insured is a partner or member, when such partnership or joint venture is not designated in the policy as the named insured. The purpose of this provision is to prevent covering a liability exposure not contemplated by the basic premium charge of the policy. If coverage is desired for additional partnersips or joint ventures that arise during the policy period, they must be specifically declared and added to the policy by endorsement.

The definition of the term insured in the policy jacket states: "The insurance afforded applies separately to each insured against whom claim is made or suit is brought, except with respect to the limits of the company's liability." This provision, commonly referred to as the "severability" clause, serves to clarify that each person or entity which seeks protection, as an insured, will be protected as if each of them has separate coverage under the policy. So, if one insured is determined to be without coverage, this has no effect on other insureds seeking protection. However, the limits of liability are not cumulative, regardless of the number of different insureds which may be involved in any one claim or suit.

Named Insured. The term named insured means the person or entity named in the policy declarations and may include an individual, a partnership, a corporation, or an unincorporated association. It could also include two or more partnerships involved in a joint venture, a parent company and its subsidiaries, or a corporation and the individual shareholders who have a controlling interest. Each such person or entity must be specifically designated in the policy declarations if they are to be covered as named insureds. If a corporation acquires a subsidiary during the policy period, for example, the subsidiary is not automatically protected. The subsidiary must be declared to the insurer and listed on the policy as an additional named insured.

Occurrence. Occurrence is used to mean "an accident, including continuous or repeated exposure to conditions, which results in bodily injury or property damage neither expected nor intended from the standpoint of the insured." An occurrence can be any adverse condition that continues over a long period and eventually results in bodily injury or property damage, or it can be an event that occurs suddenly. In either case, the resulting bodily injury or property damage must be "neither expected nor intended from the standpoint of the insured." Thus, if a firm has a serious premises liability hazard and fails to take steps to eliminate it, any subsequent bodily injury or property damage loss could conceivably be denied as not coming within the definition of an occurrence.

Policy Territory. The policy jacket definition of policy territory consists of three sections. The first two concern the territorial scope of all liability exposures. The third section is limited to the policy territory of products liability exposures.

As defined in the first two sections, policy territory means "the United States of America, its territories, possessions, or Canada, or international waters or air space, provided the bodily injury or property damage does not occur in the course of travel or transportation to or from any other country, state or nation."

The definition makes coverage applicable while an insured is upon international waters or in air space between the United States and its territories, possessions, or Canada, between the continental United States and Hawaii or Alaska, or between the United States, its territories, possessions, or Canada and off-shore towers, regardless of their location in international waters. No coverage applies during the course of travel or transportation between two foreign countries or between either the United States or Canada and a foreign country.

Products Hazard. The term products hazard is defined to include bodily injury or property damage arising from (1) the named insured's products or (2) reliance upon a representation or a warranty made at any time with respect to products. It is a further requirement that bodily injury or property damage not only must occur away from owned or rented premises of the named insured, but also after physical possession of those products is relinquished to others.

Note the two conditions that generally must be met before a loss is considered to be one of products liability. First, bodily injury or property damage stemming from a product (which either is defective or does not serve the purpose for which it was warranted or represented by the named insured) must occur *away* from the owned or rented premises of the named insured. And, second, the product must be in the physical possession of one other than the named insured at the time of injury. Both of those conditions must be met. One or the other will not do. For example, if a person purchases a product and sustains an injury from its use at any location other than the seller's owned or rented premises, the loss is one of products liability insurance. But if a person is injured while handling a product on the store premises, the loss is the subject of premises and operations liability coverage.

However, only one of the two products hazard's conditions is applicable when food, beverages, and other kindred products are sold for consumption on business premises. Restaurants, confectionary stores, and caterers, for example, may have as much (or more) exposure to products liability on their premises as they do away from the premises. The rate for premises and operations coverage does not include the products liability exposure of businesses which sell products for consumption on their premises; therefore an endorsement must be attached to the liability policies of those businesses to redefine the term "products hazard" to include injury or damage occurring on premises of the products seller. The effect of the endorsement is to extend the scope of the products hazard (and, hence, create the need for products liability insurance) to *any* location on or off premises, provided physical possession of the product, at the time of injury, had been relinquished by the seller.

Named Insured's Products. The definition of named insured's products is important because it describes the exposures subject to the products hazard, as well as those exposures not within that hazard. The "named insured's products" are goods or products manufactured, sold, handled, or distributed either by the named insured or by others trading under the insured's name. The term also includes any containers of products other than vehicles. Excluded from the term, however, are vending machines or other property (exclusive of containers) that, instead of being sold, merely are rented or situated at various locations for the use of others.

The term named insured's products refers to goods or products manufactured, sold, handled, or distributed, not to the performance of operations, such as the completion of work or service by the named insured. A firm hired solely to perform a service, such as the installation of a heating system purchased from a wholesaler or a retailer, does not require products liability insurance. Such businesses require completed operations coverage, which deals with losses following the completion of work or service. A firm that both sells and installs heating equipment needs both products liability and completed operations insurance.

Containers of goods or products such as bottles, cardboard cartons to hold bottles, cans, jars, boxes, oil drums, propane tanks, or cylinders, and wood crates also are considered to be subjects of products liability insurance. This is because containers are not only devices used to hold products, but also are goods or products themselves, capable of producing harm. For example, a court held that steel bands and straps keeping steel coils in place on a skid, which came apart and injured a person, were considered to be a container.

Containers may be the subject of products liability insurance even though they remain the property of the manufacturer, distributor, or retailer. Returnable beverage bottles and refillable propane gas cylinders are examples. As previously mentioned, one of the keys to most products liability exposures is that injury or damage occurs after *physical* possession of goods or products has been relinquished by the named insured. Legal title to goods or products has been relinquished by the named insured. Legal title to goods or products does not have to pass. Nor does ownership of such products necessarily have to be relinquished by the named insured as a prerequisite of any products liability exposure. Returnable fuel oil drums are as much a product liability exposure, for example, as the oil contained in them. Vehicles are not considered to be containers for purposes of the term "named insured's products."

Vending machines, as goods or products manufactured, sold, handled, or distributed by an entity, come within the meaning of the term "named insured's products" and, hence, are appropriately within the scope of the term "products hazard." However, when the owner retains the vending machines following their purchase from the manufacturer or the distributor, and either rents them to others or places them at various locations for the convenience of patrons, the machines are outside the meaning of the term "named insured's products." Products liability insurance, therefore, is not necessary. But these vending machines sometimes produce exposures to loss by their very existence. The machines may malfunction, for example, and may cause fire or water damage to the premises in which they are located. In addition, vending machines may be responsible for the injury of a person when they are situated in places that hinder the thoroughfare of premises. Such exposures to loss, dealing with the existence hazard of vending machines, are the subject of premises and operations insurance.

The contents dispensed by vending machines can also represent a products liability exposure, whether injury or damage arises on or away from premises owned or rented by the named insured. Therefore, when products liability insurance is obtained for the contents of vending machines, the products hazard must be redefined as it is for restaurants and similar businesses, to include damage arising from a product on the premises of the named insured and away from the premises. When products liability insurance is not obtained for the contents of vending machines, the same procedure must be followed as would apply to a restaurant that does not obtain products liability insurance. Thus, an exclusion must be attached to the policy so that no coverage applies for injury or damage arising from the named insured's products (vended from those machines) either on premises owned or rented to the named insured or elsewhere.

Finally, the term "named insured's premises" does not encompass liability exposures of businesses that rent or lease their property, exclusive of containers, to others. Businesses in this category are covered against injury or damage arising from such rented or leased property under their premises and operations coverage, subject to a separate premium charge in some cases. If rental of property is incidental to a business, e.g., a hardware store that handles wallpaper and paints and also rents a wallpaper removing machine to its customers, no additional charge is required. But when a business's principal function is to rent or lease equipment or appliances, such as lawn mowers, lawn rollers, ladders, post hole diggers, floor polishers and sanders, refrigerators, stoves, and machines—on a short or long-term basis—a separate premium charge is necessary either at policy inception, or, if the operation arises during the policy period, upon audit at expiration of the policy period.

Completed Operations Hazard. The term "completed operations hazard" is described in two parts. The first part defines the characteristics of operations included within the hazard, as well as the time periods operations are deemed to be completed. The second part deals with operations that are not considered to be within the scope of the completed operations hazard.

Completed operations hazard is defined to include bodily injury and property damage arising out of (1) operations, including materials, parts, or equipment which are furnished in connection with such operations; and (2) reliance upon a representation or a warranty made at any time with respect to those operations.

The completed operations hazard, like the products hazard, makes loss contingent upon two criteria. First, bodily injury or property damage must arise (1) from work improperly completed, (2) from the use of defective or improper materials, parts, or equipment, or (3) from a completed operation properly performed or free of defects that nevertheless fails to serve its purpose as warranted or represented by the named insured. Second, bodily injury or property damage must arise from operations which have been completed or abandoned at premises other than those owned or rented to the named insured. Both of those criteria must be met. Otherwise, loss is not within the completed operations hazard.

Suppose, for example, part of a building under construction collapses because of a contractor's negligent act or omission and an adjoining building is damaged by falling debris. The resulting damage to that adjoining building is considered to be within the "operations" hazard of premises and operations insurance, not completed operations insurance. However, if that structure were to partially collapse *following its completion,* the resulting damage to the adjoining building is the subject of completed operations insurance, even though the underlying cause of that loss was created while operations were still in progress. It does not matter when a defect is created. What matters, instead, is when bodily injury or property damage occurs. The CGL policy, including completed operations insurance, of course, must be in force at the time of injury or damage, because the terms "bodily injury" and "property damage," as defined in the policy jacket, only apply to losses which occur during the policy period.

Location of loss also is important. For example, if a person is injured by a premises defect after work is completed by the *owner* of the premises, the bodily injury is the subject of premises and operations insurance, because work was performed by the named insured at its own premises. But, when a person is injured by a premises defect at someone else's premises following completion of work by a contracting firm, the resulting bodily injury is the subject of completed operations insurance.

Completed Operations Hazard Versus Products Hazard. Some characteristics of the completed operations hazard are so similar to those of the products hazard that their precise differences sometimes are difficult to detect. Both hazards impose somewhat similar criteria for losses to be covered, for instance, losses emanating from both must occur away from premises owned by or rented to the named insured. Manual classifications and general rules of both hazards also are contained in the product liability manual of ISO.

In spite of these similarities, there is a distinct difference between the two hazards. The products hazard involves losses resulting from goods or products that are manufactured, sold, handled, or distributed by a firm. Such goods or products, furthermore, either are defective or they do not serve their purposes as warranted or represented by the seller. An appliance store that sells but does not install gas ranges needs products liability insurance in the event that bodily injury or property damage emanates from the gas ranges, its products. The completed operations hazard, on the other hand, includes situations in which a firm is engaged in rendering services, rather than being in the business of manufacturing, selling, distributing, or handling goods or products. Such work or service either is performed incorrectly or it simply fails to serve its purposes as warranted or represented by the one who completes the operation. An excavation contractor, for example, furnishes its services in terms of labor and equipment to perform its work under contract. No product is involved. The result of its services, say, is an open trench that may or may not be shored, depending upon its depth.

There are numerous occasions, however, when contractors must physically handle products and even supply them in order to perform their services. A carpenter sometimes recommends and supplies lumber, an electrician supplies wiring and other components, a mason supplies bricks and mortar, a plumber supplies the piping, and the heating contractor supplies the equipment to be installed. The primary exposures of these contractors are concerned with the manner in which work is performed. But if their work results in losses because of defects in lumber, wiring, bricks, pipes, or heating equipment (materials, parts or equipment furnished with such work), those losses still are the subject of the completed operations hazard, rather than the products hazard. This is because the contractors deal in services, not with the manufacture, sale, or distribution of products. The matter of defective products used in any work ultimately must be settled, usually by subrogation, between the insurers of those contractors and the manufacturers or distributors of the allegedly defective products.

On the other hand, an appliance store that sells and installs its products needs both products liability and completed operations insurance. The former coverage will protect the store in the event bodily injury or property damage arises from a defective product it has sold, or from failure of its product to serve its purpose as warranted or represented at the time of sale. The latter coverage protects that store against bodily injury or property damage arising from the manner in which work was performed in installing its product.

Time of Completion. The time at which an operation is considered to be completed is important because it can determine whether premises and operations coverage or completed operations coverage is applicable. Thus, when loss occurs after an operation is completed or abandoned and away from premises owned or rented to the named insured, it comes within the scope of the completed operations hazard. Completed operations insurance is therefore the appropriate form of protection. But when a loss occurs while an operation is still in progress, it is the subject of the premises and operations hazard. Premises and operations insurance is therefore the appropriate form of protection.

To avoid any argument in determining precisely when a particular operation is deemed completed, the definition of "completed operations hazard" lists three time periods, and specifies that an operation is considered to be completed by whichever of the following three periods occurs first:

1. when all operations to be performed by or on behalf of the named insured under contract are completed;
2. when all operations to be performed by or on behalf of the named insured at the site of operations are completed; or
3. when the portion of work out of which injury or damage arises has been put to its intended use by anyone other than another contractor or subcontractor who is engaged in performing operations at the same project.

Each of those time periods requires additional comment, because they are not always as clear as they sometimes first appear.

TIME PERIOD (1). The provision of time period (1) requires that all operations to be performed under contract must be completed, whether the work is performed in whole or in part by the named insured or by someone else (such as a subcontractor) on behalf of the named insured. When a subcontractor performs all or part of the work under contract, it needs completed operations insurance just as much as the general contractor. If loss should occur from the subcontractor's completed work, and suit is brought against the general contractor, the latter would be protected under its completed operations insurance, if loss is not otherwise excluded. The subcontractor also would be protected under its completed operations insurance if the general contractor's insurer should decide to seek reimbursement of its damages from the subcontractor through subrogation.

If certain work is only partially done and the one performing it intends to return at a later date to finish it, such work as is already performed is not deemed to be completed. For example, suppose an electrical subcontractor is hired to do the wiring and other related work on a newly constructed one-story building. The contractor does the rough work, but is unable to install the switches, plugs, and light fixtures until the walls and ceilings are finished. If someone on the work site, such as a carpenter, should sustain injury from an electrical shock, or if a fire should start from within the circuit breaker box before work is fully completed, loss is the subject of the premises and operations hazard rather than the completed operations hazard.

TIME PERIOD (2).   The provision of time period (2) specifies that, regardless of all operations to be performed under contract by or on behalf of the named insured, work is considered to be completed as soon as all work that has to be done at the site of operations is finished. Work under this second category usually involves the performance of two or more like operations at different sites. For example, each utility pole removed by a contractor is considered to be a completed operation at each site no matter how many such poles must be removed under contract. Or, each sewer line laid and connected to a newly constructed dwelling is considered to be a completed operation at that site, even though such work must be performed on a whole tract of new dwellings. Each newly constructed and completed story of a high-rise building could conceivably be considered as a separate site of operations. Much depends on how the term "site of operations" is interpreted, because it is not defined in the policy provisions.

As each utility pole is removed, each sewer line is laid and connected, and each story of a building is finished, contractors will need completed operations insurance against any bodily injury or property damage arising from such completed work. They also will need premises and operations insurance against any bodily injury or property damage stemming from operations while the poles are being removed, the sewer pipes are being laid and connected, and work is being performed on the upper levels of a building.

TIME PERIOD (3).   The provision concerning time period (3) considers operations to be completed when some portion of work, out of which bodily injury or property damage arises, has been put to its intended use by anyone other than another contractor or subcontractor who is performing operations on the same project. Occupancy or use of work for its intended purpose therefore takes precedence, even though the work in question has not been officially inspected and accepted.

Thus, if a boiler is put to use by its owner before work on the entire heating system is completed and the boiler causes bodily injury or property damage, loss is considered to be the subject of completed operations insurance. The same results are intended to apply when bodily injury or property damage arises from a portion of a newly constructed highway that the public is permitted to use before it is officially opened, and from a building that is partially occupied before it is officially opened, and from a building that is partially occupied before it is fully completed. However, when the boiler, the highway, or the partially completed building is being used by other contractors on the same project, the operation is not considered to be completed.

As explicit as the provision of time period (3) may appear, it nonetheless is a source of argument for at least two reasons. First, it is not work used by others that is the controlling factor. It is work that is put to its *intended* use by others. Second, bodily injury or property damage must arise out of that portion of the work which has been put to its intended use by others.

Completed Operations Requiring Service, Maintenance, or Repair Work. Another important provision of the term "completed operations hazard" deals with operations that require continuous service or maintenance, as well as repair work. The relevant provision states that any operation requiring further service or maintenance work, *or* correction, repair, or replacement because of any defect or deficiency, but which otherwise is complete, is considered to be completed.

Were it not for this provision, firms under a continuing obligation to service, maintain, and repair work would never need completed operations insurance. Firms simply could maintain that operations requiring further service or repair work would be considered still in progress (and covered under premises and operations insurance).

The conjunction "or" of that provision separates service and maintenance work from correction, repair, or replacement work. This means that service or maintenance work does not have to be made necessary because of any defect or deficiency. Operations concerning correction, repair, or replacement work, instead, must be necessitated by a defect or a deficiency. In either case, however, operations are deemed to be completed at the earliest of the three time periods previously mentioned. For example, assume a firm installs an elevator and promises to inspect and service it periodically, as well as to repair it when necessary. As soon as the elevator is installed and accepted by its owner, it is considered to be a completed operation, unless one of the other time periods occurs first. The fact that the elevator must be inspected and serviced periodically or repaired has no effect on such operation. It still is completed. The elevator firm, of course, needs premises and operations insurance as protection against any bodily injury or property damage that may result while it is inspecting, servicing, or repairing the elevator. However, if the elevator should subsequently malfunction, fall, and injure its passengers because of the way it was installed or because of neglect in servicing it properly, loss is considered to be within the scope of completed operations insurance.

Operations Not Within the Scope of Completed Operations Hazard. Bodily injury or property damage arising out of the following operations are not within the scope of the term "completed operations hazard," unless otherwise excepted:

1. operations in connection with the transportation of property, unless bodily injury or property damage arises out of a condition in or on a vehicle created by its loading or unloading;
2. the existence of tools, uninstalled equipment, or abandoned or unused materials; or
3. operations for which the classification stated in the policy or in the insurer's manual specifies "including completed operations."

Operations in Connection with the Transportation of Property. The policy covers bodily injury or property damage stemming from any automobile, aircraft, or watercraft that is not owned, not operated by, not rented, nor loaned to any insured. An example of a covered exposure within that meaning is the automobile, aircraft, or watercraft of an independent contractor.

If bodily injury or property damage arises out of a condition in or on a vehicle of an independent contractor created by its loading or unloading, loss is the subject of coverage under the completed operations hazard. The vehicle must be one that is not owned, not operated by, not rented, nor loaned to any insured. And, in line with the definition of completed operations hazard, bodily injury or property damage must occur away from premises owned by or rented to the insured. The exposures in question are those allegedly caused by an insured, or by a person for whom the insured is responsible, who improperly loads or unloads cargo and causes dangerous conditions that result in bodily injury or property damage to others.

The completed operations hazard of the CGL only applies to losses stemming from such conditions which exist on nonowned vehicles. Such conditions which exist on owned vehicles must be handled under the auto liability policy.

Existence of Tools, Uninstalled Equipment, or Abandoned or Unused Materials. Bodily injury or property damage arising from the existence of tools, uninstalled equipment, or abandoned or unused materials is the subject of premises and operations insurance rather than completed operations insurance. This is the case even though such tools, equipment or unused materials were used or were intended to be used in performing operations which have since been completed or abandoned away from premises owned or rented to the insured.

Manual Classifications Automatically Including Completed Operations. For some classifications in the OL&T and M&C manuals, there is no separate premium charge for completed operations insurance; the coverage is automatically included along with an entity's premises and operations insurance. Among such OL&T classifications are churches, clubs that have no buildings or premises of their own, convalescent and nursing homes, electronic data processing centers, and self-service laundries and dry cleaners. Examples of such M&C classifications are cleaning and renovating outside surfaces of buildings, detective and patrol agencies, engineers and architects who do consulting but no actual construction work, engravers, oil or gas lease operators of natural gas, geophysical exploration, and car washes.

Since the policy provisions govern the terms of coverage between the insured and the insurer, it is necessary that the policy term state specifically that operations classified in the policy declarations, policy schedule, or manual as including completed operations are not subject to the completed operations hazard, as defined. Through this provision, the policy is stating, in effect, that the completed operations hazard, as an exposure which can be separately noted, does not apply to OL&T and M&C classifications that include completed operations. Instead, the completed operations hazard, as included within those classifications, applies as a combined exposure included in the rate for premises and operations insurance. This means the insured has completed operations insurance without having to purchase it for an additional premium. So, for example, if a club assists in building a park and playground and someone is injured because of work performed by it, the club has protection under its premises and operations insurance, even though such work has been completed. The only requirement, of course, is that the club have insurance at the time of the injury or damage.

Policy Jacket Conditions There are twelve conditions within the policy jacket.

Premium. In the premium condition, the statement is made that all premiums are to be computed in accordance with the insurer's rules, rates, rating plans, premiums, and minimum premiums. The named insured also must maintain such records as are necessary for premium computations. The "advance premium" is a deposit premium, with the final premium determined by audit at the end of the policy period.

Inspection and Audit. The inspection and audit condition puts special stress on disclaiming any implication that an inspection constitutes an undertaking, on behalf of or for the benefit of the insured or others, to determine or warrant that property or operations are safe. It also stipulates the insurer shall be permitted to examine and audit the named insured's books and records at any time during the policy period.

Financial Responsibility Laws. The purpose of the condition entitled "financial responsibility laws" is to certify that the policy will meet the requirements of any motor vehicle responsibility law which requires proof of financial responsibility. For example, a firm whose automobile is involved in an out-of-state accident may be required to show proof of insurance for at least the minimum limits of liability required by the state where the accident occurred. If the financial responsibility limits to be certified are higher than the limits specified on the firm's policy, the higher limits apply. However, it is stipulated that the insured shall reimburse the insurer for any payment made in excess of the specified policy limits. There are two reasons why the financial responsibility condition appears in the policy jacket. A coverage part concerning automobile liability insurance may be attached to the policy jacket by some insurers, and there may be times when an insured needs certification of financial responsibility for mobile equipment operated on public roads.

Insured's Duties in the Event of Occurrence, Claim, or Suit. In the event of an occurrence, the insured will give the insurer written notice as soon as practicable, as well as particulars concerning time, place, and circumstances of any loss. In the event of claim or suit, the insured agrees to forward every demand, notice, or summons immediately to the insurer, and to cooperate and assist the insurer in attending hearings and in making settlements.

Action Against Company. Sometimes an insured may wish to bring an action against the insured's insurer. This is not permissible until the insured is in full compliance with all terms of the policy, or until the amount of the insured's obligations have been determined, either by judgment after trial or by written agreement of the insured, claimant, or insurer. The condition also states that bankruptcy or insolvency of the insured or of the insured's estate will not relieve the insurer of its obligations.

Other Insurance. The purpose of the "other insurance" condition is to specify how an insurer will contribute to the payment of loss when an insured has more than one applicable policy. When the insurance of the coverage part attached to the policy jacket is on a "primary basis," the applicable limit will be paid without requiring any contribution from another insurer whose limits are stated to be excess or contingent on the absence of other applicable insurance. But, if all policies are written on the same basis, i.e., all primary, all excess, or all contingent, settlement will be made in one of the following two ways:

1. If all policies provide for "contribution by equal shares," each insurer will contribute equally to the loss until the limit of liability of the lowest policy is reached or the loss is paid. For example, assume Company Y provides limits of $100/100/300 ($100,000 per occurrence bodily injury, $100,000 per occurrence property damage, $300,000 aggregate property damage). Company Z provides limits of $50/50/100, and a $25,000 bodily injury liability judgment is rendered against the insured who has insurance with both companies. Under contribution by equal shares, each insurer will contribute equally up to the lowest applicable limit or the amount of loss, whichever is the lesser of the two. In this case, since the $25,000 loss is less than the lowest applicable limit ($50,000), each insurer will contribute $12,500. Going one additional step, assume the same limits as above but a bodily injury liability judgment of $125,000. In this situation, Company Z will pay $50,000, which is its maximum limit, and Company Y will pay the remaining $75,000.

2. If all policies do not provide for contribution by equal shares, e.g., one policy provides for contribution by equal shares and the other provides for contribution by limits, settlement will be made on the basis of "contribution by limits." This means each insurer's contribution will be calculated on the basis of the ratio between its limit and the total limit of all valid and collectible insurance. For example, assume that Company A provides limits of $50/25/50 and Company B provides limits of $100/100/300. The judgment amount for a bodily injury liability loss is $54,000. Since Company A's limit is $50,000 and the total limit of both policies for bodily injury is $150,000 ($50,000 Company A and $100,000 Company B), Company A is liable for $50,000/$150,000 of the $54,000 loss or $18,000. Company B is liable for the remainder of the loss or $36,000. An additional example appears in Exhibit 2-1.

Subrogation. In the event that any payment is made by the insurer in a situation where another person's tortious conduct contrib-

Exhibit 2-1
Payments Based on Other Insurance Provision of CGL

		A	B	C	Total
		Policy			
Limits		$ 50,000	$100,000	$300,000	$450,000
Judgment	$300,000				
Contribution by equal shares		$ 50,000	$100,000	$150,000	$300,000
Pro-rata by total limits		50/450 ($33,333)	100/450 ($66,667)	300/450 ($200,000)	450/450 ($300,000)

uted to the loss, it is a condition of the subrogation clause that the insurer may, to the extent of its payment, take over its insured's right of recovery against that negligent third party. If a judgment award were to exceed the insurer's limit of liability, the insurer may exercise its right of subrogation in an attempt to recover the amount of its payment, and the insured also may proceed against the negligent third party in an attempt to recover at least a portion of any amount the insured had to pay in excess of the insurer's limit of liability.

Changes. It is a condition that the terms of the policy may not be waived or changed except by endorsement attached to the policy. Any notice to or knowledge by the producer or any other person concerning a change has no effect on the policy and does not prevent the insurer from exercising any of its rights.

Assignment. Any assignment of interest under the policy is not binding without the insurer's consent. However, in the event of the named insured's death, coverage applies to the named insured's legal representative or to a person who has temporary custody of the named insured's property until a legal representative is appointed and qualifies for that role.

Three Year Policy. If a policy is written for a period of three years, any limit stated in the policy as an "aggregate" shall apply separately to each consecutive annual period.

Cancellation. Under the "cancellation" provision, the named insured is given the right to cancel the policy at any time by mailing notice to the insurer and specifying when cancellation is to be effective. The insurer also has a right of cancellation, if not otherwise prohibited by law. However, the insurer must specify when, not less than ten days following the mailing of its notice to the named insured, cancellation is to be effective. When the named insured requests cancellation, the insurer's earned premium is calculated on a "short-rate" basis, and when the insurer requests cancellation, its earned premium is calculated on a pro-rata basis.

Declarations. The named insured agrees, under the final condition in the policy jacket, that (1) all statements made in the policy declarations are considered to be the named insured's agreements and representations, and (2) the policy is issued in reliance of those representations.

Since the CGL coverage part is considered to be the broadest of the standard liability coverages for nonautomobile liability exposures, its basic characteristics, coverages, and exclusions will be discussed first.

Checkpoints

1. List the supplementary payments provisions within the liability policy jacket.
2. List the incidental contracts covered by the policy jacket.
3. Distinguish between "an insured" and the "named insured."
4. What are the critical elements necessary for coverage under:
    a. the products hazard?
    b. the completed operations hazard?
5. What are the insured's duties in the case of loss or claim?

COMMERCIAL LIABILITY INSURANCE COVERAGE

Comprehensive General Liability Coverage Part

The comprehensive general liability (CGL) policy is the broadest standard form of protection available to business. In its basic form, the CGL coverage part is broader than the other forms to be discussed. The CGL is used for either premises or operations exposures. It is not the type of business that suggests usage of the CGL, but rather the necessity for coverage for specified exposures such as independent contractors, products, and completed operations liability, and the coverage in the CGL for unknown exposures and newly acquired operations and property. Since products and completed operations liability will be treated in a separate section, this analysis will not include those coverages.

Besides covering more liability exposures, the CGL has another broadening feature. Subject to all other terms of the policy and particularly the exclusions, it covers unknown insurable exposures as well as any exposures that may arise during the policy period including newly acquired locations without a provision for reporting that new location.

In addition to the broad scope of protection in its basic form, the CGL can be broadened by more extensions and added coverages than any other coverage part. This broad coverage part should always be the first recommended by the producer.

Insuring Agreement The insuring agreement expresses the insurer's promises:

> The company will pay on behalf of the insured all sums which the insured shall become legally obligated to pay as damages because of bodily injury or property damage to which this insurance applies, caused by an occurrence, and the company shall have the right and duty to defend any suit against the insured seeking damages on account of such bodily injury or property damage, even if any of the allegations of the suit are groundless, false or fraudulent, and may make such investigation or settlement of any claim or suit as it deems expedient, ...

Note there are no restrictive terms like "designated premises" and "operations necessary or incidental." The key words in the first part of this insuring agreement are "legally obligated," "bodily injury," and "property damage" (when referring to both terms, the word "injury" will be used). This is not goodwill insurance, such as medical payments coverage discussed later. The insured must be legally obligated for the insurer to pay the claim, and it must be for bodily injury or property damage.

Important in the agreement is the insurance company's duty to defend suits against the insured and its right to investigate and settle any claim. Note the insurer will defend even those suits whose allegations are groundless, false, or fraudulent.

Finally, the right of the insurer to settle a claim is well founded in theory and has always existed. Yet it is a source of dissatisfaction to many insureds. For some insureds it is instinctive to disclaim liability. Seldom does the insured believe in or admit fault. When insureds think that payment of a claim will cause the premium to increase, they may become even more adamant against settlement of the claim and more dissatisfied when it is paid. Then there is the other extreme, the insured who feels morally responsible for an injury but has no legal liability. In either instance, the insurer will exercise its right and pay according to the policy terms—when there is legal liability despite an insured's disclaimer and then for legal liability only, not moral responsibility. The best a producer can do is explain the coverage when the policy is sold and, should a loss occur, try to make the insured understand that the insurance company is within its rights granted by the policy including both defense and settlement for experience based on the insurer's broader experience and ability to handle claims. Additional coverage provided in the policy jacket was discussed earlier under the section entitled "Supplementary Payments."

Exclusions The insuring agreement is most affected by the policy's exclusions and to some degree by the definitions discussed earlier. Exclusions are a necessary part of every insurance policy and the most important part of the CGL for a producer. Understanding them completely can help to avoid disagreements over policy coverage. They have the same degree of importance as exclusions do in property policies covering against "all-risks." The "all-risks" property policy insuring agreements cover against "all-risks" of loss except as "hereafter provided," meaning excluded. Without such limitations the policy would cover everything which is not affordable or reasonable.

The CGL may be termed an "all-risks" liability policy. There is a broad insuring agreement without limitations as to premises and operations covered and the CGL covers unknown exposures, even those that existed at policy inception so long as they are unknown, and exposures arising out of newly acquired locations and operations after inception of the policy. Understanding the exclusions is necessary in order to understand the CGL coverage.

The purposes of exclusions may be arranged in three categories:

1. They eliminate coverage for exposures that require additional premiums such as contractual liability (other than from incidental contracts).
2. They eliminate coverage for exposures provided in other policies such as automobile, aircraft, watercraft, workers' compensation, nuclear energy, and products recall.
3. They eliminate coverage for exposures not generally considered insurable such as war, pollution, and faulty workmanship.

In the following review of CGL policy exclusions, note how each falls into one of the above categories.

Contractual Liability Exclusion. This exclusion falls into the "additional premium" category. The exclusion provides that liability assumed under incidental contracts is covered, and that liability from warranties of fitness, quality, or workmanship will not be excluded here. The purpose of the exclusion is to avoid providing coverage for the nonincidental contractual exposure without receiving the appropriate additional premium. Contractual liability is not confined to construction operations, but it is in connection with such activities that the exposure is found most often.

In the case study of R. P. Davis, Contractor, he will probably find a contractual liability provision (a hold-harmless agreement) in most contracts with the owners for whom he works. This additional liability exposure will not be covered by his CGL without adding contractual liability coverage. Similarly, Davis may require subcontractors to hold him harmless in his agreement with them. But it will be useless if the subcontractors do not have sufficient assets or obtain the additional contractual coverages. For instance, if the negligence of the subcontractor plumber causes flooding that damages the work of other trades such as electrical wiring, flooring, painting, and papering, the damaged party may seek to recover from the plumber and Davis. Though the agreement is in effect, the plumber's CGL, without appropriate endorsement, will not respond.

Automobile and Aircraft Exclusion. The purpose of this exclusion is to eliminate coverage for exposures more properly insured in other policies. Examples are automobile and aircraft liability forms. The intent is to avoid almost all claims relating to automobiles and aircraft. The exclusion applies not only to automobiles and aircraft owned, operated by, rented, or loaned to the insured but also to any other automobile or aircraft operated by a person in the course of employment by the insured. In addition to excluding claims arising out of ownership, maintenance, operation, or use, the CGL does not cover losses resulting from loading or unloading of automobiles and aircraft. As broad as this exclusion is, there may be coverage in the CGL for contingent liability from loading or unloading of nonowned vehicles such as those owned or used by independent contractors, discussed earlier.

An automobile related exposure for which coverage is granted in the CGL by an exception in the exclusion is that arising out of parking of an automobile on premises owned by, rented to, or controlled by the insured, including the ways immediately adjoining. This is important to insureds who park customers' automobiles such as restaurants and hotels. Even with this coverage there may be a need for garagekeepers' insurance in the garage policy insurance because of the "care, custody, or control" (CCC) exclusion, discussed below, in the CGL. In a CCC case, the CGL would insure against bodily injury and property damage resulting from operation of the vehicle but not for damage to the customer's vehicle itself.

For instance, a restaurant may park customers' automobiles at a lot located away from the premises. Depending upon the location and distance, the entire route may not qualify as "ways immediately adjoining," creating an uninsured exposure. If the insured does not obtain the garage keeper coverage, the lot location should be specified in the CGL schedule of classifications. This will not give as broad protection, but it will provide premises coverage automatically included in the garagekeepers' insurance form.

Liability for the Use of Mobile Equipment During Certain Activities Exclusion. This exclusion slightly limits coverage in the CGL for mobile equipment. Mobile equipment, defined earlier, usually does not include cars and trucks. The intent of coverage is to include equipment of the type generally insured for physical damage in the contractors equipment floater discussed in Chapter 5. The CGL provides liability coverage for ownership, maintenance, or use of the equipment not for physical damage to the equipment. The exclusion limits bodily injury and property damage coverage arising from mobile equipment in two categories: (1) while being used in any prearranged or organized racing, speed, or demolition contest, or in any stunting activity, or in practice or preparation for such contest or activity; or (2) the operation of any snowmobile or trailer designed for use with a snowmobile. In part one of this exclusion there is a "while clause." There is coverage for equipment intended for use in the named activities except *while* it is so being used. The entire exclusion is intended to avoid coverage of activities deemed too hazardous and not covered by standard liability rates. Specific coverage may be added for additional cost, but most often such coverage is provided by specialty insurers and usually at surcharged rates.

Mobile Equipment Being Transported by Automobile Exclusion. The purpose of this exclusion is to avoid coverage of the automobile liability exposure insured elsewhere. Although bodily injury and property damage liability from use of mobile equipment is covered in the CGL, mobile equipment is considered part of the auto while being transported, and the auto liability policy provides coverage in this circumstance. The exclusion applies to bodily injury and property damage in the course of transportation by an auto owned, operated by, rented or loaned to any insured. This suggests that the CGL would provide liability coverage for mobile equipment transported by other than an insured, but in all likelihood, it would not. The previously discussed exclusion relating to automobiles and aircraft bars coverage for automobiles operated by those employed by the insured.

Watercraft Exclusion. This exclusion is similar to the exclusion of bodily injury or property damage relating to automobiles and aircraft. It pertains to the ownership, maintenance, operation, use, loading, or unloading of owned or nonowned watercraft both owned, operated by, rented to or loaned to any insured or operated by any person in the course of employment by any insured. A difference between the watercraft and automobile exclusions is that there is coverage of watercraft while ashore on premises of the named insured. However, there is no coverage for damage to the watercraft itself. The CCC exclusion eliminates coverage for nonowned watercraft and because the CGL is a liability and not physical damage coverage, there is no coverage for damage to owned watercraft.

Pollution and Contamination Exclusion. This excludes coverage for pollution and contamination claims, unless attributable to *sudden* and *accidental* pollution or contamination. Manufacturing and other industrial plants are examples of those with this exposure, but the producer should remember that pollution is common but not limited to such operations as it can occur in small as well as large businesses. Oil dealers and sewage plants are examples that may not be as obvious as fertilizer plants, chemical manufacturers, and steel mills. The exclusion refers to "smoke, vapors, soot, fumes, acids, alkalis, toxic chemicals, liquids or gases, waste materials or other irritants, contaminants or pollutants. . . ." There are good reasons for such broadly sweeping language. They are to avoid insuring catastrophic losses of a nonaccidental and nonsudden nature and to avoid insuring contrary to public interest. The pollution exclusion limits coverage only to pollution that is sudden and accidental. It is not likely that the CGL insurer wll eliminate this exclusion, but broad coverage (not limited to sudden and accidental pollution) is available from excess and surplus lines insurers.

War and Allied Perils Exclusion. Bodily injury or property damage due to war, declared or not, civil war, insurrection, rebellion, or revolution is not covered with respect to (1) liability assumed by the insured under an incidental contract, or (2) expenses for first aid. The reason incidental contracts are specified is that they are the only contracts automatically insured in the CGL. Expenses for first aid are excluded to avoid the coverage provided without limit in the supplementary payments section of the policy. First aid expenses normally are small, but potentially large claims exist in connection with war. As it is unlikely an insured would be legally liable for such acts as war, the exclusion, in practice, applies to the supplemental coverages.

Liquor Liability Exclusion. The exclusion states that insurance does not apply to alchohol-related injury of various entities in or connected with the alcoholic beverage business. The exclusion mentions both the insured or the insured's indemnitee; in measuring the extent of the exclusion any hold harmless agreements that may exist must be considered.

The exclusion is aimed at any person or organization in the business of manufacturing, distributing, selling, or serving alcoholic beverages, but it also excludes coverage for an owner or lessee of premises used for such purposes. Both categories are denied coverage for liability from violation of alcoholic beverage laws. However, the exclusion part dealing with providing alcoholic beverage to a minor, a person under the influence of alcohol, or contributing to the intoxication of any person applies only to those in the alcoholic beverage business, not owners or lessees. Even so, the exclusion is very broad, and the need for familiarity with applicable state laws cannot be overemphasized.

For example, in most states a business that serves liquor in entertaining clients or at a company party is not considered to be in the alcoholic beverage business, so the exclusion does not apply. The exclusion probably would apply to caterers and it certainly would for taverns and many restaurants. But does state law impose liability? Producers must check local law for the answer.

Host liquor liability insurance may be advisable for businesses not affected by the exclusion. It would eliminate the danger of uninsured liability from ambiguity in application of the exclusion. Host liquor liability insurance will be discussed in the next chapter; however, it is not available to firms in the alcoholic beverage business.

Should there be a need for coverage, firms may obtain liquor liability insurance by deleting the exclusion or obtaining it from specialty insurers. Producers should be careful in recommending coverage as policies are not standard and liquor liability insurance does not include premises or products coverages and a CGL policy is still needed. It is best to have host liquor liability insurance with the same insurer as the CGL. There may be a question as to which policy—liquor or premises liability—applies if a customer falls off a bar stool.

Exclusion Relating to Workers' Compensation and Similar Laws. This exclusion appears in almost all commercial liability policies. It excludes coverage for liability under any workers' compensation, unemployment compensation, or disability benefits law or under any similar law. The intent is to avoid duplication of benefits provided by policies specifically designed to protect employees. Since statutory provisions almost always apply, the specialty forms are more appropriate than the CGL.

Bodily Injury to Any Employee Exclusion. The purpose of this exclusion is basically the same as the workers' compensation exclusion. It reinforces the intent, however, that the CGL does not cover bodily injury to an employee of the insured arising out of the course of employment. This exclusion reaches employers exempt from workers' compensation laws whereas the previous exclusion does not. One exception to the exclusion is that liability assumed by the insured under an incidental contract is covered.

Care, Custody, or Control Exclusion. While this is one of the best known exclusions among producers, it is one of the least recognized among insureds. When any loss is denied because of this exclusion, more often than not insureds will complain that they have never heard of it. Producers should always explain this vital exclusion and, if possible, have the insured acknowledge the explanation in writing. The acknowledgment may not help retain the account when an insured has no coverage, but often it will. Also important, the acknowledgment is the first step toward avoiding an errors and omissions claim. A more positive step would be to provide coverage. This will not always be possible, but there are countermeasures to the exclusion to be discussed in the next chapter.

This exclusion relates to property damage only and has three sections:

(1) property owned or occupied by or rented to the insured,

(2) property used by the insured, or

(3) property in the care, custody or control of the insured or as to which the insured is for any purpose exercising physical control.

Least controversial is the part of the exclusion relating to the insured's own property. Most insureds understand the CGL is a legal liability contract and an entity cannot be liable to itself. As for the rest of the exclusion, one only need consider the numerous possibilities of uninsured loss, and the dissatisfaction of insureds becomes clear. Leased property (perhaps an entire building), borrowed property (and large values often are at stake), and property left for safekeeping on processing are all in the care, custody or control of insureds who are without coverage in the CGL. Rarely if ever do insurers eliminate the care, custody, or control exclusion.

There is a modification in the exclusion that provides coverage for liability under a written sidetrack agreement and for property damage arising out of use of an elevator at premises owned by, rented to, or controlled by the named insured. The sidetrack coverage includes damage to the sidetrack spur itself for which the insured is liable. But for elevators, only damage arising out of elevator use—not damage to the elevator—is covered. Elevator collision insurance is needed to cover damage to the elevator.

Premises Alienated Exclusion. Without this exclusion, the CGL would provide a form of products or completed operations coverage not intended without premium charge. The exclusion states that insurance does not apply to premises alienated (sold) by the named insured.

It is important to remember three points. First, only property damage coverage, not bodily injury, is excluded. Second, the property excluded is the alienated premises, not other property, such as an adjoining building. Third and most important, there is no coverage of any kind unless a CGL is in effect at the time of loss. Since insureds usually request cancellation of coverage with respect to a property as soon as that property is sold, this point merits emphasis.

The exclusion affects a property owner who, for example, makes repairs to a property and then sells the property. If, after the sale, the repairs cause damage to the property, there would be no coverage under the CGL.

Failure to Perform Exclusion. The exclusion prevents the CGL from providing guarantees that are more appropriately furnished by surety bonds or that are otherwise uninsurable. There is no coverage for loss of use of property that has not been damaged resulting from delay, or lack of performance, or failure of the insured's products to work or otherwise meet expectations.

Damage to Products Exclusion. All commercial liability policies exclude damage to the named insured's products. The purpose of the exclusion is to avoid paying for repair or replacement of defective work. If products or completed operations coverage applies, resulting property damage to other property is covered, and the exclusion concerns only property damage not bodily injury. In interpreting this exclusion, the insured's product is regarded as a unit including all components. This exclusion will be reviewed in the next chapter on products and completed operations liability.

Thought should be given to the interaction of exclusions. Only one policy exclusion needs to apply to a loss situation to bar coverage for that loss, but often there is a relation between various exclusions. This is illustrated by noting the connection between this damage to products exclusion, and the CGL exclusions relating to failure to perform, injury to work performed, and withdrawal.

Exclusion of Injury to Work Performed. This exclusion, property damage to work performed by or on behalf of the named insured arising out of the work, relates closely to the damage to products exclusion in the preceding discussion. Its purpose is the same: to avoid paying for redoing faulty work. These are companion exclusions, one relating to products and the other to completed operations.

As noted, the work is regarded as a single unit including all of its parts. It includes work performed "on behalf of" the named insured (as by subcontractors) "arising out of the work or any portion thereof, or out of materials, parts or equipment furnished...."

Damages for Withdrawal, Inspection, Repair, Replacement, or Loss of Use Exclusion. The purpose of this so-called "sistership liability" exclusion is to prevent payment for expenses in connection with withdrawal of products known or suspected of being defective.

Most often this exclusion is applied in situations involving spoiled food products. In such cases, food manufacturers, packers, distributors, and other suppliers may be called upon to clear store shelves of such products. The CGL will not pay for withdrawal or for expenses associated with the withdrawal such as inspection, repair, replacement, or loss of use. Like the preceding property damage exclusions, this exclusion contains broad terms extending the exclusion to products or work "completed by or for" the insured or any property "of which such products of work form a part."

The "sistership liability" exclusion directly affects products and completed operations liability. However, since withdrawal is named in addition to inspection, repair, replacement, and loss of use, it is possible that a loss may arise out of the premises-operations exposures as well. The insured may have defective inventory undelivered which must be inspected, repaired, or replaced. Products liability is not involved unless the loss occurs away from premises and physical possession has been relinquished to others. Therefore, the exclusion should not be regarded as applying only to the products-completed operations exposures.

In order to avoid the exclusion, an insured may purchase products recall expense coverage. In addition to spoiled food, typical claim situations involve pharmaceuticals, chemicals, and automobile parts. Perhaps no incident has gained more attention or involved greater cost than the one involving the inspection of all DC-10 airplanes in 1979.

"X, C, U" Exclusions. There is a set of exclusions that apply to the CGL on a selective basis. They are known as the "x, c, u exclusions," "x" for explosion, "c" for collapse, and "u" for underground. These exclusions (1) have no effect on bodily injury liability, (2) only apply to property damage, and (3) apply only to classifications so designed in the manual by one or more of the letters "x, c, u." When the automatic coverage provision of the CGL policy includes operations affected by these exclusions, the coverage is picked up with the exclusion(s) intact; that is, the exclusions apply. Finally and equally important, these exclusions almost always may be removed for additional premium. However, sometimes special deductibles and reduced limits of liability may apply in granting the broader coverage.

Explosion Exclusions. Damage to or loss of use of property that results from blasting or explosion is not covered when the exclusion applies. The intent of the exclusion is to avoid loss within the explosion hazard as it relates to construction operations. The meaning of "blasting" is generally agreed upon while "explosion" is less clear. The exclusion clearly states that not included in the "x" hazard (and therefore covered) is property damage from explosion of steam vessels, piping under pressure and various other equipment, or arising out of operations of independent contractors, or from completed operations or the underground property damage hazard, or from liability assumed by the insured under an incidental contract.

Collapse Exclusion. The collapse (c) hazard includes structural property damage, as defined, and property damage to any other property at any time resulting from collapse. The effect of the exclusion is that there is no coverage for collapse of or structural injury to any building or structure due to grading of land and many similar operations including excavating, burrowing, filling, and pile driving or moving, shoring, underpinning, raising or demolition of any building or removal or rebuilding of any structural support of said building or structure.

As with the explosion hazard, the collapse hazard does not include property damage from operations or independent contractors, completed operations, or liability assumed by the insured under an incidental contract. Therefore, liability of the named insured arising out of such activities is covered even when the collapse exclusion applies.

Underground Exclusions. The underground (u) hazard includes property damage to underground property from the use of mechanical equipment for the purpose of grading land, paving, drilling, burrowing, filling, back-filling, or pile driving. The property specified includes wires, conduits, pipes, mains, sewers, tanks, tunnels and similar property under ground or under water.

The underground exclusion, as with the explosion and collapse counterparts, does not apply to liability from operations of independent contractors, completed operations liability, or liability assumed under incidental contracts.

Application of "x,c,u" Exclusions. The "x," "c," and "u" exclusions may apply individually or in any combination. For example, the manual classification for excavation is 15111xcu. For this classification and several others that include all three symbols there is no property damage liability coverage from explosion, collapse, or underground operations as defined when the exclusion is in the policy. Among such classifications are grading of land, certain pile driving, sewer construction, street construction or paving including repair and water mains construction. This is not a complete list, and the classification section of the manual should always be referred to in determining the need for coverage.

Classifications containing only the "xc" designation include building raising or moving, salvage operations, and wrecking. The "xu" symbols apply to the classification for irrigation or drainage system construction. Other examples are earth moving "cu," sand or gravel digging "x," and plumbing domestic "u."

There are other more highly specialized operations that have classifications followed by letters designating that special exclusions

Exhibit 2-2
Lettered CGL Exclusions

"x"—Explosion or blasting
"c"—Collapse—property damage by excavation, etc.
"u"—Underground—property damage by mechanical equipment
"d"—Underground resources and equipment
"e"—Blowout or cratering
"v,k,l"—Professional services—care, custody and control
"z"—Contamination
"o"—Work performed—care, custody and control

apply. They do not appear nearly as often as the "xcu" exclusions, but merit attention. They are:

1. exclusion d—underground resources and equipment exclusion;
2. exclusion e—blowout or cratering exclusion;
3. exclusions j, k, and l—professional services exclusions; and
4. exclusion z—contamination exclusion

The "d," "e," and "z" symbols are used with many oil-related classifications. Exhibit 2-2 summarizes the nature of the "lettered" exclusions.

Nuclear Exclusion. There is one other exclusion that should be mentioned, the nuclear energy liability exclusion (Broad Form), which usually appears away from the standard exclusions of the CGL. This exclusion seldom causes a problem. Most insureds involved with nuclear facilities know that nuclear energy liability insurance is available to cover what is excluded in the CGL regarding nuclear exposures. This exclusion affects a very small percentage of insureds. Its purpose is to eliminate coverage more appropriately furnished by another policy.

Exclusion Summary. The CGL, as broad as it is, does not cover all of the many liability exposures a business may have. That is not possible, but most coverage gaps created by exclusions can be filled when the need exists. Perhaps it is a greater problem for the producer to recognize or identify the insured's liability exposures than to provide offsetting coverage. Exposure identification is a growing responsibility of the producer. Exhibit 2-3 contains a summary of CGL exclusions and why the exclusions exist. Producers may refer to the exhibit either to explain the reasons or to find a way to provide coverage.

For additional premium, insurance can be provided for coverage lacking due to the exclusions relating to contractual liability and the

Exhibit 2-3
Purposes of CGL Exclusions

CGL Exclusion	Require Additional Premium for Coverage	Intended to be Covered Elsewhere	Generally Uninsurable
Contractual Liability	X		
Auto/Aircraft		X	
Mobile Equipment Use	X	X	
Mobile Equipment Transport		X	
Watercraft		X	
Pollution	X		X
War			X
Liquor Liability		X	
Workers' Compensation		X	
Employee Bodily Injury		X	
CCC		X	X
Premises Alteration		X	
Failure to Perform		X	
Injury to Work Performed			X
Withdrawal, Inspection, etc.			X
X,C,U, etc.	X		
Nuclear		X	X

"x,c,u" hazards. Other policies fill the gaps caused by the exclusions relating to automobiles, aircraft, watercraft, pollution, employees, alienated premises, delay or lack of performance or product failure, and products recall. The exclusions of liability for hazardous activities and alcohol related activities can be effectively eliminated either for additional premium or by other policies.

Of all the exclusions in the CGL, only those relating to war and allied perils (first aid expenses) and the business risks of damage to product and work performed are uninsurable generally.

The care, custody, or control exclusion can be handled in a number of ways such as (1) purchase of broad form property damage liability insurance to be discussed later; (2) bailee policies (discussed in Chapter

5); (3) purchase of an umbrella liability policy; (4) purchase of fire legal liability insurance; (5) owner's purchase of first party property coverage and a waiver of subrogation agreement with the bailee.

Checkpoints

1. When may an insured need garagekeepers' insurance in addition to a CGL?
2. Explain pollution coverage in the CGL.
3. List the three parts of the "CCC" exclusion in the CGL.
4. Describe the effect of "X, C, or U"
   a. appearing on the CGL.
   b. not appearing on the CGL.

Owners, Landlords, and Tenants Coverage Part

The owners, landlords, and tenants (OL&T) form was devised to provide liability coverages to individuals and firms whose exposures are centered primarily on premises. The only coverages automatically provided by the OL&T coverage part are premises and operations, including contractual liability for "incidental contracts," and liability for structural alterations performed by or on behalf of the named insured, provided alterations *do not* involve changing the size of or moving an existing structure or building. The OL&T form is not intended for use when an exposure exists for either products or completed operations. This form is suited only for firms which do not have a products or completed operations exposure, such as lessors and lessees of building office complexes, firms which operate automobile parking lots, municipal exposures concerning firehouses, golf courses, street signs and banners, and individuals who rent one or more private dwellings or apartment houses to others.

The OL&T form's premises and operations coverages are narrower in scope than the same coverages of the CGL and are best understood by examining the definition of insured premises, the operations liability coverage, and the exclusions.

Insured Premises Defined The premises coverage of the OL&T is limited to the ownership, maintenance, or use of the insured premises. The term "insured premises," as used in the OL&T form means:

1. Premises designated in the policy declarations. (Whether the premises is designated as a store, an office located within a building complex, or a building leased in whole or in part to others, the owner, tenant, lessee or whoever purchases the

OL&T policy will have protection for any liability suits arising from the physical exposures of such premises as are described in the form.)

2. Premises alienated (sold) to others—other than those constructed for sale. (Premises constructed for sale are insurable exposures customarily covered under completed operations insurance, and the OL&T policy cannot be written to include completed operations insurance.)

3. Newly acquired premises and the ways immediately adjoining on land, provided notice is given to the insurer within thirty days following any acquisition. (A firm that acquires a new building can be at a disadvantage under the OL&T policy if it fails to report such acquisition as there is no similar restriction under the CGL.)

Operations Liability Coverage   Coverage for operations under the OL&T policy is limited to operations specified in the policy declarations, plus those which are necessary or incidental to the insured premises. What is "necessary or incidental" could very well be a source of argument. It is clear, however, that a firm will not be automatically covered under the OL&T policy (but it would be covered under the CGL) if it decides to expand its operations to an entirely different type of business venture. Furthermore, because completed operations insurance is not available under this form, only operations in progress are covered, subject to the applicable exclusions.

Exclusions   All of the exclusions which apply to premises and operations coverages of the CGL are contained in the OL&T. However, the OL&T has two additional exclusions not found in the CGL.

The first of these excludes bodily injury or property damage arising out of operations on or from premises owned, rented, or controlled by the named insured—other than insured premises, as defined in the OL&T coverage part. This exclusion reinforces that the only premises and operations covered are those reported and insured. Thus, if a store owner obtains a second location and sustains a liability claim thirty-one days after acquiring the new premises, it will not be covered unless its location has been reported and insured within thirty days of its acquisition.

The second exclusion peculiar to the OL&T policy precludes coverage for claims arising out of (1) structural alterations which involve changing the size of or moving an existing structure or building and (2) new construction or demolition operations, regardless of their nature, whether all such operations are performed by or for the named insured. The purpose of this exclusion is to require that such hazardous exposures be specifically declared and insured for an additional premium. Examples of alterations not considered to change the size of a structure or building include the replacement of an old heating system, the rewiring of electrical outlets, the resurfacing of floors, and the paneling of office walls. Examples of alterations which involve changing the size of an existing structure or building include the construction of an additional room onto a dwelling or a new wing to a building office complex, the construction of new interior walls to make additional offices, and the construction of a new dormer on a dwelling. Structural alterations which involve a change in size of a structure or building can be covered for an additional premium.

Manufacturers and Contractors Coverage Part

The OL&T is predominately a premises-oriented coverage which includes operations coverage of an incidental nature; the manufacturers and contractors (M&C) form is just the reverse. The M&C form was devised to provide various liability coverages to enterprises whose exposures are predominantly away from premises. Among those for whom coverage may be written under the M&C are auctioneers, marine divers, funeral directors, fire fighters, and sales and service organizations. Presently, the only coverages automatically provided by the basic M&C coverage part are (1) premises coverage, (2) contractual liability for "incidental contracts," (3) liability for operations performed by the named insured away from its premises, and (4) liability for operations performed by the named insured or by independent contractors involving maintenance and repairs at premises owned by, or rented to, the named insured, and structural alterations at the named insured's owned or rented premises which do not involve changing the size of or moving buildings or other structures. The M&C cannot be written to include products liability and completed operations insurance and hence makes this unsuitable for manufacturers and contractors, since the former usually requires products coverage and the latter usually requires completed operations coverage.

The scope of the M&C premises and operations coverages is much narrower than the CGL but is somewhat broader than those of the OL&T.

Premises and Operations Coverage The premises coverage of the M&C encompasses exposures relating to premises without restricting the premises by definition, as is the case with the OL&T. The reason the premises coverage of the M&C is not defined is that the primary exposures of firms written on an M&C seldom are concerned with the physical nature of the insured's own premises. Instead, the primary exposures are associated with operations emanating from premises, as well as away from premises.

Construction contractors, for example, ordinarily have comparatively little exposure to liability loss on their own premises. Most liability losses occur at construction sites of others. However, if a premises liability claim were to occur at a construction contracting firm's office or grounds or at a construction site to which the firm holds title until work is completed, the firm has coverage. An OL&T rated on an area basis would not properly price the off-premises exposure of a contractor or other firm whose exposure is predominantly away from its premises; nor would the coverage of the OL&T suffice, since it is designed for the on-premises exposures of the insured. The M&C rated on the basis of payroll or receipts is more appropriate.

Manufacturers, on the other hand, seldom operate from premises other than their own, but it is not the premises exposure to the public that is hazardous. It is the potential vicarious liability of manufacturers, resulting from the negligent acts and omissions of its employees who work away from the manufacturing premises, which is the major exposure to liability loss. Hence, an M&C rated on the basis of payroll more clearly and fairly reflects the exposure than would an OL&T rated on the basis of area.

Coverage of the M&C applies to all operations, i.e., the operations are not in any way limited to those which are necessary or incidental to the insured business. If a firm decides to undertake an unrelated type of operation, it will be covered. However, the scope of such coverage again depends upon the exclusions. The exclusions of the M&C are virtually identical to those of the OL&T with two exceptions.

The first exclusion peculiar to the M&C policy precludes bodily injury or property damage arising out of (1) operations performed for the named insured by independent contractors and (2) acts or omissions stemming from the general supervision of such operations by the named insured. It makes no difference whether such claims occur on the premises of the named insured or on the premises of others. If an insured anticipates using independent contractors and decides that insurance is desirable or necessary, independent contractors coverage must be specifically added to the M&C and an additional premium paid.

Specifically excepted from the foregoing exclusion is bodily injury or property damage that occurs in the course of (1) maintenance and repairs at premises owned by or rented to the insured, or (2) structural alterations at such premises which do not involve changing the size of or moving buildings or other structures.

Two points of coverage can be inferred from the two exceptions. First, claims emanating from maintenance and repair work at premises of the named insured are covered under premises and operations coverage of the M&C whether they are performed by the named insured or by independent contractors. Second, structural alterations which do not involve significant changes or do not involve the moving of buildings or other structures are covered by the M&C whether they are performed by independent contractors or not. More important, claims stemming from alterations which involve changing the size of or moving a building or structure also are covered by the M&C premises and operations coverage part when they are performed by the named insured's employees. But when they are performed by an independent contractor, additional coverage is required, whether such operations take place on premises of the named insured or on premises of others.

The second exclusion applicable to the M&C (also identical to that of the CGL) excludes property damage including the explosion, collapse, and underground property damage hazards, unless a firm doing work within the scope of those hazards has the appropriate x, c, or u exclusion deleted from the policy for an additional cost.

Storekeepers Liability Form

The storekeepers liability form is an indivisible package of liability coverages designed for retail stores which meet the eligibility requirements prescribed in the OL&T Manual. Retail stores which sell more than 50 percent of their goods by mail order are not eligible; nor are auction stores, barber shops, beauty salons, chain stores having more than ten locations, cleaning and dyeing establishments, certain department stores, drug stores, mail-order houses, and open-air markets. Stores in the supermarket class are also ineligible if their total sales annually exceed $500,000 and their store area exceeds 3,000 square feet.

The storekeepers liability form provides premises and operations coverage and exclusions almost identical to those of the OL&T. The form also includes coverage for the elevator liability exposure, premises medical payments, products and completed operations, and independent contractors coverage, excluding only the demolition hazard.

However, since firms covered under the storekeepers form are less likely to have off-premises mobile equipment liability exposures than firms which are covered by CGL, OL&T, and M&C forms, the persons insured provision of the storekeepers form is considerably shorter than the other forms.

Persons Insured Under the Storekeepers Form In brief, the term "persons insured," as it appears in the storekeepers liability form, means:

1. An individual, when such person is designated in the policy declarations as the named insured, but only to the extent of that person's business activities as a sole proprietor.
2. A partnership or joint venture, when such firm is designated in the policy declarations as the named insured, and including any partner's or member's liability during the conduct of a partnership or joint venture activity.
3. Any organization, other than a sole proprietorship, partnership, or joint venture, such as a corporation, when such organization is designated in the policy declarations as the named insured, including the liability of any executive officer, director, or stockholder while such person is acting within the scope of his or her duties.
4. Any person or organization while acting as a real estate manager for the named insured, other than employees of the named insured.

Owners and Contractors Protective Liability Coverage Part

Like the CGL, owners and contractors protective liability insurance (OCP) provides owners with coverage against exposures arising from their supervisory duties with a contractor and for the acts of contractors, as well as providing coverage to contractors against exposures arising from the acts of subcontractors. Coverage in the separate OCP policy is the same as it is when written as part of the CGL policy. The separate policy is used more often by owners than by contractors as when someone is having a building constructed.

This independent contractor's coverage is automatically included in the CGL policy. Premium is based on the amount paid to independent contractors (or to subcontractors by a contractor). Coverage of the independent contractors hazard protects the named insured against liability for bodily injury and property damage caused by others performing work in the insured's behalf. This is important protection for a contractor or for one for whom work is performed and who is subject to vicarious liability because of negligent acts of a subcontractor or other delegate. Even though the subcontractor is insured, the general or prime contractor could and probably would be sued in the event of damage. While it is probable that liability would fall on the subcontractor, not the prime contractor, the latter would still need to finance the costs of legal defense. Sometimes OCP is referred to as "defense coverage" since it is used in this way more often than as indemnity. The relatively low cost of this coverage recognizes that in practice it is more of a defense than a liability coverage.

Independent contractors are not the same as employees even though the one for whom work is performed may be liable for the acts of both employees and independent contractors. The OCP may also apply, for example, when a merchant or building owner may have repairs or renovations performed. The OCP in this case would protect the merchant or building owner.

Another purpose of OCP coverage is to protect against the strict liability that may be imposed on contractors for failure to exercise proper supervision or even for selection of unqualified subcontractors. Most of this discussion of independent contractor's coverage has concerned vicarious liability, the liability imputed to another because of the acts of one performed in his or her behalf. On the other hand, strict liability is liability imposed through inherently dangerous activities, even though a reasonable degree of care was exercised. Production of dangerous products such as chemicals and operations or the performance of dangerous activities such as blasting are examples of inherently dangerous activities. When such activities are performed in behalf of others, independent contractor's coverage protects against the strict liability that may be imposed on the hiring party.

Checkpoints

How does coverage under the following forms differ from the CGL?
- a. OL&T
- b. M&C
- c. Storekeepers
- d. OCP

SUMMARY

Whether one liability form should be recommended over another depends upon the needs and qualifications of the firm. Since the CGL provides a number of coverages, including products liability and completed operations, as well as automatic coverage for new exposures that arise during the policy period, it is recommended for any firm, except those eligible for garage liability forms. Even if products liability or completed operations coverage is not desired or is unavailable, the CGL is still recommended because of its automatic coverage for newly acquired exposures. Furthermore, the cost of a CGL without products liability and completed operations coverages is approximately the same as an OL&T or an M&C policy.

If a store has a relatively small growth potential and requires products liability insurance, the storekeepers liability policy should seriously be considered as an alternative to the CGL. Products liability insurance is automatically included as part of the storekeepers package premium without the requirement of an audit on product sales. However, when a store does not qualify for the latter form, the CGL should be recommended.

Automobile dealers, repair shops, and other similar operations should select one of the garage liability forms because they contain coverages for exposures usual to those businesses. In addition, garage liability forms provide the convenience of automatic coverage.

Both the OL&T and the M&C are limited in scope and they should be used only when operations are so limited that coverage is needed simply for premises or operations. The OL&T is suited for individuals whose dwellings do not qualify for the homeowners program or for separate CGL policies, for individuals and commercial entities whose rental properties do not qualify for the commercial multi-peril package programs, or for firms which do not need the broader coverage provided by the CGL, particularly products and/or completed operations insurance, such as lessors of apartment houses or mercantile or office buildings. The M&C may be suited for the supervisory exposures of architects and engineers, detective agencies, and fire fighters who have no need for products and/or completed operations insurance.

At one time, the M&C was commonly written for the individual contractor who specialized in small operations. But with the broad insurance requirements now demanded by owners of projects, the M&C appears not to serve a useful purpose. Therefore, it would be better for a contractor to purchase a CGL with or without products and/or completed operations coverage, rather than an OL&T or M&C, to get the extra benefits provided at little, if any, additional cost.

CHAPTER 3

General Liability Insurance (Continued)

INTRODUCTION

The comprehensive general liability policy (CGL) is the broadest policy available to meet the liability insurance needs of all kinds of businesses (except those engaged in the automobile business). Even the coverage provided by a form as broad as the garage liability policy is improved by adding the CGL coverage part. The CGL form covers insurable exposures that *arise* as well as insurable exposures that are *discovered* during the policy period. Covered exposures in the CGL are (1) premises and operations, (2) independent contractors, (3) products, and (4) completed operations. Yet, as broad as the CGL is, some organizations face additional exposures that need treatment. Most of these additional exposures can be insured by use of the broad form CGL endorsement.

BROAD FORM CGL ENDORSEMENT

A number of insurance companies use their own broad liability endorsements to expand the CGL. They are known by different names such as Multi-Cover, Supplementary Liability, Ten Pac, Comp Plus, and Roll-on Coverage. There may be wide differences among the various insurance company endorsements. They are generally similar, but far from uniform in detail. They also differ in some ways from the broad form comprehensive general liability endorsement developed by Insurance Services Office (ISO). The ISO form is used by many insurers that do not have their own endorsement and even some that have their own but allow the use of either form.

Producers and others responsible for selling, selecting, or explaining coverages should be aware of the lack of uniformity in the various broad or extended liability endorsements. First of all, such knowledge is needed to tailor coverages to loss exposures. Perhaps equally important, when replacing coverage, it is necessary to identify any reductions of coverage that may result from substituting one broad liability endorsement for another and to inform the insured of such reductions. This may help a producer avoid an errors and omissions loss, and as always, notice should be in writing in order to be most effective.

Coverages

The standard broad form CGL endorsement provides the following twelve coverage extensions for a premium equal to a fixed percentage of the premiums for basic limits of the bodily injury and property damage liability coverage:

1. blanket contractual liability,
2. personal injury liability and advertising injury liability,
3. premises medical payments,
4. host liquor liability,
5. fire legal liability on real property,
6. broad form property damage, including completed operations,
7. incidental medical malpractice,
8. nonowned watercraft liability,
9. limited worldwide coverage,
10. additional persons insured,
11. extended bodily injury coverage,
12. automatic coverage on newly acquired organizations.

Space limitations will permit only a very brief explanation of each coverage, including the need for each coverage and selling points when applicable.

Most of the coverages included in these broad form liability endorsements are available separately. Since the cost of the package of coverages is often less than one or two coverages purchased individually, price is not usually the deciding factor. More often the decision is dictated by underwriting considerations. Because the broad form liability endorsement is so comprehensive, an underwriter may not be willing to write some of the included coverages in certain business situations.

Contractual Liability Coverage The CGL covers five types of incidental contracts. By definition, incidental contracts must be in writing and include: (1) lease of premises; (2) certain easement agreements; (3) indemnification of a municipality required by municipal ordinance, except in connection with work for the municipality; (4) sidetrack agreements; and (5) elevator maintenance agreements.

Many business situations involve contractual agreements other than those defined as incidental contracts. Businesses frequently agree to hold harmless or indemnify others, notably customers and suppliers. Small retailers frequently sign contracts with alarm companies containing hold harmless agreements. When such agreements do not fall within the definition of incidental contracts, contractual liability coverage is needed. Unlike incidental contracts coverage, contractual liability covers *any* contract or agreement including oral contracts. Only written agreements qualify as incidental contracts. This considerable broadening of coverage is also found in many independently filed forms. Blanket contractual coverage may be purchased separately. The separate blanket contractual coverage is the same as coverage in the broad form CGL endorsement. Separate coverage is also available for designated contracts. When designated contract coverage is desired, the underwriter will probably want to inspect each contract.

CGL Exclusions. The CGL exclusions apply to the contractual liability coverage and all of the other included coverages, except as modified or deleted. The exclusions deleted in the contractual liability provisions are those relating to automobiles and aircraft, snowmobiles and trailers designed for use therewith, watercraft, and transportation of mobile equipment. The forms used by many insurance companies may not delete these exclusions. Producers should assess the need for contractual liability coverage in these areas. When the need exists or is probable, and if the form used does not delete the appropriate exclusion(s), producers should attempt to modify it or use the ISO endorsement or one similar in this regard.

In addition to the nondeleted CGL exclusions, there are five specific contractual liability exclusions added by endorsement.

Additional Contractual Exclusions. The first additional exclusion eliminates coverage for liability assumed under contract for damages occurring prior to the execution of the contract. The second and third exclusions relate to professional liability assumed by architects, engineers, or surveyors in contracts. The fourth contractual exclusion relates to damage to third-party beneficiaries to a contract with a public authority. For instance, if a municipality by contract requires a contractor to be responsible for damage to all property along the work site, the exclusion denies coverage to the contractor if sued for damages by a "third party" or a party not engaged in the project. The final contractual exclusion is for damage from operations within fifty feet of any railroad property or affecting certain railroad property such as trestles and bridges. The exclusion does not apply to sidetrack agreements.

Exposure Identification. Producers should ask, and when possible insist, that they be given copies of all agreements entered into by their insureds. This should be standard practice and not just limited to contractors. Coverages should be provided for insurable contractual liability exposures, and insureds should be informed of any exposures they have assumed that cannot be insured. Such notices should be conveyed in writing. Examples of typical obligations assumed by contract but not covered by contractual liability are fines, taxes imposed, and finance charges. Contractual liability, like the CGL itself, covers only loss caused by bodily injury or property damage.

Personal Injury and Advertising Injury Liability Coverage
These two coverages are combined in the ISO form, but not all insurance company forms include advertising injury coverage. Also, treatment of exclusions is not uniform. These coverages can be purchased separately. However, individually, advertising injury liability insurance is considered a specialty coverage obtainable from excess and surplus lines insurers or from a small number of other insurance companies. On the other hand, personal injury liability insurance is written by almost every insurance company that writes liability insurance. Of the two exposures, the personal injury exposure is more common.

Personal Injury. Personal injury is a broader term than bodily injury. Personal injury adds to coverage in the CGL's bodily injury coverage usually with the addition of libel, slander, wrongful entry or eviction, false arrest, detention, defamation or malicious prosecution coverage. It is hard to imagine any business that does not need personal injury liability coverage. Some of the most obvious examples are hotels, motels, and apartments for wrongful entry or eviction, and retail and wholesale stores for false arrest, detention, or malicious prosecution. Newspapers, magazines, and radio and television stations immediately come to mind for the libel and slander exposures, but they usually are covered by Broadcasters' or Publishers' Liability insurance designed for these specialty situations.

Claims arise out of various kinds of situations. Tired or tactless sales people may insult customers in such a way as to damage their reputation. Individuals may be embarrassed by the acts of others. Incidents can occur in public confrontation or from communication by telephone or mail. Losses may result from credit inquiries and employment references, even those that seem innocent. Acts of an insured or the insured's representative (employee or other person) may embarrass another in front of a crowd, as in false arrest or detention, or in the presence of just one other person, friend or stranger.

Telephone communications may cause losses as when insulting messages are left with others. The same is true of misdirected mail or a falsely accusing letter that may be opened and read by an employer's secretary. Angry creditors frustrated by unsuccessful collection attempts sometimes announce to others, intentionally or otherwise, dim views of "the scoundrel" beyond the alleged credit indiscretions. Should the allegation be false and damaging, a personal injury claim may result.

LIBEL AND SLANDER. One defense for libel or slander is truth, with different standards applying for public figures. For most individuals, if the pronouncement is untrue, it constitutes libel (a written communication) or slander (an oral communication). In many cases damages may be hard to prove, but necessary legal defense may be costly. A CGL without personal injury coverage added would not respond to a claim or defend the insured, so even if only to provide defense, personal injury liability insurance is vital.

Personal injury liability insurance is available separately by endorsement to the CGL or as part of the coverage in the broad form CGL endorsement. Cost of the separate coverage is usually based on a percentage (often 10 percent) of the bodily injury liability premium.

BROAD FORM VERSUS SEPARATE COVERAGE. There are three improvements in the broad form endorsement over coverage in the separate personal injury liability endorsement. Two have little or no effect in actual practice while the third is very important. In the separate personal injury liability endorsement there is a provision for insured participation. This participation is expressed as a percentage of the limit of liability. Participation is not mandatory; in fact, it is used infrequently. An underwriter may request insured participation in a loss when the nature of the insured's business makes the exposure to loss much greater than average.

In the separate endorsement, the hazards insured by the broad form are divided into three groups (A, B, and C). This allows both underwriter and insured to select the specific coverages desired. Some may consider this advantageous; however, with today's increasing consumer activity, generous juries, and greater emphasis on individual rights, the all-inclusive coverage approach of the broad form endorsement seems preferable. In practice, this feature, like insured participation, has little effect; separate personal injury liability coverage, when provided, usually includes all of the hazards in groups A, B, and C of the endorsement. Even so, producers should discourage buyers from omitting any of the coverages. Also, they should be alert to issuance of less coverage than desired, accidental or otherwise, when separate coverage is used instead of the broad form endorsement.

The remaining difference between the two methods of providing this coverage concerns an important exclusion. In the separate coverage endorsement there is no coverage for personal injury resulting from an offense relating to employment of someone by the named insured. This exclusion does not appear in the broad form liability endorsement, so employment-related offenses are covered.

In the separate personal injury liability endorsement the employment exclusion may be deleted for additional premium. The advantage of using a form without the exclusion is not only that the surcharge is avoided but also there is no danger of omitting this needed coverage because of oversight or lack of knowledge.

In addition to some lack of knowledge about existence of the exclusion, there is also confusion as to its effect. Some erroneously believe that excluding offenses "related to the employment" is intended to deny coverage for acts of personal injury committed by employees of the insured. That is not correct. The exclusion eliminates coverage for liability for personal injury *to* a former or present employee of the insured.

An employer may falsely accuse an employee or cause him or her to be unjustly detained or arrested. A job reference may contain incorrect, damaging information. On-the-job situations may result in an invasion of privacy. If anything, the nature and closeness of the employer-employee relationship increases the exposure of the employer to liability for personal injury. Increased equal opportunity in employment laws have brought emphasis to the need of providing personal injury liability coverage without the employment exclusion. Producers should take care to delete the exclusion when using the separate endorsement or when using a broad form other than the ISO edition that contains the exclusion.

PERSONAL INJURY EXCLUSIONS. Exclusions that appear in the broad form endorsement relate to contractual liability, injury occurring before inception date of the policy, losses involving information known to be false by the insured, and injury arising out of willful violation of a penal statute or ordinance committed by or with the knowledge or consent of the insured. Also, there is no coverage for personal or advertising injury arising out of partnerships or joint ventures not designated as a named insured in the policy. It may be confusing to note that personal injury liability assumed (contractual liability) is excluded after stating the broad form CGL endorsement includes coverage for contractual liability. The purpose of the exclusion is to avoid coverage for assumption of the personal injury liability exposure of others which underwriters consider to be unmanageable. As in most multi-coverage insurance forms, exclusions are inserted as the coverage builds in order to control the exposure.

Advertising Liability. While the exclusions reviewed so far apply to both the personal and advertising injury liability coverages, there are additional exclusions applicable only to advertising injury liability:

- failure of performance of contract;
- infringement of trademark, service mark, or trade name, other than titles or slogans;
- incorrect description or mistake in advertised price of goods sold, offered for sale or advertised;
- advertising injury to any insured in the business of advertising, broadcasting, publishing, or telecasting; and
- injury arising out of any act committed by the insured with actual malice

What is covered in the advertising injury liability section is "injury arising out of an offense committed during the policy period occurring in the course of the named insured's advertising activities, if such injury arises out of libel, slander, defamation, violation of right of privacy, piracy, unfair competition, or infringement of copyright, title or slogan."

Advertising injury liability is paired with personal injury because the exposures insured are similar. It is possible to libel someone in an advertisement (a nonsmoker shown smoking) or by a written statement ("Karen smokes Camels"). However, advertising injury liability is not errors and omissions coverage for advertising agencies or advertisers. That type of coverage is usually available only from excess and surplus lines insurers and a limited number of standard insurers.

Premises Medical Payments Coverage Of all the coverages in the broad form endorsement, medical payments coverage is probably the best known and most often used as a separate endorsement. Often it is called the "good will" coverage and although a companion to liability insurance, it is not liability insurance. It pays without regard to fault for medical expense incurred within one year from the date of an accident arising out of a condition in the insured premises or operations covered by the named insured's bodily injury insurance.

Broad Form Versus Separate Coverage. While coverage provisions in the broad form endorsement are the same as separate medical payments coverage, there is a difference in how the limits of liability are provided. The broad form provides a basic per person limit of

$1,000. The aggregate limit for all persons is the same as the occurrence limit of the bodily injury coverage in the policy. Basic limits in the separate coverage are $250 per person and $10,000 per accident.

Insufficient medical payments coverage is not as serious a problem as insufficient liability insurance limits. If the insured is not negligent, and therefore not legally liable, the medical payments amount to goodwill damages (although an unhappy customer may be lost along with goodwill). On the other hand, if the insured is liable for the accident causing the injury, the bodily injury liability coverage will protect the insured up to the limit of liability, which will be considerably in excess of the medical payments limit. Despite this apparently safe situation, producers should inform insureds of the goodwill that may be salvaged by adequate medical payments limits.

Exclusions. Many of the medical payments exclusions relate to exclusions in the CGL. There is no coverage for accidents relating to automobiles, to mobile equipment while used in connection with racing, demolition, or stunting activities, to operation of snowmobiles, or to watercraft. Also excluded are medical payments for (1) bodily injury within the products or completed operations hazard, (2) certain operations performed by independent contractors, (3) resulting from activities involving alcoholic beverage, or (4) due to war.

Certain persons are excluded from coverage such as the named insured, and any partner or tenant, employees, people engaged in maintenance and repair or construction, anyone covered by workers' compensation, unemployment compensation, or disability income insurance, participants in athletics of any kind, club members (if the insured is a club), and guests (if the insured is a hotel, motel, or tourist court).

Host Liquor Liability Coverage This coverage is more a reinforcement than an extension of coverage. The CGL excludes alcohol-related activities of various kinds but does not directly exclude liability from incidental activities such as office parties. It may be said that host liquor liability coverage specifically provides protection that may already exist in the CGL to which the broad form endorsement is attached.

The coverage "modifies" or clarifies the CGL exclusion, allowing coverage for serving alcoholic beverages incidental to the named insured's business. Whether or not such incidental activities are excluded in the CGL, the specific host liquor coverage has value if it does no more than establish that coverage does exist where before there may have been uncertainty.

Host liquor liability coverage does not remove or modify in any way the policy exclusion relating to alcohol activities if the insured is engaged in the business of manufacturing, distributing, selling or serving alcoholic beverages. Coverage for such activities is not provided in the broad form endorsement. In fact, coverage applies only if the named insured is *not* engaged in such businesses. This is not the so-called "dram shop" coverage for restaurants, taverns, or anyone otherwise engaged in the business of manufacturing, distributing, selling, or serving alcoholic beverages. The repetition is intentional—this point cannot be made too strongly. Host liquor liability coverage is available from excess and surplus lines insurers for those engaged in the businesses named above.

Fire Legal Liability Coverage—Real Property   This is another of the coverages in the broad form CGL endorsement also available separately. As a separate coverage, it is found in the Fire and Allied section of the Commercial Lines Manual. However, it is legal liability insurance and is needed by a large number of insureds.

Without fire legal liability coverage, some tenants do not have protection for damage to the leased premises in their care, custody, or control resulting from fire caused by the tenant's negligence. The CGL policy contains an exclusion for damage to property (1) owned or occupied by or rented to, (2) used by, or (3) in the care, custody, or control of the insured. There is a remedy to this problem other than or in addition to providing fire legal liability insurance discussed later.

Need for Coverage.   The liability covered by fire legal liability insurance is specified as to structures or portions thereof rented to the insured, including fixtures permanently attached. The wording "portions thereof" and "including fixtures permanently attached" is significant. In a building with multiple occupancy "portions thereof" would include hallways, entryways, rest rooms, and similar common use areas. Without this broadened language, damage to such areas might not be covered, since it may be held that the insured had care, custody or control. Even if that premise would not disallow coverage, the CGL exclusion for damage to property used by the insured would.

The benefit of "including fixtures permanently attached" is more obvious. It avoids the possibility that fixtures owned by the landlord might not be considered part of the building and therefore not covered.

Limit of Liability.   The limit of liability in the broad form endorsement is $50,000 and usually can be raised for additional premium. Producers should be alert to the need for increase. Also, producers should check the limit and the use of special deductibles if a broad form endorsement other than ISO's is used because there is not uniformity between the various broad form CGL endorsements used. Many insurance companies use a $25,000 limit, some provide limits higher than $50,000, and a few specify no limit, meaning the policy property damage limit applies. One insurance company's form does not provide fire legal liability coverage at all.

Exclusions and Limitations. The fire legal liability provision deletes all exclusions in the policy, as they may apply to fire legal liability, except the nuclear exclusion, but adds a contractual liability exclusion more restrictive than in the CGL. The problem is that the added exclusion applies to all contracts including incidental contracts which include leases of premises, leaving an insured without coverage if the insured assumed damage in the lease. Since leases frequently contain contractual liability clauses, the problem is not unusual, and it can be quite serious. Producers should try to have the exclusion modified so as to apply only to contractual agreements other than incidental contracts. This may not be easy, so alternative courses of action should be prepared. Another less serious restrictive provision is that fire legal liability insurance is excess over the insured's other collectible insurance. It is not so-called "good will" insurance and should not be represented to an insured as such.

Alternatives. While considering alternatives, all parties involved should be aware that fire legal liability *covers only real property* and only against loss by fire. Insureds frequently lease expensive personal property such as office machines, furniture, and furnishings. Personal property is exposed to perils other than fire, particularly burglary and theft. The purchase of separate property insurance covering the property for which liability is assumed may be necessary to solve the problems caused by the limitations of fire legal liability coverage. However, even with its limitations, fire legal liability is an important coverage.

A noninsurance solution that eliminates the problems discussed here is waiver of subrogation. Most fire insurance and package policies automatically permit the insured to waive, in writing prior to a loss, the insurer's right of recovery against any party. The advantages are that the perils are not limited to fire, the agreement applies to contents as well as real property, and there are no problems with contractual agreements or excess insurance provisions. Even if the tenant insured is required to insure the building for the landlord, a waiver of subrogation agreement should be entered into by the parties as the waiver then applies to any personal property of the landlord and the fire insurance protects the landlord's real property.

Some nonstandard policies may not permit waiver of the insurer's right of subrogation. In such cases most insurers will grant permission upon request without charge. This requires attachment of a subrogation waiver to the policy. Of course, the need to be certain that policies

Exhibit 3-1
Sample Waiver of Subrogation Agreement

> "Landlord and Tenant and all parties claiming under them mutually release and discharge each other from all claims and liabilities arising from or caused by any casualty or hazard covered or required hereunder to be covered in whole or in part by insurance on the premises or in connection with property on or activities conducted on the premises, and waive any right of subrogation which might otherwise exist in or accrue to any person on account thereof."

permit the waiver is incumbent upon producers, particularly before they recommend this course to an insured.

Seeing that the policy involved permits waiver of subrogation is only part of the job. There must be an agreement in writing between parties to a lease or real or personal property, and it should be of mutual benefit. That is, each party should agree to waive its insurer's right of subrogation against the other. Some agreements are written to benefit only one party and should be discouraged.

There are various forms of waiver of subrogation agreements and it is best to let attorneys prepare them. There is no standard agreement; Exhibit 3-1 is used only to acquaint the reader with the possible format and provisions.

Broad Form Property Damage Liability Coverage (Including Completed Operations) For many insureds the inclusion of this coverage may be of no benefit but it can be to contractors. Some manufacturers, processors, and service organizations also have need for this coverage.

Broad form property damage coverage removes the exclusions referred to generally as the "care, custody or control" and the "work performed" exclusions in the CGL and replaces them with other language. The exclusions are both removed and restated; they are not eliminated. In restating the exclusions, the effect of the CGL exclusions is narrowed somewhat. It cannot be stressed too strongly that broad form PD insurance does not provide total care, custody, or control coverage.

Care, Custody, and Control Modifications. In the restated language, property owned or occupied by or rented to the insured is still excluded. Also excluded is property more appropriately covered elsewhere, such as property held by the insured for sale or entrusted to the insured for storage or safekeeping. Property on the insured's premises to be worked on by the insured, tools or equipment while being used by the insured in his operations, and property in custody of the insured to be installed, erected or used in construction by the insured are excluded. Broad form PD coverage does not cover the insured's own property insurance exposures; nor does it provide bailee coverage.

The change in application of the CGL exclusion has to do with care, custody, or control away from the insured's premises. For example, if a plumber is working in a house and negligently causes flooding that damages carpeting, furniture, and furnishings, the unextended CGL will provide no property damage coverage if conditions show that the plumber had care, custody, or control of the premises. The broad form property damage exclusion refers "to that particular part of any property" away from the insured's premises upon which operations are being performed, or out of which property damage arises or the restoration, repair, or replacement of which is caused by faulty workmanship by or on behalf of the insured. Thus the damage caused by the plumber is covered by the broad form property damage coverage. This illustrates an interesting feature of broad form PD liability: the coverage is inferred from the exclusions rather than stated affirmatively. The words "particular part" are highly significant and have the effect of confining the area of custody.

Although it may be an oversimplification, the narrowing of the exclusion (and therefore broadening of coverage) perhaps is best explained by pointing out that the phrase "care, custody or control" does not appear in the substitute exclusion, having been replaced by one that focuses on the specific area of operation rather than a more general area of care, custody, or control. The result is to give an insured liability coverage for damage to property in its care, custody, or control, except the particular part of the property on which the insured is performing work at the time of an occurrence.

Frequently activities at construction sites as well as repair and service operations cause claims that illustrate the need for broad form PD coverage. For example, a contractor who installs faulty columns that cause collapse would not have coverage for replacement of the columns, but with broad form PD coverage the resultant damage caused by the collapse would be covered.

Reference to "upon which operations are being performed" and "faulty workmanship" reinforces the long held position that liability insurance, when applicable, will pay for resultant damage caused by faulty work but not for repair or replacement of the fault itself.

Broad form PD liability coverage mainly benefits contractors, but many others have need of this insurance. Whenever there is exposure to damage to property of others away from insured's premises that the

CGL would not cover because of the care, custody or control exclusion, broad form PD coverage is the solution if the insured's circumstances can be improved by narrowing applicability of the exclusion. Food caterers, interior decorators, installation, repair or servicing contractors—in fact, anyone who works on the premises of others—may have need of broad form PD liability coverage.

Work Performed Modifications. This part of the discussion applies only to the completed operations coverage. While the broad form PD coverage in the ISO broad form CGL endorsement always includes completed operations coverage, the CGL coverage may be written without completed operations. At the beginning of the discussion on broad form property damage, it was stated that broad form PD coverage modifies two exclusions in the CGL policy. The final exclusion is the work performed exclusion, which eliminates coverage for "property damage to work performed by or on behalf of the named insured arising out of the work or any portion thereof." In the broad form PD coverage, when completed operations coverage is included, the words "or on behalf of" are omitted.

The need for modifying the work performed exclusion exists for any contractor who employs subcontractors. For homebuilders and general contractors it is obvious. Without broad form PD coverage including completed operations, the insured contractor cannot be protected against liability for damage to the buildings constructed by the insured even though completed operations insurance is included in the CGL. Damage to the buildings caused by faulty work of electricians, plumbers, heating and air conditioning contractors, roofers, any other subcontractors, as well as work performed by the builder, is not covered. As far as the general contractor is concerned, the entirety of each structure fits within the phrase of "work performed by or on behalf of the insured" and is thereby excluded from coverage in an unendorsed CGL. Considering the likelihood of damage by fire (faulty wiring), explosion (defective heating), water damage (improper plumbing), and a myriad of other loss possibilities, including completed operations in broad form PD coverage seems essential. However, without broad form PD completed operations coverage, there is liability coverage for damage to other property such as neighboring structures, personal property, and automobiles. Still, by covering all subcontracted work through the elimination of "on behalf of" in the exclusion, the insured contractor's coverage is broadened considerably. Of course an insurmountable problem remains for the builder who subcontracts little or no work, but this is rare. The coverage is so important that broad form PD liability insurance should be recommended to all insured contractors and others as conditions warrant.

Importance of Broad Form Property Damage. Aside from the effect this coverage has on care, custody, or control and the work performed exclusions in CGL coverage and the importance of including completed operations for certain insureds, broad form PD liability causes other confusion because of the name itself.

Because the separate coverage and the broad CGL endorsement both begin with the words "broad form," some producers and insureds confuse the two. This is dangerous. The problem that results from providing specific broad form PD coverage when the insured expects the package of coverages in the broad form CGL endorsement is obvious.

The automatic inclusion of completed operations with broad form PD liability in the ISO form also may cause a problem, since it can be attached only to a policy including completed operations coverage. An unendorsed CGL coverage includes products and completed operations protection; however, it can be deleted from the policy. When this has been done, a broad form CGL endorsement that automatically includes completed operations, such as the ISO form, cannot be used.

The producer then has three choices, using a broad form CGL endorsement that either (1) omits broad form PD liability coverage, (2) includes it without completed operations, or (3) provides the desired supplemental coverages individually. Usually the pricing is such that two or three of the individual coverages found in the broad form CGL endorsement cost as much or more than the complete broad form CGL endorsement. Finding the appropriate separate form may be difficult.

Incidental Medical Malpractice Liability Coverage Insureds who provide medical services incidental to their business operations (a nurse in a factory) need this coverage. The exclusions applicable to bodily injury in the CGL make no mention of incidental malpractice so there already may be coverage for liability arising out of the exposures. The extension of coverage in the broad form endorsement assures coverage, eliminating potential dispute and litigation.

The word "incidental" explains the intent of this coverage. The definition of bodily injury in the CGL is amended to include medical malpractice injury defined as:

> injury arising out of the rendering of or failure to render during the policy period, the following services:
>
> (A) medical, surgical, dental, x-ray or nursing service or treatment or the furnishing of food or beverages in connection therewith; or
>
> (B) the furnishing or dispensing of drugs or medical, dental or surgical supplies or appliances.

It is not the intent of this coverage to provide professional liability insurance. Any insured or indemnitee engaged in the business or occupation of providing such services is excluded. This prevents unintended assumption of coverage should the insured agree to indemnify or hold harmless a doctor, dentist, hospital facility, or other professional medical entity or individual. Also not covered are expenses incurred by the insured for first aid to others at the time of an accident, thus altering the coverage provided in the "Supplementary Payments" portion of the CGL. This avoids extending the coverage to incidental medical operations.

Nonowned Watercraft Liability Coverage (under twenty-six feet in length) This coverage modifies the watercraft exclusion in the CGL. It provides bodily injury and property damage liability insurance resulting from operation of watercraft under twenty-six feet in length neither owned by the named insured nor used to carry persons or property for a charge. What is covered is liability incurred by the insured from use of watercraft owned by others, such as employees entertaining insureds' customers.

Most individual insurance company forms cover use of watercraft larger than the twenty-six feet limitation in the ISO form. In addition to this difference, producers should exercise caution in making sure that in the form of coverage selected, nonowned watercraft means craft not owned by the *named* insured, not just *an* insured. Often employees are named as additional insureds in CGLs (as they are in the broad form CGL endorsement). Therefore, if the form covers watercraft not owned by an insured (instead of the named insured), the insurance is severely limited and does not cover the employee-customer exposure described.

The watercraft coverage will not pay any part of a loss when the insured is protected otherwise. For instance, if the owner's insurance pays, the nonowned watercraft liability coverage does not apply, even if the owner's insurance is inadequate to pay the loss.

Limited Worldwide Liability Coverage The CGL provides that insurance applies only to bodily injury or property damage which occurs within the policy territory which includes the United States, its territories or possessions, or Canada. This extends coverage for bodily injury, property damage, personal injury, and advertising injury to a worldwide basis. Insurance applies for injury arising out of the activities of any insured permanently domiciled in the United States who is temporarily outside the policy territory. The original suit for injury or damage must be brought within the United States, its territories or possessions, or Canada.

This is not the coverage needed by insureds with foreign operations. That coverage is readily available from several sources, such as the American Foreign Insurance Association (which acts as the foreign department for a group of American stock insurance companies), excess and surplus lines insurers, and in the foreign departments of a few domestic insurance companies. What is provided in the broad form CGL endorsement is coverage for liability arising out of foreign travel by insureds who are permanently domiciled in the United States or elsewhere within the CGL's policy territory. For example, there is liability coverage for the actions of a salesperson or other employee of the insured that take place outside the policy territory and result in bodily injury, property damage, or personal or advertising injury.

Specifically excluded are bodily injury and property damage losses arising out of completed operations or products. This is not an absolute limitation, as there is worldwide products coverage subject to certain conditions in the CGL. However, it is preferable to delete this products exclusion when possible so that losses arising out of this hazard under the limited worldwide liability coverage are covered.

In the CGL, the definition of policy territory is expanded to anywhere in the world for damages arising out of the products hazard if the original suit is brought within the United States, its territories or possessions, or Canada, and the product is sold for use within this territory. When the exclusion in limited worldwide liability coverage does not apply, the CGL requirement that intended consumption or use be in the United States is avoided.

Premises medical payments coverage also is excluded from the limited worldwide liability coverage.

Additional Persons Insured This provision adds as insureds under the policy the insured's spouse (if the insured is a partnership) and employees of the insured. A spouse is covered only with respect to conduct of the business, and employees are covered only while acting within the scope of their duties.

There are three exclusions regarding the coverage of employees:

1. to bodily injury or personal injury to another employee of the named insured arising out of or in the course of his employment,
2. to personal injury or advertising injury to the named insured or, if the named insured is a partnership or joint venture, any partner or member thereof, or the spouse of any of the foregoing,
3. to property damage to property owned, occupied, or used by, rented to, in the care, custody, or control of, or over which physical control is being exercised for any purpose by another employee of the named insured, or by the named insured or, if the named insured is a partnership or joint venture, by any partner or member thereof or by the spouse of any of the foregoing.

The exclusion relating to care, custody, or control broadens the similar exclusion in the CGL to exclude damage to property in the care, custody, or control of an employee, a partner's spouse, and any partner as well as in care, custody or control of an insured. While this is a restriction of coverage, it merely makes the policy coverage uniform by making the care, custody or control exclusion apply to the additional insureds.

The additional insureds coverage is desirable. It reduces the possibility of subrogation against employees, although becoming an additional insured does not make one "suit-proof." Recently, there have been successful attempts to subrogate against additional insureds such as subcontractors. Generally insurers have not exercised their subrogation rights against negligent employees, but the possibility does present a potential problem to employees. Adding them as insureds reduces the possibility of employees suffering an uninsured loss.

Extended Bodily Injury Coverage   This coverage protects the insured against liability for an intentional act causing bodily injury at the direction of the insured if injury results from the use of reasonable force for the purpose of protecting persons or property.

In the insuring agreement of the CGL, coverage is granted for bodily injury and property damage arising out of an occurrence which is defined as "an accident...neither expected nor intended from the standpoint of the insured." Extended bodily injury coverage broadens the protection to include the intentional act. The requirements of reasonable force and purpose of protecting persons or property must be met if coverage is to apply. Since reasonable force depends on the circumstances of each case, disagreement over interpretation is not unusual.

The activities of security guards, "bouncers," and watchmen frequently result in claims that come under extended bodily injury coverage. A guard who injures an intruder or shoots an assailant would have coverage if a lawsuit results from the injury if the action constituted reasonable force. The requirement for protection of person or property would have been met. Without the extended protection there would be no coverage as the act causing injury would be deemed intentional.

Automatic Coverage—Newly Acquired Organizations (Ninety Days)   This automatic coverage gives the insured liability protection for newly acquired organizations. The CGL, according to its terms, covers liability arising out of unknown exposures and newly acquired operations and property, but it does not provide for automatic additions of new entities as named insured. This automatic coverage provision provides such added liability protection for any organization acquired

Exhibit 3-2
Additional Coverages Provided by
Broad Form CGL Endorsement

```
1.   Contractual Liability
2.   Personal Injury and Advertising Liability
3.   Premises Medical Payment
4.   Host Liquor
5.   Fire Legal
6.   Broad Form PD/including Completed Operations
7.   Incidental Medical Malpractice
8.   Nonowned Watercraft
9.   Limited Worldwide
10.  Additional Persons Insured
11.  Extended Bodily Injury
12.  Automatic Coverage-Newly Acquired Organization
```

or formed by the named insured for up to 90 days. The named insured must maintain ownership or majority interest, and there is no coverage for joint ventures. Further, if the new organization is protected by any other liability insurance, this extension of coverage does not apply even if the policy limits of liability in the other insurance have been exhausted.

Value of Broad Form Endorsement

The broad form CGL endorsement is a valuable liability coverage addition. Few insureds will need each of the coverages included, but most insureds will need several of them. The cost of packaged coverages almost always will be less than furnishing even two or three of the coverages separately because of a reduction in policywriting expense and the popularity of the broad form endorsement.

Providing the broader coverages obligates producers to explain them particularly with regard to exclusions and limitations. Producers should be specific and when outlining noncoverage (exclusions and limitations), do it in writing. Exhibit 3-2 lists the additional coverages available under the broad form CGL endorsement.

Producers should remember this discussion is based on the ISO broad form CGL endorsement; many other forms of this coverage are available and there is great similarity but little uniformity among them.

Checkpoints

1. What is the major distinction between personal injury and advertising injury liability?
2. Why is premises medical payments coverage called "good will" insurance?
3. When is fire legal liability insurance needed?
4. How do "broad form property damage" and the "broad form CGL endorsement" differ?
5. How does limited worldwide liability coverage expand coverage under the CGL?
6. Why would automatic coverage-newly acquired organization coverage be necessary?

UNDERWRITING INFORMATION

Knowledge of any product is essential; knowledge gives confidence and a competitive edge in selling. Furthermore, because the financial security of most individuals and businesses can be destroyed by inadequate or improperly written insurance, technical knowledge of insurance is essential.

The application or proposal for insurance is important not only to obtain insurance but also to fit coverages with needs. The section that follows will discuss submissions by producers for CGL coverage.

Underwriting the Commercial Liability Risk

There are many aspects to be considered in underwriting the liability exposure. One is that the basic coverages concern both bodily injury and property damage, each representing separate sets of exposures. A second is that large sums of money are potentially involved. Coverage limits of $500,000, particularly for bodily injury liability, are not unusual. Third, when the broad form CGL endorsement coverages are included, the additional exposures must be considered.

As the first-line underwriter, the producer's knowledge is relied on by the insurance company. Usually the producer is the individual who has the most contact with the insured, at least when the insurance is sold, and often producers are the only ones who see the premises and the operations. Therefore, it is important for producers to recognize favorable conditions as well as hazards in order to capitalize on a client's strengths and offer suggestions to correct weaknesses.

The role of the producer in this regard may be less important when the insurer involved has strong field inspection facilities, but producers who earn the confidence and trust of underwriters through dependable performance often will enjoy valuable competitive advantages. There are many insurance companies without adequate inspection capability. Also, many times premium quotations will be needed too quickly to permit even the best staffed insurance companies to make necessary inspections. Producers who can be relied upon by underwriters often will be able to take advantage of these situations, like obtaining higher rate credits or lower debits, while less able rivals withdraw from competition.

Typical Loss Exposures

The conditions that give rise to liability losses are so numerous and diverse it is impossible to generalize about them. The following discussion will identify typical hazards for various classes of business and suggest some loss control measures.

Construction and Equipment Construction activities, perhaps more than any other, entail exposure to liability for both bodily injury and property damage, and loss control engineers pay close attention to them. The underwriter will require information concerning the levels of supervision and training involved, how well equipment is maintained, whether safety gear is provided (and used), and whether the use of dangerous materials is avoided as much as possible. In addition, evidence of financial strength should be available. Providing a well documented submission will increase the likelihood of a favorable underwriting decision. Making sure the submission is complete will avoid a possibly harmful delay necessary to obtain additional information. Perhaps most important for the producer, in those jurisdictions where rating flexibility is permitted, a competitive price edge may be gained by means of a complete, accurate submission.

Special Hazards The nature of some businesses invites special hazards. Where crowds are present, such as in hotels, department and discount stores, theaters, sports arenas, large restaurants, and nightclubs, crowd control, fire prevention, and the ability to vacate the premises in an orderly and prompt fashion take on added importance. Special considerations are sufficient exits, wide, clear aisles, evacuation plans, security, and auxiliary emergency lighting. Fire presents a particular bodily injury loss exposure where large numbers of people congregate, so loss control devices such as sprinkler systems, extinguishers, and good housekeeping are frequently required. Insurers will want to know that sprinkler systems are operable and maintained or that there is a suitable number of workable fire extinguishers strategically located and readily visible. As for housekeeping, the loss hazards created by poor cleaning and maintenance are numerous.

Common Hazards Certain premises conditions present loss hazards no matter what the business. Examples are poor lighting, loose handrails, unsafe wiring, tripping hazards in parking areas and walkways, and defective stairs. Slip-and-fall injuries are possible anywhere but they are particularly common to supermarket and restaurant occupancies. Since slip-and-fall claims are sometimes contrived, it is important an insured has adequate inspection procedures and customarily keeps floors clean and free of hazardous material.

Individual characteristics of some businesses present special hazards. Certain manufacturing plants are more likely than others to present the threat of sudden and accidental pollution (not excluded in the CGL). Pest control procedures are considered to increase the liability exposure. More obvious are the exposures that accompany inherently dangerous operations like blasting for construction, munitions manufacture and handling, and chemical plants.

The best solutions to the problems of underwriting insurance for such businesses are implementation of effective safety programs, experienced workers, and interested ownership and management. Even so, when the inherent danger is excessive or perceived to be so by underwriters, the producer may encounter class underwriting or judging the proposed insured not on individual merit but rather on characteristics of the class of business. A broad knowledge of insurance companies, particularly the specialty insurance companies, may be more effective than all of the foregoing suggestions in solving the problem of class underwriting. Even so, any submission for insurance will be strengthened by citing the presence of safety practices, other loss control measures, and able and interested management.

Safety

OSHA regulations have introduced a new dimension to underwriting the business liability exposure. Most insurance companies disclaim any responsibility for including in their inspections conditions that violate OSHA requirements, but their inspectors and underwriters are familiar with the regulations and demonstrating compliance with OSHA is a plus factor in the underwriting process. Security is another factor.

The increase in crime has caused hotels and motels to strengthen security in order to provide a safer environment for guests. Peepholes, door chains, and dead bolt locks are now commonplace, as are security patrols. The absence of measures that increase safety may either increase premium or prompt an underwriter to decline the application for insurance.

This underwriting discussion has focused on adverse liability characteristics and the problems more frequently experienced in providing insurance for them. However, the majority of liability insurance submissions are readily accepted and written as requested in the application for insurance. Frequently all that the insurer requires is honest and informative answers to all of the questions contained in the application.

The Application for Comprehensive General Liability Insurance

Most insurance companies will accept the standardized ACORD forms, conceived by Independent Insurance Agents of America, Inc., as applications for insurance. While some insurance companies still use their own forms, most of the information required is uniform among various insurance company forms and the ACORD forms, which will be the basis of this discussion.

The ACORD Application Completion of two ACORD forms is necessary when applying for a CGL policy, the commercial insurance application (Applicant Information Section), and the general liability section (reproduced in the PRO 82 Course Guide). The commercial insurance application contains general information. It may be used for all kinds of business insurance and when application is being made for two or more kinds of insurance at the same time, only one commercial insurance application is completed. A separate form, such as the general liability section, is attached for each type of insurance requested. The general liability section pertains to information related specifically to the liability insurance exposure.

Commercial Insurance Application. Much of the information in this form is the same as that found on the policy declarations page or "daily" report. Included are names of producer (in this case the submitting production office, not the producer), the proposed insurance company called the "carrier," the applicant's name, address, and type of entity (individual, partnership, corporation, joint venture, or other), and proposed effective and expiration dates.

Rather detailed information is requested in sections dealing with the prior insurer and loss history. Both sections request data for the previous five years. The size and complexity of applicants' operations often determines the amount of information required. Other information required includes locations and descriptions of premises owned and/or occupied by the applicant and nature of business and description of operations.

General Liability Section.   While the commercial insurance application provides general information, the general liability section relates specifically to the liability exposures of the applicant. The front of the form includes limits of liability desired and the information that will be shown in the schedule of hazards. The hazards scheduled are premises/operations, escalators, independent contractors, contractual, and products/completed operations. For each hazard the information to be provided includes description, liability classification code, premium basis, territory, rate, and premium. The rates and premiums do not have to be furnished as they will ultimately be determined by the insurer. However, since policies issued from an application should be checked as to coverages and cost before they are delivered to the insured, providing this information in the application will save time later.

Included in the schedule of hazards is space to indicate number of escalators, if any, and number of floors serviced by them. The insurer requires this since a liability premium charge is made for passenger escalators even though liability coverage is automatically included for escalators and elevators. Elevator collision is shown as an option on the form. Since that coverage is not automatically included, it should be selected whenever the exposure exists.

The general liability section form is used for all basic commercial liability coverages, not just the CGL. Therefore, it should be completed carefully. This is needed to obtain proper coverage as well as for rating information. In some firms, producers are responsible for completing applications. Even when it is completed by others, use of the application forms is valuable as an information gathering tool.

The reverse side of the general liability section deals with supplemental underwriting information for the contractor, contractual and products/completed operations hazards. For producers without their own exposure identification survey form, this is an excellent substitute. Producers should use this form in interviewing the client or prospect. The extent of the information required is an aid to the producer, not a nuisance, and completion of the form should not be regarded lightly. If information is unknown or unavailable, it should be so indicated to the underwriter. Producers should not guess or fabricate information.

Supplemental Information.   The commercial insurance application with general liability section attached completes the liability insurance application. Other information may be helpful though not required. The producer should offer any other pertinent information that has been learned from contact with the client or inspection of the premises and operations. Photographs may be useful, but pictures should be taken on a nice day whenever possible with color film. Financial information may be important. Demonstrating the ability to purchase good equipment, maintain it, and to provide safety measures will favorably impress an underwriter.

Often, the more information the producer submits, the less information the underwriter will have to obtain from outside sources. In addition to saving time, this may reduce the likelihood of misleading information the underwriter might otherwise obtain.

Underwriter Relations

Producers should become acquainted with the underwriters who handle their applications. Periodic personal visits by producers are helpful even in larger production offices where a "placer" handles the insurance application submission and subsequent negotiations. This does not conflict with the growing and welcome trend of divorcing producers from procedural paper work. Rather, it establishes rapport with underwriters, an important part of the sales function.

Finally, a sense of trust must be developed with underwriters. The underwriter needs to know that the producer knows how to interpret the information obtained competently and honestly.

PRODUCTS AND COMPLETED OPERATIONS AND PROFESSIONAL LIABILITY INSURANCE

Two of the most difficult liability exposures are products and completed operations and professional liability. This section describes those exposures and the insurance for the exposures.

Products and Completed Operations

The exposure of businesses to liability for products and completed operations is as great if not greater than their premises and operations exposures. First, the insured has no control over the exposure once the product is sold or after completing and abandoning work to its owner. Improper use or abuse by the consumer and other adverse conditions are unpredictable. If the nature of use is inherently dangerous, the seller's liability may be absolute, even making consumer misuse an invalid defense.

The possibility that a single loss can affect so many people increases the amount of damage a seller or supplier may suffer from the products exposure. It is likely that tainted food products will cause sickness or death to a large number of people. The same is true of injury from defective products. Pressure from attorneys has weakened legal defenses and inflation of jury awards has added to the sellers' problem. Many well publicized cases involving products liability in recent years have been affected by one or more of these elements.

Products liability cases are not always widely publicized; nor do they usually result in verdicts of millions of dollars. Still, the exposure exists for all manufacturers, distributors, and retailers, and the amount of liability can be substantial. Insuring this liability and that arising out of completed operations will be the subject of this discussion. Since the CGL is the only coverage that offers products and completed operations insurance as an option, the CGL will be used in this analysis.

In other business liability policies, either products and completed operations coverage cannot be added (OL&T and M&C policies for example) or it is automatically included (such as in the storekeepers or druggists liability policies). While the CGL automatically includes products and completed operations, an additional premium is charged and the coverage can be excluded if not needed or wanted.

Certain manual classifications include products liability insurance as part of the premises and operations coverage. In most cases the exposure is incidental to primary operations but if coverage were not included, camps, nursing homes, theaters, schools, and civic and fraternal clubs would have to buy specific coverage. Not all classifications that include products coverage involve food service. For example, the classifications for exterminators, laundries and cleaners, and photo processors include the coverage. There are relatively few classifications which automatically include products and completed operations, but those businesses that fit into them have a form of automatic coverage for products liability. Still, insurance for products and completed operations liability usually is purchased specifically or obtained as an automatically included coverage.

Products and Completed Operations Review   The CGL, unless endorsed, includes products and completed operations coverage. Failure to include a products or completed operations classification in the policy's schedule of hazards or to charge a premium has no effect. The CGL automatically includes exposures that exist at policy inception and exposures that arise during the policy term, a feature that applies to liability for premises and operations as well as products and completed operations.

When coverage for products and completed operations is requested, a change in expressing the amount of bodily injury liability protection is necessary. In addition to a limit per occurrence, there is a

"We the jury award the plaintiff all the gold in Fort Knox."

Drawing by Ed Fisher; © 1981 The New Yorker Magazine, Inc.

separate annual aggregate limit that applies separately to each year of the policy. The basic bodily injury limits are $25,000 for all damages suffered by one or more persons from an occurrence and $50,000 aggregate. Increased limits of liability may be provided for an additional premium. Basic property damage liability limits are the same as for the premises/operations coverage: $5,000 per occurrence and $25,000 aggregate.

Exclusions. Four exclusions in the CGL deal with products and completed operations insurance: (1) failure to perform, (2) damage to products, (3) exclusion of injury to work performed, and (4) damages for withdrawal, inspection, repair, replacement, or loss of use, the so-called "sistership" exclusion. Only the sistership exclusion can be removed for an additional premium. However, coverage for products recall is obtained more often from specialty insurers than by removal of the exclusion from the CGL. All four exclusions apply to property damage only, not bodily injury.

While these exclusions may distress some insureds, particularly those unaware or who do not understand them, without exclusions, insurers would be guarantors of product workmanship. Product quality is a speculative risk and is neither intended as part of insurance nor contemplated in the premium charged.

FAILURE TO PERFORM EXCLUSION. This exclusion eliminates coverage for loss of use of undamaged tangible property resulting from failure of the insured's products or work performed to meet a standard warranted or represented by the named insured. The exclusion does not apply to loss of use of other tangible property resulting from damage to or destruction of the products of or work performed by or on behalf of the insured. An important condition of this liberalizing feature of the exclusion is that it applies only after the products or work have been put to use by others than the insured. As this exclusion applies *only* to property damage, bodily injury caused by failure of a product to perform is covered.

As an example of a loss excluded by the failure to perform exclusion, consider a steam turbine that fails to produce power to a guaranteed specified level and causes its owner to lose the use of related machinery dependent on the power. Since the related machinery is undamaged, there is no insurance coverage for the loss.

However, if the turbine blew apart causing sudden and accidental damage to other equipment, that damage would be covered including loss of use. Damage to the turbine, being the named insured's (manufacturer's) product, would be excluded in the CGL. The purpose of the exclusion is to prevent liability insurers from covering performance guarantees.

DAMAGE TO PRODUCTS EXCLUSION. Damage caused by the insured's product to other property is covered; however, the intent of the exclusion is to avoid paying for damage to any part of the product supplied by the insured.

Two aspects of the exclusion should be understood. First, if damage to any part of a product makes the entire product useless, the exclusion applies to the entire product, not just the part causing the damage. Second, there is no coverage for any damage to the insured's product even if caused by a component part manufactured or supplied by someone other than the insured. Losses involving damage to products made up of component parts supplied by other than the principal manufacturer can be complicated. Fortunately, however, many cases are relatively clear-cut.

For example, Able Generator Manufacturing Company supplies electric generators to Baker Steam Products, Inc. for use in Baker's steam turbines. A defective generator burns out and damages a steam turbine used by Baker's customer. Baker has no liability coverage for damage to either the generator or the turbine, since the entire unit is Baker's product. Able, manufacturer of the generator, would have coverage for damage to the turbine since it was not manufactured, sold, handled, or distributed by Able.

The applicability of coverage does not necessarily determine the respective obligations of the parties involved. Baker probably will be responsible to its customer for the entire loss irrespective of any recourse it has against Able, supplier of the defective generator. For instance, if Able has no products liability insurance, that will not relieve or mitigate Baker's liability.

Of course, as Baker has no coverage for damage to the steam turbine including the generator, neither does Able have coverage for damage to the generator, each being the product of the respective insured. Sometimes, manufacturers may otherwise protect themselves by providing physical damage (first party) coverage, such as boiler and machinery insurance, for the duration of a warranty period. Unfortunately, there is not always a form of insurance for insuring every product as appropriately as boiler and machinery for generators and steam turbines. For example, protection would not be possible for food products. Yet the same circumstances of loss might exist and if the food product contains many different ingredients supplied by separate entities, difficulty in determining coverage will be immense. Loss of use of the product will not be covered, but the policy will pay for loss caused by bodily injury from food poisoning.

INJURY TO WORK PERFORMED EXCLUSION. This exclusion is the same in concept as the preceding damage to products exclusion. Its purpose is the same: to prevent payment for redoing faulty work. While the damage to products exclusion relates to products liability coverage, the injury to work performed exclusion relates to completed operations insurance. It excludes work performed by, as well as on behalf of, the named insured, including materials, parts, or equipment furnished in connection with the work.

Because of the extent of this exclusion it can be extremely troublesome to general contractors. Since "work performed by or on behalf of the named insured" could include an entire building, the injury to work performed exclusion leaves a very large exposed area uninsured for many general contractors. Also, coverage is needed for protection against liability for damage to other property such as adjacent buildings, vehicles, and the personal property of tenants.

The effect of the exclusion is not as damaging to subcontractors. For example, a mechanical subcontractor who negligently installs a heating system that later explodes and severely damages a building would have completed operations coverage for damage to property other than the heating system. The exclusion provides no such limitation of liability for a general contractor. A partial remedy is to provide broad form property damage liability protection discussed earlier.

EXCLUSION OF DAMAGES FOR WITHDRAWAL, INSPECTION, REPAIR, REPLACEMENT, OR LOSS OF USE. The sistership liability exclusion is unique among the four exclusions discussed here, because it has an effect upon the premises and operations and products liability coverages. Products liability involves loss that occurs away from the insured's premises and after possession of products has been relinquished to others. Since the exclusion covers not only withdrawal (which would fulfill the location and possession conditions of products liability) but also inspection, repair, and replacement, it is possible that loss, were it not otherwise excluded, could arise out of the premises and operations coverage also.

The possibility of loss caused by withdrawal, inspection, repair, replacement, or loss of use of products is great, and the financial consequences can be catastrophic. Unfortunately, incidences involving contaminated or spoiled food, defective automobile and airplane parts, and harmful pharmaceuticals, contraceptives, and hygiene products have become all too familiar. Severity of loss has been increased by the wide distribution made possible by modern production and transportation systems. Coverage, while excluded in the CGL, is available.

The sistership liability exclusion is the only one of the four products and completed operations exclusions that may be deleted for additional premium. The nature of the product, loss control procedures, and size of the business are factors that may persuade the underwriter to provide coverage by deleting the exclusion in the CGL. This alteration of the CGL, while permitted, is not made very often, and producers should become familiar with excess and surplus lines insurers that more frequently provide needed protection through a separate products recall expense policy.

A review of the CGL policy's definition of "property damage" illustrates the need for the sistership liability exclusion:

> "property damage" means (1) physical injury to or destruction of tangible property which occurs during the policy period, including the loss of use thereof at any time resulting therefrom, or (2) loss of use of tangible property which has not been physically injured or destroyed provided such loss of use is caused by an occurrence during the policy period. . . .

In addition to *loss of use* of damaged or destroyed property, the definition of property damage also includes *loss of use of property* which has not been physically injured or destroyed. This explains the need for the sistership liability exclusion. Without it the CGL would provide unintended coverage for damages associated with products recall.

Review of Related Definitions. Four other definitions in the CGL policy should be reviewed in order to have a better understanding of products and completed operations liability coverage: completed operations hazard, products hazard, named insured's products, and policy territory.

COMPLETED OPERATIONS HAZARD. This definition establishes that completed operations coverage applies to liability for bodily injury or property damage occurring *after* operations have been completed or abandoned and away from the insured's premises. The inclusion of abandonment is important. While operations are completed much more often than abandoned, this clearly settles the status of abandoned property as not being within the premises and operations hazard.

The definition establishes an operation as being complete at the earliest of:

1. all operations to be performed under the contract have been completed,
2. all operations to be performed at the site of operations have been completed, or
3. when the portion of the work out of which the injury or damage arises has been put to its intended use by other than a contractor or subcontractor engaged in the project.

Another provision in this definition is that operations shall be deemed completed if they are otherwise complete except for required service or maintenance or repair of a deficiency. This painstaking attempt to define the assignment of hazards in the CGL to either category, premises-operations or products-completed operations, may seem excessive. It is not. Because products and completed operations coverage can be deleted from the policy, the division of hazards is absolutely necessary.

Finally, the policy definition of completed operations hazard does not include losses arising out of:

(a) operations in connection with the transportation of property, unless the bodily injury or property damage arises out of a condition in or on a vehicle created by the loading or unloading thereof,

(b) the existence of tools, uninstalled equipment or abandoned or unused materials, or

(c) operations for which the classification stated in the policy or in the company's manual specifies including "completed operations. . . . ."

The provision regarding manual classifications that include completed operations is related to the discussion of some insureds with a form of automatic coverage when their operations are assigned to such manual classifications. This provision merely clarifies that policy coverage, though it exists in such cases, comes under the premises and operations portion of the CGL.

PRODUCTS HAZARD. The definition of products hazard is much shorter and simpler than the definition of completed operations hazard. They are similar, but there is not the same need to establish the dividing line between premises-operations coverage and products coverage.

The similarity is that the products hazard also includes bodily injury and property damage that occurs away from the insured's premises. The difference is that loss must arise out of the insured's product (instead of operations) or reliance upon a representation or warranty. An added requirement is that loss occur not only away from premises but also after possession of products has been relinquished to others.

The provision that loss occur away from the insured's premises creates the need for a modification, by endorsement, when coverage applies to restaurants, refreshment stands, and some other food service operations. The endorsement redefines products hazard *to include* loss occurring on premises. The requirement that physical possession be relinquished by the insured still applies. The modification is needed to assign coverage and premium to the same categories. The rate for premises and operations coverage does not contemplate the products liability exposure of businesses that sell products for consumption on premises.

NAMED INSURED'S PRODUCTS. This broad definition includes goods or products manufactured, sold, handled or distributed by the named insured or others trading under the same name. It is broad enough to meet the needs of all of the participants in the selling process—manufacturers, distributors, wholesalers, and retailers. However, it does not include vending machines or other property rented or furnished but not sold by the insured.

POLICY TERRITORY. A portion of the CGL policy's definition of policy territory applies to the products liability coverage. With regard to premises and operations coverage, policy territory is defined as the United States, its territories or possessions, or Canada. The definition expands coverage for products liability to anywhere in the world subject to two conditions: (1) the product was sold for use in the United States, its territories or possessions, or Canada, and (2) original suit for damages be brought within such territory. The words "original suit" are used instead of "claim." Therefore, it is possible an insurer will pay for a claim arising in a foreign country for bodily injury or property damage provided it arises out of a product sold for use in the narrower territory.

Two additional points regarding this feature of coverage must be mentioned. First, the broadened territory does not apply to completed operations coverage. Second, even though it does apply to products liability, this coverage does not protect export operations in foreign countries. Producers who need to provide coverage overseas will find it available from several sources including some domestic insurers, excess and surplus lines insurers, and various pools of insurers. In addition, some insurance agencies have facilities for placing coverage directly with underwriters at Lloyd's and other foreign insurers.

When Coverage Applies Coverage, while usually on an occurrence basis, may be on a "claims made" basis.

Occurrence Coverage. Coverage in the CGL, including protection against products liability, is on an *occurrence* basis. This means the policy will pay for bodily injury or property damage that occurs during the policy period. It is not when the product was sold or when claim is made that determines whether insurance is in force or which insurer or policy will respond to a loss. It only matters which policy was in force on the date of the occurrence.

On an occurrence basis an insurer may have to pay a claim long after expiration of its policy. The period of time between the occurrence and when the claim is made is known as the "tail." The longer the "tail" the greater the problem.

PROBLEMS OF THE "LONG TAIL." There are problems with the "long tail." First, there is the inability to match premiums in any given year with losses for that year, since losses may not be known that year or perhaps for several years. Another problem is that the amount of premium dollars available to pay losses is decreased by inflation. The results may be inequitable premium pricing and decreased capacity.

INTERRUPTION IN COVERAGE. An insured who, after carrying products liability insurance for many years, without an occurrence, decides not to renew coverage and subsequently is sued for a loss that occurred after coverage was discontinued has no protection. It does not matter when the product was manufactured, distributed, or sold. Conversely, an insured who has never had coverage and then purchases it will be protected against liability for loss that occurs during the policy period arising out of products whenever they were manufactured, distributed, or sold in the past.

The problems that may result from a decision to discontinue products liability coverage must be considered when an insured is discontinuing business operations. Even though a business is dissolved, there may be liability for losses that occur after dissolution. Products liability insurance can be purchased in a so-called "tail policy" to cover a period after business operations cease. Usually premium is based on sales during the last year of full operation and reduced each subsequent year coverage remains in effect.

Claims-Made Coverage. Reduced to the simplest terms, a claims-made policy covers "claims made" during the policy period. It makes no difference when the occurrence giving rise to the bodily injury or property damage takes place. While claims-made coverage has become common in professional liability policies, it is not generally used in products and completed operations insurance. However, producers should be aware of the effects of claims-made coverage. One reason is that products liability insurance on a claims-made basis may be found in independently filed and excess and surplus lines insurers' policies. Also because of the apparent success of the claims-made basis in insuring professional liability, it would not be surprising if it gains widespread use in products and completed operations coverage.

In claims-made policies, the problem of delay or "long tail" between occurrence causing a loss and submission of the claim is solved. Such claims are referred to as incurred but not reported (IBNR) claims. With a claims-made policy, an insurer need not estimate the amount needed to settle claims covered by any policy for years after expiration. Because a claims-made insurer at the end of each policy year knows of all claims for which it may have to pay, it can determine future rate adjustments more accurately. This permits more equitable

Exhibit 3-3
"Occurrence" Replacing a "Claims-Made" Policy

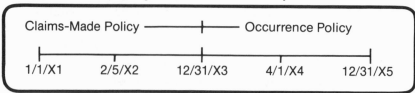

premiums for insureds by tying premiums received and claims paid more closely together. An advantage to insureds is that when coverage applies only to claims made during the current policy period, it is easier to estimate the amount of coverage needed in a given policy year.

A disadvantage to insureds that is magnified both by increased competition among producers and recurring restrictive insurance underwriting standards is the danger of insurers switching from a claims-made to an occurrence basis. Unless either policy is modified, an insured would not have coverage for unreported losses (occurrences) that took place during the term of the claims-made policy but were not reported.

For example, in Exhibit 3-3, during the three years 1/1/X1 to 12/31/X3, a manufacturer was covered by a claims-made policy. An "occurrence" happens on 2/5/X2 but neither is a report filed or a claim made. On 1/1/X4 the manufacturer buys an "occurrence" policy. On 4/4/X4 a claim is filed for the 2/5/X2 occurrence. Because the claim was not made prior to 12/31/X3, there is no coverage under the claims-made policy. Because the occurrence happened on 2/5/X2, there is no coverage under the occurrence policy. The client is, in fact, not insured for any occurrences between 1/1/X1 and 12/31/X3 *if claims are not made* during that same period.

Producers who are faced with such situations must be certain that coverage gaps are filled with special policies and if not, that insureds knowingly assume any uninsured losses.

Products Liability Legislation and Litigation No other branch of insurance has as much adverse potential as does products liability insurance. On the legislative docket in many states are various topics that affect products liability. These include legal reforms involving some or all of the following:

1. establishing a statute of limitations from either the date of introduction of a product or from the date of an accident,
2. allowing a defense that a product met the state of the art at the time of manufacture,
3. eliminating or restricting a failure to warn claim,

4. allowing a defense that a product met government standards and
5. allowing a defense if a product were altered after it left the manufacturer.

Federal lawmakers have turned their attention to investment income earned from reserves established for products liability claims. California's Supreme Court has ruled in a landmark decision that when the maker of a defective or unsafe product cannot be identified, all manufacturers of such products can be held liable.

The California case involved the drug DES taken by thousands of pregnant women and later banned by the Food and Drug Administration after scientists linked it to cancer found in daughters of some of the women who had taken the drug. The effect of this case will spread to other states and other products. Perhaps the most important situation will involve the alleged connection between asbestos products and related lung diseases. Thousands of cases seeking damages have been filed in courts across the United States.

As the major contact with insureds, producers need to be constantly aware not only of coverage changes but also of other developments that affect protecting the assets of their customers. Considering the amount of activity under way, they will do well to keep up with developments relating to products liability insurance.

Professional Liability

The liability exposure from conduct of professional activities is at least as great as from commercial activities. For established professions such as physicians and attorneys, the standard of conduct required is high. The possibility of litigation, findings for the plaintiffs, and size of award for damages have all been affected by an increase in the public's awareness and expectations accompanied by deterioration in the professional relationship. For example, the doctor-patient and lawyer-client relationships are no longer regarded with as much reverence as they once were.

Other factors have caused just as much revolution in the professional liability marketplace:

- the change to almost exclusive use of claims-made policies
- decrease in the number of participating insurers
- increase in the types of specialized practices covered
- cost of coverage
- size of policy limits

Professional liability insurance is required to protect the professional from liability arising from professional acts or omissions. This discussion will include an analysis of the types of policies available in addition to a general coverage review. The types of policies will be divided into three categories: medical, other professions, and miscellaneous business.

Medical Malpractice Liability Medical practitioners are subject to liability arising from professional acts or omissions. Physicians, dentists, and nurses all need insurance to protect them against legal liability resulting from malpractice. This insurance differs from commercial forms of liability insurance in several important respects.

Medical malpractice insurance covers liability that results from rendering or failing to render professional services. Often, injury to a claimant results from an intentional act of the doctor even though the resulting damage was not intended—for instance, prescribing a drug which results in an injury because of a side effect of the drug.

The standard form of medical malpractice insurance insures against "injury"—not bodily injury, personal injury, or property damage. Coverage is provided for all injuries that result from professional acts or omissions including not just bodily injury but also mental anguish, humiliation, defamation, and invasion of privacy.

Most policies provide a limit of liability per claim and an aggregate limit or a maximum amount to be paid during any policy year, usually three times the limit per claim. Producers should recommend, even urge, the purchase of high limits of liability. High premiums have caused many insureds to carry less insurance. In order to avoid an errors and omissions loss of their own, producers should properly document their files in such instances.

Another unique feature is that in many professional liability policies the insurer may not settle claims without the insured's consent. Considering the value of reputation to a medical professional, this is extremely important. However, as the number and size of claims increased, many insurers have deleted or modified this provision. In some policies the insurance company's liability is limited to the amount of a proposed settlement plus defense costs incurred up to the date of refusal if the insured vetoes a settlement offer. It is important that policy provisions relating to payment, defense and consent as well as coverage be explained to the insured.

Malpractice Coverage. The policy covers the legal obligation of the insured for any injury resulting from rendering or failing to render professional services. It includes liability of any person for whom the insured is legally responsible such as employees and associates but not partners. A separate insuring agreement is used to insure a partnership.

There is an exclusion of liability of the insured as proprietor or official of a hospital, sanitarium, bed and board clinic, laboratory, or business enterprise such as for sale of medicine or medical appliances. This exposure should be insured in a concurrent hospital or products liability policy, preferably written with the same insurer.

Some policies exclude criminal acts, injury caused while under the influence of alcohol or drugs, and liability involving treatment for weight reduction. Even when these exclusions do not appear in a policy, it is contrary to public policy to insure criminal acts.

Premises Coverage. Professional liability insurance does not eliminate the need for premises liability protection, however. Some insurers are willing to include premises coverage with the professional liability policy. When premises coverage is not included, a separate CGL should be provided. Aside from the liability exposures that arise from the office premises there are borderline areas of possible claim that may arise. Insuring at the same limits and with the same insurance company when possible will avoid coverage problems in such situations.

Hospital Professional Liability Hospitals and other medical institutions, like individual practitioners, may be insured against liability arising out of acts or omissions with regard to the following professional services:

(a) medical, surgical, dental or nursing treatment for such person or persons inflicting the injury including the furnishing of food or beverages in connection therewith,

(b) furnishing or dispensing of drugs or medical, dental or surgical supplies or appliances if the injury occurs after the named insured has relinquished possession thereof to others,

(c) handling of or performing postmortem examinations on human bodies, or

(d) service by any person as a member of a formal accreditation or similar professional board or committee of the named insured, or a person charged with the duty of executing directives of any such board or committee. . . .

The phrase "to such person or persons inflicting the injury" is unique. It expresses the intent of the policy to cover all liability arising out of professional acts whether they result in injury to a patient or someone else. For example, there is coverage if a disturbed patient, through lack of supervision, injures a third party.

Furnishing food is specifically covered in connection with professional services. Therefore, food *served* to patients is covered but not food *sold* to members of the public in a cafeteria or restaurant. Liability arising out of products sold in a gift shop is also excluded.

An interesting coverage is that provided in (d) of the insuring agreement. There is coverage if the hospital or someone acting in its behalf is sued by a physician for damage to reputation from being refused staff privileges, i.e., denied the right to practice medicine in the hospital.

Some exclusions are similar to exclusions in the CGL relating to bodily injury to employees in the course of employment, obligations of the insured under workers' compensation or similar laws, and ownership or use of motor vehicles, trailers, watercraft or aircraft.

Liability of nonprofessional employees, volunteers, and board members is covered as are nonprofessional acts of medical staff members such as liability arising from committee work. Variations may exist in coverage for additional insureds, but generally individual professionals need their own coverage.

Miscellaneous Medical Professional Liability Besides the physicians, surgeons, and dentists liability professional policy and the hospital professional liability policy, there are coverages available for a number of other medical professionals including druggists (store owners), pharmacists (employed), chiropodists, chiropractors, dental hygienists, laboratory technicians, nurses, opticians and optometrists, and X-ray technicians. However, coverage is available from just a few insurers for some of these specialties which increases the demand upon producers to familiarize themselves with the malpractice insurers, to understand the policies they sell, and to explain them even more carefully than usual because of the degree of specialization.

Liability coverage for druggists is standardized and widely available. Some insurers offer professional liability coverage combined with the drug store premises coverage—in effect, a package policy for the store and malpractice insurance for the druggists. A feature of the druggists liability policy is that it includes products liability for not just medical products but for everything sold in the drug store.

Claims-Made Insurance. One of the most serious hazards producers face results from the effect on coverage of switching between the occurrence form and relatively new claims-made form as indicated in Exhibit 3-4. While claims-made is the predominant form for medical malpractice coverage, there are still some occurrence forms in use. Furthermore, given the predictable cyclical nature of the insurance business, the occurrence form may regain its prominence.

The claims-made form is not without problems. Aside from the coverage gap that exists when a claims-made policy is renewed by an occurrence form, there also can be a problem in renewing one claims-made policy with another. The policies may contain a "retroactive date" to respond to claims made but not reported during the prior claims-made policy. The retroactive date in the renewal policy must be no later than the retroactive date in the previous policy to avoid a gap in coverage. In similar fashion, an occurrence form can be modified to insure prior acts thereby eliminating the problem cited earlier regarding renewal of claims-made policies with occurrence forms.

Another gap may arise with claims-made policies when an insured retires or otherwise quits business or professional practice. Coverage may be obtained by purchasing extensions of coverage, usually for reduced premiums. A similar device may be used to solve the problem that occurs when a renewal claims-made policy contains a later retroactive date than the preceding one. Some claims-made insurers will provide an extension of coverage in this instance. This is known as the "discovery period."

In summary, producers must guard against coverage gaps, paying special attention to available extensions of coverage both prior to inception and after expiration of a claims-made policy. Extension at one end, inception, is identified by the "retroactive date" and at the other, expiration, by the "discovery period." Finally, the coverage gap that results from renewal of claims-made insurance by an unaltered occurrence basis form must not be ignored.

Other Professional Liability The other professional category includes attorneys, architects and engineers, accountants and insurance agents and brokers.

Lawyers Professional Liability. The basic format of all standard professional liability policies is similar. This is true of the lawyers professional liability policy.

The lawyers professional policy has separate insuring clauses for individuals and partnerships. Since partnerships are more common in the legal profession, this is important in the lawyers policy. In a partnership, individual attorneys must be insured as well as the partnership.

The insuring agreement is unusually broad, making no reference to "accident," "malpractice," "error," or "mistake." It covers the insured's legal liability because of any act or omission arising out of the performance of professional services for others in the insured's capacity as a lawyer. The acts of employees and others for whom the insured is responsible are covered. Normal fiduciary relationships, the financial loss of others caused by acts or omissions of the insured, are also covered. This recognizes that lawyers frequently oversee trusts and estates as a service to clients who otherwise would have to serve as executors or trustees.

STANDARD EXCLUSIONS. The standard policy for lawyers contains five exclusions. Liability arising out of any dishonest, fraudulent, criminal, or malicious act or omission is excluded. Also excluded is any claim made by an employer against an insured employee. This protects against an employer recovering loss from what is essentially a business risk—the error or incompetence of an employed attorney. There is no coverage for bodily injury, sickness, disease or death, or property damage, including loss of use. There is an exclusion related to the fiduciary coverage that prevents recovery by the insured as beneficiary of a trust or estate. The fifth exclusion is the broad nuclear energy exclusion.

Architects and Engineers Professional Liability. This coverage, while not offered by many insurance companies, is available through numerous sources, mainly "excess and surplus" lines firms. Coverage is provided by specialized insurers in the United States as well as by underwriters at Lloyd's of London. The lack of standardization of forms requires special attention from producers selling the coverage.

The policy protects against the legal liability caused by an error or omission by the insured in rendering professional service as an architect or engineer. In addition to providing defense of claims, most policies provide supplementary payments usual to most liability policies such as bond premiums and interest on unpaid judgments.

The policy limit of liability is shown as an aggregate limit; that is, it applies to all claims occurring during each annual policy term. Therefore, producers' recommendations should be made with the potential liability for a full year's activities in mind, not just one claim.

Both occurrence and claims-made policies are used so provisions regarding retroactive dates and discovery periods are especially important.

Most policies contain numerous exclusions. They will not be detailed here because of the lack of uniformity. However, certain general comments can be made.

Some exclusions relate to specific types of work such as fairgrounds, tunnels, dams, and bridges. The intent in such instances is to avoid assuming liability for highly specialized or hazardous activities without specific notice and payment of additional premium. Some insurers are willing to cover professional services connected with such activities by endorsement and additional premium.

Some exclusions eliminate coverage for ownership or management of property, business enterprises, and joint ventures. Joint venture coverage may be added by endorsement. The exclusion of business enterprises arose in part because of the fairly common practice of accepting ownership interest in a venture in lieu of professional fees.

There are exclusions for liability arising out of cost estimates, failure to effect or maintain proper insurance or bonds, and copyright infringement. The exclusions reinforce the intent that policy coverage be confined to liability for errors, omissions, or negligent acts in connection with professional services.

Other exclusions are those common to many liability insurance policies: intentional acts, workers' compensation claims, and nuclear, aircraft, watercraft, vehicle, and contractual liability exclusions.

Deductibles are regularly applied and are usually sizable. Even smaller architectural firms have policy deductibles of several thousand dollars. Often policies are written with deductibles applying to defense costs as well as the liability coverage. Care should be exercised by producers in this regard, being certain to inform insureds when the deductible applies to claim defense and investigation.

Usually policy territory is limited to the United States, its territories or possessions, and Canada. Worldwide coverage is available by endorsement; however, activities in Communistic countries are generally excluded.

Accountants Professional Liability. There is little uniformity among coverage forms offered by insurers for accountants professional liability. Accountants professional liability protects against liability for neglect, error, or omission in performing professional accounting services. Policies also usually protect against loss caused by dishonesty, fraud or misrepresentation of employees.

Generally, coverage is on a discovery basis with insurance applying not only to acts committed during the policy term but also to acts committed prior to inception date of the policy if discovered during the policy period. Such coverage applies widely in the field of professional liability insurance provided the insured has no prior knowledge of the claim or reveals knowledge of an occurrence that may give rise to a claim in the application. Claims-made insurance for accountants is gaining increased acceptance.

A unique provision in the accountants' policy is the exclusion of liability under the Securities Act of 1933. Accounting firms involved in stock offerings and other securities matters need specific coverage for this liability exposure, and coverage is available by endorsement. As might be expected, strict underwriting is applied in considering this extension of coverage.

Much of the professional liability insurance for accountants is written in cooperation with their professional associations. A high degree of risk management has been practiced to increase availability and lower the cost of coverage. For many years CPAs offered two types of accounting reports, an audit and a compilation. The audit involves more complete financial recordkeeping verification and usually costs considerably more. Recently a third form of report has been added. Known as a review, it is more extensive than the compilation and less costly than the audit. The purpose is to encourage more disclosure by clients, enabling the accountant to do a more professional job. Another device that may prove effective is the use of broad disclaimers. Also, many firms are having clients agree in writing as to the nature and expectations of services performed.

Agents Errors and Omissions. Until several years ago professional liability insurance or malpractice insurance was sold mainly to protect those engaged as physicians, attorneys, accountants, and architects and engineers. The introduction of errors and omissions insurance for insurance agents and brokers and the rapid growth of this coverage perhaps reflect the growth of insurance as a profession in the estimation of the buying public. As producers are held to higher standards of performance, the level of their practice is also elevated. This fact combined with a growing complexity of the insurance business and a claims-conscious buying public has caused an increase in the number of claims against producers. It follows naturally that most agents now regard errors and omissions protection as essential. Much of this coverage is written through producers' association sponsored plans.

COVERAGE. Policies are not standard but there is much similarity among the forms available. The insuring agreement protects the insured against loss caused by any negligent act, error, or omission in the conduct of the insurance business. "Insured" includes the named insured and any partner, executive officer, stockholder, director, or employee while acting within the scope of his or her duties.

The role of the insurance agent or broker is somewhat unique in representing both buyer and seller. Depending upon the controversy at issue and the advantage sought, both sides have at times claimed the agent to be their representative and at other times to be the agent of the other. Fortunately, most policies cover liability to either party.

An insurance company might claim that a producer has exceeded authority by issuing an unauthorized policy or binder or by insuring for an excessive amount of coverage. The types of claims an insured might make include failure to issue a renewal or new policy, inadequate or improper coverage, bad advice, and acts that might prejudice an insured's claim.

Policies are usually written with a deductible. Supplementary payment provisions are like those in most liability policies. They include defense of claims, payment for appeal bonds and bonds to release attachments, interest on unpaid judgments, costs taxed against the insured, and incurred taxes. Bonds to release attachments and interest payments are based on an amount not to exceed the policy limit of liability.

Exclusions usually include bodily injury, property damage, and libel or slander. These exclusions highlight the need an insurance production firm has for premises coverage, preferably a CGL, including personal injury or broad form CGL coverage.

As the rate of inflation and claims activity has increased, so has the amount of coverage carried by many producers. The premium volume of an office frequently determines the amount of coverage purchased, although even small offices may be exposed to sizable liability. Limits of liability exceeding $1 million are not usual, and excess errors and omissions liability policies are gaining in popularity.

EXAMPLES OF CLAIMS AND SOME SAFEGUARDS. Unfortunately, even if a producer does everything right, claim situations might arise. Certainly there is no room for carelessness and sloppy office procedures.

Producers have been held liable for nondisclosure or improper disclosure of information about insureds and for failure to reveal policy information to insureds. Many claims involve failure to effect coverage for clients or to carry out requests of insurance companies. Policy provisions relating to vacancy, coinsurance, and cancellation have led to claims. Producers have been held for not knowing insurance regulations, for being unfamiliar with coverages available, for improper completion of applications, and even for failure to provide for insurance requirements in leases and contracts entered into by insureds.

Producers have a great opportunity to practice risk management for themselves. Some general recommendations for preventing or controlling losses are:

- Make notes of conversations with insureds always noting the time and date and place this documentation in the insured's file. Send the insured a copy when the subject is likely to result in controversy.
- Confirm declinations of coverage, changes, and binders in writing.
- Be specific as to whether or not insurance is bound whenever an order for insurance is received.
- Before stating that coverage is not available be certain that is the case or at least reveal the extent of efforts to place the desired insurance.
- Report only correct information to the insured and insurer in writing.
- Do not give legal, accounting, or appraisal advice, unless qualified.

- Explain policy coverages and provisions as completely as possible, being especially careful to point out any differences between a renewal policy and a policy being replaced.
- Prepare binders immediately and show effective date, insurer, type and amount of coverage and property insured. A binder must contain an expiration date.
- Use binders to effect new coverage in existing policies if the endorsement cannot be issued.
- Keep all office personnel current as to binding authority with all insurers represented and never exceed binding authority.
- Establish a standard office procedure for renewals including sufficient cross checking to avoid accidental nonrenewal.
- A renewal must be issued unless the insured requests nonrenewal or the office notifies the insured that the policy will not be renewed. If the insured's request is oral, the producer should confirm it in writing. If the office gives notice of nonrenewal, there should be sufficient time to comply with any laws that may apply. In the absence of such laws, there should be enough time for the insured to obtain other coverage.
- Never misrepresent the applicant or withhold information.
- Honor insurance company requests promptly for cancellation or modification of coverage, or notify the insurer in writing if compliance is not possible.

These represent a skeleton list of suggestions. Attendance at seminars and reading as much as possible on how to prevent errors and omissions claims is strongly recommended. Standard procedures, well organized work habits, and doing as much as possible in writing will help avoid the seemingly countless possibilities of claim. More will be said on this topic in PRO 83, *Office Operations and Sales Management.*

Miscellaneous Professional Liability   The growth in expectations of the public has produced a number of policies designed for various occupations, such as barbers and beauticians, social workers, collection agents, members of the clergy, real estate agents, management consultants, and employment agencies. This discussion will touch briefly on some of these.

Barbers and Beauticians Malpractice.   While malpractice liability for beauty shops was once considered a greater exposure than that for barber shops, the "unisex" approach to hair styling has eroded the distinction. Many of the practices that caused greater concern for beauty shops are now common in providing services for men, including hair coloring and permanent wave.

Coverage is not standard but usually protects against liability for injury or death resulting from treatments or operations usual to a barber shop or beauty parlor. Special practices such as hair removal by electrolysis may be added by endorsement. Most policies include premises and products liability in addition to protection against malpractice. Some insurers, recognizing an increase in the popularity of wigs and hair pieces, cover the bailee's exposure or loss or damage to such items left by customers in the care, custody, or control of the shop.

Real Estate Agents Errors and Omissions. This policy protects against claims resulting from alleged negligence in the conduct of real estate negotiations for others. The possibilities of claim are numerous considering the scope of negotiations between buyer and seller. Deductibles frequently are used, and coverage is written rather freely.

Collection Agents Errors and Omissions. This policy protects against loss due to negligent act, error or omission in connection with collection of an account by the insured, including employees. Policies are underwritten carefully and use of deductibles is common. Underwriting concerns involve shoddy practices and personal injury hazards such as false arrest, libel, slander, and invasion of privacy. Most insurers who would provide premises liability for collection agents would not knowingly provide personal injury coverage. Some E&O policies do not cover these hazards, and producers should be wary in this regard.

Employment Agencies Errors and Omissions. The dislocation of workers brought about by the mobility of the work force and business cycles in the economy have created something of a business boom for employment agencies. With it have come problems from misrepresentation of jobs to applicants, of applicants to employers, and claims of defamation, often from disappointed clients. A limited number of insurers offer this coverage that protects insureds against misrepresentation through negligence, error or omission and usually against defamation as well.

Professional Liability Summary

There are numerous kinds of professional liability policies available for various businesses. Aside from the medical, legal, architectural and accounting professions, only insurance agents and brokers are widely covered by liability from malpractice or errors and omissions.

The terms "professional," "malpractice" and "errors and omissions" have been used interchangeably in this discussion. Each name denotes a liability policy designed to insure the practitioner against the consequences of misdeeds in the performance of professional activities—"professional" used here in the broad sense.

Generally, "professional liability" is the name given to all such policies with "malpractice" and "errors and omissions" used as subclassifications. The distinction that is frequently made between the two terms is that "malpractice" insurance covers an exposure to loss that arises largely from bodily injury (medical practitioners, hair stylists), and "errors and omissions" policies cover the exposure to loss that arises from damage to property, usually intangible property (lawyers, insurance agents, accountants, architects).

Insuring agreements usually are very broad. There may be no distinction between bodily injury and property damage. Coverage goes beyond the confinements of these two phrases, and care, custody, or control exclusions that are so common to other liability policies are usually not part of professional liability policies. In almost every instance (druggists liability is an exception), professional liability insurance is not a substitute for other liability insurance.

In most professional liability policies the term "caused by accident" is not used. The practitioner may have intended the act that caused the loss, but certainly not the consequence. Many claims, particularly in the medical field, involve such claims, such as from faulty diagnosis, and they are covered.

Many types of professional liability policies make regular use of deductibles, and they are frequently large. Policies for insurance agents, architects, lawyers, and accountants are examples. Deductibles sometimes apply to defense costs as well as indemnification. This is an important point—producers should alert insureds when this condition exists as it is adverse to them.

At one time almost all professional liability insurance required consent of the insured before an insurance company could settle a claim. The reputation of the professional is of such critical value that it was and is important to prevent settlement for reasons of expediency where perhaps there was no liability on the part of the insured. This is a desirable feature, and producers should seek to obtain it for clients when possible. It has been removed or modified in some instances. A typical modification is that should the insured not consent to settlement, the insurer ultimately will be liable for no more than the amount of proposed settlement with the insured paying any additional sums.

Claims-made insurance policies are being used to insure many professionals. Occurrence forms are also being used, but the trend definitely is shifting to the claims-made basis. Producers must be aware of which form applies in each given instance, exercising care as to retroactive and discovery provisions discussed earlier.

Finally, the available sources of professional liability insurance leads to a marketplace of insurers more varied as to type than that for almost any other kind of insurance. Excess and surplus lines and

Lloyd's insurers are used extensively in addition to agency companies and, to a limited degree, some direct writers. A knowledge of the insurers in the professional liability marketplace and how to operate within it are essential for producers who sell professional liability policies.

Checkpoints

1. List the distinctions between the products and completed operations hazards.
2. Which of the four CGL products and completed operations exclusions may be covered? How?
3. Describe the major difference between an "occurrence" and a "claims-made" policy.
4. How does coverage under a professional liability policy differ from a CGL?
5. What is the difference between "malpractice" and "errors and omissions" coverage?

SUMMARY

Coverage of the CGL is the broadest available for nonpersonal liability insurance. Yet many exposures are uninsured even with a CGL. Therefore, producers should recommend the broad form CGL endorsement as an addition to the CGL whenever the need arises and underwriting considerations allow.

Coverage for products and completed operations is essential to many businesses. While the CGL may cover the exposures, some insureds and clients present hazards that require greater premium and underwriting control. Producers must be aware of the hazards, coverage restrictions, and insurance techniques to handle the exposures.

Profitability problems in products, completed operations, and professional liability have led many insurers to use claims-made policies instead of occurrence policies. Producers must be aware of the differences between the two types of policies and the problems that arise when replacing one with another. Reading, understanding, and explaining policies to clients becomes even more critical in these areas because of many nonstandard policy forms being used by both standard and excess and surplus lines insurers. The bottom line for producers is not only to be sure clients have the proper coverage for their exposures, but also to protect themselves from their own growing errors and omissions exposures.

CHAPTER 4

Workers' Compensation and Employers' Liability

INTRODUCTION

Current workers' compensation laws have evolved over time. Originally, a worker was not automatically compensated for a work-related injury. The injured employee had to file a suit against the employer and prove the injury was due to employer negligence. In many firms, filing a suit meant immediate dismissal. In addition, it was very difficult to persuade a fellow employee to testify on behalf of the injured employee because of fear of dismissal. Further, under the laws of negligence, the employer had three common law defenses against a lawsuit. These made it extremely difficult for the injured employee to collect damages.

The first major defense was *contributory negligence*. If the employer could show that the employee contributed to the accident in any manner, the employee was barred from a recovery. The second major defense was the *fellow servant rule*. Under this rule, an employee injured because of the negligent actions of a fellow employee was not able to collect from the employer and had to sue the fellow employee. The last major defense of the employer was the *assumption of risk doctrine*. If the employer could show that the employee had taken the job, aware of the exposures associated with it, the worker had *assumed the risk* and was barred from recovery.

By 1900 the United States was becoming an industrialized nation, and the number of industrial accidents was increasing rapidly. It became apparent to state governments that the problem of compensation for injured workers had to be dealt with. Between 1900 and 1910, many states adopted employers' liability laws that modified or eliminated the three common law defenses. With these defenses no longer available to the employer, the injured worker had a better chance of recovery in the courts, although employer negligence still had to be proved. Suit was still an expensive, time-consuming process and, for injured persons out of work and in need of immediate medical attention, an impractical process.

The next step was enactment of workers' compensation laws. The intent of the laws was to pay medical expenses immediately and, to some degree, reimburse the injured employee's lost wages with no need for court action. The cost of industrial injury was shifted from the injured employee to the business. The individual employer was subtly encouraged to implement safety standards through the use of experience rating formulas developed by insurers to lower the cost of workers' compensation insurance, in the long run.

All states have enacted workers' compensation laws. It is impossible to review each of these different laws. This chapter will discuss provisions included by most states. The producer should become familiar with the laws of the states in which the producer's clients operate.

BASIC CONCEPTS

Right of Recovery

The basic concept of all workers' compensation laws is that the employer is responsible for paying benefits to an employee injured on the job, whether or not the employer was negligent. There is no need for court action to establish liability. The employee need only prove that the injury arose "out of and in the course of employment." In making the liability of the employer "absolute," the laws also provide basic protection for the employer because this "absolute" liability on the part of the employer is limited to benefits specifically spelled out in state workers' compensation laws. Recovery is limited to those mandated benefits and, with few exceptions, the employee cannot seek additional compensation through court action—even if negligence of the employer could be shown. Generally, the employee must accept the benefits granted by the law and consequently loses the right to recovery in a tort action.

Certain industrial injuries and occupational illnesses are not covered by law. If an uncovered injury occurs, the injured employee has full right to pursue recovery through court action. Employer protection for this type of action is covered by the employers' liability portion (coverage B) of a workers' compensation policy.

Covered Injuries

The majority of the laws state that a covered accident or illness must arise *out of and in the course of employment.* This does not necessarily mean that every accident occurring while the employee is "at work" is compensable. For example, if an employee was in the office and her estranged husband came in and severely beat her, the injury may not be compensable under workers' compensation. Although the employee was "at work," the injury did not necessarily arise out of employment.

A major problem arises when the employee is injured in a traffic accident on the way to work. The question of coverage under the law depends heavily on the circumstances. Under normal circumstances, accidents occurring "to and from work" are not compensable under the law if the place of employment is a fixed location. However, if the employer is either providing transportation or paying for transportation of the employee, the injury would come under the jurisdiction of the workers' compensation law. If employees do not have a fixed place of employment (for example, traveling salespersons), the compensation law would cover them from the time they leave home until they return.

Another "gray area" is an injury sustained by an employee while attending a company-sponsored picnic or social event, or even while playing on a company-organized sports team. Most states are interpreting these injuries as fully within the scope of the law and thus compensable. For example, a restaurant holds an annual picnic for its employees at a park. Although swimming is prohibited in the lake, an employee dives from the pier into water only twelve inches deep and suffers a broken neck. The state administrative body responsible for workers' compensation may determine that the employee was in the course of employment and the workers' compensation insurer would have to provide benefits. Workers' compensation laws are broadened through judicial, administrative, or adjustor interpretation.

Willful injury to oneself, injury caused solely by the employee's intoxication, and injury from work specifically forbidden by the employer are not compensable under the various state workers' compensation laws. However, the burden of proof is always on the employer in these cases.

Assault by Employer

In the case of battery by the employer causing injury to an

employee, most states stipulate that the act of assault breaks the employer-employee relationship. The employee has the option of either claiming benefits under workers' compensation law or pursuing recovery through tort action. However, battery by a fellow employee or a third party arising out of and in the course of employment is compensable under the workers' compensation laws. The employee has no right of action against the employer but could sue the third party for damages and, depending on the jurisdiction, sue the fellow employee.

Accident

Generally, courts have been liberal regarding what constitutes a covered "accident." The general rule is if the incident was "accidental" from the standpoint of the injured person, it is compensable. Courts have held that many occurrences fall within the jurisdiction of the workers' compensation laws and so provide benefits. A common controversy of this nature occurs when an employee has a heart attack on the job. This is construed to be a compensable accident if it can be established the employee was undergoing undue stress because of work duties. This ruling also applies to the employee who has a medical history of fainting spells. If the employee blacks out, falls down, and breaks an arm, the courts will usually rule the injury is compensable under the law.

In an actual case, an employee with a medical history of epilepsy had a seizure, fell from a three-foot stepladder and sustained fatal head injuries. The workers' compensation insurer denied the claim on the basis the injury had no relationship to the work being performed. However, the state industrial commission ruled the injury was compensable under the law.[1]

Third Party Claims

Generally, if an employee's injury arises from the negligence of a third party, the employee is still eligible for benefits under workers' compensation laws. In all but three states, the law allows the employee to collect statutory benefits *or* collect from a negligent third party. In some states, the employee may receive workers' compensation benefits and also bring court action against a third party. The laws give the employer the primary responsibility for the injury to the employee. This provides protection to the injured employee if a suit against the negligent party is not successful.

This provision of the law also affords some protection to the employer by preventing the employee from collecting twice on the same loss. In some states, if the employee collects under workers' compensation benefits, the insurance company has full rights to subrogate against the third party. If the insurance company recovers any amounts in excess of the amount paid to the employee, it must turn over a percentage (for example, two-thirds) of the excess to the employee. In other states, employees collecting workers' compensation benefits may file suit in their own behalf against negligent third parties. If an employee is successful in attaining a judgment, all sums previously paid by the workers' compensation insurer must be refunded.

For example, an employee, Betty, was driving a delivery van for a retail furniture store. As she was proceeding through an intersection Sam ran a red light and collided with Betty's vehicle. Betty collected workers' compensation benefits totaling $22,000 in medical expenses and lost wages. Since the accident occurred in a state that permitted employees to bring legal action on their own behalf, she sued Sam for the injuries sustained. The court awarded Betty $100,000 in damages. Betty was required to refund the previously paid $22,000 to the workers' compensation insurer. This example shows how Betty can receive more in tort action than under the statutory benefits of workers' compensation and also demonstrates how the employer, or in this case the insurance company, is protected.

Checkpoints

1. Explain three common law defenses available to an employer prior to the enactment of workers' compensation legislation.
2. Briefly explain the phrase "arising out of and in the course of employment."
3. Explain the rights of an *employee* injured by the assault of the *employer*.
4. Define the term "accident" in the context of workers' compensation.

WORKERS' COMPENSATION LAWS

Compulsory Versus Elective

Workers' compensation laws are either compulsory or elective. The producer should check to see which type of law is in effect in his or her marketing area. A *compulsory* law requires every employer falling within the scope of the law to provide the specified workers' compensation benefits. Noncompliance is punishable by fines and sometimes by imprisonment.

A few states have *elective* laws. In these states, the employer may reject the law without becoming liable for fines or imprisonment. If the employer engages in work covered by the workers' compensation laws and has elected to reject the law, an injured employee may bring suit against the employer. However, in this case, the employer is stripped of the three common law defenses.

Who Is Covered

"Who is covered" should be researched in state laws by the producer since it can vary in any given jurisdiction.[2]

Minors In all jurisdictions, a minor, whether legally or illegally employed, falls within the scope of workers' compensation laws. Some state laws provide extended benefits to injured minors, sometimes twice the benefits for other employees. The standard workers' compensation policy would pay only normal benefits under the law, and the employer would be held liable for any excess amount. This point should be fully explained to an insured who employs a minor. For example, assume an automobile service station owner employs a fourteen-year-old minor to pump gas during the summer. The minor-employee sustains a work related accident in which the minor loses an arm. The scheduled benefit in the state stipulates a payment of $25,000 for the lost arm. However, the law also doubles benefits for a minor. The workers' compensation insurer would be liable only for the $25,000 stipulated in the law (the normal benefit) and the service station owner would be liable for the additional $25,000.

Legal Entity The legal form of ownership of the employer has a bearing on who is covered by the workers' compensation law. It is important to determine the exact legal form of organization of the named insured since each legal entity is treated differently.

Sole Proprietor. The sole proprietor as the employer is *excluded* from coverage. All of the sole proprietor's employees would be covered by the policy. If the sole proprietor wishes to be covered by the workers' compensation policy he or she must sign a form electing coverage.

Partnership. As with the sole proprietor, individual partners are considered employers and are excluded from coverage. If coverage is desired, each partner must sign a form electing coverage. Some states do automatically provide coverage by law to "working" partners—that is, those actively engaged in working for the partnership.

Corporation. In the eyes of the law, a corporation is a "fictitious person." Thus, the corporation is the employer and everyone working for it is an employee. This being the case, all officers of the corporation, even though they may also be owners, are treated as employees under workers' compensation laws, and are covered under the workers' compensation policy. Corporate officers may not want to be covered by the policy because of the cost or because they believe they have adequate coverage under a group health and accident policy. If they wish to be *excluded*, they must sign a rejection form. If the exemption is sought because of "adequate health insurance," that coverage should be verified as most group health insurance policies exclude work related accidents and sicknesses.

Independent Contractors A true independent contractor is *not an employee* and does not come within the scope of the law. Sometimes, though, it is difficult to determine whether the contractor involved is an employee or is truly an independent contractor. A court would usually scrutinize the degree of control the principal has over the contractor to make a binding determination. Independent contractors usually furnish their own materials and equipment and are paid in a lump sum. "Independents" are responsible only for the final result and are not subject to daily supervision by the principal. If a court should decide the injured worker is an employee rather than an independent contractor, the principal's workers' compensation policy would be liable for payment of the benefits whether or not the insurance company had ever collected premiums on the independent contractor's payroll. The producer should make this point to prospects using independent contractors, as the prospect's workers' compensation premium will ultimately be affected.

A good example of the difference between the interpretations of the various states on this rule is in the field of real estate. In some states, such as Ohio, the solicitor for a real estate firm is treated as an independent contractor and would not be covered under the firm's workers' compensation policy for a work related injury. However, in South Carolina, solicitors are treated as employees by the South Carolina Industrial Commission, so they are fully covered for benefits under the workers' compensation policy of their firm.

Subcontractors A general contractor employing a subcontractor may be held liable for injuries to employees of the subcontractor. In most states the general contractor is liable for payment of all benefits prescribed by the workers' compensation laws for the injured employee of a subcontractor if the subcontractor does not provide a workers' compensation policy. The producer can help the general contractor avoid this exposure to loss by recommending that the general contractor require a Certificate of Insurance from each subcontractor verifying that each subcontractor carries workers' compensation coverage. If a subcontractor does not carry workers' compensation insurance, the general contractor's insurer will include the subcontractor's payroll on the audit, and the general contractor will have to pay the premium based on it.

Although the workers' compensation law, and therefore the policy, extends to cover employees of the uninsured subcontractors, it does not apply to an individual working as a subcontractor. The individual would be treated as an independent contractor and thus would not be covered by the general contractor's policy.

Excluded Employments Certain types of employees are excluded from workers' compensation statutes in almost every state. With exceptions in a few states, agricultural workers, domestics, and casual laborers are not covered by the law. Thus, even in states having a compulsory law, an employer of farm labor, for instance, is not required to carry a workers' compensation policy on those farm workers. The employer may wish to provide coverage for these classes of employees and may do so using a voluntary compensation endorsement (discussed later). This is done solely at the election of the employer. By doing so, the employer is providing the benefits of the law on otherwise exempt employees, but, in this situation, the employer does not lose any of the common law defenses otherwise available under employer's liability.

Methods of Providing Workers' Compensation Benefits

The most common method of providing workers' compensation benefits is through the purchase of a workers' compensation policy from a private (nongovernmental) insurer. However, there are several methods for providing benefits.

Monopolistic State Funds Presently, six states (Nevada, North Dakota, Ohio, Washington, West Virginia, and Wyoming) have established a monopolistic fund that handles all workers' compensation insurance in that state. The state fund does all administrative work such as policy insurance, inspections, and claims adjustment.

Private Insurance Except for the six monopolistic states, every state allows workers' compensation insurance to be provided by authorized private insurers.

Competitive State Funds and Private Insurers At the time of this writing, twelve states permit employers to purchase insurance either from a competitive state insurance fund or from a private insurance company.

Self-Insurance (or Retention) Self-insurance is permitted in the vast majority of states. Some states require the deposit of securities or a bond, but others require only a financial statement indicating the employer's financial ability to pay compensation benefits. Self-insurance should be used only by very large firms able to predict their losses accurately and have the necessary loss control, medical, and claims handling services. Producers should be prepared to sell excess workers' compensation insurance over the employer's "self-insured retention."

THE WORKERS' COMPENSATION POLICY

The workers' compensation policy is somewhat standardized in all states. The following discussion will use excerpts from a standard workers' compensation policy. Many states will have exceptions to this standard policy so the producer should learn the exceptions applicable to his or her marketing area.

The Declarations Page

The declarations page (Exhibit 4-1) of the workers' compensation policy contains the usual information such as the name and address of the insured, the type of entity insured, and the effective dates of coverage.

The declarations page also indicates the usual workplaces and the states involved in the insured's operation. Item 4 on the declarations page identifies the type of work codes and rates as well as the payrolls used in calculating the deposit premium. Rating of the workers' compensation policy will be discussed later.

The Insuring Agreements

Coverage A—Workers' Compensation

I. Coverage A—Workers' Compensation

To pay promptly when due all compensation and other benefits required of the insured by the workers' compensation law.

Coverage A states the policy will pay all sums required of the insured (employer) by the workers' compensation law. There are no limits in the policy, and benefits payable conform exactly to the workers' compensation law of the state, as if the law were printed in the policy. Benefits under workers' compensation states can be grouped into four categories: medical benefits, wage loss benefits, survivor benefits, and rehabilitation benefits.

Medical Benefits. Injured workers are entitled to payments for medical, surgical, and hospital services as the nature of the injury and

Exhibit 4-1
Sample Workers' Compensation Declarations Page

CROWLEY FIRE AND MARINE

WORKMEN'S COMPENSATION AND EMPLOYERS' LIABILITY POLICY NUMBER

DECLARATIONS

1. NAME OF INSURED

ADDRESS (NUMBER - STREET - CITY OR POST OFFICE - COUNTY - STATE - ZIP CODE)

☐ INDIVIDUAL   ☐ PARTNERSHIP   ☐ CORPORATION   ☐ OTHER

LOCATIONS—ALL USUAL WORKPLACES OF THE INSURED AT OR FROM WHICH OPERATIONS COVERED BY THIS POLICY ARE CONDUCTED ARE LOCATED AT THE ABOVE ADDRESS UNLESS OTHERWISE STATED HEREIN:

2. POLICY PERIOD: FROM   TO   12:01 A.M. STANDARD TIME AT THE ADDRESS OF THE INSURED AS STATED HEREIN.

3. COVERAGE A OF THIS POLICY APPLIES TO THE WORKMEN'S COMPENSATION LAW AND ANY OCCUPATIONAL DISEASE LAW OF EACH OF THE FOLLOWING STATES:

4.

CLASSIFICATION OF OPERATIONS	CODE NO.	PREMIUM BASIS — ESTIMATED TOTAL REMUNERATION ☐ ANNUAL - ☐ THREE YEAR	RATES — PER $100 OF REMUNERATION	ESTIMATED PREMIUMS ☐ ANNUAL - ☐ THREE YR.
ENTRIES IN THIS ITEM, EXCEPT AS SPECIFICALLY PROVIDED ELSEWHERE IN THIS POLICY DO NOT MODIFY ANY OF THE OTHER PROVISIONS OF THIS POLICY.				

MINIMUM PREMIUM

$

TOTAL ESTIMATED ☐ ANNUAL PREMIUM — ☐ THREE YEAR PREMIUM $

IF INDICATED BELOW, INTERIM ADJUSTMENTS OF PREMIUM SHALL BE MADE:

☐ SEMI-ANNUALLY ☐ QUARTERLY ☐ MONTHLY

DEPOSIT PREMIUM $

5. LIMIT OF LIABILITY FOR COVERAGE B — EMPLOYERS' LIABILITY:

$

SUBJECT TO ALL THE TERMS OF THIS POLICY HAVING REFERENCE THERETO.

COUNTERSIGNED AT

COUNTERSIGNATURE DATE

MONTH DAY YEAR

COUNTERSIGNATURE OF LICENSED RESIDENT AGENT

the process of recovery require. The amount of medical benefits is unlimited in all fifty states. Medical care includes the cost of such items as drugs, artificial limbs, and X rays. Coverage is also granted for any disease peculiar to a particular occupation. Diseases the public are regularly exposed to, flu for example, are excluded.

Wage Loss Benefits. The injured employee is entitled to wages lost due to work related accident or disease. This usually is a percentage of the employee's weekly wage (usually $66^2/_3$ percent) subject to maximum and minimum benefits set by law. Most states have a waiting period before lost wages will be paid, usually from three days to seven days. In most states, once the waiting period has elapsed, lost wages are paid retroactively from the first day. There are four classifications of disability: temporary total, permanent total, temporary partial, and permanent partial disability. Most cases involve temporary total disability. That is, the employee, although totally disabled and collecting benefits, is expected to recover and return to work. Each state law contains a schedule of maximum amounts for certain permanent injuries such as loss of a hand or an eye.

Survivors Benefits. Funeral expenses payable to a survivor are covered by the law for a specified amount. In addition, a percentage of the workers' former weekly wage is paid to the surviving spouse and children for a specified time period. These benefits are generally paid to the spouse until remarriage and to the children until a specified age.

Rehabilitation Benefits. Rehabilitation benefits include both medical and vocational rehabilitation in cases involving severe disabilities. In most states, reasonable board, lodging, and travel expenses are covered subject to certain limits.

Coverage B—Employers' Liability. In addition to workers' compensation benefits, the policy provides coverage for other employers' liability exposures.

Coverage B—Employers' Liability

To pay on behalf of the insured all sums which the insured shall become legally obligated to pay as damages because of bodily injury by accident or disease, including death at any time resulting therefrom,

(a) sustained in the United States of America, its territories or possessions, or Canada by any employee of the insured arising out of and in the course of his employment by the insured either in operations in a state designated in Item 3 of the declarations or in operations necessary or incidental thereto, or

(b) sustained while temporarily outside the United States of America, its territories or possessions, or Canada by any employee of the insured who is a citizen or resident of the United States or Canada arising out of and in the course of his employment by the insured in connection with operations in a state designated in Item 3 of the declarations; but this insurance does not apply to any suit brought in or any judgment rendered by any court outside the United States of America, its territories or possessions, or Canada or to an action on such judgment wherever brought.

Not all injuries or diseases sustained while in the course of employment are compensable under state laws. If the injured employee has no benefits available under coverage A, the employee may be able to bring a tort action against the employer. In addition, the employer may be sued by a third party, such as a dependent of a disabled employee. Since the comprehensive general liability policy (CGL) excludes injury to any employee in the course of employment, the employer would have no coverage under the CGL. Coverage B, employers' liability, affords coverage for these rare situations. It is a legal liability coverage, and negligence must be proved to be covered by the policy. Coverage is worldwide, but any foreign travel must be incidental to the employment in the state designated in the declarations. Employers' liability applies outside the United States only to suits brought by citizens or residents of the United States or Canada. For example, coverage B would not respond to a suit brought by a Japanese worker if he were a resident of Japan. Unlike coverage A, employers' liability has a limit of liability stated in the policy declarations. The basic limit for coverage B is $100,000. Like any other liability limit, it may be increased to a level selected by the insured.

Agreement II—Defense, Settlement, Supplementary Payments

The insurance company agrees, as in most liability policies, to defend any suit brought against the insured but retains the right to settle any claim as it elects. The insurer will pay all court costs and bond premiums required in defending a suit and agrees to reimburse the insured for all reasonable expenses, other than loss of wages, incurred at the insurance company request. All of these are supplemental payments in addition to the limit of liability.

Agreement III—Definitions

The definitions section defines the terms "Workmen's [sic] Compensation Law," "State," "Bodily Injury by Accident; Bodily Injury by Disease," and "Assault and Battery" as used in the policy. These terms have been or will be explained in this chapter.

Agreement IV—Application of the Policy

The policy specifically states it only applies to accidental injury occurring during the policy period. Thus, from a claims standpoint, the policy is on an *occurrence* rather than a *claims-made* basis. In order for occupational disease to be covered, the last exposure to a condition causing an ailment must occur during the policy period. For example, Bill Smith was employed by a firm manufacturing commercial dyes. Bill left his job at the dye manufacturer to take a job in an unrelated field in June of 19X1. In 19X2, Bill developed a skin condition called "color poisoning" often found on workers in dye manufacturing. Since Bill's last exposure to this health hazard was in June 19X1, the workers' compensation policy in effect on June, 19X1 would be liable for any benefits available under the workers' compensation laws.

Exclusions

The workers' compensation policy contains a list of exclusions from coverage.

Exclusion (a) The policy provides coverage for any location within the state or states designated in the policy declarations. Exclusion (a) excludes coverage at any location not described in Item 1 or 3 of the declarations if the insured has other insurance for that operation or is a qualified self-insurer at that location. This exclusion prevents pyramiding of benefits under two policies for the insured with two separately insured locations in the same state.

Exclusion (b) Exclusion (b) deletes coverage for certain classes of employees. In most states, domestic workers and farm employees do not come under the workers' compensation laws. There are a few exceptions so the producer should check the appropriate law.

Exclusion (c) Exclusion (c) only applies to coverage B—employer's liability and is similar to the contractual liability in the CGL policy. It specifically excludes liability assumed by contract.

Exclusion (d) Exclusion (d) applies to employment of minors and affects only coverage B.

In all states, minors illegally employed (according to child labor laws) come under the scope of workers' compensation. As mentioned, many states provide for additional or penalty compensation for injured minors. Exclusion (d) excludes any punitive damages or penalty benefits due an injured minor under the law. The employer must bear the cost of all of these additional damages directly.

Exclusion (e) Exclusion (e) places a time limit on any suit brought under coverage B. A suit brought for bodily injury by disease must be presented within thirty-six months after expiration of the policy.

Exclusion (f) Exclusion (f) states if the injury or disease is covered by workers' compensation laws, and thus covered by coverage A, coverage B will not apply.

Policy Conditions

As with all insurance contracts, the workers' compensation policy contains conditions which describe the privileges and obligations of both the insured employer and the insurance company.

Condition 1 (Premium) Condition 1 states the premium will be calculated by the rules and rates used by the insurance company at inception of the policy. It allows the insurance company to adjust the rates and calculation of premiums if state law changes the rate structure. This condition indicates that all remuneration is the basis of the premium. Rating will be discussed in more detail later in this chapter but an important point should be made.

Assume a producer or previous insurer had used an incorrect classification in developing a deposit premium. Condition 1 obligates the insured to pay the final premium based on the correct classifications determined at audit. Therefore, any mistakes made at policy inception *may* be a double source of embarrassment to a producer—first when the classification error is corrected and second when the proper premium is billed after an audit of the insured's payroll. Carefully review employee classifications to help obtain misclassified accounts and to prevent personal embarrassment.

Condition 2 (Long Term Policy) Condition 2 refers to the procedure for writing a "long term policy." This policy condition grants the insuring company the right to issue a long term policy yet adjust rates and codes on an annual basis. Insurers prefer to write a one-year contract and are generally reluctant to write a long term policy.

Condition 3 (Partnership or Joint Venture as Insured) Condition 3 assures that coverage applies only to the entity indicated on the declarations page for partnerships or joint ventures. If one partner starts another venture on an individual basis, there would be no workers' compensation coverage provided by the partnership's policy. Coverage applies only to injury while working in the scope of duties of the specified partnership.

Condition 4 (Inspection and Audit)   Condition 4 gives the insuring company and rating authority the right to make inspections of the workplace and to audit the books of the insured for the purpose of establishing the correct classification and rates for the insured. This condition contains a disclaimer. By making an inspection, the insurance company in no way warrants that the insured's working conditions are "safe" or that the employer is in compliance with any state or federal safety regulations. The inspection is said to be solely for the purpose of the insurance company. Actually, insureds benefit from insurer safety inspections, but insurers wish to avoid being held responsible for safety conditions at the insured location.

Conditions 5, 6, and 7   Conditions 5, 6, and 7 place certain obligations on the insured. The insured must give written notice of any injury (Condition 5) as soon as practicable and notice of claim or suit (Condition 6) immediately. This notice must give sufficient information for the insurance company to investigate the claim. The insured is obligated to assist the insurance company in the investigation and defense of a claim (Condition 7).

Condition 8 (Statutory Provisions)   Condition 8 relates several statutory conditions applying to Coverage A. This condition states that the policy automatically complies with workers' compensation laws of the state or states for which it is written. Bankruptcy or insolvency of the insured in no way relieves the insurance company of its statutory obligations to an injured employee. Although the insurer is bound to pay benefits for the injury, it obligates the insured to reimburse the insurance company for any amounts paid in excess of the normal benefits because of injury to an employee illegally employed, such as a minor, or for injury due to willful misconduct of the insured.

Conditions 9 through 17   Conditions 9 through 17 are common to insurance policies and a producer selling workers' compensation should be familiar with them. Briefly, Condition 9 relates to the limit of liability under coverage B—employers' liability. Condition 10 discusses an action against the insurer by the insured under coverage B. Condition 11 is the "other insurance" provision and pro-rates the policy's liability based on the proportion of benefits payable under the policy to total benefits payable under all policies. For instance, if three policies apply, and the liability for an accident is $3,000, each policy will pay $\frac{1}{3}$ or $1,000.

Condition 12 reserves the insurer's rights of subrogation, if any. Changes to the policy are discussed in Condition 13 and assignment of the policy is discussed in Condition 14. The cancellation provision of the policy, Condition 15, calls for a ten-day notice of cancellation by the insurance company. However the last paragraph of the condition allows that if the law requires a longer notice than ten days, the policy is automatically amended to comply with the law. Other terms of the policy are made to conform to applicable law under Condition 16. Finally, Condition 17 describes the declarations as a representation of the insured.

Checkpoints

1. Explain the difference between the compulsory and the elective type of workers' compensation law.
2. Identify coverages afforded by coverage A and coverage B of the workers' compensation and employers' liability policy.
3. Identify and explain three exclusions in the workers' compensation and employers' liability policy.
4. Explain the Inspection and Audit Condition contained in the workers' compensation policy.
5. What is the nature of the subcontractor problem when a producer insures a general contractor for workers' compensation?

Endorsements

Maritime Employment Endorsement State workers' compensation laws do not apply to maritime employees. Crew members of vessels are subject to Admiralty Law and may sue their employers for work related injuries. Although the state laws do not cover crew members, it is still permissible to write a workers' compensation policy for maritime workers. The policy would be sold in either of two forms.

Protection and Indemnity (P & I). The employer can purchase P & I insurance which is an ocean marine coverage. P & I would pick up the workers' compensation exposure.

Amend Coverage B. An endorsement entitled "Amendments to Coverage B Endorsement—Maritime (Masters or Members of the Crews of Vessels)" may be purchased. Technically, the territorial restriction of the policy is modified by the endorsement and the endorsement is only for Coverage B—employers' liability. Because of exclusions contained within the endorsement, only a degree of coverage is actually provided.

Longshoremen or Harbor Workers The United States Longshoremen's and Harbor Workers' Compensation Act (L&HWCA) (a compulsory law administered by the Department of Labor) covers injuries to employees on vessels or drydocks. This compulsory insurance is written on a standard workers' compensation policy to which the

United States Longshoremen's and Harbor Workers' Compensation Act Endorsement is attached. The endorsement modifies the definition of "workers' compensation law" and provides unlimited coverage as defined by the L&HWCA under coverage A and provides the usual limit of $100,000 on coverage B—employers' liability. The employers' liability limit may be increased to $500,000 or $1 million. Because of the breadth of the L&HWCA benefits, coverage may be difficult to obtain.

An endorsement is also available to provide for any incidental longshoremen's or harbor workers' exposure an insured may have. Since benefits under the federal act are usually broader than those of the individual states, this can be a valuable coverage for an employer who may have this exposure to loss. For example, a florist in a coastal state received an order to deliver a dozen roses to the stateroom of a couple going on a cruise for their honeymoon. The employee making the delivery fell down the stairs on board ship and was severely injured. The courts determined the injured employee was eligible for benefits under the United States Longshoremen's and Harbor Workers' Compensation Act which provided greater benefits than the state's workers' compensation act. The workers' compensation insurer for the florist would only pay the benefits prescribed by state law and the florist was held liable for the excess benefits provided by the Longshoremen's and Harbor Workers' Compensation Act. If the florist's policy had been endorsed for incidental Longshoremen's and Harbor Workers' Compensation Act coverage, it would have covered in full.

Broad Form All States Endorsement The workers' compensation policy will only comply with the workers' compensation laws in the state or states designated in Item 3 of the declarations page. This can cause a serious gap in coverage when an employee is traveling in the course of employment and is injured in a state not designated in the declarations. If the benefits in the state where the injury occurred are higher than those in the state of employment, the injured employee may elect to receive the benefits of the state paying the higher benefits. The employer's workers' compensation policy would only pay the benefits designated by the law of the state of employment. The employer would be held liable for the excess amount.

This gap can be closed by attachment of the Broad Form All States Endorsement. The broad form actually pays on behalf of the insured in the other states where workers may be injured (other than monopolistic fund states). The limited "All States" form will *indemnify* the employer for out of states benefits. The Broad Form "pays on behalf of" the employer.

Foreign Voluntary Compensation Foreign voluntary compensation coverage is for (1) United States nationals, (2) working outside of the country, and (3) beyond jurisdiction of compulsory workers' compensation or similar laws. Technically, such employees may receive the benefits of the Defense Bases Act, which are the same as the U.S. Longshoremen's and Harbor Workers' Compensation Act. Where an employee is under a foreign workers' compensation act, the insurer issuing the foreign voluntary compensation endorsement is responsible for the difference between local and Defense Bases Act benefits.

When attached to a workers' compensation policy, four changes to the policy are made.

1. *When not applicable.* Benefits are optional. If an eligible employee refuses *voluntary* compensation and sues the employer instead, the endorsement does not apply. The employee is protected by employer's liability coverage.
2. *Covered bodily injury.* Only bodily injury by accident is covered. Bodily injury by disease benefits are not covered unless the employee sues; then the employer's liability section responds.
3. *Repatriation expense.* Some costs to bring an injured or deceased employee back to the United States are covered up to a $5,000 per employee or body limit. For a deceased employee, only costs that exceed expenses to repatriate a healthy employee are covered up to a limit of $5,000.
4. *War exclusion.* No compensation will be paid if loss is caused directly or indirectly by war, invasion, rebellion, and so forth.

Voluntary Compensation Endorsement For employees not eligible for mandatory coverage (agricultural employees, and so on), this endorsement extends such benefits voluntarily to them. Like foreign voluntary coverage, benefits are optional to the employee (who may reject them and sue the employer instead) and this coverage is only for bodily injury by accident. Bodily injury by disease can be added, however.

Selling Voluntary Compensation Coverage. For prospects and clients with more than incidental exposures, these coverages are desirable. They show concern for employees and most workers' compensation insurers will endorse such coverage to workers' compensation policies. Producers should check for the existence and extent of foreign or excluded employees in the exposure identification process and make appropriate coverage suggestions.

Other Coverage

Stopgap Coverage. Prospects with operations in monopolistic fund states need to check state requirements to be sure they are in compliance with the appropriate laws. Most monopolistic states do not offer employers' liability as part of their policies. Except in Ohio, stopgap coverage is available to be endorsed to a general liability policy. Wording of the endorsement is exactly like employers' liability.

Aggregate and Specific Excess Coverage. For clients with a retention program for workers' compensation, two forms of excess coverage are available and essential for such clients.

AGGREGATE EXCESS OR STOP LOSS. For all losses in a year, the employer retains a specified amount from the first dollar (assume $200,000). An insurer would then pay all workers' compensation and employers' liability losses in excess of the $200,000 up to a maximum amount. Coverage above retention is not unlimited. Insurers will negotiate the amount of protection they are willing to provide over the aggregate retention limit of the employer.

SPECIFIC EXCESS. Specific excess is available as an alternative to or in addition to aggregate excess. The specific retention limit in specific excess is for any one loss or occurrence. The insurer will pay only if one loss or occurrence exceeds the retention. A maximum limit for the insurer is also included in the policy. Exhibit 4-2 shows the differences between aggregate and specific excess coverage for the same retention, maximum limit, and losses.

COMBINED AGGREGATE AND EXCESS COVERAGE. The combined form is illustrated in Exhibit 4-3. Since no one loss exceeded the specific excess retention, no losses would be paid by that portion.

However, since total losses exceeded the $200,000 aggregate retention, the employer would be indemnified for $25,000 in this case.

SELLING EXCESS COVERAGES. Whether sold singly or in combination, the risk management process will help the producer and prospect or client decide on the retention limit and maximum coverage sought. Negotiations with underwriters will determine an insurer's willingness to write those limits (or an alternative) and what the premium will be. Excess insurance will be a real service to clients who can retain a portion of this exposure. Good relations with the underwriters and proper and complete information on the client will help obtain the coverage at a proper price.

Checkpoints

1. Explain how workers' compensation laws treat minor employees.
2. Describe how the nature of a legal entity is important under a workers' compensation policy for owners of the entity.
3. Differentiate between an independent contractor and a subcontractor, and describe how coverage applies to each under the workers' compensation laws.

Exhibit 4-2

Aggregate Excess Versus Specific Excess

Aggregate Excess	Specific Excess
$100,000 aggregate retention limit $1,000,000 maximum limit	$100,000 specific retention limit $1,000,000 maximum limit

Losses		Losses	
	$ 25,000		$ 25,000
	75,000		75,000
	90,000		90,000
	35,000		35,000
Total	$225,000	Total	$225,000
Aggregate retention	100,000		
Amount of excess insurance	$125,000		

Since none of the losses exceeds the $100,000 per occurrence retention limit, the entire loss must be retained.

Exhibit 4-3

Combination Aggregate Excess and Specific Excess Coverage

Aggregate Excess	Specific Excess
$200,000 aggregate retention limit $1,000,000 maximum limit	$100,000 specific retention limit $1,000,000 maximum limit

	Losses
	$ 25,000
	75,000
	90,000
	35,000
Total losses	$225,000

4. List three classes of employment excluded from most state's workers' compensation laws.

5. Explain how coverage is provided for longshoremen and harbor workers.
6. Explain the need for voluntary compensation endorsements.

OTHER ASPECTS OF WORKERS' COMPENSATION

Occupational Safety and Health Act of 1970 (OSHA)

Although the federal government has left regulation of workers' compensation insurance to the states, it has become indirectly involved with providing safety regulation for all industry in all states. The 1970 Williams-Steiger Bill established Occupational Safety and Health Act (OSHA) regulations.

The law and subsequent regulations establish safety standards for all types of industries with which employers must comply. The law applies to all employers. These health and safety standards are set forth in a 248-page booklet. These standards cover almost every aspect of any given industry.

The Department of Labor has a staff of OSHA inspectors who regularly inspect workplaces. If a violation of standards exists, the inspector gives the employer a written report of the violations and sets a time period in which the unsafe condition must be corrected. On reinspection, if the hazardous condition has not been corrected, the employer is subject to a fine of up to $1,000 for each day the violation continues past a deadline. An employer may appeal the inspector's decision to the Occupational Safety and Health Review Commission and may appeal this commission's decision to the Federal Court of Appeals.

The employer is not only required to meet the safety standards set for the industry, but must also maintain and file periodic reports on work related diseases or accidents. An OSHA log (Exhibit 4-4) must be kept in the office of the employer and posted once a year on a bulletin board where employees may see it. This log of accidents is open for review by the OSHA inspector and any employee of the firm.

While OSHA was enacted at the federal level, permission was granted for a state to take over administration and enforcement of occupational safety and health state laws as long as the state complied with or exceeded the federal guidelines. About one-half of the states have enacted their own laws and assumed the administration and enforcement responsibilities.

Economic Opportunities Act Endorsement The Federal Anti-Poverty Program provides for programs that offer opportunities for education, training, and employment. The federal departments of Education, Labor, and Health and Welfare are involved in the administration of this act. The act places additional liability on the employer if one of the employees in the program is injured on the job. Benefits include unlimited total disability and medical expenses. If a state workers' compensation law limits either the disability or medical benefits, the employer's policy must be amended to remove all of these limitations.

These modifications are made by the Economic Opportunities Act Endorsement. It is necessary to schedule the states in which the endorsement applies for both the medical and disability benefits. Rating of the endorsement is done by applying a percentage of 2.5 to 11.5 percent of the standard premium developed on the program participant.

Assigned Risk Plans

Some employers, in either high hazard industries or with very poor loss experience, find themselves unable to obtain a workers' compensation policy through normal commercial insurance channels. For this reason, twenty-three states have workers' compensation assigned risk plans. These plans are operated by the National Council on Compensation Insurance. To be eligible for the assigned risk plan the employer must show the inability to obtain a policy through regular markets. This is usually done by producing at least two letters of declination from insurance companies licensed to provide workers' compensation coverages in the state.

Any producer can submit an application for workers' compensation to the assigned risk plan. The governmental agency that administers the plan will assign the applicant to an approved insurer, which in turn will issue the workers' compensation policy. Like any other pool arrangement, losses in excess of premiums and expenses are shared by all insurance companies writing workers' compensation coverage in the state. The insurers should provide loss control or engineering services to these insureds to improve the working conditions so the insured can move again into standard coverage.

Second Injury Funds

With the advent of the workers' compensation laws came the workers' compensation policy. Of course this meant additional insurance premiums for an employer. Employers soon learned that a bad loss record caused an increase in those premiums. Some employers instituted strict loss control programs to keep the number and size of the losses down. However, employers feared hiring an employee who already had a disability, such as a missing limb or eye. If that employee lost another limb or eye in a work-related accident, the employer would

Exhibit 4-4
OSHA Log

Bureau of Labor Statistics
Log and Summary of Occupational
Injuries and Illnesses

NOTE: This form is required by Public Law 91-596 and must be kept in the establishment for 5 years. Failure to maintain and post can result in the issuance of citations and assessment of penalties. (See posting requirements on the other side of form.)

RECORDABLE CASES: You are required to record information about every occupational **death**; every nonfatal occupational **illness**; and those nonfatal occupational **injuries** which involve one or more of the following: loss of consciousness, restriction of work or motion, transfer to another job, or medical treatment (other than first aid). (See definitions on the other side of form.)

Case or File Number	Date of Injury or Onset of Illness	Employee's Name	Occupation	Department	Description of Injury or Illness
Enter a nonduplicating number which will facilitate comparisons with supplementary records.	Enter Mo./day.	Enter first name or initial, middle initial, last name.	Enter regular job title, not activity employee was performing when injured or at onset of illness. In the absence of a formal title, enter a brief description of the employee's duties.	Enter department in which the employee is regularly employed or a description of normal workplace to which employee is assigned, even though temporarily working in another department at the time of injury or illness.	Enter a brief description of the injury or illness and indicate the part or parts of body affected. Typical entries for this column might be: Amputation of 1st joint right forefinger; Strain of lower back; Contact dermatitis on both hands; Electrocution—body.
(A)	(B)	(C)	(D)	(E)	(F)

PREVIOUS PAGE TOTALS

TOTALS (Instructions on other side of form.)

Continued on next page

☆ U.S. GOVERNMENT PRINTING OFFICE 1978—708 437 1058 2 1

FOLD

OSHA No. 200

U.S. Department of Labor

For Calendar Year 19 _____   Page ___ of ___

Form Approved
O.M.B. No. 44R 1453

Company Name

Establishment Name

Establishment Address

Extent of and Outcome of INJURY

	Fatalities	Nonfatal Injuries				
	Injury Related	Injuries With Lost Workdays			Injuries Without Lost Workdays	
	Enter DATE of death. Mo./day/yr.	Enter a CHECK if injury involves days away from work, or days of restricted work activity, or both.	Enter number of DAYS away from work.	Enter number of DAYS of restricted work activity.	Enter a CHECK if no entry was made in columns 1 or 2 but the injury is recordable as defined above.	
	(1)	(2)	(3)	(4)	(5)	(6)

Type, Extent of, and Outcome of ILLNESS

Type of Illness — CHECK Only One Column for Each Illness (See other side of form for terminations or permanent transfers.)

(a) Occupational skin diseases or disorders	(b) Dust diseases of the lungs	(c) Respiratory conditions due to toxic agents	(d) Poisoning (systemic effects of toxic materials)	(e) Disorders due to physical agents	(f) Disorders associated with repeated trauma	(g) All other occupational illnesses
(7)						

Fatalities — Illness Related

Enter DATE of death. Mo./day/yr.
(8)

Nonfatal Illnesses

Illnesses With Lost Workdays			Illnesses Without Lost Workdays
Enter a CHECK if illness involves days away from work, or days of restricted work activity, or both.	Enter a CHECK if illness involves days away from work.	Enter number of DAYS away from work.	Enter number of DAYS of restricted work activity.	Enter a CHECK if no entry was made in columns 8 or 9.
(9)	(10)	(11)	(12)	(13)

ILLNESSES

INJURIES

Certification of Annual Summary Totals By _____ Title _____ Date _____

OSHA No 200

POST ONLY THIS PORTION OF THE LAST PAGE NO LATER THAN FEBRUARY 1.

FOLD

be liable for the total permanent disability benefit provided in the law. Insurers were also reluctant to insure an employer who had disabled employees. This reluctance on the part of the employer and the insuring company made it difficult for the disabled person to secure employment.

This problem was resolved in all but two of the states with the creation of a *second injury fund* to encourage hiring of handicapped persons by relieving some of the burden of liability imposed by state workers' compensation laws. In those states the employer is only liable for the subsequent or second injury as if the previous injury did not exist. The new injury is treated on a totally separate basis by the current insurer and not compounded with previously incurred disability or injury. The second injury fund pays any excess amount to provide the injured employee with the total disability benefit prescribed by law.

As an illustration, consider an employee with vision in only one eye. In a work-related accident the employee loses sight in the second eye. Following is a summation of how the workers' compensation policy and the second injury fund would respond to the claim:

1. Workers' compensation policy:
   - Medical bills—Unlimited medical expenses in this particular state.
   - Scheduled benefit—Loss of *one* eye—$10,000.
   - Permanent partial disability—Maximum weekly benefit prescribed by law in that state for loss of one eye.
2. Second Injury Fund: Total disability benefit because the worker is now totally and permanently disabled due to the total loss of sight and the difference between scheduled benefits for loss of both eyes and loss of one eye. The employer (and the employer's insurer) is liable only for benefits available if the injured employee *had not been* previously disabled.

The second injury fund would pay sums in excess of this amount. In this manner the employer is not penalized for hiring the handicapped and the handicapped are not penalized if a total disability occurs.

Usually, second injury funds are financed by assessing all companies writing workers' compensation and self-insurers in the state. (In some states self-insurers are not assessed, but they are responsible for full benefits as they do not have access to the second injury fund.) Some states also require the payment into the fund of any otherwise payable death benefits for employees killed on the job without dependents to collect the benefits. The employer or insurer is still liable for the amount set forth for a death benefit. If it remains unclaimed, it is paid to the second injury fund.

What the Underwriter Needs to Know

A new producer entering the commercial lines insurance field soon learns that the placement of workers' compensation insurance can be difficult. Workers' compensation insurance is, in many cases, a "loss leader" for many insurers. In other words, insurers will sometime accept a loss on workers' compensation to obtain above-average property and liability lines of an employer. Workers' compensation benefits in all states have been increased tremendously in the past decade and rates for workers' compensation insurance have not kept pace because of regulatory constraint and a natural lag in the rate-making process. Most producers will encounter a negative underwriting attitude toward many workers' compensation submissions. To counter this attitude, the producer must be well equipped with the important facts on the prospective account as well as a complete list of supporting businesses. The development of full underwriting information is essential if the producer expects to obtain a positive response from the underwriter. The much used "Well, we *do* write the rest of the account" may not sell the workers' compensation line to the underwriter.

Application Information   The ACORD workers' compensation application is shown in Exhibit 4-5.

Page 1 Information.   The first page of the application identifies the insurer, producer, applicant, locations, policy, and rating information. Much of this information is mechanical and is used to aid in the issuance of the policy.

APPLICANT INFORMATION.   The name and address of the applicant is included along with the legal form of business, years in business, and other identifying information.

LOCATION.   All locations of the applicant should be indicated. By knowing all locations (owned or controlled by the applicant), the underwriter can order safety inspections if necessary. A long list of such locations can be attached as a separate schedule. The policy only responds to the state or states designated. Such designations are made here and in the following section.

POLICY INFORMATION.   Some of this information is for processing. However, in case the underwriter feels it is necessary to contact the previous insurer, the previous insurer's name and the applicant's policy number with that insurer should be listed. Also, there is a blank in which to indicate the state or states where coverage A will apply.

RATING INFORMATION.   Specific classifications of employees are listed along with other information to determine the rate. Classification and rating will be discussed later. It is extremely important to classify

Exhibit 4-5
Worker's Compensation Application

ACORD® **WORKERS' COMPENSATION APPLICATION**

SET TABSTOPS AT ARROWS

MAIL TO: (INSURER/UNDERWRITER)

DATE

PRODUCER

APPLICANT INFORMATION

NAME

MAILING ADDRESS (Include Zip Code)

☐ INDIVIDUAL ☐ CORPORATION
☐ PARTNERSHIP ☐ OTHER

Years in Business

CODE | SUB-CODE

EMPLOYER I.D. NUMBER | RATING BUREAU I.D. NO.

☐ QUOTE ☐ BOUND (Give Date Attach Copy)
☐ ISSUE

LOCATIONS°

#	STREET, CITY, COUNTY, STATE, ZIP CODE
1	
2	
3	

POLICY INFORMATION

INSURER | POLICY NUMBER | Proposed Effective Date | Proposed Expiration Date | Normal Anniversary Rating Date

PREVIOUS INSURER | PREVIOUS POLICY NO. | ☐ PARTICIPATING ☐ NON-PARTICIPATING | Dividend Plan/Safety Group | RETRO PLAN

COVERAGE A (STATES) | COVERAGE B (If Not $100,000) $ | ☐ AGENCY BILL ☐ DIRECT BILL

PAYMENT PLAN
☐ ANNUAL
☐ SEMI-ANNUAL
☐ QUARTERLY

AUDIT PERIOD
☐ AT EXPIRATION
☐ SEMI-ANNUAL
☐ QUARTERLY
☐ MONTHLY

SPECIAL COMPANY AND STATE INFORMATION

RATING INFORMATION

STATE	L O C	CLASS CODE	COMPANY USE	CATEGORIES, DUTIES, CLASSIFICATIONS	NO. OF EM- PLOYES	ESTIMATED ANNUAL REMUNERATION	RATE	ESTIMATED ANNUAL PREMIUM
						TOTAL		$

EXPERIENCE MODIFICATION	$
MODIFIED PREMIUM	$
	$
PREMIUM DISCOUNT	$
	$
	$
TOTAL ESTIMATED ANNUAL PREMIUM	$
MINIMUM $	DEPOSIT PREMIUM $

SPECIFY ADDITIONAL COVERAGES/ENDORSEMENTS

☐ BROAD FORM ALL STATES
☐ U.S.L. & H.
☐ VOLUNTARY COMPENSATION
☐ OTHER

PLEASE COMPLETE REVERSE SIDE

ACORD 130 (12/75)

Continued on next page

INDIVIDUALS INCLUDED/EXCLUDED

SET TAB STOPS AT ARROWS

PARTNERS, OFFICERS, RELATIVES TO BE INCLUDED OR EXCLUDED. Remuneration To Be Included Must Be Part Of Rating Information Section.

#	NAME	AGE	TITLE/ RELATIONSHIP	OWNER- SHIP %	DUTIES	INC./EXC.	CLASS CODE	RE- MUNERATION
1								
2								
3								
4								
5								

PRIOR EXPERIENCE

PROVIDE INFORMATION FOR THE PAST 5 YEARS AND USE THE REMARKS SECTION FOR LOSS DETAILS

YEAR	INSURER & POLICY NUMBER	ANNUAL PREMIUM	MOD.	#CLAIMS	AMOUNT PAID	RESERVE

NATURE OF BUSINESS/DESCRIPTION OF OPERATIONS

Give comments and descriptions of business, operations and products: Manufacturing—raw materials, processes, product, equipment. Contractor—type of work, sub-contracts. Mercantile—merchandise, customers, deliveries. Service—type, location. Farm—acreage, animals, machinery, sub-contracts.

GENERAL INFORMATION

PLEASE PROVIDE ALL THE REQUIRED DETAILS FOR "YES" RESPONSES BY USING THE REMARKS AREA BELOW

	YES	NO		YES	NO
(1) Does Applicant Own, Operate Or Lease Aircraft/Watercraft?	☐	☐	(11) Any Employees Under 16 Or Over 50 Years Of Age?	☐	☐
(2) Any Exposure To Flammables, Explosives, Caustics, Fumes?	☐	☐	(12) Any Employees Over 60 Years Of Age?	☐	☐
(3) Any Exposure To Radioactive Materials?	☐	☐	(13) Any Part Time Or Seasonal Employees?	☐	☐
(4) Any Work Performed Underground Or Above 15 Feet?	☐	☐	(14) Is There Any Volunteer Or Donated Labor?	☐	☐
(5) Any Work Performed On Barges, Vessels, Docks?	☐	☐	(15) Any Employees With Physical Handicaps?	☐	☐
(6) Is Applicant Engaged In Any Other Type Of Business?	☐	☐	(16) Do Employees Travel Out Of State?	☐	☐
(7) Are Sub-Contractors Used?	☐	☐	(17) Are Athletic Teams Sponsored?	☐	☐
(8) Any Work Sublet Without Certificates Of Ins.?	☐	☐	(18) Are Pre-Employment Physicals Required?	☐	☐
(9) Is A Formal Safety Program In Operation?	☐	☐	(19) Any Other Insurance With This Insurer?	☐	☐
(10) Any Group Transportation Provided?	☐	☐	(20) Any Prior Covg. Declined/Cancelled/Non-Renewed (Last 3 Yrs.)?	☐	☐
INSPECTION (CONTACT/PHONE)			ACCOUNTING RECORDS (CONTACT/PHONE)		

REMARKS

APPLICANT'S SIGNATURE

PRODUCER'S SIGNATURE

the employees correctly because it is this classification that gives the underwriter a true picture of the exposures and may have a strong influence on the underwriter's judgment.

The lower left hand portion requests any additional coverages or endorsements. The lower right hand side indicates any premium modifications, including the experience modification applying to the insured. Experience rating will be discussed later, but this too may have an impact on the underwriter. A high experience modification indicates poor workers' compensation experience. However, the poor experience may be due to one or two "shock" or large and infrequent losses, such as a freak death claim. If this is the case, it should be fully explained to the underwriter on the second page or by a separate attachment.

Page 2 Information. For underwriting, page 2 of the application is critical.

INDIVIDUALS INCLUDED/EXCLUDED. If individual proprietors or partners are to be covered, they must elect coverage, and corporate officers must elect to be excluded if they desire. If this section is left blank, the underwriter may assume no election has been made. This could result in an errors and omissions claim against the producer.

PRIOR EXPERIENCE. This section requests a five-year loss history and any remarks should be made in the "remarks" section or attached to the application. Attaching an OSHA log will reveal the number and type of accidents, but here, the underwriter wants to know the dollar amount of benefits paid or reserved for future payment by the previous insurer. The premium record indicates the change in the size of the exposure. Underwriters are particularly interested in the loss history and trends in losses. By offering solutions to loss problems in the remarks section, the producer has the potential to turn a negative fact into a positive solution. Sometimes the producer needs to elaborate on these answers on a separate sheet of paper to make sure the underwriter has all the information necessary to make an intelligent and informed decision.

NATURE OF BUSINESS. Full and complete descriptions are essential here. The more information provided, the better the underwriting decision. Pictures of processing and operations may prove helpful. Again, any unusual situations may call for comments in the "Remarks" section or an additional page attached to the application.

GENERAL INFORMATION. Any "yes" answer to questions in this section will require explanation by the producer. A "yes" does not automatically mean a problem, if explained. For instance, question (2), relative to explosives, if answered yes, with no explanation, is likely to cause rejection of the application. A note may make the applicant acceptable by explaining that explosives are a minor and infrequent exposure.

If subcontractors are used (question 7), the producer needs to explain fully what they do. If the applicant is subcontracting work and not requiring certificates of insurance (question 8) the underwriter will need to know exactly what work is being subcontracted. The underwriter will then underwrite the subcontractor's employees as employees of the applicant. For instance, suppose the application indicates the employer is involved in water main construction and has no explosives exposure. However, the application indicates all blasting work is subcontracted and no certificates of insurance are required of the subcontractor. Since the underwriter knows the policy may respond to injured employees of the subcontractor, the policy will have to be underwritten as if the applicant were doing the blasting.

Employment practices occupy a few questions. For example, a large number of part-time employees can have an adverse bearing on underwriting attitudes. Part-time employees, as a rule, are not as familiar with safety programs or with the handling of machinery. Age of employees is requested because young workers tend to be less safety conscious and elderly workers may not have the quick reaction time needed for certain types of work. Employment of seasonal workers tends to result in more claims for the insurer. Usually, seasonal employees are less experienced at their jobs. Pre-employment physicals may be a strict requirement for certain tasks. As cited, heart attack may be compensable under the policy if the job is strenuous. This being the case, the underwriter would like to know about any previously existing health conditions in all workers.

A "yes" answer to employees traveling out of state would indicate the need for the broad form all states endorsement.

Question 19 can be a plus if answered yes. As mentioned, in many states, workers' compensation insurance is not a profitable line for many insurance companies, and many underwriters will not consider issuing a workers' compensation policy unless it is supported by other business.

The last question asks if the applicant has been rejected or canceled in the last three years. An underwriter will not want to accept a submission which has already been rejected by several other insurers. If the answer to this question is yes, a detailed explanation should accompany the application. An explanation of why the applicant was in the assigned risk plan should accompany the application if the employer had been in the plan.

Checkpoints

1. Explain the operation of a workers' compensation assigned risk plan.
2. Explain the effect of a second injury fund on an employer's liability for injury to a handicapped employee.
3. Identify the major requirements placed on the employer by OSHA.
4. Explain how the underwriter uses an employer's OSHA-required records as an underwriting tool.

RATING PROCEDURES

The producer needs to be aware of facts required by the underwriter to properly rate a submission. In fact, a properly rated submission will display a greater knowledge of the account to the underwriter. First, employees must be properly classified. The National Council's workers' compensation manual contains a classification section in which most classes of employees may be found. If further classification is necessary, the manual contains an underwriting section with a more refined classification section. Once employees have been classified by type and code, it is a matter of using state rate pages and locating the rate for the appropriate code. Almost without exception, rates apply per $100 of payroll. The appropriate experience modification factor and premium discount factor are then applied to determine the deposit premium.

Proper initial classification rating is vital so the insured is not "surprised" by reclassifications and a potentially higher audited premium at the end of the policy year.

Classification

The basic classification for the applicant is identified as the *governing classification*. This would be the classification and rate applying to the largest of the insured's payrolls except for *standard exception classifications*. These standard exception classifications apply to all employees whose duties fall within those classes unless the governing classification is worded in the manual to include them. There are three National Council standard exception classifications separately classified and rated.

Clerical Office Employees—Code 8810 These employees work exclusively in clerical or bookkeeping positions. The office provided for these employees must be physically separated from all other operations by standard partitions. If such an employee has other duties, the entire payroll for that employee is assigned to the highest rated classification to which that employee is exposed.

Drivers, Chauffeurs, and Their Helpers—Code 7380   These employees must be exclusively engaged in duties involving a vehicle.

Salespersons, Collectors, or Messengers—Outside—Code 8742   These are employees engaged in such duties away from the employer's premises. If employees deliver merchandise, they cannot be included in this classification.

Proper Classification   Proper classification can be complicated. For example, the general contractor who has employees involved in almost all phases of the construction of a shopping center may have as many as twenty or thirty separate classifications on the workers' compensation policy schedule. Normally a particular employee's payroll cannot be divided between two different classifications. Generally, the entire payroll of a particular employee is assigned to the highest rated classification to which the employee is exposed; however, construction operations are an exception. An individual employee's payroll may be divided into each classification in which the employee is involved. The employer must maintain separate payroll records for each operation to support this division of payroll. If the employer cannot clearly indicate how much of the payroll goes into each classification, the entire payroll for that operation must be assigned to the highest rated classification. When in doubt, local workers' compensation inspection bureaus can offer their services to perform a proper classification.

Payroll   The payroll used is the total remuneration of the employee on an annual basis. There are a few items that may be deducted from this payroll figure to minimize the premium. Extra pay for overtime is not considered regular payroll and may be excluded. This applies only to the extra amount paid for the overtime hours. Exhibit 4-6 may help explain.

Several other items may be excluded from remuneration including tips, payments by employees for group insurance or pension plans, special awards for invention, and severance pay.

There are also limitations on the payroll of certain employees. These limitations may vary from state to state. Producers should review the state rate sheets in the manual to determine if there is an exception in their particular state. The standard payroll limitations are:

1. Executive Officers. The payrolls for executive officers of a corporation are limited to a minimum of $100 per week and a maximum of $500 per week.

Exhibit 4-6
Payroll Calculations

Regular Wage	Overtime Wage-All Over 40	Hours Worked
$4.00/hour Total Pay	1½ times regular ($6.00) 40 hours X $4.00 (regular wage) = $160 8 hours X $6.00 (overtime wage) = $ 48 $208	48
Wages to be Included in Payroll Figure for Premium Computation		
Regular wage X total hours = regular payroll $4.00 X 48 = $192		
Extra Pay not to be Included for Premium Computation		
Additional wage over regular wage for overtime X overtime hours = Extra pay not to be included $2.00 X 8 = $16		

2. Partners or Sole Proprietors. If the state allows the inclusion of a sole proprietor or partners for coverage, the payroll for each partner or sole proprietor is usually a fixed amount.

Experience Modification

To encourage employers to control losses, most states have developed a method of experience rating workers' compensation insurance. The state rating organization keeps detailed premium and loss information on each eligible insured and calculates and publishes the experience modification which must be used in policy rating. The individual employer's loss experience is measured against industry averages, and a factor, expressed as a decimal, is developed. A .75 experience modification factor means the employer pays 75 percent of the standard rate (a 25 percent credit), while a 1.30 experience modification factor means a 30 percent surcharge above the standard. Accident frequency is weighed more heavily than severity in the promulgation of the modification factor. Thus, an insured that incurred ten losses of $5,000 each for a total of $50,000 will develop a higher modification than an insured who incurred one loss of $50,000.

The experience modification is not used on smaller insureds since

Exhibit 4-7
Adapted State Times Premium Discount Table

Premium Discount Percentages—The following premium discounts are applicable to Standard Premiums:

	Stock	Non-Stock	Assigned Risks
First $5,000	————	————	————
Next 95,000	9.5%	2.0%	9.5%
Next 400,000	11.9	4.0	11.9
Over 500,000	12.4	6.0	12.4

their loss experience would not be credible—one loss might exceed the entire premium. In most states, an insured must develop an annual premium of at least $750 for the most recent two or three years to be eligible. To promulgate the experience modification, the rating organization usually uses a three year experience period and omits the year immediately preceding the current policy year. For example, the 19X5 experience modification is based on premiums and losses for 19X1, 19X2, and 19X3. 19X4 is omitted so the losses can "age"and develop fully before being included in the subsequent calculation.

Premium Discount   To reflect lower insurer expenses involved in handling larger insureds, a premium discount is allowed for premiums over $5,000. The discount may vary from state to state and may be found in each state's rate pages in the workers' compensation manual. There is a separate premium discount factor shown for stock and nonstock insurance companies. As the premium increases, the amount of the discount increases. Exhibit 4-7 is an adaptation of one state's premium discount table.

Loss and Expense Constants   The loss constant is applied per state and is an additional charge made on small accounts. Almost every classification in the workers' compensation manual has published a loss constant with the rate. If the premium for the account is less than $500, the loss constant is added. At this writing, if the addition of the loss constant increases the premium to more than $500, the loss constant will be reduced to bring the premium to $500.

To illustrate this, assume the annual premium for an insured is $320 and the published loss constant is $15.

Premium	$320
Loss Constant	$ 15
	$335

Now assume that the same insured develops a premium of $495 and the loss constant is $15.

Premium	$495
Loss Constant	$ 5
	$500

The addition of the loss constant cannot increase the premium above $500. Any expense constant is not included in this portion of the premium calculation.

If more than one classification is used in the policy, the loss constant for the classification which has the highest loss constant is used. The loss constant is not subject to the experience modification factor. If the policy is subject to a minimum premium, the loss constant does not apply since the minimum premium contains the loss constant.

An expense constant is applied similarly to all policies regardless of size and is intended to cover the administrative expenses such as issuance, auditing, and recording of the policy. The expense constant is not subject to experience rating. If the policy develops the minimum premium, the expense constant does not apply.

Rating Sample

To demonstrate the actual rating of a policy, Exhibit 4-8 is a completed "rating information" from the ACORD application for the state of South Carolina. Footnotes will explain why certain items appear.

Retrospective Rating

There are several retrospective rating plans for large premium accounts. Retrospective rating plans differ from the experience modification plan in that the experience modification is developed from previous years' experience while the retrospective premiums are developed from losses incurred during the policy year and are calculated after the policy has expired. Retrospective plans are usually priced in a "cost-plus" form. At the end of the policy year, an actual premium is developed for the year based on loss experience during the year. It is possible for the insured to receive a refund or pay an additional premium according to experience. A large premium account with good experience can realize a substantial savings in premium by using the retrospective rating formula.

There are several retrospective rating plans available. Some of these plans guarantee that the final premium will not exceed the standard premium. Some, however, may make provisions for payment of a premium in excess of the standard premium. For example, a plan may show a possible range of from 65 percent to 125 percent of the standard premium. Retrospective rating plans are fairly complicated and are designed for accounts with $25,000 or more in annual premium. Therefore, the new producer should seek the help of the insurer to tailor the plan to the individual account.

In some states, insurers compete for workers' compensation business by offering dividends instead of premium discounts or retrospective rating plans. Whereas retrospective plans are part of the policy, dividends are not. Dividend calculation depends upon the insurer's overall profit and the individual account experience. Dividends can be arranged on an individual account basis using "a sliding scale" or "a retention plan." The former is a tabular estimate of refunds based on premium size and loss experience. A retention plan is calculated by the insurer using factors for acquisition costs, administration, and so on. The retention is expressed as a percentage and losses are added to it. If there is premium remaining after the losses are added to the retention, it is returned to the policyholder following policy expiration by six to eighteen months. (This discussion is expanded in a later section.)

Sales Tips

As stated, workers' compensation insurance may be the hardest line of insurance to place in many states when insurers are experiencing adverse loss experience. The producer can, however, use a workers' compensation policy as a "wedge" to write an entire account for an organization.

The producer could start by discussing different classes of workers' compensation exposures with each available insurer. Most insurers have lists of "acceptable" and "prohibited" accounts. The producer may discover a company is very receptive to certain so-called "high risk" workers' compensation classes if they can be written as a part of a total account. The producer can then submit those types of accounts knowing there is an insurer for the workers' compensation. On the sales call the producer may find that the prospective insured is totally satisfied with the existing insurance program, but is disturbed about the difficulty in securing workers' compensation insurance. If the producer has already identified the workers' compensation insurer, he or she is ready to solve the prospective insured's problem. The producer should point out that workers' compensation can only be considered a

Exhibit 4-8
Sample Rating Information and Explanation

RATING INFORMATION

STATE	L.O.C.	CLASS CODE	COMPANY USE	CATEGORIES, DUTIES, CLASSIFICATIONS	NO. OF EMPLOYEES	ESTIMATED ANNUAL REMUNERATION	RATE	ESTIMATED ANNUAL PREMIUM
SC	1	8810		CLERICAL OFFICE EMPLOYEES	2	$15,000	.14	$ 21
SC	1	5645		CARPENTRY-DETACHED ONE OR TWO FAMILY DWELLINGS	10	$200,000	4.90	$9.800
SC	1	5606		CONTRACTOR-EXECUTIVE SUPERVISORS	2	$52,000[1]	1.58	$ 822

SPECIFY ADDITIONAL COVERAGES/ENDORSEMENTS

☐ BROAD FORM ALL STATES
☐ U.S.L. & H.
☐ VOLUNTARY COMPENSATION
☐ OTHER

TOTAL	$	10,643
EXPERIENCE MODIFICATION		.79[2]
MODIFIED PREMIUM	$	8,408
	$	
	$	
PREMIUM DISCOUNT[3]	$	-324
LOSS CONSTANT[4]	$	-0-
EXPENSE CONSTANT[5]	$	+35
TOTAL ESTIMATED ANNUAL PREMIUM	$	8,119
MINIMUM $ / DEPOSIT PREMIUM	$	8,119

ACORD 130 (12 75)

PLEASE COMPLETE REVERSE SIDE

1. The executive supervisors are officers of the corporation. Although these two employees are paid $40,000 each per year, the maximum amount for an officer is $500 per week or $26,000 annually. The payroll for both would total $52,000 for premium calculation purposes.

2. The experience modification would be obtained from the rating organization. In this case the modification is 0.79 multiplied by $10,643 ($10,643 X 0.79 = $8,408).

3. The premium discount for this stock company is 0.095 for premiums between $5,000 and $100,000. There is no discount on the first $5,000.

Total Premium	$8,408.00
Less $5,000	—$5,000.00
	$3,408.00
Premium Discount Factor	X .095
	$ 324.00

4. Since the policy premium is in excess of $500, the loss constant does not apply.

5. The expense constant of $35 applies regardless of premium size, and is not subject to experience modifications or premium discount.

part of the total account. In many cases the producer will be successful in writing all of the prospect's coverages simply because of the availability of the needed workers' compensation coverage.

There is another side to the sale of workers' compensation. Many accounts are greatly concerned about safety in their organization. This attitude toward loss control may stem from a concern over full compliance with OSHA regulations or because of a realization of the premium savings through either the experience modification dividends or retrospective rating plans. These prospects are very interested in placing their workers' compensation insurance with an insurer with a good engineering or loss control department.

The producer should check with the available insurers to see which have the best engineering or loss control departments. Some insurers may have brochures available describing the loss control services available. These loss control services may include on-site safety inspections, periodic safety meetings with employees, and assistance with establishment and administration of "in house" safety programs and contests. Usually these are extremely valuable services and are provided without additional cost to the insured. The producer should stress loss control services to a prospective client and will find on many occasions this service will "sell" the account.

Competitive Pricing Techniques In many instances, workers' compensation develops the major portion of the premium in a given insurance account. Therefore, price competition on this line of business can be a very important factor in obtaining the account. It is not intended that the producer become an expert in this study section on these pricing techniques, but it is important to know the type of techniques that exist and the basics of their operation.

One way to understand pricing techniques is to refer to the "Workers' Compensation Pricing Spectrum." (See Exhibit 4-9.) On the left side is the standard guaranteed cost program, usually for small accounts. At the opposite end is self-insurance, where an account actually funds its own losses. There are several plans or techniques in between the extremes which are discussed below. Although the class of business has some bearing on the decision regarding these plans, in most cases the overriding factor is premium size.

Sliding Scale Dividend Plans. The most common competitive technique is the practice of paying dividends to the policyholder based on loss experience. The "sliding scale" refers to a published tabular (by company) schedule of dividend percentages to be applied to standard premium which vary with the size of standard premium and the ratio of losses to standard premium. Exhibit 4-10 is a dividend scale of a representative insurance company. For example, given a loss ratio of

Exhibit 4-9
Workers' Compensation Pricing Spectrum*

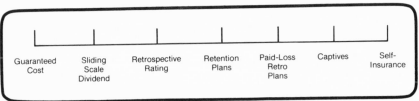

* Prepared by Ralph Hamm, CPCU.

between 20.1 and 25.0 percent and standard premium of $17,000, the insured would receive a dividend of $1,394 ($17,000 × 8.2%).

These plans are common in accounts of $2,500 premium and up and are better than retrospective plans in that the maximum premium is the standard premium less applicable premium discount, regardless of losses. Sliding dividend scale plans usually have a significant commission reduction to the producer.

Retrospective Rating.   Retrospective rating is simply a concept of determining the ultimate cost of the insurance on a "looking backwards" (retrospective) basis. That is, usually nine to twelve months after policy expiration, all incurred losses as well as other costs are totaled to determine the final premium for the policy year. The major components of this rating formula are:

- Basic Premium—company expenses, producer commissions, and insurance charges.
- Losses—actual losses incurred.
- Loss Conversion Factor—cost of adjusting losses.
- Premium Tax—applicable state premium taxes.
- Minimum Premium—the minimum amount of premium regardless of the amount of losses.
- Maximum Premium—the maximum amount of premium regardless of the amount of losses.

The total of these factors determines the final premium. Good experience will be rewarded with lower premiums and poor experience will increase premiums. In this regard, the retrospective rating technique becomes "cost plus" insurance (costs plus losses).

Several different retrospective plans are available depending on the size and other factors about the individual insured. Generally, these plans are not used for accounts of less than $25,000 and the larger the premium, the more attractive they become. It is important to note that some retrospective plans have maximum premium factors which will develop *more than* standard premium if losses so dictate.[3]

Exhibit 4-10
Schedule of Dividends—Workers' Compensation

NOTICE
Worker's Compensation Dividends

Dividends on Participating policies cannot be guaranteed and are payable only after declaration by the Board of Directors following policy expiration. The information contained herein is not a representation as to future dividend performance. However, the Board of Directors of the Company has employed schedules similar to the one above when declaring dividends on expired policies.

Loss Ratio From–Through	2500 3999	4000 4999	5000 7499	7500 9999	10000 14999	15000 19999	20000 29999	30000 39999	40000 49999	50000 74999	75000 99999	100000 149999	150000 199999	200000 299999	300000 and over
0.0— 5.0	8.2%	10.0%	10.8%	11.9%	12.6%	14.0%	15.8%	17.0%	18.2%	18.7%	19.9%	21.3%	22.5%	23.8%	24.7%
5.1—10.0	7.5	8.8	9.4	10.0	10.5	12.2	13.3	14.0	14.7	16.4	17.0	18.0	18.8	19.8	20.7
10.1—15.0	6.5	7.7	8.2	8.8	9.4	10.5	11.9	12.3	13.5	14.7	15.6	17.7	18.2	19.5	20.4
15.1—20.0	5.6	7.0	7.7	8.2	8.8	9.4	10.5	11.2	12.3	12.9	14.7	16.2	17.7	18.8	19.8
20.1—25.0	4.7	5.9	6.5	7.0	7.7	8.2	8.8	9.4	10.5	11.9	12.7	14.0	15.5	16.8	17.8
25.1—30.0	4.1	4.7	5.3	5.9	6.5	6.8	7.0	7.7	8.8	9.4	10.5	11.4	12.5	13.8	14.7
30.1—35.0	3.5	4.0	4.7	5.3	5.9	6.1	6.5	7.0	7.7	8.8	8.8	10.9	12.1	13.0	14.0
35.1—40.0	2.3	3.0	3.2	3.6	4.1	4.7	5.0	5.3	5.9	7.0	7.7	8.7	9.8	11.0	12.0
40.1—45.0	1.2	2.3	2.6	3.0	3.2	3.3	3.5	3.7	4.1	4.7	5.0	6.0	6.9	8.0	9.0
45.1—50.0	0.4	0.5	0.6	0.7	0.8	0.9	1.0	1.1	1.2	1.8	2.3	3.1	4.0	5.1	6.0
50.1 and over	0.0	0.0	0.0	0.0	0.0	0.0	0.0	0.0	0.0	0.0	0.0	0.0	0.0	0.0	0.0

Premium Size

Retention Plan. This plan is a hybrid of the retrospective rating and sliding scale plans. It operates as a "cost plus" plan, that is, it has premium components like the retrospective plan, but any returns are paid in the form of dividends. This plan has the advantages of the actual "cost plus" concept, but does not have maximum factors in excess of standard premium.

A retention plan is best used for the traditionally very low loss ratio accounts in the premium range of $25,000 to $100,000.

Cash Flow Plans. In the large attractive workers' compensation accounts, the above may not be enough. Because of the immense premium and continuing increase in the interest rates, risk managers want to retain their premium funds as long as possible rather than paying them to the insurance company. These plans can be as simple as paying the standard premium on a monthly basis or as complicated as paying only estimated monthly losses plus company expenses (paid-loss retrospective) as the premium.

Selling Workers' Compensation In many cases, the workers' compensation policy is a problem to the insured and insurer alike. Insureds may feel they pay too much for the coverage and insurers feel the premium received is inadequate. A producer who sells workers' compensation properly to the insured (downstream) and insurer (upstream) will be ahead of the competition.

Upstream Sales. Selling to the underwriter, in summary, requires four things of the producer:

1. Know what classes or types of businesses are acceptable to available insurers.
2. Know specialty markets (including Assigned Risk Plans and State Competitive Funds) available for unusual or hard to place classes.
3. Submit concise, complete information on the account.
4. Above all, know the account being submitted, including the management, processes and products.

Downstream Sales. The prospect or client needs proper protection at the lowest price. Therefore, the producer should:

1. Have a complete knowledge of workers' compensation laws in his or her own marketing territory.
2. Display to the client a knowledge of workers' compensation coverage by such activities as not having a partner, sole proprietor, or excluded corporate officer's health insurance overlap with workers' compensation or by having an acceptable relationship, with or without certificates of insurance, between general and subcontractors.

3. Have a knowledge of a particular account and the proper classifications for the account's employees.
4. Price the coverage as competitively as possible.
5. Make sure adequate service is available to the account for loss control and claims.

Checkpoints

1. Identify the three standard exception classifications in workers' compensation rating.
2. Explain the experience modification in workers' compensation insurance rating.
3. Explain when the loss and expense constants are used in workers' compensation insurance rating.
4. Explain the Workers' Compensation Pricing Spectrum as a sales tool.

CASE STUDIES

To illustrate the procedure involved in handling workers' compensation insurance, two case studies developed in PRO 81, which also appear in the Course Guide accompanying PRO 82, will be used.

J&T Appliances

Marcia Blanton, an insurance producer, has been asked by one of the partners in J&T Appliances to drop by and discuss workers' compensation insurance. Marcia's *objective on this call* is to develop the information needed to classify and rate J&T Appliances for workers' compensation.

In the discussion with the prospective client, Marcia developed the following information on employees and payroll.

1. Retail Store Operation
    a. One partner—$24,000 payroll
    b. One full-time employee—$10,000 payroll
    c. One part-time employee—$4,000 payroll
2. Service Department
    a. One partner—$26,000 payroll
    b. Two full-time employees—$12,000 payroll each
3. Bookkeeper—$8,000 payroll

Marcia discovers the retail and service departments are totally separate from each other—there is no commingling of labor from one department to another. This being the case, she knows she must

Exhibit 4-11
J&T Appliances Classifications and Payroll

Stores— Retail NOC	Code 8017	Payroll $29,600	(partner's payroll limited to $15,600)
Television service or repair	Code 9519	Payroll $39,600	(partner's payroll limited to $15,600)
Clerical	Code 8810	Payroll $8,000	

Exhibit 4-12
Selected State Workers' Compensation Rates

	Rate per $100 of Payroll	Minimum Premium
Code 8017	0.93	$ 86
Code 9519	1.65	$126
Code 8810	0.14	$ 43

classify each department in its own separate and proper classification and code for rating purposes. She then points out to the client that partners are normally excluded from coverage under workers' compensation, but that in their particular state, partners can elect to be covered under the policy. Each partner agrees to sign the proper form to be covered by the policy.

Marcia also develops all information required on the application including loss information and copies of the OSHA log. Marcia is now ready to classify J&T in accordance with the workers' compensation manual used in her state (Exhibit 4-11).

Marcia remembered the total employee payrolls are used, but there is a limitation on the payroll of the partners of $15,600 each.

Marcia then turns to her state rate pages (Exhibit 4-12) to find the appropriate rates. Then she rates J&T Appliances using the payroll information (Exhibit 4-13).

Marcia now calls the rating organization in her state to obtain the experience rating modification factor (if one has been promulgated). The rating organization informs her that the modification is .96 which indicates better than average loss experience for J&T. Marcia applies this to the standard premium ($939.00 × .96 = $901.00). Since the

Exhibit 4-13
J&T Appliances Rate Development

Code 8017	0.93 X 296 = $275
Code 9519	1.65 X 396 = $653
Code 8810	0.14 X 80 = $ 11
	$939

Workers' compensation premiums are rounded to the nearest dollar.

premium exceeds $500, a loss constant would not be used, but the $35 expense constant must be added. The total deposit premium for J&T Appliances is $936.

Marcia now explains to her client the deposit premium will be $936 based on payrolls provided. At the end of the policy year the insurer has the right to audit actual payroll records to develop the actual premium for the year. J&T Appliances may receive a return premium or have to pay an additional premium after an audit is complete.

Premier Door and Window Company, Inc.

Premier is a large account and deserves the special attention of the producer. The producer, Frank Williams, has developed a standard workers' compensation premium of $38,510, including application of the experience modification and premium discount factors. Classification and rating of Premier posed no problem for Frank, but he is greatly concerned about gaps in coverage. Frank added the following forms to the basic workers' compensation policy.

Broad Form All States Endorsement Although Premier's manufacturing operation is in one state, its sales force travels extensively as do drivers making deliveries. Frank remembers the workers' compensation policy only responds to benefits of the laws of the states designated in the declarations. Frank has now extended the policy to cover potentially higher benefits provided by any state laws where a salesman or driver may be injured.

Voluntary Compensation Endorsement The possibility of having a loss not within the scope of the workers' compensation law is remote in this case, but Frank fills the gap that could occur with the Voluntary Compensation Endorsement. With the addition of this endorsement, the policy will automatically provide voluntary workers' compensation benefits for any employee even if such benefits are not mandated by law.

Longshoremen's and Harbor Workers' Compensation Act Endorsement Frank knows Premier ships many of its products overseas. Although Premier has no employees who work as longshoremen or harbor workers, it would be possible for an injury to occur while an employee is delivering goods to a port. If the Admiralty Courts have jurisdiction over the claim, this endorsement will provide Premier with full coverage under the U.S. Longshoremen's and Harbor Workers' Compensation Act.

Foreign Voluntary Compensation Endorsement If Premier has a salesperson overseas, this endorsement would be added.

Frank has now provided a good workers' compensation insurance program for Premier, but his job does not stop here. Frank provided all the facts to his insurer to determine whether a retrospective rating plan would be feasible. If a plan can be used, the insured may realize a substantial savings in premium.

Frank works with his insurer and insured to assist in establishing and administering a comprehensive safety program to reduce loss frequency and severity. With this service, Frank is working for all three parties involved. The insurer will probably have a more profitable account with the establishment of a safety program. The insured should realize a premium savings since loss experience is reflected in both the experience modification factors and the retrospective rating plans, and will be providing a safer place for Premier employees to work. Frank may improve the profit from his commission dollars by having fewer claims to process through his office.

SUMMARY

The development of workers' compensation laws has been beneficial to American society by providing for the compensation of employees involved in industrial accidents. Commercial insurers have also responded to the needs of employers for protection against liability imposed by these laws.

Workers' compensation has become an unprofitable line of insurance in many states for most insurers, and most insurers do not aggressively seek this line of insurance. It is, however, one line that cannot be ignored by the insurance producer because it produces substantial premium. The producer should treat the workers' compensation exposure as thoroughly as any of the more profitable lines of insurance. The producer can provide a valuable service to the insured by being aware of the current state laws and providing coverages necessary to protect the insured from financial losses. The producer can also help improve the profitability of this line of insurance for the insurer by working with the insurer in emphasizing and implementing safety programs.

From a sales standpoint, workers' compensation often pays the lowest commission, requires the most service, and generates the highest loss ratio of any line of insurance. Knowledge of and use of specialty markets, including assigned risk plans and state competitive funds, where available, can be an additional lever to obtain an account and yet keep overall loss ratios for the office to a minimum. When selling a standard product that everyone must purchase, extra service, effort, and knowledge will generate other, less complicated and more profitable, business for the producer.

Chapter Notes

1. This case was heard by the South Carolina Industrial Commission. The loss occurred on May 8, 1979.
2. Chamber of Commerce of the United States, *Analysis of Workers' Compensation Laws.*
3. John R. Stafford, *Retrospective Rating,* 4th ed. (Rolling Meadows: J and M Publications), 1975 and John R. Stafford, *Workers' Compensation and Employers' Liability Experience Rating* (Rolling Meadows: J and M Publications), 1977.

CHAPTER 5

Commercial
Inland Marine Insurance

INTRODUCTION

An inland marine policy combines provisions of other lines of insurance to produce separate and distinct forms of protection. Inland marine policies often have little in common with one another, except that through custom and usage, they have come to be the responsibility of inland marine underwriters. The producer who becomes thoroughly familiar with the many inland marine insurance coverages will have an advantage—virtually every commercial insurance buyer is faced with loss exposures that can best be insured with some form of inland marine coverage. The innovative producer can arrange broad coverage at attractive premiums because of the flexibility of inland marine forms and rates.

ORIGINS OF INLAND MARINE INSURANCE

In nineteenth century America, traditional ocean (or "wet") marine policies were adequate to cover the bulk of transportation and communications exposures. Commerce in the United States moved by water—inter-coastal, river, or canal—and the transportation system was also the only form of communication. New forms of transportation and communication, however, brought new loss exposures. When the conveyances in use diversified to include railroads, motor vehicles, aircraft, and finally satellites, new forms of insurance became necessary. The insurance business had to follow the changes in the

223

transportation industry. And marine insurers, rather than fire or casualty insurers, possessed the experience and initiative to meet the new needs of the insurance buying public.

Inland marine policy forms were developed by marine insurers because they were the most knowledgeable about transportation exposures. Further, marine underwriters had a tradition of "all-risks" coverage that gave them not only a broad contract but also the flexibility to adapt to the new requirements of the insurance market-place.

THE NATION-WIDE MARINE DEFINITION

The willingness and ability of marine insurers to provide coverage for practically any type of exposure if the conditions were acceptable (and if an adequate premium could be secured) was a distinct departure from traditional fire and casualty insurance procedures. Efforts were made by fire and casualty underwriters to restrict incursions by marine underwriters into areas previously considered to be their own, and competition between the mono-line insurers and marine insurers increased dramatically in the first part of this century.

Finally, in response to demands that the lines be drawn, the National Association of Insurance Commissions (NAIC) in 1933 adopted the "Definition and Interpretation of Marine Underwriting Powers," now known as the Nation-Wide Marine Definition. The original document had the weight of law since insurers generally were licensed for only one line of insurance. Now, since most insurers are licensed for multiple lines, the Definition is used to establish statistical tabulation, rating, and policy forms for marine contracts.

The Definition is less important in states with "open competition rating" laws like California. For producers in states with strict regulation of policy forms and rates, the Definition can be used to justify writing a particular insured on an inland marine form. The inland marine forms usually allow broad coverage without the limitations of standard forms and published rate tables.

The Definition's practical importance stems from the broad classes of exposures listed as eligible for marine policies:

A. Imports
B. Exports
C. Domestic Shipments
D. Bridges, Tunnels and Other Instrumentalities of Transportation and Communication
E. Personal Property Floater Risks
F. Commercial Property Floater Risks

Although the Definition permits insuring ocean cargo (A and B), this kind of coverage traditionally is written by ocean marine underwriters; it is the remainder of the permitted classes that are insured by inland marine underwriters.

Category F, Commercial Property Floater Risks, includes a list of twenty-three separate kinds of floaters (i.e., originally policies covering property subject to constant relocation or that "floated" from place to place).

The list of exposures eligible for floaters is the principal reason it is difficult to define the scope of inland marine insurance. Inland marine eligibility is *related* to the transportation exposure, but some exposures customarily insured by inland marine underwriters have no greater transportation exposure than others insured by fire underwriters. For example, theatrical equipment belonging to a small circus might be moved daily from one open lot to another. Clearly, such equipment is subject to transit perils. However, the same form of insurance can be used to write coverage on the equipment of a Broadway show that may remain in one theater for several years before it is moved.

TYPES OF
INLAND MARINE INSURANCE POLICIES

There are many different categories of commercial inland marine insurance policies, but for the purposes of this chapter, these five categories will be discussed:

1. domestic goods in transit,
2. bailee's customers,
3. movable equipment and unusual property,
4. property of certain dealers, and
5. instrumentalities of communication and transportation.

Transportation Insurance on Domestic Shipments

Inland marine underwriters insure domestic shipments by rail, motor truck, aircraft, or while in the custody of the U. S. Postal Service. Policies covering such shipments can be purchased by the originator (shipper), the transporter (carrier), or by the recipient (consignee).

Bailees' Customers Insurance

A bailment exists when goods are left to be held in trust for a specific purpose and returned when that purpose has ended. The *bailor* is the owner of the goods, and the *bailee* is the one in possession of the goods. Bailment can be gratuitous for the benefit of the bailor ("Please keep my dog for the weekend."); bailment can be gratuitous for the benefit of the bailee ("May I borrow your lawnmower?"); but it is bailments for hire, for the mutual benefit of bailee and bailor, which are the subject of bailees' customers insurance ("Fix my watch, I'll pick it up Friday.").

General and excess liability insurance contracts almost universally exclude the bailee exposure with the so-called "care, custody, and control" (CCC) exclusion. The CCC exclusion is difficult, if not impossible, to eliminate from liability policies. Although some umbrella policies do not contain a CCC exclusion, underwriters are quick to attach one if there is a known exposure without primary (underlying) insurance. The intent of this exclusion is to eliminate coverage under the liability contract for the very kind of legal liability insurance needed by bailees. Some bailees, like trucking companies and other common carriers, are liable as virtual insurers of goods they transport. Other bailees, like laundries, are only liable for their own ordinary negilgence. Inland marine insurers provide a series of policies specifically designed to protect the bailee against claims for damage to property bailed.

Insurance on Movable Equipment and Other Property

Inland marine forms are used to insure certain types of equipment even when that equipment is situated in a fixed location. Agricultural equipment (tractors) or mobile equipment (cranes and backhoes) may be constantly moving from location to location and subject to transportation exposures. Other equipment, like physicians' and surgeons' equipment, is usually located at one site. Even computer equipment has a specialized inland marine form of coverage applicable to it. Certain kinds of property not thought of as "equipment," like livestock or fine arts, are eligible for "floaters." The difference in conditions (DIC) policy discussed later in this text is also classified as an inland marine contract.

Insurance on the Property of Certain Dealers

Dealers in mobile or agricultural equipment can buy special inland marine "block" policies to cover their stocks of merchandise. Jewelers, furriers, and dealers in fine arts and cameras also have specialized inland marine policies designed for their unique combinations or "block" of exposures.

Insurance on Instrumentalities of Transportation and Communications

Exposures related to transportation (rolling stock, bridges, and tunnels) can be insured using inland marine insurance. Inland marine insurance can also be provided on instrumentalities of communication like television towers and transmission equipment.

Examples

The following examples illustrate the kinds of prospects who have major inland marine exposures (however, few commercial insurance buyers do not have inland marine exposures).

Walnut Delivery Service is a local trucking company that delivers goods for furniture stores. If Walnut operates in more than one state, they will need to make a filing with the Interstate Commerce Commission (ICC). If Walnut only operates in one state, it will be regulated by a state agency generally called a "commerce commission" or "public utilities commission" and may need a state filing. These filings, in part, guarantee that all claims for cargo which has been lost or damaged up to a certain amount will be paid. Walnut needs to treat this loss exposure.

Big Pete's Precision Machine Repair specializes in maintenance of food packaging machinery. Although some work is done in Pete's shop (a bailee exposure), most is done on-site in customers' packing plants. In addition, Pete's installs machinery and equipment for its customers. Pete's needs an installation floater to cover the property to be installed while it is in transit, during installation and testing, and until the work is accepted by the buyer. Also Pete's can insure tools while in transit or at customers' locations using a tool floater.

Television Station, WINS, is a network station that produces shows locally. Because WINS films on location, a theatrical floater is in order to cover the scenery, costumes, and theatrical properties used in production. Further, because WINS is "an instrumentality of communications," it can insure the transmission tower and equipment like cameras, the "WINS Chopper" and WINS "Mobilecam" microphones on inland marine forms.

Overland Contracting is a builder that might require an "all-risks" builders risk policy to cover equipment, building materials, supplies and temporary structures used in construction. Further, Overland may elect to insure its "contractors equipment" like tractors, graders, and even portable handtools and scaffolding on an inland marine form.

Dr. Jason Driller, a dentist, has several exposures which can be covered with inland marine policies. The patient files would be expensive to construct and can be insured as valuable papers and records. The financial records of amounts due from patients can be insured using an accounts receivable form, and even the office furnishings, equipment, drugs and precious metals can be insured on a physicians' and surgeons' equipment floater.

French Laundry and Dry Cleaners is a retail laundry and cleaner with facilities on-premises to process laundry and dry cleaning and also to make light alterations to customers' garments. The appropriate policy to cover French's equipment, supplies, and customers' goods while French is in possession of them is the laundry and dry cleaners form. It will insure French's property and the property of others regardless of French's legal liability to them for loss or damage.

The Diamond Palace is a retail jewelry store requiring a "jewelers' block" policy. This policy covers "all-risks" of loss or damage to the stock of the store including property in the care of The Diamond Palace for display, sale, storage or repair. Coverage can be included for transit exposures while property is being shipped by parcel post, registered mail or air express.

Franklin Department Store might need several kinds of inland marine policies. An installment sales floater could be used to cover major items like furniture and appliances which have been sold on a time payment plan. The store computer can be covered by an electronic data processing form which will insure not only direct damage to the hardware, but losses involving the media, the software, and even time element exposures like extra expense or business interruption. Franklin may have merchandise which, while in the possession of Franklin, has been used as security under a bank floor plan loan. Franklin also has the exposure of transportation losses on outgoing shipments to customers, and this could be insured using a motor truck cargo-owners goods form while on owned trucks.

These accounts illustrate only a very few of the opportunities for a producer to sell inland marine insurance. When an exposure can be insured on an inland marine basis, the producer should examine the possibility because of the flexibility of form and rate available from the inland marine underwriter. This is not to say that alternative risk management techniques should not be considered in regard to inland marine exposures. On the contrary, loss control, avoidance, retention and noninsurance transfer should be explored along with other available property or liability policies.

Filed and Nonfiled Lines

The new producer or a producer relatively unfamiliar with inland marine insurance will initially have some difficulty in keeping track of all the possible coverages. Some forms are "filed" and others are "nonfiled." The former are issued on standardized forms at rates published in *The ISO Commercial Lines Manual, Division Eight— Inland Marine.* Nonfiled lines are written on nonstandard forms at rates negotiated between the producer and the underwriter. Often the nonfiled lines are insured with specially written *manuscript* policies to meet individual needs.

COMMON CHARACTERISTICS OF COMMERCIAL INLAND MARINE INSURANCE POLICIES

Policy Format

Regardless of whether the policy is nonfiled or filed, the policy is generally the foundation-plus-endorsement form similar to that used with fire insurance. There is no statutory inland marine foundation form comparable to the standard fire policy, so the policy itself must be read with care by the producer. These foundations, jackets or "backers" contain a place for declarations on one side and general policy conditions on the other side. The transportation jacket is used for policies involving major transit coverages such as cargo shipments. The scheduled property floater jacket is used to itemize insured property like agricultural equipment. To facilitate policy issuance, some insurers have developed a combined form for use with all inland marine contracts called, simply, the inland marine jacket. For policies like the electronic data processing policy, many companies use a multiple-peril policy jacket similar in appearance to a package policy. Many inland marine policies are manuscripted and typed on blank paper. But even the manuscript forms frequently are attached to one or another of the jackets.

Declarations

The declarations page is generally simple since the wide diversity of forms which can be attached to it prevent much standardized preprinting. In some cases, the front page of the policy may contain little more than the name and address of the insured, the policy period, a premium, a rate, an amount of insurance, and a place for policy countersignature. If a more elaborate declarations page is used, it may list various locations, limits, deductibles, schedules, and so on, as required by the policy.

Insuring Agreements

Perils Insured Most inland marine policies provide "all-risks" insurance. A typical insuring agreement, found in a contractors equipment floater, is as follows:

2 THIS POLICY INSURES AGAINST:

All risks of direct physical loss of or damage to the property covered from any external cause except as excluded elsewhere in this policy.

The insurer intends to cover only direct damage to the property and does not intend to pay losses arising from interruption of business.

Some inland marine policies are written on a named perils basis, such as the insuring agreement from a bailee's customers form:

THIS POLICY INSURES AGAINST DIRECT LOSS OR DAMAGE CAUSED BY:

2. (a) Fire and lightning;
   (b) Explosion;
   (c) Collision and/or overturning of transporting conveyance;
   (d) Theft, burglary and holdup;
   (e) Cyclone, tornado and/or windstorm;
   (f) Sprinkler leakage;
   (g) Flood, while in transit (meaning thereby "rising waters");
   (h) Earthquake;
   (i) Any of the above listed perils, while in the custody of public carriers or mail service (shipments to transients at hotels or temporary residences are covered if shipped by government insured parcel post or registered mail);
   (j) Confusion of goods, resulting from any of the above listed perils.

This list of covered perils is typical of many such named perils inland marine forms because it includes on-premises perils, like fire and lightning, as well as perils generally associated with transportation, like collision or overturning of a transporting conveyance.

Another named perils insuring agreement, from the motor truck cargo owners and truckmens form, covers other transportation perils:

PERILS COVERED

7. This policy covers direct loss or damage caused by:
   (a) Fire and lightning, including self-ignition or internal explosion of the vehicle;
   (b) Cyclone, tornado and windstorm;
   (c) Flood, meaning rising of rivers and waters;
   (d) Explosion, excluding explosion in the premises of the Insured originating within steam boilers, pipes, fly-wheels, engines and machinery connected therewith and operated thereby;
   (e) Collision while in the ordinary course of transportation (meaning thereby the violent and accidental contact of the motor vehicle with any other automobile, vehicle or object; but excluding loss or damage by coming in contact with any portion of the roadbed or

by striking the rails or ties of street, steam or electric railroad, or by coming in contact with any stationary object in backing for loading or unloading purposes, or the coming together of truck and trailer during coupling or uncoupling or by collision of the insured property with another object unless the transporting vehicle is in collision within the meaning of this policy) but free from all claims for loss, damage or expense by wear and tear or ordinary handling due to the mode of transportation.

(f) Overturning of vehicles on which the shipments insured are being transported; (Overturning as used herein shall mean the upsetting of the vehicle(s) to such an extent that it comes to rest on its side or top.)

(g) Collapse of bridges, docks and culverts;

(h) Stranding, sinking, fire or collision, including General Average or Salvage charges for which the Insured is legally liable on shipments being transported on or in said vehicle(s) while on any regular ferry line.

Consequences of Loss   In contrast to the three insuring agreements quoted, the following is from the accounts receivable form, and it omits the word "direct" so that the consequential loss resulting from the destruction of the records is insured:

2. Perils Insured.   All risks of loss of or damage to the insured's records of accounts receivable, occurring during the policy period, except as hereinafter provided.

In fact, the intent of the coverage is to go beyond the direct loss of the documents to include loss from the inability to collect receivables because the records were destroyed.

Other policies also provide coverage for some income lost when the subject of insurance has been damaged or destroyed. For example, the "special condition" from a bailees' customers form reimburses the insured for uncollectible charges:

This policy shall cover the customary charges that have been earned on lost or damaged goods.

Coverage on mobile or agricultural equipment may be endorsed to cover the necessary extra expenses to rent substitute equipment in the event of loss. The following clause is from a broker's manuscripted contractors equipment floater:

12. RENTAL OR EXTRA EXPENSE REIMBURSEMENT:

In Consideration of the premium charged, it is understood and agreed that in event of loss or damage to equipment insured hereunder, caused by a peril insured against, thereby preventing the necessary use of such equipment, by the insured in conjunction with normal operations, the Company agrees to reimburse the Assured for expense incurred for the rental of a substitute item of equipment or for additional expense in expediting repairs.

In the event it is necessary to rent substitute equipment this Company shall only be liable, under the provisions of this clause, for 75% of the bare rental costs, subject to a maximum of 10% of the value of such equipment.

In the event a rental or substitute item of equipment is not available, the Assured may apply up to 10% of the value of the lost or damaged items to any extra or expediting expenses as may be necessary.

Rental Reimbursement or Extra Expenses as provided under this clause shall not apply during the first forty-eight (48) hours after such loss or damage and shall terminate, regardless of expiration of the policy, on the date said loss or damaged equipment is replaced or repaired and is available for use by the Assured.

Property Covered Some inland marine policies, like the mobile agricultural equipment floater illustrated in Exhibit 5-1, cover only owned equipment and require that all equipment valued at more than $250 be scheduled for a designated amount of insurance. Policies covering a number of pieces of equipment can be written on a blanket basis with one amount of insurance covering the total exposure. Such policies often contain a coinsurance clause to assure the underwriter of insurance to value.

Bailees' forms are specifically designed to insure the property of others in the insured's case, custody, and control, whereas the insuring agreement from the motor truck cargo owners and truckmens form may provide coverage for legal liability insurance or for owner's coverage.

Territorial Limits A typical inland marine form might cover "within and between" the forty-eight contiguous states of the United States, the District of Columbia, and Canada. Others may add Hawaii and Alaska, and still others permit endorsement for coverage in Puerto Rico. Transit *to* island locations generally would not be covered because such shipments would fall into the realm of ocean marine insurance. The motor truck cargo owners and truckmen form stipulates a radius of operations, and any loss or damage occurring elsewhere would not be covered. Bailees' forms and dealers forms typically list a number of covered locations and provide for transportation coverage away from the premises within some specified territorial restrictions. Some inland marine policies offer coverage "anywhere in the world."

Conditions

The following conditions are typical of those found in many inland marine policies. Because there is no uniform wording in these policies, the conditions are often modified or even deleted through negotiations between the producer and the underwriter.

Exhibit 5-1
Mobile Agricultural Equipment Floater—Form B

MOBILE AGRICULTURAL EQUIPMENT FLOATER—FORM B

PROPERTY COVERED

THIS POLICY COVERS THE FOLLOWING PROPERTY OF THE INSURED WHILE AT THE PREMISES HEREINAFTER DESCRIBED OR WITHIN 50 MILES THEREOF

(A) MOBILE AGRICULTURAL MACHINERY AND EQUIPMENT AS PER SCHEDULE BELOW OR ATTACHED HERETO. EACH ITEM CONSIDERED SEPARATELY INSURED.

ITEM	AMOUNT OF INSURANCE	DETAILED DESCRIPTION
TOTAL (A)	$	

(B) UNSCHEDULED MOBILE AGRICULTURAL MACHINERY INCLUDING HARNESS, SADDLERY, LIVERIES, BLANKETS AND SIMILAR EQUIPMENT FOR NOT EXCEEDING $250 ON ANY ONE SUCH ITEM.

TOTAL (B)	$

Conditions Common to Insurance Policies   Many conditions in inland marine policies are similar to conditions in other insurance policies:

- Changes to the policy require an endorsement.
- Notice of loss must be given as soon as practicable and proof of loss filed within a certain number of days (usually ninety).
- The insured may be required to submit to an examination under oath.
- Loans must be paid within sixty days.
- Insurance is not for the benefit of a bailee.
- Suit against the insurer must commence within twelve months of claim.
- In case of disagreement over values, arbitration is required.

Conditions of Special Interest   A number of conditions deserve special attention by the producer.

Misrepresentation and Fraud.   The wording of this clause is similar to the standard fire policy, but legal ramifications may differ with some inland marine policies. Courts may hold insureds responsible for statements made in the application where the application is an offer or inducement to the insurer by the insured. Courts sometimes view such statements as warranties and require literal and complete truth. In situations where applications do become part of the policy, producers should seek to verify the validity of representations and statements.

Valuation.   Although this clause appears under "Conditions," it is in fact a clause limiting the amount of recovery to the actual cash value of the property while also giving the insurer the right to repair or replace. Other valuation clauses might specify how property in transit is to be valued at time of loss; for instance, shipments are often valued at their invoice cost plus incurred charges. Other policies might substitute replacement cost coverage for actual cash value, and still others are "valued policies" where a specific amount of insurance is agreed upon for each item insured. Some inland marine policies contain special valuation and settlement provisions such as "loan," loss, pairs and sets, and protection of property clauses.

The subrogation portion of this clause is similar to the provision in the fire forms—the insured cannot collect insurance and proceed against a responsible third party for a double reimbursement. The loan provision, however, is unique to inland marine insurance, and stems from a requirement in many shipping contracts (bills of lading) by which a carrier of goods attempts to make the shipper's insurance primary. Because of this wording, the insured cannot "collect" under the inland marine policy without freeing the carrier from the obligation to pay for damage or loss. Instead, the insurer "loans" the policyholder the amount of the loss, and by subrogation obtains the insured's right to collect from the carrier without negating the latter's duty to pay.

Many transportation policies add a condition called "Impairment of Recovery Rights" by which the insured cannot make any act or agreement whereby any right of the insured to recover for loss or damage against any carrier, bailee or other liable party is released, impaired or lost. Such act or agreement voids the policy.

LOSS CLAUSE. This condition clarifies the insurer's position regarding the amount of insurance and the earned premium following loss. A common loss clause refunds any unearned premium in the event of a total loss or applies it to premium due. An alternative provision declares the premium *fully earned* in the event of a total loss so that the underwriter can charge a new premium to cover the replacement property. Such an alternative might be called "Automatic Reinstatement" and might read, "Each claim paid hereunder reduces the amount of insurance by the sum paid, but the amount of such loss shall be reinstated automatically and a pro rata additional premium shall be payable from the date of the occurrence when the amount of such loss is determined."

PAIR, SET, OR PARTS. When a policy contains a "pairs or sets" clause, the insured may not claim a total loss of the pair or set where only a part of it is lost. Rather, the measure of the loss is the value of the part lost or damaged. Other similar provisions which might be called "Machinery" or "Labels" clause appear in inland marine policies stating that the insurance company is only liable for the value of the part(s) of machinery lost, or, in the event of damage to labels, capsules, or wrappers, only for an amount sufficient to pay the cost of new labels, capsules, or wrappers. These restrictive provisions may be deleted or modified by paying an additional premium.

PROTECTION OF PROPERTY. Inland marine insurance policies commonly require the insured to do more than protect property—the insured may be required to seek out and recover ("sue, labor and travel for") property. Expenses of such actions are borne by the insured and insurer "to the extent of their respective interests." For instance, if during a fire loss, a thief drives an insured's bulldozer off, the insured must, if possible, try to retrieve the bulldozer by traveling to it and recovering or protecting it.

Exclusions

Exclusions set the boundaries on the promises of the insuring agreement. In inland marine insurance they deserve the producer's careful scrutiny because many of the forms offer "all-risks" protection in the insuring agreement and limit that coverage through exclusions. Because of the wide variety of property covered by inland marine insurance and the diversity of forms used to cover that property, each policy exclusion must be read carefully. Some exclusions are discussed in this section, and the analysis of specific forms later in the chapter highlights exclusions of importance on a policy-by-policy basis.

Extraordinary Hazards Many hazardous conditions are excluded because they expand the loss exposure beyond good business practices. For example, the bailees' customers form excludes "theft of goods or packages left on delivery vehicles overnight, unless locked in the insured's private garage or a building occupied by the insured." Another example can be found in the contractors' equipment floater form which excludes loss "caused by the weight of a load exceeding the rated lifting or supporting capacity of any machine." Such losses are excluded because they are within the control of the insured. However, provisions like these may be negotiated out of policies for additional premium or when the producer suggests a substantial deductible, enough to assure the underwriter that the policyholder is equally concerned about such occurrences.

Morale Hazards Exclusions related to morale hazards attempt to limit the insurer's liability for carelessness or lack of concern about losses on the part of the insured. For instance, the bailees' customers form excludes "loss resulting from misdelivery, or careless destruction of goods or other unaccountable loss where there is no evidence that the loss was occasioned by the perils specifically insured against." The valuable papers and records form excludes "loss directly resulting from errors or omissions in processing or copying unless fire or explosion ensues and then only for direct loss caused by such ensuing fire or explosion."

Exposures More Appropriately Insured by Other Contracts The valuable papers and records form excludes fidelity crime losses: "due to any fraudulent, dishonest, or criminal act by any insured, a partner therein, or an officer, director or trustee thereof, while working or otherwise and whether acting alone or in collusion with others." The contractors' equipment floater has a similar exclusion that expands the fidelity loss exclusion: "...misappropriation, secretion, conversion, infidelity or any dishonest act on the part of the insured or other party of interest, his or their employees...."

Unusual Exposures The valuable papers and records form excludes "loss due to electrical or magnetic injury, disturbance or erasure of electronic recordings, except by lightning." This is because computer exposures require their own underwriting and rating considerations. An electronic data processing policy is available. The bailees' customers form excludes "loss or damage to goods held on storage, or for which a storage charge is made, unless endorsed hereon." If the exclusion is to be removed by endorsement, the underwriter will analyze the exposure and charge an appropriate premium for the added protection.

Commercially Uninsurable Exposures The most obvious examples of this kind of exclusion are the war and nuclear exclusions found in all inland marine policies. The word WINCE is an acronym for fire exclusions found in most "all-risks" inland marine policies.

Wear and Tear. Normal deterioration of equipment is expected and, hence, not insurable.

Inherent Vice. This exclusion is intended to eliminate coverage for losses stemming from the very nature of the subject of insurance. An example of inherent vice is the propensity of ripe tomatoes to rot when left too long in the sun. There would be no coverage under a typical transportation form for such deterioration unless the proximate cause of loss were some other peril such as breakdown of refrigeration equipment.

Neglect of the Insured. The insurer has no intention of indemnifying the insured for improper handling of the subject of insurance. The following two exclusions from an annual transportation floater exemplify typical exclusions.

> Caused by improper packing, rough handling or unexplained shortage;

> Caused by leakage, evaporation, shrinkage, breakage, heat or cold, or by being scented, moulded, rusted, rotted, soured, or changed in flavor, or by bending, denting, chipping, marring or scratching unless caused by fire, lightning, windstorm, flood, explosion, collision, derailment or overturn, or stranding, burning or sinking of ferry or lighter;

Catastrophe (Nuclear). As with most other property policies, there is no coverage in the typical inland marine form for loss caused by nuclear reaction, nuclear radiation, or radioactive contamination, except that direct loss by an ensuing fire is covered under some forms.

Enemy. This is the war exclusion which eliminates from coverage any hostile or warlike action, insurrection, rebellion, and the like. This exclusion also eliminates coverage for seizure or destruction under quarantine or customs regulations, confiscation by order of any government or public authority, or risks of contraband or illegal transportation or trade.

Miscellaneous Policy Provisions

Miscellaneous provisions deal with the mechanics of the relationship between the insured and the insurer or among them and third parties.

Mortgagee Clauses and Loss Payable Clauses These clauses are similar to those in fire insurance.

Policy Period Many inland marine forms are written on an annual or three-year basis like fire policies. Some inland marine transportation forms are written on an "open" basis and remain in force so long as the insured continues to report shipments to the insurer. Still other policies are written to cover only one shipment from its point of origin to its final destination without specific reference to the date of departure or the date of arrival.

Coinsurance and Full Reporting Clauses Insurance to value is as important to the inland marine insurer as it is to the fire insurer. Value is often established by appraisals on items scheduled. In other cases, the underwriter may know the value of the insured property (like mobile equipment) and agree with the producer and insured on an amount of insurance without an appraisal. Often policies contain coinsurance clauses or clauses that result in insurance to value by requiring the insured to report values accurately or suffer a penalty at time of loss. The reporting requirement from a bailees' customers form is an example of a reporting clause:

> Liability under this policy shall not in any case exceed that proportion of any loss hereunder, which the last reported gross receipts bear to the actual gross receipts for the period included in the said last report.

Deductibles Deductibles are often found in inland marine policies and can range from as low as $50 up to $10,000 or more.

Collateral Documents

Some documents, whether incorporated by reference or attachment, have a bearing on inland marine coverages.

By Reference The documentation associated with transportation of goods (bills of lading for example) is important to inland marine underwriters because the policies covering the transit exposure make reference to these documents.

The producer should secure copies of bills of lading, side-track agreements, and the like to analyze the exposures imposed by these kinds of contracts. The producer would benefit from reviewing the tariffs used by carriers of goods since they often include limitations on the liability of the carrier to the shipper. Tariffs are schedules of prices or rates for described services such as air fares or shipping rates.

By Attachment In the case of the jewelers' block policy, it is customary for the insured to complete and sign a proposal form (an application) which provides underwriting information to the insurer. This proposal becomes a part of the policy when issued and is considered as a warranty in the policy. The producer must be certain the information contained in the proposal is correct since any inaccuracies may void the contract. For example, if the proposal warrants a central station burglar alarm system, and if the insured discontinues the alarm service without notifying the insurer, coverage could be voided not only for burglary but for other losses as well.

Checkpoints

1. What broad categories of insurance are permitted to marine insurers by the Nation-Wide Marine Definition?
2. Why may inland marine bailee forms complement the CGL policy?
3. What are two alternative insuring agreements (perils insured) available in inland marine insurance?
4. List three bases for valuation of property in inland marine policies.

SELLING COMMERCIAL INLAND MARINE INSURANCE

Inland marine exposures exist side by side with other exposures that often may appear to the buyer to be more pressing. Because of this and because many producers do not fully understand inland marine coverages, there is a tendency to consider inland marine business to be peripheral or unimportant. For the producer competing for a new account, a knowledge of the inland marine field can offer unique opportunities to innovate. For the producer attempting to retain business, unique inland marine placements are an excellent defense against competition. This section will discuss the most frequently sold inland marine policies.

Transportation Insurance

Because of federal deregulation of the airlines and motor truck carriers, major changes are underway in the transportation industry.

While it is too soon to determine how the industry will operate in the future, the producer interested in selling transportation insurance should attempt to remain current with new developments in the field and to take advantage of sales opportunities as they arise.

Prospecting for Transportation Insurance Buyers The first place to seek prospects for transportation insurance is in the files of current clients. Because many shippers or recipients of goods assume the railroads, trucking companies, and airlines are fully responsible for damaged or lost goods, some of their transit exposures remain untreated. In fact, many common carriers promptly and fairly settle small claims as a public relations device and a gesture of good will toward regular shippers. Even clients who are aware of their transit exposure for out-bound merchandise frequently overlook their exposure with regard to incoming shipments. The question to be asked by the producer is, "Who would be responsible for loss and what would that responsibility be?"

Another frequently encountered prospecting problem is that the shipper may be unable to determine maximum values on any one conveyance. The shipper is inclined to think in terms of invoice figures and not about the possibility that all of the week's shipments from San Francisco to New Jersey might just end up on a group of vehicles piggy-backed on a single flat car in the Kansas City rail yard. It is important to determine the maximum exposure per vehicle to properly set the limits of coverage since there is usually a limit per conveyance. For little or no additional premium the insurer will grant an aggregate limit per occurrence of two, three or four times the per conveyance limit. Inter-plant or inter-location shipments are often not insured "because nothing ever happens to them." Many customers of the U.S. Postal Service are unaware of the possibility of insuring parcel post shipments through their producer even though this is certainly more convenient and often less expensive than insurance purchased from the post office.

Prospects for transportation insurance range from trucking companies to small railroads and airlines. Freight forwarding companies and freight consolidators as well as moving and storage companies need inland marine coverages since they are specialized common carriers. With the passage of the Motor Carrier Act of 1980, and the deregulation of the industry by that Act, there are certain to be many changes in the trucking business. Carriers are no longer licensed for specified routes and commodities by the Interstate Commerce Commission (ICC). Truckers are free to compete with one another. The ICC is no longer responsible for reviewing the financial condition of smaller trucking firms and there are bound to be new entrants into the field.

Small truckers may be able to challenge larger established trucking lines for profitable business, and the carriers who enjoyed exclusive routes in the past will be faced with the need to reduce overhead—including losses treated by risk management and insurance. As the trucking industry adjusts to the new competitive conditions, there will be some instability created by firms entering and leaving the trucking field. For the insurance producer these changes offer promising opportunities to develop new business and tough challenges to retain current clients.

Customs and Practices in the Transportation Business The producer interested in developing an expertise in transportation insurance must go beyond the scope of the material in this chapter. Insurers and members of the transportation business offer excellent sources of material. For a general understanding, the producer should investigate the type of carriers, their exposure for liability, and the terms of sale among buyers and sellers of goods subject to transportation insurance.

Type of Carrier

COMMON CARRIERS. Common carriers are either airlines, railroads, or trucking companies that furnish transportation to any member of the public seeking their services. Common carriers cannot discriminate among shippers and must take all loads which can be accommodated by their services. They may specialize—carrying only electronic equipment, for example—but they must accept all such equipment from any shipper.

CONTRACT CARRIERS. Contract carriers do not hold themselves out to the general public but rather furnish transportation for certain shippers with whom they have contracts.

PRIVATE CARRIERS. Private carriers haul their own goods or goods entrusted to them as bailee or lessee. This classification includes shippers who own or lease their vehicles and carry their own goods.

Liability of Carriers. Liability of a carrier is, in part, determined by the type of carrier involved.

COMMON CARRIERS. Common carriers are liable to shippers for the safe delivery of freight entrusted to them as bailees except for losses arising from:

1. acts of God or natural phenomena not reasonably foreseeable,
2. acts of public enemies,
3. acts of public authority,
4. neglect or fault on the part of the shipper, or
5. inherent vice.

Because of this liability exposure to shippers, common carriers must file a certificate as evidence that they are insured for public liability and property damage in an acceptable insurance company. Provisions are made for filing when self-insured as well.

The filing for trucking companies is made by the insurance company using an "Endorsement For Motor Common Carrier Policies Of Insurance For Cargo Liability Under Section 215, Interstate Commerce Act." Since July 1, 1976, the insurance company liability for cargo under this endorsement has been $5,000 per vehicle, $10,000 per occurrence, and the endorsement provides thirty days notice of cancellation to the ICC. Under this endorsement the insurer is *absolutely* liable for all claims for which the insured common carrier is liable even though the nature of the claim may be beyond the scope of the insurance policy to which the endorsement is attached. The insurer has a right to reimbursement from the policyholder for any claims not covered by the policy, and for this reason, the underwriter is concerned about the financial responsibility of the carrier. For example, it is possible for a trucking company in financial difficulty to withhold loss payments to shippers until the ICC requires the insurance company to settle the losses. In such a case, many uninsured claims against the carrier, amounting to substantial sums, would be paid by the insurance company. If the carrier is financially weak, the insured may be unable to recover uninsured but paid losses.

Insurers have had the advantage of being able to obtain copies of financial reports filed by the trucking companies from the ICC. Since deregulation, the smaller carriers need not make such filings and insurers must rely on other sources to verify the financial position of their carrier-insureds.

When the common carrier is liable for goods damaged in transit, the amount of the liability may be limited by the bill of lading. The bill of lading is the shipping contract between the shipper and the carrier. A straight bill of lading fixes no limit on the amount of recovery. A released value bill of lading does limit recovery to the amount specified for a particular commodity in the appropriate tariff on file with the regulatory agency. The tariff lists the shipping rates for the carrier and the rules by which the shipments are to be made. The released amounts of liability are generally low and usually quoted as dollar limits per pound or parcel. The shipper has the option to pay an "insurance charge" and declare a value for the shipment thereby increasing the limit of the carrier's liability and obtaining broader "coverage" including acts of God and breakage.

Shippers often load freight cars or containers brought to their location by side track or truck. In such cases, the bill of lading will indicate "shipper's weight, load and count." Because the shipper loaded the car, the carrier is relieved of responsibility for a short count unless it can be proven that the load was burglarized while en route.

Freight forwarders and freight consolidators generally are common carriers who combine numerous small shipments into full loads and either transport the full loads themselves or ship them using other common carriers. At the destination, the full loads are separated and delivered locally by the freight forwarder/consolidator. These specialized firms have the same responsibilities to the shippers as other common carriers.

CONTRACT CARRIERS. The liability of contract carriers is defined by the contract between the carrier and the shipper. Such contracts often release the carrier from substantial responsibility except in the case of extreme negligence. Generally it is not possible, however, for a contract carrier to totally avoid responsibility to the shipper.

PRIVATE CARRIERS. Private carriers generally are carrying their own goods and are exposed to the full value of those goods if they are damaged or destroyed.

Terms of Merchandise Sale. In ocean marine insurance, "F.O.B." means "free on board" and indicates that the shipper (seller) is responsible for arranging to have the cargo delivered on board the vessel. Once this has been accomplished, the responsibility for and title to the goods changes hands from the seller to the buyer. In domestic transactions, the term "F.O.B." is used more loosely to indicate the point at which ownership and exposure to loss shift from seller to buyer. For example, a contract of sale might stipulate "F.O.B. shipper's loading dock." In this case, the transit exposure would be that of the buyer (consignee) once goods are on the shipper's loading dock.

Transportation Exposure Identification The producer must investigate the transit exposure carefully to determine *exactly* when responsibility for shipments begins and ends. In analyzing the transportation exposure of shippers, the most significant consideration is whether there is another party who may be liable to the shipper as either a common or contract carrier. Can a client delivering its own goods on its own vehicles transfer its exposure to any other party? Can a shipper hiring a common carrier on a straight bill of lading transfer a substantial portion of the loss exposure to the carrier?

The same considerations apply to the exposures of the common or contract carrier, except that the point of view is reversed. The question becomes, "To what degree is the carrier liable to shippers for loss or damage to a shipment?"

Consideration must be given to the nature of the goods being transported, routes over which they are being carried, climatic conditions, potential crime exposures, and numerous other factors. The producer who wants the most appropriate terms and conditions in transportation insurance must fully inform the underwriters as to the relevant facts of the situation.

Insurance for Owners of Property in Transit Transportation policies and rates for owners of property in transit are not standard. Some coverage may be issued for a single trip on a trip transit policy, but most insurance is written either as an annual policy or as an open policy that remains in force until cancelled.

The insurance attaches at the time the property leaves its point of origin and is covered thereafter continuously while the goods are in the due course of transportation until delivered at the final destination. It is customary to show separate limits for various means of transportation, and the policy will often contain a separate limit for any one "disaster." The policies discussed include motor truck cargo, a transportation "floater," a parcel post, and a mail policy.

Motor Truck Cargo—Owner's Cargo on Owner's Vehicles. This is a policy designed for the shipper using owned transportation and is most commonly written as a named perils form. A typical selection of perils might include the following:

PERILS INSURED.
This policy insures, except as otherwise provided, against direct physical loss of or damage to the property insured caused by:
A. Fire or lightning;
B. Windstorm;
C. Flood (meaning the overflowing of streams, lakes, bays, ponds, or other bodies of water from their natural or man-made boundaries or barriers, and tidal wave);
D. Explosion;
E. Collapse of bridges or culverts;
F. Derailment, upset, or overturn of the transporting vehicle;
G. Accidental collision of the transporting vehicle or its load with any other vehicle or object, excluding, however, contact with any portion of the roadbed, curbing, or rails or ties of any railway, and excluding the coming together of railroad cars during shifting or coupling;
H. Theft or non-delivery of an entire shipping package;
I. The stranding, sinking, burning, or collision (including general average and salvage charges) of any regular ferry while operating on inland waterways only.

PERILS EXCLUDED.
This policy does not insure against:
A. Loss or damage caused by wear and tear, inherent vice, gradual deterioration, insects or vermin;
B. Loss by leakage, breakage, marring, or scratching, unless caused by fire, lightning, windstorm, flood, or by collision, derailment or overturn of the transporting vehicle, or by the vessel being on fire, stranded, sunk, or in collision;
C. Loss or damage caused by or resulting from delay, loss of market,

loss of use, or interruption of business;

D. Loss or damage caused by or resulting from infidelity and dishonesty, either or both, of the Insured or any person or persons in the employ or service of the Insured, whether or not such act or acts occurred during the regular hours of employment or service, or any person or persons to whom the property may be entrusted (carriers for hire excepted).

Note that certain maritime exposures are covered. *General average* arises in connection with transportation by water when there is a partial loss allocated to all interests involved. The loss is shared proportionately by all interests if a sacrifice is necessary, voluntary, and successful and made to save the venture. *Salvage charges* consist of voluntary services to save or preserve maritime property from peril. Even if the shipper does not use water transportation, it is possible to incur general average or salvage charges if there is a loss while the vehicle is waterborne on a ferry or barge.

The policy is written including a description of the property being shipped, and there is generally a schedule of vehicles, including for each the make, year, identification number, capacity, body type, radius of operations, center of operations, amount of insurance, and a rate for the insurance.

If any scheduled vehicle is withdrawn from normal use because of sale, breakdown, repair, loss, or damage, the amount of insurance applying to it can be applied, usually, to any similar vehicle operated as a substitute provided that substitute vehicles and newly acquired vehicles are reported to the insurer. When large numbers of vehicles are involved, coverage can be arranged on a reporting basis without the need to list each vehicle.

Certain property may be excluded from coverage. For instance, a typical policy may not insure such items as currency, bullion, "valuable papers," live animals, or works of art.

The producer for a shipper who routinely carries any of the excluded kinds of property would need to amend the contract to add the required coverage.

"All-Risks" Transportation Floater. The motor truck cargo form just described has a limited use but the "all-risks" transportation floater is designed to cover goods in transit on various forms of transportation as described in the policy. These contracts typically cover while the insured property is in the possession of a carrier—any railroad, railroad express company (including while on ferries and/or in cars or transfers or lighters), air carrier, air express company, public or private motor carriers, coastal and inland steamers, or while on the insured's own trucks. The coverage generally extends while the goods are on docks, wharves, piers, bulkheads, in depots, stations, and/or on

platforms but only while in the custody of a common carrier and only while such exposure is incidental to the transportation of the goods. The transportation floater is an "all-risks" form which might typically exclude (in addition to war and nuclear damage):

THIS POLICY DOES NOT INSURE AGAINST LOSS:

(a) To accounts, bills, deeds, evidences of debt, currency, money, coins, bullion, notes, securities, stamps;

(b) To jewelry, watches, silverware, furs or articles trimmed with fur, unless shipped in sealed packages by railway express;

(c) To animals, unless specifically insured hereunder, and then only against death caused by, or destruction rendered necessary by injuries due to fire, lightning, windstorm, flood, explosion, collision, derailment or overturn, or stranding, burning or sinking of ferry or lighter;

(d) Of profit, loss of use or loss of market, however caused;

(e) Caused by improper packing, rough handling or unexplained shortage;

(f) Caused by insect, vermin or inherent vice;

(g) Caused by leakage, evaporation, shrinkage, breakage, heat or cold, or by being scented, moulded, rusted, rotted, soured, or changed in flavor, or by bending, denting, chipping, marring or scratching unless caused by fire, lightning, windstorm, flood, explosion, collision, derailment or overturn, or stranding, burning or sinking of ferry or lighter;

(h) To export shipments which have been laden on board export conveyance or have come under the protection of marine insurance, whichever first occurs;

(i) To import shipments until fully discharged from import conveyance or until marine insurance has ceased to cover, whichever last occurs;

(j) To shipments by mail or parcel post;

As with any "all-risks" policy, the exclusions are critical, and the producer must be certain they are carefully reviewed and modified as necessary for each buyer of the policy.

This policy describes the property insured as "consisting principally of _____" and this description must be written carefully. A deductible is often found in the form. The premium charged is based on estimated annual shipments calculated at a rate per $100 of value. The insured is required to keep accurate records and to report all property shipped to the insurance company. The premium is then adjusted accordingly subject to a minimum annual premium. The rating for the transportation policy depends on the type of goods being shipped, the vulnerability of the property insured to damage and theft, and the mode of transportation being used.

The valuation of the property covered is the actual invoice cost, including prepaid freight, together with such costs and charges since shipment as may have accrued and become legally due. If there is no invoice, the valuation of the property is its actual cash value at the point of destination on the date of the disaster.

Cancellation of the policy does not prejudice any property in transit on the effective date of the cancellation.

Parcel Post Policy. Packages sent by parcel post can be insured at the post office, but arranging the insurance on each individual shipment and collecting any claims can be time-consuming. An alternative is the policy, which is nonfiled and works like the transportation floater with a deposit premium and reporting provisions. The limit of liability is $100 on any one package shipped by ordinary parcel post or unregistered mail and $500 on any one package shipped by registered mail or government insured parcel post. If necessary, these limits can be increased (valuable items such as gems, jewelry, or coins require high limits). The perils are broad, insuring "the safe arrival" of the package and paying for loss or damage "from any external cause whatsoever..." occurring while the package is actually in the custody of the Post Office Department. The exclusions in addition to war and nuclear loss include: types of property like currency, deeds, checks, goods on consignment, and perishable goods and causes of loss such as insufficiently addressed packages, packages with labels describing contents, or packages not stipulated "return requested." It is a condition of the policy that all packages comply with postal regulations.

Mail Policies. These policies if sold to fiduciaries are a filed line with ISO rates for registered mail and first class mail. Policies sold to nonfiduciary organizations are nonfiled and rates and forms can be negotiated. In either market, the policies can be endorsed to cover certified mail as well. Because of the security of the U.S. postal system, the policies have but two exclusions—war and nuclear damage. The policies can be written on an annual basis or as an open policy both with periodic reporting requirements. Prospects for the filed forms are fiduciaries including banks, trust companies, insurance companies, securities brokers, transfer agents, and others who mail valuable documents like securities or certificates of deposit.

The policies cover continuously in transit from the time of acceptance by the messenger or carrier until delivered to the addressee or the addressee's authorized representative. Coverage is within the continental United States but may be extended to include mail to and within the states of Alaska and Hawaii or Puerto Rico. Coverage can be arranged for shipments to Canada or even elsewhere in the world as necessary.

It is a condition that the insured "shall endeavor" to have the contents of each package verified by two persons, but failure to do so does not void the contract. The policy insures the value of the property at the time of dispatch or at the time the loss becomes known, or the cost of corresponding property purchased by the insured plus any loss of actual interest earnings, shipping and insurance charges—not exceeding a percentage such as 105 percent to 125 percent of the market value of stocks and bonds on the day of shipment. The policy limits can be quite high. For example, the published rates for First Class Mail Form A contemplate limits of liability of up to $250,000 for each shipping package and up to $1,100,000 for any one addressee on any one day. The producer should note this aggregate limit and be certain it is adequate.

Coverage for Carriers of Property in Transit   Cargo liability policies would be unnecessary if it were not for the "case, custody and control" exclusion in general liability and automobile liability policies. Since the exclusion is present, coverage for goods in the care of carriers must be insured using inland marine forms to cover the potential liability to the shipper for loss. This class of policies is nonfiled, so the producer will find independent forms and rates which vary considerably. The policies may be called "motor truck cargo—legal liability," "motor truck cargo owners and truckmens form," or simply a "motor truck cargo liability policy," but their intent is the same—to cover "the legal liability of the insured as a carrier under tariff or bill of lading or shipping receipt issued by the insured." It is to this policy that the ICC or other statutory endorsements required by the governmental agency regulations are attached.

The named perils form generally insures the liability of the insured for direct loss or damage by perils similar to those listed for Motor Truck Cargo-Owners Form.

Theft can sometimes be added as an additional peril subject to a dollar deductible and a provision that eliminates coverage for pilferage when the "entire shipping package" is not taken. Typical exclusions in the named perils form in addition to war and nuclear damage are:

(a) Loss or damage to accounts, bills, deeds, evidences of debt, letters of credit, passports, documents, railroad or other tickets, notes, securities, money, currency, bullion, precious stones, jewelry and/or other similar valuables, paintings, statuary and other works of art, manuscripts, mechanical drawings;

(b) Loss or damage to vehicles or their equipment including fittings or tarpaulins, or any property carried gratuitously or as an accommodation;

(c) Loss or damage due to inherent vice or delay whether resulting from a peril insured against or otherwise;

(d) Damage to live animals except as follows: This Company shall be liable only for claims arising from death, or from injury rendering death immediately necessary, in consequence of perils insured against;

(e) Loss or damage caused by strikers, locked-out workmen or persons taking part in labor disturbances or riots, or civil commotions;

(f) Loss or damage caused by the neglect of the Assured to use all reasonable means to save and preserve the property at and after any disaster insured against, nor for any act or omission of a dishonest character in the part of the Assured or his or their employees;

(g) Shipments by mail.

Exclusions in the "all-risks" form, in addition to a war and nuclear exclusion, would include property such as negotiable instruments, art, live animals, and warehouse receipt merchandise and perils such as fidelity, egg breakage, mysterious disappearance, and so forth. The availability and price of the "all-risks" form depend greatly on the trucking company's operations and the kinds of goods carried.

The cargo liability policy may limit the territory to "within a radius of _____ miles of _____," or the policy may list states in which the carrier operates.

In addition to providing coverage while the property is in transit, the policy can be extended for a limited period of time while the goods are held temporarily at terminals. Often these terminal locations are scheduled in the policy with a limit of liability at each location.

The limits of coverage while in transit usually apply with respect to any one vehicle, and there is frequently a catastrophe limit for any one loss.

Often the insured warrants no excess insurance over and above the primary policy, so it is important to advise the insurer if this policy is scheduled as underlying the trucking company umbrella insurance policy.

In some cases the policy will include a schedule of vehicles in the same manner as the transportation floater while permitting substitution as long as changes are reported to the insurer.

The policies contain the equivalent of a 100 percent insurance-to-value clause requiring full reporting of gross receipts. The premiums are adjusted periodically depending on the size of the policy.

Independent forms may offer various extensions of coverage such as paying for debris removal expenses, earned freight charges, or miscellaneous equipment.

A deductible is often used to eliminate smaller losses. The deductible may apply to specific perils such as collision or to all losses under the policy.

Carloading companies and freight forwarders who act as common carriers are prospects for this coverage as are warehousemen who have transportation liability exposures.

Checkpoints

1. What are the three legal classes of carriers?
2. List the responsibilities of a common and a contract carrier to a shipper for the goods being transported.
3. Describe the role of the ICC or a state agency with regard to insurance coverages purchased by common or contract carriers.
4. What is meant in domestic transportation by "F.O.B."?
5. List two transportation policies and their prospects.

Bailees' Customers Insurance

Unlike trucking companies and common carriers which are almost totally responsible for shippers' goods in their possession, other bailees are liable under common law only for the bailee's own negligence. If a loss is caused because the bailee fails to exercise the standard of care expected of the ordinary, reasonable, and prudent person, the bailee will be responsible for the loss or damage. This liability for damage to the property of others would be covered under any third party liability policy except for the care, custody, and control (CCC) exclusion. Because this exclusion is rarely deleted, bailees, like common carriers, need inland marine insurance for their liability for damage to customers' property.

Prospecting for Bailees Almost any person or enterprise that accepts the property of others for service, repair, or processing is eligible for the bailees' customers policy. Some of the policies covering the bailee exposure are written in conjunction with the liability coverages, rather than as inland marine forms per se. For example, garages and automobile repair shops have a major bailee exposure, but they are insured by a garagekeepers' legal liability form as part of a garage policy. Appliance repairers, furniture upholsterers and refinishers, and industrial equipment repair facilities are all prospects for the bailees' customers policy. Certain bailees have special bailees' customers forms tailored to their needs, such as furriers, cleaners, dyers and laundries, and warehousemen. All of these are prospects for inland marine coverages, and many will be knowledgeable about the insurance designed for them. Other prospects may have only an incidental bailee exposure when they occasionally accept the property of others for one reason or another. The producer will need to work hard to identify these less obvious exposures.

Bailees' Insurance Bailees' insurance is available in a general form or specialized to fit a unique exposure.

Bailees' Customers Form. The bailees' customers policy is a general form used to insure bailees for whom no specialized form exists. It is nonfiled, and insurance companies are free to use nonstandard forms and rates. Coverage is on all goods or articles accepted by the insured for cleaning, renovating, pressing, dyeing, repairing, or laundering while contained on the premises occupied by the insured, in the custody of the insured's agents or branch stores, and while being transported to and from the premises of customers, branch stores or agencies. The insuring agreement is not stated as a liability coverage for the bailee but rather as direct property coverage on customers' property regardless of the bailee's legal liability.

The policy can be written for small accounts on an annual basis with a fixed premium and separate limits on designated locations, on unnamed locations of the insured (for a limited period of time such as three days), at locations not owned, rented, or controlled by the insured, and on any one vehicle or messenger while in transit at the insured's exposure. On larger accounts, the policy is written on a monthly gross receipts reporting basis and sometimes without a specific limit of liability on property at locations operated by the named insured. Many bailees' customers policies permit the bailee insured to settle small losses with customers when they do not exceed $50 or $100. For larger losses, at the option of the insurer, adjustment may be with and paid to the insured, "for account of whom it may concern," or adjusted with and paid direct to customers. The insurance applies excess of other insurance—except insurance purchased by a customer.

Although an "all-risks" form is sometimes written, the named perils form is used more frequently. Typically, the named perils form might insure against:

(a) Fire and lightning;
(b) Explosion;
(c) Collision and/or overturning of transporting conveyance;
(d) Theft, burglary and holdup;
(e) Cyclone, tornado and/or windstorm;
(f) Sprinkler leakage;
(g) Flood, while in transit (meaning thereby "rising waters");
(h) Earthquake;
(i) Any of the above listed perils, while in the custody of public carriers or mail service (shipments to transients at hotels or temporary residences are covered if shipped by government insured parcel post or registered mail);
(j) Confusion of goods, resulting from any of the above listed perils.

The last peril refers to when the markings, slips, or tags on the goods are damaged or destroyed so that it is impossible to identify which items belong to which customers.

The named perils policy does not insure against (in addition to war and nuclear damage):

(a) Theft of goods or packages left on delivery vehicles overnight, unless locked in Insured's private garage or building occupied by Insured;

(b) Shortage of individual pieces or articles, unless caused by burglary or holdup;

(c) Loss or damage to goods held on storage, or for which a storage charge is made, unless endorsed hereon;

(d) Loss or damage to goods while in the custody of other dyers and cleaners or laundries, unless specifically endorsed hereon;

(e) Loss resulting from misdelivery, or careless destruction of goods or other unaccountable loss where there is no evidence that the loss was occasioned by the perils specifically insured against herein;

It is possible to purchase coverage to include goods in storage or while in the custody of other dyers and cleaners or laundries.

The policy usually covers the customary charges earned on lost or damaged goods. All thefts for which claims are made under the policy must be reported promptly to the police. When the policy is on a monthly reporting basis, it contains a full reporting clause to penalize the insured in the event of underreporting of gross receipts. Since the rates for this coverage are not filed, insurers have their own rating approaches which take the individual characteristics of the exposure into account.

Specialized Bailees' Customers Forms. There are many specialized bailees' policies but only a few will be discussed.

WAREHOUSEMEN'S LEGAL LIABILITY. These policies are nonfiled and vary considerably between insurers. Insurance generally is on an "all-risks" basis, including coverage for investigation expenses, defense, and court costs in connection with claims.

Typical exclusions include delay, loss of market, or consequential loss (except in the case of cold storage exposures where the policy generally covers spoilage from change in temperature as a result of refrigeration failure). Property must be covered by a warehouse receipt, and the policy excludes liability assumed by the warehouseman—for instance, by contract. Changes in temperature (except in the case of cold storage exposures), wear and tear, and gradual deterioration are also excluded. Forged warehouse receipts are excluded (may be covered by crime insurance) as are accounts, bills, deeds, money, and other such property. The policy also excludes loss by "trick and device" whereby the bailee surrenders property voluntarily based on a fraud of the recipient. Because the forms are not filed, many of the exclusions can be deleted or amended as necessary. In fact, much of the insurance written on warehousemen is provided by specialty insurers using tailor-made forms.

Warehousemen, like most other bailees, are held responsible for "ordinary negligence," i.e., the failure to exercise due care, and this means that the burden of proof is generally on the customer. The producer should review state statutes to determine the exact liability of the warehouseman as responsibility varies from state to state. For instance, in California the burden of proving negligence in a *fire* loss rests with the bailor (customer), but with all other kinds of losses, the burden of proof is on the warehouseman.

Warehousemen may be required by the state regulatory authorities to file a tariff including limits of liability and an insurance charge for various types of property. The three broad classes of property stored are (1) furniture and household goods, (2) frozen foods or other property requiring cold storage, and (3) general merchandise (which is anything else). When property is left with the warehouseman, a warehouse receipt is issued. An amount indicated on this receipt often limits the liability of the warehouseman. If a furniture storage customer wants insurance to value, the warehouseman can issue a certificate of insurance, which provides direct damage coverage whether or not the warehouseman is responsible for loss or damage.

The warehousemen's legal liability is excess over other insurance carried by the insured, and the limit of liability is determined by the total of the warehouse receipts issued by the insured plus the total of the amounts of insurance by certificate on household goods.

FURRIERS' CUSTOMERS POLICY. The furriers' customers policy is a filed form usually written in conjunction with a so-called furriers' block policy. It is insurance to cover the property of others made in part or wholly of furs (including imitation fur) owned by customers while in the custody of furriers or others storing such property. Other garments, textiles and similar articles can also be insured. Banks, stores, laundries, cleaners, general or fur warehousemen, cold storage concerns and other bailees, in addition to furriers, may need this form of protection. The policy can be issued on a nonreporting basis or as a monthly reporting form. The reports are of the aggregate values of the amounts set forth in all the furrier's outstanding receipts. Limits apply at designated premises or while in transit within and between the states of the continental United States, the District of Columbia, and Canada.

The liability of the insurer is limited to not more than (1) the amount stipulated in the furrier's receipt for each article, (2) the actual cash value of the property, or (3) the cost of repair or replacement of the property with materials of like kind and quality, whichever is less. Policies covering furriers issuing storage receipts may be endorsed to cover legal liability for excess valuation over the amount shown on the storage receipt. This endorsement may be needed in the case of customers who declare a lower value on the receipt than the value of the item stored. The insured may also elect to insure accrued storage and service charges, either unpaid or prepaid, or both. The insured may also arrange to issue "special fur policies" by certificates to annually insure customers' furs on an "all-risks" direct damage basis providing similar coverage but at a lower premium rate than insurance on a personal articles floater.

Coverage under the furriers' policy is "all-risks" of loss of or damage to the insured property including the insured's legal liability therefor. Exclusions in addition to war and nuclear damage are: deterioration, wear and tear, work done on the garments, and fidelity losses.

The furriers' customers policy is excess over any other insurance carried by "a named or unnamed insured or any other interested party."

It is a condition of the policy that receipts be given to customers stating values and allowing ten days to correct valuations. It is also a condition of the policy that the insured shall use "due diligence" to maintain such protective safeguards as are stated in the proposal for the policy.

CLEANERS, DYERS AND LAUNDRIES FORM. This nonfiled contract is one offered by many insurers using their own forms. Specialized forms are available for rug cleaners and for pressing and tailor shops. The form is designed to cover the dual interests of the bailee and the customer by insuring against loss or damage to customers' property regardless of the insured's legal liability. The valuation provision calls for claims to be paid on an actual cash value basis plus earned charges on demand or lost items.

Coverage can be "all-risks" or named perils but regardless of form there is usually no boiler explosion exclusion. Generally, coverage applies anywhere the customers' goods are in the possession of the insured. Coverage for theft or robbery from an insured's vehicle may exclude loss of individual items or of individual packages of laundry or dry cleaning. In fact, some forms only cover the theft of an entire vehicle load, and coverage is often excluded for theft of goods left on delivery vehicles overnight unless locked within a garage or building of the insured.

Because many laundries and dry cleaners are pickup stations that do little or no processing work on the premises, the policy can be extended to cover while the goods are in the hands of a delivery service, the Postal Service, or at the locations of processors.

Like the bailees' customers policy, the laundry and dry cleaners forms usually permit the insured to adjust small claims directly with customers.

Because the insured has little idea of the value of garments in process, many policies are written with either a fixed limit not subject to coinsurance, or with no limit at all. A deductible clause is usually included, but only applies (1) to all claims in a year and (2) only for certain perils such as loss of property and theft among others. The premiums are based on gross receipts periodically reported to the insurer.

INNKEEPERS LEGAL LIABILITY AND CLOAKROOM LIABILITY. These bailees' customers forms are designed for hotels and those businesses, like restaurants, which check customers' coats.

Each state has an Innkeepers Statute which limits the responsibility of hotels and motels for guests' property. Typically, the law sets a maximum obligation of from $500 to $1,000 per guest or per guest room. A separate statutory limit may apply to the contents of hotel safe deposit boxes unless a higher value is declared to the hotel. The producer must check local statutes to determine the exact responsibility of innkeepers on a state-by-state basis since the laws are not uniform. The policy is generally written on an "all-risks" form and is subject to a deductible.

Cloakroom exposures can be found in some restaurants, theaters, museums and other places where coats are checked. The bailee exposure can be severe, especially where one might expect to find many fur coats. Cloakroom operators are liable for ordinary negligence but usually are not protected by statute as are innkeepers. This insurance is difficult to arrange and typically includes a deductible sufficient to eliminate claims for one misplaced umbrella or raincoat.

Floaters

This section discusses policies designed to insure property with a high degree of mobility. Generally, floaters are written on equipment or other kinds of property while the property is in use. Floaters are rarely written on goods that are being manufactured or held for sale. Many floater forms and rates are filed although the contractors equipment floater which accounts for substantial premium volume, is a nonfiled line.

Contractors Equipment Floater A contractors equipment floater is designed to insure mobile equipment and machinery, such as cranes, derricks, pile drivers, tractors, graders, and scrapers. The policy can also be used to cover smaller items like hand tools. Many commercial and industrial operations other than contractors have such equipment and can insure it using this form. For example, fork lift or squeeze lift trucks owned by manufacturers, wholesalers, or retailers are often scheduled on a contractors equipment floater. Even a small apartment complex with a tractor to mow grass and plow snow is eligible. Watercraft, aircraft, and autos are ineligible for this coverage.

Prospecting for Contractors Equipment Floaters. General contractors, home builders, road builders, and other contractors are the primary prospects for this coverage because they often have large values in mobile equipment. Smaller contractors and sub-contractors are prospects for the coverage because while they have less equipment to insure, they generally cannot afford to lose any equipment. Other kinds of businesses may have mobile equipment such as fork lifts or snow removal equipment.

Perils Insured and Excluded. The policy can be written on an "all-risks" or named perils basis. The "all-risks" form, in addition to the usual war and nuclear damage exclusions, excludes losses:

(a) Caused by the weight of a load exceeding the rated lifting or supporting capacity of any machine;

(b) To any crane boom or derrick boom while such booms are being operated or used, unless directly caused by fire, lightning, windstorm, explosion or overturning of the machine of which it is a part (the term "boom" shall include any extension thereof);

(c) To dynamos, exciters, lamps, switches, motors or other electrical appliances or devices, including wiring, caused by electricity other than lightning unless fire or explosion ensues and then only for loss or damage from such ensuing fire or explosion;

(d) To tires or tubes, unless directly caused by fire, windstorm, or theft, or is coincident with and from the same cause as other loss insured by this policy;

(e) Caused by any repairing, adjusting, servicing, remodeling, or maintenance process; or resulting from structural, mechanical or electrical breakdown or failure; unless fire or explosion ensues and then only for the loss caused by such ensuing fire or explosion;

(f) Misappropriation, secretion, conversion, infidelity or any dishonest act on part of the Insured or other party of interest, his or their employees, while working or otherwise, or agents, or others to whom the property may be entrusted (carriers for hire excepted);

(g) From unexplained loss, mysterious dissapearance or shortage disclosed by taking inventory;

(h) By gradual deterioration, wear and tear, faulty design, obsolescence, latent defect, rust, corrosion, inherent vice, overheating or freezing; explosion originating within steam boilers, steam piping, pressure vessels or internal combustion engines of the property insured;

(i) Caused by delay, loss of market or loss of use.

In some ways this form is more restricting than some (Exclusion (d) for example) but in some ways it is broader. Flood is insured under the above form but is often excluded under other forms. A typical named perils form might include fire, extended coverage, and vandalism plus theft, flood, earthquake, landslide, snowslide, subsidence, and transportation hazards including collapse of bridges as well as collision or upset of the equipment itself or transporting conveyances. General average and salvage charges are often included.

Property Insured and Excluded. Covered property for smaller accounts is scheduled onto the policy including a description of the machine, the model, the identification number, and a limit of insurance for that item. The policy also contains an aggregate limit for any one loss or occurrence. For larger accounts, the contractors equipment floater is often written on a blanket basis. Policies usually provide for limited automatic coverage for additional equipment, and some of the broader forms include insurance on similar property of others which the insured may lease or be legally liable for. Most policies are on an actual cash value basis, but some extend to provide loss of use coverage or coverage for earnings lost as a result of damage to insured equipment. The following property is usually excluded:

(a) Automobiles, motor trucks, tractors, trailers, motorcycles, or similar conveyances designed for highway use; aircraft or watercraft;
(b) Plans, blueprints, designs or specifications;
(c) Property while underground, underwater, airborne, or waterborne (except while being transported on a regular ferry line);
(d) Property which has become a part of any structure;
(e) Property while leased, loaned or rented to others;
(f) Spare or replacement parts; supplies.

Other Important Policy Provisions. A 100 percent coinsurance provision is typical for contractors equipment floaters, although a lower percentage might be used in certain cases. For accounts with high values, the policy can be written with an annual adjustment without coinsurance subject to a full reporting clause.

Because of the hazardous use of much of this equipment, a substantial deductible is often required. For example, a grading contractor working in difficult terrain and bad weather might have a $10,000 or larger deductible per occurrence.

The territorial limits usually include coverage while the property is at locations within or in transit within or between the states of the United States, the District of Columbia, Puerto Rico, or Canada, although some policies might exclude Hawaii, Alaska, or Puerto Rico. The producer should be certain that clients with operations outside the forty-eight contiguous states of the United States have a proper territorial limit.

Contractors equipment floaters usually provide that the insurance does not cover loss caused by or resulting from the neglect of the insured to use reasonable means to save and preserve the property at the time of and after any loss. The policy may be voided by any act or agreement by the insured before or after the loss whereby any right of recovery against any carrier, bailee, or other liable party is released, impaired, or lost. The insurer is also not liable for any loss or damage which, without its written consent, has been settled or compromised by the insured.

Mobile Agricultural Equipment and Livestock Floaters
These are filed forms similar to the contractors equipment floater but designed for farmers and ranchers. Eligible property includes mobile agricultural machinery and equipment (not for sale, repair, or consignment, or in the course of manufacture), which has come into the custody or control of parties who intend to use such property for the purpose for which it was manufactured or created. Cattle, sheep, swine, horses, mules, and goats may be insured using the livestock forms. The ISO manual should be consulted for ineligible classes of property, but major ineligible categories include irrigation equipment, self-propelled harvester thresher combines or mechanical cotton pickers used for hire, and range animals while on ranges. Livestock used in racing or show or which are being transported to or from or while at the stockyards or commercial feed lots are also ineligible.

The policy can be written to cover equipment on a blanket basis with a single amount of insurance subject to 80 percent coinsurance. For livestock, coverage can be blanketed with a single amount of insurance applying to each class of livestock. The agricultural equipment can be written on a scheduled basis with a separate blanket amount of 10 percent or $5,000 (whichever is less) available to cover low value items of $250 or less. Newly acquired equipment similar to that scheduled is insured up to an additional 25 percent of the total amount of insurance on mobile agricultural equipment for thirty days. Livestock coverage may be provided on a scheduled basis by describing the amount of insurance applying to each type of animal. The company's limit of liability for any one animal is the lesser of $1,000, 120 percent of the average amount of insurance on each animal in a class, or the actual cash value.

The coverage is "all-risks" for agricultural equipment. For livestock, the policy covers death or destruction directly resulting from, or made necessary by, fire and extended coverage perils, earthquake, flood, collapse of bridges or culverts, collision or derailment of a vehicle on which the insured property is being transported, collision with other vehicles except those owned or operated by the insured or by any tenant of the insured, stranding, sinking, burining, or collision of vessels, including general average and salvage charges, and theft, but excluding escape or mysterious disappearance.

In addition to the usual exclusions of war and nuclear damage, the policy also excludes loss from infidelity of the insured's employees or persons to whom the property is entrusted (carriers for hire excepted). For an additional premium the livestock coverage can be extended to cover death or destruction caused by accidental shooting, drowning, artificial electricity, collapse of a building, and attack by wild animals.

Full animal mortality policies are available that provide coverage for death of animals due to sickness, disease, or accident from any cause. Animal mortality policies generally are used to insure high-value animals like thoroughbred horses, racing stock, breeding stock, and show animals.

The mobile agricultural equipment floater's exclusions are those usual for the exposures such as wear and tear, fidelity, property more than 50 miles from the premises, and so forth.

Other Floaters Space does not permit a detailed analysis of all floater policies. In fact, anything from adding machines to x-ray equipment can be insured on a nonfiled, all-purpose (either "all-risks" or named perils) policy called a "scheduled equipment floater." Some of the more popular filed and nonfiled floaters are described briefly.

Installation Floater. The installation floater is designed for contractors who specialize in the installation of machinery and equipment, including plumbing, heating, and air conditioning firms as well as manufacturers of elevators and store or restaurant fixtures. Owners for whom the work is being done or sellers who are providing materials, equipment, or supplies for installation projects are also prospects for this coverage. The insured's property is covered while in transit to the job site, at the site awaiting installation, during and after installation, until the job is accepted and title to the property passes to the purchaser. The form is nonfiled and many insurers offer either a named perils form or an "all-risks" form. Although often excluded even in the "all-risks" form, earthquake and flood coverage can be added by endorsement. The policy is frequently written on a continuous-until-canceled basis with monthly reports of insured values installed. Building materials can be covered until they become a part of a structure, and the policy can be extended to include tools and equipment used by the insured in the installation. A typical policy may not insure against any loss due to error or omission in design, faulty workmanship, or testing of equipment. The policies are often subject to a deductible and to a coinsurance or full reporting clause.

"All-Risks" Builders' Risk Form. This nonfiled form is used to cover property of the insured consisting of materials, supplies, machinery, equipment, fixtures, and temporary structures to be used in or incidental to the construction, fabrication, installation, erection, or completion of a building. The insured may be the owner, contractor, or seller of the property, or the policy may be written to cover more than one interest in the property. (Fire underwriters provide a similar policy on a named perils basis.)

Coverage begins when the insured property is moved to the job site; coverage terminates when the interest of the insured in the property ceases, when the installation or erection of the insured property is completed and accepted as satisfactory, or when the policy expires. Blueprints, plans, designs or specifications are excluded from coverage unless added to the policy by endorsement. In addition to the usual exclusions of war and nuclear damage, the policy excludes (among other causes of loss) flood and earthquake, although these may be added by endorsement. Also excluded are loss, damage, or expense caused by or resulting from subsidence, settling, cracking, shrinkage, or expansion of walls, patios, floors, or ceilings unless caused by certain named perils; loss caused by rain, hail, snow, or sleet, whether driven by wind or not, unless wind or hail first make an opening in the walls or roof of the insured building; or loss caused by error, omission, or deficiency in design or faulty workmanship. Mechanical breakdown and electrical damage are insured only for ensuing fire damage. Loss occasioned by enforcement of any ordinance or law regulating the construction, repair, or demolition is not covered; nor is breakage of certain glass by vandals.

Valuation of losses is based on the actual cash value of the property at the time of loss plus accrued labor and other charges and expenses. It is customary that the limit of insurance be designated by location, and that sub-limits apply separately to building and struc-tures; to property in the course of transit; in any one theft, burglary or holdup; and at any other location. Coverage for larger accounts is written on a monthly reporting basis of values.

Pattern Floater. This is a nonfiled form designed to cover (1) patterns, molds, dies, and forms, (2) owned by the insured or for which the insured is liable, (3) while in transit or at locations other than the insured's premises—i.e., at subcontractors' facilities to make parts for the insured's product or to process the insured's product in some way. For example, a furniture manufacturer might send partially completed metal frames to be assembled and chrome-plated. The pattern floater would cover the patterns of the insured needed to cut and assemble the frames. (The parts for the frames could be covered by a processors floater mentioned below.) The pattern floater is normally a named perils contract covering fire, extended coverage, vandalism and malicious mischief, strikers, sprinkler leakage, and transportation perils. A 100 percent coinsurance clause often applies. Sometime this policy can be extended to cover at the insured's location.

Processors Floater. The processors floater is designed to cover manufacturers that send partially completed products to contractors for processing. The perils and the policy provisions are similar to those of the pattern floater, although theft coverage is available for an additional premium from many insurers.

Garment Contractors Floater. This filed form is simply a specialized processors floater for the clothing industry where subcontracting is a standard practice. Often individual garments may be processed by numerous subcontractors who cut the fabric, assemble the garment, make button holes, attach buttons, pleat, or perform other specialized tasks. Each part of a garmant is separately insured including shipping containers, and the policy covers the property of the insured or held by the insured in trust or on commission or on consignmnet or on which the insured has made advances. Locations of subcontractors are scheduled in the policy for specific limits of insurance, and other limits apply while in transit. The insurance is "all-risks" while in transit and covers fire and lightning, sprinkler leakage, water damage, burglary, holdup, windstorm, hail, smoke, vehicle and aircraft damage, and boiler explosion while on premises. Optional additional perils include theft, strikes, riots, malicious mischief, explosion, and consequential damage to garments. The definition of consequential damage is a specialized pairs and sets clause and requires reading to avoid misunderstandings. The policy is subject to a 100 percent coinsurance clause and, unlike most similar floaters, can be extended to provide "all-risks" coverage on the insured's location including the insured's equipment, tools and fixtures as well as the garments themselves.

Exhibition Floater. This is a nonfiled form available on an "all-risks" or named perils basis to cover property owned by the insured, or property of others in the care, custody, or control of the insured, while away from the insured's premises and while in transit to, from, or on exhibition at specified locations. The named perils form covers fire, extended coverage, vandalism and malicious mischief, as well as burglary and transportation perils. Some perils excluded in the "all-risks" form are wear and tear, inherent vice, gradual deterioration, insects, vermin, freezing, dampness of atmosphere, extremes of temperature, and mechanical or electrical breakdown or failure.

Marring, scratching, breakage of glass, or other fragile articles are excluded unless caused by named perils. This exclusion can be "bought back," however. The policy is subject to a coinsurance clause and a deductible. The territorial limit of the coverage is usually the forty-eight contiguous states of the United States, the District of Columbia, and Canada.

Salesmen's Samples Floater. This nonfiled form covers samples while away from the insured's premises. The policy covers merchandise as described in the policy including

1. trunks and containers,
2. the property (a) of the insured or (b) of others held in trust or on commission or (c) for whom the insured is agent and for which the insured is liable,
3. while in the custody or control of the insured's sales representatives,
4. or while in transit between the insured and the sales representatives.

The insurance provides "all-risks" of direct physical loss or damage. The policy excludes, among other causes of loss, unexplained loss or mysterious disappearance and theft from any transporting conveyance while unattended, unless the vehicle is equipped with a fully enclosed and securely locked metal body or compartment and theft results from forcible entry evidenced by visible marks or if the entire transporting conveyance is stolen. These exclusions do not apply while the insured property is in the custody of common or contract carriers. The "trick and device" exclusion is frequently found in this form. Often the policy may warrant alarms or other security devices on sales representatives' automobiles. The limit of liability is per sales representative, and there is generally a 100 percent coinsurance clause and a deductible in the policy. The territorial limit of the coverage is usually the forty-eight contiguous states of the United States, the District of Columbia, and Canada.

Valuable Papers and Records Form. This is a filed "all-risks" form covering written, printed, or otherwise inscribed documents and records including books, maps, films, drawings, abstracts, deeds, mortgages, and manuscripts (but not including money or securities). This coverage and the accounts receivable insurance described below are necessary because of the provision in property policies limiting recovery under those policies to the value of the blank paper or other blank media. In the case of the valuable papers coverage, certain items are irreplaceable (such as first edition PRO 82 texts), and they can be insured for an agreed amount of insurance. Usually, however, valuable papers and records insurance, like accounts receivable insurance, is needed to protect the insured against the *consequences* of loss of or damage to the subject of insurance and particularly the need to recreate the records so they can be used. Coverage for valuable papers and records generally is written on a blanket basis covering their actual cash value. Coverage is provided for designated locations but applies to valuable papers and records being conveyed outside the premises or at other locations for up to 10 percent of the amount of insurance or $5,000, whichever is less. This limited transit and other location coverage can be increased.

It is a condition of the policy that coverage applies only while the subject of insurance is in described receptacles (such as a safe, vault or filing cabinet) when the premises are not open for business. Receptacles are listed in the policy showing the kind, name of maker, "Class" of "Hour Exposure" of label, and the name of the issuer of the label.

The policy does not apply to loss from war or nuclear exposures, dishonesty of the insured, directly resulting from errors or omissions in processing or copying or to loss due to electrical or magnetic injury, or disturbance or erasure of electronic recordings (except by lightning), and coverage is excluded for property held as samples or for sale.

Accounts Receivable Form. This filed form provides "all-risks" insurance on either a reporting or nonreporting basis to cover the cost of (1) reconstructing records of accounts receivable, (2) actual loss due to the inability to collect sums due as a direct result of insured loss of or damage to such records, (3) interest costs incurred because of the inability to collect accounts, and (4) extra collection expenses because of the loss. Like the valuable papers and records form, the coverage is principally on the premises of the insured subject to storage in specified receptacles.

In addition to the exclusions of war, nuclear damage and dishonesty losses, the policy excludes losses due to bookkeeping, accounting, or billing errors or omissions, electrical or magnetic injury, disturbance or erasure of electronic recordings (except by lightning), or loss due to alteration, falsification, manipulation, concealment, destruction, or disposal of records committed to conceal wrongful acts.

Physicians' and Surgeons' Equipment Floater. This filed policy covers medical, surgical, and dental equipment and instruments (including tools, materials, supplies, and scientific books) used by the insured and/or carried by the insured in the medical or dental profession. The policy is "all-risks" but excludes radium, furniture, and fixtures. (Radium used for medical purposes can be insured separately using a radium floater, also a filed form.) The physicians' and surgeons' form can replace a contents policy by an endorsement extending it to cover the furniture and fixtures as well as tenants' improvements. An optional extension of coverage endorsement is available that provides off-premises coverage for furniture and fixtures up to $1,000, up to $1,000 extra expense coverage, $250 coverage on currency, money, and stamps, and up to $500 on the personal effects of the insured. Up to $500 is provided on valuable papers and other records.

Coverage is subject to an 80 percent coinsurance clause and is limited to the continental United States and Canada. Coverage can be on an actual cash value or replacement cost basis. The insurance is usually written on a blanket basis, but individual items can be scheduled—for example, the owned microscope needed in the operating room by a neurosurgeon.

Theatrical Floater. This filed form covers scenery, costumes, and theatrical properties on a named perils basis. The policy does not insure buildings, furniture, or other property not used in the production; any conveyances not actually used on the stage; jewelry (except costume jewelry); accounts, bills, currency, deeds, evidences of debt, documents, money, notes, securities; railroad or other tickets; or animals or property shipped via the Panama Canal, or to or from Alaska, Hawaii, or Puerto Rico.

The named perils basically include fire, extended coverage, theft, burglary and holdup, and transportation perils. Optional coverage is available for water damage, sprinkler leakage, strike, riot, vandalism and malicious mischief, and earthquake. Even breakage can be insured. Insurance is on an actual cash value basis subject to a 100 percent coinsurance clause.

Sign Floater. This filed line covers fluorescent, neon, automatic, or mechanical signs which are generally excluded in standard property forms. Coverage is on an "all-risks" basis. The policy does not insure against loss or damage caused by wear and tear or gradual deterioration; faulty manufacture, installation, or occasioned by the inherent character of the insured property; loss or damage caused by breakage during installation, repairing, or dismantling; nor breakage during transportation unless caused by fire, lightning, collision, derailment or overturning of a vehicle. Mechanical breakdown and loss or damage to electrical apparatus caused by electricity, other than lightning, unless fire ensues are excluded.

A deductible of 5 percent of the amount of the insurance on an item (but not less than $10 nor more than $100) is applicable. All signs must be scheduled with an amount of insurance shown for each item.

Electronic Data Processing Policy. This nonfiled "all-risks" policy is used to cover computers, word processors, and similar electronic equipment. It is a highly specialized kind of insurance that often involves very high values in a single location. In addition to coverage on the equipment (or "hardware"), the policy also insures the "media" (magnetic tapes or discs carrying data), extra expense and business interruption. In addition to covering the property of the insured, the policy covers property leased, rented to or under the control of the insured.

Insurance can be on a blanket or scheduled basis, and on an actual cash value or replacement cost basis. A coinsurance clause is usually found in the policy, and most policies are written with a deductible ranging from $100 for minicomputers to $50,000 or more on major computer installations. The policy may be endorsed to provide valuable papers and accounts receivable insurance for computer stored records. A "difference-in-conditions" insuring agreement is included in the data processing policy to insure the policyholder's liability to the owner of leased or rental equipment subject to all policy provisions.

Policy exclusions include damage due to mechanical failure, faulty construction, error in design unless fire or explosion ensues, dishonest, fraudulent, or criminal acts by any insured, and extremes of temperature unless directly resulting from physical damage to the data processing system's air conditioning facilities. Short circuit, blow-out, or other electrical disturbance, other than lightning, within electrical apparatus except for ensuing fire or explosion is excluded, as is electrical or magnetic injury and disturbance to or erasure of electronic recordings.

Miscellaneous Floaters. Filed commercial floaters are available on cameras, film (exposed), musical instruments and fine arts. These are "all-risks" contracts designed for professionals in those areas and businesses owning such property. The items are generally scheduled and insured for a specific limit of insurance.

Dealers Policies

According to the Nation-Wide Marine Definition, most inland marine policies cover transit exposures or property with a high degree of mobility. Except for a few forms, like the electronic data processing policy, coverages reviewed to this point have primarily been for exposures away from the insured's locations. This section of the chapter, however, is devoted to "block" policies designed to insure stocks of merchandise on the premises of certain policyholders.

Lloyd's of London started writing a broad policy for jewelers around the beginning of the twentieth century in response to demands for fire and crime perils in a single contract. The policy was called the "jewelers' block." The word "block" probably is derived from the

French "en bloc," which means "all together." The jewelers' block set a precedent for other dealers policies, and special contracts were designed for furriers, camera stores, musical instrument dealers, and equipment dealers.

Jewelers' Block   This filed line is an "all-risks" nonreporting policy written for jewelry retailers, wholesalers, pawnbrokers and manufacturers. Jewelry concessions in department stores can be covered with minor modifications. Ineligible exposures include (1) bullion and precious metal dealers, (2) industrial diamond dealers, and (3) fine arts and antique dealers, unless more than 5 percent to 10 percent of their activities involve jewelry. Auctioneers and watch repairers not otherwise engaged in the jewelry trade are not eligible for the jewelers' block. Jewelry on exhibition also is not eligible.

Before prospecting for jewelers' block business, the producer should check with underwriters to determine if the policy is available. In urban areas, resort areas, or other areas of high crime, jewelers' blocks are generally written by specialty insurers. Even when the coverage is written by standard insurers, coverage may be difficult to place because of security requirements or because the underwriters lack sufficient experience with the coverage to provide the necessary service. Dealers in loose diamonds are most difficult to place with standard insurers.

Perils Insured and Excluded.   The policy covers "all-risks" of loss or damage. In addition to the usual war and nuclear damage exclusions, the policy generally eliminates coverage for loss from dishonest acts of the insured and the insured's employees or on the part of any person to whom the property is delivered or entrusted. Also excluded are loss or damage caused by delay, loss of market, gradual deterioration, insects, vermin, inherent vice, corrosion, rust, dampness of atmosphere, freezing or extremes of temperature, insufficient or defective packing, or damage sustained while the property is being processed. Loss or damage occurring in transit to shipments by mail is not covered unless the mail is registered first-class. To be covered, shipments by railway express or air express must be properly declared and in some cases sealed with wax, lead, or another approved method. The policy does not cover any shortage in goods claimed when a package is received by the consignee in apparent good order with seals unbroken, nor for loss when sent "C.O.D." with the privilege of inspection by the consignee before delivery. Unexplained loss, mysterious disappearance, or loss or shortage disclosed on taking inventory are excluded, as is breakage except when caused by certain named perils. No coverage is provided when the property is being modeled or worn socially.

Coverage is excluded for property while in or upon any automobile, motorcycle, or any other vehicle unless, at the time the loss occurs, there is a person present whose sole duty is to attend the vehicle. This exclusion does not apply while the property is in the custody of a carrier or the Post Office. Earthquake and flood are excluded but can be covered by endorsement.

Property Insured and Excluded. The policy covers the insured's property, the property of others who are not dealers in such property, and the insured's legal liability for property of others engaged in the jewelry trade or the insured's interest in property because of money actually advanced to other jewelers. The property insured includes pearls, precious and semi-precious stones, jewels, jewelry, watches and watch movements, gold, silver, platinum, other precious metals, alloys, and stock usual to the conduct of the insured's business. It is possible to exclude nonjewelry property of department stores, pawnbrokers, and others, and the producer would generally want to do so, because coverage on other property could be arranged at lower premiums on other policy forms.

The policy can be extended to include the following types of property within the premises of the insured: patterns, molds, models, and dies; furniture, fixtures, tools, machinery and fittings; and tenants improvements. Money locked in safes or vaults can be covered by endorsement, as can the exposure of property at exhibitions. Property in show windows and outside showcases may also be added to the basic policy. Property sold on an installment plan is excluded after the goods leave the insured's custody. If the insured owns the building or is legally responsible for damage to the structure, the policy will pay for building damage caused by theft in an amount up to 10 percent of the limit of liability.

Loss adjustment under the policy is on an actual cash value basis at the time of loss. Any antique or historical value attached to the property is excluded from the estimate of loss or damage.

The jewelers' block has separate limits of liability for property. Only coverage A (property on premises) is mandatory.

Jewelers' Block Limitations of Liability

The maximum liability of the Company resulting from any one loss, disaster or casualty is limited to

(A) $ in respect of property at the Insured's premises as described herein;

(B) $ in respect of property which is (1) in transit by first class registered mail, or railway express (subject to the stipulations of Exclusion (E) of Section 5), or by armored car service; (2) deposited in the safe or vault of a bank or safe deposit company; (3) in the custody of a dealer in property of the kind insured hereunder not employed by or associated with the Insured, but property deposited for safe keeping with such a dealer by the Insured or its authorized representatives while traveling is subject to the limit expressed in Clause E of this Section;

(C) $ in respect of shipments in transit by first class registered air mail or air express (subject to the stipulations of Exclusion (E) of Section 5) sent to any one addressee at any one address during any one day;

(D) $ in respect of shipments in transit by customer parcel delivery service and the parcel transportation service or railroads, waterborne or air carriers and passenger bus lines (subject to the stipulations of Exclusion (E) of Section 5);

(E) $ in respect of property elsewhere and not included in Clauses (A), (B), (C) and (D) above or otherwise limited herein.

Territorial Limits. The policy covers while the property is within or in transit between the states of the United States, District of Columbia, Puerto Rico, and Canada; however, territorial limits can be extended at the discretion of the underwriter.

Other Policy Conditions. Other policy conditions reflect the unique aspects of a jeweler's operations.

DEDUCTIBLES. A jewelers' block may be issued with a $500, $1,000, $2,500, $5,000, or $10,000 or higher deductible. A substantial deductible is available for registered mail or registered air mail shipments.

INVENTORY AND PROTECTIVE DEVICES. The insured must maintain a detailed and itemized inventory. Further, the insured must maintain the guards and other protective devices as described in the policy proposal (application) insofar as is within the insured's control during the policy period.

CONCEALMENT OR MISREPRESENTATION. The entire policy is void if, whether before or after a loss, the insured has concealed or misrepresented any material fact or circumstance concerning the insurance. For this reason, producers inexperienced in completing the jewelers' block proposal should exercise extreme care to be certain the proposal form is accurate in every detail.

POLICY LIMITS REDUCTION. The amount of insurance in the jewelers' block is reduced by the amount of any loss. For an additional premium, however, the policy can be endorsed to provide for the return of the unearned premium at the date of loss. This "premium insurance" allows the insured to "pay" the additional premium necessary to reinstate the policy limit.

LOSS ADJUSTMENT. When a loss involves the property of others, the insurance company reserves the right to adjust the loss with the owner of the property. The insurer agrees to conduct and control the defense on behalf of the named insured if legal proceedings are taken to enforce a claim for loss or damage to property of others.

Furriers' Block This filed policy follows the jewelers' block closely. The furriers' block is an "all-risks," nonreporting policy. The policy is used to insure merchants and dealers whose property consists principally of furs, fur garments, and garments trimmed with fur, but not including those firms that deal exclusively in raw or dressed skins or those who manufacture principally for the fur trade. A fur concession in a department store can be covered with minor policy modifications.

Like jewelers, furriers may buy coverage which applies away from the premises, and may include furniture, fixtures, tenants improvements, machinery, and tools. The property of others is insured for the furrier's legal liability if owned by another furrier, or on a direct damage basis if in the insured's possession for repair or alteration. Property of others accepted for storage is excluded as the furriers' customers form is specifically designed to cover that exposure.

The furriers' block excludes coverage while the property is being worn by the insured, any family member, relative, or friend, but unlike the jewelers' block it does cover property while being modeled on the premises of the insured or another dealer. The "insect, vermin" exclusion is quite important in this policy since damage to furs from these causes is a major exposure faced by the insured. Loss or damage occurring at the insured's premises is excluded if caused by flood. The flood exclusions may be removed at the discretion of the underwriter.

The proposal (application) form *is not* attached to the policy, but the insured, as a condition of coverage, must (within the insured's control) maintain protection safeguards or the coverage is suspended for the unprotected period.

The policy pays for unsold merchandise on an actual cash value basis. On sold but not delivered property the policy pays the net selling price of the insured after all allowances and discounts. On property of others, the policy pays the amount for which the insured is legally liable (not exceeding the actual cash value) including labor performed and materials expended on the property up to the time of the loss.

The policy limit is reduced by each claim, but the amount may be reinstated with a pro rata additonal premium charged to the insured.

Camera and Musical Instrument Dealers This is a filed, "all-risks" policy for any camera or musical instrument dealer (but not manufacturers) covering property of the insured including "breakage" of photographic lenses. Accounts, bills, deeds, evidences of debt, money, notes, and securities are excluded. Furniture, fixtures, tools, and machinery may be added by endorsement. The policy can be written on a reporting or nonreporting form with a full reporting clause applying to the former and an 80 percent coinsurance clause to the latter. Policy provisions follow the furriers' block form closely. The policy excludes earthquake and flood but these perils can often be bought back.

Equipment Dealers   This is a filed, "all-risks" form for dealers in construction equipment, mobile equipment (other than automobiles, watercraft, or aircraft), and agricultural equipment. Manufacturers of such equipment are not eligible for the policy. The policy can be written on a reporting or nonreporting basis. The policy can be written as a continuous policy subject to a full reporting provision. An 80 percent coinsurance clause is required when the policy is nonreporting. In addition to inventory, the policy may cover furniture and fixtures, tenants' improvements, and machinery, tools, and signs by endorsement. Flood (except in transit) is an excluded peril which can be added for an additional premium. The limits apply on premises, in transit, and elsewhere within the territorial limits of the forty-eight contiguous states of the United States, the District of Columbia, Canada, and within Hawaii.

Fine Arts Dealers   This is a nonfiled form for dealers in fine arts and antiques. It is an "all-risks" contract covering property on premises, while in transit, or while elsewhere within the territorial limits of the policy. This form can be issued on an annual or continuous basis subject to reporting of values. Unique exclusions include loss or damage caused by or resulting from insufficient or defective packaging, and loss or damage caused by breakage of articles of a fragile or brittle nature unless caused by certain named perils.

Floor Plan Merchandise   This is a filed form providing "all-risks" insurance for the single interest of the dealer or lending institution or the dual interest of both. Single interest coverage can insure for the value of the dealers' payments due or the amount of the lending institution's outstanding balances. Dual interest coverage insures the full actual cash value of the floored merchandise. It is written on a monthly reporting basis to cover merchandise in the possession of the dealer subject to a finance plan under which the dealer borrows money from a lending institution to buy the merchandise-subject of insurance. Such merchandise must be specifically identifiable (like an appliance or machine with a serial number) as encumbered to the bank or lending institution. The dealer's right to sell or otherwise dispose of such merchandise must be conditioned upon its being released from encumbrance by the lending institution. Although excluded, flood can be insured for an additional premium. Also excluded is loss to electrical appliances from electrical injury except for ensuing fire, mechanical breakdown, glass breakage (except if caused by named perils), and damage from weather to property left in the open except while in transit. The policy contains a boiler explosion exclusion.

Installment Sales Floater   This nonfiled form can be written on an "all-risks" or named perils basis (fire, extended coverage perils, flood, earthquake, and limited transit perils). The insurance is designed to be either a single or dual interest policy to insure goods sold on time payment plans. The policy may cover property loaned, rented, leased, out on approval or demonstration, and property on premises for repair. When the policy is issued on a dual interest form, a certificate of insurance is issued by the insured to the purchaser of merchandise on conditional sales contracts, deferred payment plans, or similar plans. Insurance begins at the time the merchandise passes into the shipping room of the insured for packing and delivery, or as designated in a certificate issued to the buyer. The insurance for the interest of the seller terminates when (1) the certificate expires, (2) when the amount owed is paid, or (3) when the property is repossessed or surrendered to the named insured. The policy is written on a monthly reporting form with a full reporting clause. Exclusions include loss or damage caused by dishonesty of the insured *or the purchaser*, breakage of fragile articles (except by named perils), mechanical breakdown, electrical injury, and boiler explosion. Property is not covered for more than ten days at any one time while being repaired by the insured, nor while it is shipped by mail.

Checkpoints

1. What is a bailment, and what are the responsibilities of the bailee to the bailor?
2. List three bailees' customers forms and their prospects.
3. List three floater forms and their prospects.
4. List three dealers forms and their prospects.

Instrumentalities of Transportation and Communication

Inland marine underwriters have customarily provided insurance not only on goods in transit, but also on certain types of property used in transportation and communications. The rolling stock of railroads is insured on inland marine forms. Bridges, tunnels, pipelines, power transmission lines, telephone and telegraph lines, and radio and television transmission equipment are all examples of property which can be insured on inland marine forms under the "communications" heading.

Rolling Stock   This filed policy form can be either on an "all-risks" basis or against the named perils of fire, collision, derailment, overturn, strikes, and riots. Coverage is available, scheduled or unscheduled, on all rolling stock owned in whole or in part by or leased to a railroad company. Locomotives and all other rolling stock not owned by a railroad, including trial, demonstration, and exhibition equipment, can be insured. Usually policies are issued subject to a percentage deductible based on 80 percent of the actual cash value of the property insured. Typical percentage deductibles may be 1 percent, 2 percent, 5 percent, or 10 percent per unit. Policies are written to pay losses on an actual cash value basis or using a valuation method established by the Association of American Railroads.

Bridge Property Damage Form   This filed form covers damage to vehicular or pedestrian bridges, elevated highways, and vehicular tunnels on an "all-risks" basis. A builder's risk form is available to provide coverage during construction on either an "all-risks" or named perils basis. The policy covers for direct damage to the subject of insurance with a customary deductible of 1 percent of the value insured. Other percentage deductibles are available. A special deductible for earthquake damage may be written. The policy can be extended to cover loss of revenues by using the "use and occupancy" form. The time element coverage excludes recovery of revenues for the first seven days of partial or total suspension of operation or may exclude recovery for the first fourteen, twenty-one, or thirty days of suspended operations. Optional coverage is available for debris removal either by extending the basic policy or by adding a specific amount of insurance. Subject to an additional premium, the debris removal coverage can be broadened to apply even if removal is not required by law or ordinance. Recovery is on an actual cash value basis but can be endorsed for replacement cost for steel and concrete structures. The policy contains an 80 percent coinsurance clause which can be waived by a coinsurance compliance endorsement when a statement of values determined by a qualified engineer and signed by the insured is submitted. Special exclusions include damage from strikes, lock-outs, labor disturbances, riots, civil commotion, sabotage, vandalism or malicious mischief, or damage caused by failure of the insured to keep and maintain the property in "a thorough state of repair." The policy is void if the design or construction of the property is materially altered or changed. The insurer is not liable for any increased cost of repairs or reconstruction by reason of any law, ordinance, regulation, permit, or license regulating construction or repair of the property. The amount of insurance is reduced by the amount of loss and may be reinstated by payment of an additional premium.

Instrumentalities of Communication Nonfiled policies are available to cover the property exposures of a commercial radio or television broadcaster including cable television companies. Typical policies cover radio and television transmission equipment on an "all-risks" basis including earthquake. Coverage for mobile van equipment and for the van itself is often available in the same policy. Broad coverage is written for antennas and towers including collapse from almost any cause. The policies often cover transit and off-premises exposures and many will also include business interruption insurance against loss of receipts caused by damage to the insured property or to the property of public utilities or communications services. Some unusual provisions might include coverage for tuning or retuning of towers as a result of damage, for electrical disturbances originating away from the insured's premises, or for tower damage while being worked on. Theft damage to buildings may be covered as well as personal property in the care, custody, or control of the insured. A coinsurance clause is common, and substantial deductibles may be required.

Writing Manuscript Policies

A manuscript policy, in contrast to a preprinted policy, is generally specially written for the insured by the producer or in negotiation with the underwriter. In the case of ambiguous language in a manuscript policy, the insured may not be protected by the legal doctrine of adhesion. A court of law reviewing ambiguous wording in a manuscript policy is likely to place the insured and the insurer on equal footing. Because of this shift in the legal position of the insured, a producer must take the utmost care when writing manuscript policies, and in many cases, it may be necessary to have the policy written or reviewed by an attorney.

Most producers start the process of manuscripting by analyzing existing policy forms and using the wording of the standard forms as much as possible. The intent of most manuscript policies is to broaden coverage beyond that available on filed forms or to tailor a policy for a particular exposure. In either event, the producer must be certain that the wording is appropriate and that no provisions have been inadvertently omitted or restricted. Some inland marine underwriters are comfortable with manuscript forms because many of the contracts they use are nonfiled or nonstandard. Other underwriters are noticeably more reluctant to modify standard forms. The producer attempting to place a manuscript form must be prepared to satisfy the underwriter that the broadened policy can be priced adequately to cover the exposures of the insured. The more information provided to the underwriter, the better the position of the producer in negotiating with the underwriter. The producer who can successfully negotiate manuscript forms for a client has a distinct sales advantage. Other producers may not be able to match the coverage or the price. The Appendix to the chapter is a comparison of a contractors equipment form to be attached to a preprinted inland marine backer or jacket and offers a broader manuscript alternative.

Inland Marine Forms in Package Policies

This chapter has reviewed the inland marine policies as if they existed in isolation. In fact, inland marine forms have had a great influence on property policies and on package policies in particular. Many of the property forms now available are "all-risks"—covering even such immovable objects as buildings—as a result of the inland marine "all-risks" tradition. Further, with the refinement of package policies, inland marine insurance has been integrated with other coverages. For example, many package property forms covering personal property provide extensions of coverage off-premises, in transit, or in the custody of sales representatives. In the SMP Program (Chapter 12) many of the filed, mono-line inland marine forms have been adapted and renumbered so they have counterparts specially tailored to the package concept. Signs, accounts receivable, and valuable papers and records are just a few inland marine subjects of insurance which have package forms. Because of the growing importance of package policies to insurers, it is often the package underwriter with whom the producer will be placing inland marine insurance. In smaller offices, many insurance companies have now combined the underwriting of fire coverages, inland marine insurance, and packages into one department. In larger offices or at a regional level, however, insurers have underwriters who specialize in the inland marine lines. It is to these specialists that the producer should turn for assistance.

Checkpoints

1. What are instrumentalities of transportation and communication?
2. Describe coverage for one instrumentality of transportation and one for communication.
3. Describe the legal doctrine of adhesion as it may apply to manuscripting insurance policies.

CASE STUDIES

J&T Appliances

J&T sells, installs, and services appliances from a store location. For the purposes of analyzing the exposures to be treated by inland marine insurance, the operation can be divided into a retail store and a service organization.

Retail Store   This is a relatively small store, so there is no need for many of the inland marine forms which might be required by a larger organization. For example, J&T does not need coverage on electronic data processing equipment. Further, J&T is not eligible for a filed dealers form to cover the inventory, so merchandise will probably be insured by the property portion of a package policy. The case study is not clear as to whether J&T has any merchandise on a floor plan loan. Often appliance dealers do borrow money in this way, and if this is the case with J&T, that merchandise could be insured usng a floor plan floater, although with such a small exposure, the standard package policy might be more practical. It is not clear whether J&T makes installment sales. If so, the appliances in customers' homes could be insured until they are paid for by an installment floater to cover either just J&T's interest in the items, or the dual interest of J&T and the customer.

J&T does have an identified accounts receivable exposure. The fact that records are stored in a safe will reduce the cost of the accounts receivable floater, but does not reduce the need for the coverage. A good risk management alternative would be to have duplicate records stored off-premises, but some business owners find this impractical. J&T may also have a valuable papers and records exposure, but the exposure is likely limited to inventory records. The usual extension in a package granting $500 or $1,000 valuable papers coverage ought to be sufficient, but the producer must further investigate this exposure.

J&T probably has a neon or electric sign which could be insured on a sign floater if it is not included as "property" under the package policy. The producer will need to determine the value of the sign and whether it can be covered without a separate floater. J&T does have a transportation exposure. The case study indicates no exposure for J&T on incoming merchandise, but the producer ought to investigate this completely. Even if the goods are being shipped "F.O.B. J&T's location," what actually happens if the appliances are not delivered or are damaged in transit? Has J&T paid the manufacturer? If so, how does J&T recover the value of loss? In any event, J&T may want to insure outgoing shipments on their own vehicles using an owner's goods on owner's vehicles form. The maximum exposure is $3,000 based on selling price.

Service Organization J&T has a number of exposures for which inland marine insurance is available away from the premises. An installation floater and a tool floater may be required to cover activities at customers' homes. J&T needs a bailees' customers form to cover the $6,000 of customers' television sets on premises for repair (if coverage for the property of others is not included in the package policy).

John Gale, M.D.

Dr. Gale's contents are eligible to be covered by a physicians' and surgeons' equipment floater. That policy can cover not only Dr. Gale's medical instruments, but also can be extended to cover the $60,000 in furniture, fixtures, and supplies at replacement cost. The floater can also be extended to cover some property off-premises since many surgeons carry certain of their own medical instruments. The floater can provide limited coverage on money and stamps on-premises, and even extra expense insurance or valuable papers and records coverage too. The producer will have to obtain from Dr. Gale an estimate of the cost to reproduce patient files and insure that amount as valuable papers and records. The accounts receivable can be insured on a nonreporting form since the values are low and do not fluctuate. The limit ought to be in excess of the $20,000 estimate of outstanding balances just to be certain coverage is adequate.

Dr. Gale's farming activities lend themselves to certain inland marine coverages. The Black Angus cattle valued at $200,000 can be insured on a livestock floater. It is possible that Dr. Gale would prefer complete animal mortality insurance on some or all of the herd. The farm machinery valued at $35,000 can be insured on an agricultural equipment floater.

R.P. Davis, Contractor

This firm seems to be engaged in mostly new contruction rather than renovation, so a builders' risk form will be required to cover work in progress. Davis can elect a named perils builders' risk fire policy or an "all-risks" inland marine form. The producer will need to offer both alternatives. Davis may need an installation floater if specialized jobs require one. The values of the mobile equipment, tools, and other property eligible to be insured on a contractors equipment floater require refinement by the producer to determine exactly how much should be insured as mobile equipment on inland marine forms and how much as office or shop equipment on other property forms. The transportation exposure can be covered under "all-risks" builders risk policy in most cases. Since the contractors equipment floater and the installation floater both exclude coverage for valuable papers and records, Davis will need a valuable papers and records floater to insure the $15,000 in plans and specifications if they are not duplicated and kept elsewhere.

Coverage is available on the accounts receivable records which run as high as $200,000 in value. However, since there are only a few large accounts, Davis may prefer not to insure the exposure and rather to keep duplicate records at another location. Many contractors have computers which they use to keep track of inventory accounts receivable and to bid and control jobs. If Davis has an in-house computer facility, an electonic data processing policy is in order.

Premier Door and Window Company, Inc.

This manufacturer has a number of exposures which can be treated with inland marine insurance. Transportation by company trucks seems to be a major activity, and Premier will need a transportation floater or a motor truck cargo policy. The limits should be adequate to include the possibility of more than one $15,000 load being lost in a single occurrence. Insurance on the overseas sales will need to be coordinated between the inland marine coverage and the ocean cargo policy (it might be best to have the ocean cargo policy begin at Premier's location so that the entire transportation exposure on these shipments is under one policy). Premier takes delivery of materials and supplies "F.O.B." Premier's locations, but the producer should verify the exposure carefully to be certain there is no exposure for Premier. Outgoing shipments appear to be all on owned vehicles, but the producer will need to verify this and then arrange the proper transit coverage.

The accounts receivable exposure can be covered by a reporting form with a limit of $600,000. Premier may also have valuable papers, like plans or inventory data, which could insured. Further, a company the size of Premier may have a computer, and that exposure can be insured on the electronic data processing policy. If work is done away from the premises (which does not appear likely), a processors floater could be used to cover property at the locations of contractors. Premier would perhaps also have an exposure for loss of or damage to patterns or dies at the contractors' locations and might need a pattern floater as well. A physical inspection would reveal whether Premier has a neon or electrical sign to be insured.

Appendix

A comparison of a filed contractors equipment form with an actual manuscript form used by a brokerage firm.

Insurer's Form

CONTRACTORS EQUIPMENT FORM
(All Risks)
(To be attached to Inland Marine Policy)

1 PROPERTY INSURED AND LIMITS OF LIABILITY

a This policy insures the following described property for not exceeding the amount set opposite each of the articles described.

b This Company shall not be liable for more than $_____ in any one disaster, either in the case of partial or total loss or salvage, or any other cost and expense or all combined.

c If this policy insures tools or miscellaneous items on a blanket basis, this Company shall be liable in any event for loss or damage for more than $_____ per tool or item.

Description of Property	Manufacturer	Identifying Marks and Nos.	Amount of Insurance
_____	_____	_____	_____

Producer's Alternative

ALL RISK EQUIPMENT FLOATER
PROPERTY COVERED:

This policy covers mobile machinery and equipment, tools, supplies, portable buildings, temporary buildings, sheds, portable office equipment, radio equipment and other property of a similar nature usual or incidental to the business of the Assured, property the Assured is legally liable or has assumed liability for as per schedule to be furnished to the Company.

ADDITIONAL PROPERTY COVERED:

The policy also covers additional or substitute equipment of a similar nature intended for similar use, the property of the Assured or the property of others for which the Assured is legally liable or has assumed liability including employees' personal effects for which the Assured is legally or contractually liable.

LIMITS OF LIABILITY:

The limit of liability under this policy is $_____for any one loss or occurrence.

Insurer's Form

2 THIS POLICY INSURES AGAINST:

All risks of direct physical loss of or damage to the property covered from any external cause except as excluded elsewhere in this policy.

Producer's Alternative

PERILS INSURED:

This policy insures against all risks of physical loss or damage hereinafter provided and expense incidental thereto, including General Average, salvage and debris removal costs.

Insurer's Form

3 COINSURANCE CLAUSE

In no event shall this Company be liable for a greater proportion of any loss than the sum insured bears to _____% of the actual cash value of the property described herein at the time such loss shall happen. If the insurance under this policy is divided into two or more items, the foregoing shall apply to each item separately.

Producer's Alternative

PREMIUM REPORTS AND VALUE:

(1) Without restricting the automatic and blanket coverage afforded by this policy, the Assured agrees to report any additions or deletions annually and if there is a change of more than 5% in total value a premium adjustment will be based on 50% of the rate shown in the policy. This insurance shall not be prejudiced by failure to submit reports, by unintentional delays or errors in making reports providing such omissions or errors are reported when the Assured becomes aware of any omission or error. This reporting clause pertains only to owned equipment.

(2) A corrected schedule shall be submitted on the annual anniversary date.

(3) The Miscellaneous Item on the Schedule includes values of the described miscellaneous items and also the estimated values of property of others for which the Assured is responsible.

Insurer's Form

4 DEDUCTIBLE CLAUSE

All claims for loss, damage or expense arising out of any one occurrence shall be adjusted as one claim, and from the amount of such adjusted claim there shall be deducted the sum of $_____.

Producer's Alternative

DEDUCTIBLE:

It is understood and agreed that in consideration of the premium charged, the sum of $_____ will be deducted from each and every adjusted occurrence caused by:

_____

_____

Insurer's Form

5 TERRITORIAL LIMITS

This policy insures within the limits of 48 contiguous states of the United States, the District of Columbia, Alaska and Canada.

Producer's Alternative

TERRITORIAL LIMITS:

This policy covers within the limits of the United States and Canada and in transit.

Insurer's Form

6 THIS POLICY DOES NOT COVER:

a Loss or damage to automobiles or similar conveyances, plans, blue prints, designs or specifications or to underground property or property while located underground;

b Loss or damage to any property which has become a permanent part of any structure.

7 THIS POLICY DOES NOT INSURE AGAINST:

a Loss or damage occasioned by the weight of a load exceeding the registered lifting or supporting capacity of the machine or by the collision of the boom with any part of the machine or other objects;

b Wear and tear, gradual deterioration, inherent vice, or obsolescence; breakage, rust or corrosion, unless the same be the direct result of fire, lightning, explosion, cyclone, tornado, windstorm, flood, earthquake, collision, derailment or overturn of conveyance, malicious damage or aircraft damage;

c Loss or damage to property while actually being worked upon and directly resulting therefrom, or loss by structural or mechanical failure or breakdown, unless loss by fire or explosion not otherwise excluded ensues, and then the Company shall be liable for only such ensuing loss;

d Loss of market, delay or loss of use however caused;

e Loss or damage caused by misappropriation, secretion, conversion, infidelity or any dishonest act on the part of the insured, his employees or persons to whom the insured property may be entrusted;

f Unexplained loss or mysterious disappearance or loss or shortage disclosed upon taking inventory;

g Loss or damage to electrical motors, appliances or devices (including wiring) caused by artificial electric current unless fire ensues, and if fire does ensue, then this Company shall be liable only for its proportion of loss caused by such ensuing fire;

h Loss or damage caused directly or indirectly by:

1 hostile or warlike action in time of peace or war, including action in hindering, combating or defending against an actual, impending or expected attack, (a) by any government or sovereign power (de jure or de facto), or by any authority maintaining or using military, naval or air forces; or (b) by military, naval or air forces; or (c) by an agent of any government, power, authority or forces;

2 any weapon of war employing atomic fission or radioactive force whether in time of peace or war;

3 insurrection, rebellion, revolution, civil war, usurped power, or action taken by governmental authority in hindering, combating or defending against such an occurrence, seizure or destruction under quarantine or customs regulations, confiscation by order of any government of public authority, or risks of contraband or illegal transportation or trade;

i Loss or damage caused directly or indirectly by nuclear reaction or radioactive contamination, all whether controlled or uncontrolled, and whether such loss be direct or indirect, proximate or remote, or be in whole or in part caused by, contributed to, or aggravated by the peril(s) insured against in this policy; however, subject to the foregoing and all provisions of this policy, direct loss by fire resulting from nuclear reaction or nuclear radiation or radioactive contamination is insured against by this policy.

Producer's Alternative

PERILS EXCLUDED:

This policy does not insure against loss or damage:

(1) Caused by short circuit or other electrical disturbance within any electrically equipped property unless fire ensues, and then for such loss or damage caused by fire only.

(2) By gradual deterioration, corrosion, rust, dampness of atmosphere, freezing or extremes of temperature or wear and tear, unless the same be the direct result of other loss covered by this policy.

(3) Caused by or resulting from:
    (a) hostile or warlike action in time of peace or war, including action in hindering, combating or defending against an actual, impending or expected attack
        (i) by any government or sovereign power (de jure or de facto) or by any authority maintaining or using military, naval or air forces; or
        (ii) by military, naval or air forces; or
        (iii) by any agent of any such government, power, authority or forces
    (b) any weapon of war employing atomic fission or radioactive force whether in time of peace or war
    (c) insurrection, rebellion, civil war, usurped power or action taken by government authority in hindering, combating or defending against such an occurrence, seizure or destruction under quarantine or Customs regulations, confiscation by order of any government or public authority, or risks of contraband or illegal transportation or trade.

(4) Due to disappearance of property which is conclusively proved to have been caused by infidelity of any of the Assured's employees.

(5) Due to loss of use except as provided in clause #12

(6) Caused by nuclear reaction or nuclear radiation or radioactive contamination, all whether controlled or uncontrolled, and whether such loss be direct or indirect, proximate or remote, or be in whole or in part caused by, contributed to, or aggravated by the perils insured against in this policy; however subject to the foregoing and all provisions of this policy, direct loss by fire resulting from nuclear

reaction or nuclear radiation or radioactive contamination is insured against by this policy.

Insurer's Form

8 ADDITIONALLY ACQUIRED PROPERTY

In consideration of the agreement by the Insured (1) to report additional property of the kind insured hereunder, acquired by the Insured subsequent to the attachment date of this policy, within thirty (30) days from the date acquired and (2) to pay full premium thereon from the date acquired at pro rata of the current rates of the Company for such insurance, this policy covers on each separate class of such additionally acquired property for not exceeding 25%, or $10,000, whichever is the lesser, of the amount of insurance on such class exclusive of this provision. It is specifically understood and agreed by the Insured that this policy shall cease to cover such additionally acquired property if it is not reported to the Company within the stated thirty (30) day period.

This additional coverage does not apply to property of a class not already insured hereunder.

(See Producer Wording Above: "PREMIUM REPORTS AND VALUE")

Insurer's Form

9 OTHER INSURANCE

In case other valid and collectible insurance exists on any property hereby insured at the time and place of loss, the insurance under this policy shall be considererd as excess insurance and shall not apply or contribute to the payment of any loss until the amount of such other insurance shall have been exhausted; it being understood and agreed that under this policy the Insured is to be reimbursed to the extent of the difference between the amount collectible from such other insurance and the amount of actual loss otherwise collectible hereunder.

Producer's Alternative

OTHER INSURANCE:

The company shall not be liable for loss, if at any time of loss there is any other valid and collectible insurance which would attach if this insurance had not been effected, except that this insurance shall only apply as excess and in no event as contributing insurance, and then only after all other insurance has been exhausted.

Additional Producer Provisions

REPORT AND PROOF OF LOSS:

The Assured shall as soon as practicable report to this Company or its Agent every loss or damage which may become a claim under this policy, and shall also file a detailed sworn proof of loss with this Company or its Agent as soon as practical following determination of the loss.

RENTAL OR EXTRA EXPENSE REIMBURSEMENT:

In Consideration of the premium charged, it is understood and agreed that in event of loss or damage to equipment insured hereunder, caused by peril insured against, thereby preventing the necessary use of such equipment, by the insured in conjunction with normal operations, the Company agrees to reimburse the Assured for expense incurred for the rental of a substitute item of equipment of for additional expense in expediting repairs.

In the event it is necessary to rent substitute equipment this Company shall only be liable, under the provisions of this clause, for 75% of the bare rental costs, subject to a maximum of 10% of the value of such equipment.

In the event a rental or substitute item of equipment is not available, the Assured may apply up to 10% of the value of the lost or damaged items to any extra or expediting expenses as may be necessary.

Rental Reimbursement or Extra Expenses as provided under this clause shall not apply during the first forty-eight (48) hours after such loss or damage and shall terminate, regardless of expiration of the policy, on the date said loss or damaged equipment is replaced or repaired and is available for use by the Assured.

LOSS CLAUSE:

Any loss hereunder shall not reduce the amount of the policy.

VALUATION:

Property, as defined above, shall be insured at its actual cash value at the time of loss plus cost of General Average, salvage and debris removal.

SUBROGATION WAIVER:

The Company further agrees to waive all rights of subrogation against any subsidiary, affiliated or inter-related entity of the Assured, including partners of any joint venture in which the Assured is a member.

CANCELLATION:

Thirty days prior notice shall be mailed to the named Assured in the event of cancellation by the Company.

All clauses and conditions in printed portions of this policy in conflict with the terms of this special form are waived, expect provisions required by law to be inserted in the policy.

CHAPTER 6

Ocean Marine and Aviation Insurance*

INTRODUCTION

Ocean marine insurance is one of the oldest forms of insurance. It is used to insure ships sailing among the ports of the world and their cargo and is also used to insure ships and cargo sailing in intercoastal waterways between U.S. ports.

Few activities today do not depend in part on international trade. Few businesses do not use some equipment made overseas. Many firms, whether located in New York, Los Angeles, St. Louis, or Boise, also export products. Many businesses far from any seaport import or export products and have a need for ocean marine insurance. Even a small gift shop or a novelty manufacturer may be an importer or an exporter needing ocean marine insurance.

Insurance on oceangoing ships is specialized; many producers never become involved with insurance on a commercial vessel. Few, however, fail to become involved with cargo insurance for an importer or exporter. For these reasons, the ocean marine portion of this chapter

---

* Some of the material in this chapter was developed for and used in the UND 64 text, *Commercial Property and Multiple-Lines Underwriting*, by E. P. Hollingsworth, Jr., and Robert B. Holtom, and published by the Insurance Institute of America and the CPCU 3 text, *Commercial Property Risk Management and Insurance*, by William H. Rodda, James S. Trieschmann, and Bob A. Hedges, and published by the American Institute for Property and Liability Underwriters. Used with permission.

287

will concentrate on ocean marine cargo insurance and will deal only in passing with insurance on the ships themselves.

Ocean marine insurance tends to be *different* from other lines of insurance for two reasons. First, as ocean marine insurance is one of the oldest types of insurance, the terminology used in many marine insurance contracts sounds quaint to modern ears. Change of policy language has been resisted because the language has been tested over many years of use. A second reason ocean marine insurance is different is its international character. Coverages and practices affecting cargo throughout the world are difficult to change once established.

For the producer who chooses to specialize in this area, ocean marine insurance can provide a fascinating, challenging career. The language of ocean marine policies, dealing as it does with perils such as piracy and assailing thieves, conjures images of Peter Pan, Captain Hook, and Treasure Island. There is something adventurous about the perils faced and conquered by those who brave the seas. It is to be hoped that the producer will share some of this sense of adventure.

WHOM TO INSURE

When a bulk shipment of imported Scotch does not arrive at the bottler, many firms may be involved in the loss. The shipper may bear the loss; the loss may fall on the ship line, or carrier; or the loss may be borne by the bottler who purchased the shipment. Whether the entire ship and cargo were consumed by the sea, the cargo was hijacked, or the ship was burned, stranded, or exploded—the cargo did not arrive. Even ignoring human factors, more than the value of the ship and cargo may be involved in the loss. Ocean marine losses typically also involve a substantial loss of "freight" (shipping cost). The shipper or the importer-buyer may lose the value of any freight that has been paid; the carrier may lose the chance to collect any freight not paid. In addition, there may be a substantial delay before the cargo that did not arrive can be replaced with a second shipment.

This section of the chapter analyzes the situation with respect to the shipper, the carrier, and the importer in an attempt to provide guidelines regarding whom to insure.

In general, the parties having a need for ocean marine insurance on cargo are those who will suffer a loss if that cargo is damaged or destroyed. It should be apparent that this covers a broad range of parties. Many people, besides the owner of the cargo, benefit from its safe arrival or suffer from its loss, damage, or delay.

Insurable Interests of Owners

When ocean-going cargo is involved, the "legal" owner of that cargo is not always obvious. The key question to determine ownership is, "At what point does title to property pass from the seller to the buyer?" The point when title passes depends, in turn, on the terms of sale.

Terms of Sale The terms of sale indicate when, during a shipment, the title to the property passes from seller to buyer. They therefore indicate who has an insurable interest. They may also indicate who has the responsibility for the purchase of marine insurance.

There are six terms of sale. The six terms progressively indicate the seller's increasing need for transportation insurance. For example, in the first category, Ex Point of Origin, the *seller* does not need transportation coverage since the *buyer* has ownership during the transportation of the goods. As the terms of sale tend to lengthen the duration of the seller's responsibility, the need for insurance coverage for the seller increases.

Ex Point of Origin (as "Ex Factory," "Ex Warehouse," and so forth). These terms require the seller to place the goods at the disposal of the buyer at the specified point of origin on a specified date or within a fixed period. The buyer must then take delivery at the agreed place and bear all future costs and losses. The goods are a loss exposure of the buyer from the time the buyer is obligated to take delivery, even though delivery may not actually be made at that time. The *buyer* has the need to purchase insurance.

FOB (Free on Board). Here the seller is *required* to bear costs and charges and to assume loss exposures until the goods are loaded on board a named carrier at a named point. This might be on board a railroad car at an inland point of departure or on board ship at a port of shipment. Loss or damage to the shipment is borne by the *seller* until loaded at the point named and by the *buyer* after loading at that point. Insurance protection should be arranged accordingly. Actual transfer of interest is evidenced by the carrier's furnishing a bill of lading or other transportation receipt.

FOB sales terms, specifying named points beyond the seller's premises (for example, FOB vessel), commit the *seller* to the exposures of transit until the title passes to the buyer at the point specified. The *seller* should obviously insure the cargo to the FOB point. (In actual practice, however, FOB terms are often so loosely specified that it is not easily resolved whether the seller or the buyer is exposed to the chance of physical loss or damage.)

FAS (Free Along Side—as "FAS Vessel, Named Port of Shipment"). These sales terms require the seller to place goods alongside the vessel or on the dock designated by the buyer and to be responsible for loss or damage up to that point. Insurance for the ocean voyage is ordinarily placed by the *buyer*, but the *seller* should also protect himself or herself for losses prior to the transfer of title.

C&F (Cost & Freight), Named Point of Destination. Under these terms, the seller's price includes the cost of transportation to the named point but does not include the cost of insurance for the entire trip. Insurance under these terms is the responsibility of the *buyer*. The seller is responsible for loss or damage until the goods enter the custody of the ocean carrier or, if an on-board bill of lading (defined later) is required, when the goods are actually delivered on board. Here again the *seller* needs insurance protection to that point at which the seller's responsibility for loss or damage ceases.

CIF (Cost, Insurance and Freight), Named Point of Destination. Under these terms, the selling price includes the cost of the goods, marine insurance, and transportation charges to the named point of destination. The seller is responsible for loss or damage until the goods have been delivered to the point of destination which may be in a foreign country.

In CIF sales, the *seller* is obligated to provide and pay for marine insurance and provide war risk insurance as obtainable from insurers at the time of shipment, the cost of war risks insurance being borne by the buyer. The seller and buyer should be in clear agreement on this point since in time of war or crisis the cost of war risks insurance may change rapidly.

Ex Dock, Named Port of Importation. This term is more common to U.S. import than to export practice. The seller's price includes the cost of the goods and all additional charges necessary to put them on the dock at the named port of importation, with import duty paid. The *seller* is then obligated to provide and pay for marine insurance and, in the absence of specific agreement otherwise, war risks insurance. The seller is responsible for any loss or damage, or both, until the expiration of the free time allowed on the dock at the named port of importation. Otherwise the comments under CIF terms apply here as well.

Bills of Lading

The *bill of lading* serves two primary functions: (1) it is an acknowledgment by the carrier that the goods have been received for shipment in good condition; (2) it also serves as a contract of carriage indicating the entity the goods are shipped to (the consignee), the destination, usually the route over which the shipment is to travel, and also who is to pay the charges for carriage.

Straight Bill of Lading   This instructs the carrier to deliver the goods to the consignee. The consignee is presumed in this situation to have title to the property or a right to possession of the property. This type of bill of lading is used where the goods have been paid for by the consignee, or where there is an arrangement for credit directly between the shipper and consignee, or where the shipper and the consignee represent the same interest (e.g., different offices of the same company).

A form of the straight bill of lading, called the "released bill of lading," reduces the carrier's liability to a specific amount. Sometimes underwriters refer to a straight bill of lading as one without such a release. Producers should be careful of terminology used by underwriters in insuring under "straight bills of lading."

Order Bill of Lading   This is the usual document for overseas shipments. In an "order" bill, the carrier is instructed to deliver the property to "the order of" the named consignee. This allows the order bill to be used as evidence of right to receive the goods.

Nonownership Insurable Interests

The previous sections dealt with insurable interests created by the ownership of property transported on an oceangoing vessel. In certain situations, the seller has an insurable interest even when title has passed to the buyer. In these situations, the seller has a need for insurance despite the fact that the seller does not legally own the property. For example, in some trades, the seller usually obtains insurance for the buyer as a matter of custom.

The seller certainly has a financial interest in the cargo until payment has been received. Under these circumstances, it is particularly desirable for the seller's interest to be protected by purchasing insurance. (Even if the buyer is *obligated* by the contract to make a payment, the buyer may have little incentive to pay for merchandise at the bottom of the ocean.)

There are four basic methods by which payment is made for goods purchased in international commerce.

Cash in Advance   This rather harsh method generally is required only when the prospective customer is not well known to the shipper or when the order involves custom manufacture of a special type of goods without a ready market. In a transaction of this kind on FOB terms, the exporting manufacturer, having been paid in advance, has no interest in the goods once they are shipped. Similarly, some goods are sold on terms that provide for cash payment against the shipping documents at time of shipment.

Open Account Open account is the opposite of the cash-in-advance transaction. Sales in foreign trade on open account are usually made only to very reliable customers and, as a rule, only in connection with consumer goods that can otherwise be readily disposed of. It is a charge account, the buyer arranging settlement with the seller at regularly agreed-on intervals, monthly or quarterly. In such cases, when the terms of sale are FOB, the seller still has at least a financial interest in the goods that should be protected with insurance. If a large shipment is lost en route, the buyer may be unable or unwilling to settle with the seller at the agreed time.

Draft The draft, payable either on presentation *(sight draft)* or at some specified future date *(time draft)* such as thirty, sixty, or ninety days from the date of presentation, is widely used. An example will be provided later to illustrate how a draft is used.

Letter of Credit The letter of credit is the most common payment method for exports. A purchaser contacts a local bank asking for a letter of credit for a purchase. The bank would contact its correspondent bank in the foreign country authorizing a certain credit limit and specifying the terms of shipment. The "letter" would be delivered to the seller. When all terms of the shipment, including those in the letter of credit, have been met and the shipment leaves the seller, the seller takes the letter of credit and shipping documentation to the local bank for payment. The seller's bank then collects through the international banking system from the buyer's bank. Terms of the letter of credit must be exactly conformed to and they usually have a termination date.

A Typical Transaction

Typical steps in an international cargo shipment follow. An important aspect of these steps is their indication of the parties that have an interest in the property, including the shipper, carrier, purchaser, and institutions financing the transaction.

1. The shipper delivers the goods into the custody of the ocean carrier.
2. The shipper receives an order bill of lading naming the shipper not only as the shipper but also as the consignee. The shipper is named consignee and may endorse the bill of lading to anyone at any time.

3. The shipper notifies the purchaser that the goods have been shipped and that the carrier will notify the purchaser when the goods arrive at the destination.
4. The shipper takes the order bill of lading and endorses it in blank. That is, the shipper's name appears in the space provided for endorsement, but the name of the party authorized to receive the goods is not filled in. This is equivalent to making out a check without putting in the name of the payee; it could be cashed by anyone in possession of it. If insurance is required, the shipper also obtains the type and amount of insurance required in the sales agreement.
5. The shipper also draws a *sight draft* on the purchaser. This is a written order in which the shipper directs the purchaser to pay a specified sum of money. This sight draft usually names the shipper as entity to which the money is paid.
6. The shipper takes the order bill of lading, evidence of insurance, and the sight draft to the bank and endorses them in blank, according to the procedure used by the bank.
7. The bank sends the order bill of lading, evidence of insurance, and the sight draft to a bank at the location where the goods are to be delivered. This transaction may pass through several banks in international banking channels. The order bill of lading, evidence of insurance, and the sight draft are handled with extreme care because they are endorsed in blank and could be used by anyone who filled in a name. Such documents usually are sent by registered mail in order to reduce likelihood of loss in transit.
8. The bank in the city where delivery is to be made receives the order bill of lading, evidence of insurance, and the sight draft. The bank notifies the purchaser that it has the documents and that the order bill of lading will be endorsed to the purchaser on payment of the amount named in the sight draft.
9. The carrier meanwhile is transporting the goods to the destination. The carrier will notify the purchaser that the goods have arrived and will be delivered upon presentation of the order bill of lading.
10. The purchaser pays the sight draft at the bank and receives the order bill of lading. It is endorsed to the purchaser, who can now go to the carrier's office and receive the goods upon presentation of the order bill of lading.

This method of handling payment for shipments in transit is used in connection with domestic shipments as well as in connection with ocean commerce. It appears to be a complicated method of handling cash on delivery transactions but it is used so commonly that the procedure works smoothly.

Identifying Prospects

The preceding sections described some of the complicated relationships involved when determining who has an insurable interest in cargo. Understanding this information, the producer can ask three questions to determine whether the domestic exporter or importer in question has a need for ocean marine cargo insurance:

1. Are the exporters (sellers), as owners, responsible under contract for the goods during the ocean voyage?
2. Are the exporters (sellers) responsible under contract for arranging the insurance even though they are not the owners during the ocean voyage?
3. If the importers (buyers) own the goods and bear the exposure during the ocean voyage, do the exporters collect money on delivery of the goods or thereafter?

Exporters A domestic exporter (seller) who answers any of the preceding questions "yes" is a prospect for cargo insurance. If all three questions are answered "no," the exporter is not a prospect.

The answer to the first question can be found in the purchase contract. In most cases, the exposure to loss is transferred at the location named in the purchase contract, whether it is Meridian, Mississippi, or Jerusalem, Israel. When the point named is overseas, the exporter (seller) is a prospect for insurance. If the point of transfer is located in the United States, the exporter is not a prospect for insurance unless either of the remaining two questions receives a "yes" answer.

The second question recognizes the possibility the exporter (seller) may have agreed to arrange ocean cargo insurance. As mentioned, this is sometimes done as a matter of custom. A foreign buyer may also request such an arrangement for the sake of convenience, lower premiums, or better coverage or service. When the terms of sale are "CIF Jerusalem," for example, the arrangement for insurance is required by definition. The exporter (seller) is obligated to provide the insurance because the cost of insurance is included in the selling price.

The third question is more complex and illustrates why it may be valuable to an exporter (seller) to arrange the insurance rather than relying on the buyer to insure the shipment. Suppose that True Grit Corporation (exporter-seller) makes a shipment of grits from Meridian, Mississippi, to Rome, Italy. Further assume that the terms of this sale are "FOB Meridian," and the importer (buyer) obtains an ocean cargo –

policy to cover the importer's loss exposures. Suppose also that True Grit Corporation will be paid through a draft against the importer, payable on delivery of the goods overseas. Now, suppose the importer's tastes change and a decision is made to order a shipment of canned poi from Lihue, Hawaii. The buyer therefore refuses to pay for the grits when they arrive and breaks the contract. The responsibility for this shipment of grits falls back on True Grit Corporation, which is left with an uninsured shipment several thousand miles away. If the goods were damaged during their shipment to Rome, True Grit *might* be able to collect for the loss because the importer should have had insurance on the cargo. However, this depends on whether the importer actually has insurance, whether it covers the loss in question, whether the foreign insurer resists the claim, and whether True Grit will be satisfied with payment in foreign currency. Any attempt to sue would probably cost more than it would be worth.

Clearly, it is advantageous if an exporter (seller)—True Grit, in this case—can persuade the importer (buyer) to let the exporter arrange the insurance through the exporter's own producer with a U.S. insurance company. Even if the importer refuses to let the exporter place the insurance, it is possible to obtain a contingent policy that will protect the exporter to the extent it is unable to recover for a loss from the importer's insurer.

Importers The first two of the three questions listed earlier also apply to domestic importers who may be prospects for insurance. If the foreign exporters are not responsible for insurance, the importer must purchase insurance.

Some prospects may question the need for insurance because they expect to recover from the ocean carrier for damage to cargo in transit. These prospects should be informed that the carrier and the shipowner are exempt from liability for loss due to causes including:

- act, neglect, or default of the master, mariner, pilot, or the servants of the carrier in the navigation or in the management of the ship;
- fire, unless caused by the actual fault or privity (private knowledge) of the carrier;
- perils, dangers and accidents of the sea or other navigable waters;
- act of God;
- act of war;
- act of public enemies; or
- strikes, riots, and civil commotions.

Exhibit 6-1
Summary of Who Needs Ocean Cargo Insurance*

A. The *seller,* when under the terms of sale and payment the seller has title or exposure during the ocean voyage, for example:
Terms: Ex dock—country of importation
F.O.B.—country of importation
C.I.F.—country of importation
OR has a financial exposure if the goods are not paid for until delivery or thereafter, by draft or open account, for example:
Terms: F.O.B.—domestic point, draft or open account
C.&F.—destination, draft or open account
B. The *buyer,* when under the terms of sale the buyer has the exposure and title during the ocean voyage, for example:
Terms: Ex dock—foreign point
F.A.S.—foreign point
F.O.B.—foreign point
Note dual interests may apply such as a shipment to an importer in Jacksonville, Florida, F.A.S.—Rotterdam on sight draft. The importer's exposures begin alongside the ship in Rotterdam and the exporter's exposures end with payment.

*Reprinted with permission from *Introduction to Ocean Marine,* Aetna Insurance Company, Rev. 4/77, page IOM-SW-71.

The question of who needs ocean cargo insurance is summarized in Exhibit 6-1.

Checkpoints

1. List six terms of sale that affect insurable interest in cargo.
2. List four payment methods commonly used in overseas shipments.
3. State three questions used to determine whether an importer or exporter needs ocean cargo insurance.

HOW TO INSURE

There is no standard ocean marine insurance policy. Many of the clauses used are fairly uniform, the result of centuries of experience backed by legal decisions in many countries. No laws have been passed that require standardization. Some policies contain clauses known as American Institute Cargo Clauses because they have been developed by the American Institute of Marine Underwriters.

Ocean marine insurance rates are completely competitive (not standardized). Thus, ocean marine underwriters are at liberty to work cooperatively with producers and risk managers to develop insurance coverages that meet specific needs at a price level in line with the exposures. This complete flexibility is important in a line of business where no two accounts are exactly alike. For example, cargo can be insured in one of two ways.

Cargo may be insured for a particular voyage, or under open cargo policies—a type of reporting form policy. Which type is most appropriate depends on how much is shipped and how often shipments are made.

Voyage Policies

Made to cover a single trip described in the policy, a voyage policy is used to arrange specific insurance when it is needed, and is purchased by those not regularly engaged in foreign trade.

Open Cargo Policies

The open cargo policy is basically designed for the shipper or consignee who has a large volume of overseas shipments. It is most often written without a specific expiration date, although some policies are written for a specific term, usually one year. The holder of an open policy is obligated to report all shipments covered by the policy. Premiums are based on the rates established in the policy for various shipments and paid to the insurer as shipments are made.

The open policy saves time and expense for all concerned and has particular advantages for the insured. The insured has automatic protection (up to the maximum limits stated in the policy) from the time shipments leave the warehouse at the place named in the policy for the commencement of transit. The insured warrants that shipments will be declared as soon as practicable, but unintentional failure to report will not void the insurance, since the goods are "held covered," subject to policy conditions. Under an open policy the insured knows what premium rate will be charged and thus can be certain of the cost.

For the insurer, the use of the open policy creates a business relationship that may exist over a long period of time. This permits the insurer to learn the special requirements of its clients and to provide them with individualized protection, tailor-made to fit the specific situation. This may be an important factor in loss adjustments at out-of-the-way ports around the world or in overcoming problems peculiar to a given commodity.

HOW MUCH TO INSURE

Placing a value on ocean marine cargo is not necessarily easy. Transoceanic shipments take time, and the passage of time may affect the value of a commodity. For example, consider a shipment of cut Christmas trees that reaches the buyer in January. Shipments also involve a certain amount of "freight" (the charge to transport the cargo). For a shipment that does not arrive (or arrives in damaged condition), somebody loses the "freight." If the carrier cannot collect the "freight," it is the carrier's loss. If the exporter or the importer has paid the "freight" on a shipment that does not arrive in usable condition, the exporter or importer has lost the "freight."

Another way of looking at the situation is to realize that the value of cargo when it reaches the buyer is generally increased by at least the "freight" incurred to bring it to its destination. "Freight" paid by a buyer will certainly be considered when the buyer attempts to resell the cargo; freight paid by the exporter will be built into the exporter's sales charge.

Valuation of Cargo

With single shipments of specific cargo, such as machinery or other individual items, a specific agreed value may be set for insurance purposes. However, it is seldom practical for an open cargo insurance policy to list an individual valuation for every shipment that is made— particularly for an insured sending or receiving hundreds of shipments a year. The alternative is to provide a *method* by which the value of the cargo can be determined for insurance purposes. Usual practice is valuation at the amount of invoice, including all charges such as prepaid or guaranteed freight *plus a stated percentage* and, in some cases, a duty paid or payable for import or export. This added amount above the invoice cost is intended to take care of the additional value of the cargo to the consignee at the destination. The percentage in the valuation clause depends upon the circumstances, the type of merchandise, and the anticipated value at the destination. A typical valuation clause reads:

> ...valued premium included at amount of invoice, including all charges in the invoice and including prepaid and/or advanced and/or guaranteed freight, if any, plus 10 percent.

This clause allows the insured to insure the total value on the invoice, freight charges, the insurance premium (valued premium included), plus an additional percentage of the total.

Exposure Limits

Under an open cargo policy, the insurer does not know in advance the value of any given shipment that may be declared by the insured under the terms of the open policy. The valuation clause which establishes in advance how shipments are to be valued eliminates the possibility of disagreement about the value of a shipment if loss happens to occur before the shipment is declared to the insurer.

Open policies also contain a limit of insurance showing the maximum liability the insurer is willing to accept on any one vessel. Since the exposure of cargo shipped on deck is much greater than under deck, it is not unusual to also find a separate limit in open cargo policies for "on-deck" shipments. A distinction is usually made between "on-deck" shipments and those in regular containers which are stowed by container lines either under or on deck.

Percentage of Value Lost

Coverage of loss from direct damage to the described insured property is the principal part of ocean marine insurance. A significant characteristic of this property coverage is the custom of evaluating the damage in terms of "percentage of insured value lost." Thus, if the damage is estimated to be 40 percent of what the value of the property would have been without damage, 40 percent of the *insured amount* is paid for the loss. This practice gives ocean marine insurance policies the effect of "valued policies"—in the event of total loss, the face of the policy is always paid. It also has the effect of a 100 percent coinsurance clause *when the amount insured does not exceed the value of the property.* For example, assume a property's actual value is $500, with value declared at $400; further assume a loss of $100, or one-fifth of actual value. Under 100 percent coinsurance, payment would be calculated at 400/500 times the $100 loss, producing payment of $80. Under marine practice, payment would be 100/500 times the insured value of $400, also producing $80. The producer can determine these two results will always be the same in case of underinsurance.

When the amount of insurance exceeds the value of the property, the marine computation proceeds the same way. With $600 of insurance on the $500 of property, payment for a $100 loss (one-fifth of actual property value) would still be one-fifth of the *insured amount;* that is, one-fifth of $600, or $120.

This valuation practice has arisen from a combination of need and opportunity. Part of the need comes from the fact that ocean cargo losses often must be settled in distant places, under complex market conditions, and with speed. Suppose a cargo of cotton bound for

Liverpool from Madras were lost in the Indian Ocean. If "actual cash value" were to be used as the basis of settlement, then value in what place at what time? Value in Madras, in Liverpool, or at some point in between? Value as of the day the voyage began, as of the day it should have reached Liverpool, or as of the day of the loss when that is known?

Under marine insurance practice, none of these questions has to be asked when loss is total. For partial losses, only the immediate market—the present price in the market to which the goods are delivered—needs to be known. The percentage loss in that market and the amount of insurance together determine the amount of the insured claim. The adjuster does not have to know about prices in other markets or at other times.

Marine insurers can use a method that pays some insureds more than their loss because of the special conditions of ocean marine trade. The insured usually has a very limited ability to create a loss deliberately, especially as a reaction to changing conditions. When the market for cotton collapses, the merchant with cotton en route from Madras to Liverpool may wish it at the bottom of the sea, but has little opportunity to bring about the event. Even the owner of the vessel has only limited control under those circumstances. (Of course, in the earlier days, when ship and cargo owners might have been on board their vessels and directly in charge, the exposure of their own lives was a deterrent to destroying the venture.)

Insurers are careful about the agreed amount of value set in the policy. Much of the cargo valuation is by sales invoice, of course, particularly under open cargo policies. When invoice value is not available, an agreed formula or method of valuation has to be substituted in open cargo forms.

Loss of Profit, Expense, or Income

Shippers of cargo face some unique and extensive exposures to loss of expense, profit, or income. Insurance is available to cover some of these expenses.

Loss of Profit Margin on Goods The profit margin on goods insured under ocean marine forms is covered in a manner similar to that provided by a selling price or market value clause in fire and allied lines insurance. As described earlier, the amount of insurance is set at the invoice price of the goods plus a margin for expenses not included in the invoice, and the profit margin in the invoice price is thus covered.

Interruption and Delay Profit losses caused by interruption and delay—termed "frustration losses"—are not commonly insured in ocean marine practice. However, the flexibility of the ocean marine insurance market is such that, where a demonstrable need for insurance exists, interruption and delay covers may be negotiated (although not always, of course, on terms the prospective insured considers acceptable).

Freight The freight cost is commonly prepaid, and hence the shipper is exposed to loss of "freight." This exposure can be covered by making the insured amount large enough to include it—a common practice.

Prepaid Expenses The coverage of shipper's expense for pre-paid freight was noted above. Other shipping expenses (such as prepaid premium for insurance) are similarly included in the valuation of the insured property.

Factors to Consider in Determining How Much to Insure

The reason for insuring cargo is to be "made whole" in case of loss to the cargo. Although this is commonly accomplished by using a valuation clause like the one cited earlier which added 10 percent to the amount on the invoice, there are obviously many factors that must be considered in determining whether 10 percent is adequate, inadequate, or excessive. Some factors in addition to the basic invoice cost are additional charges for export packing, inland freight, ocean freight, insurance premiums, duties paid, and miscellaneous fees. After adding all of these items, the percentage is added to the total. A commodity subject to fluctuating values may present special problems.

In certain trades, such as timber, grain, and oil, long usage has led to the standardization of special valuation clauses that should be included in an open cargo policy. An experienced marine underwriter should be aware of any such practices and form differences and should be a source of information to the producer.

OPEN CARGO POLICY COVERAGE

Duration of Cargo Coverage

Ocean marine insurance originally covered cargo only from the time it was loaded on ship until it was discharged at the port of destination. This was adequate coverage when most transportation was by water, but the development of railroads during the 1800s permitted the delivery of cargo to inland cities by means other than over water. This created a need for continuous coverage from point of origin to declared destination even though there might be many miles of land transit involved. Such coverage is commonly provided under ocean marine policies by including the *warehouse to warehouse clause.*

Warehouse to Warehouse Clause Current wording of the American Institute of Marine Underwriters warehouse to warehouse clause is:

> This insurance attaches from the time the goods leave the Warehouse and/or Store at the place named in the Policy for the commencement of the transit and continues *during the ordinary course of transit,* including customary transshipment if any, until the goods are discharged overside from the overseas vessel at the final port. Thereafter the insurance continues whilst the goods are in transit and/or awaiting transit until delivered to final warehouse at the destination named in the Policy or until the expiry of 15 days (or 30 days if the destination to which the goods are insured is outside the limits of the port) whichever shall first occur. The time limits referred to above to be reckoned from midnight of the day on which the discharge overside of the goods hereby insured from the overseas vessel is completed. Held covered at a premium to be arranged in the event of transshipment, if any, other than as above and/or in the event of delay in excess of the above time limits arising from circumstances beyond the control of the Assured.

The fifteen or thirty day limitation on coverage after discharge at final port recognizes that ocean marine insurance is generally intended to cover transit and is not ordinarily supposed to provide continuous coverage at an insured's permanent location. However, insurers recognize that circumstances beyond the control of the insured may delay the delivery of the goods for more than fifteen or thirty days.

Marine Extensions Clauses Even the coverage provided by the warehouse to warehouse clause was inadequate in many cases to fully protect cargo during transit. A ship may break down before reaching the intended destination and be forced to terminate its voyage, or the intended port of discharge may be closed by natural disaster, civil authorities, or even strikes of port workers. Under such circumstances cargo cannot be discharged. The marine extensions clauses (MEC) were developed to cover contingencies such as these. When incorporated in a cargo policy, these provisions extend the time and place of coverage.

When a cargo is sold at a port where the voyage is prematurely terminated, there may be a loss to the shipper because this sale is for less than the intended value at the destination. The difference between the intended value at destination and the amount recovered by sale at the port where the voyage is terminated would be a loss due to the change in the voyage. Such loss is not covered by the insurance policy as ordinarily written. The effect of the marine extension clauses in such a case is merely to continue the insurance on the cargo until the cargo is sold at such a port.

Lost or Not Lost Ocean marine insurance policies may be written covering the property "lost or not lost." This means that coverage applies even if the property has already been lost at the time the policy is negotiated, *provided that* the insured did not know of a loss and had no reason to suspect there had been a loss. This practice is particularly advantageous to those who are continuously engaged in overseas commerce. Open policies on cargo are written so that they cover all of the goods described while they are in transit. It is possible for a cargo to be lost before the insured knows that it had been shipped.

Perils Covered and Excluded

The perils clause of a typical ocean cargo policy reads:

Perils Clause   The adventures and perils which the said [insurance] Company is content to bear and does take upon itself, are: of the seas, fire, rovers, assailing thieves, jettisons, criminal barratry of the master and mariners, and of all other like perils, losses and misfortunes, that have or shall come to the hurt, detriment, or damage of the aforesaid subject matter of this insurance or any part thereof except as may be otherwise provided for herein or endorsed hereon.

Total losses caused by these perils are covered in full. The extent of coverage for partial losses is determined by the *average terms*, discussed later. Most of the perils listed in this clause have not previously been discussed. Although they are not defined in the policy, these perils have come to have definite meaning through decades of court interpretation.

Perils of the Seas The perils of the seas include the effects of heavy weather, stranding, foundering, collision, and other effects of the wind and waves. This is not intended to provide "all-risks" coverage, but to cover unexpected and fortuitous damage to cargo that might result *from unusual action of the oceans.* Perils of the seas does not include bad stowage, being exposed to theft or embezzlement by the master or mariners, nor seawater damage to cargo caused by a leak in the hull. Damage by rainwater is not generally considered a peril of the sea.

Fire Fire is a serious peril *at* sea but is not considered to be a peril *of* the seas. The peril is specifically mentioned in the policy in order to make clear that it is covered. Damage done by steam or water used to extinguish fire is considered damage by fire. However, use of steam or water in the mistaken belief that there is a fire in a hold when in fact none exists would not be considered fire damage.

Rovers and Assailing Thieves Damage resulting from the action of pirates and rovers is not as likely under today's conditions as it was a few hundred years ago. However, questions have arisen recently as a result of hijackings or threatened hijackings of vessels. Current practice is that hijackings would be covered by "Assailing Thieves."

Loss from "assailing thieves" includes loss from theft by violence. The policy is not intended to cover theft by stealth nor theft committed by any of the ship's company, regardless of whether the thief is a member of the crew or a passenger.

Some ocean marine policies today do cover pilferage and other theft by stealth, as well as theft from piers and wharves, without a requirement that violence be involved. This is a special coverage which is subject to rates commensurate with the exposure.

Jettisons This peril may be defined as "a voluntary throwing overboard of some property." The policy is intended to cover loss resulting from a jettison made to save the venture. Voluntary sacrifice of cargo that is carried on deck would be recognized as a jettison loss. However, cargo accidentally washed overboard would not be considered a jettison.

Barratry of the Master and Mariners Barratry includes illegal acts committed by master or crew, but not negligence or carelessness. To constitute barratry, an act must be intended to injure the goods or the ship, such as the deliberate sinking of a ship by the master or crew, the embezzlement of the cargo, or some act such as smuggling which would make the ship or cargo subject to confiscation. Insurance coverage against barratry, a fraudulent act, may be compared roughly to fidelity coverage that is issued in connection with land exposures to protect against loss by dishonesty of employees.

All Other Like Perils The concluding portion of the policy relating to the covered perils specifies, "all other like perils, losses and misfortunes, that have come or shall come to the hurt, detriment or damage" of the subject matter insured. This may appear at first glance to be comparable to the "all-risks" type of insurance commonly written to cover property on land, but it is not so intended. The term "all other like perils" under an ocean marine policy covers only perils that are *similar in kind* to the perils specifically mentioned in the policy. Originally there was uncertainty as to whether the principle applied, and, if so, which other perils were and which were not sufficiently similar to be covered. Court decisions over the years have established that the principle does apply, and have settled the classification of most perils.

Other Perils Ocean cargo policies are quite often extended to include other perils beyond those described above. Often, coverage is provided on an "all-risks" basis, subject to exclusions. Some of the perils covered by these extensions are:

- Explosion
- Loss caused by a latent defect of the ship's hull or machinery not recoverable from the shipowner because the defect could not have been discovered by due diligence
- Loss resulting from errors of navigation or mismanagement of the vessel
- Certain specified exposures on shore (such as collision, derailment, overturn, sprinkler leakage, windstorm, earthquake, flood, and collapse of docks or wharves)
- Theft
- Pilferage
- Nondelivery
- Fresh water damage
- Oil damage
- Sweat damage (caused by condensation)
- Contact with other cargo
- Breakage
- Leakage
- Hook hole damage
- Damage caused by breakdown of refrigeration machinery

Exclusions Coverage of an ocean marine policy may be limited both by exclusions written into the policy or by warranties that are either explicitly written in the contract or "read into" every marine policy by legal interpretation. These warranties are discussed later.

Two exclusions are found in almost all American cargo policies. The first of these excludes strikes, riots, and civil commotions. The second excludes a variety of perils associated with hostile action or war. Other exclusions depend on the type of cargo or voyage involved.

Strikes, Riots, and Civil Commotion. Cargo insurance policies may be extended to cover damages from strike, riot, or civil commotion. An additional premium is usually charged because of the additional exposure. The coverage ordinarily applies to physical damage to the cargo but does not cover loss from delay or loss of market.

Strike, riot, and civil commotion coverage is accomplished by a special policy or special clauses added to the ocean marine policy. The insurer as well as the insured usually has the privilege of canceling strike and riot coverage. Underwriters consider this a necessary right because a strike and riot situation can develop into severe exposure within a short period of time.

War Risks. Cargo policies can be written to cover war risks with a companion war risks only policy in the same manner that coverage is provided for strikes, riots, and civil commotions. Like strikes, riots, and civil commotion coverage, war risk coverage responds only for actual physical loss or damage to the insured property and does not cover any form of consequential loss. The war risk companion policy is normally subject to cancellation with forty-eight hours' notice, but this cancellation does not affect shipments already at sea.

Although it may be written by a different insurer, it is usually recommended that war risk coverage be placed with the same insurer that has the open cargo policy. This prevents possible questions as to liability in the case of a missing vessel or where there may be doubt as to the real cause of loss.

Other Exclusions. Some exclusions in an "all-risks" policy depend on the type of cargo involved. For example, a policy insuring a cargo of autos may specifically exclude marring and scratching of unboxed autos.

A "delay clause" is usually used to exclude claims for loss of market and for loss, damage, or deterioration resulting from delay. Sometimes this clause is modified to provide coverage that fits the special needs of a given insured, but ocean marine underwriters are understandably reluctant to cover exposures that are not entirely outside the control of the insured. In a way, these delay losses involve a speculative loss exposure related to the gambles of engaging in trade.

Other frequently used exclusions relate to foreseeable damage, involving such hazards as the tendency of perishable cargo to spoil or the tendency of fragile cargo to break if not properly packaged. A policy may also exclude or limit loss of weight caused by evaporation, referred to as "trade loss."

Losses Covered

A property loss in marine shipping is more likely to be total than a similar loss ashore. (This characteristic is shared with aviation losses, discussed later in this chapter). Even so, the vast majority of marine losses are partial rather than total. A particular terminology and set of practices pertaining to the distinction between partial and total losses has developed around marine law. Therefore, in order to explain what losses are covered by ocean cargo insurance, it is necessary to briefly examine marine law and practice, including some of the unusual terminology used in connection with marine cargo losses.

In marine practice, "total loss" means the complete loss of subject matter. If some of the property value is saved, the loss is "partial." There is a special marine term for partial losses: "average." (Although the phrase, "average loss," is sometimes used, it is redundant as the word "average" itself means "partial loss.")

Total Loss Marine terminology distinguishes between three types of total loss:

1. An *actual total loss* is one in which the subject property is totally lost or is so badly damaged that it has no value left. When there is no doubt that a vessel has sunk in deep water, total loss is clear.
2. A *constructive total loss* occurs when the cost of salvaging the cargo or ship and of making repairs is too high relative to the value saved. If a ship is ashore on rocks and the cost of recovering and repairing it exceeds its value when recovered and repaired, it would be considered a constructive total loss. There may be a constructive total loss as far as a ship is concerned without a constructive total loss to cargo. It might be possible to save the cargo even though the ship could not reasonably be saved.
3. Total loss of a part may also occur—total loss of one shipper's cargo, for example, without total loss to the ship or other shipments. There may even be total loss of a part of a single shipment—total loss of one package, say, from a shipment that contains six.

Partial Loss There are two types of partial loss in marine practice: particular average and general average. The nature and impact of these losses are discussed next with insurance coverages available for the exposures following.

Particular Average. *Average* is a loss that is not total; particular average is an average that is not general. An example of particular average would be a case in which perils of the sea caused damage to ship or cargo. There is no voluntary sacrifice of any portion of the ship or cargo but merely direct damage from the storm. Each cargo owner and shipowner would have to stand its own loss. The term particular average usually applies to the loss or damage of a specific shipment or the vessel rather than damage of multiple interests.

Particular average is said sometimes to mean partial loss. This is not entirely true. A particular average is a partial loss only in the sense that it does not involve the whole venture, the vessel and all cargo. It may involve a total loss of the property belonging to one individual interest (shipper, buyer or ship owner). Loss of the entire lot of cargo belonging to one interest without loss of the ship or loss of cargo belonging to others would still be a particular average.

General Average. When there is voluntary sacrifice of some property in order to save the rest, and certain other conditions are also met, the owners of the saved property contribute to the owners of the property that has been sacrificed. The loss, or "average," is made "general." For example, suppose a fire breaks out in one hold of a ship and it is necessary to flood that hold to keep the entire ship from burning. Only the cargo in that hold is damaged by the flooding. However, the voluntary sacrifice of that cargo has enabled the remaining cargo and the ship to survive. If a general average is declared, the owners of the ship and the other saved cargo pay a share of the value of the cargo that has been damaged. What share is paid by each party is based on the proportionate values of each party with an insurable interest in the voyage. The value of freight charges earned at successful completion of the voyage would be included in the insurable interest of the vessel owner or charter operator.

Average Terms "Particular average" terms address partial losses falling on one interest. The average terms of ocean marine policies require a change in thinking by the insured and producer when considering what covered losses will be paid. A property insurance example in marine terminology may help.

For instance, assume Patrick Roux rents space in a building. His contents are insured for their full replacement value on a standard fire policy with extended coverage in an amount of $500,000. A fire occurs that causes a loss to one-half of Patrick's contents, but no loss to the building. In marine terms there was a particular average loss. The loss was average (one-half of Patrick's contents) and particular (the loss fell only on Patrick and not the building owner or any other tenant). Customary property loss adjustment procedure would be to pay Patrick the full amount of the partial loss (average) or $250,000. In marine insurance, the *average terms* of the policy must be consulted to determine loss payment. There are many variations of average terms and the discussion here will be limited to the most common forms; total loss only, free of particular average (two variations) and with average (two variations).

Total Loss Only. This approach limits recovery under the insurance to only those cases where the cargo is a total loss as a result of the perils named in the basic perils clause, a considerable reduction in coverage.

Free of Particular Average (FPA). The American Conditions version of this clause usually used for noncontainerized cargo stored on deck (free of particular average American Conditions—FPAAC) includes the following:

> Warranted free from Particular Average unless caused by the vessel or craft being stranded, sunk, or burnt, but ... Assurers are to pay any loss ... which may reasonably be attributed to fire, collision or contact of the vessel ... with any external substance (ice included) other than water, or to discharge of the cargo at port of distress.

This clause provides that, in addition to total losses, partial losses *resulting from* perils of the sea are also covered, but only when the ship has been stranded, sunk, burnt, or in a collision. This clause still represents a considerable restriction of the coverage.

The FPAAC cover may be broadened providing an individual shipping package is covered in full, even though other parts of the same shipment were not totally lost. It is customary to provide coverage for individual packages totally damaged or lost during loading, transshipment, or discharge.

There is a second version of the FPA clause, Free of Particular Average—English Conditions (FPAEC), usually used for cargo stored below deck. Under English Conditions, stranding, sinking, or burning do not have to cause the loss, but only have to *occur during* the course of the voyage.

With Average. This approach calls for payment of any loss caused by the named perils subject, perhaps, to a deductible or franchise.

An Example. An example will show one loss adjustment under the three average clauses and two variations. The *U.S. Stephanie Evans*, a cargo ship, is transporting the cargo of Michael Roux valued and insured for $500,000. Also on the *Stephanie Evans* is the cargo of Danielle McClendon valued and insured for $1 million. During heavy weather (a peril of the sea), water damages one-half of Michael Roux's cargo. Danielle's cargo and the ship are undamaged. Michael's loss is a particular average. Will his ocean marine policy pay?

TOTAL LOSS ONLY. If Michael's average terms were total loss only (rarely sold for cargo insurance), the answer would be no.

FPAAC. If Michael's cargo were insured under the American Conditions, the answer would still be no. As indicated, the American Conditions are usually used for noncontainerized cargo stored on deck. Cargo stowed in this manner is susceptible to water damage during heavy weather and that is why the stricter conditions are used. But even if Michael's goods were below deck, there would be no coverage. FPAAC requires two conditions for particular average payment: (1) loss caused by an insured peril, *and* (2) loss caused "... by the vessel or craft *being* stranded, sunk, or burnt" or attributable to fire, collision, or contact of the vessel with any external substance other than water.

Michael's loss meets the first but not the second requirement. No loss is paid.

FPAEC. Again, there would be no payment from the insurer. The only difference in the English Conditions is that the stranding, sinking, and so forth only had to happen *during* the course of the voyage. As the example does not indicate that as the case, there is no coverage. After the following discussion of franchises, this example will continue with two more possible situations applying to Michael's cargo and possible loss payment.

Franchise and Deductible Clauses

Straight deductible clauses like those used in other types of insurance appear in ocean cargo insurance contracts. However, *franchise* deductibles are also used. With a franchise clause, the insurer pays nothing when the loss is less than the specified amount. When the franchise amount (often called just "the franchise") is exceeded, the loss is paid in full subject to average terms. The franchise amount is usually stated as a percentage (e.g., 3 or 5 percent) of the value of the insured property.

The percentage specified in a franchise type of clause varies with the type of cargo. The figure varies according to the amount of routine damage that type of cargo can be expected to suffer. Franchise and deductible clauses are used to a lesser extent in connection with package or containerized cargo because such property is better protected from the miscellaneous losses, such as leakage or errors in weighing or measuring. In general, franchise and deductible clauses are more common to policies issued to importers than on policies covering exports.

Franchises and Average Two additional average clauses of the many possible that directly interact with the franchise clauses will be examined: "With Average at a Stated Percentage," and "With Average Irrespective of Percentage." Both may pay partial losses falling on Michael Roux's interest in the previous example.

With Average, Stated Percentage. "With average at a stated percentage" clauses indicate the franchise the insured must assume before a particular average will be paid. For instance, if Michael Roux's contract was "With Average (5 percent)," his partial loss in the previous example would have been paid in full. Again, the loss must be from an insured peril (heavy weather) *and* must exceed the stated percentage of insured value. As the $250,000 loss is well in excess of 5 percent of total insured value ($25,000), the full $250,000 would be paid.

The requirement that the vessel was stranded, sunk, and so forth is not applicable in this case. The stated franchise replaced it.

With Average Irrespective of Percentage. The intent is to pay the partial losses falling on one interest. The term, "With Average Irrespective of Percentage" indicates those types of losses only need be caused by an insured peril to be paid. Hence, Michael would be treated as his brother Patrick was for Patrick's contents loss in an earlier example. Michael would be paid the full amount of his partial loss even if the loss was under the value of any stated percentage.

The Producer and Average and Franchise. Exhibits 6-2 and 6-3 summarize the interaction of average terms and the franchise. In most cases it is better for the client to have the "With Average Irrespective of Percentage" clause, but this may be expensive. Certain types of cargo will qualify, but underwriters may insist on a stated percentage for more perishable cargoes. Also, the producer should be aware of where the cargo will be stored and how it will be packed. A client's perishable cargo, such as canned goods, stowed on deck and not containerized may only be eligible for FPAAC or Total Loss Only. The more the producer can do to encourage the client to have the cargo properly packed and stowed, the better average and franchise terms can be arranged.

Checkpoints

1. List prospects for
   a. a voyage policy.
   b. an open cargo policy.
2. How is the "amount insured" determined in an ocean cargo policy?
3. For a domestic client, how is the warehouse to warehouse clause helpful?
4. List the perils covered in a typical ocean cargo policy.
5. How is the war risk exclusion covered?
6. How may partial losses to one interest be covered?

Warranties

A *warranty* is a condition of coverage that must be strictly complied with. A breach of warranty generally voids the coverage from the time of the breach, and the coverage is not reinstated when the breach is corrected. Among subjects that warranties have dealt with have been size and nature of a ship's crew, the areas in which the ship will sail, and the types of cargo it will carry.

Ocean marine insurance involves two types of warranty:

Exhibit 6-2
Examples of Average Terms*

TLO	This insurance is against the risk of total and constructive total loss only.
FPA (American Conditions)	Free of particular average unless caused by the vessel being stranded, sunk, burnt, on fire, or in collision
FPA (English Conditions)	Free of particular average, unless the vessel be stranded, sunk, burnt, on fire, or in collision.
With Average (3 percent)	"To pay Particular Average if amounting to 3 percent unless General, or the vessel be stranded, sunk, burnt, on fire or in collision."
WA Irrespective of Percentage	"To pay average irrespective of percentage."

* Adapted with permission from E.P. Hollingsworth, Jr., and J.J. Launie, *Commercial Property and Multiple-Lines Underwriting* (Malvern, PA: Insurance Institute of America, 1978), p. 449.

- *Express warranties* are written, or "expressed" in the policy.
- *Implied warranties* do not appear in the policy, but are understood to exist in connection with all maritime adventures.

Implied warranties have as much force as express warranties in ocean marine insurance.

Express Warranties   Instead of stating that loss by capture or seizure is "excluded," the common wording is that the property is "*warranted* free from capture and seizure." Ocean marine express warranties are really of two kinds:

1. those relating to *hazards* that may affect the probability of loss of the kinds insured against; and
2. those that exclude certain *perils* and *losses* from coverage such as loss of markets.

In one important way, the effect of the two types is the same—if either is violated, the insurer does not pay. The contract may be completely unenforceable.

Implied Warranties   The implied warranties generally affecting a maritime venture are subject to interpretations developed over a period of several hundreds of years.

Exhibit 6-3
A Summary of the Perils Clause and Average Conditions*

		More Limited Than Perils Clause			Equal to Perils Clause
Coverage for Total Losses	Total Loss Only (TLO)†	FPA American Conditions (FPAAC)	FPA English Conditions (FPAEC)	With Average 3 percent	Average Irrespective of Percentage
	Basic perils	Basic perils	Basic perils	Basic perils	Basic perils
Coverage for Partial Losses	No coverage	Caused by stranding, sinking, burning, on fire, in collision with another vessel	If the vessel be stranded, sunk, burnt, on fire, in collision with another vessel	Full payment if loss exceeds 3% of insured value. Under 3% only if vessel be stranded, sunk, burnt, on fire, in collision with another vessel	Basic perils

A. The Perils Clause—Perils of the Seas, Fire, Assailing Thieves, Jettison, Barratry
B. Average Conditions:

† Rarely written on cargo

*Adapted with permission from E.P. Hollingsworth, Jr., and J.J. Launie, *Commercial Property and Multiple-Lines Underwriting* (Malvern, PA: Insurance Institute of America, 1978), p. 488.

Seaworthiness. The insured under an ocean marine insurance policy warrants by implication that the ship is seaworthy at the beginning of the voyage. Seaworthiness requires a competent crew, adequate stores, and machinery and hull in condition to make the voyage.

Modern insurance policies covering loss to cargo usually waive the warranty of seaworthiness. This recognizes that many commercial shippers of cargo have no idea on what particular ship the cargo may be carried. Even where the cargo owner may arrange for carriage on a particular ship, there may be no opportunity to determine that the ship is seaworthy at the time the venture is started.

Legality. There is an implied warranty that the venture is legal. It is not considered proper nor in the public interest for insurers to protect a person against loss in some illegal enterprise. This is the only one of the implied warranties that cannot be modified by a provision in the marine insurance policy.

Not covered by a marine insurance policy would be a smuggling venture. There is an enormous traffic in the smuggling of cocaine and marijuana into the United States through the Gulf of Mexico and the Atlantic Ocean. One of the methods used is to buy an old freighter (usually obtainable for its break-up value) and bring the drugs from South America into international waters off the coast of the United States. The drugs are then off-loaded to high speed motor boats for delivery into coves along the shore. The freighter cannot be touched by the United States Coast Guard because it never enters United States waters, and the speedboats are so small and so fast that it is very difficult to catch them. Such an operation is an illegal venture. No underwriter would knowingly insure such vessels. However, should insurance be secured, it will be void because of the implied warranty that the venture is legal.

No Delay. Underwriters base their premiums for a venture and the acceptance of the exposure on expected conditions. If there is a delay in starting a voyage, there may be a seasonal shift in the weather, or a change in international conditions that would make the voyage subject to increased hazards. Some ports become congested at certain times of the year and this may increase the chance of loss or it may require that a ship stand off from a port to await a berth and thus be exposed to sea perils at a time when it otherwise would have been sheltered in port. Therefore, the underwriters covering a specific voyage or venture are entitled to assume that the voyage will start within a reasonable time.

The implied warranty of no delay may be modified in policies covering cargo. The shipper of cargo in many cases has no knowledge or control of the time at which the venture starts, so that the warranty of no delay customarily is eliminated under the terms of the policies covering cargo.

No Deviation. Deviation from the customary route may have an effect on the chance of loss. An ocean marine policy is based upon an assumption by the underwriters that there will be no deviation from the most direct or customary route for the voyage insured. Cargo insurance policies customarily contain a deviation waiver clause. The shipper or cargo owner normally has no control over the vessel's course, and may be required by the terms of the policy to notify the underwriters if a deviation is discovered. There may be a requirement that additional premium be paid because of any additional exposure that the underwriter cover because of the deviation.

Effect of Breach of Warranty. With respect to any warranty that is applicable, and whose violation would void the contract, an insured who learns that compliance will be difficult or impossible should give immediate notice to the underwriters and ask for permission to breach the warranty. The underwriters may be willing to give permission for the breach—particularly if an additional premium commensurate with the additional exposure can be secured.

For this reason, it is important that the producer inform the insured of the existence and status of warranties in an ocean marine policy. The warranties should not be breached, unless the breach is unavoidable. If a breach of warranty becomes necessary, the insured should recognize that coverage is jeopardized and should inform the producer so the producer has an opportunity to seek permission for the breach.

HANDLING A SUBMISSION

World trade conditions, weather, and other natural and human phenomena make it necessary for ocean marine insurers continuously to adapt rates and coverages to changing conditions. To cope successfully with these conditions, marine insurers use a considerable amount of judgment based on experience. The following factors might be considered in determining whether to insure a particular exposure, the rate or premium which would be charged, and what conditions would be imposed on the insured:

1. The ship or the ships in the fleet of the carrier and the general record of the shipowner in maintaining seaworthiness.
2. The route over which the ship or ships will operate, and the weather conditions at the time of the year if coverage is for a specific voyage.
3. The condition of the harbors into which calls will be made, and the world political situation in those areas.
4. The type of cargo to be insured and any inherent hazards in the cargo.
5. The coverage granted in the policy, including participations and deductibles.
6. The experience of the shipowner, operator, or cargo shipper, and whether this experience includes operations similar to the one projected for the trip or the term of the policy.
7. The competitive situation in the world insurance market.
8. The age and registry of ships.
9. The methods of packing cargo.

Ocean Marine Insurance Rates

As each exposure is proposed, the insurer must determine the rate and conditions for it. This requires great flexibility and makes regulated rates generally impractical. In addition, direct international competition for marine insurance requires that ocean marine insurers have freedom to meet changing international competitive conditions.

What the Underwriter Needs to Know

When completing a submission for ocean cargo insurance, the following types of information should be developed. The extent to which each of the following items applies depends on the particular exposures involved.

1. Commodities to be insured
   - Fragile?
   - Attractive to thieves?
   - Special trade conditions?

2. Packing
   - Export packed?
   - Packing survey required?
   - In containers?

3. Stowage
   - "On" or "under-deck"?
   - Details on loading and unloading—will a loading survey and unloading (outturn) survey be required?

4. Voyage
   - Ports and/or air terminals at point of origin, major transshipments and destinations?
   - Time of year?

5. Conveyance
   - By vessel or air?
   - Name of vessel and type?
   - Connecting land transit?

6. Past record
   - Shipper's loss experience?
   - Loss experience known on particular commodity?

7. Perils to be insured against

8. Capacity required
   - How much insurance does shipper require?

To assist the producer, the appendix to this chapter contains "Revised American Foreign Trade Definitions" which should be consulted when the producer places insurance on cargo of clients.

OCEAN MARINE INSURANCE
FOR OTHER EXPOSURES

Discussion to this point has concentrated on ocean marine insurance for cargo exposures. Many of the principles already discussed also apply when ocean marine insurance is used to insure other exposures. The purpose of this section is to briefly describe other exposures for which ocean marine insurance may be appropriate.

Many types of vessel may be insured by an ocean marine policy:

- *Ocean liners* are oceangoing carriers that run on regular schedules.
- *Tramps* are oceangoing carriers not engaged in a regular run between ports. In this case, the term "tramp" does not mean the ship is in bad condition. Even a luxurious cruise ship may technically be a "tramp."
- *Fleets* are groups of oceangoing vessels under a single owner or operator. The best examples are tanker fleets operated by major oil companies and passenger vessels such as the Cunard Liners.
- *Oceangoing cargo ships* may be of a conventional type with a large number of watertight cargo compartments or holds that contain individual packages. They may also be container ships, carrying large weather-tight boxes (containers) that resemble a truck body. Bulk carriers carry materials such as ores, coal, and chemicals in bulk. Tankers are bulk cargo ships designed to carry liquids.
- *Inland and coastal cargo vessels* are designed for inland and coastal waters, rather than for the open ocean. Barges are in this category, and may be pushed or pulled by tugboats and towboats.

There are three other types of vessel of recent origin the producer may encounter:

- *LASH* vessels (lighter aboard ship) carry barges loaded with cargo. The lighters are loaded and unloaded intact over the stern of the vessel. The lighters or barges are then towed up and down rivers to areas not accessible to the "mother ship." LASH vessels have a short turnaround time in port.
- *LNG* ships are designed exclusively to transport natural gas in liquid form. LNG ships have specially insulated tanks and refrigeration equipment to keep the gas at an extremely low temperature under high pressure.

- *"Ro-ro"* (roll-on, roll-off) vessels are specially designed to carry trucks and their trailers. They are prevalent for short hauls in Europe, the UK, and in less developed ports of the third world. Doors located on the ship open to receive or discharge the trucks and their cargo. Simply stated, a Ro-ro is an enlarged ferry boat useful in areas where there are no unloading facilities or where quick turnaround of the vessel is desirable.

Other specialty vessels, pleasure vessels, and shore installations closely associated with ocean marine operations are also often insured by ocean marine insurance. Drilling rigs, dry docks, and marine railways, ship builders' risks, and similar exposures may also be insured by an ocean marine policy.

Probably the greatest number of ocean marine policies not covering cargo are written to cover pleasure yachts.

A vessel eligible for ocean marine insurance has two exposures that should be considered. Hull insurance is needed to provide coverage for physical damage to the ship or vessel. An unusual feature of hull insurance is the *running down clause*, which provides limited coverage for liability for physical damage to other ships, as might be involved in a ship collision. Protection and indemnity (P&I) coverage is a form of liability insurance written to cover liability for bodily injury to members of the crew and to third parties and also property damage liability.

CASE STUDY 1—
PREMIER DOOR AND WINDOW CO., INC.

Premier manufactures metal doors and window frames and ships overseas approximately ten times per year with a maximum value per shipment of approximately $80,000. The exit port is located in a neighboring state 200 miles from the Premier plant.

The underwriter will need to know the ports involved and the normal route of a voyage. It is also necessary to know the nature of products being shipped to determine the susceptibility to damage. Loss experience is also an important underwriting consideration.

It should be determined if there is a need for "war risks" coverage. Remember, the policy will have a clause that excludes this peril. If shipments are going into a politically volatile area, it may be necessary to write a separate "war risks" policy to adequately cover this exposure. It may also be necessary to obtain this coverage if the shipment is financed, such as by a "letter of credit."

The producer should also inquire as to whether or not Premier's goods are shipped on deck or below deck and what deductible is desired.

Since Premier is responsible for goods from the factory until they reach the buyer, the warehouse to warehouse clause should be recommended to provide coverage for overland transportation. The underwriter will need to know how the goods are shipped from the warehouse to the port (Premier uses its own trucks).

Since Premier ships approximately ten times per year, the open cargo form with reports to the insurer at each shipment is better suited than the voyage form.

With this information in hand, the producer is ready to approach the marine underwriters to obtain a "quote." The producer now knows exactly what the prospect wants and has enough information to discuss the account. With the help of the marine underwriter, the producer prepares a proposal for insuring the ocean marine account. A good proposal for Premier would be as follows:

> We propose to insure your ocean marine exposure on an open cargo basis with a maximum of $100,000 per shipment at a rate of _____. Coverage would apply from your plant in Yourtown until it is deposited in the buyer's warehouse. The policy is an "all-risks" policy with usual marine exclusions.
>
> One important exclusion is for the peril of war. If you want this peril to be covered, or if credit terms dictate its necessity, then we can issue a separate policy with the same insurer at a rate of $_____.
>
> The open cargo policy allows you to ship at any time with no advance notice to the insurance company necessary. You will be best served if you furnish the insurance company with a report stating the value of the goods shipped at shipment date. We will not require a deposit premium. Rather you will then pay a rate of $_____ per $100 actually shipped with your report to the insurer.

This is a simple proposal, but it does point out what the producer intends to do. On the sales call, the producer can then discuss such things as the deductible plans involved or discuss more fully the valuation approach and exclusions or warranties in the policy.

CASE STUDY 2—
WINGATE EQUIPMENT CO.

Wingate Equipment Company is located in an inland state and imports industrial machinery from Europe. Wingate bought a large piece of equipment that will be delivered to a dock in Germany where Wingate will take possession. Wingate will then ship the equipment to New Orleans and transport it 1,000 miles by truck to Wingate's location. The company approached their local agent, Ellis Christian of Loventhal Bros., Inc., in Nashville, Tennessee, to handle this exposure.

Chris met with his client to get the particulars on the voyage. He gathered the necessary information on the date of the voyage, shipping line, and intended route. It was found that the ship would proceed directly to New Orleans from Germany with no other ports of call. He also found that the equipment would be shipped on deck and that the value to be insured—considering "freight" and other factors—would be $150,000.

Chris contacted the insurance companies represented by his firm and found an insurer for this type of account. He placed the coverage through the insurance company on a voyage policy. He explained the warehouse to warehouse clause would cover the land transit exposure for the one thousand mile trip from the port of entry.

Chris also informed the insured of the war exclusion and advised him of the rate for a "war risks" policy. Since this did not seem to be much of an exposure for this voyage the insured elected not to take this coverage.

With very little effort Chris had not only provided a valuable service to his client but had generated more premium dollars from an existing account. He had also prevented another producer from "getting his foot in the door."

CASE STUDY 3—
EXPORTS INTERNATIONAL

Tom, a young producer with limited experience, received a call from a total stranger. The stranger identified himself as an exporter who was looking for an alternate ocean marine insurer. Tom had never seen an ocean marine policy but considered it worth the effort to pursue. He went to the local university library and learned a little about the export business. He also checked with the insurers he represented to see if any had ocean marine facilities. He then called on his prospect.

At the interview Tom learned that his prospect would be shipping frozen meat, canned foods, office furniture, and some building materials to countries in the Middle East. The client wanted coverage from warehouse to warehouse. The meat would be coming from the Midwest and the other goods from various points in the South. The anticipated value of shipments the first year would be $10 million. Tom realized that this would be a large account and was determined that he would provide the best coverage at the best price. He contacted nine different insurers and received the best proposal through Lloyd's of London.

Coverage was on the "all-risks" open cargo form covering warehouse to warehouse. Due to the varying nature of the goods shipped, several different rates were needed for the reporting form coverage and several special warranties were applied to perils clauses.

Also, deductible provisions would be included in the policy. For an account of this size, a marine expert was sent to help Tom with the presentation of the proposal.

Important provisions of the proposal were as follows:

Rates:

Rate on frozen meat	0.85/$100
Rate on all other	0.55/$100
Rate on separate war risk policy	0.09/$100

Exclusions were:

1. Rusting or denting of canned food.
2. Damages from marring or scratching of office furniture.
3. Limited coverage to loss occurring within 24 hours of refrigeration equipment breakdown. After a 24-hour breakdown (instead of the usual 48 hour period) coverage on meat ceased.

Deductibles:

1. Per ship—A deductible of 1 percent of the value of the cargo but not less than $5,000 applied to cargo on any one ship.
2. Per vehicle—A deductible of $500 applied to all losses incurred in the course of land transportation.

The insured also chose to insure the war risk exposure since the goods were destined for the Middle East, an unsettled area of the world at the time. The account will produce an annual premium of approximately $75,000. With a little bit of study, a little bit of work, and a sincere interest in the account, Tom discovered that ocean marine insurance is not reserved for the specialty producer but can be handled locally.

COMMERCIAL AVIATION INSURANCE

Shipments by Air

Insurance for shipments by air is similar to ocean cargo insurance. In fact, all ocean marine policies provide for such shipments. Clients may use either ocean marine or aviation forms for such shipments. Generally, the air cargo policy indemnifies the insured for loss or damage to property shipped by air freight. There are some differences among the broad contracts written by the major insurers in this field. There is no one standard policy.

Exposures The air cargo exposure is one that must be carefully evaluated before a rate can be set. Most losses occur while the cargo is either in the course of ground transportation to and from the airport or in the airport terminal. Most air cargo losses are due to theft in the terminal. There is a high concentration of valuable merchandise in the terminal and security is difficult to maintain.

Regulation Regulation of air carriers is by the Civil Aeronautics Board (CAB). The CAB has authority over the *direct* air carrier, the carrier who operates aircraft, as well as the *indirect* air carrier, the company used to transport cargo to or from the airport. The CAB sets certain regulations on the maximum limit for which a carrier may be held liable. These limits change from time to time. In 1981 most air waybills (similar to bills of lading) are set at $50 per shipment or $.50 per pound limit if the shipment weighs more than 100 pounds. If the shipper can declare a higher value, the carrier is liable for the declared value or actual cash value whichever is less.

Coverage The air carrier usually carries coverage similar to that of the land common carrier to protect it from liability up to the stated limit. The shipper who wants higher values on cargo must pay for the additional amount of insurance, and the carrier issues a certificate to the shipper to cover that shipment.

The so-called Warsaw Convention also set limits of liability for cargo on international flights. It states that liability only applies while the cargo is on board the aircraft or in the terminal. No liability exists during the course of ground transportation.

Many requests are made to cover a single shipment of cargo on the insured's own plane. The rate on this type of shipment is always higher since the insurer would have no opportunity to subrogate if a loss occurred.

Since the air carrier is only liable for damage caused by negligence, and since the carrier's liability is limited by law, the shipper usually needs to provide for its own insurance protection. The air cargo policy for the shipper is usually written on an "all-risks" basis. This, among other things, provides theft coverage at the air terminal. The air cargo policy also covers the ground transportation to and from the airport. This is similar to the warehouse to warehouse clause in the ocean marine policy. The underwriter may want to cover the air transit exposure on the "all-risks" basis but only give named peril coverage on the ground transportation. If this is done, the "all-risks" coverage only applies while the cargo is either on the aircraft or in the airport terminal.

Exclusions The only significant exclusion in the "all-risks" policy is the peril of war. There often is an exclusion for loss or damage by freezing or changes in atmospheric pressure. This is not as important today with modern aircraft. Loss by strike may be excluded if the underwriter has reason to believe that this hazard is out of proportion to the rate charged.

The air cargo policy also is usually written to cover general average. This general average clause reads much like the clause in the ocean marine policy.

Air cargo coverage is subject to a per plane limit of liability and a per catastrophe limit. Limits should be set for the maximum amount that the insured would have on any one plane. The catastrophe limit is set to limit the amount in any one loss. This is done primarily to limit the aviation underwriter's exposure in an area where values may be concentrated, such as in the airport terminal or in a mid-air collision of two planes carrying the same insured's property.

Valuation The shipper can value the shipment at actual cash value plus 10 percent. The 10 percent is added to the invoice price, freight and other charges similar to ocean marine. The carrier usually has insurance to cover its own legal liability for loss of or damage to the property in his care, custody, and control.

Air cargo coverage is needed for some clients the average producer will encounter. It is one that should be recognized and placed for customers. There are no standard rates. The producer must seek the most competitive market for the coverage desired.

Other Commercial Aviation Exposures and Insurance

Any attempt for the risk management-oriented producer to identify a firm's loss exposures is incomplete unless aircraft exposures have been considered. There has been a rapid growth in the business and pleasure use of aircraft, and it is not reasonable to *assume* that the exposure does not exist for a given account. Any complete risk management exposure analysis must consider the possibility that an exposure to loss arises out of the ownership, use, or occupancy of an aircraft.

When an individual or company owns an airplane, the exposure is obvious. However, it is more difficult to identify exposures encountered when employees of a company rent or charter a plane, or use a personal aircraft on company business. This exposure must be identified so it does not remain uninsured.

Owned Aircraft If it is determined that the client owns any airplanes, the need for aircraft hull and liability coverage is obvious. If the client is a joint owner of an airplane, it is necessary to be sure all interests—including lienholders—are named in the policy.

Hull and liability insurance on aircraft are described in PRO 81, and the discussion will not be repeated here. However, when a commercial aircraft exposure exists, it is desirable to check the policy to be sure all exposures are properly covered and that the client does not have unusual operations or circumstances that are excluded by the policy.

Nonownership Coverage   It is very easy to overlook exposures due to the use of aircraft not owned by the insured. This exposure is by no means uncommon, for many businesses regularly use air travel other than scheduled airlines, but do not own any planes. Air travel enables executives and sales personnel to cover more area with less time than any other form of transportation. By using rented or charted airplanes, the individual traveler can dictate the most convenient times of departure and arrival—a luxury not possible with scheduled airlines. Employees who charter planes as a matter of course may frequently incur the potential for severe losses.

Most aircraft liability insurance policies provide *use of other aircraft* and *use of substitute aircraft* coverage, but this is not true for a business. Businesses need additional coverage when they lease or use other planes.

Other Exposures   The list of potential clients with a special need for some form of aviation insurance coverage is not limited to those who fly airplanes, helicopters, gliders, or other aircraft. Special exposures are also faced by hangar keepers and by firms that manufacture products used in aviation.

Hangar keepers legal liability insurance covers the insured's liability for damage to aircraft in the custody of the insured. Even though a hangar keeper may have general liability insurance, the general liability policy excludes coverage for damage to property in the insured's care, custody, or control. Although hangar keepers legal liability coverage resembles the garagekeepers form, it does not limit coverage to liability for damage caused by specified perils.

Aircraft products liability may be written either as part of a comprehensive airport liability policy (a form used to insure airports) or as an individual contract that closely resembles coverage for products liability in other lines. Manufacturers and repairers of airframes, aircraft components, parts, and accessories are prospects for this coverage. If an account with an aircraft products liability exposure is involved, the producer should also be sure to check the umbrella policy, if one exists, to be sure no unexpected exclusions deny coverage the insured intends to purchase.

Exhibit 6-4 contains a list of some potential aircraft insurance clients.

Because the nonownership exposure is so often overlooked, this

Exhibit 6-4
Potential Aircraft Insurance Clients*

The following are businesses with a potential need for aircraft insurance:

- aerial photography and geophysical operations
- aircraft manufacturers, dealers, or distributors
- aircraft engine, parts, or components manufacturers
- ranchers and farmers
- individuals renting or borrowing aircraft
- owners but not operators of airports
- powerline and pipe line patrol operations
- any person or organization operating any type of aircraft facility
- any business chartering or renting aircraft for business use

*Reprinted with permission from *FC&S Bulletins*, Sales Section, Surveys EA-3.

coverage in particular has proven to be a "door opener" for many insurance producers soliciting new accounts.

Aviation Insurance Rating There is no rating bureau control over aviation insurance rates. Factors that are particularly important in establishing a judgment rate are the qualifications and flying experience of the pilot, the type and value of the equipment, the use being made of the aircraft, and so on.

Completing a Submission Generally, a completed application is required to obtain a quotation. The underwriter will be particularly interested in the following information, which may be obtained even if an application is not readily available:[1]

1. Name, address, and occupation of applicant.
2. Description of aircraft by FAA number, make and model, year built, seating capacity, and type of plane (whether land plane, sea plane, or amphibian).
3. Insured value.
4. Coverages and limits desired.
5. Use of the aircraft.
6. Pilot license and ratings (such as Student, Private, Commercial, ATR, Instrument).
7. Pilot's age.
8. Total pilot time.
9. Time as pilot in command of similar make and model aircraft.
10. Is aircraft hangared or unhangared? Where?
11. Previous loss experience and citations by the FAA.

12. Amount of lien. Is breach of warranty or loss payable necessary?

Checkpoints

1. Distinguish between an implied and an express warranty.
2. List four implied warranties in ocean marine insurance.
3. Describe two ways to insure cargo shipped by air.
4. List three common exclusions to the air cargo policy.
5. List the exposures of a user of aircraft for business purposes.

SUMMARY

Most producers do not need an extensive technical background in ocean marine and aviation insurance unless they will specialize in one of these lines. Yet every producer will have the opportunity to insure such exposures occasionally. As ocean cargo is the most likely ocean marine exposure to be encountered, most of the chapter was devoted to it. Coverage for yachts, an ocean marine line, was discussed in PRO 81, *Principles of Insurance Production.*

Producers encountering hull exposures on boats, ships, or aircraft should first contact the ocean or aviation departments of their insurers or a reputable excess and surplus lines broker for technical assistance. Most such exposures encountered will be a challenge for the producer. If substantial amounts of other insurance are the reward for good ocean or aviation coverage, the effort is worth it.

Producers intrigued by ocean or aviation insurance are encouraged to learn more about the exposures and their treatment. Ocean marine or aviation insurance can be a good place to build a producer's "temporary monopoly."

Chapter Note

1. *A Guide to Aviation Insurance,* Insurance Company of North America, 7/75.

Appendix

Revised American Foreign Trade Definitions*
1941

Adopted July 30, 1941, by a Joint Committee representing the Chamber of Commerce of the United States of America, the National Council of American Importers, Inc., and the National Foreign Trade Council, Inc.

The following *Revised American Foreign Trade Definitions - 1941* are recommended for general use by both exporters and importers. These revised definitions have no status at law unless there is specific legislation providing for them, or unless they are confirmed by court decisions. Hence, it is suggested that sellers and buyers agree to their acceptance as part of the contract of sale. These revised definitions will then become legally binding upon all parties.

In view of changes in practice and procedure since 1919, certain new responsibilities for sellers and buyers are included in these revised definitions. Also, in many instances, the old responsibilities are more clearly defined than in the 1919 Definitions, and the changes should be beneficial both to sellers and buyers. Widespread acceptance will lead to a greater standardization of foreign trade procedure, and to the avoidance of much misunderstanding.

Adoption by exporters and importers of these revised terms will impress on all parties concerned their respective responsibilities and rights.

General Notes of Caution

1. As foreign trade definitions have been issued by organizations in various parts of the world, and as the courts of countries have interpreted these definitions in different ways, it is important that sellers and buyers agree that their contracts are subject to the *Revised American Foreign Trade Definitions - 1941* and that the various points listed are accepted by both parties.

2. In addition to the foreign trade terms listed herein, there are terms that are at times used, such as Free Harbor, C.I.F. & C. (Cost, Insurance, Freight, and Commission), C.I.F.C. & I. (Cost, Insurance, Freight, Commission, and Interest), C.I.F. Landed (Cost, Insurance, Freight, Landed), and others. None of these should be used unless there has first been a definite understanding as to the exact meaning thereof. It is unwise to attempt to interpret other terms in the light of the terms given herein. Hence, whenever possible, one of the terms defined herein should be used.

3. It is unwise to use abbreviations in quotations or in contracts which might be subject to misunderstanding.

4. When making quotations, the familiar terms "hundredweight" or "ton" should be avoided. A hundredweight can be 100 pounds of the short ton, or 112 pounds of the long ton. A ton can be a short ton of 2,000 pounds, or a metric ton of 2,204.6 pounds, or a long ton of 2,240 pounds. Hence, the type of hundredweight or ton should be clearly stated in quotations and in sales confirmations. Also, all terms referring to quantity, weight, volume, length, or surface should be clearly defined and agreed upon.

5. If inspection, or certificate of inspection, is required, it should be agreed, in advance, whether the cost thereof is for account of seller or buyer.

6. Unless otherwise agreed upon, all expenses are for the account of seller up to the point at which the buyer must handle the subsequent movement of goods.

7. There are a number of elements in a contract that do not fall within the scope of these foreign trade definitions. Hence, no mention of these is made herein. Seller and buyer should agree to these separately when negotiating contracts. This particularly applies to so-called "customary" practices.

---

*Issued by the National Foreign Trade Council, Inc. Reprinted with permission from *Marine Insurance: Notes and Comments on Ocean Cargo Insurance*, Copyright 1971 by Insurance Company of North America.

Definitions of Quotations

(I) EX (Point of Origin)

"EX FACTORY", "EX MILL", "EX MINE", "EX PLANTATION", "EX WAREHOUSE", etc. (named point of origin)

Under this term, the price quoted applies only at the point of origin, and the seller agrees to place the goods at the disposal of the buyer at the agreed place on the date or within the period fixed.

Under this quotation:

Seller must

(1) **bear all costs and risks of the goods until such time as the buyer is obliged to take delivery thereof;**

(2) render the buyer, at the buyer's request and expense, assistance in obtaining the documents issued in the country of origin, or of shipment, or of both, which the buyer may re-quire either for purposes of exportation, or of importation at destination.

Buyer must

(1) **take delivery of the goods as soon as they have been placed at his disposal at the agreed place on the date or within the period fixed;**

(2) pay export taxes, or other fees or charges, if any, levied because of exportation;

(3) bear all costs and risks of the goods from the time when he is obligated to take delivery thereof;

(4) pay all costs and charges incurred in obtaining the documents issued in the country of origin, or of shipment, or of both, which may be required either for purposes of exportation, or of importation at destination.

(II) F.O.B. (Free on Board)

NOTE: *Seller and buyer should consider not only the definitions but also the "Comments on All F.O.B. Terms" given at end of this section (page 45), in order to understand fully their respective responsibilities and rights under the several classes of "F.O.B." terms.*

(II-A) "F.O.B. (named inland carrier at named inland point of departure)"*

Under this term, the price quoted applies only at inland shipping point, and the seller arranges for loading of the goods on, or in, railway cars, trucks, lighters, barges, aircraft, or other conveyance furnished for transportation.

Under this quotation:

Seller must

(1) place goods on, or in, conveyance, or deliver to inland carrier for loading;

(2) provide clean bill of lading or other transportation receipt, freight collect;

(3) **be responsible for any loss or damage, or both, until goods have been placed in, or on, conveyance at load-ing point, and clean bill of lading or other transportation receipt has been furnished by the carrier;**

(4) render the buyer, at the buyer's request and expense, assistance in obtaining the documents issued in the country of origin, or of shipment, or of both, which the buyer may require either for purposes of exportation, or of importation at destination.

Buyer must

(1) **be responsible for all movement of the goods from inland point of loading, and pay all transportation costs;**

(2) pay export taxes, or other fees or charges, if any, levied because of exportation;

(3) be responsible for any loss or damage, or both, incurred after loading at named inland point of departure;

(4) pay all costs and charges incurred in obtaining the documents issued in the country of origin, or of shipment, or of both, which may be required either for purposes of exportation, or of importation at destination.

---

* See Note above and Comments on All F.O.B. Terms (page 45).

Heavy type is used to stress references to responsibility or insurance.

(II-B) "F.O.B. (named inland carrier at named inland point of departure) FREIGHT PREPAID TO (named point of exportation)"*

Under this term, the seller quotes a price including transportation charges to the named point of exportation and pre-pays freight to named point of exportation, without assuming responsibility for the goods after obtaining a clean bill of lading or other transportation receipt at named inland point of departure.

Under this quotation:

Seller must
(1) assume the seller's obligations as under II-A (page 42), except that under (2) he must **provide clean bill of lading or other transportation receipt, freight prepaid to named point of exportation.**

Buyer must
(1) assume the same buyer's obligations as under II-A (page 42), except that he does not pay freight from loading point to named point of exportation.

(II-C) "F.O.B. (named inland carrier at named inland point of departure) FREIGHT ALLOWED TO (named point)"*

Under this term, the seller quotes a price including the transportation charges to the named point, shipping freight collect and deducting the cost of transportation, without assuming responsibility for the goods after obtaining a clean bill of lading or other transportation receipt at named inland point of departure.

Under this quotation:

Seller must
(1) assume the same seller's obligations as under II-A (page 42), but deducts from his invoice the transportation cost to named point.

* See Note (page 42) and Comments on all F.O.B. Terms (page 45).

Buyer must
(1) assume the same buyer's obligations as under II-A (page 42), including payment of freight from inland loading point to named point, for which seller has made deduction.

(II-D) "F.O.B. (named inland carrier at named point of exportation)"*

Under this term, the seller quotes a price including the costs of transportation of the goods to named point of exportation, bearing any loss or damage, or both, incurred up to that point.

Under this quotation:

Seller must
(1) place goods on, or in, conveyance, or deliver to inland carrier for loading;
(2) **provide clean bill of lading or other transportation receipt, paying all transportation** costs from loading point to named point of exportation;
(3) **be responsible for any loss or damage, or both, until goods have arrived in, or on, inland conveyance at the named point of exportation;**
(4) render the buyer, at the buyer's request and expense, assistance in obtaining the documents issued in the country of origin, or of shipment, or of both, which the buyer may require either for purposes of exportation, or of importation at destination.

Buyer must
(1) be responsible for all movement of the goods from inland conveyance at named point of exportation;
(2) pay export taxes, or other fees or charges, if any, levied because of exportation;
(3) **be responsible for any loss or damage, or both, incurred after goods have arrived in, or on, inland conveyance at the named point of exportation;**

(4) pay all costs and charges incurred in obtaining the documents issued in the country of origin, or of shipment, or of both, which may be required either for purposes of exportation, or of importation at destination.

(II-E) "F.O.B. VESSEL (named port of shipment)"*

Under this term, the seller quotes a price covering all expenses up to, and including, delivery of the goods upon the overseas vessel provided by, or for, the buyer at the named port of shipment.

Under this quotation:

Seller must

(1) pay all charges incurred in placing goods actually on board the vessel designated and provided by, or for, the buyer on the date or within the period fixed;

(2) **provide clean ship's receipt or on-board bill of lading;**

(3) **be responsible for any loss or damage, or both, until goods have been placed on board the vessel on the date or within the period fixed;**

(4) render the buyer, at the buyer's request and expense, assistance in obtaining the documents issued in the country of origin, or of shipment, or of both, which the buyer may require either for purposes of exportation, or of importation at destination.

Buyer must

(1) give seller adequate notice of name, sailing date, loading berth of, and delivery time to, the vessel;

(2) **bear the additional costs incurred and all risks of the goods from the time when the seller has placed them at his disposal if the vessel named by him fails to arrive or to load within the designated time;**

* See Note (page 42) and Comments on all F.O.B. Terms (page 45).

(3) handle all subsequent movement of the goods to destination:
   (a) **provide and pay for insurance;**
   (b) provide and pay for ocean and other transportation;

(4) pay export taxes, or other fees or charges, if any, levied because of exportation;

(5) **be responsible for any loss or damage, or both, after goods have been loaded on board the vessel;**

(6) pay all costs and charges incurred in obtaining the documents, other than clean ship's receipt or bill of lading, issued in the country of origin, or of shipment, or of both, which may be required either for purposes of exportation, or of importation at destination.

(II-F) "F.O.B. (named inland point in country of importation)"*

Under this term, the seller quotes a price including the cost of the merchandise and all costs of transportation to the named inland point in the country of importation.

Under this quotation:

Seller must

(1) provide and pay for all transportation to the named inland point in the country of importation;

(2) pay export taxes, or other fees or charges, if any, levied because of exportation;

(3) **provide and pay for marine insurance;**

(4) **provide and pay for war risk insurance, unless otherwise agreed upon between the seller and buyer;**

(5) **be responsible for any loss or damage, or both, until arrival of goods on conveyance at the named inland point in the country of importation;**

(6) pay the costs of certificates of origin, consular invoices, or any other documents issued in the country of origin, or of shipment, or of both, which the buyer may require for the importation of goods into the country of destination and, where necessary, for their passage in transit through another country;

(7) pay all costs of landing, including wharfage, landing charges, and taxes, if any;

(8) pay all costs of customs entry in the country of importation;

(9) pay customs duties and all taxes applicable to imports, if any, in the country of importation.

NOTE: *The seller under this quotation must realize that he is accepting important responsibilities, costs, and risks, and should therefore be certain to obtain adequate insurance. On the other hand, the importer or buyer may desire such quotations to relieve him of the risks of the voyage and to assure him of his landed costs at inland point in country of importation. When competition is keen, or the buyer is accustomed to such quotations from other sellers, seller may quote such terms, being careful to protect himself in an appropriate manner.*

Buyer must

(1) take prompt delivery of goods from conveyance upon arrival at destination;

(2) **bear any costs and be responsible for all loss or damage, or both, after arrival at destination.**

Comments On All F.O.B. Terms

In connection with F.O.B. terms, the following points of caution are recommended:

1. The method of inland transportation, such as trucks, railroad cars, lighters, barges, or aircraft should be specified.

2. If any switching charges are involved during the inland transportation, it should be agreed, in advance, whether these charges are for account of the seller or the buyer.

3. The term "F.O.B. (named port)," without designating the exact point at which the liability of the seller terminates and the liability of the buyer begins, should be avoided. The use of this term gives rise to disputes as to the liability of the seller or the buyer in the event of loss or damage arising while the goods are in port, and before delivery to or on board the ocean carrier. Misunderstandings may be avoided by naming the specific point of delivery.

4. If lighterage or trucking is required in the transfer of goods from the inland conveyance to ship's side, and there is a cost therefor, it should be understood, in advance, whether this cost is for account of the seller or the buyer.

5. The seller should be certain to notify the buyer of the minimum quantity required to obtain a carload, a truckload, or a barge-load freight rate.

6. Under F.O.B. terms, excepting "F.O.B. (named inland point in country of importation)," the obligation to obtain ocean freight space, and marine and war risk insurance, rests with the buyer. Despite this obligation on the part of the buyer, in many trades the seller obtains the ocean freight space, and marine and war risk insurance, and provides for shipment on behalf of the buyer. Hence, seller and buyer must have an understanding as to whether the buyer will obtain the ocean freight space, and marine and war risk insurance, as is his obligation, or whether the seller agrees to do this for the buyer.

7. For the seller's protection, he should provide in his contract of sale that marine insurance obtained by the buyer include standard warehouse to warehouse coverage.

(III) F.A.S. (Free Along Side)

NOTE: *Seller and buyer should consider not only the definitions but also the "Comments" given at the end of this section (page 39), in order to understand fully their respective responsibilities and rights under "F.A.S." terms.*

"F.A.S. VESSEL (named port of shipment)"

Under this term, the seller quotes a price including delivery of the goods along side overseas vessel and within reach of its loading tackle.

Under this quotation:

Seller must

(1) place goods along side vessel or on dock designated and provided by, or for, buyer on the date or within the period fixed; pay any heavy lift charges, where necessary, up to this point;

(2) provide clean dock or ship's receipt;

(3) **be responsible for any loss or damage, or both, until goods have been delivered along side the vessel or on the dock;**

(4) render the buyer, at the buyer's request and expense, assistance in obtaining the documents issued in the country of origin, or of shipment, or of both, which the buyer may require either for purposes of exportation, or of importation at destination.

Buyer must

(1) give seller adequate notice of name, sailing date, loading berth of, and delivery time to, the vessel;

(2) handle all subsequent movement of the goods from along side the vessel:

(a) arrange and pay for demurrage or storage charges, or both, in warehouse or on wharf, where necessary;

(b) provide and pay for insurance;

(c) provide and pay for ocean and other transportation;

(3) pay export taxes, or other fees or charges, if any, levied because of exportation;

(4) **be responsible for any loss or damage, or both, while the goods are on a lighter or other conveyance along side vessel within reach of its loading tackle, or on the dock awaiting loading, or until actually loaded on board the vessel, and subsequent thereto;**

(5) pay all costs and charges incurred in obtaining the documents, other than clean dock or ship's receipt, issued in the country of origin, or of shipment, or of both, which may be required either for purposes of exportation, or of importation at destination.

F.A.S. Comments

1. Under F.A.S. terms, the obligation to obtain ocean freight space, and marine and war risk insurance, rests with the buyer. Despite this obligation on the part of the buyer, in many trades the seller obtains ocean freight space, and marine and war risk insurance, and provides for shipment on behalf of the buyer. In others, the buyer notifies the seller to make delivery along side a vessel designated by the buyer and the buyer provides his own marine and war risk insurance. Hence, seller and buyer must have an understanding as to whether the buyer will obtain the ocean freight space, and marine and war risk insurance, as is his obligation, or whether the seller agrees to do this for the buyer.

2. For the seller's protection, he should provide in his contract of sale that marine insurance obtained by the buyer include standard warehouse to warehouse coverage.

(IV) C. & F. (Cost and Freight)

NOTE: *Seller and buyer should consider not only the definitions but also the "C. & F. Comments" (page 40) and the "C. & F. and C.I.F. Comments" (page 40-41), in order to understand fully their respective responsibilities and rights under "C. & F." terms.*

"C. & F. (named point of destination)"

Under this term, the seller quotes a price including the cost of transportation to the named point of destination.

Under this quotation:

Seller must

(1) provide and pay for transportation to named point of destination;

(2) pay export taxes, or other fees or charges, if any, levied because of exportation;

(3) **obtain and dispatch promptly to buyer, or his agent, clean bill of lading to named point of destination;**

(4) **where received-for-shipment ocean bill of lading may be tendered, be responsible for any loss or damage, or both, until the goods have been delivered into the custody of the ocean carrier;**

(5) **where on-board ocean bill of lading is required, be responsible for any loss or damage, or both, until the goods have been delivered on board the vessel;**

(6) provide, at the buyer's request and expense, certificates of origin, consular invoices, or any other documents issued in the country of origin, or of shipment, or of both, which the buyer may require for importation of goods into country of destination and, where necessary, for their passage in transit through another country.

Buyer must

(1) accept the documents when presented;

(2) receive goods upon arrival, handle and pay for all subsequent movement of the goods, including taking delivery from vessel in accordance with bill of lading clauses and terms; pay all costs of landing including any duties, taxes, and other expenses at named point of destination;

(3) **provide and pay for insurance;**

(4) **be responsible for loss of or damage to goods, or both, from time and place at which seller's obligations under (4) or (5) above have ceased;**

(5) pay the costs of certificates of origin, consular invoices, or any other documents issued in the country of origin, or of shipment, or of both, which may be required for the importation of goods into the country of destination and, where necessary, for their passage in transit through another country.

C. &. F. Comments

1. For the seller's protection, he should provide in his contract of sale that marine insurance obtained by the buyer include standard warehouse to warehouse coverage.

2. The comments listed under the following C.I.F. terms in many cases apply to C. & F. terms as well, and should be read and understood by the C. & F. seller and buyer.

(V) C.I.F. (Cost, Insurance, Freight)

NOTE: *Seller and buyer should consider not only the definitions but also the "Comments" (pages 40-41), at the end of this section, in order to understand fully their respective responsibilities and rights under "C.I.F." terms.*

"C.I.F. (named point of destination)"

Under this term, the teller quotes a price including the cost of the goods, the marine insurance, and all transportation charges to be named point of destination. Under this quotation:

Seller must

(1) provide and pay for transportation to named point of destination;

(2) pay export taxes, or other fees or charges, if any, levied because of exportation;

(3) **provide and pay for marine insurance;**

(4) **provide war risk insurance as obtainable in seller's market at time of shipment at buyer's expense, unless seller has agreed that buyer provide for war risk coverage (See Comment 10 (c), page 49);**

(5) **obtain and dispatch promptly to buyer, or his agent, clean bill of lading to named point of destination, and also insurance policy or negotiable insurance certificate;**

(6) **where received-for-shipment ocean bill of lading may be tendered, be responsible for any loss or damage, or both, until the goods have been delivered into the custody of the ocean carrier;**

(7) where on-board ocean bill of lading is required, be responsible for any loss or damage, or both, until the goods have been delivered on board the vessel;

(8) provide, at the buyer's request and expense, certificates of origin, consular invoices, or any other documents issued in the country of origin, or of shipment, or both, which the buyer may require for importation of goods into country of destination and, where necessary, for their passage in transit through another country.

Buyer must

(1) accept the documents when presented;

(2) receive the goods upon arrival, handle and pay for all subsequent movement of the goods, including taking delivery from vessel in accordance with bill of lading clauses and terms; pay all costs of landing, including any duties, taxes, and other expenses at named point of destination;

(3) **pay for war risk insurance provided by seller;**

(4) **be responsible for loss of or damage to goods, or both, from time and place at which seller's obligations under (6) or (7) above have ceased;**

(5) pay the cost of certificates of origin, consular invoices, or any other documents issued in the country of origin, or of shipment, or both, which may be required for importation of the goods into the country of destination and, where necessary, for their passage in transit through another country.

C. & F. and C.I.F. Comments

Under C. & F. and C.I.F. contracts there are the following points on which the seller and the buyer should be in complete agreement at the time that the contract is concluded:

1. It should be agreed upon, in advance, who is to pay for miscellaneous expenses, such as weighing or inspection charges.

2. The quantity to be shipped on any one vessel should be agreed upon, in advance, with a view to the buyer's capacity to take delivery upon arrival and dis-

charge of the vessel; within the free time allowed at the port of importation.

3. Although the terms C. & F. and C.I.F. are generally interpreted to provide that charges for consular invoices and certificates of origin are for the account of the buyer, and are charged separately, in many trades these charges are included by the seller in his price. Hence, seller and buyer should agree, in advance, whether these charges are part of the selling price, or will be invoiced separately.

4. The point of final destination should be definitely known in the event the vessel discharges at a port other than the actual destination of the goods.

5. When ocean freight space is difficult to obtain, or forward freight contracts cannot be made at firm rates, it is advisable that sales contracts, as an exception to regular C. & F. or C.I.F. terms, should provide that shipment within the contract period be subject to ocean freight space being available to the seller, and should also provide that changes in the cost of ocean transportation between the time of sale and the time of shipment be for account of the buyer.

6. Normally, the seller is obligated to prepay the ocean freight. In some instances, shipments are made freight collect and the amount of the freight is deducted from the invoice rendered by the seller. It is necessary to be in agreement on this, in advance, in order to avoid misunderstanding which arises from foreign exchange fluctuations which might affect the actual cost of transportation, and from interest charges which might accrue under letter of credit financing. Hence, the seller should always prepay the ocean freight unless he has a specific agreement with the buyer, in advance, that goods can be shipped freight collect.

7. The buyer should recognize that he does not have the right to insist on inspection of goods prior to accepting the documents. The buyer should not refuse to take delivery of goods on account of delay in the receipt of documents, provided the seller has used due diligence in their dispatch through the regular channels.

8. Sellers and buyers are advised against including in a C.I.F. contract any indefinite clause at variance with the obligations of a C.I.F. contract as specified in these Definitions. There have been numerous court decisions in the United States and other countries invalidating C.I.F. contracts because of the inclusion of indefinite clauses.

9. Interest charges should be included in cost computations and should not be charged as a separate item in C.I.F. contracts, unless otherwise agreed upon, in advance, between the seller and buyer; in which case, however, the term C.I.F. and I (Cost, Insurance, Freight, and Interest) should be used.

10. In connection with insurance under C.I.F. sales, it is necessary that seller and buyer be definitely in accord upon the following points:

(a) The character of the marine insurance should be agreed upon in so far as being W.A. (With Average) or F.P.A. (Free of Particular Average), as well as any other special risks that are covered in specific trades, or against which the buyer may wish individual protection. Among the special risks that should be considered and agreed upon between seller and buyer are theft, pilferage, leakage, breakage, sweat, contact with other cargoes, and others peculiar to any particular trade. It is important that contingent or collect freight and customs duty should be insured to cover Particular Average losses, as well as total loss after arrival and entry but before delivery.

(b) The seller is obligated to exercise ordinary care and diligence in selecting an underwriter that is in good financial standing. However, the risk of obtaining settlement of insurance claims rests with the buyer.

(c) War risk insurance under this term is to be obtained by the seller at the expense and risk of the buyer. It is important that the seller be in definite accord with the buyer on this point, particularly as to the cost. It is desirable that the goods be insured against both marine and war risk with the same underwriter, so that there can be no difficulty arising from the determination of the cause of the loss.

(d) Seller should make certain that in his marine or war risk insurance, there be included the standard protection against strikes, riots and civil commotions.

(e) Seller and buyer should be in accord as to the insured valuation, bearing in mind that merchandise contributes in General Average on certain bases of valuation which differ in various trades. It is desirable that a competent insurance broker be consulted, in order that full value be covered and trouble avoided.

(VI) "EX DOCK (named port of importation)"

NOTE: *Seller and buyer should consider not only the definitions but also the "Ex Dock Comments" at the end of this section (this page), in order to understand fully their respective responsibilities and rights under "Ex Dock" terms.*

Under this term, seller quotes a price including the cost of the goods and all additional costs necessary to place the goods on the dock at the named port of importation, duty paid, if any.

Under this quotation:

Seller must

(1) provide and pay for transportation to named port of importation;

(2) pay export taxes, or other fees or charges, if any, levied because of exportation;

(3) **provide and pay for marine insurance;**

(4) **provide and pay for war risk insurance, unless otherwise agreed upon between the buyer and seller;**

(5) **be responsible for any loss or damage, or both, until the expiration of the free time allowed on the dock at the named port of importation;**

(6) pay the costs of certificates of origin, consular invoices, legalization of bill of lading, or any other documents issued in the country of origin, or of shipment, or of both, which the buyer may require for the importation of goods into the country of destination and, where necessary, for their passage in transit through another country;

(7) pay all costs of landing, including wharfage, landing charges, and taxes, if any;

(8) pay all costs of customs entry in the country of importation;

(9) pay customs duties and all taxes applicable to imports, if any, in the country of importation, unless otherwise agreed upon.

Buyer must

(1) take delivery of the goods on the dock at the named port of importation within the free time allowed;

(2) bear the cost and risk of the goods if delivery is not taken within the free time allowed.

Ex Dock Comments

This term is used principally in United States import trade. It has various modifications, such as "Ex Quay," "Ex Pier," etc., but it is seldom, if ever, used in American export practice. Its use in quotations for export is not recommended.

Entire appendix "A" quoted from "Revised American Trade Definitions—1941" issued by the National Foreign Trade Council, Inc.

CHAPTER 7

Commercial Crime Insurance

INTRODUCTION

A crime is a violation of law punishable by some governmental body. This chapter concentrates on those crime exposures of commercial or mercantile organizations insurable by either fidelity bonds (employee dishonesty) or crime insurance. Some insurance companies separate the two lines with the surety department handling fidelity insurance and the property-liability staff handling crime exposures. The distinctions between bonds and insurance are made elsewhere.

The importance of crime insurance, particularly to the small commercial establishment, is demonstrated by this fact from the U.S. Chamber of Commerce: approximately one-quarter of all bankruptcies of business firms are caused by some form of crime. Typically, property in the form of money, securities, office equipment, or inventory is taken and the business cannot recover. Some losses are caused by long time, trusted employees, while others are caused by people who make their living by crime. Not all types of crime losses are insurable. Some are covered under other insurance forms such as the vandalism and malicious mischief coverage in a fire policy.

Types of Crimes

A complete listing of the types of crimes is not possible. Neither is it possible to present a list of definitions of types of crimes because technical definitions vary from one jurisdiction to another. The terms used here are generally understood by the public and are only descriptive by the types of crime loss exposures commercial firms face.

Theft has a broad definition: it means any act of stealing. Theft can refer to picking a pocket, shoplifting, or swindling. More specific types of theft include burglary and robbery. Burglary is the taking of property by breaking into a closed premises. Robbery usually indicates some violence or threat causing the surrender of property. Extortion and blackmail are forms of robbery because they involve depriving an owner of property by some threat of violence.

In addition to theft, there are many other crimes. Deliberately passing a worthless check is common. Forgery is another crime peril affecting many commercial firms. The widespread use of credit cards has led to an increase in forgery and fraud, and the passing or acceptance of counterfeit money is another way a business may lose property to the criminal. In some cases it is not possible to determine whether some type of theft has occurred. For instance, "mysterious disappearance" refers to property that was in a known location and is no longer there.

Many firms engaged in highly technical operations are subject to industrial espionage or the theft of trade secrets. Almost all businesses now use a computer, and computer fraud is a growing area of commercial crime. Predating the computer, but in some cases made easier by its use, is the crime of embezzlement.

There are a host of other types of crimes including vandalism and sabotage. Arson is a crime, and to some degree kidnapping can be considered part of the extortion peril.

Businesses of all sizes and degrees of sophistication are subject to a wide variety of property loss, damage, destruction, or disappearance because of crimes. Crime coverage can be an important entree into an account for a producer because, in many cases, crime is the forgotten or mistreated peril. Understanding the nature of crime insurance and how it can be used to treat commercial loss exposures can help the producer become more successful and the client to stay in business.

Crime Insurance Categories

There are three general categories of crime insurance indicated by rate manuals—mercantile operations, financial institutions, and governmental entities. The majority of this chapter will address mercantile crime insurance. As a general definition, mercantile prospects are all nonfinancial institutions and nongovernmental entities. Therefore mercantile crime prospects would include large conglomerates, factories, warehouses, delivery companies, small mercantile establishments, professional firms, or any other type of business organization.

Financial institutions will also be treated in this chapter. The discussion of financial institution coverage will not be as extensive as that for mercantile coverage simply because the purchase of crime insurance by financial institutions is almost universal. The producer does not need to convince the bank, savings and loan, stock brokerage house, or other financial institution to buy crime insurance. Those organizations almost always buy the coverage in any event. It is merely a matter of deciding if optional coverages are desirable and whom to buy the coverage from.

Governmental crime insurance will not be covered in this chapter. It is treated in the bonding chapter.

Format for Analysis of Crime Policies

Crime policies will be examined in four principal areas: (1) type of property covered, (2) perils insured, (3) location of the property covered, and (4) persons causing the loss.

Property Covered As with most types of insurance, property covered by a crime policy may be either broadly or narrowly defined. For instance, the property covered by a mercantile open stock policy will include "merchandise, equipment, furniture and fixtures." Or, the property covered may be very narrowly defined, such as money orders and paper currency as in the Money Order and Paper Currency Policy. The most common types of property specifically mentioned in crime insurance policies are "money and securities," payroll funds and checks, merchandise, equipment, furniture and fixtures, and "other property."

The producer must be sure the crime policy is written to cover the specific property the client needs to insure. For instance, a travel agency would have little need for coverage on "merchandise," but it would have a substantial exposure with regard to money, securities, and checks. The problem of matching policy coverage to the property becomes difficult because in some policies some types of property covered are very specifically defined while in others, the definitions are not as precise. For instance the word "securities" has a very definite meaning in crime insurance.

Perils Insured Rarely will the definition of an insured peril match the specific definition of that word in a criminal statute. Therefore, the producer must be sure the policy definition of the peril matches the loss exposure faced by the client.

As with the types of property covered, some perils are very specifically defined within the policy while others remain undefined. Perils can be as broad as theft or narrower, such as burglary or robbery. Forgery usually is very specifically defined. At the other extreme the broadest perils insured in a crime policy, "disappearance, destruction, and wrongful abstraction," are rarely defined. Similarly, a word like extortion may or may not be defined within a policy.

Location of Property Covered Some types of crime insurance only insure property in a very specific place, such as in a safe or vault. Others may insure property while "inside the premises." With "inside the premises" coverage, another restriction may be that the property is covered only while the firm is not open for business, or it could be that the property is covered at any time. Similarly, some property is only insured while a guard is on the premises. Restrictions on "outside the premises" can vary from property being with a messenger while being conveyed to some specific location such as a bank, or the property could even be covered in a messenger's home. Some crime coverages will cover certain property while in a "night depository." For extortion coverage, property is usually covered "beginning outside the premises." Again, the producer must make sure that the coverage for property is at the location desired by the client.

Persons Causing the Loss There are generally two categories of persons causing loss, anyone or anyone but an employee.

Anyone. The culprit, or the person causing the crime loss, may be anyone, which would include employees of the named insured as well as nonemployees. When losses by employees are insured, it is usually for a fidelity coverage (bonds). Losses by employees may be covered in a number of different ways.

SPECIFIED EMPLOYEES. In many cases an individual bond is written on a specific, named employee, for instance Michael Roux. In that case, losses caused by an individual named in the bond are insured.

SCHEDULES OF EMPLOYEES. Another way losses by employees may be insured by a fidelity bond is by schedule. Scheduling employees means losses caused by a specific list of employees will be covered either by the employees' names or by a listing of their positions. For instance on a *name schedule bond,* coverage is for losses caused by all of the employees specifically listed by their names. This is a sometimes cumbersome process because as employees turn over, the bond must be endorsed to indicate the name of the individual who is replacing a terminated employee. To overcome the constant endorsement of a bond, a *position schedule bond* is available in which only the job titles are scheduled. Therefore, the only time a change in the bond would be necessary is when a new position is added to the firm.

BLANKETING EMPLOYEES. A third way losses caused by employees may be covered under bond is by blanketing. A *blanket bond* indicates that losses caused by all employees, perhaps within a department, or each and every employee, are covered by a bond. The names of bonds usually associated with a blanket coverage are the *commercial blanket bond* and the *blanket position bond.* There is one important difference between these two types of bonds in the actual coverage when a loss results from the collusion of employees. The commercial blanket bond limits recovery in such a case to the *penalty,* or limit of liability, which is selected in the bond no matter how many employees participate in the dishonest act. The blanket position bond, on the other hand, permits recovery to the named penalty, or limit of liability, for each employee who is identified as participating in the loss.

For example, assume a bond limit of liability is $10,000 and two employees participated in a dishonest act, causing a loss of $15,000. The commercial blanket bond would pay only the limit of $10,000 and the insured may suffer a loss of the balance of $5,000. A blanket position bond, in contrast, could permit recovery of the full $15,000 because each of the employees is considered bonded up to $10,000. There are other differences between the two types of blanket bonds discussed later.

"Anyone but an Employee." The second category of losses covered by people or culprits is designated "anyone but an employee." Crime coverages written on this basis are usually considered insurance rather than bonds—for example, open stock burglary or theft insurance.

Persons Always Excluded. Without exception, losses caused by two categories of persons are always excluded from crime insurance coverage; *the named insured and any partner of the named insured.* This exclusion cannot be overemphasized. The losses are excluded whether the named insured or partner acts alone or in collusion with others.

COMPREHENSIVE DISHONESTY, DISAPPEARANCE, AND DESTRUCTION POLICY (3-D)

Introduction

Only two crime policies will be discussed for mercantile establishments: (1) the comprehensive dishonesty, disappearance, and destruction policy (3-D), its variations and endorsements, and (2) the mercantile open stock policy. The broadform storekeepers policy will not be discussed, as it has been basically assimilated into the businessowners policy and discussion of it is reserved for Chapter 11.

Combinations of Coverage Forms

There are two types of 3-D policies, designated here as form A, form B, and the blanket crime policy (BC), another crime policy similar to the 3-D with respect to coverage. Each of the three policies has the same five basic insuring agreements available. However, under forms A and B, the insured may select any or all of the five coverages offered and may also select separate limits of liability for each insuring agreement. Under the BC form, the insured must take all five agreements at a single limit of liability. Other differences among the three forms will be discussed below. Primary emphasis here is given to form A of the 3-D policy.

Declarations Page The declarations page for all three forms is essentially the same. The insured and the producer are identified and the policy period is stipulated. The limit of liability for any coverage and deductibles selected is indicated, and endorsements to the form are designated. Finally, a statement is made relative to the cancellation of other similar coverages. Essentially, in the last section of the declarations page, the insured agrees that all bonds or crime policies, if any, with the insurer and as listed in the declarations page, are terminated or canceled as of the effective date of the 3-D policy, preventing overlapping coverage.

3-D Coverages

The five basic insuring agreements of the 3-D Policy are

    I. employee dishonesty;
    II. loss inside the premises;
    III. loss outside the premises;
    IV. money orders and counterfeit paper currency; and
    V. depositor forgery coverages.

In addition to the five basic insuring agreements, there are thirteen optional insuring agreements. The discussion will concentrate first on the five basic coverages, then on policy agreements, limitations, and conditions that apply to all five coverages, and finally on the thirteen optional agreements.

Agreement I—Employee Dishonesty Coverage Property covered by Insuring Agreement I includes the loss of money, securities, and other property. The maximum amount of loss insured is shown on the declarations page. Because form A is a commercial blanket bond, no matter how many employees are in collusion, the maximum amount per loss is the amount in the declarations page. Employee dishonesty is a fidelity bond coverage and protects the insured against fraudulent and dishonest acts committed by an employee. Coverage does extend, however, if the employee acts in collusion with others, including nonemployees.

Definitions. *Money* means not only those items normally associated with the word, such as coins, currency, bank notes and bullion but also includes travelers checks, registered checks, and money orders that may be held by the insured for sale to the public. The definition of *securities* excludes items defined as money but does cover negotiable and nonnegotiable instruments or contracts representing money or other property including revenue stamps in current use, tokens, and tickets. The distinction can be important because not all coverages apply to both money and securities.

Because Insuring Agreement I is for employee dishonesty, the term "employee" has a specific meaning. An *employee* is a natural person performing regular duties of the insured in a normal course of the insured's business. A trustee or officer of a corporation who is also an employee of the corporation is included. Further, the individual causing the loss must be performing these duties for the insured during the policy period and must be compensated for services. But an employee does not include a broker, factor, commission merchant, consignee, contractor, or other agent or representative. Persons other than an employee in collusion with a covered employee are also covered under the agreement.

Loss Under Previous Bond (Superseded Suretyship). Agreement I, employee dishonesty, covers losses which occurred under a previous bond with some restrictions. First, coverage under the present agreement is part of and not in addition to the amount of insurance previously in force. Second, to be covered under the present policy, the loss must have been one that would have been covered by the previous bond, had it been in force. Third, the limit of liability is the lesser of the old bond limit or the current bond limit. Fourth, the loss must have occurred within the territorial limit which includes the United States, District of Columbia, Virgin Islands, Puerto Rico, Canal Zone or Canada. However, for this agreement, the loss could have occurred while a covered employee was outside of these territorial limits for a limited period of time. Fifth, a loss under a previous bond will be covered only after the expiration of the old bond's *discovery period.*

DISCOVERY PERIOD. The discovery period is unique to bonds. Essentially the discovery period is an extension of time to "discover" a covered loss and still have it paid by the bond in force at the time of the loss. The discovery period is one year for form A and two years for form B. For example, assume an employee's dishonest act on May 9,

19X7 causes a covered loss and the bond covering the loss expired on June 30, 19X7. Under form A, the loss must be discovered by June 30, 19X8 or, under form B, discovered by June 30, 19X9 to be paid by the bond in force at the time of loss. If no other bond replaced the expired bond and the discovery period passes, the insured suffers the loss.

DISCOVERY PERIOD AND SUPERSEDED SURETYSHIP. If a new bond replaces an expired bond and all five conditions for superseded suretyship, above, are met, the new bond assumes the loss payment.

For example, an employer buys a bond effective January 1, 19X2 replacing a form A bond expiring on that date. In March of 19X3, a loss is discovered caused by an employee's act in October, 19X1. The form A insuring agreement that expired in 19X2 would have paid the loss if discovered any time up to and including January 1, 19X3 (one year discovery period). Because the loss was discovered later in 19X3, the new bond's insuring agreement would make the payment under the superseded suretyship provision. If the expired bond had been a form B, and the other facts remained the same, the old bond would pay as the discovery period (two years) had not expired.

Exclusions. An inventory shortage is not covered by the bond. Similarly, any loss discovered in the compilation of a profit and loss statement is not covered. In other words, if during an inventory, the insured discovered a shortage of $1,000 in merchandise, there is no automatic coverage under the bond per se. The insured must be able to identify a specific employee or show circumstances that can only lead to the conclusion that it was an employee dishonesty loss of insured property in order to collect under the policy. Similarly, if at the end of an accounting period the insured discovers that bad debt expenses exceeded those expected, the amount of the difference between the bad debts incurred and the bad debts expected is not covered.

The other exclusions applying to Insuring Agreement I also apply to other insuring agreements and will be discussed later.

Conditions and Limitations.

UNIDENTIFIABLE EMPLOYEES. If an insured sustains a loss by fraud or dishonesty where there is reasonable proof such loss was caused by an employee, yet no specific employee or employees can be identified as the culprit, there is coverage under Agreement I. The insured, in filing proof of loss, must supply evidence that reasonably proves the loss was due to the fraud or dishonesty of one or more employees.

PRIOR FRAUD. If the insured knows that an employee has committed a prior fraud or dishonest act or has had his or her fidelity insurance canceled, there is no coverage for the employee under

Agreement I. The provision does allow for negotiation with the insurance company to reinstate coverage for a particular employee who may have had fidelity insurance previously canceled. The entire insurance policy is not canceled. Rather, fidelity coverage is automatically canceled for only those employees whose prior fraud or dishonesty is known to the insured.

Ownership and Interest Covered. Coverage for property under the 3-D policy is extremely broad. The insured property may be owned by the insured or held by the insured in any capacity. Under Insuring Agreement I, coverage applies whether or not the insured is liable for the loss to the property. Insureds with bailee exposures, like a watch repair shop or a furrier storing customers' furs, have coverage for property in their care, custody, and control if loss is caused by the dishonesty of an employee.

NOTICE AND PROOF OF LOSS. When a loss is discovered, the insured must give notice to the insurance company as soon as practicable and also file a detailed proof of loss within four months of discovery of loss. The insured may be requested to submit to an examination under oath. The insured cannot take legal action against the insurance company until there has been full compliance with the policy conditions, and until ninety days after the required proof of loss has been filed with the insurer and unless such action is begun within two years from the date of discovery of the loss.

LIMITS OF LIABILITY. The limit of liability under Agreement I is not reduced when a payment is made. However, all losses due to a series of dishonest acts by one employee or a group of employees in collusion with each other are considered to arise out of one occurrence. For example, if over a period of a year, an employee embezzled $1,000 a month, the total $12,000 embezzlement is considered one occurrence. Where a loss has developed over a long period of time and when two or more bonds apply to the loss, the limit of liability of the multiple bonds is not aggregated. For example, if a previous bond had a limit of $25,000 per employee and the current bond has a $30,000 limit per employee, the total amount payable for losses sustained during both the previous and current bond terms is not more than the $30,000 of the new bond. The insured is not allowed to "stack" the benefits and claim a $55,000 combined limit.

OTHER INSURANCE. If other insurance is carried on the property, Insuring Agreement I will only respond to that portion of the loss which is excess over the amount recoverable from other insurance. Also, if a loss involves both Insuring Agreement I and Insuring Agreement V (forgery coverage) losses are to be paid under insuring

Agreement V until its limit is exhausted and then charged to Insuring Agreement I.

How Fidelity Coverage Can Be Written. In the 3-D policy, the insured may select Insuring Agreement I alone, in combination with other insuring agreements, or not buy the coverage. Fidelity coverage can also be sold separately as a commercial blanket bond. Losses caused by all employees are covered without specific mention of name or position in forms A and B of 3-D policy.

Agreement II. Loss Inside the Premises Coverage Loss inside the premises has four key elements: (1) loss of money and securities, (2) other property, (3) property taken from a locked cash drawer, and (4) damage to the premises.

Money and Securities. Insuring Agreement II covers loss of money and securities by "actual destruction, disappearance or wrongful abstraction" from within the premises or any banking premises. Money and securities have been defined; however, the policy does not contain any definitions of destruction, disappearance, or wrongful abstraction. The perils are extremely broad. Destruction is self-explanatory. Disappearance can be characterized by the phrase, "The money was here; it disappeared; I do not know where it is." Wrongful abstraction can be considered the same as theft. The broad perils of destruction, disappearance, and wrongful abstraction only apply to money and securities. Further, the loss must be from within the premises or from a banking premises or similar place of safe deposit.

Loss of Other Property. The perils that apply to loss of other property are narrower than for the loss of money and securities. Loss of other property is covered only for safe burglary, robbery, or attempted robbery. Similarly, loss from a locked cash drawer or cash register is covered if there was felonious entry into the container or an attempt to remove the cash register or cash box from the premises. The final coverage is for damage to the premises when a burglary, robbery, or attempted robbery occurred causing damage to the premises if the insured is the owner of the premises or is liable for the damage. Such damage might occur, for example, when a door is broken by burglars attempting to gain entry.

Definitions. Definitions play an important part in determining the scope of coverages.

PREMISES. Premises means the interior of the building or portion of the building occupied by the insured in conducting the insured's business.

PERILS DEFINED. *Robbery* means the taking of insured property by violence or threat of violence. Such violence or the threat must be inflicted on a messenger or a custodian. For Insuring Agreement II, robbery includes someone breaking a show window within the premises only while open for business. A *messenger or custodian* includes an employee or partner of the named insured if authorized by the insured to have to have custody of the insured property. A messenger exercises control outside the premises while a custodian exercises such control inside the premises. A custodian does not include a guard, porter, or janitor.

Safe burglary involves felonious abstraction of insured property from within a vault or safe. The door of the safe must have a combination lock and the safe must be located within the premises. Coverage only applies when the safe is closed, locked, and when the entry or attempted entry is evidenced by actual force or violence. Coverage also applies when an entire safe is taken from the premises. The words "felonious abstraction" are not defined in the policy. They can be held to mean that there was some intent to commit the crime of theft.

Territory Covered. Insuring Agreement II applies only in the territory of the United States, District of Columbia, Virgin Islands, Puerto Rico, Canal Zone, or Canada.

Exclusions. Any loss caused by any dishonest act of an employee is excluded. Coverage for such loss is available under Insuring Agreement I. Losses caused by war are excluded. Swindle type losses occurring in a normal commercial transaction (exchange of money for goods) or due to an accounting error or omission or loss or destruction of manuscripts or accounting records are not covered. Money inside a vending or amusement machine is not covered unless the machine is equipped with a device that automatically and continuously records the amount of money going into the machine. Without such a recording device, the magnitude of the loss would be impossible to determine. Losses caused by nuclear radiation are excluded and any losses caused by a fire are excluded except to money and securities. Fire losses would be covered by basic property insurance.

Conditions and Limitations. Coverage under Insuring Agreement II only applies to the interest of the insured in owned or nonowned property. The interest of any other person or organization in nonowned property is not covered unless specifically included in the insured's proof of loss.

The notice and proof of loss requirement is expanded for loss covered by Insuring Agreement II. In addition to notifying the insurance company and filing a detailed proof of loss, the insured must also file a report with the police if the loss was due to a violation of law.

Two restrictions are added regarding other insurance. First, any property specifically insured by other insurance is not covered. Second, any property otherwise insured is not covered unless such property is owned by the insured. For example, under the first provision, assume an art gallery insures its works of art under an inland marine form where each item is specifically described, valued, and insured. If some of these works of art are stored in a safe or vault overnight, and are lost due to a burglary, Insuring Agreement II would not provide coverage; the inland marine form would. Further, there would be no coverage if such works of art were on consignment to the art gallery and specifically insured by the consignee. But, as an example of the second restriction, if the insured owned works of art *not* specifically insured and kept the art in the safe overnight, there would be coverage for those items if taken in a safe burglary.

How Insuring Agreement II Can Be Written. An insured may purchase Insuring Agreement II alone, in combination with any other of the insuring agreements or not purchase it at all using the 3-D policy. As a separate policy, the same coverage is available under a policy called money and securities broad form—coverage A, inside premises.

Any organization that handles a substantial amount of cash is a prospect for this coverage, because coverage for loss of money and securities is extremely broad. Other property the insured may value would be covered for safe burglary or robbery while stored in a safe overnight. Cash registers and locked cash drawers are covered if an attempt is made to take them and finally, damage to the premises because of a safe burglary or robbery would be covered.

The challenge to the producer is to discover the true nature of the client's exposure. A fast food business with significant sales volume would need higher limits than a florist. But the florist may have seasonal peak money and securities exposures that need to be considered in establishing the limit of liability. The money and securities exposure of the fast food company might be more consistent over time. Similarly, a business that operates principally on a check or credit card basis, such as an insurance firm or mail order firm, would have a smaller exposure. The exposure is not to money alone, however. Any business that deals in securities, as defined within the policy, also has an exposure if tickets or tokens are used as the form of admission to a ride. Any business that deals with negotiable instruments, such as money orders, is also a prospect for Insuring Agreement II.

Agreement III. Loss Outside Premises of Coverage Insuring Agreement III is a complementary coverage to Insuring Agreement II. Similar property is insured for similar exposures but when away from the premises.

Coverage. Loss of money and securities is covered for their destruction, disappearance, or wrongful abstraction outside the premises. There are three covered locations for property. First, property is covered while being conveyed by a messenger. Second, money and securities are covered while being conveyed by an armored motor vehicle company. Third, money and securities are covered while temporarily in the living quarters of the messenger.

Other property is covered for robbery or attempted robbery in the same three places. The definitions and territory for Insuring Agreement II are the same for Insuring Agreement III.

Exclusions. The exclusions are the same as in Insuring Agreement II. Any dishonest act of an employee is excluded as is war, swindle by exchange or surrender of money and securities in a commercial transaction, nuclear radiation, and so forth. One additional exclusion does apply to Insuring Agreement III. If an insured suffers a loss of insured property while it is in the custody of an armored motor vehicle company, the policy only applies as excess over any amounts recoverable from the armored motor vehicle company. As with Insuring Agreement II, the insurance under the policy will not benefit any carrier or bailee for hire.

How Insuring Agreement III Can Be Written. Insuring Agreement III in a 3-D policy may be purchased alone, in combination with any other insuring agreements or not purchased at all. As a single policy, coverage is available in a policy called money and securities broad form—coverage B—outside premises.

As with Insuring Agreement II, the challenge to the producer is to measure the loss exposure. The organizations discussed under Insuring Agreement II have a need for Insuring Agreement III when they transport their money and securities from the business establishment to a bank. The limits selected may be the same as selected for Insuring Agreement II or may differ. For instance, a travel agency with a substantial stock of blank airline tickets has a greater exposure with regard to ticket blanks than they do when a ticket is issued and being delivered. A blank airline ticket can be filled in for first class, round trip, New York to Los Angeles, and may have, on that one ticket, a value exceeding $1,000. If, however, a ticket has been written as one way between Rockford, Illinois, and Chicago, the exposure is much less. In either case, the value of the ticket as a security can be insured.

Agreement IV. Money Order and Counterfeit Paper Currency Coverage Insuring Agreement IV covers two types of property. Only money orders issued by a post office, bank or an express company are covered if they are dishonored when presented for payment. Only those money orders accepted in exchange for merchandise, money, or securities are so covered.

The second part of the coverage is for counterfeit paper currency of the United States or Canada. Checks dishonored by the bank are not covered by Insuring Agreement IV.

Coverage Provisions. The territory, conditions and limitations on coverage are the same as for Insuring Agreements II and III.

How Insuring Agreement IV May Be Written. Money order and counterfeit paper currency coverage is available under the 3-D alone, in combination with any of the other insuring agreements or it need not be purchased. As a separate policy it is known as the money order and counterfeit paper currency policy.

Prospects for the coverage would be those who do a significant amount of noncheck business. Many people pay their utility bills by money order and hence the coverage would be appropriate for a utility company. Identifying the extent of the loss exposure is difficult. Unless the firm has records of the amounts of money orders dishonored or counterfeit currency received, it is difficult to select an appropriate limit of liability.

Agreement V. Depositors Forgery Coverage Depositors forgery coverage is a valuable addition to coverage when a significant number of checks or other negotiable instruments are written in the operations of the insured's business.

Coverage. Loss by receipt of fraudulently issued or altered negotiable instruments is covered by Agreement V. Checks, drafts, promissory notes, bills of exchange, or similar written promises or orders to pay are the only documents covered. Specifically mentioned are any checks or drafts made or drawn in the name of the insured payable to a fictitious payee and endorsed in the name of the fictitious payee. Any payroll check, payroll draft, or payroll order endorsed by someone other than the payee without the payee's authority is covered. Even if an endorsement to such a negotiable instrument is not considered a forgery by law, the policy construes such an endorsement to be a forgery and hence covered by the policy. Mechanically reproduced signatures are treated just as are handwritten signatures.

Because the Uniform Commercial Code clearly outlines the responsibility of a bank or any financial institution in the processing of a forged instrument, Insuring Agreement V provides that the insured and any bank which is included in the insured's proof of loss and with which the insured carries a checking or savings account will be covered as their respective interests may appear. In other words, while a bank may not be held liable at law for honoring a forged instrument, the insured may recover through the policy in the event of a loss. The

"Come on in, Dolores. Al got in twenty-five cords of firewood. I froze and canned a winter's supply of food. And now we're just putting the finishing touches on six months' worth of money."

Drawing by W. Miller; © 1981 The New Yorker Magazine, Inc.

insurance company limits its liability in this joint insured-bank type of loss by making the insurer's liability to a bank a part of and not an addition to the amount of insurance applicable to the insured.

Finally, certain defense costs may be covered by this agreement. If the insured or a bank refuses to honor a check as forged and a legal proceeding is brought against the insured or bank, the insurance company will give its written consent to defend such a suit. In that case, reasonable attorney's fees, court costs, and similar legal expenses will be considered part of the loss in this insuring agreement.

Loss Under Prior Policy.   As with Insuring Agreement I, the insurance company agrees to pay a loss that occurred under prior bond if three conditions are met. First, the prior coverage had to be the same as the current coverage and be continuous from the date of loss to the date of discovery. Secondly, the discovery period of the old bond must have expired. Finally, the limit of liability for the insurance company is the smaller of the old or the current policy limit.

Conditions and Limitations.   The policy period and territory are the same as Insuring Agreement I, granting coverage temporarily to employees outside of the stated territories for a limited period. While a condition stated in the policy period section clearly says that "Insuring Agreement V applies only to loss sustained during the policy period," the previous discussion of a loss under a prior policy still applies. If an insurer was not willing to pick up the loss under a previous bond for similar coverage carried continuously, few prospects would be willing to switch to the new insurer. The intent of the policy condition limiting loss to that sustained during the policy period is to clearly define the extent of coverage for an insured purchasing this coverage for the first time. In that case, a forgery loss before the policy was issued would not be covered.

EXCLUSIONS.   The exclusions applicable to Insuring Agreement V in the 3-D policy are those that apply to all insuring agreements. These are discussed below.

NOTICE AND PROOF OF LOSS.   An additional requirement to the notice and proof provisions previously discussed is added for Insuring Agreement V. The proof of loss under this agreement must include the forged or altered instrument which is the basis of the claim.

LIMIT OF LIABILITY.   There are four aspects to the limit of liability for Agreement V. First, the limitation of liability is usually the same as for Insuring Agreement I. Second, there is a provision that allocates the loss among the current and previous bonds. Third, there is a limitation on the total amount that would be paid out on the policy. For example, if one individual, over a period of time, was responsible for a series of forgeries, all such forgeries are treated as one occurrence.

Finally, in the event of coverage under a previous policy and current policy, the maximum payable will be the larger of the limit of liability in either policy.

OTHER INSURANCE. If other insurance applies, this policy will be excess over the amounts recoverable from other insurance. If a loss can be charged to either Insuring Agreement I or V, it will first be applied to Insuring Agreement V until its limit is exhausted and the balance then paid under Insuring Agreement I (assuming Insuring Agreement I is purchased).

HOW INSURING AGREEMENT V MAY BE WRITTEN. In the comprehensive 3-D policy, depositors forgery coverage is available individually, in addition to any of the other insuring agreements or need not be purchased at all. As a separate policy, it is available under a form known as depositors forgery bond.

Prospects for the coverage are any organization that uses checks or drafts in its operations. The coverage only applies to outgoing negotiable instruments and not to checks received in normal business transactions. Therefore, in identifying the exposure and explaining the coverage, it must be clearly understood by the prospect that only the *forgery or alteration of any of its own checks, drafts, and similar instruments is covered* and not the receipt of forged negotiable instruments received in the course of transaction.

Checkpoints

1. What four principal areas of analysis are used to examine a crime policy?
2. Who is *always* excluded from coverage under persons causing a crime loss?
3. Explain
   a. the discovery period.
   b. superseded suretyship.
4. List the five insuring agreements of the 3-D Policy.

Provisions Applying to All Insuring Agreements There are general agreements, policy conditions and limitations that apply to all five basic insuring agreements.

General Agreements. In the event an insured merges or consolidates with another organization, the new premises and new employees are covered providing the insurer is notified within thirty days and a new premium is paid.

Because of multiple locations and the potential for multiple insureds to be covered by one policy, there are a number of provisions that apply to these insureds. For instance, a business organization may have branch offices in three different locations. Each branch office could be insured under one policy. In any situation like this, the first named insured acts for all named insureds. Knowledge of an employee's dishonesty by an insured in a branch office is knowledge for all insureds under the policy. Payment by the insurer to the first named insured is considered payment to all insureds.

Conditions and Limitations. This section contains many definitions in addition to exclusions, conditions and limitations. Keeping accurate accounting records is only one condition of the policy.

EXCLUSIONS. Exclusions applicable to all coverages include the exclusion of any fraudulent, dishonest or criminal act by an insured or partner. Also excluded are defense costs, except under Insuring Agreement V. There is an exclusion for any indirect losses under the policy. For instance, if because of payment to a fictitious payee, the insured lost interest or dividends on the money paid out, such loss of interest or dividends is not recognized as a loss under the policy. Also not recognized as a loss are damages of any type for which the insured is legally liable except direct and compensatory damages arising from a covered loss under the policy (therefore punitive damages are excluded, for example). And finally, all costs, fees, and expenses incurred by the insured to establish the existence of a loss are not considered part of the loss.

VALUATION. The valuation and hence the amount ultimately recovered by the insured is on an actual cash value basis. Securities are valued as of the day after the loss occurs while all other types of property are valued on the day of the loss. If the insurer is obligated to a third party, a bank for instance, the insurer retains the right to settle directly with the third party. Damage to property is limited to its actual cash value or, if lesser, the amount to repair or replace the property. In the event there are differences of opinion between the insurer and insured as to the actual cash value of the loss, provision is made for settlement by arbitration.

RECOVERIES. In many instances, it is possible to recover property, money, or securities from whoever possesses it. In the event a loss exceeds policy limits, the 3-D policy allows the insured to be made whole for its loss before the insurer receives any recovery. Assume a covered loss occurs of $15,000 in the form of securities taken from a safe. The insured had limits of liability of only $10,000. The insurer was able to recover only $8,000 of the securities, the balance having been spent or otherwise disposed of by the culprit. In this case the insured sustained a $15,000 loss. Initially, the policy limit, or $10,000, would be paid to the insured. Of the $8,000 subsequently recovered, the insured would then receive up to $5,000 of that amount. The only deduction from the recovery the insurer is allowed to make are the costs of collection. If the cost of the recovery exceeded $3,000 the insured would receive less than $5,000. Once the insured is indemnified, the insurer retains the balance of recovered property.

SUBROGATION. As with any insurance policy, the insurer is subrogated to all the insured's rights of recovery against any person or organization.

CANCELLATION. Coverage of any employee under Insuring Agreement I is canceled immediately upon discovery of a fraudulent or dishonest act of that employee by the insured or any partner or officer not in collusion with the employee. Coverage may be canceled at noon standard time on the effective date specified in a written notice mailed to the insured. Such a date must not be less than fifteen days after the date of mailing.

POLICY ASSIGNMENT, POLICY CHANGES. The assignment of interest under the policy does not bind the insurance company until the insurer consents to the assignment. In the event the insured dies, the legal representative of the insured becomes the insured. Changes in the policy must be made only with the insurer's consent.

Comprehensive 3-D Policy—Form B There are two essential differences between the Form A and Form B. Under Form B, each loss under Insuring Agreement I is adjusted on a per employee rather than a per loss basis. For instance, if policy limits for Insuring Agreement I are $10,000, and five employees working together embezzle $50,000, under Form A the maximum payable by the insurer is $10,000—the policy limit *per loss*. Under form B, the full $50,000 could be paid as each employee is covered for up to $10,000.

The second major difference under Form B is that the bond carries a two-year, rather than a one-year, discovery period. An advantage of a two-year discovery period for the insured is difficult to envision unless the insured drops the coverage entirely. It does help a subsequent insurer by allowing two years from the termination of the policy for a loss to be discovered and paid under a previous policy.

As with form A of the 3-D policy, the insured may still select any single insuring agreement or any combination of insuring agreements for coverage. Also different limits of liability may be established for each insuring agreement.

Blanket Crime Coverage A Blanket Crime policy (BC) is similar to both forms A and B of the comprehensive 3-D policy in that there are the same five insuring agreements. However, under the BC policy, all five basic insuring agreements are mandatory at a single limit of liability. Therefore, if the insured selects $5,000 as the limit for Insuring Agreement I, the same limit applies to each insuring agreement. Under the BC policy, losses under Insuring Agreement I are on a per loss basis, just as in the 3-D form A. The BC uses a one-year discovery period. A final difference is that there are only five optional coverages available as endorsements to the BC policy while the 3-D policies (in both forms) have thirteen options available. Exhibit 7-1 summarizes the coverages for the comprehensive 3-D policy.

ENDORSEMENTS TO CRIME POLICIES

Introduction

No insured would ever buy a 3-D policy with all thirteen endorsements. Many of the endorsements relate to specific needs of certain types of businesses, such as a warehouse storing goods for clients. Also, some of the endorsements are similar, the only difference being the perils. All of the endorsements may be issued either as separate policies or as endorsements to separate policies. The discussion here will relate to those coverages attached to both forms of the comprehensive 3-D policy. When an endorsement can be used with the blanket crime policy it will also be noted.

Each of the endorsements to the 3-D policy is also identified by a Roman numeral and name of the insuring agreement.

Specific Endorsements to the 3-D Policy

Insuring Agreement VI—Incoming Check Forgery Coverage Incoming check forgery coverage is applicable to any business with a significant amount of its receipts in the form of checks or other negotiable instruments. The single peril insured is forgery or alteration of checks and drafts accepted by the insured during the normal course of business. Checks returned because of insufficient funds are not covered.

The endorsement only covers loss caused by forged checks received in payment or partial payment for goods purchased or services rendered. Incoming check forgery does not apply to forged checks received for the payment of goods previously sold and delivered on credit.

The limit of liability is usually a percentage, such as 75 percent of the amount of the forged instrument. This serves as a loss control device by making the insured a coinsurer. The measure of loss is the inventory value of the goods transferred in exchange for the forged instrument. Crime policies do not intend to cover indirect losses; the lost profit on the sale is not covered.

Exhibit 7-1
Comprehensive 3-D Policy Coverage Summary†

Insuring Agreement	Location of Property Covered	Property Covered	Perils	Person Causing Loss††
I Employee Dishonesty	Anywhere (USA, its possessions or Canada)	All property	Employee dishonesty (fidelity bond)	Any employee
II Inside Premises	Inside premises	Money and securities	Destruction, disappearance or wrongful abstraction	Anyone but an employee
		All property	Safe burglary Robbery	Anyone
III Outside Premises	Outside premises	Money and securities	Destruction, disappearance or wrongful abstraction	Anyone but an employee
		All property	Robbery	Anyone
IV Money Order and Counterfeiting	Anywhere (USA, its possessions or Canada)	Money orders	Forgery and counterfeiting	Anyone
		Paper currency	Counterfeiting	Anyone
V Forgery	Anywhere (USA, its possessions or Canada)	Check & drafts issued by insured	Forgery	Anyone

† Format with permission of Travelers Insurance Company
†† Named Insured and/or partner always excluded.

As a separate coverage, incoming check forgery is available as an endorsement to a depositor's forgery bond.

Insuring Agreement VII—Burglary Coverage on Merchandise Any form of crime insurance covering merchandise is known under the general heading of mercantile open stock insurance. Prospects for this particular coverage are any firms with an inventory exposure to burglary. The perils covered by this insuring agreement are narrow but can be broadened through the use of another endorsement discussed later.

Coverage. Only two perils are insured—burglary, and robbery of a watchman. Burglary essentially requires two elements: a forcible entry or exit from the premises or showcase *and* visible signs of forceful entry or exit. The burglary peril applies to the premises, a showcase, or a show window outside the premises. Robbery of a watchman is loss by violence or threat of violence. For this particular coverage, however, the robbery peril requires robbery of a private watchman employed exclusively by the named insured and while such watchman is on duty within the premises.

The premises must not be open for business when the burglary or robbery takes place. Property covered by the agreement includes the merchandise and stock of the business in its normal trade and any equipment, furniture, or fixtures. The person causing the loss can be anyone but an employee.

EXCLUSIONS. There are five major exclusions. The loss of any manuscripts, accounting books, or records are excluded. These records are extremely valuable and necessary for the insured to establish the amount of any loss. These papers should be insured separately through valuable papers insurance specifically designed for this purpose.

A second major exclusion relates to furs in a window or showcase. This exclusion can be eliminated by endorsement or the property can be covered by other primary insurance. A third exclusion is referred to as the looting exclusion. Any form of crime insurance assumes some particular level of control or security that the insured has for the merchandise. When there is a change in conditions, such as fire with temporarily boarded windows, coverage for the burglary and robbery perils is suspended.

The fourth exclusion pertains to vandalism and malicious mischief. (This exclusion can be used as a sales point to sell V&MM coverage on a basic property form.) Finally, because this insuring agreement is for burglary, any the insured sustains because of a swindle or trick or other fraudulent exchange of goods for a promised gain to the insured, is not covered.

LOSS PAYMENT. There are loss payment provisions within the coverage that require the insured to make a decision before purchasing the policy. For instance, one way to buy burglary on merchandise coverage is with blanket limits—one limit covering all locations. A second way is to schedule the locations and have different limits at each. In the case of scheduling the locations with different limits, a type of coinsurance is applied to the loss settlement. However, the coinsurance in this form is somewhat different from that used in property insurance.

Each type of mercantile establishment is categorized in the manual as to a particular class of business.

In order to obtain full coverage for a partial loss, the insured must carry insurance up to the *lesser of* (1) a dollar amount for the particular class of business, called the *coinsurance limit*, or (2) a stated percentage (usually 40 to 80 percent) of the actual cash value of the merchandise at the location at the time of loss, called the *coinsurance percentage*. The coinsurance percentage varies by territory. The coinsurance limit (the amount of insurance that always meets the coinsurance requirement) varies by class of merchandise.

Assume the client owns a clothing store located in DeKalb County, Georgia. The insured's merchandise has an actual cash value of $10,000. The retail clothing stores class has a coinsurance limit of $7,500, and the coinsurance percentage for a clothing store in DeKalb County, Georgia is 40 percent of the actual cash value of the merchandise at time of loss. In order to avoid a coinsurance penalty, the insured must carry limits of liability equal to or greater than the *lesser* of the class coinsurance limit (in this case $7,500) or the percentage (in this case 40 percent) applied to the actual cash value of the merchandise at the time of loss. The insured must, therefore, carry a limit of liability of at least $4,000 which is 40 percent of the merchandise value of $10,000 at the location.

The coinsurance provision is only important when the locations are scheduled. When an insurance company issues a blanket policy on multiple locations, the minimum permissible limits written would be the coinsurance dollar limit for that particular class of business.

A second loss payment provision includes internal limits on merchandise in a showcase or a show window. There is a specific limit on items held for pledge or as collateral and a limit per article of jewelry per loss if the window does not open into the building.

CONDITIONS. There are five important additional conditions for this burglary coverage. First, after a loss, the insured must provide the insurer with a complete inventory of all the merchandise. Second, when other insurance is in force on the merchandise, this insurance does not apply.

Third, after a loss, the limit of liability under the policy is reduced until the insured either restores the security at the location to what it was prior to the loss or employs a watchman to be on duty while the business is closed. Fourth, recoveries by the insurer are treated in a manner similar to Insuring Agreements I through V. Any costs of the recovery are first deducted, then the insured is reimbursed fully for the loss and any remaining recovery is retained by the insurer. The final condition of note is one requiring a physical inventory of merchandise at least annually. This is a reasonable requirement because to determine the amount of any merchandise lost, the insured would need to have accurate inventory records.

Insuring Agreement VIII—Paymaster Robbery Inside and Outside Premises Paymaster robbery coverage is available for those prospects who pay their employees in cash. If a prospect pays employees by check, the coverage can be modified to cover the payroll checks for a reduction in premium.

Coverage. There are two parts to paymaster robbery coverage, inside and outside the premises. The prospect must purchase both coverages with this insuring agreement (inside premises coverage is separately available with another insuring agreement). The peril insured is robbery only. The property covered are payroll funds or checks only. The culprit can be anyone except the insured or a partner.

As a separate policy, this coverage is available as a paymaster robbery policy—inside and outside premises. Broader coverage for payroll is available under Insuring Agreement IX, discussed next.

Insuring Agreement IX—Paymaster Broad Form—Inside and Outside Premises This insuring agreement is the same as Insuring Agreement VIII with the perils of disappearance, destruction, and wrongful abstraction added to the coverage for payroll funds of the insured.

Under section A—inside premises, the disappearance, destruction, and wrongful abstraction peril applies to all payroll funds. Robbery inside the premises also applies to payroll funds paid to an employee. Hence if an employee receives a check or cash and loses it in a robbery while still on the employer's premises, this policy provides protection for those funds.

Under section B, the disappearance, destruction, or wrongful abstraction of money and securities is covered outside the premises (e.g., payroll en route to the firm from a bank). The robbery peril applies not only to money and securities, but also to any satchel or container in which the funds are being transported. Some limited coverage, of up to 10 percent of the policy limits, may be applied to nonpayroll money and securities taken in conjunction with a payroll robbery.

This insuring agreement is available as a separate policy under the paymaster broad form inside and outside premises policy.

Insuring Agreement X—Paymaster Broad Form—Inside

Only If the insured has no exposure until the payroll is delivered to the location for distribution to the employees (the bank assumes the exposure until payroll is inside the insured's premises) only inside premises coverage may be required. In such a case, Insuring Agreement X would be used. The coverage is exactly the same as the section A, inside premises, discussed under Insuring Agreement IX. As a separate policy, this coverage is known as paymaster broad form—inside premises only.

Insuring Agreement XI—Burglary and Theft of Merchandise

Coverage Insuring Agreement XI is a broader form of merchandise coverage than Insuring Agreement VII (burglary coverage on merchandise).

Coverage. The essential difference between the coverage under Insuring Agreement XI and Insuring Agreement VII is that the peril is expanded to include theft and is not limited to burglary and robbery of a watchman. The policy does not contain the time restriction of "while not open for business," and because theft is covered instead of robbery, the restriction that requires "signs of forced entry or exit" are not used. Similarly, there is no requirement for a private watchman.

Other Conditions. In addition to the exclusions outlined for Insuring Agreement VII, a so-called "swindle exclusion" is added. Theft by expressed or implied authority of the insured is not covered— "The boss said I could try this out at home."

Loss payment provisions are similar to Insuring Agreement VII, but in addition, mere disappearance of merchandise is excluded. Such disappearance would show up in an inventory shortage. Where theft can be reasonably shown, such inventory shortage will be covered. In that case, however, the average inventory shortage over the last five years will be used as a deductible from the loss payment. Only normal inventory losses are excluded while those reasonably attributable to theft are covered.

As a separate policy this coverage is available as mercantile open stock theft insurance.

Insuring Agreement XII—Warehouse Receipts Forgery Coverage

erage Many businesses use warehouses to store goods when there is not sufficient room on their own premises. In such cases, the insured would issue an order to the warehouse to release a certain amount and kind of goods to someone for delivery to the store. This coverage is designed to protect the business that stores goods in a warehouse, or for the warehouse firm that receives the orders. Coverage is effected at the insured place of business and only for the peril of forgery of a receipt issued by the insured for withdrawal orders directed to an insured. The person causing the loss can be anyone but an employee.

As a separate policy, warehouse receipts forgery coverage is endorsed to a depositor's forgery bond.

Insuring Agreement XIII—Securities of Lessees of Safe Deposit Boxes Coverage This coverage is designed for businesses with a substantial amount of securities in safe deposit boxes. Many businesses purchase securities as investments to improve cash flow. Rather than keep a substantial amount of securities on the premises, many businesses choose to deposit these securities in a safe deposit box in a bank.

The peril insured is disappearance, destruction, or wrongful abstraction of securities. The securities must be housed in a bank, and the person causing the loss can be anyone but an employee. As many banks do not provide coverage for the property of their customers in safe deposit boxes, this can be a valuable addition to a client's coverage. As a separate policy, the coverage is sold as securities of lessees of safe deposit box coverage.

Insuring Agreement XIV—Burglary of Office Equipment For the office exposure with little or no merchandise on hand, the "mercantile open stock" type coverage is not appropriate as coverage is too broad and, hence, too expensive for the exposure. For insurance on office equipment only, this insuring agreement may be used. Coverage is essentially the same as indicated under Insuring Agreement VII but the property insured is office equipment only. This coverage may also be endorsed to the mercantile open stock policy.

Insuring Agreement XV—Theft of Office Equipment If the prospect described in the preceding section wishes broader coverage on office equipment for theft rather than burglary only, Insuring Agreement XV may be used. The coverage is the same as described for the mercantile open stock theft coverage in Insuring Agreement XI, but property insured is restricted to office equipment. This coverage may also be endorsed to a mercantile open stock policy as a separate coverage.

Insuring Agreement XVI—Paymaster Robbery Coverage— Inside For the prospect or client who needs inside coverage only for robbery of the paymaster, separate coverage is available. It is the same as described under Insuring Agreement VIII for section A only. The only peril is robbery. Available as a separate policy, it is known as paymaster robbery inside premises only.

Insuring Agreement XVII—Credit Card Forgery Many businesses have credit cards issued in the corporation's name and entrust those credit cards to drivers, sales representatives and officers for business expenses. This coverage is designed to protect against the forgery or alteration of sales receipts by anyone, anywhere. It protects only credit cards issued *to* the named insured and does not include any coverage for credit cards issued *by* the named insured. Available as a separate coverage, it is known as the credit card forgery bond.

Insuring Agreement XVIII—Extortion Extortion coverage applies when there is an indirect threat of bodily harm to certain individuals (with robbery, the threat is direct). Extortion covers the surrender of property, including money and securities, when bodily harm is *threatened* to a director, trustee, officer, partner, or relative of any of these individuals. The threat must be for bodily harm; there is no coverage for a threat to property.

The insuring agreement requires the person receiving that threat to *attempt* to communicate the threat to an associate and to the FBI or the local law enforcement authorities. The property must be surrendered away from the premises. The perpetrator can be anyone but an employee.

The coverage is also available as an endorsement to the money and securities broad form policy.

Optional Endorsement Summary Exhibit 7-2 summarizes the thirteen option endorsements to the 3-D policy. Essentially there are six types of coverage: (1) for forgery; (2) for merchandise, furniture, and fixtures; (3) for office equipment only; (4) for the paymaster; (5) for securities; and (6) for extortion. Forgery coverages are for different financial instruments. Merchandise, furniture, and fixtures coverages are for narrow or broad perils as are the office equipment and paymaster coverages. Paymaster coverages may have inside premises only or inside and outside premises coverage. Securities and extortion coverages are specialized.

Blanket Crime Policy Optional Coverages Only five of the thirteen optional coverages to the 3-D policy are available as endorsements to the blanket crime (BC) policy:

1. Burglary only for merchandise, furniture, and fixtures (Insuring Agreement VII).
2. Theft for merchandise, furniture, and fixtures (Insuring Agreement XI).

Exhibit 7-2
3-D Coverage Summary by Type of Insuring Agreement

Type of Coverage	Insuring Agreement	Name or Description
Forgery	VI	Incoming checks only for sales not on credit
	XII	Warehouse receipts
	XVII[†]	Credit card issued to insured
Merchandise, Furniture and Fixtures	VII[†]	Burglary only
	XI[†]	Burglary and theft
Office Equipment	XIV	Burglary only
	XV	Burglary and theft
Paymaster	XVI	Robbery inside only
	VIII	Robbery only, inside and outside
	X	Disappearance, distribution or wrongful abstraction and robbery—inside only
	IX	Disappearance, destruction or wrongful abstraction and robbery—inside and outside
Securities	XIII	Lessees of safe deposit boxes
Extortion	XVIII[†]	Threat to life only

[†] Also available with blanket crime policy.

3. Theft of office equipment (Insuring Agreement XV).
4. Credit card forgery (Insuring Agreement XVII).
5. Extortion (Insuring Agreement XVIII).

These endorsements or optional insuring agreements to the BC policy are identical to coverage offered by the noted insuring agreement endorsements to the 3-D policy.

Mercantile Open Stock

The mercantile open stock (MOS) policy has been referred to in an examination of the optional insuring agreements available to the 3-D policy. As a separate policy, mercantile open stock coverage is often sold and does contain some different provisions than discussed.

Definitions The premises as defined by the separate MOS policy is more restrictive. In the mercantile open stock policy, premises is the interior of that portion of the building at the location designated in the declarations occupied by the insured but not including either showcases or show windows not opened directly to the interior of the premises or public entrances or hallways or stairways. For robbery, coverage is limited to a private watchman employed exclusively by the insured while such watchman is on duty within the premises. If coverage is provided for burglary, the signs of forcible entry must appear on the premises just as they had to appear on the safe itself in the mercantile safe burglary policy. The mercantile open stock policy applies only inside the premises and only while the business is not open.

If endorsed for theft, coverage applies inside the premises whether the business is open or not. Also with theft coverage, the forced entry requirement does not apply.

Types of Mercantile Open Stock Policies The types of mercantile open stock policies are the narrow mercantile open stock *burglary* or broader mercantile open stock *theft* insurance. Both policies provide coverage for merchandise including stock, equipment, furniture and fixtures. The burglary, robbery, or theft can be by anyone but an employee. For those prospects or clients without a merchandise exposure, the mercantile open stock can be endorsed to apply to *burglary* coverage on office equipment only or for *theft* coverage on office equipment.

Checkpoints

1. When is coverage canceled automatically for an employee under Insuring Agreement I?
2. What are the two essential differences between form A and form B of the 3-D policy?
3. What is (are) the essential difference(s) between the 3-D form A and the blanket crime policy?
4. How may a client without a merchandise exposure cover furniture, fixtures, and office equipment?

MARKETING CRIME INSURANCE

Introduction

Crime insurance offers an important opportunity for the producer to use the risk management approach. Many prospects and clients either do not buy crime insurance or are buying it but not really understanding all of the alternatives to the insurance they may use. Even those using some risk management alternatives find that crime insurance is affordable with proper combinations of insurance and other risk management techniques.

The ACORD Crime Section Application is reproduced in the PRO 82 Course Guide. It is an effective risk management tool that can help to identify the insured's exposure to crime losses, help the insured reduce the loss potential from crime losses, and help to reduce the insurance premium.

Exposure Identification There are two major classifications of property exposed to crime losses: (1) money and securities and (2) merchandise, furniture, fixtures, and equipment. The analysis of exposures will generally relate to the type of exposure and amount thereof, and the nature of the protection for such property. For instance, money and securities have unique exposures in that money is negotiable and transferable. Securities, on the other hand, may have either unrestricted or restricted negotiability. Checks payable to cash, for instance, have unrestricted negotiability, as do postage stamps. At the other extreme, securities such as stocks and bonds payable to a named individual or to a corporation have limited negotiability.

Under the general information section of the application, one question asks if checks are endorsed "for deposit only." Such a simple loss control procedure on all incoming checks immediately restricts the negotiability of checks payable to the business. The application should be completed in the presence of the prospect so the producer may suggest some risk management alternatives to help control the exposure.

Merchandise, Furniture, Fixtures, and Equipment. There are three important aspects to identifying and analyzing the loss exposure of this type of property. The first is convertibility. It is easier for a thief to convert a color television set into cash than it is to convert a stock certificate made payable to a named corporation. The second aspect is the value of the property. The greater the value of any merchandise, furniture, and so forth, the greater the exposure. The third consideration is the relative ease of transportation of property. A 21-inch portable TV set can easily be carried by most thieves, whereas a heavy table saw of approximately the same value would be relatively more difficult to move.

PROTECTION. The protection of property is an important part of both the exposure identification and analysis process and determining risk management alternatives. For Insuring Agreement I, the fidelity exposure, prudent business practices suggested in every accounting and finance course are important. For instance, no individual should be in charge of both the receipt and dispersal of cash. In the same manner, no individual should be in charge of the receipt of cash and the recording of cash in the books or records. Secondly, employees with access to property, whether it be money or merchandise, should be directly supervised in the performance of their duties. Mandatory vacations at regular time periods and for certain lengths of time are a good idea. Finally, audits performed both by an outside accounting firm and by the inside accounting department should be carried out.

Page four of the application lists seventeen questions that can be used to determine and improve the audit procedures and internal controls a prospect uses.

For forgery coverages, Insuring Agreement V, the use of safety paper on checks, controlled use of facsimile signature machines and plates, and of course protection of blank checks are important.

In fidelity and forgery insurance, the absence of good financial management practices, accounting controls, and internal audits will not be replaced by insurance. Insurance is never designed to handle the "maintenance problems" of any business.

For theft exposures, a combination of good business practice and protection systems is ideal. Not only is it good cash management to deposit cash frequently during the day; it also eliminates a portion of the inside-the-premises exposure. The amount of money kept inside the premises overnight should never exceed the minimum amount necessary to carry on normal business transactions the following day. Physical protection will help to decrease the exposure. Bars over windows are an improvement over panes of glass. Central station alarm systems are still better burglary protection (certified systems can generate into credits ranging from 5 to 40 percent).

By far the most vital part of selling, underwriting, and rating crime insurance is gaining management assistance and cooperation. A management with a good loss history, good management practices, and strong protection systems will usually generate a lower rate. The producer who can suggest systems to improve the protection in a business and at the same time lower the insurance premium charged will be making a good impression on the client or prospect.

Rating Crime Insurance

Rating procedures for crime insurance vary depending on the nature of the insuring agreement. General rating procedures for each of the five insuring agreements in the 3-D policy will be examined.

Rating for the 3-D policy is done on an individual insuring agreement basis.

Fidelity Rating The premium for fidelity coverage is based on four principal items: (1) the limit of liability, (2) classification of employees, (3) classification of the business, and (4) loss experience.

Blanket Fidelity Premium Determination. The "published rate" for fidelity coverage is determined by the limit of liability and the classification of employees. The most intricate part of this procedure is determining the classification of employees.

As all employee dishonesty losses are covered by an employee dishonesty bond, the total number of employees is important. The employees can essentially be categorized into three types or classifications:

1. Those who regularly handle or have custody of money, securities, or merchandise.
2. Those who work outside or away from the premises with access to money, securities, or merchandise.
3. All other employees.

Through a classification procedure too detailed for explanation here, a number of so-called Class 1 and Class 2 employees are determined. These employees and the selected limit of liability determine the "published premium." The "published premium" is modified by the class of business (public utilities receive a .60 modification, for example, compared to a 3.00 modification for small loan companies). The result after applying the modification is called the "manual premium." The final premium is determined by applying an experience debit or credit to the manual premium.

Individual or Schedule Premium Determination. Every class of business has a specific rate per thousand or is rated from a Basic Rate Table. The limit of liability is multiplied by the rate per thousand to determine the final premium. For example, if the published rate is $5.00 per thousand and there are five employees, the total premium for $10,000 on each employee would be $250.00, calculated this way:

$$\left(\frac{\$5.00}{\$1,000} \times \$50,000 \right)$$

Loss Inside Premises Rating The rating of Insuring Agreement II takes into consideration the location of the business, the classification of the safe, the business classification, protective devices used, and the limits of liability selected (or the money and securities exposure).

Rating Procedure. Manual rates are determined first by the location of the business. Considered next is the classification of the safe or vault. Page two of the crime application describes safes and vaults by manufacturer, class, label, door type, combination lock type, and the door and wall thickness. Safes are rated by alphabetical letters. Safes rated G are considered the best while the absence of a safe is considered the worst. Third, on countrywide experience, a territorial multiplier is determined.

The final step in determining the manual rate is classifying the business. Liquor stores, for instance, are far more attractive to criminals than would be an employment agency. Businesses are classified as 1 through 11 with class 1 having the lowest loss exposure and class 11 having the highest loss exposure.

Protective devices, also listed on page two of the crime application, will modify the manual rate. Some protective safeguards will allow rate credits of as high as 35 percent of the premium. The type and nature of the alarm system used, the areas of the building protected, the name and type of alarm system used, the number of guards and watchmen, and other protection devices including those on doors and windows, will all help to minimize the inside crime exposure. The final premium is determined by multiplying the manual rate by the limit of liability for a 3-D policy or by multiplying the manual rate by the money and securities exposure (not the policy limit) for a BC policy.

Outside Premises Rating. There are six major factors for rating a loss outside the premise (Insuring Agreement III) coverage; location, number of guards, protective safeguards, limit of liability, money and securities exposure, and additional messengers.

Rating Procedure. As with inside premises coverage, the location establishes a territorial multiplier. The number of guards and the type of protective safeguards for messengers determine the basic or manual rate. After applying the territorial multiplier to the basic rate, the final premium is determined by multiplying the manual rate times the limit of liability for a 3-D policy or by the money and securities exposure for a BC policy. If additional messengers are used to transport property to and from banking establishments, the manual rate is reduced 50 percent and multiplied by the actual money and securities exposure for each messenger.

Money Order and Counterfeit Paper Currency Rating

The rating procedure for Insuring Agreement IV is perhaps the easiest. If a 3-D policy is applied for, the limit of liability and the number of locations will determine the rate. If a BC policy is desired, only the number of locations involved determine the rate.

Depositors Forgery Rating The limit of liability is the principal determinant in calculating the premium for depositors forgery. Most insurers allow the personal checking accounts of officers to be eligible for coverage by endorsement. If such accounts are endorsed, an additional charge is made.

Depositors forgery premiums are determined by a percentage of the fidelity premium.

Rating Other Crime Endorsements. Each of the optional thirteen insuring agreements is individually rated. The nature of each will not be discussed here. Important rating considerations are principally the location of the insured; the class of business of the insured; the protective safeguards, including guards, that may be employed to protect property; and the limit of liability.

Underwriting Information

Every item on the crime application is essential. The more supplemental information the producer can provide to the underwriter, the more helpful the underwriter can be to the producer and client in providing insurance coverage and suggestions for loss control. In some cases, a deductible will be recommended. In such cases, the insured should become even more interested in loss control procedures and accounting controls. Completing the application in the presence of the client will help the producer understand the client's business better and help the client understand where some management activity might reduce the exposure to loss.

The producer should add any information not required by the application that would be valuable to the underwriter. The producer should note that the application does not have questions for many optional insuring agreements. For instance, the application does not contain any space for questions relative to credit card forgery coverage. Any information needed to issue that insuring agreement must be attached to the application. Similarly, if Insuring Agreement XIII, Securities of Lessees Deposit Box coverage, is desired, information relative to the bank, the type and sizes of safe deposit box and the amount of securities normally kept should be appended to the application.

CASES

J&T Appliances

J&T Appliances has loss exposures that involve all five of the insuring agreements in the 3-D, or blanket crime, policies. Since J&T is a partnership, no coverage would apply to dishonest acts of either partner.

According to the information provided in the case, the following limits would be recommended if "all-risks" (including theft) property insurance coverage were in force:

Insuring Agreement	Limit
I. Form A	$25,000
II.	2,000
III.	2,000
IV.	1,000
V.	25,000

Ms. Thomas and Mr. Johnson should implement some basic financial controls over the management of cash and managerial controls over employees' access to property. The $25,000 limit on Form A applies per loss and appears to be adequate based on the most recent balance sheet. As the business grows, a $50,000 limit should be recommended in view of the relatively small additional premium. Insuring Agreements II and III (inside and outside money and securities coverage) appear to be adequate at $2,000 for each coverage.

The money order and counterfeit paper currency exposure is minimal, and a $1,000 limit is suggested. The limit of liability for depositors' forgery coverage should be $25,000. Although the exposure to loss is less than that for employee dishonesty (depositors' forgery does not cover the insured's property), the $25,000 limit is recommended due to the small premium involved.

The 3-D policy is recommended rather than the blanket crime policy due to its flexibility. The limits of liability for each of the insuring agreements reflects J&T's actual loss exposures.

If "all-risks" property insurance is not in force, a mercantile open stock theft policy with a $15,000 limit appears to be adequate, even if an entire truck load of appliances or parts is stolen. In view of the bulkiness of the inventory, this limit appears to be adequate and meets the coinsurance limit for the location involved.

John Gale, M.D.

Dr. Gale's office crime exposures can be adequately insured by the inland marine "all-risks" physicians' and surgeons' office equipment floater, extended to include money and securities to a $400 limit, and a 3-D policy with Insuring Agreements I (form A) of $50,000 and V of $50,000 (fidelity losses are excluded from the floater).

Dr. Gale's farm exposures are best covered by the "all-risks" farm equipment floater with no crime coverage needed.

If premium dollars are important, there is $250 money and securities coverage in the physicians' floater, and Dr. Gale could assume the losses in excess of $250. Tight inventory records and control of drugs stored in the office are recommended. Package treatment (Chapter 12) is also an alternative.

R. P. Davis, Contractor

The construction firm appears to be financially well run. Payroll, for instance, is handled by bank check and no payroll exposure exists. Also, the firm handles very little cash. Therefore, a 3-D with Insurance Agreements I and V, in conjunction with "all-risks" property insurance, would be correct. Recommended limits of liability are $100,000 for Insuring Agreement I and $50,000 for Insuring Agreement V.

Premier Door and Window Company, Inc.

The major crime exposures for Premier Door and Window are the fidelity and related forgery plus a cash payroll exposure. A 3-D policy with high limits ($250,000) is recommended for Insuring Agreements I and V. The cash payroll exposure can be treated in one of two ways:

- $30,000 limits on Insuring Agreements II and III or
- $30,000 limits on Paymaster Broad Form (Agreement IX).

With the financial strength of Premier, the incidental office cash exposure can be retained.

FINANCIAL INSTITUTION COVERAGE

Introduction

Establishing the need for crime coverage for financial institutions is much easier than for mercantile establishments. Nonfinancial institutions may decide they do not want crime insurance and choose instead to retain the entire exposure. Financial institutions generally do not have that choice. Certain coverages are strongly recommended by many regulatory authorities.

Therefore a producer is not really selling crime coverage to a financial institution. Rather, the producer is selling the ability to service the account and to provide the appropriate recommendations and supporting services. These financial institutions usually buy coverage but they do not need to buy it from any particular producer.

In this portion of the chapter, attention will be given principally to the bankers' blanket bond. Other types of coverage for nonbanking financial institutions will also be addressed.

Bankers Blanket Bond

One of the most important bonds for financial institutions is the Bankers Blanket Bond Form No. 24, a commonly used form and the basis of a wide variety of bonds for other financial institutions. The bankers blanket bond is more than employee dishonesty coverage; it also includes many insurance coverages.

The bond period starts with the date noted in the declarations and runs until termination or cancellation. It is not written for a specified term as is the case with the 3-D policy. A single limit of liability applies to all insuring agreements with provisions for lower limits or entire deletion of coverage for any insuring agreements that may be specified. In this respect, it resembles the comprehensive 3-D policy as separate limits may be selected for each insuring agreement.

Much of the coverage applies to named premises of the insured. The declarations page includes provision for deletion of coverage for certain offices of the insured in cases when the insured does not wish to cover them, or if the underwriter considers such locations unacceptable for coverage.

The insurance company will indemnify and hold harmless the insured with respect to loss which is *sustained by the insured at any time* but which is *discovered during the bond period.* It is important to note the act causing the loss may have occurred any time, even prior to the effective date of the bond, but that *discovery* must occur during the bond period, a major difference from the comprehensive 3-D.

Coverage The various insuring agreements have titles which indicate in general the nature of the coverage. The effect of each insuring agreement is summarized here, with notations of any special features, but the full text should be consulted for details.

Fidelity. This insuring agreement covers loss resulting from any dishonest or fraudulent act committed by any "employee" (broadly defined) anywhere and whether committed alone or in collusion with others. This includes loss of property held by the insured for any purpose and in any capacity, whether it is held gratuitously and whether or not the insured is liable for it. This is very broad fidelity coverage applying to all employees and limited only to the amount or amounts specified in the limit of liability provision. It is comparable to and in some respects even broader than the comprehensive 3-D policy.

On Premises. Property, as defined in the bond, is covered for loss due to robbery, burglary, theft, false pretenses, misplacement, mysterious unexplained disappearance, and damage to or destruction of such property. Also covered is loss from conversion, redemption, or deposit privileges because of such misplacement or loss of property, all while the property is within the offices or premises which are covered by the policy. This applies whether or not there is negligence or violence in connection with the damage to or disappearance of the property.

Coverage applies to damage to property of customers on the premises of the bank, including outside parking lots or deposit facilities, that occurs to customer's property from the perils listed.

Property includes money (currency, coin, bank notes, and Federal Reserve Notes), postage, and revenue stamps, bullion, precious metals, jewelry, gems, and a number of similar items listed in the bond. Coverage also applies to furnishings, fixtures, stationery, supplies, and equipment within the insured's offices for loss caused by larceny, burglary, robbery, or by vandalism or malicious mischief. Loss or damage by fire is excluded; a bank should have fire insurance which would apply to any such loss.

In Transit. The coverage of property in transit applies to acts of robbery, larceny, theft, misplacement, mysterious unexplainable disappearance, or property otherwise lost, damaged, or destroyed. This includes loss by subscription, conversion, redemption, or deposit privileges through the misplacement or loss of property. Coverage applies while the property is in transit anywhere in the custody of any person or persons acting as messenger, except that there is no coverage for property in the mail or in the custody of a carrier for hire other than an armored motor vehicle company.

Forgery or Alteration. A rather lengthy section provides coverage against loss from forgery or alteration of specified documents. This covers practically any loss that the bank might sustain because of a forgery or alteration in documents that pass through the custody of the bank. This, too, applies practically regardless of who is responsible for the forgery or alteration.

Securities. This, too, is a lengthy provision covering loss to the insured in connection with the handling of securities. This may occur because of counterfeit or forged securities, raised or otherwise altered securities, and a variety of other losses that can occur in the handling of securities for the bank itself or for others. This coverage is separate from forgery or alteration coverage and applies principally to the loss that might occur because of transactions involving the securities.

Redemption of United States Savings Bonds. This covers loss through the insured's paying or redeeming, guaranteeing, or witnessing any signature which has been forged, counterfeited, raised or otherwise altered, lost or stolen, or on which the signature to the request for payment shall have been forged. This protects the bank against loss that may occur from its handling the redemption of United States Savings Bonds on behalf of customers.

Counterfeit Currency. This covers loss through the receipt by the bank in good faith of any counterfeited or altered paper securities or coin of the United States or Canada.

Coverage Summary. Of the seven coverages reviewed, six are insurance coverages. Only the first is a fidelity coverage. The six insurance coverages apply regardless of whether the loss is perpetrated by an employee or by outsiders. There is no mention of what person shall have committed the various acts. If the loss does occur through a dishonest or fraudulent act of an employee, it would be considered as covered under the first agreement (fidelity coverage).

A bankers blanket bond can be written with one or more of the optional coverage paragraphs deleted from the contract. There may be situations where an underwriter would be unwilling to provide the extremely broad coverage under one or more of these coverage paragraphs. Underwriting considerations may also dictate that the limit of liability under one or more of these coverage paragraphs be less than the general limit of liability applying to the bond. Limits of liability and other features are subject to negotiation between the insured bank, producer, and the insurance company.

Exclusions Loss resulting from forgery or alteration of any instrument is excluded if it is not covered by the insuring agreements applying to fidelity, the specific provisions applying to forgery or alteration, the provisions applying to securities, the provisions applying to redemption of United States Savings Bonds, or the provisions relating to counterfeit currency. It is the intent of the underwriters to cover forgery or alteration only under the specific provisions of the agreements listed.

Loss due to riot or civil commotion outside the United States and Canada is excluded. Also excluded are described acts of war or the effects of nuclear fission or fusion or radioactivity, excepting that loss resulting from industrial uses of nuclear energy is not excluded.

Acts of directors of the insured are excluded unless they are employed as salaried, pensioned, or elected officials.

Exclusions also apply to certain nonpayment losses or defaults of loans unless covered under the fidelity, forgery, or alteration of securities provisions of the bond.

An important exclusion is that of loss of property contained in customers' safe deposit boxes unless such loss is sustained through any dishonest or fraudulent act of an employee in such circumstances as would make the insured legally liable. Thus, the bond would not cover loss resulting from a burglary or robbery of customers' property from a safe deposit box if there were no dishonesty on the part of an employee in connection with the loss. This exclusion is an important reason to suggest Securities of Lessees of Safe Deposit Box coverage to individual clients with securities stored in a bank's safe deposit box.

Loss through cashing or paying forged or altered traveler's checks and loss of traveler's checks entrusted to the insured for sale are excluded unless there is fraud or dishonesty on the part of an employee and the checks are paid or honored by the drawer.

Loss of property due to misplacement or mere loss is covered subject to an excess insurance provision when the property is in the custody of an armored motor vehicle company. The bond covers only the amount which cannot be recovered from the armored motor vehicle company or its insurer. An excess insurance provision also applies to "chattels" (property) which are specifically insured elsewhere. A shortage due to error in any teller's cash is excluded, regardless of the amount of such shortage.

An exclusion applies to any person who is a partner, officer, or employee of any processor covered under the bond after the time that the insured or an officer of the insured not in collusion with such persons learns that such a person has committed a fraudulent or dishonest act. This is comparable to the provision in the comprehensive 3-D policy that the dishonest acts of an employee are not covered from the time that he or she has been discovered as having committed a dishonest act.

Excess and Catastrophe Coverages for Banks

An important question facing the officers of a bank is how much coverage to buy. One case revealed that the loan officer of a medium-sized bank had transferred funds from an account to a fictitious organization which he had established subject to his withdrawal signature. This transfer of funds was made over a period of several years, with an aggregate loss to the bank of almost $2.5 million.

There have been other cases where bank officials have made loans which went into default, and then felt it necessary in order to preserve their reputations and positions in the bank to cover up the bad judgment in making new loans. Thus, what originated as a case of bad but honest judgment may be converted to a dishonest act. There also have been cases where the success in covering up the bad judgment initially has led the bank official to appropriate funds for personal benefit. The potential loss to the bank in spite of the bank's own auditing procedures, periodic examinations by governmental officials, and other attempts at control, can be high where fraudulent activity is perpetrated over a period of years. Therefore, the limits of liability must be set with this in mind.

One method of covering the large loss exposure from employee dishonesty is by means of an excess bond. This usually is written for high amounts, such as $1 million or more and covers as excess insurance over other applicable bonds and insurance. Lesser amounts are subject to loss from burglary and robbery, for example, so that the usual limits in a bankers blanket bond may be sufficient for such exposures. Losses due to forgery or alteration of securities are likely to include dishonest employees.

There also have been catastrophic losses from the burglary of safe deposit boxes. A bank that operates a safe deposit box facility needs to consider the purchase of a safe deposit box legal liability policy to cover any liability that the bank might incur as a result of a burglary of the facility.

Bonds for Other Financial Institutions

The bankers blanket bonds are designed to meet the extremely broad loss exposures of commercial banks. Other types of financial institutions have less exposure to loss in some respects, but they also have some greater exposures in other respects. Insurance companies have designed special kinds of blanket bonds to cover the exposures of other financial institutions. These are reviewed briefly here in order to distinguish them from the bankers blanket bond.

The divisions of coverage in the blanket bonds issued to other financial institutions generally follow those which appear in the bankers blanket bond. These include fidelity coverages, on-premises coverage, transit coverage, forgery or alteration losses, loss of securities, and loss from accepting counterfeit currency. There are some differences in the details of the coverage, depending upon the exposures and needs of a particular type of financial institution.

Common bonds available for specialized financial institution exposures include:

- stockbrokers blanket bonds
- stockbrokers partnership bonds
- finance company blanket bonds
- credit union blanket bonds
- savings bank and savings and loan blanket bonds
- insurance company bonds

Kidnap-Ransom-Extortion Coverage

A relatively new threat of loss to a bank or other financial institution is extortion under threat of kidnapping or other violence. A typical situation is where an officer of a bank receives a telephone call saying that a relative, an officer of the bank, or an employee of the bank, is being held and will be killed if a specified amount of money is not turned over to the kidnapper. The usual extortionist in such a case will instruct that arrangements must be carried out in great secrecy and that the police are not to be advised of the situation. Other types of threats against financial institutions include the threat of bombing or other catastrophe to the bank if money is not provided as instructed.

Several such cases that resulted in the payment of money for the release of a bank official or family member subsequently resulted in claims being made under bankers blanket bonds. In most cases, the money was delivered to the kidnapper away from the premises of the bank. In certain cases, the money changed hands on the bank's premises. There appears to be agreement that such payment is covered by the bankers blanket bond if the delivery of the money occurs on the bank's premises because of the wording of the bankers blanket bond relating to premises coverage. However, there is disagreement as to whether the bankers blanket bond covers the situation where the money is delivered to the kidnapper away from the bank's premises. Some insurance companies did pay such claims under the bankers blanket bond, while others denied liability. The result has been the development of an endorsement to the bankers blanket bond (and comparable bonds for other financial institutions similar to Insuring Agreement XVIII of the comprehensive 3-D policy) that covers loss incurred by the insured as the result of surrender of property because of an extortion incident to the kidnapping or alleged kidnapping of a bank official or employee. Coverage usually is also extended to the members of the household of a threatened person.

Two principles apply to this coverage. First, the financial institution, unlike a mercantile firm, pays a certain proportion of any loss from a kidnap incident. This is necessary in order to influence the bank officials to seriously consider any situation which may or may not be an actual kidnap threat. Second, a reasonable effort must be made by the threatened official to determine that the threat is genuine. It is also required that the threat be reported to at least one other officer or employee of the institution and also to local law enforcement officials or the Federal Bureau of Investigation.

Coverage of any kidnap-ransom-extortion case usually is delayed for thirty days from application. A policy may also contain a warranty that no such threat has been made at the time the extortion endorsement is added. The receipt of a real or suspected threat might influence bank officials to buy the insurance.

It is also required as a part of the coverage that the board of directors of the institution, within ninety days after the surrender of the property, shall ratify such surrender as an official act of the institution. This is to avoid any payment for an uncertain or indefinite situation.

The coverage may also be subject to an aggregate limit of liability during the bond period or the limit of liability may be for each loss that occurs during the bond period. This provision would be subject to negotiation between the insured, the producer, and the insurance company.

Bomb Threats Another form of extortion that has occurred is a telephoned or written threat to a bank or other institution that a bomb will be placed or has been placed at the premises and will be detonated unless a specified amount of money is paid. Here also such coverage, if written, would apply only if the payment is made away from the bank's premises. Payment on the premises may be considered as covered under the usual provisions of the bankers blanket bond. Loss due to payment under the threat of a bomb explosion ordinarily is not covered under the kidnap-ransom-extortion endorsement. This would have to be negotiated separately between the insured and the insurance company. Rates and exact provisions would depend on the surrounding circumstances and whether this institution or others in the area had previously been subjected to such threats or incidents.

Checkpoints

1. List the three aspects of identifying and analyzing crime loss exposures.
2. What is the difference between physical and financial protection?
3. Why is it easier to have a financial institution prospect accept the need for crime insurance?
4. List the major insuring agreements of the banker's blanket bond (No. 24).

SUMMARY

Crime insurance can be sold under a combination form policy known as either the comprehensive 3-D (form A or form B) or the blanket crime policy. The only difference between the 3-D policies form A and B is Insuring Agreement I, the fidelity coverage. Form A has a limit of liability that applies per loss no matter how many employees are involved. Form B's limit of liability for employee dishonesty is per employee so that the ultimate limit is based on the number of employees involved in a fidelity loss. Form A also has a one-year discovery period, whereas form B has a two-year discovery period. There are no other essential differences between the 3-D forms A and B in any other of the insuring agreements.

Significant differences between the 3-D policies and the blanket crime policies are with regard to selection of the insuring agreements, the limits of liability, the recovery, and additional insuring agreements available. The 3-D policy may be purchased with any one or any combination of the five insuring agreements, whereas the blanket crime policy requires all five insuring agreements. The limits of liability for a 3-D policy apply per insuring agreement with the insured being able to select a different limit for each insuring agreement. The blanket crime form has a single limit of liability per crime loss. The 3-D policy may be purchased on a per employee or a per loss basis, whereas the blanket crime policy is as stated the single limit of liability *per loss* regardless of how many insuring agreements apply. There are thirteen additional insuring agreements available to the 3-D policy, whereas only five are available for blanket crime.

The most common financial institution policy sold is the bankers blanket bond. The bankers blanket bond includes fidelity coverages, on-premises coverage for property, coverage for property in transit, forgery or alteration coverage, securities coverage, redemption of United States savings bonds, and counterfeit currency coverage. The general agreements and policy conditions differ from the 3-D policy only as the needs of a financial institution differ from those of a mercantile establishment. Just as additional coverages are available to the 3-D policy, so too do bankers have access to different bonds and different endorsements to their bonds.

Any type of financial institution, such as a stockbroker, a stockbrokerage firm which is a partnership, finance companies, credit unions, and so forth, has bonds similar to the bankers blanket bond and may have optional insuring agreements unique to their particular exposures.

CHAPTER 8

Surety Bonds

INTRODUCTION

Surety bonds are not as complex as many producers think. Most producers do not handle surety bonds every day and many believe that surety bonds should be handled exclusively by surety specialists. Admittedly, many types of surety bonds require the advice of experts, but the successful producer is one who aggressively solicits surety accounts, knowing when and how to use specialists.

Producers should have a working knowledge of surety bonds in order to provide complete service to their contractor accounts. Contractors usually prefer dealing with one producer, and this requires a knowledge of contract bonds and how they are written. Also, surety bonds such as license and permit bonds, public official bonds, and judicial bonds are profitable lines of business that may be a source of new contacts for additional business. Finally, commission rates are comparatively high in surety bonds, and since losses are not expected to occur, a substantial profit sharing or contingency commission may result.

Like compulsory automobile insurance and crime insurance on financial institutions, producers do not have to convince surety prospects of the need for coverage. Public officials are required to post bonds, and contractors are not able to bid unless a bid bond is in effect. Moreover, surety bond forms are virtually identical from one insurer to the other, so product differences are nonexistent. Therefore, the service provided by the producer is the key selling point backed up by a financially sound and experienced surety. (In this text, the terms

383

surety, surety company, or *bonding company* will be used synony-mously.) Many insurance companies are licensed to write surety bonds.

How Suretyship Operates

Two examples will be used to help to clarify the purpose of surety bonds and the parties involved. The first case involves a contractor; the second involves a probate bond, a type of judicial bond.

The township of Willistown, Pennsylvania, has obtained approval from its board of supervisors to construct a municipal building. The specifications for the building have been sent to a number of contrac-tors in the area whose qualifications have been approved by the architect. When the bids are opened, the low bidder is the B&E Construction Company. Prior to awarding the construction contract, the B&E Construction Company must furnish a contract bond guaran-teeing that the work will be done in accordance with the specifications and time schedule.

There are three parties to this (and all other) surety bonds. B&E Construction Company is the *principal*—the party whose performance is being guaranteed. The township of Willistown is the *obligee*—the party to whom the principal owes a duty and the party who will benefit from the guarantee. The third party is the *surety*—an insurance or bonding company that guarantees the work will be performed accord-ing to the specifications.

In the event that B&E Construction Company experiences financial difficulties and is unable to complete the job, the surety company may step in and hire another contractor to finish the job in accordance with the construction contract terms.

The second example involves a probate bond required by the orphans' court (a court name used to administer and distribute estates). In this situation, the *principal* is the decedent's daughter, who is named in the will as executrix of her father's estate. By law, she must follow the instructions of the court while performing her assigned duties. The *obligee* is the court that is compelled by law to carry out the terms of the will and requires a bond for faithful performance from the principal. The third party is the *surety* that guarantees that the daughter will perform her duties in a reasonable and proper manner.

Although they are not parties to the bond, two other individuals are involved. An attorney who is a friend of the family is responsible for the filing of the will and all other necessary forms. The attorney will guide the family through the judicial process and fulfill the decedent's wishes as specified in the last will and testament. Finally, the producer who issues the surety bond is called the *attorney-in-fact*. The producer executes the required probate bond so that the executrix and court may proceed with settling the estate.

If the daughter fails to properly account for and dispose of property in accordance with the will, the surety would respond and pay any damages suffered as a result of the improper performance of her duties.

Characteristics of Surety Bonds[1]

There are many different types of surety bonds. There are those that guarantee the faithful performance of public officials or fiduciaries. Some guarantee the performance of work contracts of a statutory or nonstatutory nature. Others guarantee the payment of taxes upon demand of the government, or duties upon the arrival of imports. Yet, surety bonds have some basic similarities which, taken together, set them wholly apart. One of these, as noted, is that there are three parties to the surety contract. The following paragraphs describe some of the other characteristics of surety bonds: the principal is liable to the surety; the surety theoretically expects no losses; the indeterminate length and noncancelability of many bonds; the influence of regulations and statutes; the bond penalty; the bond premium; and the bond must be in writing. In varying degrees, these characteristics distinguish surety bonds from insurance, and these distinctions will be summarized following the analysis of surety bond characteristics.

Principal Is Liable to the Surety In the event the principal should fail in the performance of its obligation to the obligee, the surety becomes answerable. This means that the surety must then fulfill that obligation and/or pay damages. However, the surety's performance does not extinguish the principal's duty to reimburse the surety. On the contrary, the principal still is obligated to indemnify the surety. This right is granted to sureties at common law and need not necessarily be specifically expressed in the bond or in the application. However, bond applications often contain indemnity agreements between principals and sureties. One such indemnity agreement found on a bond application to be signed by the principal reads:

> The Indemnitor(s) will at all times indemnify, and keep indemnified, the Surety, and hold and save it harmless from and against any and all damages, loss, costs, charges and expenses of whatsoever kind or nature, including counsel and attorney's fees, whether incurred under retainer or salary or otherwise which it shall or may, at any time, sustain or incur by reason or in consequence of its suretyship.

Surety Theoretically Expects No Losses When a bond is issued, the surety is attesting to the principal's integrity, capability, trustworthiness, financial responsibility, or whatever qualities may be required for the undertaking. Therefore, a surety will not provide a bond until it is sure that the principal has the necessary qualifications. By prequalifying the principal, the surety does not expect to become involved in any default and thus does not expect to sustain any losses. Bond underwriting requires careful analysis of the principal's character, capacity, and capital—the "three Cs." Before a surety bond will be issued, the surety considers the three Cs to determine, to its own satisfaction, that the principal is of such character, capacity, and capital that the obligation will be fulfilled. (These points will be discussed in greater detail as they apply to various types of bonds.)

Sureties frequently require the principal to post collateral of a value equal to all or part of the bond penalty (amount of the bond). Usually, the use of collateral results in a premium credit, since it reduces the surety's loss exposure. The situation with a surety bond involving collateral is similar to that of a bank charging interest on a collateral loan. The bank charges interest for the use of its money despite the fact that the loan is secured by collateral.

Joint control may also be used to reduce a surety's loss exposure, particularly when fiduciary bonds are involved. Joint control means any disbursements of assets must be with the approval of the surety. This makes it more difficult for a fiduciary administering a trust to divert some of the assets of the trust to the fiduciary's own benefit, or to use the assets unwisely. Because of careful surety underwriting, it is said the fee a surety charges for its services theoretically contemplates no losses. Nevertheless, losses do occur for many reasons, including poor judgment in underwriting and unforeseen developments in the economy. Losses are reduced by the rights of the surety in default, and by the possibilities of subrogation and salvage.

Rights of the Surety Upon Default. Should the principal be unable to perform fully, for some reason, the surety must do whatever is necessary to fulfill the undertaking. (Remember, the principal is still liable to the surety.) However, in the event of default the surety acquires no more of an obligation than the principal's original obligation, subject to the bond limit (also called the penalty). If, for some reason, damages exceed the bond limit, the surety's obligation usually ceases; but the liability to the obligee of the principal for any default or damage may be unlimited.

Significance of Subrogation and Salvage. Once having fulfilled the principal's obligation in default, the surety is subrogated to the rights and remedies of the obligee to the extent of any payment it has made. In fact, subrogation was first used in cases involving suretyship.[2] Through subrogation, the surety attempts to recover anything of value, since whatever is recovered is used to offset its losses.

Indeterminate Length and Noncancelability of Bonds
Surety bonds usually terminate when the principal's obligations have been fulfilled, so a bond could involve performance over several years. For this reason, surety bonds are considered to be indeterminate in length. This is especially true when the bond is noncancelable. This is not to say that all surety bonds are noncancelable or terminate only when performance has been completed. A public official bond, for example, cannot normally be canceled before expiration of an official's term in office, but there are exceptions in such circumstances as premature removal from office or death. License and permit bonds can usually be canceled, and are usually renewable each year. But a statutory construction contract bond cannot be either by the obligee or surety. The reasons for these variations will become more apparent as specific bond types are analyzed.

In view of the fact that many surety bonds are noncancelable and continue until completion of the principal's underlying obligation, it is difficult for a surety to determine its loss experience in the short run.

Influence of Regulations and Statutes on Bonds Surety bonds can be statutory or nonstatutory in form. A *statutory bond* is one that is prescribed by law—a municipal ordinance, or federal or state regulation or statute. Also, the law specifies the conditions of a statutory bond, so the obligations of all three parties are controlled not by the bond provisions, but by the law involved. A *nonstatutory bond,* on the other hand, is one that is controlled by the contract as drawn by the obligee.

Bond Limit (Penalty) The bond penalty is the amount for which the bond is written. It is similar to the limits of liability of an insurance policy. If, for some reason, damages exceed the penalty, the surety's obligation usually ceases at the penalty amount, although some bonds pay for court costs and interest on judgments above the bond penalty, as do most liability insurance policies. Although the bond penalty limits the obligation of the *surety,* the obligation of the *principal* for any default or damage may be unlimited.

Bond Premium When a surety gives a bond, it charges its principal a premium or service fee. This fee represents the price of the surety's guarantee that it will answer to the obligee if the principal should fail for some reason. While the *principal* pays the premium, it is the obligee who benefits from the bond. The service fee is *not* the legal consideration of the bond. Instead, the principal's consideration is the undertaking secured by the bond, and the surety's consideration is its guarantee to answer to the obligee in the event of nonperformance. Thus, a surety is obligated to fulfill the terms of a delivered surety bond even though the premium has not been paid.

Must Be in Writing A surety bond must be in writing to be binding and enforceable. As a contract of guaranty—i.e., a promise to be responsible for the debt or default of another—it is subject to the Statutes of Frauds and other common-law and statutory requirements.

General Types of Surety Bonds

Surety bonds are used for a variety of specific purposes, but will be divided into five broad categories for purposes of this analysis.

1. *Contract bonds.* These are, in general, those that guarantee the performance of certain public or private contracts. Within this category are bid, performance, payment, and maintenance bonds.
2. *License and permit bonds.* These are required by federal, state, or municipal governments as prerequisites to engaging in certain business activities. Among those who may need such bonds are contractors who work on public streets, plumbers, electricians, and real estate agents.
3. *Public official bonds.* These guarantee the honesty and faithful performance of those elected or appointed to positions in government.
4. *Judicial bonds.* These are prescribed by statute and filed in either probate courts or in courts of equity. Probate courts deal with matters such as settlement of estates and appointment of guardians. Courts of equity are concerned with disputes involving specific performance, or other equitable remedies, rather than money damages.
5. *Miscellaneous bonds.* These do not fit into any of the other classes, and may fulfill a variety of special needs.

CONTRACT BONDS

Many of those who are involved in some form of contractual relationship involving work or service to be performed by others, require bonds as a means of obtaining additional assurance that the undertaking will be performed as specified. Contract bonds are used in these circumstances, since they generally guarantee the fulfillment of certain obligations required under contracts. As a class, these bonds guarantee both public and private contracts, with the former being the more prevalent because bonds guaranteeing public contracts usually are required by law.

Types of Contract Bonds

Contract bonds may be classified into bid, performance, payment, or maintenance bonds. The nature of these contract bonds is summarized in Exhibit 8-1.

Contract bonds are not confined to construction operations. For example, contract bonds would also be required by the municipality that advertises for bids from firms which may be interested in handling its trash collections. Contract bonds in general are frequently confused with construction contract bonds, since most contract bonds are predominantly used for construction purposes and generate the most premium volume of sureties. Most contract bonds are used in public construction work; therefore the following description involves construction contract bonds.

Bid Bond A bid bond is furnished to an owner (obligee) of a project. It promises that the contractor or construction firm (principal) bidding for a contract will, if the bid is accepted, enter into a contract and furnish the other necessary contract bonds. If the bid is accepted and the contractor fails to provide such bonds or refuses to perform the work, the obligee is entitled to be paid the difference between the amount of that contractor's bid and the bid that is finally accepted by the owner.

Potential Problems. Generally, the problems with a bid bond begin when, after being awarded the contract by the obligee, a contractor refuses to enter into a contract of performance and to supply the required bonds. The contractor usually refuses for one of two reasons. Either the contractor discovers that a mistake was made in the preparation of the bid so that performance is virtually impossible at the quoted price, or the owner or the architect changes the specifications or causes a delay in awarding the contracts and economic conditions increase the cost of performing the work and make the bid price inadequate. Of these two reasons, the first—mistake in bid preparation—seems to be the more common.

CLERICAL VERSUS JUDGMENT MISTAKES. It is not unusual for contractors to make mistakes. Some are purely clerical errors, while others are the result of poor judgment. However, it is often stated that neither reason for such mistakes should be condoned. To permit a contractor to withdraw a bid without penalty, after it is opened, defeats the purpose of sealed bids. Furthermore, granting such relief may invite intentional "mistakes" in order to gain unfair advantage, or it

Exhibit 8-1
Contract Bond Comparison*

Bid Bond	Performance Bond	Payment Bond	Maintenance Bond
Obligee (Insured)			
The owner or party who is calling for the bid	The owner of the property or the person who is having the work done	Same as performance bond	Same as performance bond
Principal (Persons Bonded)			
The bidder	The contractor	The contractor	The contractor
What Is Guaranteed			
That the bidder will enter into the contract and post a performance bond if the bid is accepted	That the work will be completed by the contractor according to plans and specifications	That the project will be free of liens—that is, all bills for labor and materials will be paid	That the work will be free from defects in materials and workmanship for a certain specified period
When Required			
Public work projects; a certified check is commonly substituted for the bond on private work	Pubic work projects	Public work projects	Usually private and nonfederal jobs
Underwriting Considerations			
The character, capacity, capital, and experience of the contractor; also information on work under bid	The qualifications of the contractor, i.e., character, capacity, capital, and experience, as well as copy of work specifications	Same as performance bond	Same as performance bond; also, term of bond

*Adapted from *FC &S Bulletins*, Casualty/Surety (Cincinnati: National Underwriter Company, October 1973), pp. Bonds Con-1, 2.

may create the opportunity for collusion among two or more contractors.

Generally, errors of judgment, such as the failure to consider and to include certain costs of a project, are indefensible in the courts. But miscalculations of costs, or mistakes in arithmetic or in the transfer of figures, are sometimes considered excusable by the courts. The problem is that it can be difficult to distinguish between an error in judgment and an error in arithmetic. Of course, when an error has been made, the burden of proof is on the contractor.

CRITERIA FOR AVOIDING LIABILITY. There are occasions when the courts grant relief to contractors. Certain criteria, of course, must be met.

First, the mistake must be of a serious nature, and to require performance would be unconscionable. This means that the mistake is so large that if performance were required, it inevitably would result in an undue hardship for the contractor.

Second, the error or mistake must not be the result of gross negligence. Gross negligence can be difficult to prove, because simple mistakes are also caused by negligence. Gross negligence concerns a complete lack of good faith in preparing a bid, and involves a decision which, though erroneous, is intended by the contractor. Conversely, an error which is generally excusable is one that involves ordinary negligence, such as those involving arithmetic calculations or the transfers of figures. However, even here, all requisites must be met before an error is considered excusable.

Third, the owner must not sustain a substantial hardship if the bidder is granted relief. This refers to damages sustained by the owner which are other than those damages stemming from loss of an especially low price. For example, if the next lower bidder's estimate is still less than what the owner anticipated the work would cost, it would be difficult for the owner to argue that a hardship will exist if the lowest bidder is permitted to withdraw from performance of the contract.

Fourth, the contractor must give the owner of the project timely notice of error and notice of intention to withdraw—before the award is made. Timely notice, however, is sometimes difficult to define. Moreover, contract specifications concerning withdrawals and the procedure to follow vary by jurisdiction. Some provide that bids may be withdrawn anytime before this opening if the withdrawal is made in some form of written communication. But once the bids are opened, they cannot be withdrawn for a certain specified period, usually ranging from thirty to ninety days.

The fact that some courts allow contractors relief after weighing certain criteria should not be taken to mean that these procedures for granting relief are always followed. Even if they were, there is always the chance that a contractor will not meet all such criteria. Moreover, some courts have ruled that no mistakes are excusable. Therefore, contractors must exercise the utmost care in estimating costs and in checking figures. This is the best way to avoid expensive court costs and loss of additional valuable assets.

Performance and Payment Bonds When a bid is accepted, the contractor who is awarded the work not only must enter into a contract with the owner, but also must furnish the other bonds that may be required for completion of work. These usually include a performance bond and a payment bond, although the two are sometimes combined under one bond form. A maintenance bond may also be required as a guarantee that the completed work is free from defects for a certain period. Like the payment bond, the guarantee of the maintenance bond may also be included within the conditions of the performance bond.

Nature of Performance Bond Guarantee. The performance bond guarantees that the owner will be indemnified for any loss stemming from the failure of the contractor to perform the work according to the contract, plans, and specifications—which may or may not be subject to statutory provisions.

If a contractor defaults under a performance bond, or is in an impending stage of default, a surety has a number of options it can exercise. It can (1) complete the contract using the existing contractor, (2) complete the contract using a replacement contractor, (3) provide the existing contractor with financial assistance sufficient to avert loss, or (4) have the owner for whom work is being done make arrangements for completion of work with any losses payable by the surety up to the penalty amount.

A surety *may* elect to complete a contractual obligation, using the existing contractor or a replacement contractor. However, it is not compelled to do so, since the usual form of performance bond does not guarantee the completion of work *by the surety*. Confusion regarding a surety's obligation to complete an existing agreement of its principal probably stems from the popular use, many years ago, of completion or lender's bonds. The primary characteristic of such bonds was the "naked and unrestricted promise" of the surety to complete the contract should the principal be unable to do so. For all practical purposes, completion bonds are unavailable today.[3]

Frequently a surety exercises its second option and completes the contract, using either the existing contractor or a replacement contractor. A surety sometimes uses the existing contractor when the reason for a problem is something other than the contractor's incompetence.

Some circumstances or hardships that have led sureties to use existing contractors include a bank's refusal to grant any additional extension of credit; an improper and an insufficient estimate of contract costs; delay brought about by modification of the contract; delay in receiving necessary equipment; and delays because of bad weather or labor disputes. On the other hand, a number of circumstances have caused sureties to use other contractors to finish work. These reasons include incompetence, bankruptcy, suicide, or disappearance of the principal.[4]

Sureties have provided financial help in order to avert additional hardships and possible defaults caused by forces of nature, overcommitments, or lack of liquid assets. Sureties have assisted their principals on many occasions.[5]

Financial assistance by the surety will not always solve a performance problem. Sometimes, too, a surety will decide not to have the contract completed. It is then up to the owner or governmental body to proceed with the completion of the project. Whether a surety may become obligated for any damages depends upon the outcome of the completed work in terms of total, final costs. If the balance of funds retained by the obligee (that amount representing the unpaid balance which would have been paid to the original contractor had the work been completed) is sufficient to cover all costs of completion by others, there can be no claim against the surety under the performance bond. But, if the costs of completion exceed those originally estimated by the defaulting contractor, the excess represents the owner's loss, and is payable by the surety subject to the penalty amount of the bond.[6]

Any court costs assumed by the surety, however, are in excess of the penalty amount. Whatever the outcome in the event of default, the surety always has the right to seek reimbursement from the principal. The surety can collect from the principal (1) by an assignment of the obligee's rights to the surety, (2) by reason of the written indemnity agreement (typically included in the bond application), and (3) through the equitable right of subrogration.[7]

Since a performance bond guarantees the completion of work according to specifications, this also means that such work, when completed, will be free of any liens. This latter guarantee is especially important to owners of projects, because suppliers of labor and materials who go uncompensated usually can apply a mechanic's lien to the property. A mechanic's lien is a right granted by statute and is available to those who seek to secure the value of their work or services which have gone into the form of additions on real estate.[8] When a lien is placed on such property, the owner does not have clear title to it until all debts are settled. In fact, property has been sold in order to settle debts which have been secured by mechanic's liens.

From the owner's standpoint, therefore, the performance bond serves a dual purpose. It guarantees the completion of work as specified, and it guarantees that the work will be free of any liens. However, a performance bond does not provide total protection for suppliers of labor and materials, for the following reasons. First, a performance bond that guarantees the completion of work free of liens—without mention of any guarantee for the payment of labor and materials supplied by others—usually provides coverage only for claims that are properly liened. This sometimes means that suppliers who fail to file liens within the time period and other specifications of such mechanic's lien laws will have no protection.[9] Second, owners of projects have first claim to funds under the performance bond, while the claims of laborers and suppliers who have liens on such property have a secondary interest. In other words, the owner under a performance bond is entitled to be fully satisfied before claims of others are handled. This means that claims of others may be delayed, and there still is no guarantee that all such claims will be paid. Third, the mechanic's lien statute does not protect all suppliers. For example, the statutes sometimes limit the privilege to particular classes of workers such as plasterers or bricklayers. Furthermore, certain criteria must be met before a lien becomes effective. Finally, a mechanic's lien usually cannot be filed upon public property or public work.[10] So, if suppliers of labor and materials were to rely solely upon the performance bond of an owner for their only recourse, they could very well go without compensation for their services.

Nature of Payment Bond Guarantee. To avoid the utilization of mechanic's liens by suppliers, where such liens are permissible, and to provide a method whereby unpaid bills of creditors can be secured where mechanic's liens cannot be filed, owners of projects frequently request a payment bond in addition to the performance bond. A payment bond—often referred to as a labor and materials bond—guarantees that bills incurred by a contractor for labor and materials will be fully paid at the completion of the project.

Actually, a payment bond is often required for government work, whether the work is on a federal, state, or local level. Such a bond also is often suggested with private work when bond forms of the American Institute of Architects are used.

Maintenance Bonds Many jurisdictions have statutes, ordinances, or covenants which require that a certain degree of care be exercised in the construction of property. In addition, construction contracts often specify that contractors must remedy any work which is unsatisfactory due to faulty work or defective materials. To comply with these laws and specifications, contractors must usually provide obligees with a maintenance bond which guarantees that faulty work will be corrected or defective materials will be replaced.

Generally, a performance bond includes this maintenance guarantee, for a period of one year after completion of performance, without additional premium. Even when a separate maintenance bond is required along with a performance bond, there usually is no additional charge by the surety for the maintenance bond. But when a contractor does not have to furnish a performance bond, but still has to produce a maintenance bond, or when the contractor must guarantee certain work and materials for periods longer than one year, the maintenance bond requires an additional charge.

Sureties often are understandably reluctant to provide maintenance guarantees for periods over one year. First of all, the longer the guarantee, the greater the chance that a latent defect in materials or a faulty job will become apparent. It also becomes more difficult, after a lapse of time, to determine the cause of any defects. They could be caused by the contractor, by faulty specifications, by abnormal usage of property by the owner, or by some combination of reasons. And, finally, the reluctance of sureties to extend lengthy guarantees can be attributed in no small way to an apparent increase in contractors' vulnerability to claims after the work is completed. Part of this vulnerability is no doubt justified by a poor quality of construction workmanship and materials. The other part stems from a documentable tendency of the courts to award judgments holding contractors liable to owners on the basis of a variety of legal theories, including negligence, express and implied warranties of fitness, and strict liability in tort.[11]

There are a number of ways by which contractors can become implicated in suits involving faulty work. They may perform work which is done properly only to find out later that certain materials which had been used had latent defects. For example, green lumber can eventually warp or split, bricks of improper mix can retain moisture, and concrete products can fail to meet specifications relating to strength.

Plans and specifications prepared by the contractor or by others, such as architects, may be misleading or improper for the type of work that is being done. There may be times, too, when contractors are brought into suit because of the faulty work of subcontractors, especially when the latter are not asked to supply performance and maintenance bonds. Or, contractors may be implicated by accepting certain responsibilities under exculpatory or hold harmless agreements. And there are many situations when contractors clearly are negligent in the way in which they perform their work.

The fact that there is no relationship with products and completed operations insurance needs to be clearly stated. If the contractor is found to be responsible for defective work which is the subject of a maintenance bond, the work must be remedied at the contractor's own expense. Many contractors are not aware that faulty work is uninsurable, judging from the number of disputes and court decisions involving completed operations liability insurance claims. Nevertheless, most liability insurance policies, whether they are standard or nonstandard, exclude claims for property damage to work performed or to materials that are used in that work. Most such work is therefore done at a loss, since there is usually no insurance whatever available to treat this exposure. As a result, sureties are careful to bond only contractors that are financially capable of repairing or replacing defective work or materials, since they are in fact attesting to that capability by issuing maintenance bonds.

Miscellaneous Contract Bonds In addition to the bid bond, performance bond, payment bond, and maintenance bond mentioned above, there are a variety of types of "miscellaneous contract bonds." Complete analysis of all such bonds is beyond the scope of the Producer's Program. However, an analysis of two of the more common types of miscellaneous contract bonds—subdivision bonds and supply bonds—will illustrate their intent and scope.

Subdivision Bonds. Developers of land and real estate firms often desire to subdivide large tracts of property for housing developments. Developers must not only build suitable homes, but also handle all improvements—such as streets, sidewalks, and streetlights. They also must provide proper sewage disposal systems, a water supply, and other utilities. Before such construction can begin, developers are usually required to obtain permits and to provide subdivision bonds to the local governmental authority.

EXTENT OF GUARANTEE. The subdivision bond is considered a financial guarantee because the developer (principal) promises the municipality (obligee) that the housing development will be completed properly, along with all of its improvements. If not, the principal is responsible for the payment of any damages sustained by the obligee.

There is a marked difference between subdivision bond and a performance bond that is used for construction work. Under a performance bond, the contractor (principal) enters into a written agreement with the owner (obligee) promising to complete the work as specified, free of any liens. The obligee, of course, promises to pay the principal for services rendered as work progresses. The relationship is different when a subdivision bond is involved. The principal, here, promises to complete the project as planned, but the obligee promises nothing in return.

Only when the property has been developed and sold does the

developer begin to receive a return on its investments. Suppose, however, that the costs of building materials and labor far exceed expectations and, as a result, the land is not fully developed. Or, suppose the demand for such housing is not as great as anticipated because of the style of construction or the price range. Cyclical downturns of the economy may also have adverse effects on prospective homeowners. Any of these circumstances can create a hardship for the developer, who may face financial difficulties or even bankruptcy as a result. If bills cannot be paid so as to permit full completion of the project, or if damages ultimately assessed against the developer by the municipality cannot be paid, the surety becomes answerable under the guarantee of its bond.

Largely because of such hazards, a subdivision bond is difficult for developers to procure unless they can provide the type of qualifying credentials required by the surety.

QUALIFICATIONS OF THE APPLICANT. While the principal's character is important, capacity and capital are the most crucial factors in underwriting subdivision bonds. The capacity of a developer relates to an ability to meet the commitments underlying the work to be performed. The factors considered, therefore, are no different from those which are viewed when a construction contractor desires performance and payment bonds. The surety must determine whether the principal is qualified to perform the type of work involved, has the equipment and tools to do the work, and has the overall capabilities of completing the work as planned.

It is important in connection with subdivision bonds to learn whether the real estate firm or developer has ever handled projects of this nature before, and whether the developer has the expertise that is required in constructing houses on a large scale. When the developer has neither the knowledge nor experience for this kind of business venture, sureties certainly will not be interested in providing subdivision bonds. In such cases, satisfactory character and capital of the developer are not enough.

In cases where a developer intends to subcontract most or all of the work to another contractor who has the capacity to perform, many of the obstacles to qualifying for a subdivision bond can be overcome, particularly if the developer requires performance and payment bonds from a subcontractor which name the developer as the obligee.

The developer can still be confronted with difficulties. Nevertheless, the developer, in this type of arrangement, at least has a buffer—someone to look to for results—whether it is the contractor or the contractor's surety. Contract bonds are not total guarantees for all difficulties that may arise. There may be circumstances when the subject of any disagreement between the developer and the contractor is not within the scope of either the performance or payment bond. Should something like this arise, the burden is then shifted from the contractor to the developer's surety under the subdivision bond, if the developer is unable to meet the guarantees given to the municipality.

Capital or financial status of the real estate developer is also of extreme importance under subdivision bonds, whether the developer intends to complete the work itself or to subcontract all work. Some obligations of the developer cannot be transferred to the contractor, such as the guarantee to pay taxes and assessments on property. And, as previously mentioned, there may be occasions when the contractor is not under any obligation to the developer.

Since sureties view most subdivision bonds as precarious undertakings, sureties generally require that the developer provide collateral in the form of cash, in an amount sufficient to cover all costs of the entire project, including all costs of improvements when these are the subject of the contract, too. In lieu of cash collateral, some sureties may accept an escrow account so that money is available to pay for any costs of improvements and to pay suppliers of labor and materials.

Supply Contract Bonds. A supply contract is one that involves an agreement for furnishing and delivering materials or supplies at an agreed upon price, usually without any obligation to install whatever is to be delivered. Most such contracts are between private enterprise and federal, state, or local governmental bodies. A supply contract bond is one which is required by those governmental bodies (obligees) from their suppliers (principals) guaranteeing the performance of those supply contracts. Since, for the most part, these bonds are required by the government, they are statutory in form.[12]

EXTENT OF GUARANTEE. Those who wish to obtain supply contracts, whether they are manufacturers, wholesalers, or dealers, must submit bids, a situation like that of contractors who wish to obtain public work contracts. Typically, the lowest bidder must be selected. When a bidder fails to furnish whatever is required according to the contract specifications, the supplier is liable for the difference between the bid price of the supplier originally selected and the cost of buying those materials or supplies on the open market.[13]

Occasions may arise when the property covered by a supply contract is not readily available on the open market. Equipment made to order by a manufacturer is an example. Unless the commitment to supply the equipment can be met, the manufacturer may be subject to extraordinary damages, including costs for the delay involved in having some other firm complete the contract.

QUALIFICATIONS OF THE APPLICANT. Although character of the suppliers, that is, reputability and responsibility, is important, the capacity (ability of suppliers to meet their commitments) and their capital (financial status) are by far more important. From the standpoint of capacity, sureties must determine whether suppliers have equipment with which to fulfill the contract, as well as sufficient sources from which materials or supplies are to be obtained. Depending upon the material or commodity in question, it is also important for the surety to determine whether the supplier has a fixed price contract from the ultimate source. The price of steel and copper, for example, fluctuates from week to week, and a supplier without a fixed price contract may be confronted with financial hardship if the price for supplying that material eventually exceeds the price for which the supplier has agreed to sell it. In other words, conditions may arise whereby a supplier may have to fulfill a contract at a loss. How much a supplier can withstand in terms of losses thus becomes an important point for the surety to consider.

Checkpoints

1. List the three parties to a survey bond.
2. List the characteristics of a surety bond.
3. Describe the general nature of four contract bonds.
4. What are the surety's options in default of a performance bond?

Contract Bond Case Study—R. P. Davis

This case study involves R. P. Davis, Inc. (described in Chapter 10 of PRO 81) located in Chester County, and the Capable Insurance and Bonding Company. The project is the construction of a metal-clad storage building to be used for some of the road maintenance equipment owned by Chester County. The county commissioners have completed their preliminary work relative to letting bids and are ready to accept bids and award a contract.

Bid Bond Having dutifully met, advertised, and otherwise complied with all legal provisions of their office, the county commissioners are now at a public meeting ready to open bids. It is the appointed hour and date and in the presence of all interested parties. In this instance there were four contractors offering to perform the work, R. P. Davis among them. All bids have been sealed.

Simple formalities are dispensed with quickly and the envelopes are opened. The listing is posted on a chalkboard:

Dawn Construction Company—$119,262
Commercial Builders, Inc.—$116,987
R. P. Davis, Inc.—$112,962
Joseph Bloom & Sons, Inc.—$114,345

All bids were submitted with a bid bond (Exhibit 8-2) attached as required in the specifications set forth by the commissioners.

The purpose of the bid bond is to assure the county commissioners of the contractor's potential ability to bid and to secure a performance bond if successful in bidding. When accepting the apparent low bid, the officials want a guarantee that R. P. Davis will make good any expense incurred by the commissioners, i.e., the difference between its bid and the next lowest bid, should Davis fail to assume the job.

Bid bonds are not always necessary. A certified check in an amount prescribed by the obligee is sometimes acceptable. However, the charge for a bid bond is nominal and most contractors prefer it. There is another alternative called a bid bond service undertaking. It is an agreement between the surety company and contractor in which all bid bonds that may be required by the contractor during the ensuing year will be written for an initial nominal premium. This is done to avoid costly billings of individual bonds. Such service undertakings are granted to established contractors who have a line of credit with their surety company. Bid or proposal bond charges are nominal:

- Single Bid Bond—$25
- Service Undertaking—$50 Annual or $100 Continuous Form

While there may not be an actual agreement on the part of either party, the contract bond of performance usually is furnished by the surety that gave the bid bond.

Performance Bond Once all of the bids have been checked and analyzed and all has been found to be in order, a construction contract is awarded. This necessitates the contract of performance bond (Exhibit 8-3). Again, it is a simple form promising that R. P. Davis will do the work, at the price agreed upon, in accordance with all specifications and in the time allotted.

Qualifying the Contractor. If contract bonds are approached from the point of view of a substantial loan from a commercial bank, there should be no problem. In the final analysis, banks and bonding companies are especially interested in the same factors before providing financial backing. Specifically, surety companies insist that a contractor meet three previously mentioned criteria before providing a bond—*character, capacity,* and *capital.* In other words, the contractor must have qualities of honesty, excellent management ability with a thorough knowledge of the work, and enough money to back the undertaking even in adverse circumstances. Many things can affect contract completion or performance. A sewer project may be hampered by bad weather causing cave-ins, a building contractor may be plagued with labor problems, including indirect strikes, and almost anyone may have to face shortages or defective products and delivery delays. Naturally, some of this can be anticipated and provision should be made in the contract. Court recordings are filled with cases of bankruptcy from the unforeseen.

R. P. Davis is a cautious contractor with a quick, analytical mind. He stays abreast of current costs and always makes provision for the unexpected. Before bidding on a job, Davis makes certain that materials are available and gets price commitments to avoid unpleasant surprises.

The Davis corporation has proven itself to be a firm with integrity. Testimonials from previous customers are excellent and given freely. Davis selects the most reputable subcontractors and makes sure the entire job is done correctly. Any errors or faulty materials are voluntarily adjusted without argument or delay.

In summary, the three Cs for R. P. Davis, Inc. are:

- Character—The integrity of the company and the family behind it has been established. It appears there is little chance of dishonesty or poor moral character.
- Capacity—The experience to the Davis Company people indicates an ability to function on proper schedule. A fairly good labor pool is available for mustering of additional help if it is needed. All supervisors are competent with a wealth of construction knowledge and familiarity with local conditions, weather patterns and ordinances. The company's past record indicates it can readily perform the work that is to be bonded. Work on hand appears easily manageable.
- Capital—Capital is more difficult to ascertain since it calls for in-depth analysis of financial information. The underwriter has requested and obtained the latest audited financial statements and will render a decision after considering them and other equally important factors.

The essential financial statements follow. These are CPA-audited statements as previously shown in Chapter 10 of PRO 81. The accounting firm had performed certain accepted tests to substantiate information which might be open to questions if it were an "unaudited" statement. Additional underwriting questions are asked that go beyond the figures in the financial statements. An example is the accounts receivables of $174,315 shown on the balance sheet (Exhibit 8-4). If unaudited, the figure would have to be questioned. Who owes the

Exhibit 8-2
Bid Bond

BID BOND

Bid or Proposal Bond

BOND NO. ....

KNOW ALL MEN BY THESE PRESENTS,

That we, ... R. P. Davis, Inc. ....

of .... (hereinafter called the Principal), as Principal, and

Crowley Fire and Marine Insurance ......, a corporation, organized and existing under the

laws of the State of Illinois and authorized to become Surety in the State of ...... Yourtown

(hereinafter called the Surety) as Surety, are held and firmly bound unto ...... The County

of Chester ....

(hereinafter called the Obligee) in the penal sum of ...... 10% of the amount bid ....

.... Dollars ($ 11,297.00 ......) for

the payment of which the Principal and the Surety bind themselves, their heirs, executors, administrators,
successors and assigns, jointly and severally, firmly by these presents.

Whereas the Principal has submitted or is about to submit a proposal to the Obligee on a contract for

$112,962.00 for construction of a metal-clad warehouse as per

specifications outlined in contract 3C-13587

NOW, THEREFORE, the condition of this obligation is such that if the said contract be awarded to the Principal and the Principal shall, within such time as may be specified, enter into the contract in writing, and give bond, with surety acceptable to the Obligee for the faithful performance of the said contract; or if the Principal shall fail to do so, pay to the Obligee the damages which the Obligee may suffer by reason of such failure not exceeding the penalty of this bond, then this obligation shall be void; otherwise to remain in full force and effect.

SIGNED, SEALED and DATED this............day of...................., 19.........

R. P. Davis

I. M. Capable

WITNESS:

BY ....

Attorney-in-Fact.

FA 66-1

Exhibit 8-3
Performance Bond

CROWLEY FIRE AND MARINE INSURANCE CO.

PERFORMANCE BOND

KNOW ALL MEN BY THESE PRESENTS, That we ___R. P. Davis, Yourtown___

_____ as Principal, and _Crowley Fire and Marine_

of __Yourtown___ as Surety, are held and firmly

bound unto ___The County of Chester___ , hereinafter

called the Obligee, in the penal sum of _____ Dollars

(_$112.962.00_ for the payment of which sum well and truly to be made,

we bind ourselves, our heirs, executors, administrators, and
successors, jointly and severally, firmly by these presents.

THE CONDITION OF THIS OBLIGATION IS SUCH, that whereas the Principal
entered into a certain contract with the Obligee, dated

_____ for _____

NOW THEREFORE, if the Principal shall well and truly perform and fulfill all the undertakings, covenants, terms, conditions, and agreements of said contract during the original term of said contract and any extensions thereof that may be granted by the Obligee, with or without notice to the Surety, and during the life of any guaranty required under the contract, and shall also well and truly perform and fulfill all the undertakings, covenants, terms, conditions and agreements of any and all duly authorized modifications of said contract that may hereafter be made, notice of which modifications to the Surety being hereby waived, then, this obligation to be void, otherwise to remain in full force and effect.

IN WITNESS WHEREOF, the above bounden parties have executed this instrument under their several seals this _____ day of _____, 19____, the name and corporate Seal of each corporate party being hereto affixed and these presents duly signed by its undersigned representatives, pursuant to authority of its governing body.

ATTEST:

BY: _____ R. P. Davis

BY: _____ Attorney-in-fact

money? Is it readily collectible? How much of it is really bad debt? Another concern may be the cash figure. Which banks have the money? Is it free of assignment? In this case, for example, there might be a cash flow problem. A review of accounts receivables in the assets column and accounts payable in the liabilities column shows both to be about equal. On the other hand, the cash safety valve, consisting of savings and money in the checking account, is a plus factor.

The income statement (Exhibit 8-5) appears sound, showing a net profit of over $60,000, or better than 8 percent of sales, which is higher than industry average. It indicates good management and efficiency in operation to the surety company.

Financial statements alone, however, may not provide enough information. Many bond underwriters look for a much clearer and more perceptive analysis by means of an accurate statement of work in progress using the percentage of completion method, a way of determining a contractor's position on uncompleted contacts. Outstanding contracts are listed, showing the amount of the contract and the amount of money actually earned based on the percentage of work actually completed. Deposits or retainages are also shown. The method gives an underwriter a good picture of how much money a contractor will need to complete the work on hand.

Not all underwriters insist on the percentage of completion method. However, all will insist on a *Contractor's Work in Progress* report. The information called for includes:

- Contract Description and Location,
- Contract Amount,
- Percentage Completed to Date,
- Amount Billed to Date,
- Estimated Cost to Completion, and
- Estimated Date of Completion.

The form must be filled in accurately and is subject to verification.

The percentage of completion method is more analytical and requires the following information:

- Contract or Job Description,
- Contract Price,
- Contract Revenue to Date,
- Contract Costs to Date,
- Gross Profit to Date,
- Total Contract Costs,
- Gross Profit at Completion,
- Percent Complete,
- Partial Billings,

Exhibit 8-4
Balance Sheet—R. P. Davis, Inc.

Current Assets		
Cash		
Checking	$10,083	
Savings	50,053	$ 60,136
Accounts Receivable		174,315
Notes Receivable		37,011
Prepaid Taxes		13,515
Total Current Assets		$284,977
Properties		
Equipment	$75,158	
Land and Buildings	99,052	
	174,210	
Less: Accumulated Depreciation	68,061	106,149
Other Assets		
Due from Officers		27,899
Total Assets		$419,025
Liabilities and Stockholder's Equity		
Current Liabilities		
Accounts Payable		$178,711
Accrued Salaries		2,690
Payroll Taxes Withheld and Accrued		1,822
Accrued Profit Sharing		8,368
Notes Payable (current portion)		29,923
Mortgages Payable (current portion)		4,098
Total Current Liabilities		$225,612
Long-Term Debt		
Mortgages Payable	$66,262	
Notes Payable	952	67,214
Stockholder's Equity		
Paid in on Capital Stock Common		
—100,000 Shares Authorized 50,000		
Shares issued and outstanding $1		
Par Value	$50,000	
Additional Paid in Capital	5,452 $55,452	
Retained Earnings	71,747	56,199
Total Liabilities and Stockholder's Equity		$417,025

Exhibit 8-5
Income Statement—R. P. Davis, Inc.

Net Sales		$1,303,688
Other Revenue		3,557
		$1,307,245
Expenses		
Materials	$430,045	
Labor	56,423	
Subcontractors	547,719	
Salaries	76,826	
Advertising	2,464	
Dues and Subscriptions	667	
Draft and Engineering	2,655	
Entertainment	6,336	
Equipment Rental	6,371	
Employee Benefits	9,916	
Depreciation	12,380	
Insurance	29,178	
Gasoline and Oil	10,521	
Maintenance and Repairs	9,061	
Interest	9,188	
Taxes and Licenses	16,699	
Legal and Accounting	1,007	
Utilities	5,384	
Telephone	5,256	
Office Expense	2,328	
Supplies	308	
Travel	4,406	
Rent	300	
Miscellaneous	947	1,246,385
Net Income		$ 60,860

- Billings in Excess of Related Costs, and
- Unbilled Accounts Receivable.

The latter method will generally reveal "over and under" billings on jobs. For example, if a $100,000 job is 60 percent complete, then $60,000 should have been billed. The percent of completion method will also point up deficit spending on the part of the contractor.

The work in progress report for R. P. Davis is shown in Exhibit 8-6. While the work in progress is not as detailed or informative as some others, it does give the underwriter a fairly good understanding of how

Exhibit 8-6
R. P. Davis—Work in Progress

Description	Contract Amount	Percent Completed	Amount Billed	Estimated Cost to Complete	Estimated Time to Completion
City of Yourtown— fire station	$420,352	70%	$298,974	$ 52,210	2 mos.
Smith Co.— maintenance bldg.	78,450	90%	54,543	12,662	2 mos.
Wilson— shopping center	742,378	5%	42,318	612,000	7 mos.
Jones residence	124,300	0%	—	105,000	4 mos.

the contractor is progressing. A serious financial crisis can develop if a contractor is overextended by taking on too much work. Underwriters are careful about such items as retentions and deposits—some contractors apply them to work already in progress. If this is being done, it can easily lead to financial problems. As long as new work keeps coming, bringing a fresh supply of funds, a satisfactory cash flow can be maintained. But, as soon as that source dries up, the entire business may collapse, producing bond losses that are not supposed to occur.

"Material-intensive" jobs can be another distortion of the financial picture. Collection for materials in advance may look like work has progressed at a rapid, or at least a satisfactory, rate, but the actual work may only be in the beginning stages with the material money having gone toward another job or in payment of debts.

Accounting Knowledge Obviously, the more knowledge the producer has, the better are chances for writing an account that will be acceptable to the underwriter. Many factors affect the desirability of an account. Sometimes, a contractor's corporation is financially weak, for very good reasons. The contractor's willingness to give a personal guaranty through personal indemnity agreements can serve to strengthen the corporation sufficiently to make the bond writable. Certainly, a realistic surety will not forego premium if the contractor's personal proven wealth is used to shore up the contracting. Keep in mind, it must be *proven* wealth readily available so that legal processes are not required for the surety to collect under its rights of subrogation, should it become necessary to do so. Generally, stocks of good quality, savings accounts, bonds and other instruments of similar liquidity are acceptable. Personal indemnity agreements are an important and useful tool. They need not be limited to the owner of the business. Others may grant it.

A key element in bonding is liquidity. Assets vary in their significance and those of particular interest to surety companies are the type immediately available for conversion to cash. A piece of land in an undeveloped area or a yard full of heavily encumbered earth-moving machinery will do little to meet payrolls or pay suppliers. Buildings, such as apartments or offices, may be fine long-term investments and look good on the balance sheet, but qualified buyers must be found before money is realized.

The contractor must accept the rules of sensible underwriting and not hesitate to reveal all personal and corporate information to the producer and surety. The surety-contractor relationship should be long lasting. It calls for adept handling before consummation and full cooperation in order to continue. The producer initiates sale of the idea but should seek expert counsel from a qualified bond specialist if experience is lacking. A joint meeting with the contractor is normally a good idea. The effort may accomplish two things—sale of the contractor on the services offered and tentative acceptance by the surety. A third plus may be clearing up technical questions.

Additional Case Studies

Following are some actual cases that illustrate certain fundamental principles of contract bonding. The cases have been slightly modified for purposes of illustration and simplification.

Case Study #1—The need for liquidity A sewer contractor was fortunate in obtaining a couple of good public contracts at a proper bid level (his bids were low but only by a small amount, enough to get the jobs but not underpriced to a danger point). All went well with weather and his men performed admirably, producing more effective man-hours of work than normally expected. Upon completion, inspections were made and all work approved for payment.

In the interim, the contractor bid a considerably more extensive project. As payment was received from the previous public jobs, he immediately used the funds to purchase one new piece of equipment capable of moving more earth in a shorter period of time than the equipment already owned. He also arranged for a lease of another unit on a long-term basis. All of this resulted in heavy debt commitments impairing liquidity. An application for a bond was denied because of a profoundly weakened financial condition. He was close to being without sufficient funds to handle payrolls for the newly bid job.

Case Study #2—The contractor-surety partnership A general contractor had spent a number of years in public and private work. He and his wife amassed substantial personal wealth in excess of a half-million dollars. About 75 percent of the funds were invested in qood quality stocks and convertible debentures with the balance in Certificates of Deposit and passbook savings accounts. There had been no difficulty in obtaining corporate surety bonds for the smaller to medium-sized jobs in which he specialized. Occasionally, a large bond was approved when required. In such instances, personal indemnity became necessary; that is, the contractor and his wife had to sign agreements giving the surety immediate access to their personal wealth in the event of default by their construction firm.

Then the contractor reevaluated his financial position. The personally owned stocks were not appreciating; the contractor and his wife sold them and then purchased a gentleman's farm and 214 acres as an investment for the future. They also purchased an office building as a retirement nest egg and paid for it in cash. Regrettably, while they may have enhanced their personal goals, the timing was poor. A fairly sizable job came up for bid but the surety refused to issue the needed bid bond. The contractor's new investments may have been sound and, perhaps, even more profitable in the long run. However, his personal financial picture had changed considerably. Obviously, the funds held by the contractor and his wife had really been an integral part of the business, at least when it came to larger contracts. The contractor should have discussed his prospective transactions with the surety company before altering his position so drastically. In this case, he suffered from neglecting to consider the surety as a true partner.

Case Study #3—Working ability as an asset Four brothers had been in the excavating business for about fifteen years. Each had accumulated considerable personal assets through savings and subsequent investments in real estate. Their corporation was always properly funded with never a need for personal indemnity from any of the four active officers. An authorized line of credit for $450,000 had been granted by their surety; in other words, they could have that much work in progress at any one time. A further stroke of good fortune came when a national railroad engaged the excavating company for continual grading work along the tracts in the general area.

Things continued to go smoothly for about a year; then the railroad began to delay paying for the work performed. Before anyone could do anything, the railroad owed $75,000 to the contractor and had gone into receivership. Cash flow was seriously impaired and when an opportunity developed to accept a good job, the bond underwriter began to pressure for personal indemnity, quite a setback for a cohesive and successful contracting family. The problem was resolved amicably when the producer met with the brothers and surety company in a joint session. His recommendation was that the four work without wages for the entire contracting season in an effort to strengthen the bleak financial statement. Each had sufficient personal worth to do so and enough life insurance in the event of premature death.

Case Study #4—Proper accounting procedures Another very interesting situation involved the Patriotic Plumbing Company. In the small contractor category, Patriotic usually did public work ranging from just a few thousand dollars to about $75,000. Most contracts were with hospitals, schools, community buildings, and private corporations and businesses.

The Crowley Fire and Marine had granted a line of credit up to $150,000 to the father and son operation. Most jobs were performed by the two with supplemental labor from the local union hall. All contracts were completed on time and the business was very profitable. Repeat jobs were now common and it was not necessary to fight for every piece of work.

Patriotic's accountant kept records on a "complete jobs" basis instead of a "percentage of completion" basis. The system worked well with the Internal Revenue Service for tax purposes, but it produced a distorted picture that caused the surety to question the plumbing contractor's ability to perform. It was bid time again and facilities for surety bonds were withdrawn, at least temporarily. In effect, Patriotic was now out of business, unable to bid jobs it had been accustomed to performing over a number of years on a profitable basis.

Consultations with underwriters and the accountants brought about a revamping of procedures to the more desirable "percentage of completion" method. The result was a substantially improved financial statement resulting in restoration of the $150,000 line of credit, putting the firm back into business.

Case Study #5—Proper other insurance Not long ago, a small- to medium-sized contractor was found responsible for undermining a building next to the construction site, causing a partial building collapse and nearly $100,000 in damage. The general liability policy did not include coverage for collapse and the contractor did not carry an umbrella policy. The insurer of the collapsed building paid the loss and repairs were affected as promptly as possible. There was subrogation against the contractor who had to reimburse the insurer. It weakened the contractor's financial condition so severely that bonds were no longer available. The contractor went out of business.

Kinds of Contract Bonds for Underwriting Purposes

Surety companies have developed groupings of contracts for rating and underwriting purposes:

Class A Contracts These usually are available for operations that are not as hazardous as general contractors or subsurface earth movers such as excavators, drillers, and tunnelers. Examples of this class are: land graders; aluminum siding installers; parking area contractors; site preparation workers; map makers; playground or park work employees; ceiling installation workers; roofers; tennis court or athletic field construction workers; elevator or escalator installers; and glazers. Standard rating is $9 per $1,000 for the first $500,000, dropping to $5.60 per $1,000 for the next $2 million. Rate drops further as contract price increases.

Class A-1 Contracts This group includes technical, scientific, and data processing contracts and contracts that provide for the furnishing of facilities or personnel to perform some type of work or labor. Examples include contracts for the installation of conveyors, computers, bookbinding equipment, doors, generators, guard rails, kitchen equipment, metal windows and shutters, "qualified" oil or gas pipelines, radio towers, street and subway lighting systems, and public address and music systems. Not considered as risky as other groups, these carry a standard rate of $6 per $1,000 for the first $500,000 of contract price, dropping to $5 per $1,000 for the following $2 million and even lower thereafter.

Class B Contracts These include subsurface earth movers such as excavators, sewer contractors, general contractors, drillers, dock and drydock installers, tunnel builders, nuclear reactor contractors, and builders of garbage disposal plants. Certain other types of contracts also in this group include air conditioning systems, carpentry, coal stripping, drainage and other ditches, electrical wiring, gasoline cracking plants, golf course building, heating and ventilating systems, grain elevator construction, and landscaping. Considered the most hazardous of the contracting groups, these bonds carry a standard rate of $12 per $1,000 for the first $500,000 down to $7.25 per $1,000 for the next $2 million, scaled downward thereafter and bottoming out to $4.80 per $1,000 at $7.5 million and above.

Supply Contracts Considered the least hazardous, supply contracts have a standard rate of $2.40 per $1,000 for the first $500,000, reducing to $2.00 per $1,000 on the succeeding $2 million and even more on larger amounts. As suggested, supply contract bonds are designed to guarantee that the supplier will deliver the promised quantity at a promised price; otherwise financial reimbursement will be made by the surety to the purchaser. Such contracts can range from furnishing coal of defined quality to public utilities to supplying peach turnovers to a military encampment. Experience shows that such bonds are not very risky.

Maintenance Guarantees If the general contract calls for maintenance, no extra charge is made under the contract bond for the first twelve months. If the maintenance agreement is to run longer, premium is determined on length of maintenance agreement with certain discounts applying for stipulated conditions--i.e., 50 percent reduction in rate if the contract provides for a 10 percent retention of contract price by owner for maintenance. Standard rates are $1.80 per M per year for the first $500,000 with reductions as the amount of bond increases.

Miscellaneous Contracts This includes a varied assortment of contracts from building bridge superstructures down to grubbing and clearing a piece of land. Bonds are needed to cover contracts for advance payments, aircraft construction or repair, rental equipment, transportation of school children, snow or garbage removal, U. S. mail contracts, and many other activities many people are unaware of. Rates differ from one bond to the next, depending on degree of exposure and type of contract.

Completion bonds are frequently confused with performance bonds, but there is a clear distinction. Completion bonds are provided for lenders or lessors guaranteeing that funds loaned or paid for a specific project will be used for that project. In other words, a bond promising a bank that its money will be used for purposes for which loaned will eliminate the possibility of mechanics' liens against a building if the contractor has failed to pay the tradespeople or suppliers involved in the construction of that building.

Selling Contract Bonds

Opening the door to a sale is still a fundamental principle in any kind of selling. There is little question that much bonding results from political connections. However, there is a great deal more written by the knowledgeable and hardworking producer. There are specialists in the field who make a living doing nothing but selling contract bonds, but that is far from the norm in most areas. In some communities, there is not enough bond business available to support a specialist; yet someone must be around to handle bonds.

One way to enter the bonding arena is through other lines of insurance. Nearly every producer has small service or tradespeople insured who can serve as "centers of influence" by introducing the producer to contractors who perform work requiring bonds. If a producer has a good market for general liablility or umbrella insurance, these centers of influence might be used as a means of working into an account. Sometimes, the reverse is true—obtaining bonds results in getting the other lines.

Attendance at bid openings may be helpful as a display of interest. Attendance at building trade shows or conventions can serve to open a few doors, particularly with use of an insurance and bonding booth.

Getting to know suppliers who deal with contractors is another means of getting exposure. Their recommendation of a producer is of value. A direct method that has worked for some is a letter to known and well established contractors suggesting an interview in order to act as "backup" surety.

Accountants are a good source. It is best to time visits to accountants in late summer or fall when they are not busy with tax work. They are influential and should not be overlooked as potential centers of influence. Membership in business clubs, if available, gives good exposure. Even if it produces no bond business directly, it is likely to prove of value in other ways. Certainly, the "people" business of insurance and bonds calls for as many contacts as possible.

There are many reasons why bondable contractors may want to change surety companies or producers. Some have relocated and do not like traveling long distances for a bid bond. Others may have been pressured politically into dealing with someone who is not to their liking. Some get very poor service or may be dealing with a producer or insurance company that may not be as competent as they would like.

What the Bond Underwriter Needs to Know

It is vital that submissions be as complete as possible. Incomplete information only delays things. A general outline on procedures follows:

1. *Cover Letter.* Begin with a concise but factual letter outlining the contractor's technical background, experience, work record, and any other material data that will give the surety company an insight into the person with whom they will be dealing.
2. *Contractor's Experience and Information Statement.* This gives the underwriter a reasonably good idea of the organization and past experience relating to jobs that have been completed successfully.
3. *Work on Hand Form.* This form gives the underwriter a word picture of what the contractor is doing at the moment.
4. *Application.* This form relates to the specific job for which the bond is required. If there is not specific application being made at the time of submission, the cover letter should state that this is to pre-qualify the contractor.

5. *Financial Statements.* The latest year-end financial statements and the previous full year's statements should be submitted. If the submission is being made in the middle of the year, or later, an interim statement should be included. If the financial information is not audited and certified by a CPA, schedules of receivables and payables must be included. The names and addresses of banks should also be made known.

Supplemental data in the form of a statement of retained earnings, statement of changes in financial position, statement of jobs completed, and statement of contracts in progress can be invaluable assistance to the underwriter. If personal indemnity is to be given, statements for indemnitors should also be furnished.

The bond underwriter will look for certain characteristics, such as:

- A favorable ratio of current assets to current liabilities of approximately two to one;
- A considerable amount of bid work with more than half of the gross income derived in work requiring bonds;
- Several years in business with a fine reputation in the construction industry, even among competitors;
- A good record-keeping system with an emphasis on job costs;
- An excellent credit rating as a result of profitable operations, leaving a respectable portion of those earnings in the company to finance growth.

Surety Bond Guarantee Program for Small Contractors

There are many small contracting firms (or individuals) that, although able to fulfill job contracts, lack a certain amount of the capital or capacity necessary to meet sureties' underwriting requirements for bid, performance, and payment bonds. To many such small firms, assistance is available through the Small Business Administration (SBA) under its Surety Bond Guarantee Program. The purpose of the program is to give small, inexperienced contracting firms the opportunity to be bonded so they can compete for jobs. Having this opportunity, they can then prove themselves by performing the work specifications. A history of successful performance may in turn enable such firms to secure future surety bonds based upon their own reputation and financial ability.

Nature of the Program The SBA program is intended only for individuals or firms that are required to obtain bid, performance, and payment bonds for work including, but not limited to, construction, repair, maintenance, service, supply, and janitorial services. Only work which requires a contract bond is within the scope of the program, although work requiring another type of bond is sometimes permissible if written in conjunction with a contract bond. For example, a license and permit bond that is required of a construction contractor working on a public highway may be included under this program, since it is considered to be incidental to a contract bond.

Eligibility   The fact that the Surety Bond Guarantee Program is intended for small contracting firms that may be unable to secure financial assistance elsewhere does not mean all such firms automatically qualify for assistance. Actually, the program is not intended for blatantly unqualified contractors, but only for those that are considered borderline by normal underwriting standards. In fact, the program requires that sureties are not to lower their underwriting standards in determining contractors eligible under this program.

In order to evaluate an applicant under this program, the information sought by the surety corresponds with that required to underwrite a contractor under normal procedures. Among the data required are a financial statement no more than two months old and an annual financial statement. Furthermore, since the surety is interested in the management of the business, it will want background information on the character of the individual or on the principals of the firm.

A description of the job involved is always required. The surety, of course, requires a copy of the bid proposal, information concerning whether the applicant is required to bid for a job, and details concerning the financing of the job.

An explanation is required as to the applicant's expertise with the type of job being sought. As to previous experience, a surety needs to know about the types and amounts of contracts outstanding, and whether the applicant has ever previously served as a prime contractor or a subcontractor.

On some occasions applicants for this program are declined because they are unable to supply required financial data. However, there are other reasons for declination, such as insufficient capital and lack of technical expertise. When the reason is easily correctable, the SBA may try to assist the contracting firm in overcoming its deficiencies. Otherwise, the case is considered closed.

Even when a contracting firm is considered to be borderline, its annual gross volume must not exceed an amount established by the SBA in order to be eligible for the program. One million dollars is the maximum contract amount that may currently be bonded in the program. However, there is no limit to the number of bonds that may be guaranteed for a contractor, provided each separate contract does not exceed $1 million. For example, if an otherwise qualified contractor desires to perform two separate but related jobs and each requires a separate performance bond, the contractor may be able to secure guarantees for both, provided each contract does not exceed $1 million. On the other hand, a firm that needs a bid bond for 5 percent of a $2 million contract cannot receive an SBA guarantee even though the bond amount is $50,000.

Extent of Guarantees The SBA is not a surety, nor does it issue surety bonds. It merely guarantees a participating surety—which itself must be on the Treasury Department's list of approved sureties—up to 90 percent of any loss that is sustained under any bond of less than $250,000 and 80 percent of contracts between $250,000 and $1 million. The term "loss" in that guarantee encompasses all liability, damages, court costs, legal fees, charges, and expenses of any kind that the surety may sustain as the result of writing a bond under the SBA program.

In addition to issuing the required bond or bonds, the surety must pay the SBA a fee for guaranteeing the bonds that are written. This fee amounts to 10 percent of the bond premium, including a like percentage on any additional premiums which later may develop.

Effect of Breach In the event that any contract is breached by a contractor bonded under the program and any claim or suit is brought against the surety, the SBA must be notified within a reasonable time. Even though the SBA requires notification of any breach, it is still the surety's responsibility to handle all phases of the claim. This usually included determining the extent of the contractor's liability and taking whatever action is considered necessary in minimizing the loss, defending the contractor, and offering any settlements.

The Surety Bond Guarantee Program is a reimbursement program. This means that after the surety sustains losses it is reimbursed for those losses up to the 80 or 90 percent guarantee. However, the SBA reimburses the surety on a calendar quarterly basis, and it makes adjustments on a pro rata basis when the surety receives any recoveries through salvage or subrogation.

Checkpoints

1. Explain the "three Cs."
2. List three different financial statements that should accompany all contract bond submission.
3. What is the intent of the SBA's surety bond guarantee program?

LICENSE AND PERMIT BONDS

Licenses are required by states, counties, cities, and political subdivisions for two primary reasons: first, they are a source of revenue; second, they may help in the regulation of license holders through statutes, regulations, or ordinances which exist for the safety and general welfare of the community. Among those who must obtain licenses are auctioneers, automobile dealers, barbers, owners or operators of laundromats, commission merchants, electricians, plumbers, demolition contractors, fumigators, owners of gas stations, vendors of alcoholic beverages, grocery store proprietors, operators of parking lots, photographers, ticket brokers, and warehousemen.

Permits are somewhat like licenses. They, too, must be obtained from political subdivisions. They also serve as a means of regulation and as sources of revenue. However, they often are needed as prerequisites to performing special functions that are incidental to business operations. A licensed business, for example, may need a permit before it can use public property to park customers' automobiles. Permits are required when signs or canopies overhang public property, as well as for sidewalk elevators (invariably for freight handling) on public walkways. Truckers with oversize loads often need permits before they can legally use public roadways. Contractors who work on streets, sidewalks, and public sewer systems also need permits, as do individuals and firms who make structural alterations or improvements to their properties. Whatever the type, licenses or permits normally are not issued until those who are in need of them furnish license or permit bonds to the appropriate public bodies.

Purposes of License and Permit Bonds

License and permit bonds, though required for a variety of specific reasons, can be categorized into two general groups, according to their underlying purpose.

Under the first group are bonds which serve the purpose of holding public bodies harmless for any damages resulting from the failure of licenses to comply with statutes, regulations, ordinances, or codes that control their activities. Principals required to furnish this type not only are subject to revocations of their special privileges (licenses or permits), but also are subject to any damages and fines that may accrue as the result of their noncompliance with such laws. (The bond penalties are the maximum obligations of sureties.) What sets bonds in this group apart from the other group of bonds is that these bonds directly benefit public bodies. Members of the public do not have a direct claim under bonds per se. An example of a bond in this category is one required of merchants who agree to pay sales taxes collected on goods that are sold.

The second group of bonds serves essentially the same purpose, but also serves to provide members of the public, as third parties, with direct rights of action against the bondholders. For this reason, these are commonly referred to as indemnity bonds. In this category is the bond required of contractors who work on public sidewalks. Such bonds agree to protect and indemnify the public for any injuries or damages stemming from failure to complete the principal's obligations under the law requiring the bond.

License and permit bonds are usually written for one year, although they can terminate sooner, depending upon the reasons for their use. Since the bonds are statutory in nature, the laws are read into these bonds. This means, among other things, that whether these bonds may be cancelable depends upon the law for which they are issued. Many laws do permit cancellations.

Types of Guarantees—Examples

To achieve one or both of their general purposes, license and permit bonds may provide a number of guarantees. The guarantees can be grouped into five categories: (1) compliance guarantees, (2) good faith guarantees, (3) credit guarantees, (4) financial guarantees, and (5) indemnity guarantees.

Compliance Guarantees Consistent with their statutory nature, all license and permit bonds begin with the basic guarantee that principals will comply with those laws that affect them. Some bonds confine their guarantees to compliance with applicable laws. Among these are bonds which guarantee that principals who are to perform certain work must comply with building codes that may affect them. Licensed electricians and plumbers, for example, are required to adhere to certain specifications when installing wiring, electrical units, piping, and other fixtures. Public inspectors usually check all such work to determine whether, in fact, such work meets the required specifications.

Other bonds more specifically guarantee that principals will conduct their businesses in compliance with specified laws or codes. Vendors of alcoholic beverages, for example, must strictly adhere to alcoholic beverage control acts, or dram shop acts, which generally prohibit the sale or gift of beverages to a minor, a drunkard, or an intoxicated person. They also regulate the hours of sale, and sometimes the type of products that must be served. Others may prohibit carryout service, or entertainment, unless special permits are purchased in addition to the license to operate. Noncompliance with these laws can result in revocation of licenses and penalties.

Whether these bonds benefit only a public body in the event of default or also give third parties a right of action is sometimes difficult to determine. While the answers to many questions of this nature lie with the statutes or alcoholic beverage control acts that prescribe the obligations of these dealers or vendors of alcoholic beverages, many are questions of fact for the courts to decide.

Good Faith Guarantees   Some license and permit bonds, in addition to guaranteeing compliance with the law, also carry the guarantee that principals will perform in good faith, and thus protect the public against any harm through unfair business practices.

For example, statutes in many jurisdictions require that used car dealers obtain licenses and furnish bonds. These bonds cover not only the actual sale or exchange of used automobiles, but also other details in connection with that business. These bonds benefit persons who sustain losses, and cover any unlawful act of dealers, whether criminal in nature or merely a tort. Because they can improve the reputation of the trade, these guarantees of good faith also can benefit other dealers.[14]

As another example, real estate agents and brokers bonds also come within this good faith category in most cases. The purpose of statutes requiring license and permit bonds, here, is to protect the public against fraud in real estate transactions. These bonds have been held to cover a broker's failure to convey property or to return the purchase price, damages for the conversion of funds, and vicarious liability of subordinates.[15]

Credit Guarantees   Principals required to furnish bonds providing credit guarantees essentially promise to conduct properly their business affairs in the best interests of others, and to provide honest accountings of all funds in their possession. Auctioneers and dealers in agricultural products are among those who must obtain bonds with guarantees of this nature.

Commission merchants or factors also are required to provide the credit type of guarantee. These individuals or firms are employed to receive goods from others and to sell them for a commission. In that role, commission merchants are both bailees and sales agents for the owners of such goods. Therefore, they must be loyal to the interests of others, and they must comply with the instructions concerning time, place, and terms of sale. Generally, commission merchants who disregard or otherwise violate instructions concerning the sale of goods are held accountable for all damages specified by law. Whether this liability will present any financial hardship upon these merchants depends upon their financial status.[16]

Financial Guarantees Manufacturers, wholesalers, and retailers of goods, as well as firms which provide services, are almost always required to collect taxes on those goods and services at the time of sale. These can include amusement and sales taxes required under the laws of municipalities and/or tobacco and gasoline taxes as imposed by federal, state, and local laws.

Without a doubt, the responsibility for collecting and recording those taxes requires some additional bookkeeping expense for businesses. Some of the additional expense can be overcome through the profitable use of tax money until it is due. However, this is where much of the cause for concern lies. If the business uses tax money—which may involve many thousands of dollars—for the unsuccessful expansion of business, or if a business is confronted with financial difficulties, it may be unable to pay those taxes when due. In any case, the bonds required of those businesses guarantee the payment of those taxes, and when they cannot be paid, it becomes the obligation of the surety to pay them.

Since license and permit bonds are ordinarily written for high penalties, it becomes extremely important for sureties to determine the qualifications of their principals in terms of their capacity (their ability to meet commitments), character (reputability and responsibility), and capital (financial standing or solvency).

Indemnity Guarantees Bonds which provide indemnity guarantees are distinguishable in one important respect from those which do not. Bonds limited to good faith guarantees, such as those dealing with automobile dealers and real estate agents and brokers, and bonds limited to financial guarantees, such as those given by merchants under various tax obligations, solely benefit public bodies. On the other hand, bonds that provide indemnity guarantees benefit not only public bodies but also third parties. Third parties, in other words, are given a right of action against principals of those bonds if the third parties sustain injuries or damages to their property through the acts or omissions of the bond principals.

Bonds with indemnity guarantees are usually required of those who must obtain permits from public bodies before commencing certain activities or before using public property. Among those who must obtain permits and bonds with indemnity agreements are contractors who work on public streets, walkways, and utility systems; contractors who must perform structural alterations, improvements, demolition or blasting work in areas of public exposure; truckers conveying wide loads or excessive loads on public roadways, including house movers;

merchants who attach to their buildings signs or awnings that overhang public thoroughfares; those who construct billboards on public property; and those businesses which utilize sidewalk freight elevators.

Bonds providing indemnity guarantees should not be confused with liability insurance policies, despite the apparent similarities. If a surety is required to indemnify a third party, it will later seek to recover from the principal. Liability insurance, in contrast, promises to pay on behalf of (or sometimes to indemnify) *the insured.* Sureties usually require verification that satisfactory liability insurance is in force before they will issue a bond providing indemnity guarantees.

If, in a given circumstance involving a third-party suit, it is determined that the claim is excluded under some form of liability insurance, it then is up to the bondholder to assume the financial consequences to the extent imposed under the law governing the permit in question. An example might be the demolition contractor who does not purchase optional collapse coverage under a general liability policy, and whose negligence results in collapse damage to adjoining property. Whether the bondholder can handle any such financial burdens depends upon the nature of the claim and the extent of the damages.

Selling License and Permit Bonds

After checking with underwriters to assure that such bonds are available, the producer should make an effort to promote sales by reaching out to present customers or their friends. Premiums are usually quite low because bond amounts are not high. However, the service provided may work to the producer's advantage in obtaining or keeping other desirable lines. There are many producers who do not write such bonds but, somehow, manage to write the commercial and personal insurance. It would be a rather naive producer who provides the bond service while forgoing all of the rest of the business.

If a producer singles out or segments a market to sell, like shoe stores, he or she should try a pre-approach based on bond needs—i.e., sales tax bonds or whatever other bond may be required of that class of business.

Leads from governmental departments requiring permits have brought some business to producers. Quite often, a list of producers who handle license bonds is maintained for the convenience of tradespeople.

PUBLIC OFFICIAL BONDS

Individuals who are appointed or elected to positions of public office have the obligation to faithfully discharge their duties to the best of their abilities for the purpose of protecting public interests. What those duties may encompass, and what liabilities personally may be charged against public officials, vary with their position in government and with laws that control each situation. It can be said, however, that most such persons are obligated to act in good faith. When they hold public funds, they also have the duty of accounting for and turning over such funds to their successors in office. With few exceptions, laws generally hold public officials personally accountable for losses, shortages, or damage to public property. Some officials are even held responsible for the acts and the omissions of their subordinates.

All such obligations are placed upon a public official by the oaths of office, which is one condition precedent to acting in official capacities. The other requirement is that these individuals furnish public official bonds guaranteeing the public or governmental agency that the officials will uphold their promises to faithfully and honestly perform official duties. Any public official who fails to fulfill those promises must then make restitution to the extent of his or her liability. If the official is unable to do so, the surety then becomes answerable up to the bond penalty for any damages. Interest on any judgments incurred is payable by the surety, in addition to the bond penalty.

Public official bonds are generally noncancellable. They continue in force throughout an official's term of office, and they terminate only when successors are appointed and elected and qualify for those positions. Sometimes there is a time gap between the expiration of one official's term of office and the beginning of the succeeding official's term. This period during the gap is considered to be part of the retiring official's term of office and is covered under that person's bond. In any case, the succeeding official should see to it that the necessary arrangements are made for the transfer of office—including the full accounting of all transactions, funds and other property. When a new public official takes office, an independent audit of the predecessor's office is often advisable. This prevents the new official from being held responsible for acts of a predecessor.

When an official is reappointed or reelected, a new bond is required for the new term of office. Sometimes individuals hold an office for an indefinite period. In these cases, bonds are written without expiration, but subject to annual premiums.

Public Official Bonds Versus Fidelity Bonds

The fact that honesty of an official is guaranteed by the public official bonds leads some persons to believe that the bond is more in the nature of a fidelity bond than a contract of suretyship. However, there are at least two points that distinguish public official bonds from fidelity bonds.

First, public official bonds generally guarantee both the honesty and the *faithful performance* of their principals. A fidelity bond, on the other hand, deals solely with the honesty of its principals. Second, the principal under a public official bond has an expressed contractual obligation to the obligee (public), provided under oath, and to the principal (surety) that provides the bonds. The employee under a fidelity bond generally has no expressed contractual obligation with the employer concerning honesty and certainly no contractual relationship, expressed or implied, with the surety.

Those Who Must Be Bonded

It would be nearly impossible to list all the kinds of public officials who must be bonded by virtue of their functions within state, county, and city governments, as well as within political subdivisions. However, representative of those who frequently must be bonded are agricultural commission treasurers; alcoholic beverage commissioners; attorneys general; conservation commissioners; constables; county assessors, auditors, clerks, commissioners, judges, treasurers, and sheriffs; insurance commissioners; justices of the peace; municipal court judges; notaries public; public service commissioners; state administrative officers, auditors, tax commissioners, treasurers; supreme court clerk; and township officials.

These public officials encompass members of three broad groups: (1) those whose primary duties require them to handle public funds—such as tax collectors and treasurers; (2) those whose primary functions are administrative in nature—such as assessors, insurance commissioners, and judges; and (3) those whose duties involve direct exposure to members of the public—such as constables and sheriffs.

Those whose primary duties involve the collecting, disbursing, and safekeeping of public funds have the responsibility of accounting for all such funds and the obligation to relinquish them whenever their successors take office. To these ends, such persons are charged with honesty of purpose, and with faithfully discharging their duties as specified by law.

Laws governing officials who handle public funds tend to be stringent (and rightly so, because the potential losses to taxpayers can be enormous and because—apart from losses per se—taxpayers and other voters have a right to *know* whether tax funds are being spent efficiently and properly). Yet, losses occur. Probably most losses are caused by misappropriations, which have proved to be rather difficult to prevent. Internal controls and regular audits by competent outside personnel help to reduce both the frequency and the severity of losses, but even the best run controls will not entirely prevent all losses.

JUDICIAL BONDS

Judicial bonds are prescribed by statute and are filed in either probate courts or in courts of equity. Judicial bonds are involved with a variety of types of court actions. Generally, a judicial bond guarantees that a person or firm will fulfill certain obligations—such as faithfully performing certain duties prescribed by law or by a court, or showing financial responsibility for the benefit of another until the final outcome of a court's decision. If the principal fails to do this, the surety guarantees to answer for damages.

These surety bonds are usually noncancellable and, therefore, are continuous contracts. They are prescribed by statute and are filed in probate or in courts of equity. A probate court (or surrogate's or orphans court, as it is sometimes called) deals with settlements of estates, appointments of guardians for minors and incompetents, and so forth. Each county as a probate court which administers the transactions which are domiciled in that county. A court of equity, on the other hand, is primarily concerned with arguments involving specific performance or other situations in which money damages would not provide an adequate remedy. For example, a court of equity is used when someone seeks an injunction against another or when someone seeks to regain possession of property which is in the hands of another.

Types of Judicial Bonds

There are two general classes of judicial bonds: court bonds and fiduciary bonds.

A *court bond* generally deals with an action in equity—as opposed to an action in a court of law for money damages or an action in probate court concerning faithful disposition of property of others. The primary purpose of a court bond is to permit someone to seek a remedy in a court of equity and at the same time to protect the other party against whom claim is made for any damages sustained in the event the person seeking the remedy is unsuccessful. The person seeking a remedy is the principal under a court bond, and the person against whom action is made is the obligee. If the court decides in favor of the principal, the matter is settled and the bond terminates. But if the court decides that the principal does not have the rights or interests as claimed, the bond guarantees the obligee that the principal will pay any damages, including court costs. This bond, therefore, is principally one that is concerned with a person's financial responsibility. This will become clearer over the next several pages when specific court bonds are discussed and examples are given.

A *fiduciary bond* is required of a person who is selected by a probate court to administer the property or interests of others according to the specifications laid down by the court. It also is used in equity proceedings involving receivers and liquidators of property, among others. This bond guarantees that a fiduciary will faithfully perform as specified by the court, account for all property received, and make good any deficiency for which the court holds the fiduciary liable. When the matter is settled according to the specifications of the court, the fiduciary bond terminates. Otherwise, the bond remains in force until any deficiencies are settled.

Court Bonds Court bonds can be categorized into the following general groups: (1) bonds in civil proceedings (plaintiffs' and defendants' bonds), (2) bonds in admiralty proceedings (involving maritime questions), and (3) bonds for release of persons in criminal or civil proceedings (such as bonds used for bail).

Plaintiffs' and Defendants' Bonds. A person who commences an action against another in order to obtain some type of equitable remedy—be it the performance of a certain act, the repossession of certain property, or the fulfillment of some monetary obligation—needs a plaintiff's bond before the court will proceed with the action. This bond guarantees that if it is ultimately determined that such action was wrongfully taken, the plaintiff will pay the defendant for any damages that may have been sustained as the result of such action. If the defendant desires to continue the performance of a certain act or wishes to retain the property in question during the court proceedings, such person must give a defendant's bond. If the court decides in favor of the plaintiff, the defendant must then refrain from performing the act in question, return the property sought, or pay damages that are sustained by the plaintiff.

NATURE OF PLAINTIFFS' AND DEFENDANTS' BONDS. Bonds for actions in equity involving plaintiffs and defendants are statutory in nature, have open or fixed penalties, are noncancellable and continuous, and deal with financial guarantees. With at least one exception, explained below, each type of plaintiffs' bond has a sort of matching defendants' bond. The following paragraphs describe some of the more common bonds that are required of both parties to an action.

Before a court will attach property (take it by legal authority) at the request of another for some reason (for example, because the property is about to be removed from the state without leaving enough to satisfy the plaintiff's claim, or there is reason to suspect that the property is about to be wrongfully sold), the complainant or plaintiff must give the court an *attachment bond*. This bond guarantees that if the court decides against the plaintiff, the defendant will be paid any damages as the result of having such property attached. But, if the court decides in the plaintiff's favor, the bond automatically terminates.

However, after property of a defendant is attached, it can be released to the defendant pending final outcome of the court's decision, if he or she gives the court a *release of attachment bond*. This bond guarantees that the defendant will return the property in question and pay any damages and court costs if the court should decide in the plaintiff's favor (that is, if the court rules that the attachment was proper). The defendant is *required* to furnish a release of attachment bond only if the defendant desires to maintain possession of the property until the dispute is settled. To secure the bond, the defendant must satisfy the surety that he or she is financially responsible.

Disputes involving the attachment of property—particularly property such as merchandise of a going business or perishable commodities—can be particularly troublesome, especially when the defendant does not or cannot furnish a release of attachment bond. For example, the plaintiff may be liable in damages for any business interruption resulting from the attachment of merchandise, or the plaintiff may be liable for any decrease in value of perishables attached. Such problems are avoided when a release of attachment bond is secured, because the defendant retains possession of such goods.

Replevin is a form of action instituted by the alleged owner of personal property to recover possession of specific personal property which he or she alleges to have been unlawfully taken or unlawfully withheld. A *replevin bond* is somewhat similar to an attachment bond. With a replevin bond, the plaintiff takes immediate possession of the property allegedly belonging to the plaintiff, pending the final outcome of the court's decision. The bond guarantees the plaintiff will return property if ordered to do so, as well as pay any costs and damages.

A *counter replevin bond* is issued in a replevin procedure, and it has an effect similar to that of a release of attachment bond. When the bond is issued, the defendant regains possession of the specific personal property in question pending outcome of the court case. If the defendant should lose, the counter replevin bond guarantees that the defendant will return the property to the plaintiff.

Disputes in replevin cases sometimes involve the sale of merchandise, either with the use of a conditional sales contract or on an installment basis without a formal contract. Department stores are often involved. A conditional sales contract, when filed in the court of record where goods are sold, usually provides sufficient evidence for a seller to regain possession of personal property when a buyer fails to make payments. When such conditional sales contract is not so filed, or when a sale is made on an installment basis without a formal contract, and the buyer either fails to remit payments or sells the goods to a third person, the original seller must then institute a suit in replevin in order to secure such goods. It becomes particularly troublesome when a manufacturer sells goods to a dealer for resale and does not retain title to such goods. Most businesses should have little difficulty in establishing financial responsibility in order to purchase a replevin or counter replevin bond. But many individuals find it difficult to purchase a counter replevin bond, unless they can show that they are financially capable to pay any damages that may accrue as the result of a dispute.

When a plaintiff desires someone to perform or to refrain from performing some act or function (such as continuing a business, discontinuing a patent infringement, or removing trees from land where ownership is in dispute) a court injunction can sometimes be secured upholding the wishes of that plaintiff. Before an injunction is issued, however, the plaintiff must post an *injunction bond* guaranteeing to reimburse the defendant for any damages suffered if the court later refuses to uphold the injunction against the defendant.

The defendant in such a suit may have the injunction set aside until the dispute is settled merely by posting a *dissolve injunction bond.* This guarantees the plaintiff payment of any damages should a permanent injunction be granted in favor of the plaintiff.

An *appeal bond* is required of a plaintiff who did not obtain the remedy that was sought and desires to appeal an adverse decision to a higher court. Such bond, when posted, guarantees the payment of all court costs on the appeal. If, on the other hand, a lower court were to grant the defendant affirmative relief—instead of merely denying the plaintiff the remedy sought—then the plaintiff must post a *stay of execution bond* when the judgment is to be appealed. What the court does, in effect, is to halt execution of the lower court's decision pending outcome of the higher court's decision. The bond guarantees payment of any judgment and costs that may be awarded to the defendant by the higher court.

When the defendant desires to appeal a case to a higher court, an *appeal for defendant bond* or a *supersedeas bond,* as it is sometimes called, is required. It guarantees the plaintiff that the defendant will pay the entire judgment, plus court costs and interest, should a higher court overrule the initial judgment in favor of the defendant.

Some court bonds do not come in pairs, in the sense that there is no corollary bond available to one of the parties in an equity action. One of these is a *bond to discharge a mechanic's lien.* As was previously mentioned, it is often possible for suppliers of labor and materials to file a lien against property of an owner in the amount of debt outstanding. When a mechanic's lien is filed against property, it can be discharged by the property owner by filing a bond to discharge a mechanic's lien. This bond guarantees those who file such lien that the owner will pay the lien, if it is considered to be valid by the court.

Fiduciary Bonds   The *fiduciary* is a generic term which refers to persons or legal entities, such as administrators, guardians, and trustees who are appointed by a court under a will or a trust for purposes of managing, controlling, or disposing of property of others. Like court bonds, fiduciary bonds are a type of judicial bond used for a variety of purposes, and they are governed by statutes or by directives of probate and equity courts. Fiduciary bonds can be categorized into the following groups.

Bonds in Probate.   Bonds in this class are written for administrators and executors who handle the estates of deceased persons (or persons who are presumed to have died); guardians who are appointed to administer the estates of minors; conservators, committees, and custodians who are appointed to handle the estates of incompetents; and trustees of trust estates.

Bonds in Equity.   Included in this class are bonds for equity receivers, liquidators, trustees, and others appointed by a court to manage or to liquidate property. Also within this group are assignees, liquidators, trustees, and others, who are appointed by insolvent debtors to liquidate and to distribute property for the benefit of creditors.

Bonds in Bankruptcy Proceedings of Federal Courts.   These bonds are written, usually on a petition of creditors, for receivers who commonly are appointed in bankruptcy to collect and to protect assets of an alleged bankrupt.

Miscellaneous Fiduciary Bonds.   These bonds are required of receivers, trustees, and conservators of financial institutions and insurance companies. Fiduciaries are appointed by state or federal courts, depending upon the type of proceeding.

Nature of Fiduciary Bonds.   Bonds written for fiduciaries generally guarantee that such persons who are entrusted with the care of property belonging to others will exercise their duties faithfully, account for all property received, and make good any deficiency for which the courts—probate or equity—may hold such fiduciaries liable. Fiduciary bonds usually hold the principals and the sureties jointly and severally liable to obligees for the faithful performance of specified duties. They are continuous instruments which require no renewal, although premiums are charged annually, and they are noncancellable—usually running until the proceedings are completed and the sureties and the fiduciaries are released from further obligation.

Examples of Fiduciaries Bonded. Both individuals and corporations often are selected to act as fiduciaries. Guardians, administrators, and executors, and receivers and trustees in bankruptcy proceedings are among those fiduciaries frequently bonded, as described in the following paragraphs.

GUARDIANS. Generally, a guardian is anyone who legally has the care of a person and/or a person's property because of the inability of that person to manage his or her own affairs. A guardian is often nominated in a will and appointed by a probate court to look after the affairs of a minor or other person suffering a legal disability (ward of the court). The one appointed to act as guardian can be a parent, a relative, or some other competent person. It usually is the responsibility of the guardian to see to it that the ward is properly supported, clothed, and educated. A *curator* is a guardian who controls property of a ward. Thus, it is possible for a ward to have a guardian and a curator, although an individual guardian can fill both roles. A *conservator* or a *committee* is a guardian selected by a court to manage the affairs of an incompetent.

All jurisdictions have statutes which safeguard the rights and interests of minors and others deemed legally incompetent. One of the provisions of those statutes is that a guardian give a bond before assuming the role of a fiduciary for such minor or incompetent. That bond guarantees that the fiduciary will faithfully perform all duties, observe all directives of the court, and provide an accounting of all money and other property when required by the court to do so. Failing this, the fiduciary is liable to the court for all damages. The surety is secondarily liable, but only up to the penalty of the bond. However, a surety can be required to pay, in excess of the bond penalty, any court costs and interest that has accrued from the time any judgment is rendered against the fiduciary.

Sometimes a surety will not write a fiduciary bond unless it is given joint control over the assets of an estate. This means that the estate moneys are deposited in a joint bank account of the fiduciary and the surety, and they are disbursed only with the surety's approval. The primary purpose of joint control is to protect heirs of an estate against loss through some act of the fiduciary. This arrangement is particularly important when a large estate is involved and the fiduciary is not experienced in handling assets of that magnitude. A corporate trust company or bank, of course, would be usually excepted from this arrangement, since such firms normally have the expertise and other qualifications that are required in handling such estates.

Just as a surety will prequalify its principal for the bond, a probate court may do likewise. The court will also consider the principal's character, capital, and capacity. Generally, if a person can take care of his or her own affairs in an efficient manner, then he or she is qualified to assume the responsibilities of a fiduciary. There have been occasions when a probate court has rejected a fiduciary nominated in a will and, instead, has used a substitute who is judged more capable of managing the affairs of a minor or incompetent. In any event, once the fiduciary posts a bond, it continues in force until it terminates at some time in the future as specified by the court. Generally, the bond for an estate of a minor terminates when that person who is otherwise an incompetent may stay open until the court determines that a guardian or a conservator is no longer necessary.

There are times when a bond terminates prematurely because of the incompetence or the neglect of the fiduciary. In those cases, both the fiduciary and the surety are liable to the court for any damages. There have also been occasions when courts have permitted a surety to be relieved of liability for any future acts of its principal because the principal has been guilty of misconduct or breach of duties in handling the estate.

ADMINISTRATORS AND EXECUTORS. An *executor* (male) or *executrix* (female) is one named in a will to administer an estate. When a person dies intestate (without leaving a will), a court will appoint an *administrator* or an *administratrix* to settle the estate of the decedent. The duties and obligations of administrators and executors are generally the same, but there are distinctions. For example, administrators settle estates according to the directives of the courts, while executors settle estates as specified in the wills, subject to approval of the courts. The duties and responsibilities of these fiduciaries include collecting all assets of the estate and preserving them from loss, paying all debts which may have been incurred by the decedent and providing the court with an accounting of all transactions. Upon the court's approval of such accounting, the fiduciary is obligated to distribute the remaining assets as specified in the will or by the statute in question. Upon satisfactorily completing these duties, the fiduciary is discharged by the court.

When a court requires an administrator or an executor to post a bond (the latter may be excused from doing so, if the will so specifies), the bond guarantees the fiduciary's faithful performance as dictated by law or by the court. The surety also may require, as a prerequisite to giving a bond, that it be given joint control, along with the fiduciary, over the disbursement of certain assets.

A bond that is furnished for an executor or an administrator of an estate has the same characteristics and guarantees as a bond which is furnished for a guardian or a conservator. It is noncancelable and terminates with the court's acknowledgment that all duties required of the fiduciary have been properly discharged. Also, the fiduciary is liable to the full extent of any losses, while, in the event of default, the surety must answer only to the extent of the bond penalty—and beyond the penalty for any court costs and any interest that may accrue on any judgment that is rendered against its principal.

Although this bond is noncancellable, it may be terminated prematurely with the death, resignation, or discharge of the administrator or executor. If an administrator should die, resign, or be discharged before the estate is settled, the person appointed by the court to succeed is referred to as an *"administrator de bonis non."* The person so appointed is to complete that which was not finished by the preceding administrator.

RECEIVERS AND TRUSTEES IN BANKRUPTCY PROCEEDINGS. In situations involving bankruptcies or insolvencies, two types of fiduciaries usually require bonds. One is the *receiver* who is appointed by the court or by the *referee* (an impartial person selected by the parties or appointed by the courts). It is the receiver's responsibility to assemble and to preserve all assets of a debtor until a *trustee* is elected from among the creditors or is appointed by the court. The trustee is the second fiduciary whose duties are to reduce any assets to cash, and to determine the priority of payment among the creditors for the final distribution of those assets.

Bonds written for receivers and trustees guarantee faithful performance of duties as directed by the court in bankruptcy. The trustee works closely with the referee, since the latter is an intermediary of the court. In fact, the referee must consent to the withdrawal of any funds by the trustee, in an arrangement similar to that of an administrator under a joint control arrangement with the surety.

Common Causes of Loss. In spite of the fact that courts usually exercise care in selecting guardians, administrators, and other fiduciaries, and even though sureties also try to ascertain the qualifications of the same people, losses nonetheless occur. Most problems involving bonds of fiduciaries and their sureties deal with administrators of estates and with guardians of minors and incompetents. Some of these claims involving administrators range from allegations of simple failure to perform to charges of mismanagement of estates' affairs because of ignorance, negligence, or dishonesty.

Administrators and executors are under an obligation to exercise reasonable care in notifying all heirs of an impending probate proceeding. This is not always done, and estates are sometimes settled without notification of all heirs. Courts have held administrators and their sureties accountable in cases when all heirs could have been determined if reasonable care had been exercised by the administrators.

Administrators and executors are also obligated to give public notice of the estate proceedings for a certain period, usually six weeks, in order to give creditors of the estate an opportunity to file claims against the estate. Problems often arise when fiduciaries begin to close the estate before the expiration of this period. Related to this are cases where fiduciaries do not make payments to secured creditors and general (unsecured) creditors in order of priority.

Finally, administrators who are direct heirs sometimes conceal funds or other property of the estate, so that they are not involved in the distribution among other heirs, and fiduciaries sometimes do not make a proper accounting for tax purposes and are subsequently involved in suits by the government.

Guardians of minors and conservators of incompetents who are bonded incur difficulties for a number of reasons including:

1. Expenditures are improperly made by guardians under conditions when joint control arrangements are not required by sureties, or when certain expenditures are made by guardians without court orders.

2. Funds are misappropriated. Some fiduciaries who never before manifested dishonesty may nevertheless steal assets of an estate when an opportunity arises. Others commit dishonest acts because they are entangled in personal financial hardships of their own. Fiduciaries are tempted to recover from financial adversity of their own, such as gambling or conditions beyond their control. Whatever the reason, losses by dishonest acts of fiduciaries are extremely difficult to prevent.

3. Funds or property are mismanaged. Administrators and executors are only human and are therefore not infallible. They can make costly mistakes. For example, they may fail to collect all assets due the estate, or they may use assets or carry on the decedents' businesses without authorization. They may also delegate their duties to others for whose acts they will be held liable, or they may make improper investments. Whatever the

Exhibit 8-7
Rating of Fiduciary Bonds

Amount of Bond		Per Thousand Dollars Per Annum
Up to $2,000		$10.00
$2,000	$20 and for each additional M to $ 50,000	5.00
$50,000	$260 and for each additional M to 200,000	4.00
$200,000	$860 and for each additional M to 500,000	3.00
$500,000	$1760 and for each additional M to $1,500,000	2.00
$1,500,000	$3760 and for each additional M to	1.00

reason—incompetence, negligence, or flagrant disregard of duties—these fiduciaries are usually held personally accountable to the estate for any losses. In any event, proper underwriting should screen out bond applicants who are inept or irresponsible, so that losses are restricted to those caused by other types of errors.

4. Records are inadequate. Accountings of all transactions—which are required of the courts as conditions precedent to settling estates and to releasing guardians—are sometimes improperly prepared, and records are sometimes lacking in a number of ways. Courts or personal representatives of estates usually discover irregularities of fiduciaries because of the final accounting. However, there are times when misappropriations or other irregularities are not discovered until guardians have been released by the courts under apparently satisfactory conditions. However, sureties may still be held accountable for any losses, if guardians are unable to make restitution.

Rating Fiduciary Bonds. Rates depend on classification, amount, and locality. Typical rates for bonds of administrators, executors, trust estates, and estates of minors and incompetents are shown in Exhibit 8-7. Some courts, in certain circumstances, impose a requirement that the bond be "double the value of the estate assets," called a double penalty bond. In such instances, premium is reduced by 20 percent.

Special rates apply to other bonds:

● bonds in open penalty—$20 per thousand dollars on the amount of money paid or transferred for the term. Minimum premium is $20.

● referees or trustees in litigations concerning real estate—$4 per thousand

- referees or trustees in litigations concerning businesses—$5 per thousand

These rates are intended as examples only and are not to be read as standard. Reference should be made to the bond manual and specific exceptions discussed with a bond underwriter. Some sureties have made significant deviations in some of the more common bonds. Others adhere strictly to association rates.

In most instances, attorneys are not as interested in saving a few dollars for their clients as they are in proper service from the surety and the producer. Also, attorneys have a good idea what the charges should be. But it is wise to familiarize yourself with advantageous generalities such as:

- special discounts for advance premium payments, and
- discounts applicable on bonds written for an individual serving as a cofiduciary with a bank or where a bank is fiduciary— usually 1/3.

Selling Judicial Bonds and Developing Leads

Because premiums and rates for judicial bonds do not vary greatly from one surety company to another, business is not gained or lost on those points. Business is lost because of neglect, incompetence, or an unwillingness to provide adequate service.

Perhaps the best way to generate business is to visit local attorneys and simply ask if they are satisfied with their current bond situation. Again, thorough advance preparation is the producer's best weapon in the attempt to gain new bond business.

Some surety companies and producers have developed a "mini bond kit" consisting of an expandable folder, or legal-size envelope, filled with commonly used bond forms, proper applications, powers-of-attorney, surety company seals, execution reports, and whatever else may be useful.

A number of surety companies are agreeable to granting power-of-attorney to attorneys so they may process bonds more expeditiously. When this is accomplished, all that remains for the producer is to bill the item. It is an excellent tool openly welcomed by attorneys. Development of "mini" rate charts have been helpful. If producers' bonding companies do not have such kits, producers should consider developing one. An example of a mini rate chart is shown in Exhibit 8-8. It is suggested that the kit and chart be put together as a package and delivered personally to several attorneys.

Check on availability and cost of advertising space in local legal trade journals or bar association directories. Results on this are

Exhibit 8-8
Sample "Mini" Rate Card

Obverse

Crowley Fire and Marine Insurance Co.
Bond Rate Chart

The following are "quick reference" rates intended to help you rate the majority of bonds that you execute. If you have any doubt as to rate, you may leave that portion of the Execution Report blank, and we will fill in the rate and return the agent's copy to you by return mail.

Judicial

Fiduciary:
Your state, U. S. A.

Up to $2,000—$10 per M per year
$2,000-$50,000—$20 plus $5 per M per year on portion over $2,000
Minimum Premium $20 per year

Plaintiff:
Generally $20 per M on the penalty of the bond. Check first — these vary.
Minimum Premium $20 per year

Bonds of Administrators, Executors, Guardians and Trustees Under Will
Where the bond is double the value of the personal property, reduce final premium 20%.
Where bank is Co-Fiduciary, discount final premium 33 1/3%.

License

Range from $5 to $20 per M per year, depending on class and location
Minimum Premium $20 per year

Reverse

Public Official
Generally $3.50 per M per year for officials that do not handle tax money.
Peace officers and subordinates, $5 per M per year.
For officials handling money, see your State page in Public Official section of manual.
Minimum Premium $20 per year.

Fidelity

A. Individual and Schedule
Usually $5 per M per year for Commercial and Professional.
Use application # 625
B. Blanket
Refer to company office for rating. Premiums vary depending on class of business.
Use application F-660
Special discount when attached to a package policy— 20%

Contract

Must be prequalified.
Class B—General Contractors. Work on buildings and underground work.

First $500,000 — $12 per M
Next $2,000,000 — 7.25 per M
Next $2,500,000 — 5.75 per M

Please call if in doubt on rates.
If you are not certain which application is needed, see summary sheet in your bond kit.

mixed—some firms do well, others get little reaction. Somewhat allied is the use of envelope stuffers pertaining to bonds to regular customers informing them of bond availability.

Employees in the trust department of a bank are good contacts for probate bonds. They are also interested in good service. Even if their bonds are committed to another agent or company, bank officers change or the bank may be willing to reciprocate if a producer has an account.

Often overlooked is the opportunity to work out a bonding arrangement with other producers who do not have bonding facility. There are others who may not have time to service bonds in the way they would like to and who will pass them to a friendly competitor.

Political associations, direct and indirect, are helpful. Some present clients may have jobs somehow connected with courts, banks, or as subordinates to elected officials. They can serve as a means of introduction or may even be in a position to direct bonds to a producer who asks for the business. It pays to watch new business auto applications or to review long-standing files for hints of bond potential. Reviewing occupations of customers and their children can be of considerable benefit.

Judicial bonds are not sold, they are placed. It is largely a matter of producers' selling themselves. With whom the bonds are placed depends on factors such as competence, friendship, willingness to serve, reciprocity, knowledge, and developing a sound reputation as a bond agent.

Service After the Sale When written, a bond is identical to an insurance policy in that, at the sale, a producer begins the service. Whether it involves joint control or merely answering questions or explaining the billing, there must be a continuing contract. That does not mean that the producer has an obligation to visit the attorney or principal weekly. Rather, an occasional telephone call, perhaps on anniversary, or a personal visit when there is a legitimate reason to do so, is required. The point is that if neglect or inattention should set in, it could spoil an opportunity for the next bond.

There are times when a bond must be increased because of newly discovered assets—normally that information is conveyed to the producer. On the other hand, a reduction in bond amount may be in order because of a partial distribution of estate assets or a settlement with a ward who has reached legal age. If the producer becomes aware of circumstances that may save some premium, the attorney should be notified. The savings should make heirs happy and the attorney pleased that the producer is looking after things.

An important potential service is to provide a back-up attorney-in-fact. One particular producer may not always be available. Someone else in the firm should also be on the "qualified" list to execute bonds. It is an added service frequently overlooked by otherwise astute bond agents.

Qualifying As a Bond Representative

All that is needed to qualify as a bond representative is approval of the insurance or security companies that will be writing the bonds.

The first step is completion of a request for power of attorney. This usually consists of a one-page form calling for the name of the producer as it is to appear on the power; a three-year history of bond premiums written by the agency; names of other surety companies which may have granted a power, including date and amount and a question concerning any revocation, if any, by other sureties; and the amount of power being requested.

It is recommended that the applicant for a power of attorney personally visit the bond department of the surety company. It is necessary to gain an insight into how the bonds are underwritten and processed.

Upon approval, which is normally routine, a formal contract is drawn outlining the producer's discretionary authority to execute various classes of bonds up to certain limits. It is actually a *letter of authority* and calls for indemnity to the surety company in the event of loss resulting from any violation. It is a serious obligation and must be signed by both the surety company and producer. The standard letter of authority usually grants power to execute administrator and executor, guardian, certain bankruptcy, public official, and license bonds. Bid, contract, supply, fidelity, forgery, defendant, and miscellaneous bonds are in the "refer" category and will be authorized by specific letter when necessary. A surety company may grant more liberal authority to those possessing greater qualifications.

Once appointed, the producer becomes an attorney-in-fact, and is supplied with an adequate number of powers of attorney (Exhibit 8-9). These powers may be placed in the offices where signed bonds are ultimately filed, including city offices and with specific court clerks. Such placement reduces the need for attaching a power to each bond issued. However, a reasonable supply of powers should be retained in the producer's office for attachment to bonds when required.

Acceptance of the power of attorney carries with it the responsibility to perform in a manner displaying professionalism and good judgment. Bonds, once issued, cannot be recalled or canceled as simply as insurance policies. A mistake made in ignorance in an effort to serve a customer can be very costly.

Exhibit 8-9
Specimen Form—Power of Attorney

CROWLEY FIRE & MARINE INSURANCE COMPANY

Malvern, PA

Power of Attorney

KNOW ALL MEN BY THESE PRESENTS: That THE CROWLEY FIRE & MARINE INSURANCE COMPANY, a corporation organized under the laws of the state of Pennsylvania, and having its principal office in the City of Malvern, does hereby constitute and appoint _____ of _____ its true and lawful Attorney(s)-in-Fact to sign, execute, seal and deliver on its behalf as Surety, and as its act and deed, any and all bonds, policies, undertakings, or other like instruments, as follows:

Any such obligation in the United States, up to $ _____ .

This appointment is made under and by authority of the following resolution passed by the Board of Directors of said Company at a meeting held in the principal office of the Company, a quorum being present and voting, on the _____ day of _____ , 19 _____ , which resolution is still in effect:

"RESOLVED, that the President or any Vice-President by hereby authorized, and empowered to appoint Attorneys-in-Fact to affix the corporate seal; and may with or without writings so executed by such Attorneys-in-Fact shall be binding upon the Company as if they had been duly executed and acknowledged by the regularly elected officers of the Company."

IN WITNESS WHEREOF, THE CROWLEY FIRE & MARINE INSURANCE COMPANY has caused these presents to be sealed with its corporate seal, duly attested by its Vice-President this _____ day of _____ , 19 _____ .

THE CROWLEY FIRE & MARINE INSURANCE COMPANY

_____
Vice-President

(seal)

STATE OF PA) ss:

Checkpoints

1. List two prospects for each category of "guarantee" type license and permit bond.
2. How do public official bonds differ from fidelity bonds?
3. List four types of fiduciary bonds.
4. How does a producer proceed to become an "attorney-in-fact"?

SUMMARY

Surety bonds offer the producer high commission business opportunities, an opportunity to specialize, and a chance to round out insurance coverages for commercial clients. Surety bonds involve three parties: the party whose work is guaranteed *(principal)*, the party who is owed a duty *(obligee)*, and the party guaranteeing performance *(surety)*.

Contract bonds include bid, performance, payment, maintenance, and miscellaneous contract bonds. A contractor being bonded usually is underwritten based on the firm's character, capacity, and capital. The Small Business Administration has a Surety Bond Guarantee Program for small contractors.

License and permit bonds are used to help guarantee compliance, good faith dealings, credit, payment of financial obligations, or indemnity. Public official bonds are used to guarantee not only honesty of public officials but also their faithful performance.

Judicial bonds are categorized as court or fiduciary bonds. Fiduciary bonds offer producers a good opportunity to sell bonds to a number of specialized markets.

More than any other line of protection, surety bonds require good service by producers. Bond coverages and rates are almost uniform. Service is the key.

Chapter Notes

1. This material is drawn from Donald S. Malecki, James H. Donaldson, and Ronald C. Horn, *Commercial Liability Risk Management and Insurance* (Malvern: American Institute for Property and Liability Underwriters, 1978).
2. Ronald C. Horn, *Subrogation in Insurance Theory and Practice* (Homewood, IL: Richard D. Irwin, 1964).
3. Donald H. Rodimer, "Use of Bonds in Private Construction," *The Forum*, Vol. 7, No. 4, July 1972, p. 242.
4. *Contract Bonds: The Unseen Services of a Surety* (New York: The Surety Association of America, 1973), pp. 41-56.
5. *Contract Bonds*, pp. 15-20.
6. Luther E. Mackall, *Surety Underwriting Manual* (Indianapolis: The Rough Notes Co., 1972), p. 103.
7. Horn, p. 228.
8. 53 *Am. Jur.* (2d) Sec. 1, p. 512.
9. George J. Couch, *Couch on Insurance*, 2nd ed. (Rochester, NY: The Lawyers Co-Operative Publishing Co., 1965), Vol. 13, Sec. 47:289, p. 441.
10. Frederick A. Collatz, "Claims for Equipment Use Under Public Contract Bonds," *A.B.A. Section of Insurance, Negligence, and Compensation Law, 1969 Proceedings* (Chicago: American Bar Association), p. 60.
11. 25 *A.L.R.* 3d 383.
12. Mackall, p. 253.
13. Donald Dickinson Jenne, *Jenne's Suretymaster* (St. Paul: Suretymaster of America), p. 38.
14. Couch, Vol. 13, Sec. 48, pp. 143-46.
15. Couch, Sec. 48, p. 98.
16. 3 *A.L.R.* 3d, pp. 815-16.

CHAPTER 9

Excess Property and Liability Coverage

INTRODUCTION

Often, the producer finds a client faced with certain catastrophic loss exposures not provided for in the conventional basic or primary policies. To deal with this type of circumstance, the producer can use what is known as "excess" coverage. This discussion of "excess" coverages should not be confused with the so-called "surplus" lines coverage, commonly called "excess and surplus lines." The latter usually refers to difficult-to-place exposures.

Excess coverages serve two basic and important functions: (1) they provide *additional limits* to complete the total amount of insurance required to protect the given exposure; and (2) they provide coverage for *perils* to which the insured is exposed that are not covered or are excluded in primary policies. These excess functions are important in both the property and liability areas.

The first policy discussed in this chapter is the property "catch-all" policy, often called a "difference in conditions" (DIC) policy. For liability purposes, there are several excess types of coverage, such as "following form," or "straight excess," and "umbrella," both of which are discussed in this chapter. A form of "DIC liability" coverage exists, but it is rarely used and will not be discussed. Finally, the case studies discussed in Chapter 10 of PRO 81 are reintroduced from the standpoint of the umbrella producer.

443

DIFFERENCE IN CONDITIONS

Introduction

As an illustration of the importance of this policy, consider the following case. In 1977 a producer in the Midwest wrote a commercial multi-peril policy on a textile business. The producer did a good job on insurance-to-value and the package policy was issued on an "all-risks" basis using the special extended coverage endorsement on the building. The insured building was located in a potential flood area not designated by the federal flood program as eligible for flood insurance. The producer advised the insured that flood insurance was not available. As the result of a spring flood, the insured suffered a $200,000 loss. When the insured contacted the producer, he was again informed that flood coverage was not afforded under the package contract and that this peril was not covered under the federal flood program in this area. The insured, not willing to accept "no" for an answer, contacted an attorney. The attorney brought suit against the producer on the grounds that the producer was negligent due to the fact that flood coverage could have been provided with a DIC policy. The suit alleged the insured had assumed the producer was a professional and had accepted the producer's opinion as fact. The suit also showed the producer had stated on two different occasions that flood coverage was not available. The court awarded a judgment to the insured. The producer had never heard of a DIC policy. Due to ignorance, he incurred a financial loss and damage to his reputation. This type of story is not uncommon. Producers must be aware of the coverages available in order to cover adequately exposures to loss and to protect against potential errors and omissions claims.

The DIC Policy

The purpose of the difference in conditions (DIC) policy is to protect the insured from catastrophic losses not covered by basic property coverage. The DIC was originally intended as a "gap filler" or an "all risks" form providing coverage where more common basic property forms left off and reducing the chance of an uninsured loss. The DIC basically extends the "perils covered" and is not intended to provide coverage in excess of otherwise inadequate property limits (unless specifically designed for that purpose as will be shown in a later case study).

The (DIC) policy is relatively new. There is a problem placing the DIC policy since few insurers provide this very broad property contract. However, it is a valuable tool. The alert producer can use the DIC policy to generate new business and adequately cover many existing accounts.

There is no standard DIC policy. Insurers serving the DIC market use very similar forms, but many are written as manuscript contracts in order to tailor the DIC to fit the needs of a specific insured. This section of the chapter will discuss the coverages, conditions, exclusions, and the common use of a DIC form. Because no standard DIC exists, each policy when delivered to the producer must be carefully analyzed to see that it fits the client's needs.

Property Covered   It is important to understand what types of property of an insured may be covered under the DIC. The place to begin is on the declarations page of the contract, shown in Exhibit 9-1.

A DIC policy may cover the same property insured under a basic insurance program—that is, real and personal property, improvements and betterments, property in transit, and loss of income. Coverage is also available for (1) personal property in the care, custody, and control of the insured for which the insured may be held legally liable, or (2) property in the insured's care, custody, and control that the insured has agreed to cover.

Property Excluded   There are certain types of property specifically excluded by a DIC. Usually there are three reasons for DIC exclusions: (1) the probable loss frequency is too high on the type of property, (2) 100 percent insurance-to-value is readily available on the property on a more common form, or (3) the loss is difficult to prove or establish. Property normally excluded includes:

A) Aircraft, watercraft, vehicles licensed or designed for highway use;

B) Animals, growing plants, standing timber, growing crops, trees, shrubs or lawns;

C) Currency, money, notes, postage stamps, securities, evidence of debt, letters of credit, railroad or other tickets;

D) Jewelry, watches, pearls, precious and semi-precious stones, gold, silver, platinum, other precious metals or their alloys, bullion, furs and articles trimmed with fur except this exclusion shall not apply to industrial diamonds or precious metals or their alloys used for industrial purposes;

E) Property sold by the Insured under conditional sale, trust agreement, installment payment, or other deferred payment plan, after delivery to customers;

F) As respects Sections 4.A and 4.C of this form, architect fees, cost of excavations, grading and filling, underground flues, pipes, wiring (but not wiring on conduit), drains, brick or stone or concrete foundations, piers, or other supports below the undersurface of the lowest basement floor, land values;

Exhibit 9-1
Difference in Conditions Policy—Declarations Page

DIFFERENCE IN CONDITIONS POLICY

No. _____

CROWLEY FIRE AND MARINE

In consideration of the stipulations herein named and of the premium below specified the Company does insure the below Named Insured, hereinafter called the Insured, whose address is shown below, from the inception date shown below, at noon (standard time), to the expiration date shown below, at noon (standard time), at place of issuance to an amount not exceeding the amount(s) below specified, on property described below or in schedule attached.

Declarations

Named Insured and Address   (No., Street, Town, County, State)

Policy Period:

From   To   at noon, standard time at place of issuance.

$ _____ Premium. _____ Rate. _____ Amount

Coverage, Limits and Deductible   Limit of Liability   Deductible

☐ Real Property

☐ Personal Property

☐ Improvements and Betterments   (Single Loss Limit)

☐ Loss of Income

☐ Flood   _____   _____

☐ Earthquake   _____   _____

☐ Transit   _____   _____

COUNTERSIGNATURE DATE   COUNTERSIGNED AT   COUNTERSIGNATURE OF AGENT

This Page, when accompanied by the forms, schedules, and endorsements issued to form a part thereof, completes the above numbered policy.

G) Property eligible for insurance coverage in Nuclear Energy Property Insurance Association or Mutual Atomic Energy Reinsurance Pool;

H) Data processing equipment, and media (meaning all forms of converted data, program or instruction vehicles employed in the Insured's data processing operations).

Perils Covered The DIC policy is written to insure property and loss of income on an "all-risks" basis. While this does not increase the limit of liability written on the basic forms, it does fill in peril gaps on the "all-risks" basis. Because the DIC perils are broad, the exclusions in the "all-risks" DIC should be carefully studied.

Perils Excluded The first group excluded in the DIC are the basic perils of fire, extended coverage, vandalism, and sprinkler leakage intended to be covered by basic forms.

This policy does not insure against loss or damage:

A) Caused by or resulting from:
   (1) The perils of fire and lightning as set forth in a Standard Fire Insurance Policy;
   (2) The perils of windstorm, hail, explosion, riot, riot attending a strike, civil commotion, aircraft, vehicles, and smoke as set forth in the Extended Coverage Endorsement in use by this Company;
   (3) The perils of vandalism and malicious mischief as set forth in the Vandalism and Malicious Mischief Endorsement in use by this Company;
   (4) The peril of sprinkler leakage as set foth in the Sprinkler Leakage Endorsement in use by this Company;

   Whether or not insurance for such perils is being maintained by the Insured at the time of the loss and whether or not such loss or damage is directly or indirectly caused by or contributed to by a peril covered under this policy.

All perils excluded in a DIC because of coverage provided by basic policies should be worded identically to those perils as found in the basic property insurance contracts. Producers may want underwriters to attach copies of the basic property forms so that the wording of perils covered by basic forms can be compared to perils excluded in the DIC. For instance, if an insured qualified as a highly protected risk (HPR) and property is insured on that specified peril basis, the perils excluded on the DIC should be stated exactly as those covered in the HPR policy.

The next two excluded perils also deserve special attention:

B) Caused by or resulting from earthquake, landslide, subsidence or other earth movement;

C) Caused by or resulting from flood. The term "flood" shall mean waves, tide or tidal water, and the rising (including the overflowing or breakage of boundaries) of lakes, ponds, reservoirs, rivers, harbors, streams, or similar bodies of water whether wind driven or not;

Both earthquake and flood are specifically excluded from coverage, and both exclusions may be deleted for an additional premium. The declarations page (Exhibit 9-1) contains a space for a limit of liability and deductible for each of these perils. If the underwriter agrees to cover the flood and earthquake perils, a limit of liability and deductible amount may be established that are different from the other limits of liability or amounts. If an insured location is in a flood or earthquake-prone area, this coverage may be difficult for the producer to place. Several examples will be given later in this section.

The remaining exclusions should also be studied. Only a few are deserving of further individual comment, as most are common to "all risks" property insurance. Several are common to inland marine coverages, also generally an "all-risks" form.

D) By any fraudulent or dishonest act of omission by any Insured(s) or by any authorized representative thereof, or by any employee thereof, while working or otherwise, and whether acting alone or in concert with others; this exclusion shall not apply to robbery or to safe burglary committed by an employee of the Insured;

E) By explosion or rupture of steam pipes, steam turbines, steam engines, steam vessels or steam boilers, which are designed to be operated at pressures in excess of fifteen pounds per square inch, if owned by, leased by or actually operated under the control of the Insured;

F) By mechanical breakdown or malfunction, including rupture or bursting caused by centrifugal force;

G) For the cost of making good, faulty or defective workmanship or materials, errors in design, or latent defects, but this exclusion does not apply to loss or damage resulting from such faulty or defective workmanship or materials, errors in design or latent defects;

H) Caused by or resulting from delay, loss of market, loss of use;

I) By shrinkage, evaporation, loss of weight, contamination, change in flavor, color, texture or finish, change in temperature or humidity;

J) By deterioration, wear and tear, rust or corrosion, moth, vermin, termites or other insects or inherent vice;

K) To property while being actually worked upon and directly resulting therefrom, excepting ensuing loss from a peril not otherwise excluded by this policy;

L) By unexplained or mysterious disapperance, or shortage disclosed on taking inventory;

M) To electrical appliances or devices of any kind (including wiring,

by artificially generated electrical currents; however, this exclusion shall not apply to ensuing loss from a peril not otherwise excluded by this policy;

N) Caused by or resulting from hostile or warlike action in time of peace or war, including action in hindering, combating or defending against an actual, impending or expected attack, by any government or sovereign power (de jure or de facto), or by any authority maintaining or using military, naval or air forces; or by military, naval or air forces; or by an agent of any such government, power, authority, or forces; any weapon of war employing atomic fission or radioactive force whether in time of peace or war; insurrection, rebellion, revolution, civil war, usurped power or action taken by governmental authority in hindering, combating or defending against such an occurrence; seizure or destruction under quarantine or customs regulations; confiscation by or destruction by order of any government or public authority, or risks of contraband or illegal trade;

O) By nuclear reaction or nuclear radiation or radioactive contamination, all whether controlled or uncontrolled, or due to any act or condition incident to any of the foregoing, and whether such loss be direct or indirect, proximate or remote, or be in whole or in part caused by, contributed to, or aggravated by the peril(s) insured against in this policy;

P) By wet or dry rot; smog; smoke, fumes or vapors from agricultural or industrial operations; settling, cracking, shrinkage or expansion of pavements, foundations, walls, floors, roofs or ceilings; rain, snow, sand or dust whether driven by wind or not, to personal property in the open;

Q) By pilferage, burglary, larceny, theft or attempted theft if the described property had been vacant beyond a period of thirty (30) consecutive days immediately preceding the loss;

R) To fences, pavements, swimming pools and related equipment, retaining walls, bulkheads, piers, wharves or docks, when loss is caused by water pressure, ice or impact of watercraft;

S) Occasioned directly or indirectly by any ordinance or law regulating construction, repair or demolition of buildings or structures, nor by the suspension, lapse, or cancellation of any lease, contract, or order, nor for any claim for recovery due to interference by strikers or other persons with rebuilding, repairing, or replacing property, or with the resumption or continuation of operations;

T) Occasioned directly or indirectly by any ordinance, law, regulation, or order pertaining to the manufacture, packaging, labeling, sale, or distribution of goods, wares, merchandise or other products by the Insured.

Typically, dishonesty (exclusion D) is excluded in DIC policies as well as steam boiler explosion (exclusion E), since these coverages usually are best covered by specific policies. Losses relating to mechanical breakdown, wear and tear, and any other "maintenance" type of loss are excluded. War and nuclear losses are too catastrophic to be covered, although the nuclear peril may be added by endorsement for nuclear facilities, suppliers, or transporters. More so than with most insurance policies, producers can negotiate the elimination of exclusions for an additional premium.

Deductible Clause The DIC is intended to cover severe losses the insured may sustain. Since it is designed for large losses, the deductible is usually high—varying from one thousand to hundreds of thousands of dollars. The high deductible is used to eliminate smaller losses while still maintaining coverage of severe losses. The deductible on the DIC policy is usually negotiated between the producer and the underwriter to fit the needs of the insured. More about the use of deductibles appears in the case studies.

DIC Coverages The DIC appears to be restrictive relative to perils covered and excluded under the policy. However, some important perils not ordinarily covered by the basic property policy can be picked up by the DIC contract—some because they are not excluded (transportation), and some because the producer negotiates for elimination of exclusions. The list of perils covered could be extensive, as the DIC is "all-risks" in nature. The following are mentioned because they are more universally applicable to clients and may be used as selling points to prospective insureds.

Flood and Earthquake. Both the flood and earthquake perils can be added under the DIC policy, typically with a very high deductible, perhaps with the flood deductible to be covered through the federal government's flood program. This layered coverage is handled by the "other insurance" clause discussed later. DIC limits on these perils may carry a lower limit of liability than other perils in the policy according to the wishes of the underwriter considering the particular exposure. For instance, the general limit in a DIC policy may be written with a $5 million limit and $10,000 deductible. But flood and earthquake may be limited to $1 million with a $200,000 deductible, as shown in Exhibit 9-2.

The underwriter also may limit the insurer's exposure by endorsing the policy to cover only a percentage of each flood or earthquake loss over the deductible. In Exhibit 9-2 if the underwriter wished to limit recovery to 50 percent of each occurrence, the underwriter could manuscript the deductible portion of the flood cover to read: "The flood deductible will be $200,000 entirely borne by the insured plus 50 percent of the loss in excess of $200,000 up to the policy limit for flood." In the event of flood loss totaling $1.5 million, the adjuster would settle on the following basis:

Exhibit 9-2

Sample Coverage Section of the Differences in Conditions Policy

Coverage, Limits and Deductible	Limit of Liability	Deductible
☑ Real Property		
☑ Personal Property		
☑ Improvements and Betterments	$5,000,000 (Single Loss Limit)	$ 10,000
☐ Loss of Income		
☑ Flood	$1,000,000	$200,000
☑ Earthquake	$1,000,000	$200,000
☐ Transit	————	————

Amount of loss	$1,500,000
Less deductible	− 200,000
	1,300,000
50% clause	× .50
Total recovery	$650,000

Transit. A strong selling point of the DIC policy is that property in transit may be covered in the insuring agreement for high limits of liability. This would be written with a high deductible to eliminate small and frequent losses from coverage while covering the large loss. An importer or exporter with highly valued shipments, for instance, may be interested in this aspect of the DIC.

Burglary. Another good reason for suggesting the DIC policy to some clients would be to provide burglary coverage. The burglary limit needed by the insured may not be available from usual insurers for mercantile open stock burglary coverage or the rates may be considered too high for the limits desired. The DIC policy could cover the catastrophe burglary exposure at a lower rate because of the high deductible. This would fit the needs of the clients exposed to severe burglary losses, such as a stereo wholesaler.

Off-Premises Water Damage. There are numerous examples of this exposure, the most common being a break in a city water main resulting in water damage to the insured premises. This is excluded under a basic property form, but can be covered by the DIC.

Collapse. Collapse of a building, not covered by the fire and extended coverage contract, would be covered by the DIC policy. During the winter of 1979, a severe ice storm hit a southern city leaving five inches of ice on structures. Many buildings, particularly those of steel construction, collapsed. The DIC policy would have covered those losses.

Other DIC Policy Provisions

Coinsurance. One of the most important features of the DIC contract from a sales standpoint is that the insured is not required to carry insurance-to-value. Of course, the basic property policies underlying the DIC will be written to cover either 80, 90, or 100 percent to value, either actual cash value or at replacement cost, giving the insured adequate coverage for normal losses. To save on premium cost, the insured may want to limit the amount of insurance for "all-risks" coverage in basic property policies. There are many situations where the maximum probable loss from the "all-risks" perils is not nearly as great as from the basic perils.

For example, suppose a high-rise motel is located in an area subject to surface flooding and the value of the structure is $3 million. The producer covered the $3 million for fire and special extended coverage under a basic package policy. The insured was concerned with the flood exposure, however, which is excluded under the basic policies. The producer checked and learned that the motel was not in an approved flood zone and therefore was not eligible for the federal flood program. The only available alternative to retention was the DIC policy. The producer discussed with the insured what would be the amount subject to loss, and together they agreed that in all probability only first floor damage could occur. They set a limit of $150,000, with a $5,000 deductible. The premium for $150,000 was considerably less than for the entire $3 million. Thus, because of the lack of a coinsurance requirement, the DIC policy met the needs of this insured at an affordable premium.

"Other Insurance" Another feature of the DIC policy with which the producer should be familiar is the "other insurance" clause. This clause varies from insurer to insurer and even among insureds in one insurance company, depending on the needs of the insured. A typical "other insurance" clause in the DIC contract follows:

> OTHER INSURANCE. The Company shall not be liable for loss, if, at the time of loss, there is any other insurance which would attach if this insurance had not been effected, except that this insurance shall apply only as excess and in no event as contributing insurance, and then only after all other insurance has been exhausted.

The clause limits coverages on any loss for which other coverage is applicable through the basic property policies. It also states that the DIC policy will not be considered contributing insurance but rather as excess over other insurance. If underlying coverage is in force, the DIC policy will respond as an excess coverage after the primary is exhausted. This point will be illustrated later.

Losses Covered The DIC may be written to cover direct as well as indirect damage exposures. When named peril coverage is written on indirect damage exposures, the DIC also can be used to fill in the peril gaps. The DIC may be used to broaden the coverage to "all-risks" on earnings, loss of rents, and other indirect losses. On this basis, the DIC is usually written at the same limits as the basic policy for indirect damages. Thus the producer can provide "all-risks" indirect damage coverage for those clients desiring it.

DIC Case Studies The following cases illustrate some of the many ways in which a producer may use the DIC to "fill in the gap" left by basic policies. One preliminary observation is that the DIC is well suited for insureds with larger than average loss exposures due to larger deductibles in the DIC and the resultant catastrophe coverage of the DIC.

Premier Door and Window Co., Inc. The property values involved in this case are:

1. Owned building—$2,000,000
2. Improvements and betterments in the leased building—$300,000
3. Total contents—$1,000,000
4. Transit maximum per shipment—$15,000

Further assume Premier is located near the river in Yourtown in an earthquake-prone area.

The producer may approach this client with the DIC policy from a premium savings standpoint. The perils of fire, extended coverage, vandalism, and sprinkler leakage are covered under Premier's package policy. The producer wishes to cover other amounts subject to loss from "underinsured" or uninsured perils. Both flood and earthquake are loss exposures that may be handled. Working together, the producer and Premier's management establish a limit they feel is adequate for the exposure. Because of the absence of a coinsurance clause in the DIC, the insured may select any DIC limits.

The exposures to loss from the perils of transportation would probably be adequately covered under a basic inland marine form since the $15,000 maximum value per shipment is relatively low. Also, the burglary exposure is not great because of the class of property

Exhibit 9-3
Captain Kidd Villas—Building Schedule

Loc.	Bldg.	Description	No. of Apartments Per Building	Coverage	Coins.	Amount
1	1	Building A/101-104	4	A	80	213,000
1	2	Building A/105-106	2	A	80	187,000
1	3	Building B/107-110	4	A	80	267,000
1	4	Building B/111-114	4	A	80	266,000
1	5	Building B/115-118	4	A	80	267,000
1	6	Building E/129-132	4	A	80	318,150
1	7	Building E/133-136	4	A	80	318,150
1	8	Building F/137-140	4	A	80	294,800
1	9	Building F/141-144	4	A	80	345,900
1	10	Building D/121-124	4	A	80	312,000
1	11	Building D/125-128	4	A	80	312,000
1	12	Building C	2	A	80	189,400

involved. These two exposures would not be a consideration for the DIC policy since they do not represent large or difficult to insure exposures.

Any client refusing a coverage suggested by a producer should be requested to notify the producer of such refusal in writing for the producer's errors and omissions loss exposure. The producer should seek a DIC insurer willing to cover the perils of flood, earthquake, and collapse, the most important perils not covered by the basic package policy. Several DIC insurers may have to be contacted to secure adequate coverage with reasonable deductibles and premium charges for the insured.

Captain Kidd Villas. Captain Kidd Villas is a new apartment complex located on an east coast sea island. The management of the complex contacted a local producer, Bob Shenefield of Dubose-Stickey Insurance Agency, Inc., in Columbia, SC, and asked that he review their insurance needs and suggest an insurance program to adequately cover them. One important fact was discussed in the initial meeting—Captain Kidd Villas is highly susceptible to loss from hurricane (windstorm) or flood (wind-driven tidal waters) accompanying a hurricane. The mortgagee required full protection for these exposures.

Bob developed the schedule shown in Exhibit 9-3 while preparing a proposal for the basic package policy.

Each location was insured under a commercial package form with the special extended coverage endorsement attached giving "all-risks" coverage. However, the "all-risks" contract contained some serious peril gaps that made it inadequate for the requirements of the mortgagee.

First, as is true in most seacoast states, windstorm and hail perils are excluded from the extended coverage by endorsement when the buildings are located in a "beach area." Also, flood is not covered under the special extended coverage form. This particular location is also in a very active earthquake zone. Although there has not been a serious earthquake since 1890, minor earthquakes and tremors are recorded on a regular basis.

Bob recognized these limitations in his proposed package policy and sought ways to handle these exposures. He first went to the state "Windstorm and Hail Underwriting Association," a pool of companies set up to handle exposures to hurricane losses. Most coastal states have these pools. The pool has a maximum limit of liability they will write on a particular class. In this case, Bob could obtain limits up to $200,000 per building through the pool.

He then went to the federal flood program and found that he could insure a maximum limit of $250,000 per building for the flood exposure.

Bob had done a good job up to this point, but still had not satisfied the mortgagee's requirement of full coverage on the wind and flood exposures. He then approached DIC insurers for the rest of the coverages. With the information at hand, setting the amount of coverage and the deductible desired was a fairly simple process. Bob was primarily looking for flood and wind coverage in excess of limits available through the pool. He established the schedule of required limits shown in Exhibit 9-4.

Bob was aware that (1) there is no coinsurance problem with a DIC policy, (2) the "other insurance" clause in the DIC policy will allow him to cover DIC deductibles with basic policies, and (3) the DIC policy will act as excess over these amounts in almost all cases. Bob knew that special limits and deductibles would be set on the flood and earthquake perils. These special or "inside" limits and deductibles would not apply to other perils covered by the DIC.

Bob next discussed the potential earthquake coverage of the DIC policy with the management of Kidd. They were not too concerned about this peril but would like to cover a catastrophe loss subject to a high deductible.

Bob contacted DIC insurers and came up with a proposal, shown in Exhibit 9-5, in addition to an "all-risks" commercial package policy.

Through the use of the DIC policy, Bob met the property insurance needs of Captain Kidd Villas and he issued a package policy covering all real property. He ordered coverage through the wind pool that satisfied the $200,000 deductible on the DIC policy and also bought a flood policy through the federal flood program to satisfy the $250,000 deductible on the DIC for flood. Bob also covered the earthquake exposure for the catastrophic loss. In this case study, the DIC policy was truly an excess property insurance coverage.

Exhibit 9-4
Excess Coverage Required—Captain Kidd Villas

Bldg. #	Total Limits Required	Wind Coverage Available	Excess Wind Needed	Flood Coverage Available	Excess Flood Needed
#1	213,000	200,000	13,000	213,000	None
#2	187,000	187,000	None	187,000	None
#3	267,000	200,000	67,000	250,000	17,000
#4	266,000	200,000	66,000	250,000	16,000
#5	267,000	200,000	67,000	250,000	17,000
#6	318,150	200,000	118,150	250,000	68,150
#7	318,150	200,000	118,150	250,000	68,150
#8	294,800	200,000	94,800	250,000	44,800
#9	345,900	200,000	145,900	250,000	95,900
#10	312,000	200,000	112,000	250,000	62,000
#11	312,000	200,000	112,000	250,000	62,000
#12	189,400	189,400	None	189,400	None
TOTAL			$914,000		$451,000

Exhibit 9-5
DIC Proposal Captain Kidd Villas

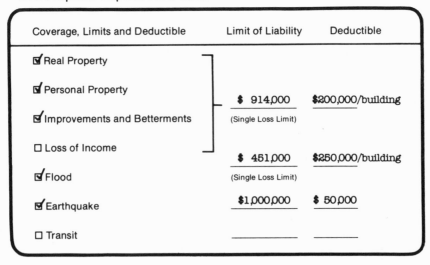

Coverage, Limits and Deductible	Limit of Liability	Deductible
☑ Real Property		
☑ Personal Property	$ 914,000	$200,000/building
☑ Improvements and Betterments	(Single Loss Limit)	
☐ Loss of Income		
	$ 451,000	$250,000/building
☑ Flood	(Single Loss Limit)	
☑ Earthquake	$1,000,000	$ 50,000
☐ Transit		

Rating and Underwriting Information

Rating Information   The rating of a DIC policy is based on the judgment of the underwriter with assistance from the producer. Underwriters look at the type of coverage desired and the frequency and severity of those types of losses in the geographical area of the insured. Even though the number of insurance companies writing DIC coverage is limited, premiums can vary drastically among them for a given submission. The producer should attempt to obtain more than one quote on each submission to make sure the premium is competitive.

Underwriting Information   Because of the extremely broad coverages involved, the DIC underwriter needs to know more than the underwriter of basic property coverage. Several items will require further explanation:

1. Construction—Although basic construction information such as joisted masonry, modified fire resistive, frame, and so forth, will be sufficient for the fire underwriter, the earthquake resistive features will be of particular interest to the DIC underwriter. Earthquake information can be secured by the producer from U.S. Geodetic Survey.
2. Geographical location—The DIC underwriter will need to know the susceptibility to flood damage of the area in which the property is located.
3. Weather of the region—The underwriter will need to have an indication of weather patterns in the region where the property is located. This will help the underwriter evaluate the exposures to loss from such perils as weight of ice, snow, sleet, or windstorm, if included under the DIC. The producer can use the U.S. Weather Service as a source for this information.
4. Transit—If the transit exposure is to be covered under the DIC, the underwriter will need the same information needed for basic transit coverage:
   - Maximum value per shipment and per conveyance
   - Catastrophe loss exposure—maximum per any one occurrence (i.e., multiple conveyances exposed simultaneously like rail cars in a single train or yard)
   - Whether goods are shipped by owned trucks or by common carrier
   - Radius of operation
   - Loss history
   - Any protective safeguards such as burglar alarms on the trucks

5. Burglary—Burglary is closely underwritten for any form of insurance. The underwriter will want information on loss history and on all safeguards employed by the insured to prevent or minimize losses, such as alarm systems, guard services, or twenty-four hour guard service.

Producers should remember that the DIC is not a commonly used form. The DIC underwriter faces the possibility of a catastrophic loss and must weight all of the facts to underwrite and rate the submission properly.

Checkpoints

1. How does the DIC accomplish the function of "excess" insurance?
2. Why does the DIC policy make use of high deductibles?
3. Is "other insurance" allowed in the DIC contract?
4. What major exclusions in a DIC are commonly eliminated?
5. Are there standard forms and rates for DIC policies?

EXCESS LIABILITY COVERAGE

Introduction

Excess coverage is used more frequently for liability than for property insurance. There are two principal reasons for this. First, an insurance company may want to limit its exposure to loss by writing relatively low limits on a liability contract. If these lower limits do not fit the needs of the insured, the producer must obtain a policy with higher limits, in excess of the primary insurance. Thus, one purpose of the straight excess liability policy is to increase the limits of liability to the level needed by a particular insured.

The second reason an insurer will not write limits in excess of a given amount is a reinsurance treaty. The insurance company's reinsurer may only be willing to go "so high" on a given class of business. The insurer could also have certain classes of business excluded from its reinsurance treaties and would want to limit the dollar amount of exposure to a low level for that class. The insurance company may also limit the dollar exposure on a class that falls within its treaty simply to protect the reinsurer from a potentially large loss.

When an insurer will not write requested limits, producers must seek the best method to layer the coverage up to the desired limits. In doing so, producers may have to approach the specialty insurers for the coverage, usually at a surcharge rate (although many insurers write excess liability insurance). When dealing with specialty insurers for excess coverages, the producer should always check on the excess insurer's financial stability—the financial rating in the *Best's* guide, the Department of Insurance in the producer's state, or a reputable excess and surplus lines broker. When dealing with unknown or unfamiliar companies, the producer should be satisfied that they are capable of paying any losses that may occur.

Straight Excess Liability Policy

The straight excess liability policy is also known as "following form" or "follow form" liability insurance. This means that the excess policy tracks the primary insurance policy in all aspects, i.e., coverage, conditions, definitions, and so forth. The excess insurer relies on the primary insurer for coverage interpretations and "follows" them. Unlike a DIC policy, the straight excess contract should never be written to try to pick up liability coverages not insured by the primary policy. It is simply a means of layering limits of liability to the level needed by the insured.

The straight excess policy can be used in all forms of liability coverage. In many instances, an excess layer of liability is used to bring the coverage up to the primary requirements of an umbrella policy. When this is the purpose, the excess policy is called a "gap" or buffer layer. (The umbrella policy will be discussed in detail later in this chapter.)

Excess Liability Case Studies The following cases illustrate the use of the straight excess liability policy.

Dean-Dempsey Lumber Company. John Courson, a producer in Columbia, SC solicited the Dean-Dempsey Lumber Company and sold the insured on his ability and service. John found the account involved a forestry operation—cutting the trees and operating a saw mill and a trucking firm. The company takes wood from the forest to the wholesaler. John wanted to write a comprehensive general liability (CGL) policy and a business auto policy (BAP) with limits high enough to qualify for a commercial umbrella policy.

John realized he had a tough account to place because the fleet included forty-four tractor trailer units, some of which are used to haul logs and lumber a long distance. His first step was to contact the primary umbrella market used by his firm to see what primary limits of liability would be required for the umbrella. He was advised that he would need limits of $500,000/$500,000 bodily injury ($500,000 per occurrence and $500,000 aggregate) and $100,000/$100,000 property damage on the CGL and $500,000/$500,000 bodily injury and $500,000 property damage on the fleet of vehicles.

John placed the CGL policy with one of his firm's insurance

Exhibit 9-6
Dean-Dempsey BAP Insurance

Company	Bodily Injury	Property Damage
A Primary	$15,000/$30,000	$5,000
B Excess	$85,000/$270,000	$95,000
C Excess or Gap	$400,000/$200,000	$400,000
Totals	$500,000/$500,000	$500,000

companies, but none of the insurance companies wanted to write the BAP. John had to go to specialty insurers to obtain three layers of coverage (two in excess of primary). (See Exhibit 9-6.) Company A wrote the primary policy with limits of $15,000/$30,000 bodily injury and $5,000 property damage. Company B agreed to the second layer (the excess layer) with limits of $85,000/$270,000 bodily injury and $95,000 property damage that would pay any claim in excess of limits provided by Company A. This brought the limits up to $100,000/$300,000 bodily injury and $100,000 property damage. Company C agreed to write a third or "gap" layer with limits of $400,000/$200,000 bodily injury and $400,000 property damage in excess of both Company A and Company B. This gave John the limits needed for the client.

Company A was the primary insurer and agreed to pay all claims up to the $15,000/$30,000 bodily injury and $5,000 property damage limits. Company B would be an excess insurer and pay only when the claim exceeded the limits under Company A's policy. Company C's policy would respond only after Company A's and Company B's limits were exhausted. Company C's policy filled the gap between primary and first excess insurance and umbrella liability requirements.

This type of layering technique should be used only when absolutely necessary. Generally, it is expensive and, as in this case, involves multiple policies and companies. Producers who must use the layering technique should be sure all policies follow form so that coverage and limits of liability are consistent (single vs. split limits).

John next called his umbrella insurer and ordered a $3 million umbrella policy. By the use of the straight excess contract, he had satisfied the underlying requirements of the umbrella and the needs of his insured.

Jacob's Gas and Oil Company. Zelda, a local producer, wanted to write the insurance business for a local gasoline and oil distributor operating in only one county using small tank trucks for delivery. One of her insurance companies offered to write the coverage, but the underwriter informed Zelda that the exposure would have to be written with two policies rather than one.

The company underwriter explained that it was because of the way the insurance company's reinsurance program was designed. The insurer's casualty department had a reinsurance treaty that excluded this class because of the catastrophic loss potential. However, the insurance company also had an excess liability department with a separate reinsurance treaty that did not prohibit gasoline and oil dealers.

The casualty department could issue a policy with limits of $25,000/$50,000 bodily injury and $25,000 property damage, but could not exceed those limits because of the lack of reinsurance. However, the excess department could issue a straight excess policy for the excess of those limits up to $1 million combined single limits of liability. In this case, the insurance company could use an excess liability policy to satisfy the needs of its producer and her client.

Rating and Underwriting Information

Rating is on the same basis as that used for the primary coverage. Usually, the excess rate is a percentage of the primary rate, giving credit for the primary layer. There are no standard rates and the underwriter uses judgment in rating.

The straight excess liability underwriter will need the same information as the primary underwriter. Usually, a copy of the application submitted to the primary insurer will satisfy the excess underwriter. The excess underwriter will usually depend on the primary underwriter's judgment about any drivers insured for the automobile fleet and will not require full driver information. Also, the excess underwriter will ask for loss history only on losses in excess of a figure like $5,000 or $10,000.

When a producer receives an excess liability policy from an insurer, the producer should carefully compare the excess liability policy to the primary policy before delivering it to the insured. In some cases, the excess insurer may not have "followed the primary," allowing a coverage gap. This gap, if not corrected, can defeat the layering effort and create an errors and omissions claim for the producer.

Checkpoints

1. What are the two purposes of straight excess liability policies?

2. What are the two reasons for companies' limiting their dollar exposure on certain accounts?
3. Explain layering as it applies to excess liability insurance.

THE COMMERCIAL UMBRELLA

Introduction

The commercial umbrella liability policy can provide limits of liability in excess of $1 million, offer broader coverage, and serve as primary coverage for uninsured exposures over a self-insured retention (similar to a property insurance deductible). With the advent of jumbo court awards in liability suits, the umbrella is a "must" for all commercial accounts.

The umbrella was developed by Lloyd's of London. The original Lloyd's umbrella was extremely broad with very few exclusions. Several U.S. companies followed Lloyd's with the development of their own umbrella contract. Competition drove premiums down and many losses were incurred that had not been anticipated. After only a few years of existence, this new line of liability coverage became unprofitable and insurers restricted their writing in the line. Finally, after Lloyd's and the domestic insurance companies began inserting exclusions and modifying other policy terms, the current-day umbrella policy evolved. Now many domestic insurance companies in addition to Lloyd's freely write the commercial umbrella policy.

All insurers writing umbrellas purport to provide broad, high-limit coverage, but standardization of policy forms and rates does not exist. This portion of the chapter describes the coverage generally available, but because of form differences among insurers, producers must carefully examine each insurer's umbrella policy. As with any contract, an apparently slight change in wording can drastically alter the scope of a policy's coverage. Further, availability of umbrella liability insurance changes with the underwriting results of insurers. A freely written class of business today may be hard to place tommorrow, and a "competitive" rate today may become "exorbitant" tomorrow.

To properly serve their clients, producers should become familiar with the umbrella's intent and types of coverage, and constantly review their insurer's policy forms, rates, and acceptable classes.

Purpose

Umbrella coverage is designed to give the insured high limits of liability protection and to grant some protection for uninsured primary exposures. The umbrella covers over and above primary general liability, commercial auto, and other liability contracts. Exhibit 9-7 shows graphically how the umbrella acts to increase limits and provide some measure of primary insurance protection.

The remainder of this chapter will discuss the umbrella policy and use as an example a representative umbrella form. However, because umbrellas vary so widely, *the producer should carefully review each umbrella policy to determine any differences*. An attempt will be made to identify those characteristics most commonly found in umbrellas.

Umbrella Requisites

Most umbrellas require underlying coverage, minimum limits of liability, and a self-insured retention (SIR) for exposures not covered by primary insurance.

Underlying Policies   Umbrella underwriters require a warranty that underlying policies be maintained for certain exposures, and usually schedule the underlying coverage in the umbrella's declarations. Primary coverages usually required, if they are to be extended by the umbrella, include:

1. comprehensive general liability (CGL)—including personal injury, contractual liability, and products and completed operations coverage;
2. business auto policy (BAP);
3. employer's liability; and
4. any other coverages necessary for a particular exposure, such as (but not limited to) aircraft, watercraft, or professional liability.

If the underlying CGL excludes, as an example, the products or completed operations hazard, the umbrella can still be written, but it would likely be endorsed to exclude this hazard or the underwriter would raise the SIR for the hazard. If the underlying CGL does not cover personal injury liability, the underwriter may either exclude this exposure or include it according to a determination of how great the exposure may be.

Underlying Limits of Liability   The underlying limits of liability required vary from insurer to insurer, and for one insurer between various classes. The minimum limits can be as low as $300,000 bodily injury and $50,000 property damage on the primary CGL and $100,000/$300,000 bodily injury and $50,000 property damage on the BAP, although most umbrella insurers now require higher primary

Exhibit 9-7
Diagram of a $5 Million Umbrella*

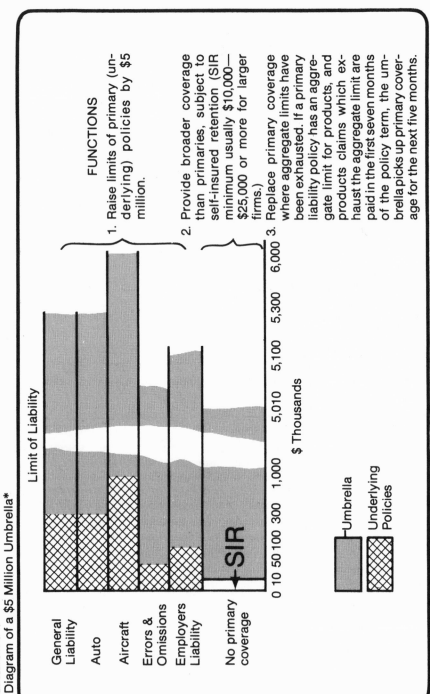

FUNCTIONS

1. Raise limits of primary (underlying) policies by $5 million.

2. Provide broader coverage than primaries, subject to self-insured retention (SIR minimum usually $10,000—$25,000 or more for larger firms.)

3. Replace primary coverage where aggregate limits have been exhausted. If a primary liability policy has an aggregate limit for products, and products claims which exhaust the aggregate limit are paid in the first seven months of the policy term, the umbrella picks up primary coverage for the next five months.

Limit of Liability

General Liability
Auto
Aircraft
Errors & Omissions
Employers Liability
No primary coverage

SIR

0 10 50 100 300 1,000 5,010 5,100 5,300 6,000
$ Thousands

Umbrella

Underlying Policies

* Excerpted from *The Umbrella Book*, Edited by James A. Robertson, CPCU. Warren, McVeigh & Griffin, Newport Beach, CA, © 1979, 1980. Used with permission.

limits. The requirement for employer's liability is usually the standard limit in the insured's state, but typically $100,000 minimum limit.

Because of the catastrophe loss potential in certain types of liability exposures, the minimum limits on the underlying policies may be extremely high. For instance, to include aviation liability for owned aircraft under the umbrella contract, it is not uncommon for the umbrella insurer to require $5 million per passenger seat for primary coverage. Medical malpractice is another class for which umbrella insurers require high primary limits (when umbrella coverage is available at all over that exposure). Higher limits for primary coverage may be required for a trucking firm hauling hazardous materials such as gasoline or volatile chemicals.

Self-Insured Retention (SIR) An umbrella policy usually is so broad that it covers many exposures not covered in primary policies. (One misleading feature about some "umbrella" forms is that many of them contain exclusions or other terms that make them more restrictive than standard primary forms.) For this reason the policy contains an SIR which operates like a deductible over exposures when underlying insurance is not required or purchased. But, the SIR does *not* apply *between* primary and umbrella coverages. The most common SIR in umbrella policies is $10,000 or $25,000, although on large accounts it may be significantly higher. This is an area of coverage the producer should closely analyze because of the defense coverage in an umbrella. The variation in defense costs is discussed later.

Checkpoints

1. What are the purposes of an umbrella policy?
2. What underlying policies are usually required before the umbrella can be written?
3. Explain self-insured retention.

Policy Structure

Insurers organize umbrellas in many ways, but the basic components of an umbrella policy are:

1. Declarations
2. Insuring agreements, including:
   a. Coverage
   b. Defense
   c. Limits of liability
3. Persons insured
4. Definitions

5. Exclusions
6. Conditions

Some parts of different policies may be classified under different headings. For example, the *policy territory* may be found (1) in a separate insuring agreement, (2) in the definitions, or (3) included in the conditions section. *Definitions* sometimes are found in the conditions section, but the *definitions of coverages* (personal injury, property damage, advertising liability) often are contained in the main insuring agreement. Exclusions often immediately follow the coverage agreement. This diversity of structure makes the producer's job difficult, since only careful study of a form will reveal the location of its many provisions.

Umbrella Policy Analysis

Declarations Page The declarations page of an umbrella policy is shown in Exhibit 9-8. The exhibit refers to the policy as a "comprehensive catastrophe liability policy." Different insurers use different names, but the generic term "umbrella" will be used in this discussion.

Items #1 and #2 identify the named insured, address, and the policy term. (The term "named insured" will be discussed in the definitions section following.) The policy term can either be one or three years. If the insured is a small business, the underwriter might be willing to write a policy for a three-year term. However, for larger business, the underwriter will usually want the option of reunderwriting and repricing on an annual basis.

Items #3, #4, and #5 identify the limit of liability, the aggregate annual limit, and the SIR. The first limit is the maximum that would be paid in any one occurrence and the aggregate limit is the limit that would be paid for all occurrences in one policy year. As mentioned, the usual minimum limit is $1 million per occurrence and the aggregate annual limit usually is the same as the occurrence limit. Some umbrella policies may provide insurance "up to" $1 million, which is less coverage than $1 million in excess of primary. An umbrella providing "up to $1 million" merely increases overall limits to $1 million, whereas "$1 million in excess of primary" adds $1 million to the underlying policy limits.

Occurrence Limit of Liability. The minimum "limit" of liability under the umbrella is $1 million (whether *excess* of underlying or *up to* the umbrella limit). However, significantly higher limits are available. Some insureds may only need an additional $1 million coverage in excess of underlying, but many exposures warrant buying limits of $50

Exhibit 9-8
Comprehensive Catastrophe Liability Policy—Declarations Page

COMPREHENSIVE CATASTROPHE LIABILITY POLICY

CROWLEY FIRE AND MARINE

COMPREHENSIVE CATASTROPHE LIABILITY POLICY

Declarations

---

1. NAMED INSURED

   ADDRESS (Number—Street—City or Post Office—Zone—County—State)

2. POLICY PERIOD: (Also State Time If Other Than 12:01 A.M.) | TO

   12:01 A.M. Standard Time at the Address of The Named Insured as Stated Herein

3. Occurence Limit: $ 6. Premium due at Inception $

4. Aggregate Limit: $ Premium due on First Anniversary $

5. Retained Limit: $ Premium due on Second Anniversary $

       Total Policy Premium $

7. Schedule of Underlying Insurance:

Type of Policy	Applicable Limits
Comprehensive General Liability Insurance including: ☐ Products—Completed Operations ☐ Personal Injury ☐ Broad Form Property Damage ☐ Employees as Add'l. Insureds ☐ Independent Contractors ☐ Blanket Contractual ☐ ☐ Insurer: Policy Number: Policy Term: To	Bodily Injury: $,000. each occurrence $,000. aggregate Property Damage: $,000. each occurrence $,000. aggregate or Combined single limit and Aggregate: $,000.
Comprehensive Automobile Liability Insurance including: ☐ Non-owned ☐ Hired Auto Insurer: Policy Number: Policy Term: To	Bodily Injury $,000. each person $,000. each occurrence Property Damage $,000. each occurrence or Combined single limit $,000.
Standard Workmen's Compensation and Employers Liability Policy: Insurer: Policy Number: Policy Term: To	Coverage B: $,000. each accident

8. Other:

   Form Numbers of Endorsements forming a part of the policy at issue:

COUNTERSIGNED AT	COUNTERSIGNATURE DATE MONTH DAY YEAR	COUNTERSIGNATURE OF LICENSED RESIDENT AGENT

Exhibit 9-9
Possible Umbrella Aggregate Applications*

Products/completed operations personal injury only
Products/completed operations property damage only
Products/completed operations bodily injury only
All products/completed operations
Professional liability or services
Advertising claims
All umbrella coverages
Occupational disease
Property damage
Underlying coverage aggregates

*Developed by James A. Robertson, CPCU, Editor, *The Umbrella Book.*

million to $100 million or more (multi-million dollar judgments are not uncommon today). The producer should at least recommend higher limits and should quote the premium for several additional $1 million layers, because they cost less per $1 million as the exposure gets farther away from the first dollar of loss.

Aggregate Limits. The aggregate policy limits apply per policy year, but insurer uniformity ends there. Exhibit 9-9 shows the possible application of aggregate umbrella limits, ranging from all umbrella coverages to just one type of paid claim, or any combination thereof. Producers should carefully check each umbrella's application of the aggregate limits.

Policy Limits and the SIR. Defense costs in umbrellas may or may not be included in the policy limits. They may or may not apply to losses subject to the SIR. Umbrellas have five basic defense coverage variations, including:

1. No coverage for defense costs at all.
2. First-dollar defense coverage, including losses subject to the SIR.
3. Coverage for defense costs after the SIR is exhausted.
4. No defense coverage if underlying policies pay (until annual aggregate liability limits are exhausted).
5. No exclusion of defense costs in the presence of underlying coverage.

For example, Roux Medical Services, Inc., is currently being sued for $500,000 in each of two suits. One suit is defended by the CGL insurer and the second is uninsured, falling under umbrella coverage excess of the SIR. Depending on its umbrella policy's terms, Roux

Medical may have no defense cost coverage in the umbrella for either suit. For the SIR suit, defense costs may be covered from first dollar *or* they may be paid only after the SIR is exhausted. For the CGL-defended suit, Roux Medical may have no umbrella defense cost protection unless and until the CGL aggregate is exhausted. Finally, Roux Medical may have defense cost coverage for both suits by the umbrella. Also, the defense cost coverage may be a supplemental payment (in addition to the policy limits) or may be included in the policy limit. The producer must know what defense coverage applies before the policy is delivered because the *insured* will be affected by the presence or absence of defense coverage.

Schedule of Underlying Insurance. Item #7 in the declarations displays a schedule of underlying policies. The CGL section shows what is covered under the primary policy, which insurance company writes the coverage, the policy number, the effective dates of coverage, and limits of liability. Insurer, policy number, and term are displayed for the BAP and workers' compensation coverage, as well.

Other Information. Item #8 of the declarations is simply called "Other." This space is provided to list any other primary liability policies in effect such as professional or aviation liability. The same policy information must be listed on these exposures if they exist. If space does not permit the listing of all underlying policies on the declarations page, a separate schedule can be added by endorsement.

Insuring Agreements

Coverage. A sample insuring agreement reads:

I. Coverage

The Company agrees to indemnify the insured for all sums which the insured shall become obligated to pay as damages, direct or consequential, and expenses, all as hereinafter defined as included within the term ultimate net loss, by reason of liability

(a) imposed upon the insured by law, or

(b) assumed by the named insured, or by any officer, director, stockholder or employee thereof while acting within the scope of his duties as such, under any contract or agreement, because of personal injury, property damage, or advertising liability caused by or arising out of an occurrence which takes place during the policy period anywhere in the world.

This agreement is broad, granting coverage for almost any personal injury, property damage, or advertising liability. To understand the limitations on the coverage, it is necessary to read and understand defined terms and exclusions later in the policy. Coverage provisions vary. Some umbrellas agree to "pay on behalf of" instead of "indemnify." Some do not pay for consequential damages. Finally, the corporate contractual provision may appear in the definitions of named insured, as may the world-wide coverage provision (which may not be world-wide in some policies, or not even mentioned).

Limits Of Liability. Part II of the insuring agreement in the sample umbrella form states the policy's intent with regard to the limits of liability.

II. Limits of Liability

Regardless of the number of persons or organizations who are insureds under this policy and regardless of the nature and number of claims made or suits brought against any or all insureds, the total limit of the company's liability for any one occurrence shall be the ultimate net loss resulting therefrom in excess of the underlying limit and then only up to the amount stated in the declarations as the occurrence limit; provided, however, the company's liability is further limited to the amount stated in the declarations as the aggregate limit, with respect to all ultimate net loss resulting from one or more occurrences during each annual period while this policy is in force commencing from its effective date and arising out of either (1) products-completed operations liability, or (2) occupational diseases of employees of insureds, such aggregate limit applying separately to (1) and (2).

Regardless of how many "named insureds" are covered under the policy or named in a suit, the limits of the policy are those stated on the declarations page of the policy. This prevents pyramiding of limits under the policy (i.e., accumulating full policy limits separately for each insured). Note also in this example that application of the aggregate limits applies separately to (1) products and completed operations losses, and (2) occupational diseases of employees. As mentioned, this aggregate application must be checked before each umbrella is delivered.

Definition of Insured, Named Insured. Part III is devoted entirely to the definition of insured and named insured.

III. Definition of Insured, Named Insured

The "named insured" means the person or organization named in the declarations and includes any subsidiary thereof and any other organization coming under the named insured's control of which it assumes active management.

The unqualified word "insured" includes the named insured and also includes:

(a) any officer, director or stockholder of the named insured while acting within the scope of his duties as such, and, if the named insured is or includes a partnership, any partner thereof but only with respect to his liability as such;

(b) except with respect to the ownership, maintenance or use, including loading or unloading, of automobiles while away from premises owned by, rented to or controlled by the named insured or the ways immediately adjoining, or of aircraft, (1) any employee of the named insured while acting within the scope of his duties as such; or (2) any person or organization acting as agent with respect to real estate management for the named insured;

(c) with respect to any automobile owned by the named insured or hired for use by or on behalf of the named insured, any person while using such automobile and any person or organization legally responsible for the use thereof, provided its actual use is with the permission of the named insured, except

(1) any person or organization, or any agent or employee thereof, operating an automobile sales agency repair shop, service station, storage garage or public parking place, with respect to any occurrence arising out of the operation thereof; or

(2) the owners or any lessee, other than the named insured, of a hired automobile or any agent or employee or such owner or lessee;

(d) with respect to any aircraft chartered with pilot by or on behalf of the named insured, any person using such aircraft and any person legally responsible for the use thereof, provided its actual use is with the permission of the named insured, except

(1) the owner, pilot or air crew thereof or any person operating the aircraft; or

(2) any manufacturer or aircraft, engines or aviation accessories, or any aviation sales, service or repair organization or airport or hangar operator or any employee of any of them;

(e) any person or organization to whom or to which the named insured is obligated by virtue of a written contract to provide insurance such as is afforded by this policy, but only with respect to operations performed by the named insured or facilities owned or used by the named insured and subject to the underlying limit applicable to the insurance for the named insured with respect to such operations or facilities;

(f) any individual who is a named insured, but only with respect to the conduct of a business which is insured by the underlying insurance policies described in the **Schedule of Underlying Insurance;**

(g) any other person or organization who is an insured under any policy of underlying insurance, listed in the **Schedule of Underlying Insurance,** subject to all the limitations upon coverage under such policy other than the limits of the underlying insurer's liability.

The insurance afforded applies separately to each insured against whom claim is made or suit is brought, but the inclusion herein of more than one insured shall not operate to increase the limits of the company's liability.

The definition in this sample policy grants coverage to the named insured identified in the declarations page and also any unnamed subsidiaries or organizations over which the named insured assumes active management control. Insured persons include directors, officers, or stockholders of the named insured while acting within the scope of their duties for the named insured. Also included as insureds are other organizations or employees acting within their scope of duties. The policy also provides coverage for any person or organization to whom the named insured is obligated by virtue of a written contract.

Definition of insured or named insured varies so widely among umbrellas as to make useful generalization impossible. Producers must verify that the definitions in any given umbrella policy provide the scope of coverage desired by a particular insured.

Other Definitions.   Part IV of the sample policy contains the other definitions. Some are self-explanatory and will not be discussed, but several require special emphasis.

PERSONAL INJURY.

> "Personal injury" means (a) bodily injury, shock, sickness or disease (including death, mental anguish and mental injury resulting therefrom); (b) injury arising out of false arrest, false imprisonment, wrongful eviction, wrongful entry, wrongful detention or malicious prosecution; or (c) injury arising out of racial or religious discrimination not committed by or at the direction of the named insured or any executive officer, director, stockholder or partner thereof, but only with respect to liability other than fines, penalties or liquidated damages imposed by law; or (d) injury arising out of libel, slander, defamation of character, humiliation or invasion of right of privacy, unless such injury arises out of advertising activities.

Personal injury is defined in very broad terms. It includes all of the elements of the traditional definition of bodily injury and includes such personal injury coverages as libel, slander, false arrest, and others.

Variations in personal injury coverage are numerous. Most umbrella personal injury definitions are at least as broad as standard primary (ISO) coverage, but some policies are much broader. Exhibit 9-10 shows these variations for only a few insurers' forms.

PROPERTY DAMAGE.

> "Property Damage" means (1) physical injury to or destruction of tangible property which occurs during the policy period, including the loss of use thereof at any time resulting therefrom, or (2) loss of use of tangible property which has not been physically injured or destroyed provided such loss of use is caused by an occurrence during the policy period.

Property damage in this policy includes physical injury to or the destruction of tangible property, including the loss of use of the property. It also includes loss of use of tangible property that has not actually been physically damaged or destroyed. Some umbrellas do not define property damage as broadly; producers should read this definition carefully.

Exhibit 9-10
Bodily/Personal Injury Perils Named in Policy*

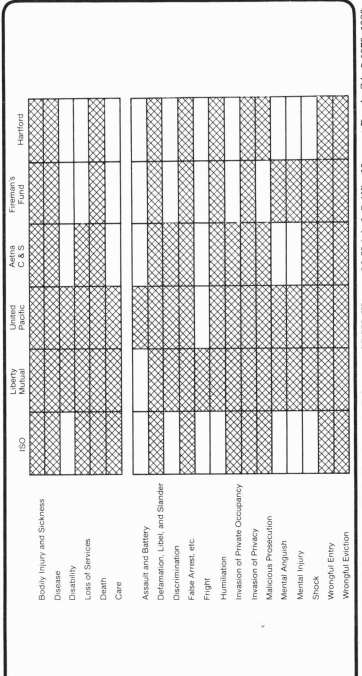

* Excerpted from *The Umbrella Book*, Edited by James A. Robertson, CPCU. Warren, McVeigh & Griffin, Newport Beach, CA, © 1979, 1980. Used with permission.

ULTIMATE NET LOSS.

"Ultimate net loss" means the total of the following sums arising out of any one occurrence to which this policy applies:

(a) all sums which the insured or any organization as his insurer, or both, become legally obligated to pay as damages, whether by reason of adjudication or settlement, because of personal injury, property damage or advertising liability; and

(b) all expenses incurred by the insured or any organization as his insurer, or both, in the investigation, negotiation, settlement and defense of any claim or suit seeking such damages, excluding only (1) the salaries of the insured's or insurer's regular employees, (2) office expenses of the insured or any insurer, and (3) all expense included in other valid and collectible insurance.

Ultimate net loss in this policy includes all sums the named insured is legally obligated to pay and all other expenses necessary to investigate and defend claims. In this policy, the cost of defense and investigation is *not* a supplemental payment in addition to the limits of liability, and there is no separate defense insuring agreement for SIR claims. All costs are added together and paid only up to the policy limits. The ultimate net loss definition varies from insurer to insurer, and relates defense costs to policy limits. The producer should check each umbrella issued for the applicable type of definition.

UNDERLYING LIMITS. In the illustrated umbrella, underlying limits are defined in the insuring agreements. They may also be defined in the "Conditions" section of policies.

"Underlying limit" means

(a) the amount of the applicable limits of liability of the underlying insurance as stated in the **Schedule of Underlying Insurance,** less the amount, if any, by which an aggregate limit of such insurance has been reduced by payment of loss; and

(b) in addition to the amount applicable in paragraph (a), the amount of any other valid and collectible insurance available to the insured, whether such other insurance is stated to be primary, contributing, excess or contingent (except insurance purchased to apply in excess of the sum of underlying limits described in paragraph (a), or the retained limit, and the limit of liability hereunder); or

(c) if the insurance afforded by the underlying insurance policies stated in the **Schedule of Underlying Insurance** is inapplicable to the occurrence, the amount stated in the declarations as the retained limit, or the amount of other insurance stated in paragraph (b), whichever is greater.

The limits of liability of any underlying insurance policy stated in the **Schedule of Underlying Insurance** shall be deemed applicable irrespective of (1) any defense which the underlying insurer may assert because of the insured's failure to comply with any condition of the policy subsequent to an occurrence, or (2) the inability of the underlying insurer to pay by reason of bankruptcy or insolvency.

The explanation of underlying limits has great significance in the policy. It states specifically that all the underlying limits stated in the declarations schedule are deemed applicable regardless of any defense the underlying insurer may assert because of the insured's failure to comply with any policy conditions, or the inability of the underlying insurer to pay by reason of bankruptcy or insolvency. This wording means the umbrella will not respond until the underlying limits are exhausted, whether the underlying policies actually pay their limits on the claim or not. In other words, if primary policies do not respond, the insured has an SIR equal to the primary limit.

OTHER DEFINITIONS. This section includes many definitions.

"Products—completed operations liability" means liability arising out of

(a) the handling or use of, the existence of any condition in or a warranty of the named insured's products other than equipment rented to or located for use of others but not sold, if the personal injury or property damage occurs after the named insured has relinquished possession thereof to others; or

(b) operations, including operations performed on behalf of the named insured, if the personal injury or property damage occurs after such operations have been completed or abandoned and away from premises owned, rented or controlled by the named insured; provided that operations which may require further service or maintenance work, or correction because improperly or defectively performed, but which are otherwise complete, shall be deemed completed; and provided further that the following shall not be deemed to be "operations" within the meaning of this paragraph: (1) pick-up and delivery, except from or onto a railroad car; (2) the maintenance of vehicles owned or used by or on behalf of the insured; or (3) the existence of tools, uninstalled equipment and abandoned or unused materials. The word "operations" as used herein includes any act or omission in connection with operations performed by or on behalf of the named insured on premises owned, rented or controlled by the named insured or elsewhere, whether or not goods or products are involved in such operations.

"Aircraft" means any heavier-than-air or lighter-than-air aircraft designed to transport persons or property.

"Advertising liability" means liability arising out of the named insured's advertising activities for:

(a) Libel, slander or defamation of character;

(b) Infringement of copyright or of title or of slogan;

(c) Piracy or unfair competition or idea misappropriation under an implied contract;

(d) Invasion of right of privacy;

committed or alleged to have been committed in any advertisement, publicity article, broadcast or telecast.

"Automobile" means a land motor vehicle, trailer or semi-trailer.

"Named Insured's Products" means goods or products (including any container thereof) manufactured, sold, handled or distributed by the named insured, or by others trading under his name.

"Occurrence" means an accident, including a continuous or repeated exposure to conditions, which results, during the policy period, in a personal injury, property damage or advertising liability neither expected nor intended from the standpoint of the insured, except that assault and battery committed by the insured for the purpose of protecting persons or property shall be deemed an occurrence.

For the purposes of determining the company's liability under the terms of Insuring Agreement II,

(a) with respect to personal injury and property damage, all such exposure to substantially the same general conditions existing at or emanating from one premises location or source shall be deemed one occurrence; and

(b) with respect to advertising liability all ultimate net loss arising out of any advertisement, publicity articles, broadcasts or telecasts or any combination thereof involving the same injurious material or act, regardless of the frequency of repetition thereof, or the number or kind of media used, or the number of persons claiming damages, shall be deemed to arise out of one occurrence.

Exhibit 9-11 contains some other definitions of the term "occurrence," including the CGL's definition. From the insured's standpoint, both an unsatisfactory definition and a more acceptable definition are included. Other variations also exist among umbrellas.

Exclusions The exclusions in the umbrella policy are important because they restrict the otherwise broad insuring agreement.

Workers' Compensation and Employer's Liability. Any obligation under the workers' compensation law usually is excluded. Excess coverage may be afforded over the employer's liability section of the workers' compensation policy, but not over the statutory benefits. Some umbrellas also exclude employer's liability.

Fellow Employee Injury. Liability arising out of injury to one employee by another employee in the course of employment is excluded.

Coverage does not apply:

to any employee as an insured with respect to personal injury to another employee of the same employer injured in the course of such employment, but this exclusion shall not apply to personal

Exhibit 9-11
Occurrence Definition

CGL

"Occurrence means an accident, including continuous or repeated exposure to conditions, which results in bodily injury or property damage neither expected nor intended from the standpoint of the insured."

Unsatisfactory Umbrella Wording*

"Occurrence means an accident, including continuous or repeated exposure to conditions which results in personal injury, property damage or advertising injury neither expected or intended from the standpoint of the insured."

More Acceptable Umbrella Wording

The term "occurrence" wherever used herein shall mean an accident or happening or event or a continuous or repeated exposure to conditions which unexpectedly or unintentionally results in personal injury, property damage or advertising liability during the policy period.

---

*Limited only to the scope of the CGL—accidents—thus not accurately describing personal or advertising injuries, which are *intentional* acts with unintentionally injurious results.

---

injury with respect to which insurance is afforded such insured by underlying insurance;

Aircraft and Watercraft.   In the sample policy, owned aircraft and aircraft chartered without crew are specifically excluded. This coverage often can be added by endorsement when the exposure is on a primary basis. This exclusion usually does not apply to nonowned aircraft. Coverage would apply for the liability of a licensed pilot who occasionally borrows an aircraft. Many forms exclude owned as well as nonowned aircraft. Aircraft coverage restrictions can be elusive because they often are incorporated into the definition of insureds.

This policy also excludes owned watercraft over fifty feet in length. Boats less than fifty feet in length and nonowned watercraft of any length are covered for watercraft liability. Owned watercraft over fifty feet in length may be covered by endorsement. Umbrellas vary in the length thresholds for excluding watercraft, and some umbrellas contain no aircraft or watercraft exclusions.

Advertising Liability. Certain exclusions pertaining to advertising liability are reasonably uniform in umbrella policies. Each policy's exclusions, however, should be reviewed by the producer.

Coverage shall not apply to advertising liability arising out of

(1) failure of performance of contract, other than the unauthorized appropriation of ideas based upon alleged breach of an implied contract.

(2) personal injury or property damage.

(3) infringement of trademark, service mark or trade name, other than titles or slogans, by use thereof on or in connection with goods or services sold, offered for sale or advertised.

(4) incorrect description or mistake in advertised price of goods or products sold, offered for sale or advertised.

"Sistership" Exclusion. Product recall or "sistership" liability is excluded, denying coverage for damages claimed when the insured withdraws products from the market because of a real, suspected, or alleged defect. This is a standard exclusion in nearly all umbrella policies.

Insured's Property or Products. Property damage to the insured's own property or products is nearly always excluded.

Contractual Liability. Contractual liability created by a war is excluded, but some policies (unlike the sample), do not contain this exclusion.

Coverage shall not apply:

to personal injury or property damage due to war, whether or not declared, civil war, insurrection, rebellion or revolution, or to any act or condition incident to any of the foregoing, with respect to liability assumed by the insured under any contract or agreement.

Delay or Lack of Performance. Liability for the loss of use of property that has not been physically injured is excluded if the loss of use is caused by a delay or lack of performance of a contract by the insured. Also excluded is liability for any loss of use caused by the failure of performance of the insured's product, to the extent or quality of performance warranted by the insured.

Coverage shall not apply:

to loss of use of tangible property which has not been physically injured or destroyed resulting from

(1) a delay in or lack of performance by or on behalf of the named insured of any contract or agreement, or

(2) the failure of the named insured's products or of work performed by or on behalf of the named insured to meet the level of performance, quality, fitness or durability warranted or represented by the named insured;

but this exclusion does not apply to loss of use of other tangible property resulting from the sudden and accidental physical injury to or destruction of the named insured's products or work performed by or on behalf of the named insured after such products or work have been put to use by any person or organization other than the insured.

Some umbrellas delete the exceptions in the final section, thus restricting coverage more than a standard CGL policy.

Limitations   There are two limitations on coverage that actually should not be called exclusions. They are almost always found in an umbrella policy, and usually cannot be deleted. They are the so-called nuclear energy liability exclusion and the exclusion for pollution.

Nuclear Energy Liability.   Not all nuclear or radiation hazards are excluded. Producers should refer to the policy kit for wording of the illustrated umbrella policy.

Pollution.   Pollution which is "sudden and accidental" is covered while that which is continuous and not accidental is excluded. Also, some umbrellas exclude pollution from certain "Described Operations," such as drilling oil and gas wells, regardless of its sudden and accidental nature. Most umbrellas, however, do not have the "Described Operations" exclusions.

Variations in Exclusions or Limitations   Umbrellas vary so widely that a complete list of the exclusions used by all insurers is not possible here. Producers should read all exclusions before delivering any policy, since many not mentioned here may appear, and the exclusions mentioned may be worded differently.

Conditions   Another section of the umbrella policy that must be carefully scrutinized by the producer contains policy conditions. Like many other components of the umbrella, this section can and does vary from insurer to insurer. An umbrella policy will contain most of the conditions mentioned here, however.

Premium Inspection and Audit.   Conditions A and B state that the premium in the declarations is an advance premium and that the insured must make records and premises available for inspection. The final premium may be determined by audit, if a variable rate is specified in the declaration.

An audit is usually required if premium is based on gross receipts. A producer should strive for a "flat" or guaranteed premium rather than an audited premium based on gross receipts during inflationary times. Inflation and subsequent product price increases can create a substantial audit premium in excess of the deposit premium. This increase may not reflect an actual change in the exposure the insurer has accepted.

Notice of Occurrence. Condition C requires the insured to give written notice to the insurer of any claim that may involve payment under the umbrella policy. It also requires the insured to forward all documents and information concerning the claim and all investigation reports. This requirement is made so that the umbrella insurer can monitor the claim in the event the insurance company becomes involved. Varying wording may make this condition onerous because of unusual demands on the insured.

Assistance and Cooperation. The insured is held responsible for the investigation, defense, and settlement of claims within the SIR. No settlement by the insured is allowed if the settlement will exceed the SIR and involve the umbrella insurer, without the prior consent of the umbrella insurer. The insurer may participate with the insured in any SIR claims situation. Finally, the insured is required to cooperate with underlying insurers as required by the terms of those policies.

Appeals. The appeals condition (E) gives the umbrella insurer the right to appeal a judgment when the underlying insurer involved elects not to appeal (when such judgment involves payment under the umbrella). If the umbrella insurer exercises this right, the umbrella insurer is responsible for all associated costs, as well as interest on the judgment. Some insurers may not pay appeal expenses in addition to policy limits, which is harmful to the insured.

Loss Payable, Bankruptcy of the Insured. These conditions explain how and when losses are paid, and affirm that bankruptcy of the insured does not relieve the insurer from its obligation to provide coverage.

Subrogation, Policy Changes, and Assignment. These conditions are straightforward and similar to corresponding provisions in all liability insurance contracts.

Maintenance of Underlying Insurance. Condition K addresses the issue of maintaining underlying insurance. It requires that the underlying policies described in the declarations section, including renewals or replacements, be maintained in full effect during the term of the umbrella policy (except for the reduction or exhaustion of their limits by loss payments). If the underlying limits are not maintained, the umbrella will respond only after the insured has paid an amount equal to the underlying limits. The insured must inform the umbrella insurer of any underlying policy changes or the exhaustion of underlying policy aggregate limits. In some policies, the insured is liable for underlying limits if the primary insurer is insolvent.

Cancellation. Condition L gives the insurance company the right to cancel the policy with thirty days' written notice of cancellation to the insured identified in the declarations section of the policy.

Agent for Named Insured. The insured identified in the declarations is the agent for all insureds with respect to the policy. The insurer need not notify all possible "insureds" to cancel, for instance; only the named insured identified on the declarations must be notified.

Declarations. The effect of this condition is to make the declaration section warranties of the insured. Some insurers do not try to make the declarations warranties (an advantage to the insured).

Checkpoints

1. Why is the definition of "named insured" in the umbrella policy important?
2. Why is the definition of "ultimate net loss" in the umbrella policy important?
3. Explain the nature of the aviation and watercraft liability exclusion in the umbrella policy.
4. What is an advantageous wording of the "appeal" condition in the umbrella policy to the insured?
5. Outline the policy conditions requirements for maintenance of underlying insurance.
6. Where may restrictions in umbrella coverage be found outside of the exclusions section of the policy?
7. Why is the definition of occurrence important, and how should it be defined in the insured's best interest?

Underwriting

The principal basis for decision making by the underwriter is the application form prepared by the producer and the insured. Each question must be answered completely in order for the underwriter to properly evaluate and rate the policy. An example of an umbrella application is shown in Exhibit 9-12.

Information About the Insured Item #1 of the illustrated application asks for the named insured and the number of years in business. The named insured and each entity over which the named insured exercises control or active management control should be listed if they are to be covered by the umbrella policy. The underwriter wants details of each operation under consideration. The number of years the named insured has operated is important because it gives the underwriter some idea of the named insured's experience and competence. Further, it may indicate products liability exposure from past production or discontinued products.

Items #2 and #3 ask for a description of the products maufactured or procured and a description of the insured's operations. If the

Exhibit 9-12
Application for Umbrella Insurance—Comprehensive Commercial Catastrophe Liability Policy

CROWLEY FIRE AND MARINE
Application for Umbrella Insurance
Comprehensive Commercial Catastrophe
Liability Policy

☐ Quotation
☐ Issue Policy
Inception Date _____
Expiration Date _____

1. Named Insured _____ No. of Years in Business _____ YRS.

Mailing Address _____

2. Description of Products _____

3. Description of Operations _____

4. Annual Payroll _____ Annual Sales—Receipts _____

5. UNDERLYING INSURANCE

a. Do underlying policies contain any special exclusions other than exclusions printed in standard bureau form? ☐ Yes ☐ No.
   If yes, please attach the wording shown in such policies.

b. Do underlying policies provide reduced limits for specific exposures? ☐ Yes ☐ No. If yes, explain: _____

c. Primary Insurance Policies

	Insurer	Policy Number	Policy Dates	Limit of Liability	Premium	Debit Credit?
General Liability BI				BI		
PD				PD		
Products—Completed BI				BI		
Operations Liability PD				PD		
Automobile BI				BI		
Liability PD				PD		
Worker Comp. &				Statutory		
Employers' Liability				$ EA. ACC.		
Liability BI				BI		

Liability		PD
	BI	
	PD	

	PD
BI	
PD	

6. Description of Coverage provided by Underlying Insurance. Indicate Coverage by ☒ Yes or No.

Hazard/Coverage	Yes	No		Hazard/Coverage	Yes	No
a. Public Liability—CGL	☐	☐		j. Incidental Malpractice	☐	☐
b. Public Liability—OLT—M&C	☐	☐		k. Personal Injury Liability	☐	☐
c. Public Liability—Storekeepers	☐	☐		l. Blanket Contractual Liability	☐	☐
d. Products—Completed Operations	☐	☐		m. XC Hazards	☐	☐
e. Auto Liability—Garage	☐	☐		n. U Hazard	☐	☐
f. Automobile Liability—Owned	☐	☐		o. Aircraft Liability Including Passenger Bodily Injury	☐	☐
g. Automobile Liability—Non-Owned	☐	☐		p. Broad Form Property Damage	☐	☐
h. Employers' Liability	☐	☐		q. Liquor Law Liability	☐	☐
i. Longshoremen or Harbor Workers	☐	☐				

7. General Information

a. AVIATION, MARITIME AND WATERCRAFT LIABILITY—Does Insured own, lease or charter aircraft or watercraft?
☐ Yes ☐ No. If yes, describe exposures: _____

b. AUTOMOBILE LIABILITY

(1) State number of units owned and leased:

	No.	Radius			No.	Radius
Private Passenger	___	___		Truck-Tractors: Heavy	___	___
				Extra-Heavy	___	___

(2) Trucks: Light ___ ___
Medium ___ ___
Heavy ___ ___
Truck-Trailer: ___
Trailers: ___

(3) Are all motor vehicles insured on underlying policies? ☐ Yes ☐ No. If no, explain: _____

c. NON-OWNED PROPERTY

(1) Does Insured own or lease any business premises? Check: ☐ All Owned; ☐ Leased—If leased, complete following:

Address	Occupancy	Part Occupied	Estimated Value

(2) Insured's protection for leased premises listed above:
(a) Fire Legal Liability Insurance ☐ Yes ☐ No. If yes, Limit of Insurance $ _____

Continued on next page

(b) Insured added to owner's fire insurance ☐ Yes ☐ No. If yes, Amount of Insurance $_____

(c) Hold harmless agreement from owner or lessor to Insured ☐ Yes ☐ No

List all personal property of others in CARE, CUSTODY or CONTROL of Insured with values in EXCESS of $10,000:

Location	Description	Estimated Value

8. Any liability losses over $5,000 in past five years? _____

9. What Excess Limit is desired? _____

AGENCY: _____   DATE: _____

IF PERSONAL UMBRELLA IS DESIRED, COMPLETE THE FOLLOWING

1. Name of Insured: _____
   Home Address: _____
   City and State: _____

2. Automobiles:
   a. Number of Automobiles Operated by Insured Including Owned, Leased and Company-Owned: _____
   b. Number of unmarried male operators under 25 _____
      Full time? _____ Part time? _____
   c. Present Automobile Liability Limits Carried: _____

3. Aircraft:
   a. Does any Insured have a Pilot's License? _____
   b. Does any Insured own or regularly fly any Aircraft? _____
      If so, describe _____
      No. of engines _____
   c. Aircraft Liability Policy carried? _____
      If so, advise limits, Carrier, Policy No. and Policy Term _____

   Submit copy of Aircraft Liability Policy.

Does any underlying policy exclude coverage or provide reduced limits for specific exposure? ☐ Yes ☐ No. If yes, describe: _____

Any losses over $5,000 in past five years? _____

What Excess Limit is desired? _____

AGENCY: _____   DATE: _____

4. Personal Liability:
   a. Number of Residences or Farms–Owned: _____
   b. Present Personal Liability Limits Carried: _____
   c. Any Recreational Motor Vehicles? _____
      Number and Type: _____
      Liability Limits Carried: _____

5. Watercraft:
   Any Watercraft over 26 feet in length? If so: _____
   Number: _____
   Length: _____
   Liability Limits: _____

6. Investment Property:
   Description of Property: _____
   Primary Carrier: _____
   Policy Number: _____
   Liability Limits Carried: _____

products hazard is not excluded, it is covered under the umbrella. As discussed in the chapters on general liability insurance, this particular exposure is closely underwritten by primary insurers and it is just as closely underwritten for umbrella coverage. It is always helpful, and sometimes required, that the insured send all sales brochures describing the products manufactured or sold by the insured, as well as quality control records, or manuals. If a variety of products are involved, the producer should break down the gross sales by product or number of units. Discontinued products should be listed if they were hazardous. This is always helpful to the underwriter in determining the acceptability and premium. If the insured is involved in manufacturing a hazardous product, the underwriter may look more favorably upon the submission if the producer can show that a particular operation or product represents only a small portion of the total operation or products.

Item #4 requests annual payroll figures and sales or receipts. The producer should indicate which payroll figure is being used—workers' compensation or general liability. As indicated in those chapters of this book, each of the payroll figures has certain limitations or exceptions to certain classes of employees, so the underwriter needs to know which figure to work with. For a large operation, the underwriter will require the payrolls and sales by classification and/or state so the exposure can be determined more accurately.

Schedule of Underlying Policies   Item #5 asks for underlying insurance policy information. The underwriter needs to know underlying limits, primary insurer, policy number and policy dates. This information is made part of the declarations of the policy and a policy condition may state that the umbrella applies in excess of the named policy limits or their renewal or replacement.

The primary insurer is important to the umbrella underwriter. The insurance company issuing the umbrella policy may refuse to issue the umbrella when the underwriter is not satisfied with the financial stability of the underlying insurer. A space is left for additional underlying policies such as professional liability.

Premium Information.   Item #5 also asks for the premium on the underlying policies, and what credit or debit has been used in rating of the underlying premiums for umbrella rating purposes. There are no standard rates for umbrella policies but some underwriters base their premiums on a percentage of the underlying premium charges. This percentage can range from 15 percent on less hazardous risks to 35 percent or more on larger or more hazardous operations. The percentages, and minimum charges per million dollars of coverage very widely as conditions change.

SALES POINT. This section of the application can be used as a sales tool for the producer. If the producer is soliciting an umbrella policy on an account that is not now written, the umbrella application can be used as a stepping stone to the rest of the account. If umbrella application information is successfully obtained, the producer has the expiration dates, premiums on the underlying policies and underlying insurers. The producer can then solicit the entire account at its expiration date (as well as recommend that any noncurrent liability anniversaries be made concurrent). For a producer to protect his or her own own account and the insured, no excess or umbrella policy should be written without common (concurrent) expiration dates with primary liability coverage. If concurrent, a competitor cannot quote an umbrella only and return with a competitive bid later on the balance of the account.

Description of Underlying Coverages. A description of the coverage provided by the underlying insurance is required. The insuring agreements of the umbrella are usually so broad that they would cover all underlying exposures, except possibly aviation, either over primary coverage or the self-insured retention. For this reason the underwriter can either require the insured to cover exposures under the primary, or exclude them from the umbrella if the underwriter feels the exposure cannot be accepted over the SIR.

General Information

Water and Aircraft. If the insured owns, leases, or charters aircraft or watercraft, the underwriter will need a full description of these exposures. Nonowned watercraft and aircraft usually are covered in the umbrella policy, but coverage for owned or chartered aircraft, or watercraft in excess of a variable length limitation (the maximum is 75 feet), is severely restricted. If such exposures exist, the underwriter will require underlying policy information to include coverage under the umbrella policy. If there is an owned aircraft policy in force, the underwriter may ask for a copy of the policy to determine exactly what coverage exists.

Autos. Also requested is full information on automobile exposures. The underwriter wants the number of units in the fleet, and the use and radius of operation of each unit. To evaluate the potential for catastrophic loss, the underwriter wants any information on flammables or explosives hauled. If the insured hauls hazardous materials, the underwriter may require higher limits on the primary BAP.

Nonowned Property. Another exposure that will be evaluated carefully is liability for the property of others. This includes any property for which the insured may be held legally liable, such as leased premises, leased equipment, or property of others in the care, custody, or control of the insured. Although policies vary, the umbrella usually does not contain the standard care, custody or control exclusion found in the primary CGL. Therefore, coverage could be provided by the umbrella policy. For this reason, the umbrella underwriter needs to know the exposures present. If this exposure has not been adequately provided for in the underlying policies, such as fire legal liability insurance or a bailee form, and if the values greatly exceed the SIR, the underwriter may exclude coverage under the umbrella policy.

Loss Information. In evaluating the limits of liability requested for the umbrella policy, umbrella underwriters consider past losses in excess of some figure, usually $5,000 or $10,000. If there is a high frequency of losses in excess of this amount, the underwriter may refuse to issue the policy; a better alternative is to price the umbrella accordingly higher, or require higher underlying limits for "working" loss layers (limits of liability with a high probability of loss).

Personal Umbrella Application The last section of the sample application is for a personal umbrella to be attached to the commercial umbrella. The personal umbrella was discussed in PRO 81. In many cases, the commercial umbrella is issued with a personal umbrella endorsement added for the principals of the named insured. This can be a good premium builder for the producer. Also, if both the personal and commercial umbrellas are placed with the same insurer, some gaps in coverage for an owner-insured can be reduced or eliminated.

Professional Umbrella Coverage

The umbrella policy may not contain an exclusion for professional liability. In that case, any professional exposure is automatically picked up under the umbrella insuring agreements. However, no umbrella underwriter would knowingly accept a professional liability exposure over the SIR. This exposure must be covered by underlying policies, or the umbrella underwriter will specifically exclude professional liability.

Occurrence form umbrellas create insolvable coverage problems over claims made primary forms. Therefore, a straight excess liability program layered over claims made primary professional liability coverage is the cleanest way to solve the problem.

Underlying limits of liability required for an umbrella will vary from underwriter to underwriter and from one professional class to another. With the increasing numbers of large court judgments in the professional liability area, underwriters are requiring higher primary limits of liability. Rating the professional portion of an umbrella policy usually is not based on a "floating" percentage of the underlying premium (as in the other coverages). The premium usually is a flat charge.

Producers' Errors and Omissions Exposure from Umbrellas

As in the placement of all lines of insurance, an errors and omissions exposure is created when producers arrange umbrella coverage. One particularly dangerous subject in umbrella coverage terms is in the maintenance of the underlying limits of liability. An actual case illustrates the point.

Case Study A producer had written an SMP contract for a local surgeon and included the medical malpractice coverage with limits of $250,000 per occurrence and $500,000 aggregate per policy year. The package policy was written effective January 1. On June 15, the producer pointed out the need for higher limits and "sold" the insured a professional umbrella policy. The umbrella was issued effective June 15 and the declarations page showed the insurer of the underlying coverage, policy number, policy dates, and policy limits for the professional coverage.

The following January the producer "renewed" the SMP with another insurance company. The new package also covered the medical malpractice exposure but the limits of liability were reduced to $100,000 per occurrence and $300,000 aggregate. The producer failed to notify the insurance company writing the umbrella policy of the reduction in limits (required by Condition K in the illustrated policy). On May 15, the surgeon made a serious mistake in a surgical procedure and was sued for $750,000. The producer immediately notified the primary insurer of the claim and also sent a notice to the umbrella insurer.

After investigating the claim to determine coverage and exposure to loss to facilitate setting an adequate loss reserve, the umbrella underwriter declined coverage to the producer. Citing the conditions of the umbrella policy, the umbrella underwriter informed the producer that the umbrella would respond only over the original $250,000/$500,000 limits.

Underlying limits must be maintained on all renewals of the original existing primary policy. Of course, the umbrella would respond once the claim exceeded $250,000, but not before. The primary policy, in this example, would pay only $100,000. The producer, through his errors and omissions (E&O) insurer, will pay the $150,000 gap in coverage. This case also illustrates the importance of concurrent policy dates for all policies.

The possibility of creating a gap in coverage when primary limits of liability are reduced is greater when the primary liability policy and the umbrella policy do not have common expiration dates. This problem can be avoided by prorating the first term of an umbrella to coincide with the primary policies. Then both files will be pulled at the same time for renewal and any necessary changes will be made on both policies.

If common expiration dates are not possible, the producer should document both files to alert the office staff to the effect that both policies are in effect and should be consistent at renewal. One suggested method is to have a rubber stamp that reads "Review Umbrella Policy." Each policy daily report can be stamped, thus alerting the producer to check the umbrella policy whenever a change is made in the primary liability coverage. Another way to avoid any problems is to have the primary, excess, and umbrella policies written by the same insurer. However, this may not be the best solution for the insured if the primary insurer will not provide a satisfactorily worded umbrella policy.

Sales Points The producer can use several approaches to the sale of umbrellas. For example, the producer can cite articles in trade journals or local newspapers to point out to prospective clients inflated court judgments in liability cases, graphically illustrating the need for the high limits offered by an umbrella policy. Many umbrella underwriters will furnish the producer with an umbrella sales kit that contains reproductions of many such articles that are useful in the sales process.

The producer should look first to his or her own accounts to build a book of umbrella business. All the information needed to obtain quotes on an umbrella should be in the files on the commercial liability and package policies he or she already writes. This approach, suggesting the unbrella and knowing the price on the initial call, has proven successful in many cases. Some umbrella underwriters will issue an umbrella policy prior to getting a firm order from the insured. The producer then approaches the insured, outlines the need for higher limits, and presents a completed policy that will satisfy the outlined need. If the insurer will allow the producer to take this approach, a clear understanding with the umbrella underwriter is needed so policies can be sent back for flat cancellation when not accepted. (This approach works best with small commercial accounts with limited products exposure and no aviation or professional liability exposures because of the paper work involved and the possibility of flat cancellation.)

Once the producer has learned the umbrella markets from a pricing and coverage standpoint, he or she is ready to pursue the large commercial umbrella accounts in the marketing area. As stated, the umbrella application provides the producer with the needed information to solicit the remainder of the account at a later date. Also, if the producer establishes the need for higher limits of liability and fills it with an umbrella policy, the prospect should gain enough confidence in the producer to allow him or her to handle other insurance.

Case Studies

To illustrate the application of terms and coverage of the umbrella policy, the cases outlined in Chapter 10 of PRO 81 will be used here.

J&T Appliances   Assume that a sound insurance program has been worked out on the primary liability exposures for J&T Appliances. The primary policy covers J&T for premises liability, products and completed operations, and BAP coverage including nonowned and hired car liability. Limits of liability on the CGL are $300,000 combined single limits. A combined single limit of $300,000 is also written on the BAP. There are several examples of loss situations indicating why a business as small as J&T would be an excellent candidate for an umbrella policy. For example:

1. J&T wrongly accuses a customer of shoplifting. This is a personal injury claim perhaps not covered by the primary liability policy. The umbrella would pay any judgment over the self-insured retention, or if there were primary coverage, over the underlying insurance limits.
2. One of J&T's drivers ignores a warning signal and crosses a railroad track, resulting in the derailment of the train, property damage to the train, and loss of use damages totaling $500,000. The BAP would respond to the claim, but its limits would be exhausted at $300,000. The umbrella policy would pay the next $200,000.

These examples indicate the need in even the small business for the broad coverage and the high limits afforded by the umbrella policy. In today's market a million dollar umbrella policy for J&T might cost approximately $350 per year, a small price to pay for the catastrophe coverage.

John Gale, M.D.   Dr. Gale is a prime prospect for the umbrella policy. He needs the catastrophe protection not only for premises and automobile liability but also for his farming operation. Doctors are normally affluent and therefore targets for lawsuits. The professional producer would certainly recommend the umbrella policy to this account.

R. P. Davis, Contractor   R. P. Davis has several exposures that deserve special consideration. Naturally, a good primary liability policy should be worked out for Davis. Davis owns a boat that probably would be covered by the umbrella over the self-insured retention since it is an owned watercraft less than fifty feet in length. However, the underwriter will probably require that the primary coverage be carried to at least $100,000 combined single limits. Also, the nonowned aircraft exposure may be covered by the umbrella over the SIR. However, the umbrella underwriter will probably require a primary nonowned aircraft liability policy.

A contractor like R. P. Davis has many exposures to loss in the liability area. The umbrella underwriter will check carefully to make sure that underlying insurance covers these exposures. Producers should be certain that the umbrella issued covers all of Davis' exposures as desired.

In Conclusion

The umbrella is one of the most important developments in the insurance business. In the face of inflated court judgments, it can provide the high limits needed to cover adequately the liability exposures faced by all commercial enterprises. Umbrellas can provide from $1 million to $100 million and more in coverage. The producer should strive to fill the needs of all commercial accounts with the use of the commercial umbrella policy.

Pricing depends on many factors and because of a high degree of underwriting judgment, quotations vary significantly. Exhibit 9-13 shows how prices of umbrellas and a total package of liability protection can vary among insurers. Producers should check prices as well as coverage. Total protection for quotations A and B is the same, yet quotation B saves the insured more than $10,000.

Finally, because policy standardization is nonexistent in umbrella coverage, the producer must be constantly alert to be sure umbrella policies actually cover exposures as desired.

MARKETING EXCESS COVERAGES

Any producer who has a good working knowledge of the "excess" coverages and the catastrophic exposures that necessitate the use of "excess" can be a good producer of this type of business. The coverage may well sell itself if the exposures are there. Finding insurers for those coverages can be a much more difficult endeavor, however.

As indicated in past discussion, "excess" is inherently specialized (i.e., wind, flood, high limits). Therefore the insurers offering specialized coverages must also be specialized. Generally, standard insurance

Exhibit 9-13
Umbrella Pricing*

PICKING THE RIGHT PRIMARY LIMIT

Grading Contractor
$3,000,000. Payroll $15,000,000. Receipts
80 Automobiles

Quotation A.	$1,000,000	CSL GL	$54,000	
	$1,000,000	CSL AL	22,000	
			$76,000	
	$4,000,000	Umbrella	10,300	= 13.6%
			$86,300	

Quotation B.	$500,000	CSL GL	$46,500	
	$500,000	CSL AL	17,290	
			$63,790	
	$5,000,000	Umbrella	12,000	= 18.8%
			$75,790	

In Quotation B.

1) Primary carrier wanted $12,210 for $500,000 excess $500,000.

2) Umbrella carrier willing to write $5,000,000 excess $500,000 for $12,000.

3) Insured saves over $10,000. Though $500,000 in coverage was lost at the top, the goal of $5 million was achieved. Additional amounts of umbrella coverage now can be purchased for less than the original incremental price.

*Example provided by Marilyn Thomas, Vice President & Casualty Manager, Stewart, Smith, West, Inc., Los Angeles.

companies will not handle these coverages as they are excluded from their reinsurance treaties. In response to consistently increasing needs for "excess" coverage, the "excess and surplus line" (E&S) brokers began to specialize accordingly. The E&S brokers are wholesalers who align themselves with the specialized and unusual type of insurer. Care must be exercised in dealing with unfamiliar and/or foreign companies to be sure they are financially stable and will pay claims promptly. Another important factor is that selection of the E&S broker should be made on the basis of the broker's expertise and experience, the broker's ability to arrange the best coverage at the most economical price.

SUMMARY

In some cases, catastrophic losses can originate from perils not insured under existing policies from judgments rendered in court. But all exposures can be covered for the insured by the professional producer. In many instances, bringing these exposures to the attention of the insured or potential insured, and offering a solution, can generate new business. But just as the original producer may have overlooked an exposure, care must be taken so that the creative producer "closes those same doors" to the competition.

Use of the "excess" insurance products examined in this chapter in many cases requires the use of specialty brokers and insurers. In any new area, "quicksand" must be located and avoided. This is not to say that the new producer should avoid these areas. Instead, a systematic, risk management approach outlined in PRO 81 should be diligently followed in order to completely protect the insured and also to avoid the possibility of an errors and omissions claim.

The excess coverage for property is the differences in conditions policy (DIC). Insurers who will accept this coverage are hard to find, and producers who do place this coverage provide a valuable service to their clients. In most cases, the DIC will pick up additional perils but not increase overall coverage limits. In other cases, limits are increased.

In the liability lines, straight excess insurance means that the policy provides additional limits of liability that will come into play after primary coverage is exhausted. In cases where liability insurance is layered, it will apply after primary and other excess policies. No exposures uninsured in the primary layer are contemplated or accepted. Usually, excess liability insurance is used to "fill a gap" between primary limits and underlying umbrella underwriting requirements.

The umbrella liability policy increases overall limits of liability and also covers additional exposures. The producer who will take the time to provide full and complete information to the underwriter will be ahead of the competition and will also preserve an umbrella market in times of tight markets.

CHAPTER 10

Other Commercial Coverages

INTRODUCTION

There are a wide variety of insurance coverages designed for specific loss exposures. This chapter highlights glass, boiler and machinery, credit, FAIR plans, federal crime, national flood, windstorm and hail pools, and business life insurance. Each of these specialized coverages offers the producer opportunities to cover a prospect's unique loss exposures and to generate greater commission income.

COMPREHENSIVE GLASS POLICY

Insurance for a firm's glass exposures can be provided in several ways. For example, some types of fancy or unusual glass may be covered under inland marine forms such as a fine arts floater (stained glass). Coverage on plate glass may be provided under the special extended coverage or "all-risks" form used to insure a building. However, a large plate glass show window is a valuable asset not only in monetary terms but also as an advertising medium. The comprehensive glass policy provides insurance on the glass and also guarantees prompt and efficient replacement service.

Declarations Page

The comprehensive glass policy is one of the least complicated insurance contracts. The first portion of the declarations lists the usual information relative to effective dates, named insured, and insured location. The balance of the page describes the specific glass insured.

The type and condition of the frames in which the glass is set and the loss history for the past three years is required.

A very important question asked is if the glass is free of any imperfections. If the answer is no, the underwriter will require a full description of the imperfections as well as a diagram of the particular plate containing the imperfection. Glass with existing damage can be included in the glass policy using the "cracked glass endorsement." This endorsement simply lists the damaged plates and specifically excludes loss that results as an extension of the previous damage. For example, if a large plate was described in the endorsement as having a crack in the left corner and at a later date the crack caused the plate to shatter, the loss would not be covered.

Glass is described by type (plate glass, safety glass, and so forth), location in the building, and size. Unless glass is described as "type E" no dollar limit for glass is set in the schedule. Type E glass includes stained glass, high-value glass, lettering, ornamentation, and burglar alarm tapes. A specific value has to be placed on any of these items, and a percentage of that value is charged for the coverage. Lettering, burglar alarm tapes, or ornamentation must be described specifically in the schedule and a dollar limit set if they are to be insured. Types of glass and lettering will be discussed later. Each item of glass in this category must be specifically scheduled or no coverage will apply. The producer must be careful to measure and list each plate.

Insuring Agreement

The insurer agrees to pay for all damages to described glass and to separately described lettering or ornamentation by breakage of the glass or by chemicals accidentally or maliciously applied. For glass breakage to be a covered loss, the crack must extend through the entire thickness of the plate; therefore, mere scratching or marring of the glass is not covered. For example, suppose that during a windstorm a piece of metal flashing bends and scratches two large display windows. Although the windows must be replaced, the comprehensive glass policy would not respond to the claim because there was no "breakage."

The insuring agreement grants supplemental coverages when breakage occurs:

1. The cost of repairing or replacing frames containing the glass when necessary.
2. The cost of installing temporary plates or boarding openings containing the glass when necessary because of delay in repairing or replacing damaged glass.

3. The cost of removing obstructions (other than window displays) necessary in replacing or repairing damaged glass.

Each of these is subject to a limit of $75 per occurrence (not per plate of glass) at any one location but may be increased by endorsement and payment of an additional premium.

Exclusions

There are only three exclusions to the comprehensive glass policy:

1. Loss by fire—Fire is covered by insurance on the building itself or under the tenants improvements and betterments form if the tenant is required by a lease agreement to replace the glass.
2. War—War is not insurable.
3. Nuclear reaction, radiation, or contamination—Nuclear reaction is generally not insurable.

Conditions

Policy conditions of the comprehensive glass policy are those normal to insurance.

Limits and Settlement Options The settlement options of the policy grant the insurance company the option either to repair or replace damaged glass, or to pay the loss in money. In practice, the insurance company will elect to "repair or replace the damaged glass with like kind or quality" in most cases. The "like kind or quality" wording is important. For example, suppose a large plate is broken and the insured learns the glass cannot be replaced with similar plain plate glass because a new building code in the insured's location requires safety glass. The comprehensive glass policy will then only pay the cost of replacing the plain plate and the difference in price for safety glass is borne by the insured. For an approximate 10 percent surcharge, the producer can add the "Safety Glazing Material Endorsement" to the glass policy. This endorsement provides coverage for the additional cost of replacing plain plate with safety glass.

Insured's Duties at Loss The insured is required to give notice of the loss as soon as practical and on request to file proof of loss (under oath if requested).

Other Insurance The "other insurance" condition states that if other insurance exists for the loss, the loss payable will be *prorated* by the total of all policy limits. For instance, Camille Casualty Company and Crowley Fire and Marine each insure a plate glass window for $1,000 in separate compehensive glass policies. If damage of $600 occurs, each would pay $300. If Camille Casualty's limits were $2,000, it would pay

$$\$400\left(\frac{2,000}{3,000}\right) \text{ or } \frac{2}{3}$$

and Crowley Fire and Marine would pay

$$\$200\left(\frac{1,000}{3,000}\right) \text{ or } \frac{1}{3}$$

Other Conditions The remaining conditions are normal to insurance. There are provisions for: Action Against the Company, Subrogation, Cancellation Assignment, Changes, Terms of Policy Conformed to Statute and Declarations.

Rating

Size and Type First the producer should measure the plates of glass involved. Each plate must be measured and scheduled for coverage to apply. In measuring, some allowance should be made for glass within frames. Also, the glass must be classified as to type. The glass division of the Commercial Lines Manual contains a glass dictionary that displays the name of the glass and assigns a type for policy classification. Types are classified either A, B, C, D, or E and each type takes a different rate based on its damageability. Exhibit 10-1 is a reproduction of one page from the glass dictionary in the Commercial Lines Manual.

Location The location of glass in the building also must be described. Glass is described as exterior, upper exterior, semi-interior, or interior. The Commercial Lines Manual clearly defines these terms and several special use classifications are also defined. Special use classes include such things as showcases, refrigerator cases, counter tops, and skylights.

Rate Determination Once the type of glass and exact use in the building are determined, the Commercial Lines Manual is used to find the appropriate modification to apply to the glass table rates. Exhibit 10-1 is a reproduction from the Commercial Lines Manual showing the appropriate rate modification by glass type and use. Glass rates are displayed in a rate table according to size. This rate is then modified by the factors found in Exhibit 10-2 and that rate is further modified by a territorial multiplier. For instance, if the insured wanted $1,500 of coverage on type E, lower exterior glass with lettering, the Commercial Lines Manual charge for type E lower exterior glass coverage is 20 percent of the value insured. The premium for that coverage would be $0.20 \times \$1,500 = \$300$. The final rate would be modified by the territorial multiplier.

Underwriting

In addition to all of the rating information outlined above, the underwriter will also need loss information to underwrite the exposure properly. If the insured has suffered many losses in the past, the underwriter will want to know what caused those losses. The producer may find that losses relate to the insured location or use of the glass in the building. For instance, the building may be located in a neighborhood prone to vandalism, or may be located on a gravel street with truck traffic. The glass may be located in a door or adjacent to a door used for shipping or delivering presenting a hazard from cargo bumping into the glass.

Sales Tips

It is difficult to place a comprehensive glass policy without supporting business. Glass is usually written when the insurer writes at least a part of the account or within an SMP. When soliciting a commercial account, the producer should explain that although a package policy on the building is proposed, the glass coverage in the SMP has certain limitations, usually $50 per plate with a $250 aggregate per occurrence. If only fire, extended coverage, and VMM are being provided, the VMM endorsement excludes damage to glass. Only a comprehensive glass policy provides full coverage, including any lettering or ornamentation.

When writing a commercial package policy for a tenant, the producer should check the client's lease agreement. Many leases require the tenant to be responsible for the glass in the building. The insured may not even be aware of this lease condition, so the producer is again establishing evidence of his or her professionalism. Perhaps an insured can negotiate a change in the lease, wherein the tenant agrees to be responsible for repair of glass without the necessity of providing insurance. This would provide the insured with the risk management option to determine whether to retain the exposure or transfer it by purchasing insurance. Eliminating such a lease provision would eliminate much of the exposure.

On some larger accounts the glass premium may be substantial, and the 50/50 retention endorsement can be a valuable competitive tool. With this endorsement, the premium for the policy is calculated as described previously. However, the insured pays only 50 percent of the

Exhibit 10-1
Commercial Lines Manual Division Seven—Glass*

H. Directory Of Glass. The classification of each kind of glass for rating purposes is shown on pages G-3 through G-4.

Kind of Glass	Class	Kind of Glass	Class
Acid Etched	C	Fabric	A
Actinic	C	Factrolite	A
Aklo	See "Heat Absorbing"	Figured Glass (NOC)	A
Amber Plate	See "Heat Absorbing"	Finger Grips	C
Antique (Trade Name)	A	Flashed	A
Apex	A	Flesh Colored Plate	See "Heat Absorbing"
Aqueduct	A	Flexglass	See "Structural"
Architectural Plate	C	Floor	C
Argentine	See "Structural"	Florentine	A
Artex	A	Florex	A
Art Glass	E	Flutex	A
Aurora	A	Furniture—Glass	E
		Fyrart	C
Bandlite	A	Glass Blocks	See "Structural"
Barber Poles—Glass	E	Glass Bricks	See "Structural"
Bent	D	Glass Furniture	E
Beveled	C	Glass of Special Ornamentation or Manufacture	
Bevelite	A	Valued at $7.50 or Less Per Sq. Ft. (NOC)	C
Blocks	See "Structural"	Glass—Tile	C
Blue Plate	See "Heat Absorbing"	Glass Valued in Excess of $7.50 Per Sq. Ft. (NOC)	E
Bretlet	C	Glued	B
Bricks	See "Structural"	Gold Veining	E
Broadlite	A	Golden	See "Heat Absorbing"
Bulbed Edge	B	Golden Plate	See "Heat Absorbing"
Bullet Resistive	See "Laminated Glass"	Ground	A
Burglar Alarm Foil	E		
Carnation	A	Half Tone Screens	Rule 7.B.
Carrara	E	Hammered	A
Carved	C	Heat Absorbing up to and Including ¼"	
Cemented	B	in Thickness	C
Chipped	C	Heat Absorbing Over ¼" in Thickness	E

Clamped .... B
Clear—Set in leaded sections
Cobweb .... A
Colonial .... A
Color Span .... See "Laminated Glass"
Colored (Not Stained)—Set in leaded sections ...... D
Colored Plate Glass Not Leaded
  (NOC) .... See "Heat Absorbing"
Coolite .... See "Heat Absorbing"
Corex C
Corrugated C
Crepe .... A
Crepeline .... A
Crystal .... A
Crystalex .... A

Demi-Plate .... A
Designs .... E
Dewlite .... A
Diffusex .... A
Double Strength .... A
Doublex .... A
Duolite .... See "Laminated Glass"
Duo-Pane .... E
Duplate .... See "Laminated Glass"
Dusklite .... See "Laminated Glass"

Edges, one or more unprotected by a frame .... B
Embossed C
Enameled C
Etched C

Helioglass C
Herculite .... See "Tempered"
Holviglass C
Holly .... A
Huetex .... See "Tempered"
Hylite .... A

Ideal .... A
Imperial .... A
Industrex .... A
Insulating Unit, Multiple Plate Factory Fabricated
  Hermetically Sealed .... E
Invisible Glass .... E

Jalousies .... Rule 4.B.2.a.

Laminated Glass up to and Including ¼" in
  Thickness C
Laminated Glass Over ¼" in Thickness .... E
Leaded Colored .... D
Leaded Prism .... D
Leaded Sheet .... D
Leaded Stained .... E
Lenses .... Rule 7.B.
Lettering .... E
Liberty .... A
Linex C

Locke .... A
Louvrex .... E
Lucite .... A
Luminex .... A
Luxlite .... A

Exhibit 10-2
Commercial Lines Manual Division Seven—Glass

Use of Glass and Its Position in Building					
Exterior		Semi-Exterior Interior		Special Classifications (Wherever Located)	
(1)	(2)	(3)	(4)	(5)	(6)
Grade floor and basement glass not within the outer permanent entrance doors of a building, with lowest edge less than 12 feet above sidewalk level and with any part less than 6 feet from the building wall line. (Except columns 4, 5, 6)	Upper glass in the outside walls of a building, the lowest edge of which glass is 12 feet or more above the sidewalk level. (Except columns 4, 5, 6.)	Interior glass, including glass in wall cases, wholly within the outer permanent entrance doors of a building.	Showcases (excluding refrigerator show cases).	Refrigerator cases and refrigerator store fronts.	Canopies
			Portable bulletin or poster boards.		Marquees
		Semi-exterior glass in grade floor entrances with no part less than 6 feet from the building wall line.	Shelves and shelving of all kinds.		Penthouse roofs and skylights.
			Counter, desk, furniture and table tops.		
Glass which is a part of the building structure in greenhouses and conservatories.		Glass in arcades, corridors, lobbies and vestibules on or below grade floor, within the outer permanent entrance doors	Furniture		
			Venetian blinds		

Class	Immovable showcase glass which is part of the general store front construction and permanently located in an entrance or vestibule which does not extend beyond the building wall line and NOC.		of a building. (Except columns 4, 5, 6.) Immovable showcase glass described in column (1) with plates no part less than 6 feet from the building wall line.	Removable glass such as fronts of doors which is customarily removed from its normal position and stored during business hours.		
A	1.00	.25	.33	1.50	2.00	1.00
B	1.25	.50	.50	2.00	2.00	1.25
C	2.00	.75	.75	2.00	2.00	2.00
D	5.00	3.00	3.00	5.00	5.00	5.00
E	.20	.08	.08	.20	.20	.20

premium at inception and then pays all insured losses until the other 50 percent is paid, when the insurer pays all losses in excess of that amount. For instance, if the insured's premium is calculated at $1,000 per year, with the 50/50 retention the insured would pay a $500 premium at inception. Assume that three months later the insured suffers a $350 covered glass loss and two months later another $400 covered glass loss. The insured must pay all of the first loss and $150 of the second loss. The balance of the second loss, $250, and all other glass losses subsequently incurred during the policy year are fully covered by the policy.

An alternative to the 50/50 retention would be placing a deductible on the glass policy; however, rate credits are very small in glass insurance for higher deductibles.

Checkpoints

1. What two broad perils are covered under the comprehensive glass policy?
2. Name the three exclusions in the comprehensive glass policy.
3. Why is marring or scratching of glass not covered under the glass policy?
4. Describe the three supplemental coverages and the limits for each in the comprehensive glass policy.
5. How can lettering on the glass be covered by the glass policy?
6. What is the 50/50 retention endorsement?

BOILER AND MACHINERY INSURANCE

Boiler and machinery insurance began because of an interest in preventing boiler accidents. With the advent of steam power came boiler explosions resulting in damage and injury. In 1860, a group of engineers in Hartford, Connecticut, met to investigate the causes of boiler explosions. By 1866 these engineers established a regular inspection service and guaranteed their service by affording insurance against such loss. Boiler and machinery insurance has expanded to cover not only pressure vessels but also air conditioning, refrigeration equipment, electrical motors and other equipment.

One of the most important aspects of the boiler and machinery policy continues to be the inspection service. Many state and local governments require that boilers be inspected annually and will accept the certification of a qualified boiler inspector employed by an insurance company. Without the boiler policy, an insured would have to contract for the inspection service. About forty cents of every premium dollar paid to a boiler insurer goes toward the inspection service.

The basic policy is written to insure both boiler and machinery "objects." A schedule attached to the policy defines "object" and the "accident" insured by the insuring agreement.

In general, the boiler and machinery policy intends to cover "sudden and accidental tearing asunder or mechanical breakdown" of insured "objects." The policy excludes general maintenance items, such as wear, tear, erosion, corrosion, and so forth. A steam boiler explosion would be a sudden and accidental tearing asunder or mechanical breakdown of the "object." However, the definition intends to cover much more than explosion. Common losses usually covered under a boiler and machinery policy are overheating and leakage of boilers, short circuit of electric motors, and breaking of mechanical parts of an air compressor, such as a crankshaft or valves. Definitions of "objects" and "accident" will be discussed later.

The basic boiler and machinery policy consists of a declarations page, policy jacket, and endorsements. Within the policy, coverage is available for both the property of the insured and for some liability exposures arising out of the ownership, maintenance or use of "objects."

Declarations Page

The declarations page of the policy (shown in Exhibit 10-3) contains the usual information relative to the named insured, location, effective dates of coverage, and premium. The limit, per accident, for boiler and machinery coverage is always written on a single limit basis. How the limit applies will be discussed under the loss settlement provisions section. The schedules and endorsements that apply to the policy are listed also. The bottom of the page is intended to be used for a description of the "objects" covered under the policy. Objects may either be described individually or may be written on a blanket basis. Comprehensive descriptions can also be used to insure all boilers, pressure vessels and machinery objects.

Policy Jacket

The policy jacket contains the insuring agreements, exclusions, and conditions.

Insuring Agreements There are six coverages in the insuring agreements:

Coverage A Loss to Property of the Insured
Coverage B Expediting Expenses
Coverage C Liability for Property of Others

Exhibit 10-3
Boiler and Machinery Declarations Page

CROWLEY FIRE AND MARINE

GENERAL BOILER AND MACHINERY

DECLARATIONS

POLICY NUMBER

(Prior Policy Number)

Name of Insured

Address of Insured

Policy Period From 12:01 A.M. of _____ to 12:01 A.M. of _____ Standard Time as to each of said dates, at the place where the Accident occurs. To the extent that coverage in this policy replaces coverage in other policies, terminating NOON Standard Time on the inception date of this policy, coverage under this policy shall not become effective until such other coverage has terminated.

Limit Per Accident $

Producer The word "Loss" in the first paragraph of the Insuring Agreement means loss under Coverages A1, A2, B, C, D, E and F of the Insuring Agreement except as otherwise stated herein:

Policy Premium

Schedules and Endorsements Schedules numbered _____ Endorsements numbered _____ are hereby made a part of this policy at inception date.

Producer Code | Name | Branch Office

Countersignature Countersigned at _____ | Countersignature Date | Countersignature of Licensed Resident Agent

SCHEDULE NO. 1

Location of objects below	Section Numbers	Description of Object

The number in the column entitled "Section Numbers" identifies the Definitions and Special Provisions Endorsement and Sections thereof which are applicable to the object described opposite said number.

Paragraphs bearing these Section Numbers printed on the Definitions and Special Provisions Endorsement are hereby made a part of this Schedule.

If "Blanket" is entered under "Description of Object", the Blanket Group Plan applies to all objects of the group described.

If Code CCE-I or CCE-II is entered under "Description of Object", then the Definition of Object, Definition of Accident and Special Provisions thereof are hereby made a part of this Schedule.

Coverage D   Bodily Injury Liability
Coverage E   Defense, Settlement, Supplementary Payments
Coverage F   Automatic Coverage

Loss to Property of Insured.   Coverage A will pay for direct loss to the boiler and machinery objects and also to all other property of the insured. The extended coverage endorsement used in property insurance excludes explosion of a steam boiler, steam piping, steam engines, or steam turbines. When a boiler or steam-type object is owned by, leased by, or operated under the control of the insured, the boiler policy is necessary to obtain this coverage for potential catastrophic steam explosions.

Coverage A has a provision to adjust losses on an actual cash value basis or an alternate method to upgrade the coverage to settle losses on a replacement cost basis.

Expediting Expense.   Coverage B agrees to pay up to $1,000 of any extra cost of speeding up permanent repairs or reasonable cost of temporary repairs after an accident. This amount can be increased for an additional premium. Increases in expediting expense limits are relatively inexpensive. Producers with clients having a large boiler and machinery exposure will find increasing the limit to $10,000 costs about an additional 3.5 percent and an additional 10 percent for $50,000 limit.

Liability for Property of Others.   Coverage C is a legal liability coverage. It will pay any sum the insured is legally obligated to pay for damages to property of others in the care, custody, or control of the insured. Boiler explosion is not excluded under the CGL; however, the CGL excludes from coverage property in the insured's care, custody, or control. The boiler policy assumes coverage for this under coverage C. This would be important for the tenant who maintains a boiler. For example, if the boiler exploded, the damage to the building would be excluded in the CGL since the building is in the care, custody, or control of the insured. The boiler policy would respond to the claim.

The "other insurance" condition, discussed later, makes coverage C excess over other valid and collectible insurance.

BODILY INJURY LIABILITY.   Coverage D provides bodily injury liability for any nonemployee injured in an accident. This agreement specifically excludes injury to employees. Bodily injury, as with property damage, is covered under the insured's CGL. *This coverage part often is automatically excluded from the policy* and only available for an additional premium. Like coverage C, if coverage applies, it is excess over other valid and collectible insurance. Also, in some policies, coverage D is *an option* under coverage C. Producers should check their insurer's forms and procedures if this coverage is desired. Bodily injury liability is inexpensive because it is excess over all other valid and collectible insurance, including the umbrella, which makes the insurer's exposure low.

Supplemental Payment. Coverage E agrees to defend any liability claim under either coverage C or D. It also covers court and appeal expenses against the insured for any legal proceedings. These costs are paid in addition to the per accident limit.

Automatic Coverage. Coverage F grants automatic coverage for any "object" similar to objects directly insured. Coverage applies for a period of ninety days. However, the insured must report the new exposure to the company within that period, and agree to pay any additional premium, and coverage is subject to three other relatively minor conditions.

Loss Settlement Procedures. The method of loss settlement under the boiler and machinery policy is unique. Payment is made on a sequential basis beginning with coverage A and continuing in order for coverages B, C, and D until the limit is exhausted. When an accident occurs, the policy limit is applied to coverage A first. If any of the limit remains, it is applied to losses under coverage B, then C, and finally D.

Assume an insured has a boiler and machinery policy with a limit of $100,000. Boiler explosion causes $75,000 property damage to the object and other property of the insured. Temporary repairs cost $1,500 and claims of $20,000 for damage to property of others in the insured's care, custody and control are presented. Several people were injured and bodily injury claims amount to $30,000. Settlement is made in the following manner.

Coverage A has first priority and is totally satisfied first. The entire $75,000 of the insured's property damage is paid to the insured. Expediting expenses of $1,500 were incurred, but the maximum limit for coverage B is $1,000 so $1,000 is paid to the insured. Property damage to property in the insured's care, custody, and control is covered (coverage C) and the $100,000 limit has not yet been exceeded so the entire amount of $20,000 is paid to claimants. Bodily injury claims amount to $30,000, but $96,000 of the policy limit has already been paid. Only $4,000 is available for coverage D claims. The insured's CGL would probably respond to these claims first and coverage D would be excess in that case. If a $100,000 loss occurred to the insured's property, that would have been paid and nothing would have been available for other claims as a result of the accident.

Exclusions The policy contains only four exclusions. The first two exclude war and nuclear related losses. These are common to most property and liability insurance policies.

The third excludes coverage for any loss necessitated by any ordinance, law, rule, regulation, or building code. If a new building code causes increased cost in the repair of the "object," the policy only pays the cost of repairing or replacing the "object" with like kind and quality. Any additional cost must be assumed by the insured. The final exclusion applies only to coverages A and B. Specific causes of loss are listed. Generally, losses intended to be covered by fire insurance are specifically excluded under the boiler and machinery policy. Flood, explosions outside the object, and indirect losses are excluded.

Conditions As in all insurance policies, the conditions section further defines the intent of the policy and spells out requirements and rights of both the insured and the insurer.

Notice and Adjustment. The notice and adjustment condition contains wording similar to other property and liability insurance policies. The insured must give notice as soon as practicable, furnishing help in investigation and adjustment, and must submit to examination and interrogation by the company. The insured must not voluntarily assume any liability or make any payment without company consent. The condition also includes a procedure for appraisal if the insured and insurer do not agree as to the amount of loss.

Inspection. The inspection condition is interesting. Boiler insurance originated as an inspection service and today is sold largely on the service feature to satisfy inspection laws. The boiler policy, however, in no way obligates the insurance company to render this service or, if the service is performed, no guarantee of safety or compliance with safety laws given.

Suspension of Coverage. If a dangerous condition is discovered on inspection, the insurance company can suspend coverage on that object by written notice to the insured. When the condition is corrected, the suspended insurance may be reinstated by endorsement and the insured will be given a pro-rata return premium for the period of suspension. The inspection and suspension of coverage conditions are unique to boiler and machinery policies.

Limit per Accident. This condition prevents the "stacking of limits" in the event that more than one object is involved in a single loss.

Property Valuation. Valuation of property is on an actual cash value basis. The policy will not pay for repairs or for replacement of parts in excess of the actual cash value of the entire object. The policy may be endorsed to value property on a replacement cost basis.

Other Insurance. There are two conditions relative to other insurance. The first is for coverage A (property insurance) and the second for coverages C and D (liability).

PROPERTY INSURANCE. The policy defines a loss where two or more policies apply as a "joint loss." The (a) provision of the "other insurance property" condition states that each applicable policy is first adjusted as if no other insurance applied. Then, each applicable policy pays in proportion to the total of all separate policies. For example, a $15,000 loss is covered by both a property policy with an extended coverage endorsement and a boiler and machinery policy. The fire policy has a $75,000 limit and the boiler policy has a $50,000 limit. In this example both the fire and the boiler policy have sufficient limits to pay the entire loss. Each would pay one-half the loss or $7,500 under the joint loss provision.

The (b) provision of this condition provides for loss adjustment proportioned to policy limits if other insurance policies do not contain a provision similar to (a). If, in the example above, the policies had different limits so the fire policy would pay

$$\$9,000\left(\frac{\$75,000}{\$125,000}\times\$15,000\right)$$

and the boiler policy would pay

$$\$6,000\left(\frac{\$50,000}{\$125,000}\times\$15,000\right)$$

if both policies did not have a provision similar to (a).

LIABILITY INSURANCE. Coverage under "liability for property of others" (coverage C) and "bodily injury liability" (coverage D) is excess over any other insurance. If the insured has a CGL, the CGL would be primary and the boiler policy would be in excess over the CGL policy limits.

Deductibles. The policy mandates a $250 deductible for coverages A, B, and C. A lower deductible may be negotiated for additional premiums.

Schedules, Definitions, and Endorsements. A condition makes provision for the attachment of necessary schedules. Without the schedules the boiler and machinery policy would be incomplete because it contains no definition of "object" or "accident." Because the definitions of "object" and "accident" are important, a discussion of them is reserved for later.

Malicious Mischief. This condition grants coverage for losses caused by vandalism and malicious mishcief, strike, riot, sabotage, and civil commotion to clarify that the war and governmental action exclusion does not delete this coverage except in time of war, insurrection, and so forth.

Blanket Group Premium. This condition describes the blanket group plan which is normally used for larger boiler and machinery exposures, but there is no restriction on size for this plan. Group descriptions are scheduled on the declarations page in place of specifically describing each object. The boiler engineer makes an annual survey of equipment. This survey is not a part of the policy but any new objects acquired during the year are charged for on basis at audit. Objects disposed of generate a pro-rata return premium in the same manner. The blanket plan makes coverage certain on all objects and eliminates the need for endorsements when an object is either added or deleted. There is no extra premium for blanket descriptions.

Earthquake. The final condition limits the insurer's loss payment in case of an accident occurring as a result of an earthquake and all after-shocks within seventy-two hours. If policy limits are less than $100,000, no coverage for earthquake is provided. If limits are greater than $100,000, the minimum earthquake limit is the greater of $100,000 or 20 percent of policy limits. The maximum earthquake limit is $2.5 million in any case. Coverage applies separately at each location.

Other Conditions. Several other conditions are common to many insurance policies and will not be explained here. The conditions relate to cancellation (a short rate table appears in the policy), subrogation, two clauses regarding actions against the insurer, assignment, and policy changes.

Checkpoints

1. List and briefly describe the six insuring agreements of the boiler and machinery policy.
2. Which of the insuring agreements may be omitted from the policy?
3. Describe the unique loss settlement priorities of the boiler and machinery policy.
4. Explain the suspension of coverage condition of the boiler and machinery policy.
5. Explain both types of "other insurance" conditions of the boiler and machinery policy.

Schedules

The purpose of the schedules is to identify and define the insured "object" and "accidents." Definitions of "object" are necessary in schedules since it would be cumbersome to have all of the types of boilers and machinery eligible for this coverage included under one definition in the policy jacket. All of the different schedules cannot be covered in this chapter, but major ones will be discussed.

Boilers The first schedule discussed is used for insuring boilers. Boilers are defined as fired vessels or electric steam generators. Boilers can be covered under either a broad form or a limited form of coverage. Each contains a different definition of "accident" to be explained later. The definition of "object" is the same under both the broad and the limited form coverages.

"Object." An "object" can either be described in the schedule or can meet one of six specific definitions contained in the policy. The definition then states that "object" does not include any part of the vessel or piping not containing water or steam or any rotating machinery or electrical apparatus. There is latitude in describing object.

Definition of Object. "Object" shall mean any complete vessel designated and described in the Schedule and shall also include

1. any condensate return tank used with such vessel,
2. any steel economizer used solely with such vessel,
3. any cushion tank or expansion tank used with any such vessel which is designated and described in the Schedule as a hot water heating boiler,
4. any indirect water heater used for hot water supply service which is directly in the water circulating system of such vessel and which does not form a part of a water storage tank.
5. any piping on the premises of the Insured, or between parts of said premises, with valves, fittings, traps and separators thereon, which contains steam or condensate thereof, generated in whole or in part in such vessel, but not including any such piping which forms a part of any other vessel or apparatus, and
6. any feed water piping between such vessel and its feed pump or injector; but

Object shall not include

a) any part of such vessel which does not contain steam or water;
b) any boiler setting;
c) any insulating or refractory material;
d) any piping which does not contain steam or condensate thereof;
e) any piping not on the premises of the Insured, used to supply any premises not owned by, leased by or operated under the control of the Insured;
f) any other piping, radiator, convector, coil, vessel or apparatus except as included in Sections 1, 2, 3, 4, 5 and 6 above;
g) any reciprocating or rotating machine; nor
h) any electrical apparatus.

"Accident." The limited form of coverage requires "a sudden and accidental *tearing asunder* of the object" (explosion) while the broad form accepts "any sudden and accidental *breakdown*" for the definition of accident.

LIMITED FORM. "Accident" is limited to a sudden and accidental tearing asunder of the object caused by the pressure of the steam or water. This definition of accident is used to insure explosion only. Normal wear and tear, cracking, leakage of a valve, or furnace explosion are excluded, as is the normal functioning of a safety device. When pressure builds to a dangerous level in a vessel, the safety valve opens, relieving the pressure and preventing an explosion. This is the intended function of the safety valve and is not considered an accident.

BROAD FORM. The broad form definition of an accident assumes more coverage, and in practice is the more commonly used. The broad form grants coverage for *any* sudden and accidental breakdown, which causes damage to the object which manifests itself at the time of its occurrence. This definition excludes the normal wear and tear and leakage of a valve or fitting. It also excludes breakdown of vacuum tubes and of data processing equipment.

Special Provisions. The required schedules and endorsements needed to complete a boiler and machinery policy contain some special provisions to clarify coverage. Since explosion of unconsumed fuel and gasses is generally covered under property lines, it is excluded in the boiler and machinery policy. Furnace explosion can be endorsed to a boiler and machinery policy for a premium.

Another special provision excludes coverage for objects when they are under tests, such as hydrostatic tests of boilers and insulation breakdown tests of electrical objects.

Unfired Vessels This schedule is used on pressure vessels not directly heated by fire or flue gas, such as, but not limited to, air and hot water tanks. Even clients without boilers per se may be prospects for this coverage if they use compressed gases in operations or even if they just have a hot water heater. The broad definition of "accident" is used in this schedule.

Refrigeration and Air Conditioning Another frequently used schedule is for refrigeration and air conditioning systems. This schedule is used for most objects that contain a refrigerant—the vessels, coils, piping, valves, and fittings through which the refrigerant is circulated. The broad definition of "accident" is used. The form also grants coverage for ammonia contamination and water damage up to a limit of $1,000. The pressure test exclusion applies to this form of coverage.

A common problem with this form of coverage is when the insured treats the policy as a form of maintenance for air conditioning equipment. The broad definition of "accident" lends itself to this possibility. The producer should be sure to check and communicate to the underwriter the normal maintenance schedule of the insured for such objects. A well-maintained system will be more acceptable to the underwriter.

Machinery and Electrical Equipment Just as boilers are subject to sudden and accidental breakdown, machinery and electrical equipment may break down also. For instance, hospitals may have emergency internal combustion engines driving electric generators to produce electricity during a power failure. This type of equipment can suffer costly mechanical breakdowns. Also, electrical switching and distribution systems are needed. Many other prospects will have similar equipment—high rise buildings have extensive electrical equipment to regulate and distribute electricity. All of these may be insured on a machinery endorsement. The objects are scheduled and accident is usually defined as in the broad form. Producers should look beyond boilers and pressure vessels for boiler and machinery exposures.

Comprehensive Coverage All possible objects of boiler and machinery may be written on a so-called comprehensive coverage endorsement. In this type of form, "object" is defined to include all of the equipment mentioned in separate endorsements. Accident is defined as in the broad form. Because of the broad definitions of "object" and "accident," the special provisions are extensive. Deductibles are used to eliminate smaller and low valued equipment.

There are three forms of coverage under the comprehensive form: (1) including production machinery, (2) excluding production machinery, and (3) public utility equipment.

Indirect Damage

The producer should recognize that indirect damage losses can be as staggering as a result of a boiler and machinery accident as they can be from a fire loss. As is the case with property insurance policies, the unendorsed boiler and machinery policy covers only direct damage losses. The boiler and machinery policy can be endorsed to include three indirect damage type coverages:

1. business interruption (use and occupancy),
2. extra expense, and
3. consequential damage. (Many boiler insurance companies will treat consequential damage as part of direct damage coverage.)

Business Interruption Business interruption or use and occupancy insurance is the most important form of indirect damage coverage. This is usually an endorsement to the direct damage boiler and machinery policy. There are several forms available and they can be tailored to meet the specific needs of the insured.

Valued Form. The business interruption valued form agrees to pay the insured a fixed amount called "daily indemnity" for each day the business cannot operate because of an "accident" to an "object" covered by the policy. The endorsement also agrees to pay a part of the "daily indemnity" for partial interruption of business. A total limit of indemnity is set in the endorsement by multiplying the "daily indemnity" by the number of days the insured believes the business may be interrupted by an accident.

The endorsement explains the loss settlement procedures and exactly how partial losses will be settled. The endorsement may either assume daily indemnity payments immediately after the accident occurs or may require a specified number of days' waiting period, which serves as a deductible on the business interruption coverage. The insured is required to use "due diligence and dispatch" to resume operations as soon as possible. Also, the daily indemnity is not paid on days the insured is not normally open for business.

Actual Loss Sustained. The actual loss sustained endorsement does not stipulate a daily indemnity like the valued form, but instead agrees to pay the actual loss, which is defined as similar to the gross earnings form in commercial property coverages. Actual loss sustained means loss of net profits, fixed charges and expenses, and expenses necessarily incurred to prevent or reduce the loss. This endorsement contains a coinsurance clause and, as with gross earnings insurance, the insured must maintain accurate records to prove a loss.

Extra Expense Extra expense can be added by endorsement to the boiler and machinery policy. It is needed by those service type businesses (such as banks, savings and loans, and newspapers) that must maintain operations in event of a boiler and machinery accident. Extra expense works like additional living expense in a homeowners policy. The extra cost of doing business at the same or a temporary location is the loss, subject to a predetermined limit and period of time.

Consequential Damage Boiler and machinery accidents can cause the loss of steam, heat, or refrigeration power which may in turn cause the loss of product, manufacturing goods in process or storage. A predetermined limit can be selected to protect the insured against consequential loss such as food stuffs in cold storage, flowers in greenhouses, and so on.

Underwriting

The underwriter needs information concerning location, age, loss history, and use of the boiler. Most of the information needed for underwriting and rating can be developed only by a qualified boiler inspector; for this reason, the underwriter needs ample time to quote a boiler account. For a quick quote, subject to a satisfactory inspection, the producer can get the necessary rating information by examining the name plate on the side of each object. The underwriter will want the name of the manufacturer and the date the object was built. A brief description of the object, stating whether the object is steel or cast iron and the diameter of the boiler, usually will be sufficient. The underwriter will also want to know how the boiler is fired, the pounds per square inch (PSI) rating, and the National Board number. This procedure can only be used on uncomplicated boiler and machinery exposures. There is much room for error unless the producer has been trained to do such inspections.

On older equipment, the underwriter may only write the limited form. On newer objects the underwriting may be willing to provide replacement cost coverage under coverage A rather than actual cash value.

Sales Tips

Unlike many of the property and liability coverages, boiler and machinery insurance has to be "sold," since most equipment seems, to the uninitiated, to be indestructible. One of the hardest jobs in selling boiler and machinery coverage is making the insured aware of the loss potential, both direct and indirect. This can be accomplished partially by the use of newspaper clippings describing explosion losses. Many examples of such losses may also be obtained from publications such as the FC&S Bulletins or from insurers.

Once the insured is convinced of the need for coverage, the producer should call a boiler inspector to help establish which objects should be covered and to make sure that the coverage will be acceptable to the insurer. Acceptability should always be established before the producer quotes or takes an order for the coverage.

Once the survey has been made and the inspector has approved the submission, the producer must then help the insured establish the policy limit per accident. If the insured has adequate limits of liability with the CGL, the only other liability concern would be for property of others in his care, custody, and control. If bodily injury liability is included, catastrophic exposures should be considered. Limits for damage to the property of the insured are established by figuring the value of the object, the building, and contents. The producer should explain to the insured the pressure vessel explosion exclusion in the extended coverage endorsement of the property coverage. The producer may discuss the business interruption coverages available under the policy so that the endorsement may be ordered at the same time.

Sometimes the boiler and machinery exposure is not immediately evident even to producers. Even on a small retail account the producer should always ask how the building is heated. Additionally, most modern buildings, including churches, shopping centers, and office buildings, have very expensive air conditioning systems. However, proceed with caution in soliciting air conditioning accounts. Many boiler underwriters feel that the use expectancy of an air conditioning compressor is only seven to eight years. Older equipment is difficult to insure.

Insurers

The producer will find that relatively few companies write boiler coverage. However, many have an agreement with a specialty boiler insurer to handle their boiler and machinery coverage for them. If the coverage is placed outside of the package policy—even if it is with a different insurance company—most boiler underwriters will allow a package discount on the boiler coverage. The producer will need to reference the package policy and request the discount.

Checkpoints

1. Explain the need for the attachment of a schedule to the boiler and machinery policy.
2. Define "object" in the boiler schedule.
3. Explain the major differences between the broad and limited definitions of "accident" in the boiler and machinery policy.
4. Describe the valued use and occupancy endorsement.
5. What precautions should the producer take in soliciting the boiler and machinery account?

CREDIT INSURANCE

Introduction

The credit system is the basis for commerce in the United States today. It is estimated that less than 5 percent of all commercial transactions are made on a cash basis. It may be expected that losses will be encountered because of the inability or refusal of some debtors to pay.

There are three noninsurance treatments for this exposure: (1) loss control, (2) retention, and (3) noninsurance transfer. The firm may elect to extend credit for only a few "select" customers (loss control). Selective credit may not be feasible; in today's economy, even "select" customers are subject to the possiblity of financial failure.

Another noninsurance treatment of this loss exposure is retention. The creditor can estimate the probable losses and add them into the cost of the goods sold. If a seller can estimate "bad debt" losses accurately from experience, this method can work. However, it can work only when the credit losses do not exceed a small percentage of total sales or the cost of the goods will be excessive and sales would suffer. "Bad debts" usually are figured into the budget and simply must be expensed as a cost of doing business.

The third technique, noninsurance transfer, is called "factoring" in this case. The creditor sells the accounts receivable to a "factor," usually a bank or specialized financial institution. The factor assumes the responsibility for collection of debts. A complete noninsurance transfer would have the factor accept the accounts receivable "without recourse" or without the originating creditor responsible for uncollectible accounts.

While noninsurance treatment of credit losses may be adequate for the normal losses expected by the firm, many businesses extending credit face the potential of tremendous and unusual losses. For these unusual losses, the creditor may purchase credit insurance. Credit insurance promises to reimburse the wholesaler, manufacturer, or jobber for the unusual losses incurred through the failure of customers to meet their credit obligations. Credit insurance is not available to retailers.

Type of Policy

Credit policies are either *general* or *specific*. The general policy covers all debtors who have prescribed credit ratings. The policy will contain a schedule of "mercantile ratings" covered (discussed below) and a maximum coverage on each class of rating. If accounts with good ratings only are to be covered, the policy is called "regular." If the business owner wants to include debtors with inferior credit ratings, the policy is known as "combination." The "combination" form will take a much higher rate than the "regular" form and coverage will be more limited as to recovery.

The specific policy covers only one or a few special customers approved by the credit insurance company and specifically named in the policy.

Policy Analysis

Exposures Covered   One form of credit insurance is written to cover all sales occurring during the policy period. This "term" policy is suitable for temporary protection and would usually be written to cover one large transaction during a given year. A second form agrees to cover defaults during the policy period. This is a "continuing" type policy and is expected to be renewed annually to cover normal credit transactions.

Mercantile Ratings   Nearly all credit insurance policies depend on a table of mercantile ratings, selected by the insured and incorporated into the policy. Most policies use the Dun & Bradstreet ratings (as shown in Exhibit 10-4). The insurance company will not cover a debtor not rated in the selected mercantile ratings. The policy will specify which ratings are covered. For example, the general policy may state that coverage will apply only to debtors with 5A and 4A ratings. If the insured extends credit to a customer who has a 3A rating, the policy will not cover that exposure. Thus, the insurer is imposing a loss control criterion on the insured, and putting the insured on notice that customers without adequate rating are to be retained by the insured. In such a situation, most creditors will adjust their credit-granting practices accordingly.

Primary or Normal Loss   The primary or normal loss is that amount usually lost because of bad debts and is set forth in the policy. The primary loss is usually stated as a percentage of annual gross receipts; it is a form of a deductible and such losses are deducted from the amount of payment for credit losses during the year.

Coinsurance   The coinsurance in the credit insurance policy is a stipulated percentage that also serves as a deductible from the total net amount of annual losses. It is not an insurance-to-value device but is the amount of loss that the insured must bear. The coinsurance provision is intended to induce the insured to be more careful in granting credit and to reinforce the normal or primary loss provision.

Loss Settlement Example.   Assume the insured had two covered losses during the policy period of $10,000 each, 10 percent coinsurance, and a normal loss of $2,500. The loss would be settled:

Net Covered Loss	$20,000
Less coinsurance	$ 2,000
	$18,000
Less Normal Loss	$ 2,500
Net Recovery	$15,500

Exhibit 10-4
Dun & Bradstreet, Inc. Key to Ratings*

Estimated Financial Strength			Composite Credit Appraisal			
			High	Good	Fair	Limited
5A	Over	$50,000,000	1	2	3	4
4A	$10,000,000 to	50,000,000	1	2	3	4
3A	1,000,000 to	10,000,000	1	2	3	4
2A	750,000 to	1,000,000	1	2	3	4
1A	500,000 to	750,000	1	2	3	4
BA	300,000 to	500,000	1	2	3	4
BB	200,000 to	300,000	1	2	3	4
CB	125,000 to	200,000	1	2	3	4
CC	75,000 to	125,000	1	2	3	4
DC	50,000 to	75,000	1	2	3	4
DD	35,000 to	50,000	1	2	3	4
EE	20,000 to	35,000	1	2	3	4
FF	10,000 to	20,000	1	2	3	4
GG	5,000 to	10,000	1	2	3	4
HH	Up to	5,000	1	2	3	4

*Reprinted with permission from Dun & Bradstreet, Inc.

Collection Service The most valuable service of the credit insurance company to the insured is the collection service. The insurer will attempt to collect past due accounts rather than pay the loss. Each policy may contain different wording regarding reporting past due amounts and collection procedures, so this section should be carefully read in each contract. This service relieves the insured of the time and expense involved in attempting to collect bad debts.

Rating and Underwriting

This is a highly specialized coverage; only a very few credit insurance companies are in existence. The producer should always contact the insurance company for their help in rating and properly underwriting the account. Coverage may vary widely.

Checkpoints

1. Name three noninsurance treatments of credit losses.
2. Explain the difference between the general form and the specific form of credit insurance.
3. Identify the types of "occurrence of loss" provisions used in credit insurance policies.

4. Define (1) coinsurance and (2) primary (normal) loss in credit insurance.

GOVERNMENT PROGRAMS

Introduction

Private insurers often are not willing to cover perils that do not meet the criteria of commercial insurability due to either the catastrophic loss potential involved or the probability of adverse selection against the company. Because of the enormous potential losses the insuring public faced from certain perils, the federal and state governments have set up programs that are administered, and in some cases subsidized, by the governmental agencies involved. These government programs play an important part in providing for the insurance needs of many insureds. The producer should be aware of how the programs are administered and how to apply for and obtain coverage.

FAIR Plans

During the late 1960s, riots and civil commotions caused severe property losses in many of the nation's larger cities. Many insurance companies began canceling, nonrenewing, or refusing to issue policies covering properties located in "riot-prone" areas of these cities. In 1968, Congress passed the Urban Property Protection and Reinsurance Act. Under this act, the Federal Insurance Administration (FIA), part of the Federal Emergency Management Agency, administers the National Insurance Development Fund, which sells riot reinsurance against catastrophe losses to private insurers.

By early 1975, twenty-six states, Puerto Rico, and the District of Columbia had FAIR (Fair Access to Insurance Requirements) plans. Under the FAIR plan, any insured is entitled to apply to an Insurance Placement Facility for property insurance. The Insurance Placement Facility is a joint reinsurance association or pool supported by all property insurers in the state who share in the FAIR plan business in proportion to their total writings in the state. When an application is rejected by the pool, the pool must file a rejection report with the federal government. The pool cannot decline to insure on the basis of neighborhood or any environmental hazard beyond the control of the insured.

Policies are either issued by a servicing insurer or the association or pool establishes a servicing agency to administer policies. Rates are usually higher than "normal" and may be surcharged for hazardous conditions existing in the property. The FAIR plans make insurance available to insureds who cannot otherwise secure insurance protection. With the sharp decrease in riots in the last ten years, FAIR plans have decreased in importance but they do still exist. Producers may contact the plans where they exist if a client has difficulty in placing a property insurance submission.

Federal Crime Insurance

During the same period, a problem of availability developed regarding crime coverages in the inner cities. Because many private insurers refused to assume these exposures, Title VI of the Housing and Urban Development Act of 1970 established the Federal Crime Insurance Program. The program is available in about twenty states and is administered by FIA through a contract with a servicing organization.

Commercial applicants can purchase robbery, burglary, or a package burglary and robbery policy. The policy can be written to cover either merchandise or money and securities. The maximum amount of coverage available is $15,000. The policy contains a deductible of 5 percent of the loss or, if greater, an amount that varies from $50 for a business with gross receipts under $25,000 to $200 if the gross receipts are $300,000 or over.

To be eligible for burglary insurance, the applicant must have its doorways and other openings adequately protected during nonbusiness hours. A prior inspection, made free of charge by the servicing agency, is necessary to establish whether the applicant qualifies.

Any producer in a state where the Federal Crime Insurance Program is in effect can secure applications from the FIA's servicing organization and will receive a commission for business produced. The program is intended to be self-supporting, but when losses are incurred above expenses, the program is subsidized by the federal government.

National Flood Insurance Program

Flood has been a universal exclusion for property insurance. Insurance companies have been reluctant to provide protection for this peril because of its catastrophic nature and the limited number of persons exposed. Even in those instances where an underwriter has agreed to provide the coverage, a high premium and deductible are demanded of the insured.

Unable to find coverage through the insurance mechanism, individuals and businesses often turned to the federal government in the wake of a flood for relief. That aid was usually in the form of low-interest disaster relief loans which did nothing to control the exposure or discourage people from settling back in the flood-prone area. Alarmed over rising flood-related disaster loans, Congress sought to remedy the situation through the National Flood Insurance Act of 1968. Initially, the flood program was designed as a partnership between the federal government and private insurers, which had committed more than $42 million in capital. The program has been solely underwritten by the federal government since 1978. Essentially, this legislation enabled insurance to be made available to residents and businesses in communities whose governing officials agreed to take steps to lessen or eliminate flood problems within their area. A subsequent amendment to the enabling law, called the Flood Disaster Protection Act of 1973, expanded the law by making flood insurance a mandatory requirement for certain loans made under certain conditions.

There are over 15,000 "flood prone communities" in the nation and most have joined the National Flood Insurance Program, enabling the purchase of more than 1.9 million flood insurance policies. A producer must be aware of flood program details. Familiarity with the National Flood Insurance Program will provide the producer with another marketing tool to use in developing total insurance protection for the client.

Underwriting Rules Flood insurance cannot be written anywhere in the country nor can coverage be placed on any type of building or contents. Flood Insurance can only be written on an *eligible building* or on *eligible contents* within an eligible building located within an *eligible community*.

Community Eligibility. Under the National Flood Insurance Program, the federal government, through the FIA, notifies those communities it deems to have a flood problem. The government expresses a willingness to assist in dealing with those flood problems should the community elect to join the National Flood Insurance Program.

Should the community join, it does so under the initial program phase called the *emergency program*. Under this emergency program, a limited amount of insurance at standard rates is available. The amount of coverage available is based on the type of building or contents (see Exhibit 10-5 under the heading of *"basic amounts."*)

While the community is eligible under the emergency program, the FIA arranges for a detailed study of the community and its flood problem. This study results in the publication of a map called a Flood Insurance Rate Map (FIRM).

The publication and acceptance of the FIRM and passage of local flood plain ordinances designed to lessen or eliminate future flooding by appropriate community officials, allows the community to be "promoted" to the second and final phase of the National Flood Insurance Program, called the *regular program*.

From an insurance standpoint, the regular program means more insurance is available. The *additional amount,* as well as the basic amount available under the emergency program, are rated on an actuarial basis (shown in Exhibit 10-5).

Building Eligibility.   Once the status of the community has been determined, attention turns to the building or contents to be insured. Under current rules of the National Flood Insurance Program, insurance can only be written on the building or the contents therein if the building is walled and roofed (although there is no requirement for a minimum number of walls), affixed to a permanent site, and principally above ground (i.e., at least 51 percent of the building's ACV is above ground). Mobile homes are also eligible for coverage, but they must meet anchoring requirements established by the FIA.

Contents Eligibility.   Most types of personal property are eligible for coverage under the National Flood Insurance Program, provided they are within a fully enclosed building or, in the case of a building with one or more open sides, sufficiently ties down at the time of a flood to prevent flotation.

Some of the items most commonly damaged by a flood are ineligible for coverage: trees, lawns, shrubs, driveways and walkways, bridges and docks, as well as any other open structures located on or over water.

The residential form also excludes business property, requiring the individual who has business property in the residence to obtain coverage through the separate general property flood insurance policy.

Waiting Period.   The general rule for the national Flood Insurance Program is that there is a five-day waiting period between the time that the individual completes the application and pays the annual or three-year premium and when the coverages go into effect. However, there are three exceptions to this five-day waiting period:

1. If coverage is desired to coincide with the acquisition of a building, it can be made effective the day of closing.
2. During a community's first thirty days of eligibility under both the emergency and regular programs, coverage can be made effective 12:01 A.M. (*local time*) the day following the date of application and premium payment.
3. Increases or additions in coverage on existing policies are effective 12:01 A.M. (*local time*) the day following the date of application and premium payment.

When discussing waiting periods and effective dates of coverage, producers should keep two points in mind: (1) the National Flood Insurance Program uses 12:01 A.M. *local time* in lieu of 12:01 A.M. *standard time*; and (2) under the regulations issued by the FIA the applicant/insured is required to make the full premium payment at the time of application.

Policy Term. The National Flood Insurance Program permits a policy to be issued on a one- or three-year prepaid basis. There is no deferred premium payment plan.

Minimum Premium. The minimum premium for either a one- or three-year policy is $50.

Important Policy Terms and Conditions The drafters of the flood insurance policy used in the National Flood Insurance Program essentially took the standard fire policy and where the word "fire" appeared, it was erased and the word "flood" was inserted.

Definition of "Flood." The policy defines "flood" as a general and temporary condition of partial or complete inundation of normally dry land areas caused by the overflow of inland or tidal waters or the rapid and unusual accumulation or runoff of surface waters from any source. The definition also includes accelerated erosion of coastal areas and mudslides which are caused by accumulations of water on or under the ground.

To better understand what is meant by "flood," the producer must be familiar with the first exclusion. Among other things, the policy will not cover flooding which is confined solely to the insured premises and those premises immediately adjacent. While this limitation of the term "general" fits nicely into an urban situation, it is usually overlooked when there is rural flooding with a considerable distance between the insured premises and those immediately adjacent.

Sewer Backup. Sewer backup is covered only when the proximate cause of the backup is a flood as defined in the policy.

Removal Provision. Like the standard fire policy, the flood insurance policy provides coverage for property moved to a temporary location. However, the coverage remains only for flood and only for forty-five days at a temporary location.

Preservation of Property Coverage. The policy will reimburse the insured for those reasonable expenses incurred when the insured takes measures to preserve and protect personal property when flooding is imminent. The flood does not have to occur, but a very real threat must be present to cause the insured to act. In addition, this coverage extention is only applicable when there is contents coverage on the policy and incurred expenses are figured as part of the total contents loss subject to any deductible.

Loss in Progress. The flood insurance policy does not cover a loss which is in progress at the time of the inception of the policy.

Replacement Cost. Under its proposed dwelling form the National Flood Insurance Program makes replacement cost available to the owners of one-to-four family dwellings, but applies two standards to determine the amount of insurance needed to qualify.

1. *Principal residence* (insured lives in the dwelling at least 80 percent of the time): building loss is adjusted on a replacement costs basis, subject to policy limits, *without* regard to an insurance-to-value requirement.
2. *Nonprincipal residence* (insured lives in the dwelling *less* than 80 percent of the time): insured must carry the maximum amount of flood insurance available or 80 percent of the building's replacement cost at the time of a loss if the loss is to be adjusted on a replacement cost basis subject to policy limits. If the insured does not carry 80 percent insurance to value, the loss is adjusted in a manner similar to the replacement cost provisions of a homeowners policy.

Under the National Flood Insurance Program mobile homes can be insured on a replacement cost basis in the same manner.

Any other building and all contents losses, whether personal or business property, are adjusted on an actual cash value basis.

Other Insurance Clause. There is no coinsurance in the National Flood Insurance Program. There is, however, an other insurance clause which works like coinsurance if (1) the insured does not carry the maximum amount of flood insurance available through the program at the time of loss, and (2) there is other flood insurance on the property. For example, a client obtains a difference in conditions (DIC) policy to provide flood coverage in the amount of $1.5 million. The underwriter agrees to write the coverage with a $25,000 deductible on flood. To cover this deductible, the client selects the National Flood Insurance Program for $25,000 (subject to a proposed $250 NFIP deductible). The community in which the property is located is eligible under the emergency program, which means that up to $100,000 coverage could have been purchased. A $15,000 flood loss occurs. The DIC policy would not respond because the loss is within the deductible. The National Flood Insurance Program would apply a formula based on its other insurance clause:

$$\left(\frac{\text{Amount of NFIP coverage held}}{\begin{array}{c} \text{Total amount of} \\ \text{flood insurance} \end{array} - \begin{array}{c} \text{Excess insurance} \\ \text{maximum available} \\ \text{NFIP coverage} \end{array}} \times \text{Loss} \right)$$

$$- \text{Deductible} = \text{NFIP payment}$$

In the example outlined, NFIP would pay:

$$\left(\frac{25,000}{1,525,000 - 1,425,000} \times 15,000 \right) - 250 = \$3,500$$

In this example the insured would collect only $3,500 on a $15,000 loss from the national flood insurance policy and may look to the producer for the remainder because the insured thought full coverage up to $1,525,000 (with only a $250 deductible) was in effect.

Deductible. The national flood insurance policy has a mandatory deductible applicable to both building and contents but uses two standards to determine how that deductible should be applied:

1. nonresidential buildings and contents and residential buildings with five or more dwelling units
   - $250—building
   - $250—contents (nonresidential only)
2. one-to-four family residential buildings and all residential contents disappearing deductible: if the amount of loss is less than $2,500, the policy pays 111 percent × (loss − $250); if the loss is in excess of $2,500, no deductible applies. The disappearing deductible is applied separately to each building and its contents.

Cancellation/Reduction of Insurance Clause. The insured may cancel or reduce coverage at any time during the policy term but the premium is considered *fully earned* so long as the insured retains an interest in the property covered at the location described on the declarations page. Since the insured is required to make the full payment at the time of application, the producer cannot use nonpayment as a reason for cancellation and expect to get a refund back from the National Flood Insurance Program in those cases where the producer advanced the premium. Cancellation for nonpayment does apply in the case where the producer received a bad check from the insured.

Other Policy Conditions.   The list of other policy conditions is extensive and tracks with the standard fire policy.

Marketing Set-Up and Other Considerations   The FIA has contracted with a private computer firm to service the National Flood Insurance Program from a central location in Bethesda, Maryland, but it relies on producers to market the program. Producers can write the National Flood Insurance Program, P.O. 34294, Bethesda, Maryland, or call 1-800-638-6620 to obtain information on community eligibility, order manuals, forms, and specially designed advertising materials available at little or no cost.

Adjusting Flood Losses.   In addition to marketing the program, producers are also responsible for handling the initial reporting and assigning of losses to qualified flood adjusters. A qualified flood adjuster is one who has (1) prior flood adjusting experience, *or* (2) two years of wind and water adjusting experience, *or* (3) five years of general property adjusting experience, and, in all cases, (4) the competency to execute own small property damage estimates (up to $3,000) without resorting to a separate appraiser for such work.

On those occasions where there is serious flooding, the National Flood Insurance Program may elect to set up an on-site adjusting office. In those cases the producer would receive the notice of loss from the insured and send the notice to the NFIP storm office for the actual assigning of the adjustment.

Marketing Tips.   For many producers the National Flood Insurance Program can represent a new marketing tool that can lead to other sales. However, producers have been successfully sued by clients for failing to advise properly on flood insurance. Thus, a producer should consider implementing some or all of the following to serve client insurance needs and protect against an errors and omission claim:

- Include "stuffers," available at little or no charge from the National Flood Insurance Program, in routine mailings
- Include mention of flood insurance in advertising (e.g., Yellow Pages ad)
- Review flood files in a manner similar to other insurance lines
- When developing a proposal for a client, include a quote on flood insurance.

Mandatory Purchase Requirement.   When Congress passed the Flood Disaster Protection Act of 1973, it decreed that any loan secured by real property located in an area identified as flood-prone and within a community participating in the National Flood Insurance Program must be covered by flood insurance. While the law brings almost every type of secured loan under this heading, the most common is a

Exhibit 10-5
Limits of Insurance for National Flood Insurance Program

	Basic Amount	+ Additional Amount (1)	= Total Coverage
Building			
Single family	$ 35,000	$150,000	$185,000
All other residential	100,000	150,000	250,000
Small business (2)	100,000	150,000	250,000
All other structures	100,000	100,000	200,000
Contents (Per Unit)			
Single family	10,000	50,000	60,000
All other residential	10,000	50,000	60,000
Small business (2)	100,000	200,000	300,000
All other structures	100,000	100,000	200,000

(1) *Additional amounts* of coverage are available only in those communities eligible under the regular program

(2) "Small Business" for the purpose of the National Flood Insurance Program describes any concern having (with its affiliates) assets not in excess of $5,000,000, net worth not in excess of $2,500,000 and an average net income, after Federal income taxes, for the preceding two years not in excess of $250,000 (computed without carryover loss).

Remember that the above amounts of coverage are set by law; rates are set by Federal Insurance Administration.

mortgage secured at the sale of a building. The lending institution will normally require the bare minimum of flood coverage for the loan and then only on the building.

For the producer this represents a unique opportunity. The producer should encourage the client to protect more than the lender's investment with higher limits on contents. While the flood insurance policy does not automatically provide contents coverage, the most severe loss exposure to flood is not to the building but to the personal property within.

Windstorm and Hail Pools

Introduction The coastal portions of southern states along the Gulf of Mexico and the Atlantic Ocean are subject to extensive hurricane damage, and insurers exclude the perils of windstorm and hail from their standard property policies. In seven of these states, wind and hail pools have been formed by statutes of the individual state legislatures to provide windstorm coverages for property located in coastal areas. Participation is mandatory for each insurance company writing property and liability insurance in the state, with each insurer sharing the losses according to its volume of business written in the state. Following is a discussion of a typical windstorm pool policy. Each state's plan differs slightly, so the policy must be analyzed carefully by the producer.

Typical Program The South Carolina Windstorm and Hail Underwriting Association program is administered by an underwriting committee appointed by the participating insurance companies. Each producer in the state may submit applications to the association and receive a 10 percent commission for policies issued. Eighty percent coinsurance is required on each submission and the underwriting committee will not accept an applicant who is obviously underinsured.

Eligibility. All buildings and/or contents located in the coastal zone are eligible for wind and hail coverage. Most states recognize as the coastal zone that which is identified in the extended coverage section of the Commercial Lines Manual as Zone 3. Farm property and automobiles are not eligible for coverage. Also excluded from coverage are any properties located over water.

Policy Handling. The producer has no binding authority on wind pool business. Coverage is effective twenty-four hours after payment is received at the servicing office. The application asks for the usual information relating to the structure whether residential or business.

The application must be accompanied by a photograph of the front and rear of the building. Renewal is not automatic, and a new application must be submitted each year. The underwriting manager can either accept or reject the application. If a hurricane is in progress, each state has exact latitudinal coordinates designated as "cut off" limits for accepting new applications. Once the hurricane has reached the designated coordinates no applications will be accepted for coverage until after the storm has passed.

Maximum Limits of Coverage. As with the federal flood program there are maximum amounts of coverage available under the pool. The maximum amount on dwelling properties is $500,000 per building including contents, and the limit for commercial property is $1 million on building and contents. If coverage is desired above these limits, the producer must either seek excess windstorm coverage or secure the coverage through a difference in conditions contract.

Deductibles The windstorm coverages are subject to deductibles. The mandatory deductible is 1 percent of the actual cash value of the property at the time of loss but not less than $250 nor more than $25,000. For a premium credit, the insured may select a 2 percent deductible with an amount not less than $500 nor more than $50,000.

The percentage applies to the actual cash value at the time of loss and not the amount of insurance.

Checkpoints

1. Where may flood or windstorm coverage be written?
2. Define "flood" as covered by the flood policy.
3. What property may be covered by the flood policy? the windstorm policy?
4. List the property not covered by (a) the flood policy and (b) the windstorm policy.
5. What deductibles apply to flood policies? to windstorm policies?
6. Explain the maximum amounts of coverage available under the flood program and under the windstorm program.

BUSINESS LIFE INSURANCE

Introduction

Protecting the assets of a firm involves not only providing coverage for premises, equipment, and so on, but also for the lives of people who work there. Producers with files on commercial establishments have an advantage over the full-time life insurance producers in that almost all financial information necessary to write business life insurance is on hand. Further, the commercial client has shown trust in the producer's judgment by placing the firm's property-liability insurance with the producer. Life insurance is a logical part of total account selling.

This portion of the chapter will discuss business continuation problems of the sole proprietor, partners, and owners of closely held corporations (the "close corporation"), with special emphasis on sales opportunities with professional corporations. Use of life insurance as a selective fringe benefit for key personnel and general employee benefits also will be discussed.

Why Sell Business Life? Business life insurance is good business for the producer. Life insurance sold to business firms tends to have a lower lapse ratio (it "stays on the books longer") and higher premiums due to the age of insureds and the higher face amount purchased. Higher premiums generate higher commissions.

There is one additional advantage to selling commercial life insurance—generally the property and liability producer does not have to be an expert to be involved in the sale. Many organizations have "life producers" who only need a prospect. Many life insurance affiliates have field representatives who are happy to accompany the producer and help with the technical aspects of the sale.

Importance of Tax Expertise If there is one area in business life insurance that demands special attention, it is the myriad of tax laws affecting the business life insurance purchase. For that reason, the organization's attorney and accountant should be involved in any business life insurance purchases. Contracts sometimes must be written and accounting assistance may be needed to measure the impact of a life insurance purchase decision on the business and personal lives of those involved. If a qualified life insurance producer handles life insurance for the agency, he or she will know of expert attorneys and accountants who can help. A life insurance company field representative may ask the producer for names of tax professionals in an area. It is a good idea for a producer to become acquainted with tax attorneys and accountants who can be called in to help in a sales situation.

Taxation and Business Life Insurance

Plans for the continuation of business or special benefits for selected employees can have tax effects on the business and the individuals involved. In some cases, different tax laws, rules, and regulations may conflict. This is especially true with business life insurance because at least three sets of tax law may be involved: (1) federal income tax laws and regulations; (2) laws that affect the distribution of personal assets prior to death—federal gift tax laws and regulations; and (3) laws of the federal and state governments relative to taxes on distribution of estates—estate and inheritance laws. It is important to keep these three sets of laws in mind; any one set or combination of laws may affect a decision. For instance, one general federal *income* tax concept is that premiums on life insurance are *not* deductible for federal income tax purposes. The nondeductibility is seen as a negative by some producers; yet because premiums are nondeductible, the proceeds at death are not subject to the federal income tax—a potentially positive benefit.

Another example, illustrating multiple impact of tax laws, is a corporation's purchasing life insurance on a key officer-stockholder. Presumably, the corporation purchases the life insurance to offset corporate income losses at the officer's death. While the officer lives, premiums are not income tax deductible for the corporation. At the officer's death, the proceeds are not income taxable to the corporation, but the *value* of the corporation has increased. The value of the officer's share of the corporation has also increased and therefore the value of the officer's estate has increased. As federal estate taxes are graduated, increasing tax rates on larger values, the officer's estate now has an increased need for liquidity. The increased need for liquidity, cash, or its equivalents, is felt in two areas by the estate. First, the estate will have to pay federal *income* tax on the appreciation in value of the shares owned (capital gains). Part of the capital gain comes from the death proceeds paid to the corporation. Second, the deceased stockholder-officer's estate has an asset, the stock, with a higher value, increasing the federal *estate* tax payable. The purchase of life insurance may have been a good financial decision for the corporation, but it may have adverse effects on the individual and the individual's estate.

Business Continuation Life Insurance

There are three major opportunities for business continuation life insurance sales and one special case based on the legal form of the enterprise. The organizational forms of business addressed in this section are sole proprietorships, partnerships, and close corporations. The special case is a professional corporation or a corporation that generates the majority of its income from the owner's professional services rather than manufacturing or retailing. A professional corporation may be a group of physicians, accountants, attorneys, architects, insurance producers, or other groups offering specialized professional services.

Sole Proprietorship The sole proprietorship is the easiest business to organize. Someone decides to go into business and sets up shop. Often, no legal documents are filed. From a practical and tax standpoint, the assets of the business are also personal assets of the owner—at the owner's death, the business assets become part of the owner's estate. The estate normally must pay all federal estate taxes in cash within nine months of death. The Internal Revenue Service does not accept merchandise or furniture and fixtures in payment. The ideal situation for a sole proprietor is to have someone waiting with cash to buy the business as a going concern at the owner's death or permanent disability. The purchaser could be a son or daughter, key employee, competitor, or other interested party. If there are no interested buyers, the executor of the estate, the individual or organization charged with settling and distributing the estate, must sell the business's assets. As with most sales of inventory, fixtures, and other business assets that must take place within a short period of time (nine months in this case) the amount received from the sale generally is between 25 and 50 percent of the true value of the items sold. This has a dual effect on the estate. First, the value of the business may be high based on its previous income-producing capacity. Second, the cash actually received for the sale of the business is far less than the going concern value. Therefore, the estate pays taxes on an inflated amount and may have insufficient cash to cover the estate tax. The survivors can be hurt, too, if they have relied on the business for their livelihood. After the owner's death, they have no income.

A purchaser is needed who will buy at death and/or the estate needs liquidity to meet the estate taxes and provide the surving heirs with a reasonable level of income.

Sale of a Sole Proprietorship at Death. The ideal situation is for a businessowner to have pre-arranged the sale of the business *automatically* at death to someone with the interest and ability to operate the business. The business is continued and the estate is compensated with cash.

Assuming there is someone with the willingness to buy, the funds can be provided with life insurance on the sole proprietor's life payable to the buyer. In this way purchase of life insurance on the sole proprietor's life makes certain that funds are available for the purchase. *A buy-sell agreement* between the purchaser and owner legally binds the purchaser to buy the business.

Buy-Sell Agreements. When the sole proprietor has a viable purchaser, the buy-sell agreement is vital. The essence of the agreement is a legal and binding commitment on the part of the businessowner that *requires* the estate to sell the business to the person stated in the agreement. The purchaser is also bound to purchase the business at a fixed or determinable price. Life insurance owned by the purchaser on the life of the seller provides most or all of the funds to effect the purchase. A competent attorney should draw such an agreement.

BENEFITS. The properly drawn buy-sell agreement has advantages for the purchaser, the seller, and the heirs of the seller. From the purchaser's standpoint, the business future is assured. The purchaser knows what business he or she will be in and presumably is aware of key customers and operating practices. The estate receives payment in cash at once, helping with estate liquidity. This means the estate can be settled quickly and efficiently. Heirs who are not purchasers are relieved of business conerns and, because the value of the business has been pre-established, receive the true value of the business.

The proprietor benefits from knowing that customers will continue to be served after the proprietor's death. The purchaser is building a semi-compulsory account to buy the business; that is, the proprietor knows the money will be available at death. If an employee is the purchaser, the proprietor has a more interested employee when the employee knows the business ultimately will be his or hers.

ELEMENTS. The buy-sell agreement should not only bring about the sale of the business but also protect the interests of both parties prior to the owner's death. In that regard, a number of elements should be in every agreement:

- what assets and liabilities are being sold from the business;
- prior to death, if the business is to be sold, the owner must offer the business for sale first to the other party to the agreement;
- a binding commitment of the owner's estate to sell and the purchaser to buy at the owner's death;
- a purchase price stated or a method to determine the price;
- an agreement to fund the purchase price with life insurance;
- provisions relative to disposal of life insurance if the agreement is terminated before death;
- a provision describing how additional payments will be made if life insurance is inadequate;
- a hold harmless agreement relieving the owner's estate of purchaser-assumed liabilities after the sale;
- a power of attorney allowing the purchaser to continue the business until title transfers; and
- provisions relating to amending or ending the agreement.

Two of these need additional comment. For more complete information, producers are referred to the life insurance companies as they have complete descriptions of possible agreement contents, as well as advantages and disadvantages to each alternative.

One vital area is the price to be paid. Establishing a set price in the buy-sell agreement allows coordination with life insurance face amounts. But such prices may need to be periodically updated. If a formula is used to establish the price at death, the formula must be set with an eye toward keeping the agreement "at arm's length." A formula that grossly understates the true value may destroy an attempt to use the sale price as the value of the business for estate tax purposes.

No matter how well written, any buy-sell agreement is only as good as its funding source. If the purchaser must rely on future income, for example, to make payments, the purchaser's ability to use business earnings for growth can be impaired. If the purchaser fails in the business, the estate and heirs may not receive the money they expect.

Life Insurance Without a Purchaser. Life insurance on the sole proprietor's life is still essential even if the proprietor plans to have the business liquidated after death. The business may still be valued "high" by the Internal Revenue Service and the sale of the business assets may account for less cash than the IRS established value. The business may well represent the greatest portion of the owner's estate, and a quick sale may not be possible. Cash must be in the estate to pay death taxes. Finally, without the business producing an income for the heirs, cash may be needed for normal living expenses while and after the business is sold.

Partnership There are far more sole proprietorships in existence than partnerships or corporations. The opportunities for selling sole proprietors life insurance are many. Life insurance companies will provide producers with volumes of sales materials including direct mail campaigns, envelope stuffers, and so on.

Before beginning the discussion of partnership business continuation insurance, some of the legal aspects of this form of business should be explained.

Partnership Law. A partnership is a *voluntary* association of individuals to carry on a business. Voluntary is the key word—no one may force another into a partnership. The second important legal consideration is the role of surviving partners at the death of one partner. When one partner dies, the remaining partners are called "liquidating partners" because at law, a partnership is automatically dissolved at the death of one partner. There is no choice. The surviving partners cannot take on new business on behalf of the firm. They must finish work-in-progress, generate an accounting, sell assets, and distribute the assets to the surviving partners and the estate of the deceased partner.

Liquidation Alternatives. One extreme alternative is as described—sell everything and distribute the assets. A second alternative is to form a new partnership with the surviving partners and the heirs of the deceased. A third is to accept as a partner a third party who would buy the deceased partner's interest in the firm from the deceased's estate. The fourth and final alternative is to reorganize after death with only the surviving partners as the new partners.

Since a partnership is a voluntary association, alternatives two and three cannot be required—only the first alternative can be required by partnership law. But forcing a liquidation involves the forced sale of assets that usually bring less than full value at sale. It would be to the best advantage of all for the surviving partners to liquidate the firm by buying out the deceased partner's interest from the estate and form a new partnership with the surviving partners (alternative four). To do so requires advance planning and, again, a buy-sell agreement.

Partnership Buy-Sell Agreement. The partnership buy-sell agreement has the same elements as the sole proprietorship. Each item mentioned in the earlier section should be included in the partnership buy-sell. However, there are two different approaches to funding a buy-sell agreement with a partnership. The buy-sell may be on a *cross-purchase* or *entity* basis.

CROSS PURCHASE AGREEMENT. The essence of a cross purchase agreement is that the partners individually agree to buy from a deceased partner's estate and the partners agree the estate of any partner who dies will sell its partnership interest *before* any one partner dies. Each partner would then buy life insurance on the other partners' lives to the extent of their share of the other partners' interest. For instance, Exhibit 10-6 shows a partnership made up of Partners H, J, and K. The value of the firm is $300,000 with each partner owning one-third of the partnership. Under the cross purchase agreement, each partner purchases $50,000 on the others' lives. At *J*'s death, in this case, both *H* and *K* use their $50,000 of proceeds to purchase one-half of *J*'s interest in the firm. *H* and *K* then form a new partnership, HK and Associates, still with a value of $300,000, but with a one-half interest in the firm by *H* and *K* (see Exhibit 10-7). They can continue the business while *J*'s family has immediate cash for estate taxes.

Also shown in Exhibit 10-7 is the need to purchase additional insurance in the amount of up to $100,000 each on *H*'s life and *K*'s life by each other. (It is possible to purchase *J*'s policies on *H* and *K* for part of the additional insurance if the buy-sell agreement dictates and law allows.)

ENTITY AGREEMENT. As Exhibit 10-8 shows, under the entity agreement, *the firm* purchases $100,000 each on *H*, *J*, and *K*. At *J*'s death (Exhibit 10-9) the firm uses the proceeds to purchase *J*'s interest and then has an additional need for $50,000 each on *H*'s interest and *K*'s interest.

ENTITY VERSUS CROSS PURCHASE METHODS. The detailed advantages of either method are left for further study and consultation with a prospect's attorney and accountant. Under each, the surviving partners are assured the business can continue without liquidation. The deceased's estate is compensated for the partnership interest. The heirs receive full value for the deceased's business interest and cash to help with estate settlement. Two differences between the methods are that the entity approach requires fewer policies and the transfer of the deceased's policies on the survivors' lives is not necessary. Under either plan, the amounts of life insurance sold will be the same.

Exhibit 10-6
Cross Purchase Agreement—HJK and Associates, a Partnership

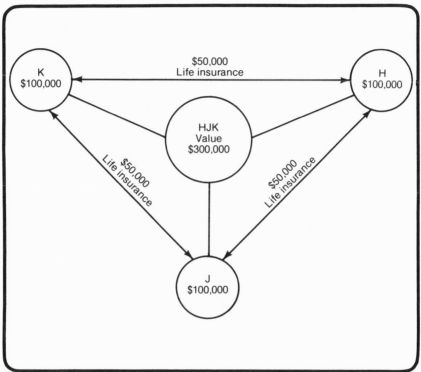

Close Corporation A corporation is legally "a person." When one owner or stockholder dies, the corporation continues, but the other owners may prefer to buy out the deceased stockholder's interest.

In a close corporation the shareholders typically are also key employees and officers of the company. They are making contributions to the success of the firm. The stockholder-employee's family have come to look on the company as the source of their income. But in close corporations, dividends are rarely paid; the employee-stockholders take salary instead. With the income of the deceased cut off, the survivors may look to the stock for income, but the surviving owners may desire to plow earnings back into the firm and not pay dividends. A conflict among the shareholders may result. If the deceased owned controlling interest, the heirs, who inherit the controlling interest, can vote to force the corporation to pay dividends and thus possibly frustrate the business operations of the firm. If the deceased was a minority owner, the heirs will have to rely on the goodwill of the surviving stockholders

Exhibit 10-7
Cross Purchase—HK and Associates After J's Death

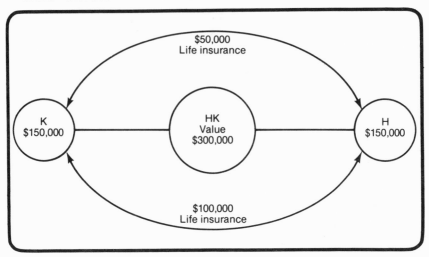

for any income. If the deceased owned a one-half interest, neither side has control and the firm may have to be dissolved.

To avoid this situation, owners of the close corporation can execute a buy-sell agreement similar to that discussed for partnerships. The heirs are relieved of an investment they may not know anything about, they get immediate cash to settle the estate, and they are paid an assured amount for the stock. The surviving owners control their own business without frustration, impasse, or raiding of income or capital. They have their own business futures assured.

The producer with agency files on close corporations can draft proposals for buy-sell agreements without much additional information. Again, the life producer in the office or the life insurance company field representative can assist in the proposal and the sale.

Professional Corporations The major difference between a professional and a commercial corporation is that the professional corporation relies on the services of its owners to generate income rather than on processing, manufacturing, or retailing. The assets of the professional corporation are relatively small in value compared to the income produced. A buy-sell agreement among the owners would generate relatively small values for the estate; yet there may be great "goodwill" values not addressed in the buy-sell agreement. It would be fair to the heirs to provide some money for the goodwill portion of the professional corporation.

Exhibit 10-8
Entity Agreement—HJK and Associates

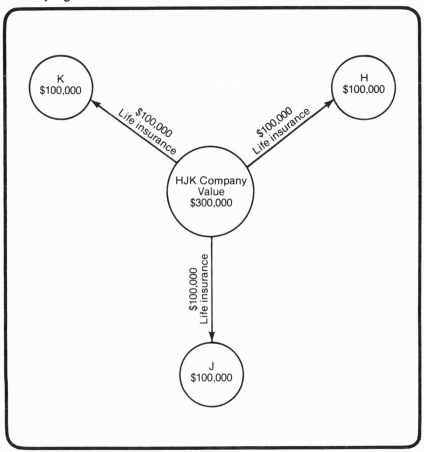

Example of a Professional Corporation Buy-Sell Agreement. Physicians M and D each have a 50 percent interest in a professional corporation that generates $200,000 in profits and cannot expand. Both doctors have as many patients as they can handle. The office and medical equipment in their leased office cost about $50,000. If Dr. M dies, many of her patients would stay with Dr. D (the goodwill); yet a normal buy-sell agreement would only compensate Dr. M's estate for the one-half interest in the corporation or $25,000. Dr. D would end up with all of the patients for only a $25,000 payment.

To solve a number of problems, Drs. M and D enter into a buy-sell agreement on the *entity* method to sell their interests at death to the corporation. They also enter into an agreement with the corporation to

Exhibit 10-9
Entity Purchase—HK and Associates After J's Death

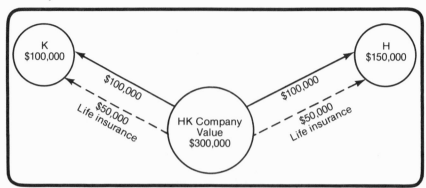

continue income to the heirs for a three-year period—paying 75 percent of normal income the first year, 50 percent the second, and 25 percent the third year. In this way, not only are the assets transferred, but also the heirs are partially compensated for goodwill in the professional corporation.

Using the entity approach gives the professional corporation the death benefits free of federal income taxes. A properly drawn income continuation agreement will make the payments for three years federal income tax deductible to the firm. If the amount of life insurance purchased on each physician's life is sufficient, the professional corporation can also use some of the proceeds to stabilize the firm's income while the surviving doctor searches for a new partner to take over the deceased's practice.

The buy-out of the deceased's interest is vital to the firm in any event. Another aspect of a professional corporation is that the owners *must* be members of the profession. For example, a nonphysician cannot be a stockholder in a medical professional corporation.

By selling a buy-sell agreement funded with life insurance, the producer is doing a real service for the professional corporation. In addition, by adding the income continuation agreement, again funded with life insurance, the producer is doing the heirs a service and earning commissions on high quality life insurance business.

Special Uses of Business Life Insurance

As noted earlier, the human as well as the physical assets of a business can benefit from business life insurance coverage. Many businesses would suffer substantial losses if one or more of their key employees died or became disabled. This exposure to loss can be minimized by the purchase of *key employee life insurance.*

Key Employee Life Insurance A key employee is an employee whose loss to a firm through death or disability before retirement would result in a loss of profits, a decreased credit rating, or the expense of recruiting and hiring a replacement, or a combination of these economic effects. Property-liability producers, with their files on business clients, are in a position to spot clients that need to insure their key personnel.

The definition of a key employee gives clues as to the types of firms that need the coverage. Usually there will be (1) a small group of men and women within the company doing the work of many, (2) with no sufficient backup for key personnel, and (3) working in a close corporation or a small publicly held company. Additionally, there may be a lack of corporate liquidity, making financial emergencies a particular hardship. Finally, the firm usually must obtain the cosignature of key personnel for its business loans.

The death of one or more of the key personnel would possibly result in a period of uncertainty until new people can be recruited, hired, and trained. Without adequate working capital, the company will have trouble finding and hiring such a person. Certainly if the deceased personally guaranteed a loan, had been a co-signer, future business loans may be hard to secure.

Life insurance on such key personnel would provide the company with adequate capital to replace the deceased, increase working capital, and provide some degree of financial solidity.

The amount of life insurance can be determined from an adaptation of the Human Life Value (HLV) approach (PRO 81, Chapter 7) or by use of another formula. An alternative formula to HLV is to determine how much each key person contributes to annual gross income, subtract the amount that would be paid to a replacement for the deceased's purely administrative duties, and multiply the remainder by the number of years it would take the replacement to become as productive as the key person. There are other variations of this formula.

The company, as employer, is the owner and beneficiary of the policy. Premiums are not income tax deductible, but neither are the proceeds paid to the company taxable at the key employee's death.

Business Life Insurance for Key Employees Another use of life insurance is to provide extra benefits for key employees to help them with their personal estates.

Deferred Compensation. A highly paid key employee may be interested in deferring some portion of income to retirement, when the employee may be in a lower tax bracket. Such an agreement may require the employer to build a fund to pay the extra retirement benefits at death (funded) or may allow the employer to pay the deferred benefit from its earnings at retirement (unfunded). There are intricate tax implications with these plans, and a document or contract has to be drawn. Professional advice from attorneys and accountants is necessary.

Basically the contract tells the key employee that due to his or her importance to the firm, extra moneys will be made available at retirement and perhaps some extra death benefits payable to the employee's spouse if death occurs prior to retirement. In exchange for this deferred compensation, the employee will work for the firm until retirement. If the employee leaves prior to retirement, some or all of the deferred benefits may be forfeited.

If the plan is funded and contains some life insurance benefits for the employee's heirs, life insurance is one obvious choice as the funding vehicle.

Deferred compensation is also an idea for an organization to pursue with any independent contractors it uses. The firm's attorney, accountant or other professional may be interested in deferring some income on a prearranged basis. The procedures and tax implications for independent contractors are different than for employees. Producers should be sure to check with tax and legal professionals when selling this type of plan.

Split Dollar Plans. A split dollar life insurance plan gives a key employee the financial ability to purchase additional life insurance by using the company's funds.

BASIC SPLIT DOLLAR PLAN. Usually the employer is the owner and a partial beneficiary under a split dollar plan. The insured employee's heirs are beneficiaries, too. The plan contemplates that the employer will pay that portion of the premium equal to the cash value increase in any year. The employee pays the balance. Corporate contributions are returned to the firm at the employee's death by deducting the amount of premiums paid by the employer from the amount otherwise payable. The employee's beneficiaries receive the balance of the death benefit.

There are two problems with the basic plan. First, as most life insurance has no or small cash values in the early years, the employee pays most of the premium at the beginning. In later years, the employee's premiums become smaller. Second, the death benefit payable to the employee's beneficiary decreases each year as the cash value and amount of employer contribution increases.

ALTERNATE SPLIT DOLLAR PLANS. Almost all life insurance companies have plans to overcome either or both of these deficiencies. For instance, the employer could waive all premium payment by the employee, or level an assumed twenty year total of the employer's payment over twenty years. For instance, if the employer anticipates paying $10,000 toward the plan over twenty years, each year the employer would pay $500 of the premium no matter what the cash value increase that year. Thus the employee pays the premium less $500 each year.

Secondly, the life insurer may offer a dividend option whereby the dividend is used to purchase additional life insurance to increase the employee's beneficiary's death benefit. With a life insurer who does not pay dividends, an increasing term life insurance option that increases by the increase in the cash surrender value can be added to level the employee's beneficiaries' death benefits.

As with all special employee benefit plans, the split dollar plan has income and estate tax implications that require consultation with tax experts. The producer will have access to the employer's accountants and attorneys as well as the life insurance field representative of the life insurer. Many life companies have attractive computer-issued proposals for split dollar presentations.

General Employee Benefits

Split dollar and deferred compensation plans are generally known as *nonqualified* employee benefit plans. They are called nonqualified plans because they receive special income tax considerations. But, benefit plans including all employees are generally "qualified." That is, they fit Internal Revenue Service rules which permit employer contributions to the plans to become deductible expenses for the firm and such expenses are not taxable income to the employees.

The market for such plans is broad and potentially profitable. No detailed discussion of group insurance or the implications and requirements of the many plans that could qualify for the IRS can be undertaken here. A few plans will be outlined in the remaining paragraphs. Producers should check with their life insurance companies to see what production assistance the producer can expect from the life insurer.

Group Life and Health Insurance In a group plan, the individual is usually acceptable to the insurer with a minimum of underwriting. The life insurer will underwrite the group rather than the individual. That means that sales to individuals are not necessary, but the covered employees as a group must meet certain underwriting standards.

The employer may pay all, part, or none of the premiums on behalf of employees. If the employer pays all, the plan is called "noncontributory" and all eligible employees must participate. If the employer and employees share the premium, the plan is "contributory" and a certain high percentage (around 75 percent) of the employees must participate. If the employer only makes the plan available but does not participate in the cost of the plan, it is probably a "franchise" insurance plan and not true group insurance.

Under group plans, employees usually do not have a say in benefit levels. Benefits are either uniform or predetermined by salary, position, seniority, or a combination of these. The employer usually does some of the administrative work for the insurer and the insurer usually operates such plans on a "cost plus" basis. Many of these plans are competitive as life insurers have qualified sales and service staffs to help the producer with an account.

Disability Income   Disability income plans are designed to fit into a particular employer's salary continuation or sick leave plans. Disability income plans may be for short or long-term disabilities.

One valuable use of disability income is to fund a "disability buy out" in conjunction with a buy-sell agreement. In many cases, a partner or stockholder in a close corporation can represent a considerable drain on the firm if he or she is totally and permanently disabled, but still receiving a salary. Disability income insurance, in conjunction with a buy-out agreement, can provide the firm with the funds to buy out the disabled owner prior to death. Life insurers offering such plans can provide producers with sales material for disability buy outs.

Sole proprietors are prospects for disability income insurance for their individual needs as well as so-called "business overhead" plans. In the latter case, when a sole proprietor is disabled, the disability income policy provides funds to pay on-going expenses of the business that may otherwise close down the business.

Group Travel Accident   Group travel accident insurance may be added to another group plan or sold separately. While these plans do not generate the premium volume that group health or life insurance generate, they can be a way for the producer to "get a foot in the door."

Pension and Profit Sharing Plans   There is room for the property-liability producer in pension and profit sharing plans. A great many small firms have or want pension and profit sharing plans but do not want to take the time and energy to qualify as a plan administrator under ERISA (Employee Retirement Income Security Act of 1974) rules of the federal government. Use of life insurer prototype plans and the life insurers' insurance and investment abilities will allow an employer to offer such a plan to its employees without large administrative expense.

Because of the complications of ERISA and the implications of federal income taxes, producers should work carefully with life field representatives and the employer's attorney and accountant.

Individual Pension Plans There are two such plans currently available, called the HR 10, or Keogh Plan, and Individual Retirement Account, or IRA. These plans allow self-employed, Subchapter S shareholder-employees, and those not covered by another qualified plan, to place a certain amount of money aside for retirement on a tax-deferred basis.

Life insurance companies have many prototype plans, specimen plan documents, and attractive brochures available to help producers sell this type of business. There are federal income and estate tax implications including rules relative to the maximum amounts that can be contributed to receive income tax benefits and penalties for early (pre-retirement) withdrawals. These tax laws are not as complicated as for qualified pension plans, so many property-liability producers find HR 10 and IRA plans easy to sell.

One way to make a proposal occurs when a producer has the opportunity to audit a particular property or liability coverage for final premium determination at or near the end of a client's fiscal year. The producer will then have access to financial information of the firm. Proposals could be made based on the firm's profits or other eligible criteria. The property-liability producer, who has periodic access to a client's financial information, is in a favorable position to handle this kind of business.

Checkpoints

1. How can business life insurance help with the business continuation problems of:
   (a) a sole proprietor?
   (b) a partnership?
   (c) a closely held corporation?
2. What types of taxes must be taken into consideration when working with business life insurance?
3. Why is life insurance an ideal product to fund a buy-sell agreement?
4. Explain and illustrate a buy-sell plan for a close corporation on:
   (a) a cross purchase basis.
   (b) an entity basis.

5. Briefly explain the following plans using business life insurance:
   (a) key employee life insurance
   (b) split dollar life insurance
   (c) deferred compensation plans
6. List the specialists who may be involved in the sale of business life insurance.

SUMMARY

This chapter discussed a variety of specialized, potentially important, coverages available to meet the unique needs of prospects and clients. In the case of glass, credit, or governmental programs, these coverages may be used to show prospects why they are not adequately covered by a competitor. In the case of boiler and machinery and business life insurance (in addition to the other coverages), the producer can round out or complete an insurance program.

A business needs to insure its physical and human assets. Life insurance can be used in a business setting to insure the human assets as well as assist in business continuation and employee benefits. The application of life insurance to a particular situation and the tax implications of plans require expertise on the part of the producer or the use of life insurance specialists of the producer's firm or life insurer. Great commission potential exists in the agency files for business life insurance. Every producer should look to business life insurance as a portion of a total insurance marketing plan. The commission dollars are large and the producer will provide service on the client's total account.

For producers seeking a specialty line of insurance, each coverage treated in the chapter offers an opportunity. For producers desiring to sell all lines of insurance, each coverage will be applicable to some insureds. In every case, assistance can and should be sought from the insurer to be sure exposures are adequately insured.

CHAPTER 11

Businessowners Policy

INTRODUCTION

The businessowners policy (BOP) of the Insurance Services Office is designed to meet most insurance needs of most small- to medium-sized retail stores, offices, or apartment complexes. The BOP is a standardized package policy; most smaller businesses share many common characteristics, and, generally speaking, lack the types of loss exposures that require individualized treatment. Like the Homeowners 76 program, the BOP is a simplified, easy to read, indivisible package policy that features broad protection, a limited number of optional coverages, and a simplified rating procedure at a competitive price.

Even though the BOP may be used for many clients for which the special multi-peril policy program (SMP) could be used, the BOP was not developed to replace the SMP. In fact, the SMP program will still be needed to treat the insurance needs of larger organizations, of businesses ineligible for the BOP and where complexity of the exposures involved requires greater flexibility in coverage forms and endorsements.

The BOP was first introduced in 1974 by an independent insurer. This innovative lead was followed quickly by other insurers with similar product offerings. In 1976, the ISO filed a BOP program. Because of its widespread use, the ISO version of the BOP program will be used as the basis of discussion and analysis in this chapter. However, many insurers have developed their own BOP programs. The producer should, therefore, expect to encounter differences and variations in terminology, eligibility rules, coverages, optional limits of liability, and the rating procedures published by different insurance companies.

549

The ISO version of the BOP program features two self-contained policies, the *standard policy* and the *special policy*. The principal difference between these two policy forms is in the property perils and crime coverage. The standard policy is a "named perils" contract to which an insured may add burglary and robbery coverage as an option. The special policy is an "all-risks" contract with theft coverage, which also includes automatically money and securities coverage without an additional charge. Otherwise, both policies are essentially the same with property coverage available for (1) buildings, (2) business personal property, (3) loss of income, (4) other optional property coverages, and (5) comprehensive business liability coverage. Both policy versions of the BOP program will be discussed following the BOP eligibility section.

It is necessary to know the basis of each type of coverage discussed in order to benefit from this chapter. Detailed analysis of such things as definitions of *objects* (in boiler and machinery coverage) or burglary and robbery are not given. These details can be obtained from the specific chapters dealing with the coverages and from the policy kit.

ELIGIBILITY

Eligibility for the BOP program is determined by reference to the nature of the business being operated (certain types of businesses, as noted, are ineligible) and by the size of the building in which the business is housed. Of course, insurers with independent BOP filings may impose different eligibility criteria, such as a specific limitation on sales volume. The ISO eligibility requirements related to the size of the building(s) are summarized in Exhibits 11-1 and 11-2. Exhibit 11-1 applies when the building is to be insured under a BOP. Exhibit 11-2 is applicable to businesses that do not own the buildings occupied and, therefore, will be insuring only business personal property under a BOP.

The BOP program may be used to insure apartments, office buildings, and retail stores if they satisfy the eligibility guidelines related to size, and if the type of business being conducted is not specifically ineligible for coverage under the BOP program. The types of businesses or property *ineligible* for BOP coverage are:[1]

1. Operations centered on automobiles, motor homes, motorcycles, or mobile homes. Parking lots and garages are acceptable when incidental to an otherwise eligible operation, such as a store that has parking facilities on the premises. While dealers in watercraft, snowmobiles, or other recreational motor vehicles

Exhibit 11-1

BOP Eligibility Guidelines for Owner-Occupied Buildings

Buildings			
Type of Occupancy	Maximum Height	Maximum Units/Area	Retail Area Restrictions[†]
Apartment Building(s)	Not to exceed 6 stories	No more than 60 dwelling units	Limit of 7,500 sq. ft. mercantile space
Office Buildings	Not to exceed 3 stories	No more than 100,000 sq. ft. total area[†]	Limit of 7,500 sq. ft. mercantile space
Retail Stores (At a single site)	No limitation	No limitation	Limit of 7,500 sq. ft. for total area

[†]Basement areas not open to the public are not counted in the area calculations.

Exhibit 11-2

BOP Eligibility Guidelines for Nonowner-Occupied Buildings

Business Personal Property	
Type of Occupancy	Maximum Area (Excluding basement areas not open to the public)
Office Buildings	10,000 sq. ft. (in any one building
Retail Stores	7,500 sq. ft.

are eligible for coverage, the BOP does not respond to most claims involving liability for or physical damage to owned boats or motor vehicles.

2. Bars, grills, or restaurants.

3. Condominiums. ISO's Condominium program is available for this class.
4. Contractors. However, a store "wherein the principal business is the buying and selling of merchandise" is not automatically ineligible merely because the operation involves some incidental contracting exposure—a hardware store might sell and install fences, for example, without taking away from its essential character as a hardware store.
5. Buildings which have any portion of their occupancy devoted to manufacturing or processing.
6. Operations involving "one or more locations used for manufacturing, processing, or servicing." A retail outlet for the products of an owner-manufacturer is thus not eligible, even if the manufacturing operations are conducted at another location.
7. Household personal property of the owner of the business.
8. Private dwellings. Garden apartments that group one- or two-family units within a single area are eligible, assuming all units are under one ownership, management, and control. Duplexes, for example are not eligible, but triplexes are.
9. Places of amusement—fairs, carnivals, amusement parks, theaters, bowling alleys. None serves a principal function in the "buying and selling of merchandise."
10. Wholesalers. The nature of wholesale operations differs from that envisaged for BOP.
11. Financial institutions—banks, savings and loan associations, credit unions, stock brokers, and so on. The crime exposure lies beyond that contemplated for the average small- to medium-sized business.

In summary, landlords may insure their buildings under the BOP program provided, of course, the building satisfies the eligibility guidelines set forth in Exhibit 11-1, and the type of business occupying the building is not one of the eleven ineligible types. If the building owner and the businessowner are one and the same, the BOP *must* cover both the building and its contents in the same policy. Businessowners who are tenants of an office or mercantile building may cover their business personal property, provided the maximum area restrictions presented in Exhibit 11-2 are not exceeded.

PROPERTY COVERAGES

As noted, there are two versions of the BOP, the standard policy and the special policy. Both policies may be used to provide coverage for a business building, business personal property, or both, as well as loss of income, other optional property coverages, and comprehensive business liability coverage. The principal difference, again, between the two BOP policies in property coverage is that one is a "named-perils" policy (the standard form) while the other is an "all-risks" policy (the special form).

Two distinctive characteristics of both BOP policies are (1) their replacement cost coverage for both buildings and business personal property and (2) property insurance without a coinsurance provision.[2] These two features are strong selling points. The absence of a coinsurance clause is rather unusual, especially when offered in conjunction with automatic replacement cost coverage for a building *and* its contents. This places the responsibility for full insurance-to-value on the producer and the underwriter.

The property coverage provided by the standard BOP will be discussed in the section below, followed by a description of the special BOP property section. Liability coverages, section II of the BOP, will then be reviewed. The liability coverage offered by both versions of the BOP is the same. The only difference to be found in the liability area is that some independently filed plans offer higher limits of liability with their special BOP.

Standard Form BOP

The property section, section I of the standard BOP, insures against direct loss caused by fire, lightning, the extended coverage perils, vandalism or malicious mischief, and sprinkler leakage. For property in transit, the following additional perils apply:

1. collision, derailment or overturn of a transporting conveyance;
2. standing or sinking of vessels; and
3. collapse of bridges, culverts, docks or wharves.

Direct property losses are subject to a $100 per occurrence deductible. This deductible applies separately to each location with an overall aggregate of $1,000 per occurrence for all locations. A higher per loss deductible amount ($250) applies separately to two of the optional BOP coverages: (1) employee dishonesty and (2) burglary and robbery. No deductible clause applies to loss of income claims, i.e., indirect losses.

Building Section I, coverage A, provides for "the replacement cost of the building(s) at the premises described in the Declarations for which a limit of liability is shown, including, all while on the premises, the following:

1. all garages, storage buildings and appurtenant structures usual to the occupancy of the insured;
2. fixtures, machinery and equipment constituting a permanent part of and pertaining to the service of the building;
3. personal property of the insured used for the maintenance and service of the building, including fire extinguishing apparatus, floor coverings, and appliances for refrigerating, ventilating, cooking, dishwashing and laundering;
4. outdoor furniture and yard fixtures;
5. personal property owned by the insured in apartments or rooms furnished by the insured as landlord;
6. trees, shrubs and plants at the described premises for not more than $250 on any one tree, shrub or plant, including expense incurred for removing all debris thereof, however, the total liability of the Company shall not exceed $1,000 in the aggregate for any one loss.

In addition to these items, the building coverage part provides for "debris removal" and for quarterly automatic increases in limits, the exact percentage to be shown in the policy declarations. The "debris removal" coverage is provided as an additional amount of insurance without a specified limit.

Business Personal Property   Section I, coverage B provides for replacement cost coverage of business personal property owned by:

the insured, usual to the occupancy of the insured, at the premises described in the Declarations for which a limit of liability is shown, including:

1. similar property held by the insured and belonging in whole or in part to others but not exceeding the amount for which the insured is legally liable, including the value of labor, materials, and charges furnished, performed or incurred by the insured; and
2. tenant's improvements and betterments, meaning the insured's use interest in fixtures, alterations, installations or additions comprising a part of the building occupied but not owned by the insured and made or acquired at the expense of the insured, exclusive of rent paid by the insured, but which are not legally subject to removal by the insured.

This coverage applies while the insured's property or property of others is (1) in or on the building(s), or (2) in the open within 100 feet of the building, specifically including property in vehicles.

Another strong sales feature of the business personal property coverage is the *seasonal automatic increase* provision. This effectively increases the amount of insurance specified for coverage B by 25 percent, to provide for seasonal fluctuations, without requiring the insured to specify in advance the dates for those peak seasons. This can be a highly beneficial provision for a merchant like a toy store owner with seasonal sales peaks. The BOP "peak season" feature differs from the one available with the SMP in two ways: (1) the BOP peak season provision is automatically included in the policy whenever business personal property is being insured while the comparable SMP provision is optional; and (2) the BOP peak season does not require the dates of the peak season(s) be specified while the comparable SMP feature does require advance specification of the peak period(s). It should be noted however, that:

> . . .[this] increase shall not apply unless the limit of liability shown in the Declarations is 100% or more of the insured's average monthly values for the 12 months immediately preceding the date of loss, or in the event the insured has been in business for less than 12 months, such shorter period of time.

Note the limit of liability must equal or exceed the average values for the twelve months preceding *the loss*. This could be considerably more than the average values for the 12 months preceding the effective date, particularly for a growing firm in inflationary times.

The business personal property of the insured, as well as any *similar* property of others in the insured's care, is covered while in transit or otherwise temporarily away from the described premises. This is another of the BOP's "extra coverage provisions" highly favorable to the insured. Care should be taken when an exposure exists where the insured has property of others in his or her care, custody, or control that is *not similar,* such as a merchant with consigned goods unlike those normally sold.

Business personal property at newly acquired locations is also covered for up to 30 days for amounts not to exceed $10,000.

Loss of Income Section I, coverage C provides for "loss of income" coverage. This coverage is *not subject* to the BOP deductible provision, nor to any coinsurance requirement, nor to any maximum stated dollar limitation. Coverage is on an "actual loss sustained" basis. Loss of income coverage is limited to the period it would take to repair, rebuild, or replace the damaged property and in no event shall the loss period exceed twelve consecutive months from the date of loss. Some independently filed BOPs limit the time period to eight months under the standard BOP.

Coverage C states:

> This policy covers the actual business loss sustained by the insured and the expenses necessarily incurred to resume normal business operation resulting from the interruption of business or the untenantability of the premises when the building or the personal property is damaged as a direct result of an insured peril. The actual business loss sustained by the insured shall not exceed:

1. the reduction in gross earnings less charges and expenses which do not necessarily continue during the interruption of business; and

2. the reduction in rents, less charges and expenses which do not necessarily continue during the period of untenantability.

The insured is required to resume normal operations as promptly as possible and to use all reasonable means to preclude any delays in reopening. The BOP will not respond to any increase of loss caused by the interference of strikers or by the cancellation of any lease or contract unless that loss results directly from the interruption of business. Finally, the insured is expected to minimize any income loss by resuming full or partial operations at the insured location or elsewhere if that is practical. An extended period of indemnity is not available in the BOP program.

Property Not Covered   The standard BOP does not provide coverage for the following items:

1. exterior signs unless insured under Optional Coverages;
2. growing crops and lawns;
3. aircraft, automobiles, motortrucks and other vehicles subject to motor vehicle registration, or watercraft (including motors, equipment and accessories) while afloat;
4. bullion, money and securities.

Property Subject to Limitations   The standard BOP limits the coverage for two principal classes of property:

1. valuable papers and records meaning books of account, manuscripts, abstracts, drawings, card index systems and other records (except film, tape, disc, drum, cell and other magnetic recording or storage media for electronic data processing) are covered for not exceeding the cost of blank books, cards or other blank material plus the cost of labor incurred by the insured for transcribing or copying such records; and
2. film, tape, disc, drum, cell and other magnetic recording or storage media for electronic data processing are covered for not exceeding the cost of such media in unexposed or blank form.

This limited coverage is similar to that available through a valuable papers and records endorsement to an SMP. While the BOP provision includes this coverage as any other part of a loss, without a specific dollar limitation, it does not cover the cost of any research necessary to reproduce the records in question.

Exclusions   The standard BOP does not provide coverage for losses:

1. occasioned directly or indirectly by enforcement of any ordinance or law regulating the construction, repair or demolition of buildings or structures;

2. caused by or resulting from power, heating or cooling failure, unless such failure results from physical damage to power, heating or cooling equipment situated on premises where the property covered is located, caused by perils not otherwise excluded. Also, the Company shall not be liable under this exclusion for any loss resulting from riot, riot attending a strike, civil commotion, or vandalism or malicious mischief;

3. caused by any electrical injury or disturbance of electrical appliances, devices, fixtures, or wiring caused by electrical currents artificially generated unless fire as insured against ensues and then this Company shall be liable for only loss caused by the ensuing fire;

4. caused by, resulting from, contributed to, or aggravated by any of the following:

    (a) earth movement, including but not limited to earthquake, landslide, mudflow, earth sinking, earth rising or shifting;

    (b) flood, surface water, waves, tidal water or tidal waves, overflow of streams or other bodies of water, or spray from any of the foregoing, all whether driven by wind or not;

    (c) water which backs up through sewers or drains;

    (d) water below the surface of the ground including that which exerts pressure on or flows, seeps or leaks through sidewalks, driveways, foundations, walls, basement or other floors, or through doors, windows or any other openings in such sidewalks, driveways, foundations, walls or floors;

    (e) delay or loss of market;

    unless fire or explosion as insured against ensues, and then this Company shall be liable for only loss caused by the ensuing fire or explosion.

Optional Coverages   The standard BOP makes several types of property coverages available to the eligible businessowner on an optional basis. The businessowner may select any one or more of these optional coverages by paying the appropriate additional premium. When any optional coverage is effective, is it will be indicated on the declarations page.

Employee Dishonesty.   When the declarations page indicates a limit for employee dishonesty coverage, the policy covers any losses of money and other forms of business personal property when caused by the dishonest or fraudulent acts of the insured's employees. There are several conditional aspects of this form of crime coverage and the producer should explain these to the businessowner to avoid any possible misunderstanding. The first condition with respect to employee dishonesty coverage states:

the limit of the company's liability for loss shall not exceed the replacement cost thereof at the time of loss, provided, however, at the option of the insured, payment of the cost of replacing securities may be determined by the market value at the time of such settlement.

Another condition excludes coverage for any losses due to dishonest or fraudulent acts by the insured or by any partner, officer, director, or trustee. A third provision limits the amount of loss on any employee to that sustained at the time of its discovery. Once discovered, the BOP will pay for the loss up to that date, but not for further loss caused by a known culprit.

For example, an employee has embezzled from a covered business for two years. On February 12, 19X3, the employer discovers $12,000 of a total $20,000 embezzled. The total amount, $20,000, is covered, less the $250 deductible. Any amount embezzled after February 12, 19X3 is not covered.

Also, a series of acts by one or more employees is considered as one occurrence for the purpose of applying the limit of liability and the $250 deductible. The producer should acquaint the newly insured businessowner with the discovery period (losses discovered up to one year after the policy expires are covered if the act was committed during the policy term) and the policy superceded suretyship provisions that apply if this BOP coverage replaces a prior coverage.

Exterior Signs. This coverage insures all exterior signs located on the premises whether they are the property of the insured or belong to others and are in the care, custody, and control of the insured. This coverage applies for "all-risks" of loss excluding wear and tear, latent defect, rust or corrosion, or mechanical breakdown. The perils and exclusions of the standard BOP do not apply to this coverage, except for the war risk, governmental action and nuclear exclusions, which do apply.

Exterior Grade Floor Glass. When this optional coverage is selected it provides replacement cost coverage for:

> all exterior grade floor and basement glass, including encasing frames and all lettering or ornamentation thereon, which are the property of the insured or the property of others in the care, custody or control of the insured in the building described in the Declarations, for direct physical loss excluding wear and tear, latent defect, corrosion or rust.

This coverage also includes reimbursement for the expense of "boarding up damaged openings, installing temporary plates, and removing or replacing obstructions when necessary."

As was the case with exterior signs coverage, the perils and exclusions of the standard BOP do not apply to exterior glass coverage, except for the war risk, governmental action, and nuclear exclusions. The BOP glass coverage is one of the broadest, most comprehensive glass coverages available.

Burglary and Robbery. When this optional coverage is selected it provides insurance against burglary and robbery losses. The producer should be careful to point out the extent of these coverages:

When coverage is designated in the Declarations for Burglary and Robbery, this policy covers loss by burglary and robbery to:

1. business personal property, (excluding money and securities) on the described premises for an amount not to exceed 25% of the limit of liability of Coverage B—Business Personal Property; and
2. money and securities while in or on the described premises or within a bank or savings institution for an amount not to exceed $5,000;
3. money and securities while enroute to or from the described premises, bank or savings institution, or within the living quarters of the custodian of such funds for an amount not to exceed $2,000.

Burglary means the abstraction of insured property from within the premises by a person making felonious entry or exit therein or therefrom by actual force and violence, evidenced by visible marks made by tools, explosives, electricity, chemicals, or physical damage to the exterior or interior of the premises at the place of such entry or exit.

Robbery means the taking of insured property:

1. by violence inflicted upon a messenger or custodian;
2. by putting him in fear of violence;
3. by any other overt felonious act committed in his presence and of which he was actually cognizant, provided such other act is not committed by an officer, partner, or employee of the insured; and
4. from the person of a messenger or custodian who has been killed or rendered unconscious when such property is in his direct care and custody.

Certain types of property are subject to limited burglary and robbery coverages. These are:

1. fur and fur garments are covered for not exceeding loss in the aggregate of $1,000 in any one occurrence;
2. jewelry and watches, watch movements, jewels, pearls, precious and semi-precious stones, gold, silver, platinum and other precious alloys or metals are covered for not exceeding loss in the aggregate of $1,000 in any one occurrence. This limitation shall not apply to jewelry and watches valued at $25 or less per item.

It is also important for the producer to be cognizant of the insurer's underwriting criteria for issuing burglary and robbery coverage. Insurers frequently require certain types of businesses to have an acceptable burglar alarm system (usually a central station) in order to obtain this coverage.

Boiler and Machinery. When selected, this provides coverage for loss to an *object* (boilers, pressure vessels, and air conditioning equipment, as defined in the policy) when caused by an *accident* as defined in the policy. Coverage is for all such objects owned, leased, or operated under the control of the insured. As with several other coverages not well known to the general public, the producer should be careful to point out how the BOP defines *object* and *accident*, and to note the exclusions that apply to this coverage. For instance, "object" for air conditioning equipment has a minimum (60,000 BTU/hr) and maximum (600,000 BTU/hr) capacity requirement, among others, and an object is not covered, for example, when undergoing hydrostatic, pneumatic, or gas pressure tests. Finally, this optional BOP coverage gives the insurer the right (but not the obligation) to inspect the equipment insured and to suspend coverage by written notice if dangerous conditions are found to exist.

Other Optional Coverages. Some insurance companies offer other types of optional property insurance coverages. Two of the most common available by endorsement are accounts receivable coverage and earthquake assumption.

When accounts receivable coverage is included in a BOP, it is normally subject to a separate deductible provision as well as to a separate limit of liability set forth on the policy declarations page. Accounts receivable coverage will pay sums owed a business by its customers, provided those sums become uncollectible due to loss or damage to the firm's records of accounts receivable by a covered peril. This coverage also recognizes reasonable expenses incurred in re-establishing and collecting any of the firm's accounts receivable following a loss. Interest charges on any loans to cover accounts receivable are normally included when determining the amount for which the business is to be indemnified.

The earthquake peril may be added to most BOPs by endorsement. Some insurers, however, limit the availability of this extension of coverage to the special BOP. When added to a BOP, the earthquake assumption endorsement provides coverage for the building(s), personal property and loss of income. The limits of liability are the same as those for the other perils, but the deductible amount is a percentage of the applicable limits of liability, usually between 2 and 10 percent.

Checkpoints

1. What classes of business generally are eligible for a BOP?
2. What classes of business are *ineligible* for a BOP?
3. What are the principle sales points of BOP property coverage?
4. Describe what is covered by section I of the BOP standard form.
5. List optional coverages available for the BOP standard form.

Special Form BOP

The special BOP is similar to the standard BOP. For example, the policy wording that provides coverage for buildings, business personal property, and loss of income are identical in both policy forms. However, there are significant differences. For example the special BOP makes section I, coverages A, B, and C available on an "all-risks" basis while the standard policy provides "named perils" coverage for these property items.

The standard BOP has a $5,000 "inside" and $2,000 "outside" money and security limit while the special BOP has limits selected by the insured for both. Definitions of money and securities basically are the same in both forms.

There are three essential differences with money and securities between the standard and special BOP. With a special BOP:

1. Coverage is "all-risks."
2. Coverage is automatic.
3. The insured selects limits applying to both inside and outside coverage.

Finally, and primarily because of the difference between the "all-risks" and "named perils" approach to coverage, there are differences between the special and standard BOP in terms of the property excluded from coverage as well as property subject to limitations. The following pages will focus on the differences found in the special BOP.

Property Covered As noted, coverages A, B, and C of the special BOP define the building(s), business personal property, and loss of income to be insured in precisely the same way as does the standard BOP. The special BOP lists sixteen different possible causes of loss for which the policy will not respond:

1. occasioned directly or indirectly by enforcement of any ordinance or law regulating the construction, repair or demolition of buildings or structures;
2. caused by or resulting from power, heating or cooling failure or due to change in temperature or humidity unless the change results from physical damage to the building or to equipment contained therein caused by a peril not otherwise excluded; also the Company shall not be liable for any such loss resulting from riot, riot attending a strike, civil commotion, or vandalism or malicious mischief;
3. caused by any electrical injury or disturbance of electrical appliances, devices, fixtures or wiring caused by electrical currents artificially generated unless fire as insured against ensues and then this Company shall be liable for only loss caused by the ensuing fire;

4. caused by pilferage, appropriation or concealment of any property covered or any fraudulent, dishonest or criminal act done by or at the instigation of any insured, partner or joint venture, including any officer, director, trustee, employee or agent thereof, or any person to whom the property covered may be entrusted;

5. caused by leakage or overflow from plumbing, heating, air conditioning or other equipment or appliances (except fire protective systems) caused by or resulting from freezing while the described building is vacant or unoccupied, unless the insured shall have exercised due diligence with respect to maintaining heat in the buildings or unless such equipment and appliances had been drained and the water supply shut off during such vacancy or unoccupancy;

6. caused by:
   (a) wear and tear, marring or scratching;
   (b) deterioration, inherent vice, latent defect;
   (c) mechanical breakdown of machines, including rupture or bursting caused by centrifugal force;
   (d) faulty design, materials or workmanship;
   (e) rust, mold, wet or dry rot, contamination;
   (f) dampness or dryness of atmosphere, changes in or extremes of temperature;
   (g) smog, smoke from agricultural smudging or industrial operations;
   (h) birds, vermin, rodents, insects or animals;

   unless loss by fire, smoke (other than smoke from agricultural smudging or industrial operations), explosion, collapse of a building, glass breakage or water not otherwise excluded ensues, then this policy shall cover only such ensuing loss.

   If loss by water not otherwise excluded ensues, this policy shall also cover the cost of tearing out and replacing of any part of the building covered required to effect repairs to the plumbing, heating or air conditioning system or domestic appliance but excluding loss to the system or appliance from which the water escapes;

7. due to any and all settling, shrinking, cracking, bulging or expansion of driveways, sidewalks, swimming pools, pavements, foundations, walls, floors, roofs or ceilings;

8. caused by explosion of steam boilers, steam pipes, steam turbines or steam engines (except direct loss resulting from the explosion of accumulated gases or unconsumed fuel within the firebox, or combustion chamber of any fired vessel or within the flues or passages which conduct the gases of combustion therefrom) if owned by, leased by or operated under the control of the insured, or for any ensuing loss except by fire or explosion not otherwise excluded, and then the Company shall be liable for only such ensuing loss;

9. to steam boilers, steam pipes, steam turbines or steam engines caused by any condition or occurrence within such boilers, pipes, turbines or engines (except direct loss resulting from the explosion of accumulated gases or unconsumed fuel within the firebox,

or combustion chamber of any fired vessel or within the flues or passages which conduct the gases of combustion therefrom);

10. to hot water boilers or other equipment for heating water caused by any condition or occurrence within such boilers or equipment, other than an explosion;

11. to property in the open caused by rain, snow, ice or sleet;

12. caused by, resulting from, contributed to, or aggravated by any of the following:

    (a) earth movement, including but not limited to earthquake, landslide, mudflow, earth sinking, earth rising or shifting;
    (b) flood, surface water, waves, tidal water or tidal waves, overflow of streams or other bodies of water, or spray from any of the foregoing, all whether driven by wind or not;
    (c) water which backs up through sewers or drains;
    (d) water below the surface of the ground including that which exerts pressure on or flows, seeps or leaks through sidewalks, driveways, foundations, walls, basement or other floors, or through doors, windows or any other openings in such sidewalks, driveways, foundations, walls or floors;

    unless fire or explosion as insured against ensues, and then this Company shall be liable for only loss caused by the ensuing fire or explosion; but these exclusions shall not apply to loss arising from theft;

13. due to voluntary parting with title or possession of any property by the insured or others if induced to do so by any fraudulent scheme or false pretense;

14. due to unexplained or mysterious disappearance of property, or shortage of property disclosed on taking inventory;

15. due to delay or loss of market;

16. to property sold by the insured under conditional sale, trust agreement, installment payment or other deferred payment plan, after delivery to customers.

The special BOP automatically includes coverage for theft losses with a $250 theft loss deductible. The producer should be careful to explain the deductible to the insured. This deductible is consistent with the $250 deductible applicable to certain closely related optional coverages under the standard BOP, e.g., employee dishonesty and burglary and robbery.

Money and Securities. Coverage D of the special BOP provides "all-risks" on and off premises coverage for money and securities used in the insured's business. The amount of insurance applicable to this category of coverage is set forth in the space provided on the declarations page.

The automatic inclusion of this form of coverage is one reason a producer should be knowledgeable in the underwriting requirements different insurers may use to help determine eligibility for the special BOP. Some insurers have minimum or maximum limits not appropriate for a client. Similarly, money and securities coverage is one that must rely upon the accuracy of records maintained by the insured in the event of loss. The producer has a responsibility to point out these aspects of coverage when a policy is ordered, not after a loss. The balance of the burglary and robbery coverages in the standard BOP are covered by the "all-risk" contents coverage in the special form.

Optional Coverage. With the exception of burglary and robbery, the special BOP offers the same optional coverages as does the standard BOP—employee dishonesty, exterior signs, exterior glass, and boiler and machinery. Coverage for accounts receivable and earthquake may be offered by some insurers.

Property Not Covered The three categories of property specifically excluded under the standard BOP are also excluded under the special policy.

Bullion, money, and securities, however, are specifically covered under the special BOP coverage D, discussed earlier.

Property Subject to Limitations The special BOP has two different sets of limitations. The first of these limits coverage for valuable papers and records (including film, tape, and other forms of electronic data storage media) to the cost of blank cards or other media forms. In the case of a manual records system, the coverage recognizes the cost of labor needed to transcribe or copy such records, but not to reproduce the data electronically. These limitations are the same as those found in the standard BOP.

The following limitations are exclusive to the special BOP and *do not apply* to losses caused by fire, lightning, any of the extended coverage perils, or sprinkler leakage:

1. glass constituting a part of the building is not covered against loss for more than $50 per plate, pane, multiple plate insulating unit, radiant heating panel, jalousie, louver or shutter, nor for more than $250 in any one occurrence.

2. glass, glassware, statuary, marbles, bric-a-brac, porcelains and other articles of a fragile or brittle nature are not covered against loss by breakage. This limitation shall not apply to bottles or similar containers of property for sale, or sold but not delivered, nor to lenses of photographic or scientific instruments.

3. fur and fur garments are covered for not exceeding loss in the aggregate of $1,000 in any one occurrence; and

4. jewelry and watches, watch movements, jewels, pearls, precious and semiprecious stones, bullion, gold, silver, platinum and other precious alloys or metals are covered for not exceeding loss in the aggregate of $1,000 in any one occurrence. This limitation shall not apply to jewelry and watches valued at $25 or less per item.

LIABILITY COVERAGES

The liability coverages provided by the standard BOP and the special BOP are identical. While some insurers may permit higher limits of liability under the special BOP, there is no difference in the types of liability covered nor in the definitions and other provisions used in section II of either form. The liability coverage is quite broad. The only decision the insured needs to make with respect to this section of the BOP is whether to select the $300,000 or the $1 million limit of liability.

Business Liability

Coverage E of the BOP states that it "will pay on behalf of the **insured** all sums which the **insured** shall become legally obligated to pay as damages because of **bodily injury, property damage** or **personal injury** caused by an **occurrence** to which this insurance applies."

The BOP liability insuring agreement provides comprehensive general liability insurance on an occurrence basis. Of course, this includes the usual liability coverage for a business's "premises and operations." Coverage for "completed operations" and "products" liability are also specifically included, as well as "personal injury" liability. The latter protects the insured against liability caused by real or alleged false arrest, libel or slander, and wrongful entry or eviction or other invasion of privacy. A fire legal liability provision provides up to $50,000 of coverage per occurrence for all damages resulting from *fire or explosion* which damages structures rented to or occupied by the named insured for which he or she is liable.

The BOP also covers other forms of liability including employers' nonowned automobile liability, blanket contractual liability, and host liquor law liability.

Most insurers also provide druggists' professional liability coverage by endorsement when the insured operates a retail drug store. This coverage specifically protects the named insured, including partners, executive officers, and so on, and the pharmacists employed by the named insured. This coverage applies to all claims arising out of goods or products prepared, sold, handled, or distributed by the drug store. Another extension of liability coverage nearly always found in the BOP is broad form property damage coverage. This coverage is valuable to businesses that service or install items away from their business location. In essence, this coverage relaxes the usual "care, custody, and control" exclusion to specifically cover damage to property caused by the negligent installation or replacement of some part of some piece of equipment or system. The cost of the negligently installed item itself is excluded from coverage.

Limits of Liability As noted, the insured may select liability insurance limits of either $300,000 or $1 million.[3] These limits of liability are "per occurrence" and are not reduced by any "supplementary payments" (discussed below). The "per occurrence" limit is also an *aggregate limit* for *all occurrences* during the policy period stemming from the completed operations and/or products liability hazards. And, as noted, fire legal liability claims are limited to no more than $50,000 per occurrence.

As with other forms of liability insurance, the insurer is obligated to defend any claim or suit against the insured seeking damages covered by the BOP even if the suit is false, fraudulent, or groundless. However, the BOP gives the insurance company the right to make investigations and settlements of claims as the insurer deems expedient. Finally, once the BOP limits of liability have been exhausted by payment of judgments or by settlements, the insurer is released from any further obligation to defend or to make payments on behalf of the insured. Liability insurance coverage applies separately to each "insured" against whom a claim is made or a suit filed, but this does not serve to increase the total amount of insurance available as a result of any single occurrence. It merely allows all "insureds" to have access to the BOP liability coverage. The BOP's limit of liability serves as an upper limit on the insurer's liability with respect to any particular occurrence, regardless of the number of insureds involved.

Supplementary Payments The BOP, like other liability contracts, promises to make certain supplementary payments that do not affect the policy's limit of liability:

1. all expenses incurred by the Company;
2. all cost taxed against the **insured** in any suit defended by the Company and all interest on the entire amount of any judgment which accrues after entry of the judgment and before the Company has paid or tendered or deposited in court that part of the judgment which does not exceed the limit of the Company's liability;
3. premium on appeal bonds in any such suit;
4. premiums on bonds to release attachments in any such suit for an amount not in excess of the applicable limit of liability of this policy;
5. expenses incurred by the **insured** for first aid to others at the time of an accident for **bodily injury** to which this policy applies; and
6. reasonable expenses incurred by the **insured** at the Company's request in assisting the Company in the investigation or defense

of any claim or suit, including actual loss of earnings not to exceed $50 per day.

Medical Payments

The BOP automatically includes medical payments coverage (coverage F) in the amounts of $1,000 per person and $10,000 for all persons requiring medical attention as a result of a single accident. Medical payments coverage is provided on an "accident" as opposed to an "occurrence" basis. This form of coverage is subject to several exclusions:

Under Coverage F, this policy does not apply:
1. to **bodily injury** excluded under Coverage E—Business Liability;
2. to **bodily injury** to any person while engaged in maintenance and repair of the insured premises or alteration, demolition or new construction at such premises;
3. to **bodily injury** arising out of operations performed for the **named insured** by independent contractors other than (a) maintenance and repair of the insured premises, or (b) structural alterations at such premises which do not involve changing the size of or moving buildings or other structures;
4. to **bodily injury** to the **named insured,** any partner therein, any tenant or other person regularly residing on the insured premises or any employee of any of the foregoing if the **bodily injury** arises out of and in the course of his employment;
5. to **bodily injury** to any other tenant if the **bodily injury** occurs on that part of the insured premises rented from the **named insured** or to any employee of such tenant if the **bodily injury** occurs on the tenant's part of the insured premises and arises out of and in the course of his employment for the tenant;
6. to **bodily injury** to any person if any benefits for such **bodily injury** are payable or required to be provided under any workers' compensation, unemployment compensation or disability benefits law, or under any similar law;
7. to any **medical expense** for services by the **named insured,** any employee thereof or any person or organization under **contract** to the **named insured** to provide such services;
8. to **bodily injury** to any person practicing, instructing, or participating in any physical training, sport, athletic activity or contest;
9. to **bodily injury** included within the **completed operations hazard** or the **products hazard**.

The producer should always point out exclusions to the policyowner.

Named Insured

The "named insured" is the person or organization set forth as such in item 1 on the declarations page. The BOP defines the word "insured" to mean any of the following:

1. if the **named insured** is designated in the Declarations as an individual, the person so designated but only with respect to the conduct of a business of which he is the sole proprietor, and the spouse of the **named insured** with respect to the conduct of such a business;

2. if the **named insured** is designated in the Declarations as a partnership or joint venture, the partnership or joint venture so designated and any partner or member thereof but only with respect to his liability as such;

3. if the **named insured** is designated in the Declarations as other than an individual, partnership, or joint venture, the organization so designated and any executive officer, member of the board of trustees, directors or governors or stockholder thereof while acting within the scope of his duties as such;

4. *any employee* of the **named insured** while acting within the scope of his duties as such;

5. any person or organization while acting as real estate manager for the **named insured**.

Even with such a broad definition, item 1 on the declarations page should be written as specifically as possible. For instance, "J&T Appliances" (a named insured), is better designated in item 1 "Robert Johnson and Joan Thomas, partners, d/b/a J&T Appliances, as their interests may appear." Under the second designation, personal property of Johnson or Thomas used in the business—a set of tools, for example—are offered coverage by the BOP. Under the first designation only property of the partnership receives such protection.

Checkpoints

1. How does the special BOP form differ from the standard form?
2. What are standard liability limits for the BOP?
3. What professional liability exposure may be insured by a BOP?

GENERAL CONDITIONS AND OTHER PROVISIONS

The BOP program does not include the exact language or format of the well-known 165 lines of the New York standard fire policy. The essence of those provisions, however, is contained in both policy versions of the BOP program. These conditions and other provisions are found in the BOP sections labeled "War Risk, Governmental Action and Nuclear Exclusions," "General Conditions," "Conditions Applicable to Section I (Property)," or "Conditions Applicable to Section II (Liability)," which follow the description of coverages and appear in the policy in that order. These various provisions and conditions will be discussed briefly. When appropriate, the discussion will indicate the comparable segment of the "standard 165 lines" discussed in PRO 81.

War Risk, Governmental Action, and Nuclear Exclusions

Virtually all insurance policies contain wording which excludes coverages for losses caused by war, governmental action, and nuclear catastrophies. In this section, the BOP, like most other insurance policies, intends to exclude losses caused by hostile or warlike action in time of peace or war, insurrection, rebellion, revolution, civil war, usurped power, contraband, illegal transportation or trade, nuclear radiation, and radioactive contamination.

General Conditions

This section of a BOP policy contains thirteen different provisions dealing with general matters that normally would be found in most insurance policies. Several of these provisions have been reworded to simplify the language but the meaning and substance of these provisions remains unchanged.

Comparable Provisions to SFP   Comparable provisions include the following:

1. "Concealment or Fraud" has the same meaning as lines 1-6 of the standard fire policy (SFP).
2. "Subrogation"—the subject of lines 162-165 of the SFP.
3. "Waiver or Change of Provisions" can only be done by written endorsement as similarly stated in lines 49-55 of the SFP.
4. "Liberalization" states that future extension or broadening of BOP coverage will benefit this particular policy as though the policy were altered by written endorsement.
5. "Replacement of Forms and Endorsements" states that the insurer may convert "old" contract forms to "new" at the policy's anniversary date, even if it is a continuous policy without a specific termination date.
6. "Inspection and Audit" gives the insurer the right but not the obligation to inspect and audit the business insured.
7. "Assignment" provides that the insured cannot assign an interest in the BOP to another party without the written consent of the insurer. If, however, the *named insured* should die within the policy period, the coverage provided by the policy would apply:

(a) to the **named insured's** legal representative, as the **named insured,** but only while acting within the scope of his duties as such; or

(b) to the person having temporary custody of the property of the **named insured** but only until the appointment and qualification of the legal representative.

8. "Premium" states that the premiums for the BOP policy are to be computed in accordance with the insurer's applicable rules, rates, and minimum premiums then in effect and that the policy may be continued by payment of successive one year premiums.

Different Provisions   Some of the "general conditions" found in the BOP are different from comparable provisions found in other insurance contracts. Each of these, therefore, deserves a brief comment.

Cancellation.   The *cancellation* provision of the BOP gives the named insured the right to cancel the policy at a future date, if specified in writing in advance of the desired effective date of cancellation. The insurer may cancel by giving the named insured and the mortgagee at least thirty days advance written notice. This is a much improved provision for the insured compared to the SFP's five days notice and the SMP's ten days notice. The return premium is computed on a pro-rata basis if the insurer cancels the policy. If the named insured should cancel, the return premium is calculated as 90 percent of the unearned premium, as determined on a pro-rata basis.

Policy Period, Territory, and Inception.   Two other provisions found in the general conditions section of the BOP define the *Policy Period, Territory,* and *Time of Inception.* The usual time of inception for a BOP is 12:00 noon, but if the BOP is replacing a policy that expires at 12:01 A.M., the BOP inception shall be 12:01 A.M. to avoid a lapse of coverage. The policy territory includes the fifty states of the United States of America, the District of Columbia, and Puerto Rico.

Other Insurance.   The BOP "Other Insurance" provision differs from most other insurance contracts because the BOP provision makes the property coverage *excess* rather than pro-rata with other applicable policies. The BOP general liability coverage is implicitly primary coverage. This allows the producer to suggest purchase of excess liability or umbrella coverage. Property in the care, custody, or control of the insured is insured as excess coverage over any other valid and collectible insurance. The final provision states if there is a loss covered by more than one part of an endorsement to the BOP, the insurer's limit of liability is the amount of the loss. This provision is included to enforce the fundamental principle of indemnity.

Conditions Applicable to Section I

This section of the BOP enumerates fourteen different provisions applicable to property coverage. These provisions include the usual insurance clauses:

1. The "Duties of the Named Insured After A Loss" are essentially the same as those in the SFP, lines 90-122.
2. "Appraisal" outlines procedures to be followed in the event the insured and the insurer fail to agree on the amount of a loss. The procedures are the same as those described in the SFP, lines 123-140.
3. The "Company Options" provision, as in the SFP, lines 141-147, gives the insurer the following rights:

   > If the Company gives notice within thirty (30) days after it has received a signed, sworn statement of loss, it shall have the option to take all or any part of the property damaged at an agreed value, or to repair, rebuild or replace it with equivalent property.

4. The "Abandonment of Property" like the SFP, lines 148-149, states that the insurer need not accept abandoned property.
5. The "Payment of Loss" clause of the BOP stipulates that property losses are to be paid within thirty days (as opposed to sixty days in the SFP, lines 150-156) of the date that an acceptable proof of loss has been presented.
6. The "Suit" clause states:

   > No suit shall be brought on this policy unless the insured has complied with all the policy provisions and has commenced the suit within one year after the loss occurs.

   This provision is the same as the one contained in the SFP, lines 157-61.
7. The "Mortgage Clause" of the BOP essentially replaces the one in the SFP and the "standard mortgage clause" usually attached to the SFP. Additional mortgagees or mortgagees added after the policy is issued receive protection as if named on the declarations page. Mortgagee rights and duties similar to those in the "standard mortgage clause" are also in the BOP mortgage clause.
8. The "Recoveries" clause states that if any recoveries are realized on loss or damaged property, the insured shall be entitled to all recoveries in excess of the amount paid by the company, less only the actual cost of effecting such recoveries.

9. The "Loss Clause" states that the amount of insurance provided in a BOP will not be diminished by the payment of a loss. This generally is true of all property insurance policies.

10. The "No Benefit to Bailee" clause states:

    This insurance shall not inure directly or indirectly to the benefit of any carrier or other bailee.

11. The "No Control" provision states that coverage provided by a BOP will not be prejudiced:

    (a) by any act or neglect of the owner of any building if the insured is not the owner thereof, or by any act or neglect of any occupant (other than the insured) of any building, when such act or neglect of the owner or occupant is not within the control of the insured; or

    (b) by failure of the insured to comply with any warranty or condition contained in any endorsement attached to this policy with regard to any portion of the premises over which the insured has no control.

Three other clauses found in this section of the BOP require a little more attention. The first of these is the "Replacement Cost" provision. Note how the first half of this provision (part a) defines the limits of replacement cost while the second half (part b) states that property damage must actually be repaired or replaced before the insurer is obligated to pay on a replacement cost basis. The producer should be careful to point out these important details concerning replacement cost. The full replacement cost provision reads:

(a) With the exception of loss to Money and Securities, loss shall be adjusted on the basis of the replacement cost value of the property insured hereunder, but the limit of liability of the Company shall not exceed the least of:

    (1) the full cost of replacement of such property at the same site with new material of like kind and quality without deduction for depreciation; or

    (2) the cost of repairing the insured property within reasonable time; or

    (3) the limit of liability applicable to such property shown on the Declarations; or

    (4) the amount actually and necessarily expended in repairing or replacing said property or any part thereof.

(b) The Company shall not be liable for payment of loss on a replacement cost basis unless and until actual repair or replacement is completed.

    The insured, however, may elect not to repair or replace, in which event loss settlement shall be made on an actual cash value basis rather than on a replacement cost basis. Should the insured elect this option, the insured's right to make further claim on a replacement cost basis shall not be prejudiced provided the

Company is notified in writing within 180 days after loss of the
insured's intent to make such further claim.

The "Privilege to Adjust with Owner" provision gives the insurer
the right to settle losses with the owner of lost or damaged property,
even if that person should not be a party to the contract. For example,
if J&T Appliances has a TV owned by a customer in the shop for repair,
and the TV is damaged by a fire at the store, the insurer may settle
directly with the TV's owner.

The final provision in this section of the BOP deals with the subject
of "Vacancy and Unoccupancy." *Vacancy* means the building is empty;
it has no contents or activities customary to its usual type of occupancy.
An *unoccupied* building would lack the people and activities, but it
would not be empty; it would have contents. The BOP "Vacancy or
Unoccupancy" provision grants blanket permission for unoccupancy,
but limits coverage during periods of vacancy to no more than 60 days.

Conditions Applicable to Section II

These are three provisions contained within this section of the
BOP. The first of these is concerned with "Action Against the
Company." This provision states:

No action shall lie against the Company unless:

(a) there shall have been full compliance with all of the terms of this
policy; and

(b) the amount of the **insured's** obligation to pay shall have been
finally determined either by judgement against the **insured** after
actual trial or by written agreement of the **insured**, the claimant
and the Company.

Any person or organization or the legal representative thereof who
has secured such judgement or written agreement shall thereafter be
entitled to recover under this policy to the extent of insurance
afforded by this policy.

The two remaining provisions set forth the "Insured's Duties in the
Event of Occurrence, Claims or Suits" and that the BOP *shall not*
serve as proof of financial responsibility under that type of law in any
state. The procedure should take care in pointing out where the duties
of the insured are enumerated for property and liability losses.

RATING AND UNDERWRITING

Careful selection and proper classification and rating of businesses
under the BOP are the responsibility of the producer. To this end, the
producer should always make at least one fact-finding visit and on-site

inspection, as the rating and underwriting of BOP business depend on the information gathered by the producer.

BOP rating and underwriting will be discussed briefly in the following sections. A BOP application and worksheet are included as Exhibit 11-3.

Rating

A noteworthy feature of the BOP rating procedure is its simplicity. The entire indivisible package premium is developed from the amounts of insurance to be placed on the building (if applicable) and the business personal property. If any of the optional coverages are desired, they can be added for an additional charge.

The first step in rating a standard BOP is to obtain the 80 percent coinsurance fire and extended coverage rates on the building and/or the contents, depending on whether building, contents, or both, are to be insured. The procedure is the same with other property insurance policies. With this information, the applicable BOP rate can be determined easily by referring to the appropriate table.

For example, assume a producer is calculating the rate for a standard BOP on an eligible gift shop leasing space within an office building. Assume the 80 percent fire rate plus the extended coverage rate on contents at this location equal 0.85, and the classification table in the Commercial Lines Manual shows that, for a gift shop, rate number 8 is appropriate. By referring to the rate page for the territory in question, as shown in Exhibit 11-4, across from 0.85 and below rate number 8 you will find the rate per $100 for this policy is 1.59. If $50,000 contents coverage and $300,000 liability coverage is desired, the premium would be $1.59 \times 500 = \$795$.

The premium for the special BOP is developed by adding a loading to the standard BOP rates. The special BOP business personal property premium is developed from a table indicating "increments" to be added to the corresponding standard BOP rates. The "increments" vary with the amount of coverage. For example, the special BOP building rate is the standard BOP rate plus $ .05.

Additional charges for optional BOP coverages are developed separately. For example, "Employee Dishonesty" coverage may be added to the BOP for a flat extra charge based on the number of employees. Up to five employees carries one rate, and any additional employees adds a flat amount to that rate. Exterior signs may be added to coverage for a flat rate per $100 of value. Exterior glass coverage has a per square foot of area that varies by public protection classification and business category (apartment, office, or mercantile). Premium amounts are set forth separately for boilers and pressure

Exhibit 11-3
Businessowners Application/Worksheet

SET TAB STOPS AT ARROWS

BUSINESSOWNERS APPLICATION/WORKSHEET

BU 16 01
(Ed. 05 76)

AGENCY CODE	NAME	ACC'T. NO.	☐ RENEWAL OF	☐ NEW

1. APPLICANT
   MAILING ADD.
2. LOC. OF PREM.

3. BUSINESS OF APPLICANT   (If more than one location, complete an application for each location)

4. BUILDING OCCUPIED AS   ☐ **APARTMENT**—no more than 15% office occupancy   ☐ **MERCANTILE**   ☐ **OFFICE**—15% or more office occupancy

5. INTEREST OF APPLICANT IN PREMISES   ☐ OWNER OCCUPYING 75% OR MORE OF BLDG. AREA   ☐ OWNER OCCUPYING LESS THAN 75% OF BLDG. AREA   ☐ **TENANT**

6. APPLICANT IS   ☐ INDIVIDUAL   ☐ CORPORATION   ☐ PARTNERSHIP ☐ OTHER

7. MORTGAGEE
   ADD.

8. EFFECTIVE DATE ☐ ☐ MO. ☐ ☐ DAY ☐ ☐ YR.   POLICY DESIRED ☐ SPECIAL   ☐ STANDARD
   (10 11)   If SPECIAL enter Trade Group from Class. Page ☐ ☐

9. CONSTRUCTION ☐ FRAME   ☐ MASONRY   ☐ FIRE RESISTIVE ☐ STEEL

10. PROTECTION CLASS ☐ (40)   NBFU DESIGNATION   RISK SPRINKLERED ☐ YES   ☐ NO

11. BLDG. INFLATION GUARD OPTION ☐ BASIC 2%   ☐ %   (OPTIONAL) SPECIFY QUARTERLY PERCENT INCREASE

12. COMP. GEN'L. LIAB. LIMIT DESIRED   ☐ BASIC ($300,000)   ☐ OPTION ($1,000,000)

13. 80% COINS. FIRE RATES   ☐ ☐ ☐ ☐ (46 47 48) BLDG.   ☐ ☐ ☐ ☐ (46 47 48) CONTENTS

    80% COINS. EC RATES   ☐ ☐ ☐ ☐ (49 50 51) BLDG.   ☐ ☐ ☐ ☐ (49 50 51) CONTENTS

    TOTAL (ENTRY RATE)

14. STATE NUMBER ☐ ☐ (18 19)   TERRITORY (see manual) ☐ ☐ (33 34)   CLASSIFICATION ☐ ☐ ☐ ☐ ☐ (25 26 27 28 29)

15. PREMIUM COMPUTATION

	REPLACEMENT VALUE	RATE	PREMIUM
COVERAGE-A BUILDING APPURTENANT BLDG.	☐ . ☐ ☐ . ☐ ☐		

☐ ☐ . ☐ ☐ . ☐ ☐ ☐ ☐ (53 54 55 56 57 58)

OPTION: $1,000,000 CGL (for Lessor's Risks only)   +
SPECIAL POLICY ONLY: add .05 to rate.   +
OPTION: B'LDG. INCREASED INFLATION GUARD FACTOR   ×
TOTAL COVERAGE-A RATE   ☐ ☐ . ☐ ☐ ☐ . ☐ ☐ ☐ (59 60 61 62 63 64 65 66)

APARTMENTS ONLY: $25 additional charge per swimming pool   ☐ ☐ . ☐ ☐ ☐ . ☐ ☐ ☐

COVERAGE-B PERSONAL PROPERTY

I. Development of Standard Policy Rate   REPLACEMENT VALUE   RATE   PREMIUM
   ☐ ☐ . ☐ ☐ . ☐ ☐ ☐ (54 55 56 57 58)

OPTION: $1,000,000 CGL   +
DRUGGISTS LIABILITY INCREMENT
(class 59116 only: see state rate pages)   +
ADD'L. DRUGGISTS LIAB. INCR. FOR OPTIONAL $1,000,000 CGL   +
TOTAL STANDARD POLICY RATE   ☐ ☐ . ☐ ☐ ☐ . ☐ ☐ ☐ (59 60 61 62 63 64 65 66)

II. BURGLARY OPTION (Standard Policy Only) ☐ Yes ☐ No   ☐ ☐ . ☐ ☐ ☐ . ☐ ☐ ☐
    Enter Trade Group from Classification Page ☐ ☐
    Premium for Trade Group and Coverage-B Replacement Value (see State Burglary Option Table)

BU 16 01 (Ed. 05 76)

576—Multiple-Lines Insurance Production

TOTAL STANDARD POLICY PREMIUM FOR COVERAGE-B (I + II)

☐ ☐ . ☐ ☐ . ☐ ☐ ☐ ☐
59 60 61 62 63 64 65 66

III SPECIAL POLICY ONLY: Development of Increment
Premium for Trade Group and Coverage-B Replacement Value (see State Special
Policy Table)

☐ ☐ . ☐ ☐ . ☐ ☐ ☐ ☐

TOTAL SPECIAL POLICY PREMIUM FOR COVERAGE-B (I + III)

☐ ☐ . ☐ ☐ . ☐ ☐ ☐ ☐
59 60 61 62 63 64 65 66

16 OPTIONAL COVERAGES

1. EMPLOYEE DISHONESTY   (Number of employees)

☐ ☐
57 58

_____

☐ . ☐ ☐ ☐
63 64 65 66

2. EXTERIOR SIGNS   (Replacement cost)

☐ ☐ . ☐ ☐ ☐
55 56 57 58

_____

☐ . ☐ ☐ ☐
63 64 65 66

3. EXTERIOR GRADE FLOOR GLASS   (Number of sq. ft.)

☐ ☐ ☐
55 56 57 58

_____

☐ . ☐ ☐ ☐
63 64 65 66

4. BOILERS, PRESSURE VESSELS AND AIR CONDITIONING EQUIPMENT

(a) Boilers and Pressure Vessels ☐ YES ☐ NO _____
(Pressure Vessels without Boilers, use Minimum Charge)

☐ . ☐ ☐ ☐
63 64 65 66

(b) BUILDING AIR CONDITIONED ☐ YES ☐ NO _____

☐ . ☐ ☐ ☐
63 64 65 66

5. EARTHQUAKE DAMAGE ASSUMPTION _____

☐ . ☐ ☐

COMPANY USE ONLY

☐ ☐ ☐
30 31 32

☐ ☐ ☐
43 44 45

17. TOTAL POLICY PREMIUM

☐ ☐ . ☐ ☐ . ☐ ☐ ☐

18. GENERAL INFORMATION

(a) AGE OF BUILDING _____ NUMBER OF STORIES _____

(b) SQ. FT. AREA OF BLDG. ☐ ☐ ☐ ☐ SQ. FT. AREA OCCUPIED BY APPLICANT _____
(Merc. and Off. Only) 37 38

(c) PRESENT CARRIERS AND LOSSES LAST THREE YEARS (Whether or not loss was covered by insurance) _____

(d) IF APARTMENT, NUMBER OF APARTMENTS ☐ ☐
37 38

COVERAGE	CARRIER	PREM	DATE & AMT. OF LOSS	CAUSE & DESCRIPTION OF LOSS

YES NO

(e) HAS THE ELECTRICAL SYSTEM BEEN CHECKED IN THE LAST THREE YEARS BY A QUALIFIED ELECTRICIAN? ☐ ☐

(f) HAS THE HEATING SYSTEM BEEN CHECKED IN THE LAST THREE YEARS BY A HEATING CONTRACTOR? ☐ ☐

(g) ARE STORAGE AREAS AND AISLES CLEAN AND TRASH DISPOSED OF PROPERLY? ☐ ☐

(h) IS THERE EVIDENCE OF WATER DAMAGE, BROKEN WINDOWS OR BREAKS IN PAVEMENTS OR FLOORS? ☐ ☐

(i) DOES APPLICANT OWN OR OPERATE ANY OTHER BUSINESS PROPERTY? ☐ ☐

(j) GROSS EARNINGS (12 MONTHS) $ ☐ ☐ ☐ ☐ ☐ ☐ . ☐ ☐ ☐

(k) 100% ANNUAL RENTS (12 MONTHS) $ ☐ ☐ ☐ . ☐ ☐ . ☐ ☐

(l) HOW MUCH MONEY IS KEPT ON THE PREMISES OVERNIGHT? $ ☐ ☐ ☐

(m) DESCRIPTION OF SAFE	(BRAND NAME)	U.L. APPROVED	TYPE OF LOCK	THICKNESS OF DOOR
		☐ YES ☐ NO		

(n) LOCAL GONG ☐ YES ☐ NO CENTRAL STATION ☐ YES ☐ NO UL. CTF NO. EXP. DATE

(o) HOW FREQUENTLY ARE DEPOSITS MADE? HOW MUCH MONEY CARRIED AT ONE TIME?

(p) DOES THE TIME OF DEPOSITS VARY? ☐ YES ☐ NO IS THE ROUTE CHANGED? ☐ YES ☐ NO

(q) DISTANCE TO BANK HOW CONVEYED?

_____   _____

INSURED OR AUTHORIZED REPRESENTATIVE   COMPANY

    _____

    DATE

BU 16 01 (Ed. 05 76)

Exhibit 11-4

Commercial Lines Manual, Division Nine—Multiple Line
Businessowners Subdivision Standard Policy Rates *

**COMMERCIAL LINES MANUAL
DIVISION NINE - MULTIPLE LINE
BUSINESSOWNERS SUBDIVISION
STANDARD POLICY RATES⋆**

RATES PER $100 TO BE APPLIED TO CONTENTS VALUE
$300,000 LIABILITY LIMITS (LIABILITY LIMITS CODE 6)

80% COINS. FIRE+E.C. RATE RANGE	RATE NUMBER								OFFICE CLASS
	1	2	3	4	5	6*	7	8	
0.00-0.049	0.33	0.39	0.45	0.60	0.70	0.81	0.75	0.98	0.32
0.05-0.099	0.37	0.43	0.49	0.63	0.74	0.84	0.79	1.01	0.35
0.10-0.149	0.41	0.46	0.53	0.67	0.77	0.88	0.84	1.05	0.38
0.15-0.199	0.44	0.50	0.56	0.70	0.81	0.92	0.88	1.09	0.41
0.20-0.249	0.48	0.54	0.60	0.74	0.84	0.95	0.92	1.12	0.44
0.25-0.299	0.51	0.57	0.64	0.78	0.88	0.99	0.96	1.16	0.47
0.30-0.349	0.55	0.61	0.67	0.81	0.92	1.03	1.00	1.20	0.50
0.35-0.399	0.59	0.64	0.71	0.85	0.95	1.06	1.05	1.23	0.53
0.40-0.449	0.62	0.68	0.74	0.88	0.99	1.10	1.09	1.27	0.56
0.45-0.499	0.66	0.72	0.78	0.92	1.03	1.13	1.13	1.30	0.59
0.50-0.549	0.70	0.75	0.82	0.96	1.06	1.17	1.17	1.34	0.62
0.55-0.599	0.73	0.79	0.85	0.99	1.10	1.21	1.21	1.38	0.65
0.60-0.649	0.77	0.83	0.89	1.03	1.13	1.24	1.26	1.41	0.68
0.65-0.699	0.80	0.86	0.92	1.07	1.17	1.28	1.30	1.45	0.71
0.70-0.749	0.84	0.90	0.96	1.10	1.21	1.31	1.34	1.48	0.74
0.75-0.799	0.88	0.93	1.00	1.14	1.24	1.35	1.38	1.52	0.78
0.80-0.849	0.91	0.97	1.03	1.17	1.28	1.39	1.43	1.56	0.81
0.85-0.899	0.95	1.01	1.07	1.21	1.31	1.42	1.47	1.59	0.84
0.90-0 ᵒ	0.98	1.04	1.11	1.25	1.35	1.51	1.63		0.87
0.ᵒ˸	ᴖ2	1.08	1.14	1.28	1 ˉ	ˉ5	1.67		0.90
			1.13	1.20.	1.34		1.72		0.ᵒ
				1.27	'				
				ᵎ.34					

---

*Reprinted with permission from *Commercial Lines Manual*, Insurance Services Office, Georgia Rate Page ML-R-1-BP, 2nd Edition 8-79, Copyright 1979.

vessels and air conditioning equipment, each according to the values involved. Burglary coverage may be added to the standard BOP by calculating an incremental premium charge in the same manner used to calculate the special BOP contents premium. Separate burglary incremental rate tables are in the Commercial Lines Manual. The BOP rate tables also set forth the extra charges applicable to increased liability insurance limits (these are added to the coverage A and coverage B premium amounts as applicable) and druggists professional liability coverage.

The final point relative to BOP premium development is the possibility for premium modification for as much as a 15 percent deviation based on certain underwriting factors. (See Exhibit 11-5.) The schedule of special credits and debits can be applied to accounts that develop a BOP premium of $500 or more (before applying these credits or debits). These credits and debits are intended for use when the

Exhibit 11-5
BOP Premium Modification Table*

Risk Characteristics	Range of Modifications		
	Credit		Debit
1. Management—Cooperation in matters of safeguarding and proper handling of property covered.	8%	to	8%
2. Location—Accessibility and environment.	7	to	7
3. Building Features—Age, condition and unusual structural features.	5	to	5
4. Premises and Equipment—Care, condition and type.	5	to	5
5. Employees—Selection, training, supervision and experience.	3	to	3
6. Protection—Not otherwise recognized	2	to	2

*Reprinted with permission from *Commercial Lines Manual*, Insurance Services Office, Copyright 1979.

special characteristics of the business in question do not seem to be fully recognized in the basic BOP rate structure.

Underwriting

The producer has the opportunity to inspect the business premises to gather all underwriting, rating and supporting information needed. The producer has a responsibility to preunderwrite as well as possible, to act within binding authority, and to communicate all needed and pertinent information gathered to the insurance company underwriter.

The first consideration for the "producer-underwriter" is to determine whether the prospect is eligible for the BOP program. The second is to gather information about the business prospect. The information should include, but not necessarily be limited to, the following:

1. The nature of the business activity being conducted. Are there other locations? Is any service or repair work performed? If so, what percentage of the firm's revenue does the activity represent? Is there cooking on the premises? (Recall from the earlier discussion of eligibility that a significant degree of service or repair work will make the business ineligible for the BOP, and of course, any food preparation or service will make the firm ineligible for a BOP.)

2. Information about the building and its contents is necessary for rating and underwriting. For example, of what type construction is the building? What are its dimensions? Does the businessowner own it or lease it? What portion of the building does the business occupy? Is there an external sign? How much exterior grade floor glass is there? What is the replacement cost of the building? Of its contents? Is there any boiler and machinery exposure? What is the general condition of the property and its housekeeping? Does the business have a safe? Safety door locks? A burglar alarm system?

3. How does the producer feel about the management? Are they experienced? Do they seem qualified? Are they actively engaged in operating or supervising the business? How many employees are there? What is the history of employee turnover? Is employee morale good?

4. The "producer-underwriter" should seek out any other relevant facts about this prospect such as the loss history of the business. Do employees regularly use their own vehicles in the course of their employment?

The final responsibility of the "producer-underwriter" in this stage of securing the business is to communicate accurate information to the insurance company underwriter. The completed BOP application is, of course, the principal tool in this communication process, but it should not be the only one. Additional information about this business and how the producer gathered it is helpful to the insurance company underwriter. The producer's job is not only to market insurance products to the public, but also to market applicants to the most appropriate insurer. If the producer can get photographs of the business, they will help tell the producer's and the prospective clients' story. A narrative description of the risk is also very helpful.

CASE STUDIES

Four case studies are used throughout the commercial portion of PRO 81 and 82: (1) J&T Appliances, (2) John Gale, M.D., a general surgeon who also owns a farm, (3) R. P. Davis, Contractor, and (4) Premier Door and Window Company. Of these four, the BOP is clearly suitable only for the first case, J&T Appliances. The other three case situations are either ineligible for or not best served by a BOP. As a contractor, Mr. Davis is specifically ineligible for a BOP coverage. Premium Door and Window Company is ineligible as it is engaged in manufacturing. Since Dr. Gale's case is not clear-cut, it will be discussed.

John Gale, M.D.

While the BOP is intended to insure office buildings as well as mercantile stores and apartments, it is not the most suitable insurance product for all types of offices. As noted in the earlier section of eligibility, there are size restrictions for buildings. These do not rule out BOP coverage for Dr. Gale's building. Some insurance companies specify the types of offices they will insure with the BOP. Such lists typically, but not always, include the offices of accountants, architects, and engineers (unless they are engaged in actual construction), attorneys, insurance agencies, real estate agencies, and travel agencies. Some insurance companies will consider dentists, physicians, and veterinarians on a case-by-case basis. Other insurers will not consider any of these offices eligible. The principal reason for this wide variation of attitudes with respect to eligibility lies in the greater-than-average liability exposures. BOP business liability coverage is inadequate when there is clearly a professional liability exposure. The BOP is generally not intended to serve in such cases. In summary, it can be said that some insurers would issue a BOP for a physicians' office, but many others would not.

In Dr. Gale's case, if (1) he owned an office building strictly as an investor/landlord, (2) he did not occupy one of the office suites within that building, (3) the building met the BOP size guidelines, and (4) the building did not contain any prohibited occupancies, such as a restaurant, he could certainly purchase a BOP to insure that building and the general liability associated with it. Since Dr. Gale is not only the building owner, but also an occupant, any BOP would have to cover his business personal property as well as the building. Dr. Gale might find the BOP coverage inadequate compared to the more conventional "physician's and surgeon's equipment floater." Of course, Dr. Gale, as a surgeon, has a considerable professional liability exposure that must be dealt with outside the BOP, and Dr. Gale's farming operation is not covered at all by a BOP. Thus, even if an insurer might be interested in providing Dr. Gale with a BOP for his office, Dr. Gale would probably consider it too inflexible for his varied and special needs. The SMP package would probably be a superior approach to Dr. Gale's insurance needs. He would also need medical malpractice insurance either as part of the SMP or as a separate policy.

J&T Appliances

The J&T Appliances case is particularly well suited for the BOP. The building leased by J&T meets the BOP eligibility requirements, and the type of business conducted by J&T is specifically eligible. The installation and servicing of appliances is a necessary and incidental part of the business activities accounting for less than 25 percent of the firm's gross revenue ($75,000 of $325,000). J&T could obtain the standard BOP or, if all underwriting criteria were met, the special BOP. Whichever form the J&T partners select, it will insure all of the following exposures:

1. Business Personal Property. On a replacement cost basis, without a coinsurance clause would be insured for the sum of a, b, and c below.
   a. Inventory. This ranges in value from a low of $30,000 to a high of $60,000 during the year with an average value of $45,000. In view of the inflationary trends and the non-reporting 25 percent peak season provision, J&T should probably insure its inventory for at least $48,000 ($48,000 × 1.25 = $60,000 maximum contents exposure).
   b. Furniture, Fixtures, and Equipment. This category of business personal property has an estimated replacement cost of $20,000 and should be insured for this amount.
   c. Leasehold improvements. This has an estimated replacement cost value of $15,000 which should be its insurable value even though its book value is only $6,000 ($10,000 cost less $4,000 depreciation).

   In addition to the coverages outlined above, the BOP will provide J&T Appliances with *transit* coverage for its goods while they are being delivered and with coverage for the property of others in J&T's care, custody, and control (appliances held for repair). In both cases, however, these added coverages are limited to no more than $1,000 per occurrence which is less than J&T's exposure on many occasions. An inland marine floater (Radio, TV, and Appliance Dealer's) would be appropriate for this exposure.
2. Loss of Income. The BOP will cover J&T's actual loss for up to twelve months. This coverage is more than adequate for J&T's

needs inasmuch as it has been estimated that the building they occupy could be rebuilt in approximately five months.

3. Money and Securities Coverage. If J&T chooses to purchase the special BOP form, this type of coverage will be included for the amount set forth in the declarations. J&T has indicated a need for $2,000 of inside and outside money coverage.

4. Optional Property Coverages.

   a. Employee Dishonesty. J&T Appliances has four full-time employees and one part-time employee. While the cash on hand is rarely more than $2,000, the checking account sometimes has as much as $20,000 in it. J&T should try to manage its cash flow more tightly and in addition, its owners might be interested in this form of coverage.

   b. Exterior signs, if any, and the exterior floor grade glass can also be insured under the BOP. Since J&T's lease makes the company liable for glass breakage, glass breakage coverage should be added to their BOP.

   c. The case situation does not reveal if boiler and machinery is needed; but a producer would want to check this possibility.

   d. Burglary and robbery coverage may be added to the standard BOP and J&T would probably be interested in the coverage. The insurer will undoubtedly make the availability of this coverage or the special form BOP contingent upon the quality of the firm's door locks, whether it has a burglary alarm, and so forth. J&T does have a Class B fire resistive safe.

5. The BOP offers J&T Appliances a comprehensive business liability insurance program which includes employer's non-owned automobile coverage and fire and explosion legal liability coverage, another exposure confronting J&T under the terms of its building lease with Mr. Anderson. The products and completed operations coverage provided by the BOP is another highly valuable coverage for a firm engaged in the installation, service, and repair of gas and electrical appliances. And, J&T employees are covered as additional insureds.

All in all, the BOP appears to fit the property-liability insuring needs of J&T Appliances rather well. Of course, the BOP cannot treat the firm's workers' compensation exposure nor its commercial automobile exposure (it uses two panel trucks for delivery and service calls), but most other property-liability insurance needs seem to be well taken care of.

Checkpoints

1. Describe the return of premium provisions for the BOP in case of cancellation.
2. How may a client obtain "replacement cost" adjustment of BOP property losses?
3. Outline the voting procedure for a standard BOP without optional coverages.
4. Generally, why is J&T Appliances the only case that "fits" the BOP?

SUMMARY

The BOP is designed for the average needs of small- and medium-sized businesses. However, a BOP may also be used to offer the professional producer an opportunity to service his or her clients' special needs. For instance, in the J&T Appliances case, in addition to the BOP, workers' compensation, business auto, and life insurance policies, the producer may determine needs for an inland marine floater for the "in-transit" and "care, custody and control" exposures. Perhaps the fire legal liability limit is inadequate for the exposure and a noninsurance transfer of the exposure could be suggested.

The BOP is an excellent product for its intended market. It offers the consumer-businessowner the advantage of broad coverage (replacement cost without coinsurance; loss of income; property of others in the insured's care, custody, and control; transit, peak season, and broad business liability coverage including employees as additional insureds; and much more) in an easy to read policy at a competitive price. For the producer, the BOP offers the advantages of a highly competitive product with wide marketability which is easy to quote (short, simplified applications and one complete reference manual).

Chapter Notes

---

1. Adapted from *F.C.&S. Bulletins*, Fire and Marine Section, Commercial Multi-Peril, pages PB-2 and 3.
2. The replacement cost provisions are discussed more fully in a subsequent section of this chapter under the heading "General Conditions and Other Provisions." It should be noted, however, that some companies permit the BOP to be written on an *actual cash value* basis if that is the request of the insured.
3. Some insurance companies offer other limits of liability, often $500,000, as well as the limit cited in the text.

CHAPTER 12

Special Multi-Peril Policies

INTRODUCTION

The special multi-peril (SMP) program offered the first package of monoline coverages to become generally accepted in the United States and has become the primary "bureau" program for combining property, liability, crime, and boiler and machinery insurance into one contract for the buyer of business insurance. When the SMP program was introduced, eligibility was severely limited and the program was reserved for "superior" exposures. As the SMP program matured, the eligibility requirements broadened, so that today the SMP is one of the most frequently written insurance contracts. Other package policies are similar to the SMP, and many insurers now have independent policy forms.

This chapter will concentrate on the SMP forms; there are so many independent programs that space does not permit adequate review of them all. The producer can benefit from studying the SMP program because almost all insurers still write SMP policies for some accounts, and, more importantly, knowledge of standard forms allows the producer to evaluate alternatives against that standard.

The name "special multi-peril" is not entirely accurate. First, there is no longer anything "special" about the program because there are so many different package programs. Second, it is in fact a multiple-line program—not just a multi-peril plan. Certain policies (like the blanket crime policy) have been multi-peril in form for many years. However, until restrictions prohibiting insurers from combining different lines of insurance in one policy were lifted in the years following World War II, only monoline policies were permitted in most states. Some insurers

585

circumvented these regulations and issued "combination policies." One such contract appeared to be a single automobile insurance policy, but was, in fact, a property policy and a liability policy combined in one policy jacket. The property insurance (automobile physical damage) was insured by one company while the liability insurance was separately insured by a companion company. The combination automobile policy could be referred to as "first generation" package contracts.

The SMP program provides a "second generation" package which integrates monoline forms into a comprehensive insurance program. Since the 1977 revision, when all of the forms were to some extent rewritten, there is more homogeneity to the contract and there is now one section dealing with general provisions.

The package policy is common; most desirable business is now being written on package forms with so-called "residual business" insured on monoline forms. The problem accounts, jumbo accounts, unusual exposures and products liability problems are handled by monoline underwriters. Many insurance companies will use the SMP policy to provide packaged protection for enterprises, large and small, hazardous or not, well-protected or not, and loss-free or not, simply by adjusting the price.

Most producers quickly realize the advantages of package underwriting. For the insurer, the package offers a spread of exposures over more than one line of business and reduced adverse selection. The package offers reduced expenses in policy issuance and administration and expedites premium collection. For the producer the package offers the same advantages and the producer can process one policy rather than having to deliver a stack of separate policies to a client. For the insured there is ease of administration and a premium discount.

A package policy by itself will not eliminate gaps or redundancies in coverage. If only half of a client's exposures are insured by a package, there will be gaps. If the producer orders duplications of protection (for instance, between inland marine and property forms), there will be redundancies in coverage. The SMP program is nothing more than one set of building blocks from which the producer can create an appropriate insurance program. There are other solutions to providing adequate coverage, and the producer who has studied the alternatives will be in the best position to protect the client and to master the competition.

General Requirements

The Insurance Services Office (ISO) Commercial Lines Manual, Division Nine—Multiple Line describes how the SMP policy is to be rated and issued. Many states have exception pages with a few changes from the norm, and the producer will need to investigate such deviations. This chapter cannot cover all state exceptions. Many states have amendatory forms which require study by the producer since these forms often materially alter the coverage in the countrywide forms. Where possible this chapter follows the sequence of the ISO Manual.

General Rules

Application of Rules and Rating Procedures for the SMP. The SMP policy provides both property and liability coverage for eligible applicants, and crime and boiler and machinery may be added optionally. Cancellation of mandatory coverages is not permitted unless the entire policy is cancelled. For each coverage not specifically provided for in the SMP Section of the *ISO Commercial Lines Manual*, the appropriate division of the Manual will provide rates, rules, forms and codes. The SMP policy is divided into four major sections:

Section I—Property Coverage (mandatory)
Section II—Liability Coverage (mandatory)
Section III—Crime Coverage (optional)
Section IV—Boiler and Machinery Coverage (optional)

The rules and rating procedures applying specifically to each major section are treated separately.

Policy Term and Minimum Premium. Policies may be written on a three-year basis or they may be renewed annually by a renewal certificate. The minimum annual premium for Section I is $100 ($300 for reporting form coverage or $2,500 for clients rated under the Multiple Location Premium and Dispersion Credit Plan). The minimum premiums for Section II are the standard general liability minimums subject to package modfications.

Policy Eligibility. Businesses, institutions, and governmental or nonprofit organizations are eligible. Exhibit 12-1 contains a general list of eligible exposures. Not eligible are boarding or rooming houses, other residential premises containing fewer than three apartment units, farms or farming operations, or exposures involved in selling, servicing, or repairing automobiles, motor homes, mobile homes, or motorcycles. Parking lots or garages are ineligible for SMP treatment unless they are incidental to an otherwise eligible class of business. Grain elevators, grain tanks, and grain warehouses are ineligible for the SMP, as are so-called "highly protected risks." Petroleum properties, petrochemical plants, electric generating stations or natural gas pumping stations are ineligible because they have access to separate programs.

Exhibit 12-1
SMP Eligible Exposures

1. Motel-hotels
2. Apartments
3. Offices
4. Mercantile businesses
5. Institutional exposures
6. Service businesses
7. Industrial and processing businesses
8. Contractors

Mandatory Coverage, Conditions, and Provisions. Insurance must be written under both Section I-Property and Section II-Liability unless the coverage is divided among two or more insurance companies. Where liability is written, both bodily injury and property damage liability must be provided.

Policy Form Numbers. There are hundreds of forms in the SMP program. In addition, the SMP "enabling" rule provides that many monoline forms may be used in SMP policies to provide coverage where no SMP form exists. It is possible to request a set of specimen forms from an insurer using SMP forms.

Coinsurance Requirements. The minimum permitted coinsurance in Section I is 80 percent on buildings or personal property written on a specific basis. Blanket insurance requires at least 90 percent coinsurance.

Premium Development. The premium is separately computed for each exposure using monoline rates found in the appropriate section of the *ISO Commercial Lines Manual.* An Individual Risk Premium Modification (IRPM) Plan and a Multiple Location Premium and Dispersion Credit Plan are available as well. Package premium credits are determined by applying package modification factors which vary by state, coverage and eligible class.

The Policy Declarations The declarations page of the SMP policy contains space for the named insured and mailing address, the policy period, the legal form of the insured entity, the premises designated as covered, the insurance provided by Section I and Section II, the applicable forms by policy section, the mortgagee, and an indication of how the premium is to be paid. At the bottom of the declaration page a space is provided for the countersignature of the authorized representative of the insurer.

SMP Conditions and Definitions

The conditions and definitions form must be attached to every SMP policy. It contains those clauses, conditions, provisions, and definitions necessary to the policy not contained in other forms. Ten general conditions will be discussed here while the specific conditions and definitions applicable to Sections I and II will be reviewed later.

Premium If the policy term is longer than one year, and the premium is payable annually, the policy will be rerated on the anniversary date. If the policy is issued without a specified expiration date, it can be continued by payment of the required premium to the insurer prior to each anniversary date. Thus, direct billing is possible for an SMP. The policy expires on the anniversary date if the premium has not been received by the insurance company.

Inception The SMP's coverage begins at 12:01 A.M. Standard Time at the location of the insured. The producer must be careful in replacing an SMP or other package policy with monoline coverage, because there is a potential twelve hour gap from expiration at 12:01 A.M. until the inception of replacement insurance at noon the same day. Many states have a uniform policy inception law stipulating all insurance begins and expires at 12:01 A.M. Standard Time to alleviate the problem.

Cancellation This is a standard cancellation clause allowing the insured to cancel at any time subject to a short rate earned premium and the insurer to cancel with ten days' written notice to the mailing address of the insured as shown in the declarations. Except in cases of nonpayment of premium, many producers have this notice period extended to thirty days or longer. Further, some producers request personal notice of nonrenewal or proposed material change in the contract to allow the client time to replace the coverage should it be canceled by the insurer.

Concealment or Fraud The policy is void if any insured has intentionally concealed or misrepresented any material fact or circumstance relating to the insurance.

Assignment The SMP contract cannot be assigned without consent of the insurer endorsed to the policy.

Subrogation This clause is also standard in stating the insurer's right to subrogation and that the insurer need not pay a loss if the insured has impaired any right of recovery of a loss. The insured may, prior to the loss, release others in writing from liability for loss as respects property while on the premises of the insured, and, as respects property in transit, the insured may ship by released bills of lading.

The SMP amendatory endorsement may replace this entire subrogation clause allowing the insured, prior to the loss, to waive in writing subrogation against any third party. After a loss, the insured can still waive subrogation in writing against a third party insured under the policy or any corporation, firm, or entity which is owned or controlled by the named insured or in which the named insured owns capital stock or other proprietary interest. The insured may waive subrogation following the loss against a parent entity owning or controlling the named insured or owning or controlling capital stock or other proprietary interest in the named insured, and the insured may waive subrogation in writing following a loss against a tenant of the named insured.

Inspection and Audit This provision permits, but does not obligate, the insurer to inspect the insured's property and operations. The insurer does not warrant by an inspection that the property or operation is safe, healthful, or in compliance with any law, rule, or regulation. This attempts to prevent the insured from suing the insurer in the event that a company inspection fails to identify something like a serious fire hazard or an OSHA violation. The insurance company also has the right to audit the books and records of the named insured as they relate to the subject matter of the insurance. In other words, the insurer has the right to verify reports of inventory value and to determine payroll and gross sales figures or other data for claims or rating purposes.

Liberalization Clause If a provision beneficial to the insured is approved in the insured's jurisdiction, the insured's policy automatically contains such beneficial language without need for endorsement or cancellation and reissuance of the policy.

Insurance Under More than One Coverage Part or Endorsement This clause prevents the pyramiding of limits if more than one coverage part or endorsement insures the same loss. For example, should there be a loss covered under both Section I—Property and Section IV—Boiler, the insurer would pay the actual loss sustained and not more than that amount.

Waiver or Change of Provisions This is the typical clause which states that the terms of the insurance are not waived, changed or modified except by endorsement to the policy.

SECTION I—PROPERTY

There are four basic property forms. The alternatives available among the forms are (1) named perils coverage on buildings, (2) named perils on personal property, (3) "all-risks" coverage on buildings, and (4) "all-risks" coverage on personal property. In addition, there are dozens of additional forms which can be used to broaden Section I to include coverage against various exposures. The SMP is designed to be written without a statutory standard fire policy. However in states mandating inclusion of such a contract, an endorsement is available. Because property insurance was treated in PRO 81, a detailed review of property coverages is presented.

Before turning to the specific forms for insuring property, the conditions applicable to Section I are reviewed.

Property Conditions

The conditions of property insurance in the SMP are essentially similar to those studied in Chapters 10 through 12, *Principles of Insurance Production* (the PRO 81 text).

Policy Period, Territory   Section I of the policy applies only to loss during the policy period while within or between the fifty states of the United States, the District of Columbia, and Puerto Rico.

Deductible   The property coverage of the SMP program may be more restrictive than monoline property forms because a standard $100 deductible applies *separately* to each building or location subject to an aggregate in any one occurrence of $1,000.

Thus, if vandals cause $100 damage to each of ten buildings in a townhouse complex, the insured would recover nothing. The producer, using one of various available endorsements, can increase the amount of the deductible, modify the deductible to apply per occurrence rather than per building or location basis, or establish an annual aggregate deductible for each policy year.

Coinsurance Clause   This is a standard coinsurance clause which refers to the percentage stated in the declarations. Inventory and appraisal of undamaged property are waived when the aggregate claim for any loss is both less than $10,000 and less than 5 percent of the limit for all contributing property insurance. The insured can elect to suspend the coinsurance provision regarding buildings by filing a signed SMP statement of values form. If these values are accepted by the insurer, the SMP agreed amount endorsement form is attached to the policy. This form substitutes an agreed dollar amount as the basis for insurance to value.

On valued personal property the insurer is not liable for a greater proportion of any loss than the amount applying under the policy to the property involved bears to the amount for the property as shown in the schedule of the endorsement. Institutional and condominium exposures may extend coverage to apply an agreed amount provision to personal property. The endorsement includes an expiration date, and if it is not extended by endorsement, the coinsurance clause is automatically reinstated, so the producer must suspense for this form just as if it were a policy renewal.

Removal The policy covers *loss by removal* of the insured property from a premises endangered by the perils insured. The insurance applies pro rata for five days at each "proper" temporary location.

Debris Removal The policy covers the expense of debris removal occasioned by any of the perils insured against up to the limit of insurance. The charges for debris removal are not considered in the determination of actual cash value for coinsurance purposes.

War and Nuclear Exclusions These are standard exclusions of loss caused by war or nuclear perils.

Other Insurance Other insurance is divided into two types—*contributing insurance* and *noncontributing insurance.* If insurance is on the same plan, terms, conditions, and provisions as the SMP policy, it is contributing and all such policies participate in a loss on a pro-rata basis. If the insurance is not the same, the SMP is excess over other insurance whether collectible or not.

A form is available to indicate how Section I coverage is shared between insurance companies. It shows the percentage of total limits for all contributing insurance policies and the form has a space to indicate the policy number of the SMP policy providing Section II coverage (liability coverage cannot be shared among insurers).

Duties of the Named Insured After a Loss In case of loss, the named insured must perform those duties usual to property insurance including notifying the insurer, protecting property, preparing an inventory of goods and so forth. The producer should note that one duty requires police notification if the loss is due to a violation of law.

Appraisal This clause is similar to one found in the standard fire policy. Appraisals apply only to *differences* between the insured and insurer concerning the amount of loss and *does not apply* to disputes over the actual cash value of the property.

Company Options and Abandonment of Property These conditions make it clear that the insurer has the right to take all or any part of the property damaged at an agreed value, or to repair, rebuild, or replace it with equivalent property and need not accept any property because the insured has abandoned it.

Payment of Loss The insurer must pay all adjusted claims within thirty days after presentation and acceptance of proof of loss.

Privilege to Adjust with Owner This condition applies to the property of others held by the named insured. The insurer has the right to adjust loss or damage with the owner, and in the event of legal proceedings against the insured, the insurance company reserves the right (at its option and without expense to the insured) to conduct the defense on behalf of the insured.

Suit The insured cannot sue the insurer unless the insured has complied with all policy provisions and has commenced the suit within one year after the loss.

Permits and Use This clause gives the insured permission to make alterations and repairs and, in the event of loss, to take reasonable steps to protect the property from further damage.

Vacancy, Unoccupancy, and Increase in Hazard This clause suspends insurance while a building is vacant (i.e., contains no contents pertaining to operations or activities customary to occupancy of the building) beyond a period of sixty consecutive days. An SMP amendatory endorsement is less restrictive, imposing a 15 percent reduction in the amount of loss payment otherwise due while the building is vacant beyond sixty days unless the period of permitted vacancy is extended by further endorsement. These two provisions do not apply to the perils of vandalism or malicious mischief or to sprinkler leakage, because those forms contain a more restrictive thirty day vacancy condition. Another endorsement grants permission for increased hazards and for change in use or occupancy.

Protective Safeguards This clause suspends the insurance (only as respects the location affected) if, as a condition of the insurance, the insured has agreed to maintain, so far as is within the insured's control, such protective safeguards as are set forth by endorsement (an alarm system, for instance), and the safeguards are not in place.

Mortgage Clause—Applicable Only to Buildings This clause is similar to that found in the standard fire policy and provides broad protection to the mortgagee in the event of any act or neglect of the mortgagor or owner, any foreclosure, any change in title or occupancy of the premises provided that the mortgagor pays the premium if the mortgagee fails to do so. This clause provides that the mortgagee must notify the insurer of any change of ownership or occupancy or increase of hazard. The insurance company can cancel but must provide ten days notice to the mortgagee. The insurer becomes subrogated to any rights of the mortgagee in the event of payment to the mortgagee of claims for which no liability existed under the policy.

Recoveries This clause entitles the insured to all recoveries in excess of the amount paid by the insurance company, less only the actual cost of effecting such recoveries.

Loss Clause The policy limits are not reduced by the amount of any loss (as is often the case with inland marine contracts).

No Benefit to Bailee The insurance does not inure directly or indirectly to the benefit of any carrier or other bailee. This provision is included to make the bailee's insurance primary.

No Control This clause says that the insurance will not be prejudiced by any act or neglect of any building if the insured is not the owner or by any act or neglect of any occupancy other than the insured when such act or neglect is not within the control of the insured. For example, if another occupant of the building commits arson and the insured's property is destroyed, the insured's policy still applies.

Failure of the insured to comply with any warranty or condition will not prejudice the insurance with regard to any portion of the premises over which the insured has no control.

Property Forms

There are four basic property forms: (1) general building form (named peril coverage), (2) general personal property form (named peril coverage), (3) special building form ("all-risks" coverage) and (4) special personal property form ("all-risks" coverage). In addition, special forms are provided for condominiums and additional coverages.

General Building Form (Named Perils Coverage) This form provides building coverage on a named perils basis and can be used in conjunction with either of the personal property forms or with other Section I endorsements. What follows is a detailed presentation of the general building form. Essentially it is similar to the general property form building coverages.

Property Covered. "Building(s)" or "structure(s)" include attached additions and extensions; fixtures, machinery, and equipment consitituting a permanent part of and pertaining to the service of the building(s); materials and supplies intended for use in construction, alteration, or repair; yard fixtures; personal property of the insured used for maintenance or service of the building(s), including fire extinguishing apparatus, outdoor furniture, floor coverings, and appliances for refrigerating, ventilating, cooking, dishwashing, and laundering (but not including other personal property in apartments or rooms furnished by the named insured as landlord); all while at the designated premises.

Property Not Covered.   The policy does not cover:

A.   Outdoor swimming pools; fences; piers, wharves and docks; beach or diving platforms or appurtenances; retaining walls not constituting a part of a building; walks, roadways and other paved surfaces.

B.   The cost of excavations, grading or filling foundations of buildings, machinery; boilers or engines when such foundations are below the undersurface of the lowest basement floor, or where there is no basement, below the surface of the ground; pilings, piers, pipes, flues and drains which are underground; pilings which are below the low water mark.

C.   Outdoor signs, whether or not attached to a building or structure.

D.   Lawns; outdoor trees, shrubs and plants except as provided in the extensions of coverage.

E.   Property which is more specifically covered in whole or in part by this or any other contract of insurance, except for the amount of loss which is in excess of the amount due from such more specific insurance.

Extensions of Coverage.   Except with respect to replacement cost, each of the limits specified in this section applies as an *additional amount of insurance*, and the coinsurace clause *does not* apply to the extensions.

NEWLY ACQUIRED PROPERTY.   For thirty days from the date construction begins, the insured can apply up to 25 percent of the limit specified for buildings to cover direct loss in any one occurrence to new buildings and structures being built on the described premises and intended for similar occupancy. The insured also has thirty days automatic coverage on buildings acquired at any location within the territorial limits of the policy and used for similar occupancies or warehouse purposes. Additional premiums are due and payable for the added values. The form contains a limit of $100,000, but an SMP amendatory endorsement may remove this ceiling.

OFF PREMISES.   The insured can apply up to 2 percent of the limits of liability specified for building(s), but not exceeding $5,000, to cover property while removed for the purposes of cleaning, repairing, reconstruction, or restoration. The extension does not apply to property in transit nor at any premises owned, leased, or controlled by the insured.

OUTDOOR TREES, SHRUBS, AND PLANTS.   The insured may apply up to $1,000 to cover outdoor trees, shrubs, and plants at the designated premises against direct loss by the perils of fire, lightning, explosion, riot, civil commotion, or aircraft damage subject to a limit of $250 for any one tree, shrub, or plant including the expenses for debris removal.

REPLACEMENT COST. Coverage is for replacement cost if (1) the damage to the building structure is less than $1,000, (2) the loss was not to outdoor furniture, outdoor equipment, floor coverings, awnings, and appliances, and (3) the amount of insurance satisfies the coinsurance clause. A replacement cost coverage endorsement, discussed later in this chapter, is available to change the policy valuation in this or other forms from actual cash value to replacement cost for all property losses.

Perils Insured. The general building form is a named perils form. The coverage is for the perils of fire, lightning, windstorm or hail, explosion (subject to the usual "boiler" and sonic boom exceptions), smoke, aircraft or vehicles (subject to normal limitations), riot, riot attending a strike or civil commotion, and vandalism and malicious mischief.

The insurer is not liable for loss to glass or outdoor signs or loss caused by crime (except damage caused by a burglar), boiler and machinery "accidents," depreciation or deterioration, nor losses if the building is vacant or unoccupied beyond thirty days.

Exclusions. In addition to exclusions for earthquake, flood, and certain other kinds of water damage, the policy contains exclusions for enforcement of any ordinance or law regulating the use, construction, repair or demolition of buildings or structures. The policy does not cover loss occasioned by any electrical injury or disturbance to electrical appliances, devices, fixtures, or wiring caused by artificially generated electrical currents except for ensuing fire. The policy excludes loss caused by interruption of power or other utility service away from the designated premises except for ensuing loss from an insured peril.

Valuation. All property is valued at actual cash value (ACV) at the time of loss. Loss payments may not exceed the amount to repair or replace the property with materials of like kind and quality within a reasonable time after such loss nor for more than the interest of the named insured.

General Personal Property Form (Named Perils Coverage)
This form provides personal property coverage on a named perils basis. It can be used alone or with any of the building forms.

Property Covered. Property covered included personal property of the insured and of others.

PERSONAL PROPERTY OF THE INSURED. The form covers business personal property owned by the insured and usual to the occupancy of the insured. An SMP amendatory endorsement deletes the words "and usual to the occupancy of the insured" from the form. Property covered includes the insured's interest in personal property owned by others to the extent of the value of labor, materials, and charges furnished, performed, or incurred by the insured. Coverage is in or on the buildings or in the open (including within vehicles) or within 100 feet of the designated premises. Coverage includes the insured's use interest in fixtures, alterations, installations or additions comprising a part of the building occupied but not owned by the insured and made or acquired at the expense of the insured exclusive of rent paid, but which are not legally subject to removal by the insured.

PERSONAL PROPERTY OF OTHERS. The policy covers personal property of owner(s) of such property, other than the named insured, in the care, custody, or control of the insured. Loss is adjusted with the named insured, but the insurer reserves the right to adjust any loss with the owners. This is not legal liability or bailee's customers coverage for the insured. For clients with minor or infrequent bailee exposures, it can provide adequate coverage. A limit must be declared on the declarations for coverage to be in force.

Property Not Covered. Property not covered refers to those kinds of property usual to property insurance forms (animals, vehicles, outdoor signs, money, and so forth). Many of the kinds of property not covered are insured using other forms of insurance.

Extensions of Coverage. The amounts of insurance for extensions apply as an additional amount of insurance, and the coinsurance clause does not apply to loss under the extensions of coverage. The insured may apply up to 10 percent of the limit of liability for personal property of the insured, not exceeding $10,000, to cover (1) new and similar property acquired for thirty days from the date of acquisition, (2) direct loss at any location (except fairs or exhibitions) acquired by the insured for similar occupancies, or (3) for warehousing purposes. The insured may apply up to 2 percent, but not exceeding $5,000, to cover personal property of the insured (other than merchandise or stock) while removed from the designated premises for cleaning, repairing, reconstruction or restoration. This extension does not apply to property in transit or at any other location owned, leased, operated, or controlled by the insured.

The insured may apply up to $100 for any individual and $500 in the aggregate per loss to cover personal effects of the insured, officers, partners or employees of the insured. The insured may apply up to $500 to cover valuable papers and records to pay the cost of research or other expense necessarily incurred by the insured to reproduce, replace, or restore such records. Up to $250 on any one tree, shrub, or plant and $1,000 per occurrence applies to outdoor trees, shrubs, and plants. One thousand dollars may be applied to cover extra expense incurred by the insured in order to continue as nearly as practicable the normal operations of the insured's business immediately following damage. The insured may apply at each location up to 2 percent, but not exceeding $2,000, to cover for the account of the owner's personal property *similar to that covered by the policy* belonging to others while in the care, custody or control of the insured.

Perils Insured and Exclusions. The covered perils and exclusions are the same as those in the general building form.

Valuation. Valuation is determined by the type of property damaged (stock, tenant's improvements and betterments, valuable papers and records, and other property).

STOCK. The value of stock sold but not delivered is the selling price less all discounts and unincurred expenses.

TENANT'S IMPROVEMENTS AND BETTERMENTS. If repaired at the expense of the insured, tenant's improvements and betterments are covered for their actual cash value. If not repaired, they are covered for that proportion of the original installation cost which the unexpired term of the lease or rental agreement bears to the period from the date such improvements or betterments were made to the expiration date of the lease. The policy will not pay if the tenant's improvements and betterments are repaired or replaced by others.

VALUABLE PAPERS AND RECORDS. Books of account, manuscripts, and other records (except film, tape, disc, drum cell, and other magnetic recording or storage media for electronic data processing) are covered for the cost of blank books, cards, or other blank material plus the cost of labor incurred by the insured for transcribing or copying such records. Film, tape, disc, and so forth are covered up to the cost of such media in unexposed or blank form.

ALL OTHER PROPERTY. Other property is insured at actual cash value but not exceeding the amount to repair or replace the property with materials of like kind and quality.

Special Building Form

Property Covered and Excluded. The property covered and property excluded by the "all-risks" building form is the same as the named perils form.

Property Subject to Limitations. The comprehensive nature of an "all-risks" form dictates the necessity to limit coverage for some types of property. Plumbing, heating, or air conditioning equipment is not covered for freezing while the building is vacant or unoccupied unless the insured takes positive action to keep them from freezing. Boiler "objects" are not covered for "accidents." Glass is covered for limited dollar amounts from damage caused by specified perils. Fences, pavements, swimming pools, and the like are not covered for freezing, thawing, or weight of ice or water. Coverage for smokestacks and awnings and antennas is restricted. Interior damage to the building is restricted unless caused by perils outlined in the policy. Buildings under construction receive limited coverage. Finally, property under repair is not covered for loss caused by the work performed on the property.

Extensions of Coverage. Extensions of coverage in the special building form (except the replacement cost extension) are additional amounts of insurance and are identical with the general building form.

Perils Insured Against. The policy insures "all-risks" of direct physical loss.

Exclusions. The first four exclusions are identical to those found in the general building form relating to building ordinances, electrical injury, interruption of power, and earthquake and flood losses. The form goes on to eliminate certain other losses typically excluded in "all-risks" form:

- wear and tear, settling and cracking, animal damages,
- boiler systems,
- V&MM or theft if vacant or unoccupied for thirty consecutive days,
- leakage after a heating or cooling system freezes,
- theft of building materials
- mysterious disappearance, and
- continuous seepage.

Valuation. All losses are subject to actual cash valuation not exceeding the amount which it would cost to repair or replace with material of like kind and quality within a reasonable time after the loss, nor in any event for more than the interest of the named insured.

Special Personal Property Form

Property Covered and Not Covered. The property covered by the special personal property form is the same as that covered by the general personal property form with a few exceptions. In addition, this form covers animals and pets when held for sale. The special forms do not cover property sold by the insured under conditional sale, trust agreement, installment payment, or other deferred payment plan, after delivery to customers.

Property Subject to Limitations. Except for loss by the "specified perils" for fire, lightning, aircraft, explosion, riot, civil commotion, smoke, vehicles, windstorm, or hail to property contained in any building, vandalism and malicious mischief, leakage or accidental discharge from automatic fire protective systems, some kinds of property receive limited coverage because they are better covered by other forms.

FURS AND FUR GARMENTS.   Recovery is limited to a maximum of $1,000 in any one occurrence.

JEWELRY.   Jewelry and watches, watch movements, jewels, pearls, precious and semi-precious stones, bullion, gold, silver, platinum, and other precious alloys or metals are covered for an amount not exceeding $1,000 in any one occurrence (this limitation does not apply to jewelry and watches valued at $25 or less per item).

PATTERNS AND DIES.   Property of this kind is covered up to $1,000 per occurrence.

VALUABLE PAPERS.   Valuable papers and records are covered only against loss caused by the "specified perils" listed above.

ANIMALS AND PETS.   When held for sale or sold but not delivered, animals and pets are covered only against death or destruction directly resulting from or made necessary by "specified perils."

OUTDOOR TREES, SHRUBS, AND PLANTS.   This kind of property is not covered except when held for sale or sold but not delivered, and then only against direct loss by "specified perils."

GLASS AND OTHER ARTICLES OF FRAGILE OR BRITTLE NATURE. This property is covered against loss by breakage only if directly caused by "specified perils," but this limitation does not apply to bottles or similar containers of property for sale nor lenses or photographic or scientific instruments.

BOILERS AND MACHINERY.   This equipment may be covered for explosion and related perils by the optional SMP boiler and machinery section IV.

Extensions of Coverage.   Some of the extensions are identical to those contained in the general personal property form. Coverage for (1) property at newly acquired locations, (2) the property of others, and (3) personal effect, valuable papers, and extra expense is identical.

There is no extension of coverage in this form for property while removed from the designated premises for cleaning, repairing, reconstruction or restoration.

The form excludes losses (except by fire or explosion) to property owned or controlled by the insured caused by a crime.

There is an extension of up to $1,000 to covered personal property (other than personal property in the care, custody or control of salesmen) during transportation by motor vehicles owned, leased, or operated by the insured for loss caused by specified perils.

Perils Insured Against.   The policy insures against "all-risks" of direct physical loss.

Exclusions. Loss caused by enforcement of any ordinance or law regulating construction, against electrical injury or disturbances, against interruption of power, and except for ensuing fire or explosion, against earthquake and flood are excluded as they are in the general personal property form.

Additional exclusions are similar to the general property form plus loss by fraud, infidelity, or to property in the open caused by snow, sleet or rain.

Valuation. The valuation provisions are identical to the named perils form.

Special Form Ineligibility. The special personal property form generally cannot be used to insure dealers in livestock, live poultry or animals, florist greenhouses, nurseries, plant or shrubbery dealers, or wholesale fresh fruit and vegetable dealers. The following categories of business personal property, more appropriately insured on other forms, may be excluded from coverage by endorsement:

1. construction or agricultural equipment
2. fine arts
3. fur, fur garments, and garments trimmed with fur, jewelry and watches, watch movements, jewels, pearls, precious and semi-precious stones, gold, silver, platinum, and other precious alloys or metals
4. glass
5. live animals, birds, or fish
6. musical instruments
7. photographic equipment and supplies
8. property of others
9. scientific equipment
10. signs inside the premises
11. tenants improvements and betterments
12. trees, shrubs, or plants
13. valuable papers and records
14. vending machines and contents

Condominium Forms A condominium is a building or group of buildings with a number of owners who each own one or more units within that building outright and own an undivided interest in a portion of the property called the common area. The common area can be the structural elements of the buildings, parking, and recreational areas, landscaping, or virtually any other facility owned in common by all of the unit owners. Originally, the unit was defined as a "box of air" bounded by the unfinished ceiling, floor, and four exterior walls. Units may also be defined as consisting of the interior space as originally constructed. The difference is important because usually the condominium association is responsible for maintenance or loss to the common area, and the unit owner responsible for maintenance or loss within the unit. Each condominium association has a condominium agreement which defines where the common area ends and the unit begins. In many states this agreement is called the covenants, conditions, and restrictions (or "CC&Rs").

Insuring condominium associations can be complex because the insurance on the interests of the association in the common areas must be carefully coordinated to be certain that what goes on inside the individual units does not affect association coverage. For instance, the coinsurance clause and the amount of insurance must only take into account the values of the assets of the association, and any increases in values within the units (being the responsibility of the unit owners) should not jeopardize the association program by exposing it to inadequate limits or a coinsurance penalty at time of loss. The producer must carefully read the CC&Rs to be certain the insurance is properly coordinated.

Coverage can be provided under the SMP program for condominium associations and for individual condominium unit owners. Individuals may also separately insure their residential interests with a homeowners form.

SMP Condominium Additional Policy Provisions Endorsement. When coverage is provided for a condominium association, this form amends the general conditions with regard to subrogation (the insurer waives its rights to subrogate against any unit owner), to other insurance (the association policy is primary with regard to any other insurance in the name of a unit owner covering the same property), and with regard to loss settlement (insurance losses can be adjusted with and paid to an insurance trustee designated by the named insured).

SMP Condominium Building Forms. There are named perils and "all-risks" forms available. Both parallel the building forms described earlier, except the property covered includes outdoor furniture and fixtures, improvements and alterations composing a part of the building, and refrigerators, air conditioners, cooking ranges, dishwashers, and clothes washers and dryers contained within units and owned by the named insured or unit owners. If the named insured condominium association is not responsible for interior fixtures and improvements in the units, they must be excluded from the policy (an SMP condominium endorsement does that with regard to the equipment and appliances within the units).

Property owned by, used by, or in the care, custody or control of a unit owner, except equipment and appliances as indicated, is excluded from the form.

SMP Condominium Personal Property Forms.   There are named perils and "all-risks" forms for condominium associations. This insurance covers personal property of the named insured and personal property in which each of the condominium unit owners has an undivided interest including personal property owned by others to the extent of labor and materials expended thereon by the named insured. The section of the policy listing property not covered excludes coverage for personal property owned by a unit owner except when a specific limit of liability for personal property in the care, custody, or control of the named insured is shown in the declarations.

There are also named peril and "all-risks" forms for condominium unit owners. These forms are designed to cover business personal property owned by the unit owner. Personal property of unit owners is insured using a personal lines form.

Builder's Risk Insurance   The SMP program can be used for insuring buildings in the course of construction for the owner on a *completed value* basis. The coverage can be provided if the building, when completed, will be eligible for SMP policy forms. The interest of the contractor, in addition to that of the owner, may be included in Section I only on a named peril or "all-risks" form. The amount of insurance shown as the "Provisional Limit of Liability" may not be less than the full contract value less the value of any property such as foundations and other such property which can be excluded. When buildings, structures, or additions in the course of construction are either completed or occupied, such property becomes the subject of a new SMP and is no longer insured by builder's risk. These forms parallel the basic policy forms with regard to the major aspects of the coverage.

Both the named peril and "all-risks" policies include an occupancy clause which makes it a condition of the policy that the buildings, additions, or structures in the course of construction shall not be occupied without obtaining the consent of the insurer endorsed onto the policy with proper rate adjustment (machinery may be set up and operated solely for the purpose of testing without prejudice to the policy).

A deductible of $500 applies to vandalism or malicious mischief in the named perils form. A $500 deductible applies on the "all-risks" form to any peril other than fire or extended coverage.

The forms do not contain a coinsurance clause per se but have a condition (Provisional Limit of Liability) which establishes the insurer's liability to no greater proportion of a loss than the provisional limit of liability to the value of the property at completion.

Reporting Form Coverages If insurance is to be arranged on a reporting basis, either the reporting endorsement—average rate or the reporting endorsement—specific rate, must be attached to the policy. Most experienced producers consider reporting forms to be advantageous if fluctuations in exposures over the year vary by more than 10 to 15 percent. If the exposures do not change more than that amount during the year, any savings in premium is generally offset by the administrative expense of reporting inventory figures.

The two reporting forms are indentical except that the average rate form calls for premium adjustment based on an average rate per $100 of insurance set at inception, while the specific rate form adjusts premiums based on specific rates at each reported location.

Property Covered. Both forms must indicate whether the form applies to personal property of the insured, to personal property of others, or to both by specifying an "X" in the box(es) on the form.

Locations Covered. The forms show a schedule of locations with a provisional limit of liability for each. The form provides for a limit for "any other location" declared at the inception of the insurance and a limit for "any other location" acquired by the insured for similar occupancies or warehouse purposes, if reported in the next report of values following acquisition. The "any other location" limit declared at inception can be used by the insured to cover minor exposures which need not be listed in the policy schedule. Insurance can also be written on a blanket basis with one limit of insurance applying over more than one location.

Reporting Provisions. There are three clauses affecting the reporting of values.

PROVISIONAL AMOUNT CLAUSE. Although a provisional limit of insurance is established, it is the intent of the insurance to cover only the total actual cash value of the property described. Thus if the provisional limit was set at $100,000 but the ACV of property at time of loss was $80,000, only $80,000 would be paid in the event of loss.

VALUE REPORTING CLAUSE. This clause makes provisions for the reporting of values and states the penalties for late reporting or failure to report at all.

FULL REPORTING CLAUSE. This clause is the equivalent of a 100 percent coinsurance clause in its effect on loss settlement. Because of this provision and because sprinkler leakage is a peril often insured for a lower limit and a lower percentage of insurance to value, separate forms are available to permit a lower coinsurance percentage to apply to that specific peril. The forms are sprinkler leakage reporting form—average rate and sprinkler leakage reporting form—specific rate. They do not require separate reports of value, but merely provide the mechanics to apply a different rate and a different coinsurance percentage to the sprinkler leakage peril.

Premium Adjustment Clause. This clause states how the final adjusted premium for the policy is to be determined through averaging the monthly reports of value at the expiration of the policy. Because some policies are written for a three-year term and the insured and insurer prefer an adjustment of the premium annually, endorsement for annual adjustment of provisional premium is available. The premiums may be charged periodically during the term of the policy if this clause is modified by endorsement specifying the interval(s) at which such adjustment is to be made. The premium adjustment clause requires the insured to report *full values* at each location and to *pay premiums on such values* even though the values are greater than the limit of liability of the policy. The producer must establish a system to monitor the reports and be certain that the policy limits are increased if the report values exceed the limit.

Debris Removal Clause (Limited Coverage). Debris removal expense is covered by the policy, but not in excess of the actual cash value of the property covered and not if occasioned by enforcement of any ordinance or law regulating the use, construction, repair, or demolition of property. Although covered, debris removal is not considered as part of the actual cash value for determining compliance with the full reporting clause.

Time Element Coverages This section will summarize the SMP time element forms which provide insurance against loss of gross earnings, loss of earnings, extra expenses, combined business interruption and extra expense losses, tuition fees losses, and loss of rents. Students are encouraged to reread Chapter 12 of PRO 81, *Principles of Insurance Production,* for further details of coverages.

General Characteristics of the SMP Time Element Forms. Each form has a distinctly different insuring agreement which defines the broad scope of the coverage, and contains definitions, exclusions or conditions related to the insuring agreement. No deductible applies to time element losses.

ACTUAL LOSS SUSTAINED. The insurance company is liable only for the actual loss sustained on the described premises by the insured. There is no provision in the SMP program for valued business interruption coverage, nor for contingent coverage away from the premises.

DUE DILIGENCE AND DISPATCH. The insurance applies only for such length of time as would be required, with the exercise of due diligence and dispatch, to rebuild, repair, or replace the property damaged or destroyed. Coverage extends from the date of the damage or destruction and is not limited by the expiration of the policy.

ORDER OF CIVIL AUTHORITY. Most of the forms extend coverage for up to two weeks when access to the premises is specifically prohibited by order of civil authority as a direct result of damage to or destruction of property adjacent to the insured location.

ELECTRONIC DATA PROCESSING LIMITATIONS. Because separate insurance is available on a computer and related equipment as well as loss of use, most of the forms limit losses resulting from damage to or destruction of media for, or programming records pertaining to, electronic data processing equipment to a maximum of thirty consecutive days.

EXPENSES TO REDUCE LOSS. Under most forms the policy pays such expenses as are necessarily incurred for the purpose of reducing loss; however, this amount cannot exceed the amount by which the loss is reduced. This aspect of the coverage poses serious problems in loss adjustment, because often the expenses are incurred before it is known to what extent a loss may be reduced. For example, advertising of a fire sale must be arranged before it is known whether the proceeds of the sale will exceed the advertising cost.

RESUMPTION OF OPERATIONS. The insured is generally required to resume operations as quickly as possible by making use of merchandise, stock (raw, in process, or finished), or other property at locations described or elsewhere.

CONTRIBUTION CLAUSE. All of the forms contain one or another form of insurance-to-value (contribution) clause which replaces the coinsurance clause related to direct damage. The gross earnings form, for example, contains the following clause:

> 4. Contribution Clause: The company shall not be liable for a greater proportion of any loss than the limit of liability specified above bears to the amount produced by multiplying the Contribution Clause Percentage specified above by the Gross Earnings that would have been earned (had no loss occurred) during the 12 months immediately following the date of damage to or destruction of the described property.

The loss of earnings endorsement encourages insurance to value because it contains a limit of liability for each thirty-day period and an aggregate limit as well. This encourages the insurance buyer to determine a maximum monthly exposure and to multiply that amount times the number of months that the business could possibly be interrupted to establish the aggregate limit. A penalty is imposed if the insured does not establish the appropriate limit.

The extra expense endorsement encourages insurance to value by setting a limit of recovery for each successive one-month period. The limit is 40 percent for the first month, 80 percent in the aggregate for a period of restoration of two months, and 100 percent when the period of restoration is in excess of two months.

The loss of rents endorsement is written on a contribution basis and requires use of a 50, 60, 80, 90, or 100 percent contribution clause based on annual rents. Blanket insurance can only be written subject to the 90 percent contribution clause or higher. Tuition fees insurance is written subject to an 80 or 100 percent contribution clause.

ALTERATIONS AND NEW BUILDINGS. Permission is granted in most forms to make alterations in or to construct additions to any described building and to construct new buildings on the described premises.

ADDITIONAL EXCLUSIONS AND LIMITATIONS. The insurer is not liable for any increase of loss by (1) enforcement of any local or state ordinance or law regulating construction, repair or demolition of building or structures, or (2) for interference at the described premises by strikers or other persons with the rebuilding, repairing, or replacing of the property or with the resumption or continuation of business.

Gross Earnings Endorsement. Coverage in the SMP program is virtually identical with that provided by monoline forms (*Principles of Insurance Production,* Chapter 12). The gross earnings endorsement—ordinary payroll exclusion endorsement, and ordinary payroll—limited coverage endorsement, have counterparts in monoline forms. Coverage extends to loss resulting directly from necessary interruption of business at the premises described, but not exceeding the reduction in gross earnings less charges and expenses which do not necessarily continue during the interruption. Due consideration is given to the continuation of normal charges and expenses, including payroll expense (unless excluded or limited), to the extent necessary to resume operations with the same quality of service which existed immediately preceding the loss. The policy pays such excess expenses as would be necessarily incurred in replacing any finished stock used by the insured to reduce the loss.

If an entity has been in operation for over twelve months, it is possible to eliminate the effect of the contribution clause by attaching an agreed amount endorsement. The producer must establish a suspense on this endorsement since it expires annually unless a new application for agreed amount endorsement is filed with the insurer.

DEFINITION OF GROSS EARNINGS. The definition of "gross earnings" poses problems because it is framed in insurance terminology little understood by the insured or the insured's accountants. It is critical for the producer to be able to "translate" this definition so that the proper amounts of insurance are arranged.

a. For the purposes of this insurance, "gross earnings" are defined as the sum of:
    (1) total net sales value of production, and
    (2) total net sales of merchandise, and
    (3) other earnings derived from operations of the business,

less the cost of:
    (4) raw stock from which such production is derived, and
    (5) supplies consisting of materials consumed directly in the conversion of such raw stock into finished stock or in supplying the services sold by the insured, and
    (6) merchandise sold, including packaging materials therefor, and
    (7) services purchased from outsiders (not employees of the insured) for resale which do not continue under contract.
NO OTHER COSTS SHALL BE DEDUCTED IN DETERMINING GROSS EARNINGS.

In determining gross earnings, due consideration shall be given to the experience of the business before the date of damage or destruction and the probable experience thereafter had no loss occurred.

By endorsing the policy to limit or exclude ordinary payroll, the definition of gross earnings is amended accordingly. Ordinary payroll is defined as the entire payroll expense for all employees of the insured, except officers, executives, department managers, employees under contract, and other important employees.

Using monoline forms, the producer can extend the period of indemnity under the policy to cover beyond the date that repairs are completed, and thereby cover reduced earnings that may result after resumption of operations until normal business levels are attained.

OTHER DEFINITIONS. Other definitions important to business interruption include "directly," "normal," "raw stock," "stock in process," "finished stock," and "merchandise," all discussed in PRO 81.

OTHER EXCLUSIONS. The insurer is not liable for the suspension, lapse or cancellation of any lease, license, contract, or order unless resulting directly from the interruption of business and then for only such loss as affects the insured's earnings during the period of indemnity covered by the policy. The insurer is not liable for any other consequential or remote loss, or for loss resulting from damage to or destruction of finished stock. The loss of profit in finished stock can be insured using the manufacturers' selling price endorsement. The insurer is not liable for loss resulting from theft of any property which at the time of loss is not an integral part of a building or structure (except direct loss by pillage and looting occurring during and at the immediate place of a riot or civil commotion), unless loss by a peril not excluded ensues, and then only for such ensuing loss.

Loss of Earnings Endorsement. This is a form that may be used for smaller accounts, providing coverage for loss of earnings without a contribution clause. The definition of "earnings" is net profit plus payroll expense, taxes, interest, rents, and all other operating expenses of the business.

Extra Expense Endorsement. "Extra expense" means the excess (if any) of the total cost incurred during the period of restoration chargeable to the operation of the insured's business, over and above the total cost that would normally have been incurred to conduct the business during the same period had no damage or destruction occurred. The insured must resume normal operations of the business as soon as practicable.

Exclusions and limitations of the extra expense form are those reasonable for insurance that pays extra expenses to stay in business. For example, direct loss to property or loss of income is not covered. Extra expenses are insured, not direct or indirect losses.

Combined Business Interruption and Extra Expense Endorsement. This form combines gross earnings and extra expense coverages into one form for those accounts who need both. The terms and conditions are the same except a single amount of insurance applies at each location. The extra expense insurance to value continues to be enforced by limiting the monthly recovery for the first, second, and succeeding months. However, the endorsement allows the client to select the proper percentages. A contribution clause still applies to the gross earnings aspect of coverage.

Tuition Fees Endorsement. This form provides coverage at specified locations for loss of the sum of tuition, fees, and other income from students, less the cost of merchandise sold and materials and supplies consumed in services sold to such students. In determining tuition fees, consideration is given to the experience of the insured before the date of damage or destruction and the probable experience had no loss occurred.

Loss or Rents Endorsement. The insurer is liable for loss resulting directly from necessary untenetability, but not exceeding the reduction in rents less charges and expenses which do not necessarily continue during the period of untenetability.

Checkpoints

1. List the four sections of the SMP policies.
2. List eight classes that may be covered by the SMP program.
3. List and distinguish among the four basic property forms.
4. List the common business interruption forms available for the SMP.

Miscellaneous Property Endorsements A number of property endorsements have been reviewed. This section highlights some other Section I endorsements frequently used by producers.

Automatic Increase in Insurance. This form, often referred to as the "inflation guard" form, automatically increases insurance by a specified percentage amount, on building items only, personal property items only, on both, or to specified scheduled items at the end of each period of three months after inception of the policy. The percentges of increase can be selected from those listed in *Division Five—Fire* of the ISO manual.

Household and Personal Property. This form amends the general personal property form to include household and personal property usual or incidental to the described apartment that is part of a building covered by the general personal property form. The endorsement sets a limit of liability for the location and permits the insured to apply up to 10 percent of the limit to cover such property located elsewhere within the United States and Canada and the State of Hawaii. Coverage is on a named perils basis. The insured would be better off, in most cases, to insure such an exposure with personal lines forms.

Glass. This form brings the traditional coverage for loss to scheduled glass and to lettering and ornamentation separately described, by breakage of the glass, or by chemicals accidentally or maliciously applied. Loss by fire is excluded.

The insurer pays up to $75 for (1) repairing or replacing frames when necessary because of damage, (2) installing temporary plates or in boarding up when necessary because of unavoidable delay in repairing or replacing damaged glass, and (3) removing or replacing any obstructions, other than window displays, when necessary in replacing such damaged glass, lettering, or ornamentation.

Optional Perils. This endorsement provides five additional named perils. The additional perils can cover buildings, personal property of the insured or personal property of others, as specified by an "X" in appropriate box(es) on the form. The perils are (1) breakage of glass up to $50 per plate ($250 in any one occurrence), (2) falling objects with usual exceptions to interior damage and property in the open, (3) weight of snow, ice, or sleet, (4) water damage, and (5) a collapse. In fact, the coverage is quite limited and for a small additional cost, "all-risks" insurance offers more protection.

Outdoor Signs. This form adds coverage for scheduled signs subject to a $100 deductible on named perils building or personal property policies. "All-risks" coverage on neon, automatic, or mechanical electric signs is obtained by using the neon signs endorsement.

Peak Season Inventory. When there is one identifiable period of time with significant increases in the value of personal property (October, November, and December for a toy store), the reporting forms may be excessively demanding. This endorsement can be used to provide additional insurance for the specified periods. The premium for the additional insurance is figured on a pro rata basis.

Replacement Cost. This form is more restrictive in the SMP program than in monoline property policies. The endorsement provides for an optional replacement cost basis for valuation of buildings or personal property. Underwriters generally require some substantiation of the estimated replacement cost of structures by an appraisal or construction information to justify the amount of insurance. With regard to personal property, underwriters grant replacement cost coverage freely on equipment like office machines while coverage may be difficult to obtain on property such as plant equipment, since replacement values are more difficult to estimate without expert assistance. An appraisal of such equipment may be necessary before the coverage can be arranged.

The form merely substitutes the phrase "replacement cost" without deduction for depreciation for "actual cash value" wherever it appears in the policy. The coinsurance paragraph is amended to reflect replacement cost and to allow for waiver of inventory or appraisal of undamaged property when the loss is both less than $10,000 or less than 5 percent of the limit of liability. The insured retains the right to make an ACV claim under the policy and later, after notification to the insurer, file for the balance of a replacement cost claim. If the insured elects a replacement cost loss settlement, the insurer is not liable for the replacement cost unless and until the damaged or destroyed property is actually repaired or replaced by the insured.

The endorsement does not cover some property on a replacement cost basis, such as stock or merchandise, property of others, valuable papers, works of art, and so forth.

The monoline form, replacement cost endorsement, is broader because some of the property not subject to replacement cost in the SMP form is not excepted from the replacement cost monoline provisions.

Specified Power Failure Loss Assumption. This form insures property for loss by a change in temperature or humidity resulting from physical damage by fire, lightning, windstorm or hail, aircraft, explosion, smoke, vehicles, or by leakage from an automatic sprinkler system to certain equipment such as that used for refrigerating, heating, or generating power when the equipment is within a described building.

Sprinkler Leakage. This endorsement is designed to add the perils of leakage or discharge of water or other substance from within any automatic sprinkler system or direct loss caused by collapse or fall of a tank forming a part of such system. The form can be used to cover buildings, including the cost of repairs and replacement of the automatic sprinkler system when the damage sustained is caused directly by breakage or freezing, or personal property of the insured or personal property of others. Exclusions and limitations are the same as the monoline forms.

Earthquake Extension. This form adds the peril of earthquake, subject to a separate deductible of up to 10 percent of the value of the property (not the amount of insurance) at the time of loss. The "other insurance" provision makes this policy excess over other earthquake insurance. A masonry veneer clause will apply when the construction dictates (the insurer is not liable for any loss to exterior masonry veneer, other than stucco, on wood frame walls, and the value of such veneer is not considered in the determination of the actual cash value when applying the deductible and coinsurance clauses).

The endorsement can also be applied to time element coverages subject to a 168 hour waiting period deductible for buildings over four stories in height. There is no package discount for the earthquake insurance.

Garagekeepers Insurance Endorsement. This form provides legal liability coverage for autos in the care, custody, or control of the insured for safekeeping, storage, service, or repair. In some ways the form is broader than monoline forms, and in other ways it is more restrictive. The producer will need to make a detailed analysis of the differences when changing from the monoline to the SMP forms or vice versa. The insured may elect physical damage coverage in three forms: (1) comprehensive; (2) specified perils of fire, explosion, theft, larceny, riot, civil commotion, and malicious mischief or vandalism; or (3) collision coverage. A schedule on the endorsement is used to indicate which coverages have been selected, the deductibles, the covered locations and the limits of liability at each location.

The deductible for comprehensive and specified perils applies for each automobile and in the aggregate per loss when the loss is caused by theft, malicious mischief, or vandalism. The collision deductible applies per automobile.

Two exclusions which do not appear in the monoline automobile forms are automobiles in the custody of the insured for demonstration or sale and automobiles damaged by an elevator or automobile hoist. Repairs by the named insured are adjusted at actual cost to the insured for labor and materials. This provision is often broader in other garagekeepers legal liability endorsements. It is not uncommon to find a form which permits either a prcentage add-on or one which pays the insured's selling price less some specified discount.

SMP Garagekeepers Insurance—Direct Coverage Options Endorsement. This form changes the garagekeepers insurance endorsement to apply without regard to legal liability. The insured can elect to make the insurance primary or excess over any other collectible insurance regardless of whether the other insurance covers the interest of the named insured, any other insured's interest, or the interest of the owner of the covered automobile.

Vandalism or Malicious Mischief Exclusion. On rare occasions it may be desirable that an SMP policy provide only fire and extended coverage, on a fraternity house, for example. This endorsement can be used with any of the named perils forms to achieve this result by excluding the perils of vandalism or malicious mischief.

SMP Optional Theft Exclusion. This endorsement excludes theft from "all-risks" personal property forms.

Manufacturers' Selling Price. This form defines the actual cash value of finished stock manufactured by the insured to be the sales price less all discounts and unincurred expenses for which the stock would have been sold had no loss occurred. This form is necessary for manufacturing firms to close the gap between the property coverage and the business interruption forms, because the latter will not pay for the profit in finished goods.

SMP Deductible. This form provides a schedule of designated locations of buildings and personal property of the insured and is used to increase the standard deductible at those specific locations.

SMP Deductible Endorsement with Annual Loss Aggregate. This form may also be used to increase the standard deductible at designated locations. The form provides an annual loss aggregate deductible. Once the aggregate of the insured's proportion of losses reaches the stated amount during any one policy year, the insurer is liable for all subsequent losses. Losses of less than 10 percent of the deductible are disregarded in arriving at the aggregate. The insured must report all losses in excess of 10 percent of the deductible amount so the insurer can determine when the aggregate is reached.

Inland Marine Coverage The SMP program provides a number of inland marine coverages to be written as part of the property coverage. The eligible coverages are as described in this section of the chapter. Rating for these coverages in accordance with *Division Nine—Inland Marine* of the *ISO Commercial Lines Manual.* Nonfiled inland marine forms are not eligible for inclusion in the SMP policy. Discussion of inland marine here will be less extensive than the preceding material, as inland marine was covered extensively in Chapter 5 of this text.

Accounts Receivable Endorsement. This form provides "all-risks" insurance on a reporting basis to cover the cost of reconstruction of records of accounts receivable as well as actual loss due to the inability to collect sums due the insured as a direct result of insured loss of or damage to such records. The coverage is principally on the premises of the insured subject to storage in specified receptacles. At loss, the policy pays the same as the monoline form (Chapter 5).

In addition to exclusions of war, nuclear damage, and dishonesty of the insured, the policy excludes losses due to bookkeeping, accounting, or billing errors or omissions, electrical or magnetic injury, disturbance or erasure of electronic recordings (except by lightning), or fidelity. If the insured prefers nonreporting coverage, an accounts receivable—nonreporting endorsement can be used to delete the reporting requirements.

Camera Floater. This form and the floaters covering musical instruments and fine arts are similar except for the description of covered property. The camera form provides "all-risks" coverage on scheduled cameras, projection machines, films, and related articles of equipment. The property can belong to the insured or to others and be in the care, custody, or control of the insured. The only exclusion in addition to the usual war and nuclear losses is for loss or damage caused by wear and tear, gradual deterioration, insects, vermin, or inherent vice. Coverage is on an actual cash value basis, worldwide, and a provision is made to insure additionally acquired property not to exceed 25 percent of the schedule or $10,000, if the insurer is notified within thirty days. Other typical inland marine clauses like pairs and sets, loss to a part, and no benefit to bailee are incorporated into the endorsement.

Fine Arts Floater. This form covers scheduled fine arts of the insured or the property of others in the custody or control of the insured while on exhibition or otherwise within the limits of the continental United States and Canada (excluding the premises of fair grounds or of any national or international exposition unless endorsed onto the policy). The insured must file a statement of values with the insurer, and the endorsement has a place for specific addresses and amounts of insurance showing where the property is located at the inception of the coverage. The endorsement has a schedule showing an amount of insurance, a title, and the artist or maker for each insured item. Coverage is "all-risks" with all of the exclusions in the camera form plus loss sustained due to and resulting from any repairing, restoration, or retouching process. Loss or damage occasioned by breakage of fragile articles, unless caused by certain named perils, is excluded unless endorsed to the policy for an additional premium. The valuation is agreed to be the amounts as specified in the schedule. Additionally acquired property is covered if reported within thirty days and if valued at less than 25 percent of the schedule or $10,000. In addition to the typical inland marine conditions, the insured agrees that the property insured will be packed and unpacked by competent packers.

Musical Instruments Floater. This form covers scheduled musical instruments and equipment on the same basis as the camera floater covers camera equipment. In addition, the insured represents and agrees that none of the instruments will be played for remuneration unless the policy is endorsed and an additional premium paid.

Neon Signs. This form covers on an "all-risks" basis scheduled neon, automatic, or mechanical electric signs. The endorsement does not insure against loss or damage caused by wear and tear or gradual deterioration, by faulty manufacture, installation, or occasioned by the inherent character of the property, loss or damage caused by breakage during installation, repairing or dismantling, nor breakage during transportation unless caused by fire, lightning, collision, derailment, or overturn of a vehicle. Mechanical breakdown and loss or damage to electrical apparatus caused by electricity, other than lightning, unless fire ensues are excluded. A deductible of 5 percent of the *amount of insurance* on an item (but not less than $10 nor more than $100) is applicable. All signs must be scheduled with an amount of insurance shown for each item.

SMP Physicians' and Surgeons' Equipment Floater. This form, different from the filed monoline form, covers medical, surgical, and dental equipment and instruments (including tools, materials, supplies, and scientific books) used by the insured in the medical or dental profession. The form covers office equipment, including furniture and fixtures and tenants improvements and betterments while within the premises. The form excludes radium, which can be insured separately using the SMP radium floater. The endorsement includes extensions of coverage for theft damage to buildings, $1,000 off-premises coverage for furniture and fixtures temporarily away from the premises, $1,000 extra expense coverage, $250 coverage on currency, money and stamps, up to $500 on the personal effects of the insured or others on premises against certain named perils, and up to $500 coverage on valuable papers and other records. Coverage is subject to an 80 percent coinsurance clause and is limited to the continental United States and Canada and within Hawaii and Puerto Rico, unless otherwise endorsed. Coverage is on an actual cash value basis and is written blanket at specified locations.

Exclusions in the endorsement in addition to the usual war and nuclear damage clauses are loss or damage caused by wear and tear, gradual deterioration, insects, vermin, inherent vice, mechanical breakdown, or breakage of glass or other fragile items (except lenses of scientific instruments) unless caused by certain named perils. Loss or damage by any process or while the property is being worked upon is excluded as is damage from electrical currents artificially generated.

Valuable Papers and Records. This endorsement provides "all-risks" coverage on written, printed, or otherwise inscribed documents including books, maps, films, drawings, abstracts, deeds, mortgages, and manuscripts (but not money or securities). Specific documents may be scheduled but usually coverage is on a blanket basis covering the records for their actual cash value. The insurance applies at designated locations but is extended to cover valuable papers and records being conveyed outside the premises or at other locations for up to 10 percent of the amount of insurance or $5,000, whichever is less. It is a condition of the policy that when the premises are not open for business, coverage applies only while the subject of insurance is in described receptacles (safes or filing cabinets). Receptacles are listed in the policy showing the kind, name of maker, "class" or "hour exposure" of label, and the name of the issuer of the label. The form does not apply to loss from war or nuclear exposures, dishonesty of the insured, directly resulting from errors or omissions in processing or copying, or to loss due to electrical or magnetic injury, or disturbance or erasure of electronic recordings (except by lightning), and coverage is excluded for property held as samples or for sale.

SMP Inland Marine Deductible. This endorsement can be used to apply a higher deductible to coverages under the camera floater, fine arts floater, musical instruments floater, valuable papers and records, and physicians' and surgeons' equipment floater forms.

Theft Coverages When insurance on buildings and personal property is written on an "all-risks" basis, there is no need for the following endorsements. When, however, a named perils approach is used, the forms outlined in this section can be used to cover such property against the perils of burglary, robbery, and theft. These endorsements are not substitutes for crime insurance, discussed later.

Church Theft. This endorsement adds coverage for loss of money, securities, and other property by theft or attempted theft (1) within the premises, (2) within a night depository safe provided by a bank or trust company on its premises, or (3) while in the care or custody of a person duly authorized by the insured. Insurance on "other property" can be on specified articles such as a chalice or vestment with specific values or on a blanket basis. Exclusions include a criminal act by the insured or theft loss during a fire. The contents of an alms box, nonowned property, and manuscripts or accounts are not insured.

Premises includes not only the church but also any other building owned by or leased to the insured used exclusively for conducting the religious, educational, recreational, or social activities of its congregation, and any residence occupied by the rector. A chapel or mission which is not located at or adjacent to the location designated in the declarations is not covered. If the insured is the owner of or responsible for the premises, damage caused by a theft or attempted theft is covered.

Liability for Guest Property. This endorsement provides innkeepers' liability and is really a bailee's form. It is treated here, however, since the SMP section of the *ISO Commercial Lines Manual* includes the form in the burglary coverages. Each state has an Innkeeper Statute which limits the responsibility of hotels and motels for guests' property. Typically, the law sets a maximum obligation of from $500 to $1,000 per guest or per room. A separate statutory limit may apply to guests' property within a hotel's safe deposit boxes unless an alternate value is declared by the guest to the hotel. This endorsement obligates the insurer to pay on behalf of the insured all sums which the insured shall become legally obligated to pay as damages because of loss to property belonging to a guest at the insured premises if such loss occurs while the property is within the premises or in the possession of the insured. The limit is $1,000 for loss of property of any guest, and the insurer's liability for any one policy year is $25,000. The insurer has the right and duty to defend any suit even if the allegations of the suit are groundless, false or fraudulent, and may make such investigation and settlement of any claim or suit as it deems expedient. Specific types of losses, such as contractual liability, to guest autos, or guest property held for dry cleaning, are not covered.

Mercantile Open Stock Burglary. This endorsement pays for loss by burglary or robbery of a guard, while the premises are not open for business, of merchandise, furniture, fixtures, and equipment, as well as for damages to the premises if the insured is the owner of the premises or is liable for such damage. Coverage is also provided for loss from within a showcase or show window located outside the premises, but inside the building line attached to such building. Monoline mercantile open stock exclusions apply. Burglary must be evidenced by visible marks made by tools, explosives, electricity, or chemicals upon, or physical damage to, the exterior of the premises. The mercantile open stock endorsement is subject to the same coinsurance requirement discussed in Chapter 7.

Mercantile Open Stock Burglary and Theft. This form provides the same coverage as above, but broadens the peril to theft or attempted theft, whether or not the premises are open for business to the extent each loss is in excess of $50. The form contains additional exclusions similar to the monoline form.

Mercantile Robbery and Safe Burglary. This endorsement has three insuring agreements. Coverage A—robbery inside the premises agrees to pay for loss of money, securities, and other property by robbery or attempted robbery within the premises and to pay for damage to the premises by robbery provided the insured is the owner or liable for such damage. Coverage B—robbery outside the premises agrees to pay for the same kinds of property while being conveyed by a messenger. Coverage C—safe burglary pays for loss of the property from within a vault or safe by safe burglary or its attempt as well as for premises damage in the same manner as coverage A. Loss due to fraudulent, dishonest or criminal acts by any insured or a partner is excluded as are loss of manuscripts, books of account or records or loss, other than to a safe or vault, by fire. The policy territory includes within any of the states of the United States, the District of Columbia, the Virgin Islands, Puerto Rico, the Canal Zone, or Canada. The endorsement contains separate declarations relating to limits of liability, premises locations, description of safe(s) and vault(s), information related to custodians and messengers, and a statement of losses during the five years preceding the policy.

Storekeepers Burglary and Robbery. This form offers a package of seven crime-related insuring agreements for storekeepers.

I   *Robbery Inside the Premises.* To pay for loss of money, securities, merchandise, furniture, fixtures and equipment by robbery within the premises.

II   *Robbery Outside the Premises.* To pay for loss of money, securities and merchandise, including the wallet or bag containing such property, by robbery while being conveyed by a messenger outside the premises.

III   *Kidnapping.* To pay for loss of money, securities, merchandise, furniture, fixtures and equipment within the premises by kidnapping.

IV *Burglary; Safe Burglary.* To pay for loss of money, securities and merchandise by safe burglary within the premises and for loss, not exceeding $50, of money and securities by burglary within the premises.

V *Theft—Night Depository or Residence.* To pay for loss of money and securities by theft within any night depository in a bank or within the living quarters in the home of a messenger.

VI *Burglary; Robbery of Watchman.* To pay for loss of merchandise, furniture, fixtures and equipment by burglary or by robbery of a watchman within the premises, while the premises are not open for business. Under this insuring agreement, the actual cash value of any one article of jewelry shall be deemed not to exceed $50.

VII *Damage.* To pay for damages to the premises and to money, securities, merchandise, furniture, fixtures and equipment within the premises, by such robbery, kidnapping, burglary, safe burglary, robbery of a watchman, or attempt thereat, provided with respect to damage to the premises the insured is the owner thereof or is liable for such damage.

The coverage does not apply to loss due to any fraudulent, dishonest, or criminal act by any insured, a partner, or an officer, employee, director, trustee, or authorized representative except for kidnapping, safe burglary, or robbery by other than an insured or a partner.

Broad Form Storekeepers. This form provides eight separate insuring agreements including employee dishonesty, loss inside the premises of money, securities, or other property from a safe burglary or robbery, loss outside the premises of money and securities, merchandise burglary, robbery of a guard, money orders and counterfeit papers currency, theft of money and securities while within the living quarters of a messenger, depositors fogery, damage to the premises by vandalism or malicious mischief following entry into the premises by one or more burglars, and other damage caused by robbery, burglary, or safe burglary provided the insured is the owner of the premises or liable for such damage.

SECTION II—LIABILITY COVERAGE FORMS

Section II of the SMP policy must include a liability form which at least provides premises and operations coverage. Section II is mandatory except when the policy is written to participate with other insurance in Section I.

SMP Liability Conditions and Definitions

As was the case with Section I, a form with general conditions and definitions is part of the policy.

Supplementary Payments Supplemental payments are those in addition to the limit of liability and include

- Costs of defense
- Premiums on required bonds
- First aid expenses at the time of the accident
- Expenses incurred by the insured at the insurer's request

Premium The premium designated in the policy for Section II is a deposit premium to be credited to the actual premium earned based on an audit.

Financial Responsibility Laws When the policy is certified as proof of financial responsibility under the provisions of any motor vehicle financial responsibility law, the insurance will comply with the provisions of the law to the extent of the coverage and limits of liability required. The insured agrees to reimburse the insurance company for any payment made which would not have been required under the terms of the policy had the certification not been made.

Insured's Duties in the Event of Occurrence, Claim, or Suit The insured's duties are to notify the insurer (1) of an occurrence within a reasonable time and (2) of a claim or suit immediately, and forward all notices to the insurer, and to cooperate with the insurer in the defense of a suit.

Medical Reports; Proof and Payment of Claim This condition applies to the medical payments coverage and requires an injured person to (1) give written proof of claim, (2) execute authorization to enable the insurance company to obtain medical records, and (3) submit to examination by physicians selected by the insurer. Payment does not constitute an admission of liability.

Action Against the Company This provision prohibits any action against the insurance company unless there has been full compliance with all of the terms of the policy, and until the amount of the insured's obligation to pay shall have been finally determined either by judgment after a trial or by written agreement of the insured, the claimant and the insurer. Any person or organization which has secured a judgment or written agreement is entitled to recover from the insurer to the extent of the insurance afforded.

Bankruptcy or insolvency of the insured or of the insured's estate does not relieve the insurer of any of its obligations under the policy.

Other Insurance The SMP policy is intended to be primary insurance. If other policies call for equal shares, the SMP pays in equal shares, or the same dollar amount as other insurance until the loss is paid or policy limits are exhausted. If all other policies do not pay on equal shares, the SMP will pay its pro rata share of a loss based on all applicable limits of liability.

Annual Aggregate The policy aggregate limits apply separately to each consecutive annual period.

Nuclear Exclusion This is an exclusion of liability for bodily injury or property damage or for loss under any medical payments coverage or under any supplemental payments provision relating to first aid or to expenses incurred caused by the nuclear perils.

SMP Condominium Additional Policy Provisions

Under Section II—Liability Coverage, this endorsement amends the "Persons Insured" provision to include as an insured each individual unit owner of the described condominium, but only with respect to liability arising out of the ownership, maintenance, or repair of that portion of the premises which is not solely owned by the unit owner.

SMP Liability Insurance Form

The SMP liability insurance form contains the descriptions of coverages used most commonly with the SMP.

Insuring Agreements Coverage is provided for bodily injury and property damage liability with a combined single limit for occurrences arising out of the ownership, maintenance, or use of the insured premises and all operations necessary or incidental to the business of the insured conducted at or from the insured premises. The coverage is tied to declared locations but includes the products and completed operations hazards but is not "comprehensive general liability." Products liability and completed operations liability may be excluded by attaching the appropriate endorsement. The policy will require a general schedule—Section II showing the hazards and locations covered.

Medical Payments If a premium is charged, this insuring agreement is activated. Medical payments is a "no-fault" agreement to pay medical expenses incurred within one year from the date of an accident arising out of a condition in the insured premises or operations. Coverage is excluded for bodily injury arising out of autos (except parking of a nonowned auto on the insured premises), aircraft, mobile equipment while being raced or transported by auto, and watercraft (except while ashore on the insured premises). Coverage is also excluded when injuries arise from completed operations or products or result from operations performed for the insured by an independent contractor. The liquor and war exclusions apply, as do the exclusions relating to workers' compensation or other injuries arising out of and in the course of employment. Coverage is excluded for any person while engaged in maintenance and repair of the insured premises or alteration, demolition, or new construction at the insured premises. Any person involved in any athletic activity or contest is excluded. Injury to the named insured, any partner, tenant, or other person regularly residing on the insured premises or any employee of any of the foregoing if the injury arises out of and in the course of employment is excluded. To any other tenant or tenant's employee if the injury occurs on that part of the premises rented from the named insured is excluded.

Liability Exclusions The form contains the normal general liability exclusions:

- Contractual liability and warranties of fitness or performance
- Auto or aircraft ownership, maintenance, or use
- Racing of mobile equipment
- Transportation of mobile equipment
- Watercraft ownership, maintenance, or use
- Pollution
- Operations from undeclared premises
- Dramshop liability
- Workers' compensation exposures
- Care, custody, and control
- Property damage to premises sold by an insured arising out of the property
- Loss of use of property by products or completed operations hazards
- Property damage to the insured's products caused by the product or a part of the product
- Workmanship faults causing property damage
- Products recall
- War
- Demolition operations
- Damage caused by "xcu" hazards

Persons Insured This section of the policy defines who is covered as an insured, and extends the coverage to the spouse of a sole proprietor, partners, or members of a partnership or joint venture, and executive officers, directors, or stockholders of a corporation while those individuals are acting within the scope of their duties. Any person other than an employee of the insured or organization while acting as real estate manager for the named insured is covered, as is any employee or other person operating mobile equipment registered under any motor vehicle registration law for the purposes of locomotion on a public highway. No person or organization is insured in connection with mobile equipment with respect to bodily injury to a fellow employee injured in the course of employment or property damage to property owned by, rented to, in the charge of, or occupied by the named insured or the employer of any other person operating mobile equipment with the permission of the named insured.

Limit of Liability This section defines the limits of liability as a combined single limit and the intent is that the limits not apply separately to insureds in spite of the numbers of parties insured. This paragraph also establishes how annual aggregate limits apply. Split limits can be provided by attaching Amendment of Limits of Liability Endorsement.

Other Liability Endorsements

A number of endorsements are available to meet an insured's requirements.

Comprehensive Personal Liability Coverage The SMP program permits the inclusion of personal liability coverage by using the monoline form for the named insured, any partner, executive officer or manager who resides on the premises. The package modification factor does not apply to the premium for this endorsement.

Employers Nonownership Automobile Liability Insurance Endorsement This endorsement provides a combined single limit of liability for bodily injury and property damage covering an employer's interest in a nonowned auto used for business purposes. For instance, an employee's auto used by the employee while on an errand for the employer. Coverage is excess over any other valid and collectible insurance available to the insured. "Nonowned automobile" means an auto not owned by, registered in the name of, hired by (or used under contract on behalf of) or loaned to the named insured. If the named insured is a partnership, an auto owned by or registered in the name of a partner is not covered. In order to get coverage on behalf of the partnership for partners' cars, the standard partnership nonownership liability form must be used.

It is necessary to purchase separate coverage for hired cars (in the monoline forms, this coverage is included). The producer must be careful when packaging accounts to be certain the hired car coverage is not lost.

There are a number of exclusions:

- contractual
- workers' compensation
- bodily injury to employees
- property damage to property owned or being transported by the insured
- property to or in the care, custody or control of the insured other than property damage to a residence or private garage by a private passenger automobile
- liability arising out of partnerships or joint ventures not named
- pollution
- war

The package modification factor does not apply to the premium for this endorsement. To provide split limits for bodily injury and property damage, amendments of limits of liability endorsement can be attached.

Other Liability Coverages The SMP program rules permit the use of any other general liability policy form such as comprehensive general liability; the broad form comprehensive general liability endorsement; fire legal liability; or personal injury liability. Products and completed operations can be excluded from the SMP by using appropriate forms.

SECTION III—CRIME COVERAGE FORMS

Section III of the SMP policy is optional and contains crime coverages. Basic crime coverage is obtained by using the SMP comprehensive crime coverage form, SMP blanket crime coverage form, or SMP public employees blanket coverage form. These forms parallel comparable monoline forms, and a number of additional forms and endorsements are available to extend or restrict coverage as necessary.

SMP Comprehensive Crime Coverage

This form is different from others used in the SMP in that no provisions, stipulations, or other terms of the SMP apply to the form.

Coverage Coverages in the form are identical to those in the monoline comprehensive 3-D policy extensively discussed in Chapter 7. Because of the earlier discussion, only a review will be given here. As with the 3-D policy, the insured may select any one of the five insuring agreements alone or in combination with the others.

Insuring Agreements. The SMP comprehensive crime coverage form combines the coverages of forms A and B of the 3-D policy. The insured may select either insuring agreement IA or IB if employee dishonesty coverage is desired. Agreement IA limits losses to a per loss basis while IB applies the limit per employee. Agreement IA has a discovery period of one year (the same as agreements II through V) while IB has a two-year discovery period. The final difference of note between the IA and IB agreements is the minimum and maximum limits of liability. Under agreement IA, the manual has a minimum limit of $10,000 with no maximum limit. Agreement IB has a minimum of $2,500 and a $100,000 maximum limit.

Insuring agreements II through V are identical to the 3-D policy and cover:

- II—Loss inside the premises
- III—Loss outside the premises
- IV—Money and counterfeit paper currency
- V—Depositor's forgery

Balance of the Policy. The general agreements, conditions, and limitations of the SMP form are the same as the 3-D monoline form.

Endorsements to the SMP Comprehensive Crime Coverage. Endorsements to the form are not limited to those with SMP numbering. Any standard 3-D or blanket crime endorsement can be attached as long as it does not overlap any of the coverages in Sections I and II of the SMP policy.

Eligibility The form may be written for an insured eligible for SMP except federal or public officials, their deputies or employees, or any organization eligible for a banker's or broker's blanket bond such as banks, stockbrokers, or similar financial institutions. The form may be written for insurance companies, personal finance companies, small loan companies, foundations, and endowment funds, although these are also eligible for certain forms of financial institution blanket bonds. The form may also be written for a single state university or state college, except when (1) faithful performance of duty coverage is required, (2) the insured is a state department or board, and (3) the officials or employees to be covered are required by law to be bonded.

SMP Blanket Crime Coverage

SMP blanket crime coverage provides essentially the same coverages as the comprehensive crime form except that one limit of insurance applies for all five insuring agreements as a single limit; the fidelity insurance is on a blanket position (limit applied per loss) basis; and all five coverages are mandatory. In some respects this form is preferable because the total limit of liability is available for money and securities losses, but underwriters are reluctant to offer blanket crime because premiums for money and securities are based on the actual money and securities exposure rather than the blanket crime limit. Underwriters feel the premium is rarely adequate to cover the risk of the "unusual" money loss in excess of the "average."

Eligibility for blanket crime is similar to the comprehensive crime coverage. The form has a minimum limit of $1,000. The producer should compare the rates and limits for the two forms and decide which best protects the client.

SMP Public Employees Blanket Coverage

This form has four insuring agreements. The perils covered may be either dishonesty (a form of fidelity coverage) or unfaithful performance of duty (fidelity coverage plus a form of performance bond). The limit of liability may apply in two ways—on an aggregate basis (like a commercial blanket bond) or on a multiple basis (like a blanket position bond). Insuring Agreement I is honesty blanket coverage similar to commercial blanket coverage (aggregate limits), and Insuring Agreement II is honesty blanket position coverage (multiple limits) similar to the blanket position bond. Insuring Agreement III is faithful performance blanket (aggregate limits) coverage and covers:

> Loss caused to the Insured through the failure of any of the Employees, acting alone or in collusion with others, to perform faithfully his duties or to account properly for all monies and property received by virtue of his position or employment during the effective period of this endorsement to an amount not exceeding in the aggregate the amount stated in the Table of Limits of Liability applicable to this Insuring Agreement 3.

Insuring Agreement IV is faithful performance blanket position (multiple limits) coverage. Coverage is excluded for any loss sustained by, or caused to, the insured under circumstances whereby and to the amount which the insured voluntarily undertakes or is obligated by law to exonerate or indemnify any of the employees against liability incurred by them in the performance of their duties. The minimum limit for Agreements I and III is $10,000, and for Agreements II and IV it is $2,500.

Eligibility Public employees blanket coverage may be written for a state, county, city, town, township, village, or borough. It may be written to cover school, water, irrigation, power, bridge, fire, and similar districts or authorities as well as state universities or state colleges. A separate policy form is required for each department, division, office of any state, county, city, or other eligible political subdivision. The bond may cover the employees of any subordinate department, division, office or institution which the insured is authorized by statute to manage, govern or control. For example, the division of the state department of transportation selling license tags may be covered in addition to the executive officers of the department.

Excluded Employees Some employees may be excluded; for example, members of boards and commissions, an individual whom the insurer is unwilling to bond, an officer or employee who is otherwise bonded, peace officers and process servers, and operators of automotive equipment. Any person who is required by statute to provide an individual bond to qualify for office *must* be excluded.

Additional Crime Forms and Endorsements

There are a number of available endorsements to broaden or restrict coverage in the three basic forms. There is a good deal of flexibility in selecting various deductible options. In addition, all standard comprehensive 3-D policy endorsements and blanket crime endorsements (Chapter 7) may be used.

Certain classes of employees can be excluded from the fidelity coverage. Payroll checks or all checks can be excluded from the money and securities coverage. The excess indemnity endorsement can be used to provide additional limits on fidelity coverage for employees in certain positions. Personal accounts coverage may be used to extend the depositors forgery coverage to the personal accounts of listed individuals.

It is possible to add extortion coverage with either the extortion coverage endorsement or the personal extortion coverage in the selective amounts endorsement. The insured or the individual may be required to be responsible for a certain percentage of loss in excess of the deductible. Insurance is provided for loss due to the surrender of property away from the premises as a result of a threat to do bodily harm to the insured, a director, trustee, officer, partner, proprietor, or employee of the insured or a relative or invitee of any such person who is, or allgedly is, being held captive. Prior to the surrender of property, the person receiving the threat must make a reasonable effort to report the extortionist's demand to an associate, the Federal Bureau of Investigation, and to local law enforcement authorities.

Exhibit 12-2
Insuring Agreements—Boiler and Machinery

Agreement Name	Corresponding Agreement Monoline Form
I — Loss to Property of Insured	Coverage A
II — Expediting Expense	Coverage B
III — Liability For Property of Others	Coverage C
IV — Defense, Settlement, Supplementary Payments	Coverage E

SECTION IV— BOILER AND MACHINERY COVERAGE

Some insurers writing an SMP do not write boiler and machinery business. For that reason, some boiler insurers will allow a package credit when issuing a monoline boiler and machinery policy, if an SMP policy is also in effect.

SMP Boiler and Machinery Coverage Endorsement

This is the basic SMP form for boiler and machinery coverage. It is used in conjunction with the declaration form which lists the various covered object groups and locations together the applicable premiums. As this material was covered in Chapter 10, only differences will be discussed.

Insuring Agreements The SMP boiler and machinery coverage endorsement only contains four insuring agreements as opposed to six in the monoline form. Exhibit 12-2 lists the insuring agreements and their corresponding monoline agreements. Details of the coverages for each agreement can be found in Chapter 10.

Exclusions. The exclusions for losses caused by certain perils are contained within the insuring agreements of the SMP form. In the monoline form, they were in a separate exclusions section. The exclusions are the same, only the physical location of the exclusions in the SMP is different.

Priority of Payment. Both the monoline and SMP forms prioritize payment among the insuring agreements. The total losses under Insuring Agreement I are paid first. If any of the limit of liability remains after such payment, losses under Agreement II are paid. The process continues through Agreements III and IV.

Conditions The conditions section of the SMP form contains not only all of the conditions found in the monoline form but also three exclusions. The conditions are:

- A limit of liability per accident
- An earthquake limitation
- Other insurance provisions for Agreements I, II, and III
- Property valuation for Agreement I
- Repair or replacement option of the insurer for Agreement I
- Inspection
- Suspension of coverage
- Cancellation, subrogation and policy change conditions
- Notice of accident and loss adjustment condition
- Action against the company conditions
- Premium adjustment
- Assignment of policy
- Deductible

The three exclusions contained in the conditions section are for nuclear energy, war damage and increased costs of construction. These are similar to those in the monoline form.

Definitions The definitions section of the SMP form contains the definitions of "objects" and "accident." These definitions were found in separate monoline endorsements.

Objects. Objects are defined by "groups" or similar types of equipment. For instance, Group I objects include various types of "fired pressure vessels" such as boilers, while Group 2 is made up of "unfired pressure vessels" such as water heaters. While the declarations page allows for sixteen different possible groups of objects, this form only defines three groups of objects. When using the SMP boiler and machinery forms, in keeping with the packaging concept of insuring all items in one policy, each individual object a client may have that falls within a group definition must be insured or none of the objects may be insured. For instance, if a client has two boilers, they must both be insured or not. The client may not select only one boiler for insurance and leave the other uninsured.

Accident. Accident in the SMP form is the broad form definition—sudden and accidental breakdown (as opposed to sudden and accidental tearing asunder). The usual exclusions of loss for the broad form definition of accident are found in the definitions section of the SMP form.

Special Provisions   Special Provision A expands the definition of object to include certain tanks and water heaters. Special provisions B and D establish that the insurer is not liable for loss from an explosion of gas or unconsumed fuel within the furnace of the object or within the passages from the furnace to the atmosphere which is covered by Section I of the SMP. Special Provisions C and F state the insurer is not liable for loss while an object is undergoing a hydrostatic, pneumatic or gas pressure test. Special Provision E equates a heat transfer medium other than water and its vapor with the words "water" and "steam" whenever such words are used in the definitions. Special Provision G clarifies that any object which is used for the storage of gas or liquid and which is periodically filled, moved, emptied, and refilled in the course of its normal services is considered as "connected and ready for use."

Additional Objects Group Endorsement   This endorsement is used to extend the coverage to the additional thirteen groups of objects for all clients except industrial, processing and contractors. Space does not permit a detailed analysis, but the form allows for coverage to refrigerating equipment, to machinery of various types, and to electrical equipment. Each object group is defined in the endorsement. Certain objects have special provisions applicable to them, like the ammonia contamination limit of $1,000 applying to refrigerating and air conditioning equipment.

Schedule Definitions and Special Provisions Endorsement
This endorsement is used to extend the coverage to additional objects for industrial and processing risks. Objects like refrigerating and air conditioning vessels and piping, auxiliary piping, engines, pumps, compressors, fans and blowers, gear wheels and enclosed gear sets, wheels and shafting, rotating electrical machines, transformers, miscellaneous electrical apparatus, deep well pump units, and turbine units can be covered as additional objects using this endorsement.

Boiler and Machinery Time Element Coverages   Because the breakdown of a boiler often disrupts all business activity, two series of time element endorsements are available. One series is for all classes except industrial, processing and contractors, and the other is for industrial and processing risks. Time element coverage on standard SMP endorsements is not available for contractors. In each case there are several business interruption options, an extra expense endorsement, and a consequential damage endorsement. For other than industrial, processing, and contractors, there is also a prevention of occupancy endorsement. Because the two series of forms are similar, they will be considered together.

Business Interruption Forms. Two valued daily indemnity forms are available for all classes except contractors: a valued weekly indenmity form is available for all classes except industrial, processing and contractors; and an actual loss sustained form is available for industrial processing risks. These forms agree to pay indemnity, either valued on a daily or weekly basis at a specific amount, or on an actual loss sustained basis for total prevention of business. A part of the indemnity is payable for a partial prevention of business, and the forms pay that amount of expense which is reasonably incurred by the insured to reduce or avert prevention of business, but only to the extent the total amount otherwise payable is thereby reduced. The forms require certain kinds of objects be designated for coverage. In addition to the normal exclusions regarding boiler and machinery loss, the insurer is not liable for any time during which the business would not or could not have been carried on if the accident had not occurred. The insurer is also not liable for any prevention of business resulting from the failure of the insured to use due diligence and dispatch and all reasonable means in order to resume business, when the object is not in use or connected ready for use, nor in excess of the limitation established for earthquake. If, following an accident, any lease, license, or order is suspended, lapsed, or canceled, the insurer is not liable for any prevention of business occurring after the time when business could have been resumed if the lease, license or order had not lapsed or had not been suspended or canceled. The insured must send notice of accident by telegram at the insurer's expense or by letter to the insurance company, and commencement of liability under the endorsement is the time of the accident, or twenty-four hours before the notice of the accident is received, whichever is later. A time or dollar deductible may apply, and each loss is subject to a maximum limit of loss. A coinsurance clause applies to the actual loss sustained form.

Extra Expense Forms. Extra expense is available for all classes except contractors by using one of two forms. Subject to conditions virtually identical with those applying to business interruption losses, the insurer agrees to pay the insured the amount of extra expense necessarily incurred to continue as nearly as practicable the normal operation of the insured's business. The limits of payments do not exceed a specified percentage of the limit of liability for loss for a designated period of restoration. The term "extra expense" is defined to mean expenses to resume operations at a level as near normal as possible and does not include lost income.

Consequential Damage Forms. Consequential damage is available for all classes except contractors by using one of two forms. The insurer agrees to pay the insured the amount of loss to specified property of the insured, or of others which the insured becomes legally obligated to pay, on an actual cash value basis, and to pay that amount of reasonable expense incurred to reduce or avert loss to the extent the loss that would have been paid is reduced. Consequential loss includes loss due to spoilage from lack of power, light, heat, steam, or refrigeration. The insured must declare certain objects and coinsurance applies. The insurer agrees to defend the insured against claims or suits alleging liability together with paying the associated expenses.

Prevention of Occupancy. For classes other than industrial, processing, and contractors, the prevention of occupancy endorsement can be used to pay a monthly indemnity for total prevention of occupancy, to pay a proportionate part of the monthly indemnity for each month of partial prevention of occupancy, and to pay reasonable expenses incurred to reduce or avert prevention of occupancy, but only to the extent the total amount that would have been paid is reduced. Conditions similar to those found in the business interruption and extra expense forms apply. Total prevention of occupancy means the prevention of the use of the premises so that neither the insured nor any of those persons who were occupying the premises at the time of the accident (except a caretaker or a watchman required for the protection of the property) is able to use the premises. This form is not unlike the loss of rents endorsement in Section I of the SMP.

INDEPENDENT FORMS

The SMP program is one of several standard "bureau" package policy programs for commercial accounts. It is a flexible program which can accommodate a wide variety of clients and most of the appropriate coverages for many accounts. The series of forms examined was selected for analysis because it is the industry standard, although many insurers use some or all of their own policy forms to provide packaged commercial insurance. In fact, the independent forms are often considerably broader than and easier to read than the SMP forms. Some independent forms are shorter and clearer than SMP forms and many provide not only broader definitions but various free extensions of coverage not found in the SMP contracts. New programs are constantly emerging and the producer must be in a position to regularly evaluate forms and rates. Using the SMP program as a "yardstick" is one approach. It is important when a producer replaces one insurance program with one using alternative policy forms, that the key differences be analyzed in detail and carefully explained, in writing, to the insured.

IDENTIFYING AND QUALIFYING SMP PROSPECTS

The SMP program is so all encompassing, very few commercial clients do not qualify for coverage on standard forms. However, most underwiters are looking for preferred accounts for this program because of the discounted rates. Some insurance companies, however, write SMP policies at manual or surcharged rates for the average or poor business in a class. The producer should be cautious when using the SMP forms because sometimes they are not the broadest available contracts. Several examples of more restrictive SMP forms are included in this chapter, but there are many other instances where monoline forms may actually provide more preferable terms and conditions. In fact, the producer should be most concerned with the coverage and pricing and less concerned with the name of the package program offered by the underwriter.

Checkpoints

1. Give three approaches to insuring outdoor signs in the SMP program.
2. Compare the replacement cost endorsement available on monoline forms to the coverage available in the SMP program.
3. Explain the garagekeepers' insurance endorsement and the direct coverage option available in connection with that coverage.
4. List the inland marine coverages available in the SMP program.
5. List three crime coverages available in the SMP program.
6. How may comprehensive general liability be provided in the SMP program?
7. List the five basic insuring agreements in the SMP comprehensive crime coverage form.
8. Explain the priority of payment in the SMP boiler coverage.

CASE STUDIES

J&T Appliances

J&T Appliances sells, installs, and services appliances from a single store location. Depending on underwriting judgments, this client might fit into mercantile or service category. The reason for concern is that different categories may receive different package modification factors.

J&T would need coverage on the physical assets of the store. The special personal property form ("all-risks" coverage) form would be suitable to cover the insured's stock equipment and tenants improvements for a blanket of $95,000. Because of the fluctuation in inventory, reporting form—specific rate is recommended.

Because coverage on the property of others is limited in the SMP program, the insured might be better off in buying a bailee customers form to insure the units being serviced at J&T. Building coverage in Section I of the SMP should be on a replacement cost basis using the replacement cost endorsement and limitation (f) should be deleted to make the form equivalent to the monoline replacement cost form. J&T may also need coverage on outdoor signs, and coverage can be written "all-risks" using the neon signs endorsement. J&T may elect earthquake coverage and since in the lease J&T is held responsible for plate glass losses, J&T may schedule the larger plates and any lettering on SMP glass endorsement. Another option for J&T to consider is automatic increase in insurance endorsement. J&T will need to arrange separate transit insurance since the SMP program provides essentially on-premises coverage for insured personal property.

J&T should buy business interruption insurance using combined business interruption and extra expense endorsement. If possible, the period of indemnity should be extended 180 days. Using a 50 percent contribution, the amount of insurance would be $85,000 for gross earnings and $4,000 for extra expense; however, to be safe, these figures should be increased to reflect the future, and if possible, an agreed amount endorsement should be added to avoid a potential coinsurance penalty.

J&T can insure the accounts receivable and should do so or make duplicate records for storage off-premises.

J&T will insure the general liability in Section II on the SMP liability insurance form. Further, a comprehensive general liability endorsement should be added. A few insurers will also add the automobile exposures, and this may be possible for J&T; if not, J&T will need a separate automobile policy and the employers' non-ownership automobile insurance and hired car coverage should be written in conjunction with the owned vehicles rather than in the SMP policy. The limit of liability for Section II ought to be $500,000 so an umbrella can be purchased separately in excess of the package policy. J&T may elect to insure $1,000 in premises medical payments, and various monoline liability endorsements should be added to the policy to provide personal injury coverage, contractual liability coverage, and so forth. The monoline broad form comprehensive general liability endorsement can best provide the needed coverage for J&T. J&T will also need to buy excess fire legal liability coverage.

Section III of the J&T package policy should include SMP

Comprehensive Crime Coverage with a limit of at least $50,000 on Agreement IA, $2,000 on Agreements II and III, $1,000 on Agreement IV, and $50,000 on Agreement V.

The case study is silent on boiler and machinery exposures, but air conditioning equipment could be insured against accident in Section IV of the policy.

John Gale, M.D.

Dr. Gale's medical office is eligible for an SMP policy but his farm should be written on more appropriate forms. The office policy could include $125,000 on the building subject to a 100 percent coinsurance clause on an "all-risks" basis using the special building form. The perils insured could be broadened by adding the SMP earthquake extension endorsement; coverage should be endorsed to replacement cost (with limitation (f) deleted) and the agreed amount endorsement and the automatic increase in insurance endorsement should be added to the policy.

Dr. Gale's business personal property can be insured on the physicians' and surgeons' equipment floater for $60,000, and this form includes an extension for $250 on currency, money and stamps. Dr. Gale will also need $20,000 coverage on the accounts receivable endorsement, and although the case study does not identify an exposure, some amount of insurance for his patient files on the valuable papers and records endorsement.

Dr. Gale may need the extra expense endorsement in an amount sufficient to provide for temporary office space if his building is untenable. He can also insure the $10,000 annual rental income on the loss of rents endorsement with a 100 percent contribution clause.

Most underwriters would be unwilling to provide more than premises liability coverage for Dr. Gale in Section II, and he will need to arrange his malpractice insurance with a separate policy. Dr. Gale should carry separate umbrella liability.

Section III of Dr. Gale's SMP policy might include the SMP comprehensive crime coverage form at least covering Agreements IA and V as the suggested equipment floater provides some money coverage.

If Dr. Gale's building is heated by steam, the SMP boiler and machinery coverage endorsement would be in order in the amount of $125,000. The time element exposures could also be covered using the business interruption endorsement (valued daily indemnity) form and the extra expense endorsement.

R.P. Davis, Contractor

Section I of Davis's SMP policy should include blanket coverage of $70,000 over the office building and warehouse on an "all-risks" plus earthquake basis similar to that described for Dr. Gale's building. The same extensions and broadening endorsements should apply. The office furnishings, supplies, and equipment should be insured also on an "all-risks" basis on a reporting form as outlined for J&T. Coverage also should be arranged on the $200,000 in accounts receivables and $15,000 of valuable papers (the plans and specifications) as described in the previous cases. The valuable papers form should list the safe as the receptacle for the documents.

Davis probably has no business interruption exposure, although some extra expense coverage on the office and the warehouse might be in order. The contractor's mobile equipment will need to be separately insured as will other inland marine exposures like an installation floater. The builder's insurance needed when Davis is required to secure and maintain property insurance on the structures being built cannot be made a part of the SMP using the SMP special builders' risk completed value form ("all-risks" coverage) because the form is limited to use by the owner of the property.

Section II of the policy should be on a comprehensive general liability basis deleting "XCU" exclusions and various extensions including the broad form comprehensive general liability supplement, although the owned, nonowned, or hired cars ought to be insured using a separate automobile policy. A separate umbrella contract is in order in excess of the package policy.

Davis's employees should be bonded with SMP comprehensive crime coverage form.

It is doubtful that Davis faces a boiler and machinery exposure so there will be no Section IV of the policy.

Premier Door and Window Company, Inc.

Section I of the Premier SMP package will insure buildings and equipment, tenants improvements, and stock on a replacement cost basis, "all-risks," blanket, and subject to an agreed amount endorsement, all as outlined in the previous cases. Premier may elect an automatic increase endorsement as well. The manufacturers selling price endorsement is necessary to be certain that Premier can recover the profit in finished goods if they are destroyed before being sold. The accounts receivable should be insured in the SMP policy, but separate insurance will need to be arranged for the transit and ocean marine exposures.

The business interruption exposure will need study but the combination business interruption and extra expense endorsement may be in order. Further, the rental income exposure may be treated separately with the loss of rents endorsement. There is also an apparent contingent business interruption exposure at Acme Mobile Home which may need to be insured separately.

Section II of the policy ought to provide adequate limits of comprehensive general liability insurance including necessary extensions of coverage to underlie an umbrella contract. Excess fire legal liability will need to be purchased to cover the $1,000,000 leased building which is in the care, custody, and control of the insured. A separate automobile policy will need to be written on owned, hired, and nonowned automobiles.

Section III of the Premier policy should include SMP comprehensive crime coverage with adequate limits of fidelity coverage. Agreements II and III will have to be in adequate amounts to cover the cash payroll on and off premises.

Section IV of the Premier policy will include direct and indirect damage coverage for the boiler and machinery exposure as there is apparently at least one boiler on the premises. Premier may elect to cover their production machinery as well, and consideration will have to be given to various extensions of coverage.

SUMMARY

The SMP combines property, liability, crime and boiler machinery coverages for eight eligible classes of clients. Property and liability coverages are mandatory while crime and boiler coverages are optional. Important exposures such as auto liability and physical damage, workers' compensation and umbrella liability must be insured with separate policies.

Coverage provisions in the SMP are similar to monoline policies. However, enough differences between package and monoline coverages exist that the producer must carefully examine SMP forms to be sure exposures desired to be covered under an SMP are covered. The essential production idea is to control the entire account. A good job on the SMP and necessary additional policies will help the producer cover a client's exposures and also protect the account from competitors.

CHAPTER 13

Case Studies

INTRODUCTION

This chapter contains six actual case situations reasonably typical of producers selling commercial lines insurance. These cases do not describe how producers wrote accounts such as Exxon or Procter and Gamble. Multinational businesses and their risk management needs are beyond the scope of the Producer's Program. Rather, the six cases are "main street" accounts similar to the cases presented in Chapter 10 of *Principles of Insurance Production*. They are the types of accounts producers will come across time and time again.

Except for changing the names of the producers, the businesses, and the locations, the cases are real. The decisions made by producers, their thought processes, and the results are presented *as they happened* (in some cases, technical errors are obvious). To that extent, these cases represent how some producers sell insurance. No attempt is made to say the results were "good or bad" for either the producer or the client. The indicated result is not presented as a model, as an example of a producer's good or poor selling efforts. Because actual situations and results are given and because each producer may approach a similar client or prospect in a different way, the checkpoints of this chapter will be used differently than those in other chapters. Instead of asking the student to review content material, questions will be asked about the case and how the student would have reacted in the same situation. Questions will also be asked about the marketing approach the student would have used or devised in a similar situation. The Course Guide also presents cases for study, but the results are not given. The student is encouraged to develop a personal approach to the client in each case, determine the exposure identification method to use, and decide on the selling strategy which should obtain the account.

The purpose of the first two courses in the Producer's Program is to prepare the producer technically to apply the appropriate insurance product to a client's exposures. The cases here and in the Course Guide are the logical conclusion to this portion of the Producer's Program. The emphasis is on application of the acquired knowledge of insurance and selling.

Ben's TV Sales

Ben Williams opened his own television and stereo business in 1968 and since that time has developed a thriving retail operation. Ben has three full-time employees who assist him in sales. One of these employees also makes deliveries of television sets and stereo units. The retail operation has been financially successful, but Ben never believed he should expand into the television repair business. Presently, Ben contracts with others to do warranty repairs.

Ben has built the business to the point where it is well-known in town, and he has many regular customers. For that reason, Ben sometimes sells TVs or stereos on a monthly payment plan to "repeat" customers. Ben also rents TV sets for a short term to students at the local college and to patients at the community hospital.

Charlie Jackson, a young producer in town, has decided to solicit Ben's TV Sales but knows very little about the operation other than the facts presented. Charlie called Ben to set up an appointment. Charlie received the appointment but had the impression that Ben was only being polite.

At the initial meeting, Charlie was informed that Ben was very satisfied with his present producer and insurance coverages. However, Charlie noticed that Ben was very open and talkative, so Charlie used the non-leading questioning technique to keep Ben talking. In the course of the conversation, it became apparent to Charlie that Ben had built a profitable business with considerable earning power. It was at this point that Charlie saw a possibility for a sale.

Charlie mentioned that he had both heard of and read about TV firms that had been put out of business by extremely large liability court judgments. Charlie asked whether Ben believed his present liability limits were adequate to protect him from the loss of everything he had worked for if a catastrophic loss occurred. Charlie pointed out that although Ben was satisfied with his present basic program he, Charlie, could provide the needed commercial umbrella coverage at an economical cost. Ben agreed to allow Charlie to quote on an umbrella liability policy.

Charlie had accomplished his goal on the first meeting with the prospect. He had established a rapport with Ben and Ben had displayed a certain amount of trust in Charlie by allowing him to work on a portion of the account. Charlie gained trust by listening to Ben, eventually identifying an inadequately handled exposure to loss, and suggesting a way of providing insurance coverage to protect Ben from the possible consequences of this exposure. Ben had expressed satisfaction in his present producer and insurance program. If Charlie had attacked them, pointing out deficiencies, Ben might have become defensive and never allowed Charlie to quote the umbrella. Charlie did not ask to look over the existing program. He simply showed an interest and offered to provide an additional service.

Charlie was now in a position to discuss insurance coverages with his prospect. Charlie explained to Ben how the commercial umbrella would provide liability coverage of at least $1 million over and above the existing liability policies. He also pointed out that the commercial umbrella would provide liability protection for exposures where Ben has no primary coverage but that a self-insured retention of $10,000 would apply like a deductible to any judgment in these areas. However, this particular umbrella would provide full defense coverage if Ben had no coverage under a primary liability policy.

Ben apparently liked what he heard so he asked Charlie what information would be needed to provide the quote. Charlie explained to Ben that the umbrella insurer required that certain primary exposures be covered up to certain limits of liability. To write the coverage, the umbrella insurer would need to know coverages, premiums, expiration dates and the names of the primary insurers. Charlie suggested that the best way to acquire this information would be to review the existing policies. Ben agreed and handed Charlie a large manila envelope containing the policies. Charlie jotted down the policy information, thanked Ben for his time, and advised Ben that he would be back with the umbrella quote in a week.

Charlie returned to his office pleased that not only had he acquired a qualified umbrella prospect but he now also had the policy information and expiration dates of the existing primary insurance program. He would diary that information and be in a position to offer Ben a quote on the entire account. Charlie filled out a commercial umbrella application and submitted it to his most competitive umbrella insurer explaining the need for the quote within one week.

Charlie received the umbrella quote and arranged another appointment with Ben. Charlie wanted to do more than simply hand Ben a quote for this coverage. He wanted Ben to fully understand the umbrella protection that would be provided as well as presenting himself and his firm as professionals in the insurance business. Charlie

Exhibit 13-1
Ben's TV Sales—Liability Insurance Proposal

Coverage	Primary Limits	Umbrella	Total
OL&T Liability	$300,000 CSL	$1,000,000	$1,300,000
Products Liability	$300,000 CSL	$1,000,000	$1,300,000
Auto Liability	$500,000 CSL	$1,000,000	$1,500,000
Uninsured Exposures	($10,000 Retention)	$1,000,000	$1,000,000

knew that doing a good job at this meeting could open the door to the entire account. He provided Ben with a chart (Exhibit 13-1) to graphically display the coverages provided by the commercial umbrella he proposed.

Charlie met with Ben and again explained the coverages and highlighted uninsured exposures, where a loss could occur and the umbrella would respond. Ben was impressed with the presentation and satisfied with the price. Charlie closed the sale by stating that coverage could be made effective that day. Charlie stated that the umbrella would be written so that its term would be the same as the underlying liability policies. Ben accepted the proposal and told Charlie to order the policy and send a bill for the premium.

Charlie had closed one sale and now used the opportunity to open the conversation for the next sale. Charlie was now established as one of Ben's insurance sources so Ben was receptive. Charlie was careful to keep comments on a positive basis rather than pointing out deficiencies he found in the primary program. He had no way of knowing whether the other producer had pointed out these deficiencies to Ben earlier and Ben had elected not to buy those coverages. Charlie simply stated he had noticed that the primary coverages would expire next June and he would be pleased to have the opportunity to work on the account. Ben expressed an interest and agreed to let Charlie quote on the entire account. Charlie thanked Ben and said he would be back in touch near the expiration date.

When the file on Ben's TV Sales came out of diary, Charlie reviewed the information he had obtained while developing the umbrella coverage. Charlie wanted to avoid the pitfall of using old information to provide a new proposal. He also realized that while Ben might not be aware of some of his exposures, they should be pointed out to Ben. Charlie decided the best approach would be to use a survey to help him identify the exposures. Charlie then set up a meeting with

Ben to develop the information needed to properly underwrite and rate the entire account.

At this meeting Charlie began the survey process by discussing the exposures to loss from owned buildings. Ben said he did not own the building; instead, it was leased from another businessowner in town. In discussing the value of the contents of Ben's store, Charlie learned the normal inventory value was consistently at $150,000 except for the last three months of the year. During those months the inventory would increase to a maximum of $200,000 due to new model introduction and the Christmas season. Ben stated that his present coverage was on a reporting form but that he found it difficult to keep up with the time-consuming reporting process.

Charlie asked Ben if he was concerned about the burglary exposure. Ben replied he had a good central station burglary alarm system and he felt he did not need to insure that exposure. However, he was concerned about theft from his van while making deliveries. The maximum value of merchandise in the one van at any one time, when Ben picked up shipment to the store, was $20,000. Ben also stated he was not concerned about the loss of one of the TVs he rented because he could easily absorb a $250 to $500 loss. This gave Charlie an indication that a deductible program would be attractive to Ben. In the conversation, Charlie mentioned that he had noticed the sign in front of the store. Ben told him he did own the sign and that it was valued at $1,500.

From the information developed, Charlie believed the present producer had adequately provided for the exposures mentioned. Charlie had noted, though, that Ben had no coverage for accounts receivable. Rather than point to the deficiency in the program, Charlie elected to highlight the need for this type of coverage and explain that he could provide the coverage in his proposal. Ben listened to Charlie's explanation of the coverages provided by the accounts receivable policy and stated that he would be receptive to this type of coverage. He also told Charlie that the maximum accounts receivable at any one time was $50,000.

Charlie also inquired about the physical damage loss to the TVs and stereos sold on installments. Charlie again identified an exposure and explained the method of affording coverage with a single interest installment sales floater policy. Ben was not receptive to this coverage, because, as he explained, his maximum loss would only be about $700 in any one incident.

Charlie's next objective was to identify any exposure to loss Ben might have to nonowned property. Charlie explained to Ben the legal implications of a fire negligently started by Ben or an employee that would cause damage to the leased building. He told Ben that fire legal liability would be included in the final proposal. Rather than ask Ben for an opinion of the building's value, Charlie chose to rely on personal knowledge that a building such as Ben occupied would be appraised for about $30 per square foot. Along this same line, Charlie checked to be sure that Ben did no repair work and did not have a bailee's exposure for customer's property.

At this point, Charlie felt that he had done a good job of surveying the exposures to direct property losses so he launched a discussion of the possibility of exposure to indirect loss. He asked Ben what the longest period of time would be before Ben could be back in complete operation if he had the worst possible loss. Ben thought that three months would be the maximum time required. Ben's opinion was that $30,000 was a figure sufficient to maintain business needs and personal income for the period of shutdown. Charlie realized that Ben had not considered the possibility of the loss occurring during the last three months of the year when sales are high. They discussed this possibility and reevaluted the situation, deciding that earnings loss during the peak period would be $15,000 per month.

Charlie then began to survey the liability exposures. He measured the square footage of the store and knew the limits of liability needed to satisfy the underlying limits of liability required of the umbrella insurer. Charlie asked for the estimated gross sales figure for the coming year to adequately rate the products liability coverage. He then discussed with Ben the need for personal injury coverage indicating that this coverage was provided in Ben's umbrella policy but that the $10,000 self-insured retention would apply to a settlement or judgment. Charlie knew that this coverage was needed from information already established so he would include this coverage in his proposal.

In a discussion of automobile liability, Charlie learned that Ben, in addition to the owned van, had the exposure of employees occasionally running errands in their own vehicles. He noted this information then went on to secure the needed information for the quotation on the owned van (the make, model, serial number, size of vehicle, cost new and radius of operation). The final task was to obtain payroll information for worker's compensation.

Charlie felt the job of surveying the loss exposures was complete and that he was in a position to provide a good insurance program. Just to be sure all the appropriate information was developed, Charlie asked Ben if he could review the lease agreement. In doing so, Charlie discovered two things. First, Ben, much to his own surprise, discovered that he was liable for glass in the building and that he held the landlord harmless for any liability involving maintenance of the premises. Charlie explained to Ben that the hold harmless in the simple lease agreement was no problem and would be covered by the premises and liability coverage. However, the glass exposure was another problem. Charlie measured the glass and told Ben that he would include the glass coverage in his proposal.

The last type of information Charlie obtained was general information about the business which he knew the insuring company would be interested in to properly underwrite the exposure. This included such things as the age of the building, the type and age of the wiring and heating systems, driver information on Ben and his employees, and loss history. Charlie thanked Ben and set a date to review the finalized proposal.

Charlie began to fill out the necessary applications and realized that he had not thought to identify any exposure for money or employee dishonesty. He was not too concerned because he believed in the survey type of interview. The producer sometimes feels too much of the prospective insured's valuable time is being taken and, in haste, forgets to investigate a possible area of exposure.

Charlie had several options which could have prevented this type of omission. He could have taken the appropriate applications with him on the interview, but this approach sometimes has a negative effect. The prospective insured is overwhelmed by the mass of applications and is less responsive to questions. The "application-survey" approach also causes the producer to appear stiff and formal rather than the more desirable personal interview atmosphere. Another option was a check-list of the possible exposures Ben might have to be discussed at the interview. This method tends to keep the interview on a more personal level.

If the checklist method is used, the producer should review the insurance company applications carefully so the appropriate questions can be asked. It would be a mistake to identify the exposures but not obtain adequate information to complete the applications.

Charlie was embarrassed about the oversight but felt the discussion of the employee dishonesty and money exposure was too important to handle by telephone. He arranged another appointment with Ben and emphasized the importance of recognizing the exposure to loss caused by dishonest acts of employees handling money or merchandise. Ben said that although he had never had this coverage it should be included in the proposal. Ben and Charlie agreed that a limit of $25,000 would be adequate. They also agreed the only other exposure to be covered would be on money and the maximum exposure was approximately $2,500. Charlie then developed the information for the fidelity application, the alarm system, and safe information for the money coverage.

With this additional information, Charlie completed the applications and submitted them to the insurance company, confident that he could respond to any additional information the underwriter might require. Upon receipt of the quotation from the insurer, Charlie prepared a written proposal for review with Ben. When the proposal was completed, he reconfirmed the appointment with Ben. The complete proposal appears in Exhibit 13-2.

Charlie took copies of the proposal to his meeting with Ben so that Ben could follow the proposal as Charlie explained the coverages. Charlie also asked Ben to initial on Charlie's copy any parts of the proposal he elected to delete from coverage, explaining this request by saying that it would make it easier for him to accurately order the policies if he had a written record. Charlie did not mention that this would also provide an initialed copy for his file to indicate that he had offered coverages and Ben had elected not to purchase them. This technique would be helpful if, in the future, there was any controversy or errors and omissions claim based on a non-insured loss. The initialed proposal would be a positive indication that the coverages were offered but not accepted by the insured, defeating a possible allegation that the insured was not aware that the coverage was available.

Charlie explained each item of the proposal and the reasons for suggesting the coverages and forms. The explanation included the following important points:

1. The contents coverage would also include Ben's interest in the improvements to the building. Since Ben had indicated that he was not concerned by the burglary exposure, Charlie had recommended "all-risks" excluding theft coverage. At this point, he also explained the normal "all-risks" exclusions. Since Ben had indicated that he would be able to absorb small losses, Charlie pointed out the deductible options, showing the premium savings realized by incorporating higher deductibles in the insurance program.

2. Remembering that Ben was not happy with his present reporting form coverage, Charlie proposed peak season coverage. It would increase the contents limit by $50,000 for the three peak months, providing adequate coverage but eliminating the monthly reports.

3. Since Ben had expressed concern about theft from the van, Charlie proposed transportation coverage with two deductible options. He explained the "locked car warranty" meant that any loss would have to be evidenced by visible signs of entry.

4. Charlie proposed insuring the sign and showed a deductible option, but pointed out that, in this case, the savings were not considerable.

5. The accounts receivable coverages were again explained to Ben.

6. Charlie explained that although Ben had not expressed an interest in the past, he wanted to show the costs of the installment sales floater. Charlie knew that sometimes the lack of interest initially was due to the lack of cost information on the prospect's part.

7. The fire legal liability coverage was included and Charlie explained that he had based the $75,000 limit on the 2,500 square foot area of the building multiplied by an estimate of $30 per square foot appraisal value.

8. Charlie explained that although they had agreed that the average monthly earnings were approximately $10,000, the earnings coverage should be written anticipating the loss occurring during the peak months of October, November, and December when the monthly earnings were $15,000. He explained that the limit was shown as $45,000 but this limit was collectible at a maximum of $15,000 per month for a period of three months.

9. Charlie explained the coverage in the CGL and pointed out that the sales figure would be audited at the end of the policy term. He explained the premises medical payments coverage. He had also included the personal injury coverage and premium since Ben had expressed an interest in covering this exposure on a primary level. Charlie also assured Ben that the proposed $300,000 combined single limit was sufficient to meet the requirements of the umbrella policy already in force.

10. Charlie reviewed the automobile coverages in the proposal for the owned delivery van.

11. The need for coverage provided by the employers' non-owned auto was explained to Ben since Charlie had noted employees were occasionally using their personal cars to run company errands, creating an exposure.

12. Charlie proposed a glass policy to cover the previously unknown exposure that he and Ben had discovered in the lease agreement.

13. Charlie briefly reviewed each proposed coverage.

Charlie was not able to sell all of the coverages proposed, but he was successful in writing the insurance program for Ben's TV Sales. Charlie used the umbrella coverage as a wedge to obtain the entire account. Even with the error, initially missing the employee dishonesty and money coverage, Ben felt he had done a good job of identifying the loss exposures and proposing insurance protection for those exposures. Charlie's success had stemmed from his own desire to make a sale and provide a valuable service. He had accomplished his goal by using a positive sales approach and product knowledge.

Exhibit 13-2
Insurance Proposal—Ben Williams d/b/a Ben's TV Sales

Coverage	Amount	Annual Premium
1. Contents including improvements and betterments "All Risk"—excluding theft		
$100 deductible	$170,000	$1400.00
$500 deductible	$170,000	$1146.00
2. Peak Season Endorsement applying October, November, and December		
$100 deductible	$50,000	$103.00
$500 deductible	$50,000	$93.00
3. Transportation—"All Risk" with locked car warranty		
$100 deductible	$20,000	$200.00
$500 deductible	$20,000	$150.00
4. Outdoor Sign—"All Risk"		
No deductible	$1500	$48.00
2% deductible	$1500	$40.00
5. Accounts Receivables		
No deductible	$50,000	$322.00
6. Installment Sales Floater "All Risk"		
No deductible	$1000 per item $25,000 per catastrophe	$250.00 deposit
7. Fire Legal Liability	$75,000	$180.00
8. Earnings Insurance 33 1/3% limitation "All Risk"		
No deductible	$45,000	$130.00
9. Comprehensive General Liability including premises/operations, products, personal injury, and $1000/10,000 premises medical payments	$300,000 CSL	$935.00
10. Automobile including liability, comprehensive physical damage and collision $100 deductible comprehensive $250 deductible collision	$500,000 CSL	$380.00
11. Employers Nonowned Automobile Liability	$500,000 CSL	$40.00

12. Comprehensive Glass	per schedule	$58.00
13. Comprehensive Crime		
Agreement IA—Fidelity	$25,000	$194.00
Agreement II—Money-Inside	$2500	$158.00
Agreement III—Money-Outside	$2500	$35.00
14. Worker's Compensation	Statutory 100,000 Employees Liability	$916.00
15. Umbrella	1,000,000	$225

Checkpoints

1. What problems were created because Charlie did not use a complete exposure identification survey method? What problems were avoided?
2. Did Charlie have objectives for each call on Ben Williams? Did they or would they have helped?
3. What exposures did Charlie miss in his proposal?
4. What aspects of the sale did Charlie handle well? Poorly?
5. Relative to the insurance coverage and ignoring price:
    a. Was the program proposed adequate?
    b. How else could the liability exposures have been insured?
    c. Should an SMP have been recommended? Why or why not?
    d. Should a BOP have been recommended? Why or why not?
6. If Charlie were interested in specializing in retail audio-visual dealers:
    a. Design an exposure checklist for the dealers.
    b. Design a letter to be sent to prospects.
7. Design the insurance proposal for Ben's TV Sales you would present.

Joseph R. Richards, D.D.S.

Vic is a producer in a medium-sized town. The field representative for a property liability insurance company Vic represents called to announce a new product. Vic listened as the field representative described a new dental professional package policy. The insurer had already assisted producers by purchasing a full-page advertisement explaining the new program in the state dental association's quarterly trade journal. The advertisement listed the firms in the state who represented the insurance company.

Vic had never solicited dentists before because he felt he could not

Exhibit 13-3
Dental Plan Form Letter

Dear _____

Your practice is in Reidville, your home is in Reidville, and your patients live in Reidville. Why shouldn't your insurance program be written in Reidville?

My firm has a very competitive and comprehensive insurance package for all of your professional insurance needs. Not only will this insurance package provide you with comprehensive protection, but all service will be handled by our capable staff here in Reidville.

Please drop me a note or give me a call at 865-2800 to arrange an appointment to discuss this program.

Yours truly,

Vic Bonner

---

compete favorably with the dental association's approved plan which was written through another producer in the state. He recognized the merits of the new plan and committed himself to selling it because he was the only producer in town who could offer the local dentists an alternative to the dental association's plan. He knew, though, that this would be a tough market to penetrate since the dental association plan had cornered the market for the past five years.

Vic's first objective was to get appointments. He knew several local dentists personally but felt he should devise a sales plan to contact more than personal acquaintances. He created a form letter to generate prospects for the new program. In his conversation with the field representative, Vic learned that the pricing of the new program was very close to that of the dental association's plan, so he felt the form letter would have to sell something other than price.

Vic's form letter emphasized service rather than price. The producer for the dental association's plan was located in a city 150 miles away. This meant dentists on this plan would have to discuss service or claims problems either by letter or by long distance telephone calls. If Vic could sell the dentists on the idea of local, convenient service, it could open the door to the dentists' accounts. With this objective in mind, Vic devised the letter shown in Exhibit 13-3.

The letter seemed simple in its content but Vic had not intended to totally explain or sell the program with the letter. His only intent was to let the dentists know that an insurance program was available locally. Vic did not mention the dental association's plan, but knew the local service he was offering would be a positive factor in obtaining response and appointments from his letters. Vic had the letter printed on his letterhead and mailed to all of the dentists listed in the Yellow Pages of the telephone book. Vic enclosed a copy of the advertisement that had appeared in the dental association's journal with each letter. This, he felt, would identify the insurance company involved in the new program and display to the dentist that this was an alternative to the dental association's plan.

Vic knew from experience that the normal rate of response from the form letter approach was slight—often less than five percent. Nonetheless, this approach could at least be used to get the new program off the ground. He was reasonably sure that at least a few of the local dentists would generate referrals which could lead to more new business.

Vic's next approach was a second technique for obtaining referrals called networking. Networking involves making contact with one prospect. Whether or not that prospect is interested in the program, Vic would ask for the names of two of the prospect's contemporaries who might be interested in the program. On each successive call Vic would ask for two more names. Vic hoped this technique would be more successful than the form letter, particularly if Vic could get the initial prospect to make the contact with the two referrals for him and help to arrange the appointments with them.

Vic made contact first with his family dentist to initiate the networking technique and, meanwhile, started to receive a small response from the form letter. Vic had then achieved his objective of making appointments with a few prospective clients—an essential first step for a producer with a new product. The most competitive product will be of no use to a producer who cannot present the product to the appropriate prospective buyer. The producer must first develop an organized plan to obtain the initial appointments.

One of Vic's first face-to-face contacts was Joseph R. Richards, D.D.S., a local dentist who had responded to the form letter because he was interested in the local service aspect of the program. In the past, someone had burglarized Dr. Richards' office, and he had experienced considerable difficulty with the claims adjusting primarily because of the need for long distance calls to the producer from the dental association to settle the claim. This was the first concrete evidence to Vic that the local service-sales approach had merit.

Knowing that this was the primary point of interest to this particular prospect, Vic launched first an introduction of his staff and an explanation of their capability to handle, in a proper and efficient manner, the insurance program for Dr. Richards. Since this was a solid prospect, Vic felt if he could sell Dr. Richards on his firm's ability to handle the program, he could make the sale. The initial interview was on the day when Dr. Richards was extremely busy and there were numerous interruptions. Dr. Richards finally told Vic that he did not really have time that day to discuss the program fully but that he would like Vic to develop a quotation based on the coverage he now had in the dental association plan. He handed Vic the policies currently in force so that Vic could duplicate the coverage. He asked Vic to telephone the receptionist if he needed additional information.

Vic left Dr. Richards' office with mixed feelings about the success of the call. He knew the policies would provide him with enough information to develop the premium quotation, but he was concerned about the acceptability of the submission, particularly the dental professional liability. He knew the insurance company had fairly strict underwriting requirements for professional liability coverages and would also require an application signed by the dentist. Vic decided that it would be best to provide the requested quotation, but also to explain to Dr. Richards that the proposed quote was subject to the approval of the insurance company upon receipt of the proper application. He also wanted to be careful to explain that his proposal was for *comparison* purposes only and was not necessarily a representation of the coverages of limits of liability he would recommend. Vic did not want another producer, in this case the producer for the dental association plan, to perform, in effect, Vic's risk management job. Vic felt that a professional job of risk identification cannot be accomplished by duplicating the coverages in another producer's insurance program. The mistake of omitting an important coverage is easy enough to commit without duplicating another's omission.

When Vic reviewed the existing policies on Dr. Richards' dental practice he found:

1. $45,000 Physicians & Surgeons Equipment Floater—"All-Risks" with $100 deductible
2. $10,000 Extra Expense "All-Risks" with no deductible
3. $6,000 Practice (Business) Interruption-Valued Form "All-Risks" at $200 per day for 30 days
4. $10,000 Account Receivables "All-Risks" with no deductible
5. $5,000 Valuable Papers "All-Risks" with no deductible
6. $10,000 Employee Dishonesty
7. $300,000 Premise Liability
8. $1,000/10,000 Premises Medical Payments
9. $100,000/300,000 Dental Professional Liability

10. $300,000 Employers Nonowned Automobile
11. $1 million Commercial Umbrella with $10,000 SIR
12. Workers' Compensation not covered

Vic quickly realized the dental association's package plan was very comprehensive, but still felt he should survey the account for any additional exposures that might exist.

After obtaining the additional information he needed to complete the application from Dr. Richards' receptionist, Vic called the underwriter and said the professional liability portion of the application was not completed but that he would like to present the proposal subject to insurance company approval. The underwriter agreed to issue a quotation on that basis.

Vic prepared a proposal displaying the exact coverages in Dr. Richards' current policies, then telephoned Dr. Richards to set up an appointment. Remembering the numerous interruptions in his last interview with Dr. Richards, Vic decided to ask Dr. Richards to meet at Vic's office. The purpose was twofold: first, to gain Dr. Richards' undivided attention; and second, to introduce Dr. Richards to the staff who would be servicing the account if his sales presentation was successful. This introduction to the staff would be the best reinforcement for the concept of good local service. Dr. Richards agreed to meet Vic during lunch.

The first point Vic made during the meeting was that the proposal was subject to the insurance company's approval after they had received and reviewed the completed and signed dental professional liability application. He went on to present the proposal, which duplicated the present coverages exactly and noting that there was very little difference in the premium he was proposing versus the premium Dr. Richards was now paying. Vic added that he was offering efficient, convenient local service.

Dr. Richards was pleased with the presentation and asked Vic to have the package issued. At this point, Vic emphasized that the proposal was based solely on replacing coverages of the policies and that he felt they should more fully discuss other exposures that may exist. Dr. Richards indicated he felt that the current limits of liability were adequate for the existing exposures. Vic's job now was to identify uncovered exposures, since Dr. Richards made it clear that the present coverages were adequate.

The first item Vic pointed out to Dr. Richards was that although the coverages were well written, they did not include primary coverage for fire legal liability. He recommended that this coverage be included in the package to provide protection against the possibility of loss arising from fire damage to the building which Dr. Richards leases caused by Dr Richard's negligence or that of one of his employees. They agreed on a limit of $100,000 for the fire legal liability coverage.

The second area of exposure was money and securities. Vic discussed this exposure with Dr. Richards and proposed a money and securities broad form policy. Vic estimated the premium for the fire legal liability and money and securities coverages. Dr. Richards agreed that these coverages should be provided in the package.

Vic also identified the personal injury exposure. He explained to Dr. Richards that although the professional liability coverage included personal injury, it was limited to personal injury related to a professional act. This, Vic explained, could leave a gap in coverage if a claim occurred related to a non-professional incident. He explained, using as an example a bookkeeper making an error in an account, resulting in the account being turned over to a collection agency. If the patient involved could show injury to the patient's reputation or credit standing in the community, Dr. Richards could be held liable, and the question of whether this was related to the dental profession could be raised. To avoid the possibility of exclusion under the dental professional liability policy, Vic proposed adding personal injury to the liability coverages. Dr. Richards agreed the coverage was needed and asked Vic to add it.

Vic and Dr. Richards were in agreement that the exposures to loss were now adequately covered in the insurance program Vic was proposing. Dr. Richards signed and completed the dental professional liability application and provided some additional information for completion of the other applications. Vic was now able to submit the applications for the dental plan for approval and policy issuance.

Vic had achieved his primary objective of selling the new dental program. But since his sale of the program was based on service and professionalism, he felt an obligation to be sure all of Dr. Richards' exposures not covered by the dental plan were identified and provided for. He had noted there was no worker's compensation policy in the file containing the other existing policies. He asked whether there was a policy currently in effect and Dr. Richards replied that he had been told that he was not required to carry workers' compensation coverage since he had only three employees. Vic explained that although the state law did not require employers with fewer than five employees to purchase a workers' compensation policy, the law did still hold the employer responsible for any benefits proscribed under the law for work-related injuries or disease. Vic explained this exposure and recommended that Dr. Richards very seriously consider the purchase of this coverage. In this jurisdiction, if he chose to purchase the coverage, as a sole proprietor, he could elect to be covered under the policy.

Dr. Richards concluded the interview by telling Vic that all of his personal coverages, including his personal umbrella policy, were written by another local producer but that he would be happy to allow Vic to review these policies before their expiration dates. Vic's professional approach and desire to provide a service on the commercial coverages had opened the door to the possibility of providing all of Dr. Richards' insurance.

Dr. Richards made it very clear to Vic he was pleased he could purchase his commercial insurance locally at a competitive price with the dental association's plan. He also appreciated the interest Vic had taken in providing the additional coverages for which he had not previously seen a need, since the producer for the dental plan had not identified those exposures.

Vic asked Dr. Richards for two referrals for his networking technique. Dr. Richards readily agreed to help Vic in making contact with some other dentists.

Eventually, Vic wrote many of the dental package accounts in the area. His success was due primarily to his organized approach to contacting prospects. He had not relied on just one sales technique but instead had used both form letters and networking. He sold local service in a positive manner in order to get the initial appointments. Vic's desire to provide the necessary coverages rather than matching the competition's program enhanced his professional standing in the eyes of his prospects.

Checkpoints

1. What are the advantages of a special insurance package to targeted markets:
    a. for producers?
    b. for prospects?
2. What were the strengths and weaknesses of Vic's sales plan?
3. Devise an exposure checklist for a professional other than a dentist.
4. Was Vic's idea of meeting Dr. Richards in Vic's office a good idea for a busy prospect? Why or why not?
5. Without a "special" plan for professionals, would an SMP or BOP be used? Why or why not?
6. Assume you wanted to develop a "special package" for a targeted group. What would you do and where would you go for help?

The Shopper

This case study involves a producer named Sharon Lawson, an associate of Vic Bonner's from the previous case study. Vic had become involved in the new dental package program and hired Sharon to service some existing accounts as well as to acquire new clients. One day, during this period, Sharon received the following form letter from a local shoe store:

> Dear Agent,
>
> Please provide us with a premium quotation on the following insurance coverages:
> > Contents—$20,000-Fire, E.C., V & MM with $100 deductible
> > Earnings—$8,000-25% monthly limit
> > OL&T—$100,000 Combined Single Limit
>
> Quotations from all agents will be reviewed and a decision will be made on June 15.

Sharon read the letter and showed it to Vic. He remembered reviewing a similar letter from the same establishment every year since he had been in the insurance business. He told Sharon this businessman purchases insurance solely on the basis of price and was not inclined to cooperate with any recommendations made by insurers. Vic also said the same letter had been sent to every producer in the area. He suggested that Sharon review her schedule. She elected not to pursue this prospect's insurance account.

Although Sharon could not ignore prospects and expect to generate new business, she had made a commitment in time and expense to become a successful producer and felt time would be better spent on other prospects rather than on this low-bid-only account. First, she reasoned, even if she were successful in writing the shoe store this year, she would probably lose it the next year since the insured shopped exclusively for price each year. She would rather work on prospects and programs like Vic's new dental program which was profitable and had a high sales and retention ratio. If Sharon had more time and had not been involved in developing another proven, successful sales program, her decision may have been different.

There is a rather simple economic lesson in this case study: the producer should sometimes choose not to quote on an account. If the indications are clear that the quotation is being requested on a "price only" basis, the producer should make the decision whether or not the time involved in the preparation of the quote is available. If there is certainty on the producer's part that he or she has a highly competitive insurer for the account, then it may be pursued.

There are also other factors that can influence the producer's decision whether or not to quote on certain accounts. If, for instance, the producer learns the prospect has been historically uncooperative about insurance company safety recommendations and that is one reason the prospect wishes to change insurance companies, the producer should be reasonably sure the insurance companies he or she represents would not also require the same adherence to the same recommendations before spending the time to pursue the account. Another factor to be considered by the producer is the credit standing of the prospect in the community. An account would not be an asset to the producer if many commission dollars had to be spent in an attempt to collect the premium.

Even with her firmly based reasoning for not quoting on the shoe store account this year, Sharon was careful how she responded to this request for a quote. She did not want to alienate the prospect for future years when she might have more time to provide the quote. Sharon knew all accounts are small at one time and did not want to close the door on any potential commercial account.

Checkpoints

1. Draft a letter to the shoe store which allows you to "bid" again at a future date.
2. List the attributes of what you consider:
    a. A "good" prospect to pursue.
    b. A "poor" prospect not to pursue.
3. Two weeks after your letter is sent, you meet the owner of the shoe store who asks you, "Why didn't you bid on my business?" Give three reasons why you did not bid that point out deficiencies in a "low bid" only account from the standpoint of the prospect.
4. If you were in Sharon's situation what type of commercial prospect would you pursue? Why?
5. What role, if any, do the insurers you represent have in your decision in question 4?

Ellenburg Furniture Store

Janet's firm had handled all of Mr. Ellenburg's insurance for the last thirty-five years. On December 1, Mr. Ellenburg called Janet to say that Ellenburg's was going out of business on December 31 and would like to cancel all of the insurance policies as of that date. Mr. Ellenburg explained to Janet that he was retiring. He would hold a "going out of business" sale and then would return any unsold merchandise to the manufacturers. His lease would expire on December 31 and he had already sold his delivery vans. Janet agreed to cancel all of his commercial insurance policies and arrange for a check for any return premium but asked if she could drop by the store and talk for a few minutes.

Janet reviewed the Ellenburg file to determine if there was any exposure that could continue after the business closed its doors for the last time. Janet knew all property would be disposed of as the fleet of vans had been, so those exposures had been eliminated. Remembering that products liability insurance responded to any property damage or bodily injury loss that occurred during the policy period due to defective products sold by the insured, she realized that a loss could occur after the policy was cancelled and Mr. Ellenburg would be without any liability coverage.

Janet called the insurance company and asked if coverage could be provided for the exposure. The insurer agreed to issue a products liability policy using the liability code for "discontinued operations." The underwriter explained to Janet that the premium would decrease each year the coverage continued. The next week, Janet met with Mr. Ellenburg and recommended the continuation of the products liability coverage.

Although Janet was losing a good commercial account, she was still able to identify an exposure and offer coverage to protect her insured from that exposure to loss. The legal entity under which the insured is operating would make no difference. Even if Mr. Ellenburg had been personally liable for a loss because he was heir to the assets of the now dissolved corporation.

The exposure can also exist if one firm sells out to another. The producer would have to read the contract of sale carefully. Sometimes the purchaser only buys the assets and does not assume any of the liabilities of the seller.

Checkpoints

1. What is the disturbing feature of this case? How would you have prevented it?
2. The case revolves on a continuing exposure of a business that is closed. Is there any other insurance that Janet could ask Mr. Ellenburg about?
3. Do you think Janet's firm controlled this account's total insurance program? Why or why not?
4. How could Janet still have been able to do business with Mr. Ellenburg if her firm had truly been an all-lines agency or brokerage house?

J-R Mechanical, Inc.

Tom Ferguson, business manager for J-R Mechanical, Inc., heard from some of his friendly competitors that Jeff Greene, a local producer, had done a good job on their insurance programs. Tom was not satisfied with his present insurance program and decided to give Jeff a call to discuss the possibility of Jeff handling J-R's coverages.

Jeff was excited about this opportunity and was eager to set an appointment. Jeff knew J-R Mechanical was a large firm but was not familiar with their entire operation. He believed the best thing to do at the first interview was to gather as many facts about the operation as possible, identify J-R's loss exposures, then go back for any necessary rating information to prepare a proposal. Tom Ferguson had given Jeff plenty of time to work on the account properly. The information he developed in that meeting follows.

J-R Mechanical was founded in 1956 as a residential heating and air conditioning contractor. Since that time it had entered the commercial heating and air conditioning field and had grown into one of the largest heating and air conditioning contractors in the state. J-R had retired from residential jobs and now specialized in the installation of large commercial units in textile plants, apartment complexes, shopping centers, schools, and government buildings.

J-R obtained as many local jobs as possible but did occasionally contract jobs in neighboring states. For these out-of-state jobs, J-R would usually send a couple of their supervisors to the job site but would subcontract the actual installation work to a local contractor. J-R would purchase the heating or air conditioning units directly from the manufacturer and have the units shipped to the job site by common carrier.

J-R Mechanical, Inc., also serves as a subcontractor doing installation work for large general contractors involved in larger commercial projects. For these jobs J-R would usually fabricate the duct work in its own metal shop and transport the duct work to the installation site in its own fleet of vehicles. The general contractor usually required an appropriate certificate of insurance with varying limits of liability.

J-R Mechanical, Inc., actually has three divisions and one wholly owned subsidiary. The first division, is the Contract Installation Division. The second division is the Service Department. The service department of the company seeks annual contract service agreements with textile plants to service and maintain the plant's heating and air conditioning systems. Service work is restricted to local plants only.

The third division of J-R Mechanical, Inc., consists of engineers who design air conditioning and ventilating systems for the textile industry. Many of J-R's competitors use this division to design and plan systems for their projects. J-R's engineers are known nationally and fly all over the United States in a corporate-owned jet to discuss designs with clients.

In 1975 the directors of J-R Mechanical, Inc., accurately forecast the growing interest of the homeowner in woodburning heating systems. They established a subsidiary corporation, Fuelsaver, Inc., to develop a woodburning fireplace insert. The investment has paid off, and Fuelsaver, Inc., was in full operation and production by 1978. Another building had been constructed to house the manufacturing subsidiary. Fuelsaver, Inc., manufactures the insert device and sells it to distributors. Although the Fuelsaver label is on the product, this corporation does no installation. It is strictly a manufacturing concern, selling the finished product F. O. B. at its loading dock behind the building. Fuelsaver, Inc., owns no vehicles.

J-R Mechanical, Inc. and its subsidiary Fuelsaver, Inc., has grown rapidly and, to help finance the operation, stock in the parent corporation has been sold to many investors in the community. The company has attained a very good financial and credit rating.

Tom Ferguson told Jeff he was not satisfied with his present insurance program because he was not confident that J-R was adequately covered. He told Jeff he wanted recommendations for coverage for all exposures to loss. This put Jeff in a dangerous situation from an errors and omissions standpoint. Jeff knew he would have to identify all of the possible exposures to loss so he returned to his office to review the information obtained. Jeff knew he would need additional information eventually, but could start with information in his preliminary survey. Jeff compiled the following list of exposures and tentative recommendations for covering them for J-R Mechanical, Inc., to discuss with Tom on the next interview:

1. Building and Contents—The building is owned by J-R and occupied by corporate offices and the sheet metal shop. Jeff recommends replacement cost coverage on the building on an "all-risks" form. He would like to delete two "all-risks" exclusions by suggesting flood and earthquake coverage. He would, of course, recommend the same perils on contents.

2. Accounts Receivable—Jeff had no details on this exposure but knew it must exist. He needed to discuss this further on the next interview.

3. Valuable Papers—Since Jeff learned J-R was active in the design of the systems, he felt sure there would be a valuable papers exposure. He would recommend that J-R be protected for loss of blueprints on and off the premises by some type of risk management techniques.

4. Off Premises Property—Another exposure to loss that Jeff identified was loss to insured property away from the premises. He would suggest transportation coverage for the property while being transported to the job site as well as an installation

floater to protect J-R from the potential loss to property while on the job site and in the course of installation.

5. Bond Exposure—Jeff recognized several different bond exposures which J-R faces that could be provided for by bond.

    a) J-R performs work for public buildings such as schools and government building projects. Jeff knew that most of these projects would require both bid and performance bonds.

    b) Employee dishonesty is an exposure. Jeff would suggest a Comprehensive Dishonesty, Destruction, and Disappearance Policy (3-D Bond). In that way the money and securities exposure, the depositors forgery, counterfeit money, and money orders coverage could all be covered under one policy form.

    c) Jeff knew that he could also include the required coverage for a pension and profit sharing plan under the fidelity insuring agreements of the 3-D if there was need to do so.

6. General Liability—Jeff recognized that the legal liability exposures of J-R were tremendous so it would be extremely important to identify and provide coverage for all of them.

    a) Premises/Operations—Jeff would recommend the premises and operations exposure be written on the M&C form. This would provide liability protection both on and off the premises for operations of all three divisions of the corporation. Jeff would provide coverage for certain exclusions in the M&C form suggesting the following additional coverage forms.

    b) Contractual Liability—By handling the insurance for other contractors, Jeff learned that many construction contracts contained "hold harmless" agreements whereby the contractor may be assuming financial responsibility for someone else's legal liability. Jeff's recommendation would be to try to write this coverage on a "blanket" basis. If this was not possible, it could be written on a "specific contract" basis with each contractual agreement reported to the insurance company.

    c) Owner's and Contractor's Protective—Jeff had learned that J-R would subcontract out-of-state installation jobs. Even if J-R required a certificate of insurance from the subcontractor, J-R could still be drawn into legal liability claims due to the negligent act of the subcontractor. Jeff would suggest owner's or contractor's protective liability coverage to protect J-R from this type of loss.

d) Broad Form Property Damage—By including this coverage, Jeff could, to a certain extent, remove the "care, custody, and control" exclusion from the liability coverages. This would be an important extension of J-R's liability protection particularly for the service division where they are constantly performing work on the property of others.

e) Personal Injury—Jeff could also see the possibility of a personal injury claim. He would suggest a full personal injury protection with the employee and contractor exclusion deleted.

f) Products and Completed Operations—This was an enormous exposure for J-R. Jeff would recommend that J-R buy this coverage part to be protected from this exposure.

g) Medical Payments—Jeff knew this coverage was fairly inexpensive and would recommend it so that these voluntary payments might help to avert a more serious bodily injury suit by someone who might be injured either on the insured's premises or on a job site.

7. Auto—Since J-R operated a fleet of owned vehicles, Jeff was able to identify several exposures in this area.

a) Owned Auto—Jeff would propose a business automobile policy to cover all vehicles for liability and the owned vehicles for physical damage exposures. He would include the uninsured motorist, *under* insured motorist and the limited no-fault coverages required by state law.

b) Non-Owned Auto—Jeff would emphasize that the BAP would include employer's non-owned auto coverage. Jeff had not developed this exposure on the first interview but knew that with a few rare exceptions, almost all businesses had this exposure. The hired automobile coverage would provide coverage to automatically cover any vehicle that J-R had to rent or lease for a short term to supplement the fleet.

8. Architect's and Engineer's Professional Liability—Since J-R had an engineering division that performed design work for both its own jobs and for others, Jeff felt that this was an essential coverage. Jeff knew professional liability was excluded from the other liability coverages he had suggested, so he knew this would have to be written specifically and, hopefully, with the same insurer as the general liability.

9. Aviation Coverage—On the first interview, Jeff found J-R owned a corporate jet. He knew aviation liability and hull

coverage were required for the aircraft since this coverage is specifically excluded from the general liability policy.

10. Director's and Officer's Liability—Jeff would suggest that J-R consider buying this coverage to protect its board of directors in legal liability situations. Jeff knew these individuals could be held personally liable for negligent acts that damaged in some way the stockholders of the corporation. This coverage could be written to cover the board as a whole and also to include each board member individually.

11. Commercial Umbrella—Jeff would recommend limits of liability on all of the previously mentioned coverages sufficient to satisfy minimum requirements for an umbrella policy. Jeff learned J-R was required to furnish certificates of insurance to various concerns at varying limits of liability. Jeff would recommend a minimum limit on the umbrella of $5 million. In recommending this limit Jeff would point out that J-R needed to protect itself against the catastrophic loss. All of the underlying liability policies could be covered by the umbrella, and any uninsured primary loss would be covered after a self-insured retention.

12. Workers' Compensation—J-R was located in a state that required a Workers' Compensation policy so, of course, Jeff would recommend this coverage. Jeff knew that occasionally J-R's employees worked in all parts of the United States, so he would recommend that the "Broad Form All States" endorsement be added to adequately protect J-R from an injured employee electing to collect benefits under another state's workers' compensation benefits.

13. Business Interruption—Jeff had not developed information on this exposure but knew it must exist. He decided to fully discuss this exposure with Tom Ferguson on their next interview to determine the exact needs of the corporation. From that conversation, he could determine which of the business interruption forms would be most appropriate—gross earnings, earnings, extra expense, or a combination of coverages. Whichever he and the insured decided would be most appropriate, Jeff knew that all businesses have a time element exposure.

Jeff then did the same type of exposure survey for Fuelsavers, Inc., and developed a similar list of their exposures. The property and general liability exposures were essentially the same. Fuelsavers, Inc., though, would not need the architect's and engineer's professional liability, aviation, or director's and officer's liability coverage. They did not own a fleet of vehicles but would still have the exposure to loss of employer's non-owned auto and possibly of the hired automobile exposures. He was sure, however, they would also need the workers' compensation coverage and umbrella protection.

Jeff met again with Tom Ferguson and discussed the list of loss exposures and recommendations that he had developed. At this meeting with Tom, Jeff gathered the necessary rating information, such as the values of property, payrolls, receipts, and so forth, to complete the applications. They came to an agreement on the proper way to cover loss of earnings of the corporation. Jeff was then able to and did request quotations from various insurance companies.

Jeff prepared a formal proposal and presented it to Tom Ferguson the following month. Jeff was successful in writing the J-R Mechanical, Inc., insurance program because of his willingness to take the time to identify exposures. In doing his survey of the business, Jeff was able to identify several exposures J-R had not previously been aware of or protected against.

Checkpoints

1. If you had a chance to work on the J-R account:
    a) How many appointments would you plan to complete the sale?
    b) What would your objective be on each call?
2. Jeff used the exposure identification process. How would you improve on the process he used?
3. How would you have used the following types of exposure identification methods:
    a) Surveys?
    b) Flow Charts?
    c) Financial Statements?
    d) Personal Inspections?
4. Which potential exposures of J-R in the case would you like to pursue that Jeff may have missed?
5. Jeff suggested separate policies for J-R and Fuelsaver, Inc. He also suggested an M&C with multiple endorsement for both.
    a) Do you have an alternative way of issuing the policies?
    b) Do you have other recommendations for the liability exposures?
6. What specific suggestions would you make to Jeff to improve his:
    a) Exposure identification process?
    b) Proposal for insurance on the J-R Mechanical account?

Casey Fishing Equipment Company

Larry Horne is the owner of his own agency in a medium-sized city. He has two other producers in his firm who traditionally emphasized personal lines and small retail commercial accounts. One morning Larry read a newspaper article concerning an old friend:

MAJOR LEAGUER RETURNS HOME

John Casey, former major league outfielder, has decided to return to his home to reside now that his baseball career has ended. Casey, 35, four times elected to the American League All-Star Team, stated that he has decided "to return home and join my father's firm as his partner." His father, James Casey, is the owner of the Casey Fishing Equipment Company, the city's largest manufacturing concern. When contacted, James Casey stated that, "I am pleased to have my only son come home to help manage the business. He will be a full partner and in charge of all financial matters. Hopefully, in five years, I will be able to retire with John completely in control."

The Casey Fishing Equipment Company has recently begun construction on a large new addition to their manufacturing plant. The new building will allow for increased output of the new "Grass Wacker" electric weed cutter they have recently developed.

Because Larry and John attended high school together and were teammates on the school's baseball team, Larry believed he might have an advantage in dealing with John concerning the company's insurance needs. In fact, two years earlier Larry had attempted to obtain the Casey account. He had interviewed James Casey and obtained information on their insurance policies. He submitted an unsuccessful quote. Larry decided to pull out the Casey file and do some background work before contacting John for an interview.

Larry knew that James Casey's business was specialized—for years its only product was a line of rods and reels. It produced no other fishing equipment. Its rods and reels had a reputation for durability and high quality. Larry was not aware of the company's new construction or expansion into the Grass Wacker, all of which had taken place since his interview.

In reviewing notes from his interview with James Casey, Larry remembered the account as being a large premium account with no unusual insurance coverages. The quotation Larry submitted had included an SMP with "all-risks" building and contents coverage, a CGL, 3D coverage, boiler and machinery coverage, adequate business interruption coverage, and automobile coverages for 6 company autos. This review also reminded him of the size of the worker's compensation exposure, which two years ago had generated a $300,000 premium.

Larry's only new recommendation had been a $2 million commercial umbrella policy.

John Casey was happy to grant Larry an interview. They met in John's office and John immediately said they should tour the plant. Larry was especially interested in the new expansion project.

John was proud of the new building which the firm was scheduled to occupy in nine months. Larry did little talking, allowing John to talk at length about the need for the new building arising from the huge success of the Grass Wacker. With only 18 months of production, the Grass Wacker accounted for 15 percent of company sales with projected sales doubling in the coming year. The product, while a diversification, was a perfect complement to the fishing equipment manufacturing because it used the same fishing line as their rods and reels. The new building would house expanded manufacturing of the fishing line used in the Grass Wacker. The casing for the Grass Wacker was imported from Japan.

Larry noticed that a railroad sidetrack connected the old manufacturing plant to the main line, but he did not see a sidetrack running to the new building site. When asked about this, John said, "Our fishing equipment is sold in a fifteen state area, so that we use the rails exclusively for shipping those products. Our Grass Wackers are being sold only in the immediate tri-state area, so we've been using common carriers to haul the Grass Wackers. We have never owned any trucks of our own."

When they returned to John's office, John mentioned that the work force had expanded twenty percent in the past two years and stated, "The workers' compensation premium will probably exceed one-half million dollars this year. That's why I am considering joining the state manufacturer's association workers' compensation self-insurance pool. I will give you a copy of the brochure describing their program." Before Larry left he received a summary of current insurance policies and a recent survey of building and property values completed before drawing up the partnership agreement between John and his father.

Larry knew that this account, if obtained, would represent 20 to 25 percent of his agency's premium volume. He wanted to do a careful analysis. His overall impression of the account was that the company was in the midst of significant changes. One product line was expanded into a new product area; the new product was rapidly increasing sales; and a new building, the first for Casey's in twenty-five years, was underway. Larry believed significant operating changes would generate new exposures. Larry knew he would need to be careful about exposure identification.

Exposure Identification

1. Based on the information given, list (i) the exposures that do exist and (ii) the exposures that you feel may exist for Casey in the following insurance lines:
   a) direct damage
   b) indirect damage
   c) auto including garage & truckers
   d) general liability (other than auto or workers' compensation) including products
   e) inland marine
   f) ocean marine
   g) crime, fidelity and other bonds
   h) miscellaneous exposures
2. How would you handle John's interest in the worker's compensation self-insurance pool?
3. At Larry's next interview with John, what should he do to:
   a) uncover exposures not clearly identified so far?
   b) develop information needed to place the account?
4. How would you involve insurance company personnel in this case?
5. How should Larry use the following to write this account:
   a) friendship?
   b) exposure identification?
   c) placing insurance with the "right" insurer?
   d) lack of experience?
6. Do you think it is wise for an agency the size of Larry's to attempt a sale this large? Do you think the agency can adequately service the account? List pros and cons concerning this issue.
7. What recommendations would you have for Larry if he decides to pursue other large commercial accounts?

SUMMARY

The first objective of the producer is to gain the opportunity to write insurance accounts. Once that initial objective is obtained, the producer must be capable of identifying the prospect's exposures to loss and providing insurance or other risk management techniques for those exposures. The intent of this chapter was to show through case studies how some producers approach and accomplish the task of risk identification and coverage determination. The purpose of the Checkpoint section was to give other producers the opportunity to examine alternate ways to accomplish the same task.

Bibliography

Chamber of Commerce of the United States. *Analysis of Workers' Compensation Laws.* Washington, D.C.

Collatz, Frederick A. "Claims for Equipment Use Under Public Contract Bonds." *A.B.A. Section of Insurance, Negligence, and Compensation Law, 1969 Proceedings.* Chicago: American Bar Association.

Contract Bonds: The Unseen Services of a Surety. New York: The Surety Association of America, 1973.

Couch, George J. *Couch on Insurance,* 2nd ed. Rochester, NY: The Lawyers Co-Operative Publishing Co., 1965.

F.C.&S. Bulletins, Fire and Marine Section, Commercial Multi-Peril.

A Guide to Aviation Insurance. Philadelphia: Insurance Company of North America, July 1975.

Horn, Ronald C. *Subrogation in Insurance Theory and Practice.* Homewood, IL: Richard D. Irwin, 1964.

Jenne, Donald Dickinson. *Jenne's Suretymaster.* St. Paul, MN: Suretymaster of America.

Mackall, Luther E. *Surety Underwriting Manual.* Indianapolis, IN: The Rough Notes Co., 1972.

Malecki, Donald S.; Donaldson, James H.; and Horn, Ronald C. *Commercial Liability Risk Management and Insurance.* Malvern, PA: American Institute for Property and Liability Underwriters, 1978.

Rodimer, Donald H. "Use of Bonds in Private Construction." *The Forum,* Vol. 7, No. 4, July 1972, p. 242.

Stafford, John R. *Retrospective Rating.* 4th ed. Rolling Meadows, IL: J and M Publications, 1977.

_____. *Workers' Compensation and Employers' Liability Experience Rating.* Rolling Meadows, IL: J and M Publications, 1977.

Index

A

Absolute liability, *170*
Accident, *172*
   definition of, *513*
Accident (broad form), *514*
Accident (limited form), *514*
Accountants professional liability, *161*
Accounting knowledge, producers', for contract bond agreements, *409*
Accounts receivable endorsement, SMP, *614*
Accounts receivable form, *263*
ACORD application, *142*
Action against company, *96*
Action against the company provision, in the SMP, *620*
Actions, tort, *72*
Actual loss sustained, SMP time element form coverage of, *605*
Additional limits, *443*
Additional objects group endorsement, SMP boiler and machinery coverage form, *630*
Additional persons insured, *136*
Adjusting flood losses, *529*
Administrator de bonis non, *433*
Administrators and executors, *432*
Advertising injury liability, *124*
Advertising liability, *127*

Advertising liability exclusion, in the umbrella policy, *478*
Agent for named insured condition, in the umbrella policy, *481*
Agents' errors and omissions liability, *162*
Aggregate and specific excess coverage, workers' compensation, *188*
Aggregate limit, *468*
Agreement, cross purchase, *538*
   entity, *538*
   trailer interchange, *44*
Agreement I—employee dishonesty coverage, *344*
Agreement II—defense, settlement, supplementary payments, workers' compensation, *181*
Agreement II—loss inside the premises coverage, *348*
Agreement III—definitions, workers' compensation *181*
Agreement III—loss outside premises coverage, *350*
Agreement IV—application of the policy, workers' compensation *182*
Agreement IV—money order and counterfeit paper currency coverage, *351*
Agreement V—depositors forgery coverage, *352*
Agreements, buy-sell, *535*

personal indemnity, *409*
sidetract, *83*
surety, *75*
Agreements required by municipalities, *73*
Air, shipments by, *321*
Air carrier, direct, *322*
indirect, *322*
Air carrier coverage, *322*
Air carrier exclusions, *322*
Air cargo exposures, *321*
Air conditioning, refrigeration and, *514*
Aircraft, owned, *323*
Aircraft and watercraft exclusion, in the umbrella policy, *477*
All other like perils, *304*
"All-risks" builders' risk form, *260*
"All-risks" transportation floater, *245*
Alternate split dollar plan, *545*
Amendatory endorsement, SMP, *590*
Amend Coverage B, workers' compensation, *185*
American Foreign Insurance Association, *135*
Annual aggregate, SMP, *621*
Annual policy, *244*
Any auto, symbol, *21*, *10*
Any auto liability, Symbol 41, *39*
Appeal bond, *429*
Appeal for defendant bond, *429*
Appeals condition, in the umbrella policy, *480*
Application, ACORD, *142*
commercial insurance, *142*
workers' compensation policy, *197*
Application for comprehensive general liability insurance, *142*
Application information, for the workers' compensation policy, *197*
Application of rules and rating procedures for the SMP, *587*
Application of "x,c,u" exclusions, *109*
Appraisal clause, SMP, *592*

Architects and engineers professional liability, *160*
Assault by employer, *171*
Assigned risk plans, *195*
Assignment, *98*
SMP policy, *589*
Assistance condition, in the umbrella policy, *480*
Assumption of risk doctrine, *169*
Attachment, incorporation by, *239*
Attachment bond, *428*
Attorney-in-fact, *384*
Audit, inspection and, *96*
Authority, letter of, *439*
Auto, any, *10*
Auto exposure, *1*
Auto exposures, unusual, *13*
Auto liability exposures, garage, *8*
Automatic coverage, boiler and machinery policy, *509*
Automatic coverage—newly acquired organizations (ninety days), *137*
Automatic increase in insurance, SMP, *610*
Auto medical payments, truckers policy, *57*
Auto medical payments insurance, *21*
Automobile, definition of, *80*
Automobile and aircraft exclusion, in the CGL, *102*
Autos, consigned, *25*
hired, *12*
hired or borrowed, *50*
no-fault coverage for owned, *11*
owned, *10*
compulsory uninsured motorists (UM) coverage for, *11*
owned nonprivate passenger, *11*
owned private passenger, *11*
Autos information, for the umbrella policy, *486*
Average, *307*
general, *308*
particular, *307*
Average and franchise, producer and, *311*

Average terms, *308*
Aviation insurance, *287*
  commercial, *321*
Aviation insurance rating, *325*

B

"Backup" surety, *415*
Bailee, *225*
Bailees, prospecting for, *250*
Bailees for hire, *32*
Bailees' customers form, *251*
  specialized, *252*
Bailees' customers insurance, *225*,
  250
Bailees' insurance, *250*
Bailment, *225*
Bailor, *225*
Bankers blanket bond, *375*
  coverage of, *375*
  exclusions to, *377*
Bankruptcy proceedings of federal
  courts, bonds in, *430*
Banks, excess and catastrophe
  coverages for, *378*
Barbers and beauticians
  malpractice, *164*
Barratry of the master and
  mariners, *304*
Basic concepts of workers'
  compensation laws, *170*
Basic split dollar plan, *544*
Benefits, wage loss, workers'
  compensation, *180*
  workers' compensation, methods
    of providing, *176*
Bid bond, *389*
Bid bond service undertaking, *400*
Bid bonds, clerical versus judgment
  mistakes with, *389*
  criteria for avoiding liability with,
    391
  potential problems with, *389*
Bill of lading, *242*
  order, *291*
  released, *242*

straight, *242*, *291*
Bills of lading, *290*
Blanket bond, *342*
  bankers, *375*
Blanket coverage versus specified
  car, *27*
Blanket crime coverage, *357*
  SMP, *625*
Blanket crime policy optional
  coverages, *265*
Blanket group premium condition,
  boiler and machinery policy,
  512
Blanketing employees, *342*
Blanket position bond, *343*
Block policy, *265*
  furriers', *269*
  jewelers', *266*
Bobtailing, *57*
Bodily injury, definition of, *81*
Bodily injury coverage, extended,
  137
Bodily injury liability, boiler and
  machinery policy coverage of,
  508
Bodily injury to any employee
  exclusion, *105*
Boiler and machinery, standard
  BOP coverage of, *559*
Boiler and machinery coverage,
  SMP, *628*
Boiler and machinery insurance,
  504
Boiler and machinery policy,
  conditons in, *510*
  consequential damage
    endorsement to, *516*
  declarations page of, *505*
  exclusions to, *509*
  extra expense endorsement to,
    516
  indirect damage endorsements to,
    515
  insurers handling, *518*
  policy jacket of, *505*
  selling, *517*
  underwriting, *516*

Boiler and machinery policy schedules, *512*

Boiler and machinery time element coverages, SMP, *630*

Boilers, *513*

Bomb threats, *381*

Bond, appeal, *429*

  appeal for defendant, *429*

  attachment, *428*

  bid, *389*

  blanket, *342*

  blanket position, *343*

  commercial blanket, *343*

  counter replevin, *428*

  dissolve injunction, *429*

  injunction, *429*

  name schedule, *342*

  nonstatutory, *387*

  position schedule, *342*

  release of attachment, *428*

  replevin, *428*

  statutory, *387*

  stay of execution, *429*

  supersedeas, *429*

Bond limit (penalty), *387*

Bond premium, *387*

Bond representative, qualifying as, *439*

Bond to discharge a mechanic's lien, *430*

Bonds, contract, *388*

  court, *426*

  defendants', *427*

  fiduciary, *427, 430*

  judicial, *388, 426*

  license and permit, *388*

  maintenance, *394*

  miscellaneous, *388*

  payment, *392*

  performance and payment, *392*

  plaintiffs' and defendants', *427*

  public official, *388, 424*

  subdivision, *396*

  supply contract, *398*

  surety, *383*

Bonds for other financial institutions, *379*

Bonds in bankruptcy proceedings of federal courts, *430*

Bonds in equity, *430*

Bonds in probate, *430*

BOP. *See* businessowners policy.

Borrowed trailers, *50*

Breach, material, *77*

Breach of warranty, effect of, *314*

Breach of warranty damages, *72*

Bridge property damage form, *272*

Broad form all states endorsement, *186*

Broad form CGL endorsement, *121*

  value of, *138*

Broad form CGL endorsement coverages, *122*

Broad form products coverage, *20*

Broad form property damage, importance of, *134*

Broad form property damage liability coverage (including completed operations), *131*

Broad form storekeepers endorsement, SMP, *619*

Broad form versus separate coverage, *125, 127*

Buffer layer, *459*

Builder's risk insurance, SMP, *603*

Building coverage, standard BOP, *553*

Building eligibility, *525*

Burglary, *340*

Burglary and robbery, standard BOP coverage of, *559*

Burglary coverage, in the DIC policy, *451*

Business continuation life insurance, *534*

Business interruption endorsement, to the boiler and machinery policy, *515*

Business invitees, *68*

Business liability, *565*

Business life insurance, *532*

  reasons for selling, *532*

  special uses of, *542*

  taxation and, *533*

Business life insurance for key employees, *543*

Business personal property coverage, standard BOP, *554*

Businesses or property ineligible for the BOP, *550*

Businessowners policy (BOP), *549*
 business or property ineligible for, *550*
 case studies in, *579*
 conditions applicable to Section I of, *571*
 coverage E of, *565*
 coverage F of, *567*
 eligibility for, *550*
 fire legal liability in, *565*
 general conditions and other provisions in, *568*
 general conditions in, *569*
 limits of liability in, *566*
 medical payments coverage of, *567*
 named insured in, *567*
 optional coverages of, *557*
 property coverages in, *552*
 provisions comparable to the SFP in, *569*
 provisions different from those in other contracts of, *570*
 rating and underwriting of, *573*
 rating of, *574*
 special form, *561*
 special policy, *550*
 standard policy, *550*
 underwriting of, *578*
 war risk, governmental action, and nuclear exclusions in, *569*

Buy-sell agreement, partnership, *538*
 professional corporation, example of, *541*

Buy-sell agreements, *535*
 benefits of, *535*
 elements of, *536*

C

Camera and musical instrument dealers policy, *269*

Camera floater, SMP, *614*

Cancellation, *98*
 SMP policy, *589*

Cancellation provision, BOP, *570*

Cancellation/reduction of insurance clause, flood insurance policy, *528*

Care, custody, and control (CCC) exclusion, *105, 226*

Care, custody, and control modifications, *131*

Cargo, valuation of, *298*

Cargo coverage, duration of, *301*

Carriers, common, *241*
 contract, *241*
 liability of, *241*
 private, *241*

Case studies, BOP, *579*
 crime insurance, *372*
 DIC, *453*
 excess liability, *459*
 general commercial lines, *639*
 inland marine, *275*
 ocean marine, *318*
 SMP, *633*
 umbrella, *490*
 workers' compensation, *216*

Case study, contract bond, *399*
 producers' errors and omissions, *488*

Cash flow plans, workers' compensation, *215*

Cash in advance, *291*

Catastrophe (nuclear), in inland marine policies, *237*

C&F (Cost & Freight), named point of destination, *290*

CIF (Cost, Insurance, and Freight), named point of destination, *290*

Changes, *98*

Character, capacity, and capital, *400*

Charges, salvage, *245*

Church theft endorsement, SMP, 617
Claims, third party, 172
Claims-made coverage, 153
Claims-made insurance, 158
Class A contracts, 413
Class A-1 contracts, 413
Class B contracts, 413
Class I (Employees), 34
Class II (nonemployees), 34
Classification, workers' compensation, 204
Clause, delay, 306
  omnibus, 84
  running down, 318
  warehouse to warehouse, 302
Clauses, marine extention, 302
Cleaners, dyers, and laundries form, 254
Clerical office employees—Code 8810, 204
Clerical versus judgment mistakes, 389
Close corporation, 539
Coinsurance, credit insurance policy, 520
Coinsurance and full reporting clauses, in inland marine policies, 238
Coinsurance clause, SMP, 591
Coinsurance provision, in the DIC policy, 452
Coinsurance requirements, SMP, 588
Collapse coverage, in the DIC policy, 452
Collapse exclusion, 109
Collateral documents, and inland marine policies, 238
Collection agents errors and omissions, 165
Collection service, credit insurance company, 521
Collision coverage, 26
  dealers' driveaway, 30
Combination credit policy, 519
Combinations of coverage forms, 3-D, 344

Combined aggregate and excess coverage, workers' compensation, 188
Combined business interruption and extra expense endorsement, to the SMP time element form, 609
Commercial aviation insurance, 321
Commercial blanket bond, 343
Commercial coverages, other, 495
Commercial crime insurance, 339
Commercial inland marine insurance, 223
  selling, 239
Commercial inland marine insurance policies, common characteristics of, 229
Commercial inland marine insurance policy format, 229
Commercial insurance application, 142
Commercial liability exposures, 66
Commercial liability insurance, 78
Commercial liability insurance coverage, 99
Commercial liability risk, underwriting, 139
Commercial umbrella, 462
Commercial umbrella requisites, 463
Commercially uninsurable exposures exclusion, in inland marine policies, 237
Committee, 431
Common carriers, 241
  liability of, 241
Communication, instrumentalities of, 273
Community, eligible, 524
Company, action against, 96
Company options and abandonment conditions, SMP, 592
Compensation, deferred, 543
  foreign voluntary, 186
Competitive pricing techniques, workers' compensation, 212
Competitive state funds and private insurers, 176
Complete performance, 77

Completed operations, deletion of
$100 deductible for, *20*
examples of losses from, *73*
garage policy coverage of, *8*
manual classifications
automatically including, *95*
products and, *144*
Completed operations exposures, *73*
Completed operations hazard, *89,
150*
operations not within the scope
of, *94*
Completed operations hazard versus
products hazard, *90*
Completed operations requiring
service, maintenance, or repair
work, *93*
Completion, time of, *91*
Compliance guarantees, *420*
Comprehensive coverage, *26*
boiler and machinery policy, *515*
Comprehensive crime coverage,
SMP, *624*
Comprehensive dishonesty,
disappearance and destruction
policy (3-D), *323*
Comprehensive general liability
coverage part, *99*
Comprehensive general liability
exclusions to contractual
liability coverage, *123*
Comprehensive general liability
insurance, application for, *142*
Comprehensive general liability
(CGL) policy, *99*
Comprehensive glass policy, *495*
conditions of, *497*
declarations page of, *495*
exclusions to, *497*
insuring agreement of, *496*
rating of, *498*
sales tips for, *501*
underwriting of, *501*
Comprehensive personal liability
coverage, SMP, *623*
Comprehensive 3-D policy—Form B,
357
Compulsory law, *173*

Compulsory uninsured motorist
(UM) coverage, Symbol 45, *42*
Compulsory uninsured motorists
(UM) coverage for owned
autos, Symbol 26, *11*
Concealment or fraud, and the
SMP policy, *589*
Condition 1 (premium), workers'
compensation, *183*
Condition 2 (long term policy),
workers' compensation, *183*
Condition 3 (partnership or joint
venture as insured), workers'
compensation, *183*
Condition 4 (inspection and audit),
workers' compensation, *184*
Conditions 5, 6, and 7, workers'
compensation, *184*
Condition 8 (statutory provisions),
workers' compensation, *184*
Conditions 9 through 17, workers'
compensation, *184*
Conditions, boiler and machinery
policy, *510*
comprehensive glass policy, *497*
inland marine, *232*
policy jacket, *95*
SMP boiler and machinery
coverage endorsement, *629*
umbrella policy, *479*
Conditions and definitions, SMP,
589
Conditions and limitations, *349*
3-D, *346*
Conditions applicable to Section I,
BOP, *571*
Conditions common to inland
marine insurance policies, *234*
Conditions of special interest to the
producer in inland marine
policies, *234*
Condominium additional policy
provisions, SMP, *621*
Condominium additional policy
provisions endorsement, SMP,
602
Condominium building forms, SMP,
602

Condominium forms, SMP, *601*

Condominium personal property forms, SMP, *603*

Consequences of loss, inland marine, *231*

Consequential damage endorsement, to the boiler and machinery policy, *516*

Conservator, *431*

Consigned autos, Symbol 31, *25*

Construction and equipment, *140*

Construction contracts, *74*

Constructive total loss, *307*

Contents eligibility, *525*

Contract, incidental, *82*

Contract bond case study—R.P. Davis, *399*

Contract bonds, *388*
  miscellaneous, *396*
  selling, *414*
  supply, *398*
  types of, *389*

Contract bonds for underwriting purposes, kinds of, *412*

Contract carriers, *241*
  liability of, *243*

Contractor, qualifications of, *400*

Contractor-surety partnership, case study on, *410*

Contractors, small, surety bond guarantee program for, *416*

Contractors equipment floater, *255*
  prospecting for, *256*

Contracts, Class A, *413*
  Class A-1, *413*
  Class B, *413*
  construction, *74*
  incidental, *6*, *74*
  miscellaneous, *414*
  supply, *413*

Contracts with tort liability assumption, examples of, *74*

Contractual actions, *70*

Contractual and protective liability exposures, *74*

Contractual exclusions, additional, *123*

Contractual liability coverage, *123*

CGL exclusions to, *123*

Contractual liability exclusion, in the CGL, *101*
  in the umbrella policy, *478*

Contractual liability exposures, *74*

Contractual obligations of a professional, *76*

Contributing insurance, *592*

Contribution by equal shares, *97*

Contribution by limits, *97*

Contribution clause, in the SMP time element form, *606*

Contributory negligence, *169*

Control, joint, *386*

Corporation, close, *539*

Corporations, coverage of, under workers' compensation laws, *174*
  professional, *540*

Cost & Freight (C&F), *290*

"Cost-plus" form, *208*

Counter replevin bond, *428*

Court bonds, *426*

Coverage, air carrier, *322*
  claims-made, *153*
  collision, *26*
  comprehensive, *26*
  excess liability, *458*
  garagekeepers direct, *33*
  interruption in, *153*
  nature and scope of, under garagekeepers insurance, *32*
  occurrence, *152*
  specified perils, *26*
  suspension of, *510*

Coverage A—Workers' Compensation, *177*

Coverage B—Employers' Liability, *180*

Coverage E, BOP, *565*

Coverage F, BOP, *567*

Coverage characteristics, garage policy, *3*
  truckers policy, *37*

Coverage for carriers of property in transit, *248*

Coverage for dealers, *27*

Coverage for nondealers, *27*

Coverage part, commercial liability, *78*

Coverages, broad form CGL endorsement, *122*

Covered autos, insureds of, *16*

Covered autos and symbols, truckers policy, *38*

Covered injuries, *171*

Credit, letter of, *292*

Credit guarantees, *421*

Credit insurance, *518*
  exposures covered by, *520*

Credit policies, types of, *519*

Credit policy, combination, *519*
  general, *519*
  regular, *519*
  specific, *519*

Credit policy analysis, *520*

Creditor, *519*

Crime, *339*

Crime conditions and limitations, *356*

Crime coverage forms, SMP, *624*

Crime insurance, *339*
  marketing, *367*
  rating, *369*

Crime insurance categories, *340*

Crime insurance exposure identification, *368*

Crime insurance underwriting information, *372*

Crime policies, endorsements to, *358*
  format for analysis of, *341*
  location of property covered by, *342*
  perils insured by, *341*
  persons causing the loss under, *342*
  property covered by, *341*

Crime policy insuring agreements, provisions applying to all, *355*

Crimes, types of, *339*

Criteria for loss, for completed operations, *73*

Cross purchase agreement, *538*

Curator, *431*

Custodian, *349*

D

Damage, property, *81*

Damage to products exclusion, *107*, *148*

Damage to the named insured's products, *7*

Damages, breach of warranty, *72*

Damages for withdrawal, inspection, repair, replacement, or loss of use exclusion, *107*

Dangerous instrumentalities, *67*

Deadheading, *58*

Dealer, *2*
  franchised, *2*
  new car, *2*
  nonfranchised, *2*
  used car, *2*

Dealers, coverage for, *27*
  insurance on the property of, *226*

Dealers policies, *265*

Dealers' class plan, *34*

Dealers' driveaway collision coverage, *30*

Debris removal, SMP coverage of, *592*

Debris removal clause (limited coverage), SMP reporting form, *605*

Deceit, fraud, or misrepresentation, intentional, *72*

Declarations, *99*
  garage policy, *4*
  inland marine insurance policy, *229*
  SMP policy, *588*

Declarations condition, in the umbrella policy, *481*

Declarations page, of the boiler and machinery policy, *505*
  of the comprehensive glass policy, *495*
  3-D, *344*
  umbrella policy, *466*
  workers' compensation policy, *177*

Deductible, flood insurance policy, *528*

SMP policy, *591*

Deductible clause in the DIC policy, *450*

Deductibles, boiler and machinery policy, *511*
  garage policy, *30*
  inland marine policy, *238*

Default, rights of the surety upon, *386*

Defendants' bonds, *427*

Deferred compensation, *543*

Definitions, *80*
  conditions and, SMP, *589*
  SMP boiler and machinery coverage endorsement, *629*
  truckers policy, *38*
  umbrella policy, *472*

Delay clause, *306*

Delay or lack of performance exclusion, in the umbrella policy, *478*

Deletion of $100 deductible for completed operations, *20*

Depositors forgery rating, *372*

Description of underlying coverages, for the umbrella policy, *486*

Difference in conditions, *444*
  case studies in, *453*

Difference in conditions (DIC) policy, *443, 444*
  coverages of, *450*
  deductible clause in, *450*
  losses covered by, *453*
  perils covered by, *447*
  perils excluded by, *447*
  property covered by, *445*
  property excluded by, *445*
  provisions of, *452*
  rating and underwriting information for, *457*

Direct air carrier, *322*

Direct coverage—excess basis, *34*

Direct coverage—primary basis, *34*

Disability income insurance, *546*

Discovery period, *159, 345*

Discovery period and superseded suretyship, *346*

Dissolve injunction bond, *429*

Doctrine, assumption of risk, *169*

Downstream sales, *215*

Draft, *292*

Drivers, chauffeurs, and their helpers—Code 7380, *205*

Duties, legal requirements and, *68*

Duties of possessors of land, *68*

Duties of the named insured after a loss, in the SMP, *592*

Duties to those on the premises, *68*

Duties to those outside the premises, *68*

E

Easements, *83*

Earthquake condition, boiler and machinery policy, *512*

Earthquake extension endorsement, SMP, *612*

Economic Opportunities Act Endorsement, *190*

Elective law, *173*

Electrical equipment, machinery and, *515*

Electronic data processing policy, *264*

Elevator, definition of, *82*

Elevator collision insurance, *106*

Elevator maintenance agreements, *83*

Eligible building, *524*

Eligible community, *524*

Eligible contents, *524*

Eligibility, BOP, *550*
  building, *525*
  contents, *525*

Eligibility for the SMP comprehensive crime coverage form, *625*

Emergency program, flood, *524*

Employee, *342, 345*

Employee benefit plans, nonqualified, *545*
  qualified, *545*

Employee dishonesty, standard BOP coverage of, *557*

Employee Retirement Income Security Act of 1974 (ERISA), *546*

Employees, schedules of, *342* specified, *342*

Employer, assault by, *171*

Employers nonownership automobile liability insurance endorsement, SMP, *623*

Employers' liability, workers' compensation and, *169*

Employment, out of and in the course of, *170*

Employment agencies errors and omissions, *165*

Endorsement, broad form CGL, *121* broad form all states, *186* individual named insured, *20* SMP boiler and machinery coverage, *628*

Endorsements, garage policy, *20* SMP liability, *623* workers' compensation, *185*

Endorsements to crime policies, *358*

Endorsements to the SMP comprehensive crime coverage form, *625*

Enemy exclusion, in inland marine policies, *237*

Entity agreement, *538*

Entity versus cross purchase methods, *538*

Equal shares, contribution by, *97*

Equipment, mobile, *80*

Equipment dealers, *270*

Equity, bonds in, *430*

Ex Dock, named point of importation, *290*

Ex point of origin, *289*

Exceptions to duties owed to those on the premises, *69*

Excess and catastrophe coverages for banks, *378*

Excess basis, *33*

Excess coverages, *491*

Excess coverages, workers' compensation, selling, *188*

Excess liability case studies, *459*

Excess liability coverage, *458*

Excess lines, *443*

Excess property and liability coverage, *443*

Excluded employments, under workers' compensation laws, *176*

Exclusion, automobile and aircraft, in the CGL, *102* bodily injury to any employee, *105* care, custody, or control, *105* collapse, *109* contractual liability, in the CGL, *101* damage to products, *107, 148* damages for withdrawal, inspection, repair, replacement, or loss of use, *107* failure to perform, *107, 147* injury to work performed, *148* liability for the use of mobile equipment during certain activities, *103* liquor liability, *104* mobile equipment being transported by automobile, *103* nuclear, *110* pollution and contamination, *104* premises alienated, *106* sistership liability, *107, 149* war and allied perils, *104* watercraft, in the CGL, *103*

Exclusion (a), workers' compensation, *182*

Exclusion (b), workers' compensation, *182*

Exclusion (c), workers' compensation, *182*

Exclusion (d), workers' compensation, *182*

Exclusion (e), workers' compensation, *183*

Exclusion (f), workers'
compensation, *183*
Exclusion of injury to work
performed, *107*
Exclusion relating to workers'
compensation and similar laws,
105
Exclusion summary, *110*
Exclusions, *147, 349, 356*
air carrier, *322*
boiler and machinery policy, *509*
CGL, *101*
comprehensive glass policy, *497*
explosion, *108*
in inland marine policies, *235*
ocean cargo policy, *305*
OL&T, *113*
personal injury, *126*
physical damage insurance, *28*
standard BOP, *556*
3-D, *346*
trailer interchange insurance, *55*
truckers policy, *47, 53*
umbrella policy, *476*
underground, *109*
"x,c,u," *108*
Exclusions and limitations, fire
legal liability coverage—real
property, *130*
Exclusions in the workers'
compensation policy, *182*
Exclusions to the bankers blanket
bond, *377*
Exclusions to the SMP general
building form, *596*
Exclusions to the SMP special
building form, *599*
Exclusions to the SMP special
personal property form, *601*
Executors, administrators and, *432*
Exhibition floater, *261*
Existence of tools, uninstalled
equipment, or abandoned or
unused materials, *95*
Expediting expenses, boiler and
machinery policy coverage of,
508
Expense constant, *207*

Expenses, prepaid, *301*
Expenses to reduce loss, SMP time
element form coverage of, *606*
Experience modification factor, *206*
Explosion exclusions, *108*
Exporters, *294*
Exposure, auto, *1*
general liability, *1*
Exposure identification, *124*
crime insurance, *368*
transportation, *243*
Exposure limits, *299*
Exposures, air cargo, *321*
commercial liability, *66*
completed operations, *73*
inland marine, examples of, *227*
ocean marine insurance for other,
317
operations, *66*
operations liability, *69*
premises, *66*
premises liability, *67*
unique, *26*
Exposures excluded, garage policy,
17
Exposures more appropriately
insured by other contracts
exclusion, in inland marine
policies, *236*
Express warranties, *71, 312*
Extended bodily injury coverage,
137
Extensions of coverage, in the SMP
general personal property form,
597
in the SMP special building form,
599
in the SMP special personal
property form, *600*
SMP general building form, *595*
Exterior grade floor glass, standard
BOP coverage of, *558*
Exterior signs, standard BOP
coverage of, *558*
Extra expense endorsement, to the
SMP time element form, *609*
to the boiler and machinery
policy, *516*

Extraordinary hazards exclusion, in inland marine policies, *236*

F

Factor, *519*
Factoring, *519*
Failure to perform, *7*
Failure to perform exclusion, *107, 147*
Fair Access to Insurance Requirements (FAIR) plans, *522*
Faithful performance, *425*
False pretense coverage, *30*
FAS (Free Along Side), *290*
Federal Anti-Poverty Program, *190*
Federal crime insurance, *523*
Fellow employee injury exclusion, in the umbrella policy, *476*
Fellow servant rule, *169*
Fidelity bonds, public official bonds versus, *425*
Fidelity coverage, *348*
bankers blanket bond, *375*
Fidelity rating, *370*
Fiduciaries bonded, examples of, *431*
Fiduciary bonds, *427, 430*
miscellaneous, *430*
nature of, *430*
rating, *435*
Filed lines, *228*
Financial guarantees, *422*
Financial institution coverage, *374*
Financial institutions, bonds for, *379*
Financial responsibility laws, *96*
SMP, *620*
Fine arts dealers, *270*
Fine arts floater, SMP, *614*
Fire, in ocean cargo policies, *303*
Fire legal liability, BOP, *565*
Fire legal liability coverage—real property, *129*
limit of liability, *129*

need for coverage, *129*
Fire legal liability insurance, *22*
Fitness for a particular purpose, warranty of, *71*
Fleets, *317*
Floater, contractors equipment, *255*
exhibition, *261*
garment contractors, *261*
processors, *261*
Floaters, *255*
installation, *259*
installment sales, *271*
miscellaneous, *265*
mobile agricultural equipment and livestock, *258*
pattern, *260*
physicians' and surgeons' equipment, *263*
salesmen's samples, *262*
sign, *264*
theatrical, *264*
Flood, definition of, *526*
Flood and earthquake coverage, in the DIC policy, *450*
Flood insurance mandatory purchase requirement, *529*
Flood insurance policy, important policy terms and conditions of, *526*
Flood insurance policy marketing tips, *520*
Flood Insurance Rate Map (FIRM), *524*
Flood insurance underwriting rules, *524*
Flood losses, adjusting, *529*
Floor plan merchandise, *270*
FOB (Free On Board), *289*
Follow form liability insurance, *459*
Following form liability insurance, *459*
Foreign voluntary compensation, *186*
Forgery coverage, incoming check, *352*
Forgery or alteration coverage, bankers blanket bond, *376*
Form, nonreporting, *28*

reporting, *28*
Forms, independent, *632*
Franchise, *310*
Franchise and deductible clauses, in ocean cargo policies, *310*
Franchised dealer, *2*
Franchises and average, *310*
Fraud, prior, *346*
Free Along Side (FAS), *290*
Free of particular average (FPA), *308*
Free of particular average American conditions (FPAAC), *309*
Free on board (FOB), *243*, *289*
Freight, *301*
Full reporting clause, SMP, *604*
Funds, monopolistic state, *176*
Furriers' block policy, *269*
Furriers' customers policy, *253*

G

Garage and truckers insurance, *1*
   marketing, *61*
Garage auto liability exposures covered, *8*
Garage liability insurance, *15*
Garage locations and operations medical payments insurance, *21*
Garage operations exposures covered, *6*
Garage physical damage exposures covered, *23*
Garage physical damage insurance, *26*
Garage policy, application of symbols—liability coverages, *10*
   completed operations coverage of, *8*
   definition of the insured in, *16*
   garage auto liability exposures covered by, *8*
   garage operations exposures covered by, *6*
garage physical damage exposures covered by, *23*
incidental contractual liability under, *6*
insuring agreement for liability insurance of, *15*
liability exposures excluded by, *17*
limit of liability under, *19*
medical payments coverage under, *21*
optional coverages, *30*
out of state coverage under, *20*
owners' protective liability coverage under, *7*
Part I, *3*
Part II, *3*
Part III, *3*
Part IV, *3*
Part V, *4*
Part VI, *4*
Part VII, *4*
premises and operations coverage of, *6*
valuation under, *29*
Garage policy coverage characteristics, *3*
Garage policy declarations, *4*
Garage policy deductibles, *30*
Garage policy general conditions, *31*
Garage policy options and endorsements, *20*
Garage policy sections, *3*
Garage policy supplemental schedules, *4*
Garagekeepers direct coverage, *33*
Garagekeepers insurance, *32*
   markets for, *32*
   nature and scope of coverage under, *32*
   persons insured under, *33*
   rating—basis concepts under, *34*
Garagekeepers insurance endorsement, SMP, *612*
Garagekeepers premium, *35*, *36*
Garment contractors floater, *261*
General average, *245*, *308*

General building form (named
perils coverage), *594*
General conditions, BOP, *569*
garage policy, *30*
General conditions and other
provisions, BOP, *568*
General credit policy, *519*
General employee benefits, *545*
General liability exposure, *1*
General liability insurance, *65*
General liability section, *143*
General personal property form
(named perils coverage), SMP,
596
General requirements, SMP policy,
586
General rules, SMP, *587*
Glass endorsement, SMP, *610*
Good faith guarantees, *421*
Governing classification, workers'
compensation, *204*
Government programs, *522*
Gross combination weight (GCW),
59
Gross earnings endorsement, to the
SMP time element form, *607*
Gross vehicle weight (GVW), *59*
Group life and health insurance,
545
Group travel accident insurance,
546
Guarantees, compliance, *420*
credit, *421*
financial, *422*
good faith, *421*
indemnity, *422*
maintenance, *414*
Guardians, bonding of, *431*

H

Hazard, completed operations, *89*
products, *86, 151*
Hazards, common, *141*
special, *140*
Highly protected risk (HPR), *447*

Hired autos, Symbol 47, *42*
Symbol 28, *12*
Hired autos only, physical damage
coverage of, *24*
Hired or borrowed autos, *50*
Hospital professional liability, *157*
Host liquor liability coverage, *128*
Household and personal property
endorsement, SMP, *610*
HR-10, *547*
Hull insurance, *318*
Human Life Value (HLV) approach,
543

I

Identifying and qualifying SMP
prospects, *633*
Implied warranties, *71, 312*
Importers, *295*
Inception, SMP policy, *589*
Incidental contract, definition of, *82*
Incidental contracts, *6, 74*
Incidental contractual liability,
garage policy, *6*
Incidental medical malpractice
liability coverage, *134*
Incoming check forgery coverage,
352, 358
Incorporation by attachment, *239*
Incorporation by reference, *238*
Indemnity guarantees, *422*
Independent contractors, coverage
of, under workers'
compensation laws, *175*
Independent forms, *632*
Indeterminate length and
noncancelability of surety
bonds, *387*
Indirect air carrier, *322*
Indirect damage endorsements, to
the boiler and machinery
policy, *515*
Individual named insured
endorsement, *20*
Individual pension plans, *547*

Individual Risk Premium
  Modification (IRPM) Plan, *588*
Indivisible package premium, *574*
Inherent vice, in inland marine
  policies, *237*
Injunction bond, *429*
Injuries, covered, *171*
Injury, *156*
  bodily, *81*
Injury to work performed,
  exclusion of, *107*
Injury to work performed
  exclusion, *148*
Inland and coastal cargo vessels,
  317
Inland marine case studies, *275*
Inland marine coverage, SMP, *614*
Inland marine exposures, examples
  of, *227*
Inland marine forms in package
  policies, *274*
Inland marine insurance,
  commercial, *223*
  origins of, *223*
Inland marine insurance policies,
  types of, *225*
Inland marine insurance policy
  declarations, *229*
Inland marine insuring agreements,
  230
Inland marine policies, collateral
  documents and, *238*
  exclusions in, *235*
  miscellaneous provisions in, *238*
Inland marine policy conditions, *232*
Innkeepers legal liability and
  cloakroom liability, *255*
Inspection and audit, *96*
Inspection and audit provision,
  SMP, *590*
Inspection condition, boiler and
  machinery policy, *510*
Installation floaters, *259*
Installment sales floater, *271*
Instrumentalities, dangerous, *67*
Instrumentalities of communication,
  273

Instrumentalities of transportation
  and communication, *271*
  insurance on, *227*
Insurable interests, nonownership,
  291
Insurable interests of owners, in
  ocean marine insurance, *289*
Insurance, automatic increase in,
  610
  aviation, *287*
  bailees', *250*
  bailees' customers, *250*
  business continuation life, *534*
  business life, *532*
  commercial aviation, *321*
  commercial crime, *339*
  commercial inland marine, *223*
  commercial liability, *78*
  contributing, *592*
  credit, *518*
  garage and truckers, *1*
  garage liability, *15*
  garagekeepers, *32*
  general liability, *65*
  hull, *318*
  noncontributing, *592*
  other, *97*
  private, *176*
  trailer interchange, *54*
  transportation, *239*
  truckers liability, *46*
Insurance coverage, commercial
  liability, *99*
Insurance for owners of property
  in transit, *244*
Insurance on instrumentalities of
  transportation and
  communications, *227*
Insurance on movable equipment
  and other property, *226*
Insurance on the property of
  certain dealers, *226*
Insurance rates, ocean marine, *315*
Insurance under more than one
  coverage part or endorsement,
  in the SMP policy, *590*
Insured, definition of, *84*
  in the BOP, *568*

in the garage policy, *16*
named, definition of, *85*
Insured premises defined, in the
OL&T, *112*
Insured's duties at loss condition,
comprehensive glass policy, *497*
Insured's duties in the event of
occurrence, claim, or suit, *96*
in the SMP, *620*
Insured's operations, description of,
4
Insured's property or products
exclusion, in the umbrella
policy, *478*
Insureds of covered autos, *16*
Insureds other than covered autos,
17
Insurers, boiler and machinery, *518*
matching markets with, for
garage and truckers
insurance, *62*
Insuring agreement, CGL, *100*
comprehensive glass policy, *496*
truckers policy, *46*
Insuring Agreement IV—incoming
check forgery coverage, *358*
Insuring Agreement VII—burglary
coverage on merchandise, *360*
Insuring Agreement VIII—
paymaster robbery inside and
outside premises, *362*
Insuring Agreement IX—paymaster
broad form—inside and outside
premises, *362*
Insuring Agreement X—paymaster
broad form—inside only, *363*
Insuring Agreement XI—burglary
and theft of merchandise
coverage, *363*
Insuring Agreement XII—
warehouse receipts forgery
coverage, *363*
Insuring Agreement XIII—
securities of lessees of safe
deposit boxes coverage, *364*
Insuring Agreement XIV—theft of
office equipment, *364*

Insuring Agreement XV—theft of
office equipment, *364*
Insuring Agreement XVI—
paymaster robbery coverage—
inside, *364*
Insuring Agreement XVII—credit
card forgery, *365*
Insuring Agreement XVIII—
extortion, *365*
Insuring agreements, boiler and
machinery policy, *505*
inland marine, *230*
SMP boiler and machinery
coverage endorsement, *628*
SMP comprehensive crime
coverage form, *625*
SMP liability insurance form, *621*
umbrella policy, *469*
workers' compensation policy, *177*
Intentional deceit, fraud, or
misrepresentation, *72*
Intentional interference, *67*
Interference, intentional, *67*
Interruption and delay, *300*
Interruption in coverage, *153*
In transit coverage, bankers
blanket bond, *376*
Invitees, business, *68*
*ISO Commercial Lines Manual,
Division Eight—Inland
Marine, 229*

J

Jettisons, *304*
Jewelers' block, *266*
Joint control, *386*
Judicial bonds, *388, 426*
selling, *436*
service after the sale of, *438*
types of, *426*

K

Keogh Plans, *547*

Key employee, *543*
Key employee life insurance, *543*
Kidnap-ransom-extortion coverage, *380*

L

Lading, bill of, *242, 290*
Land, duties of possessors of, *68*
LASH vessels (lighter aboard ship), *317*
Law, compulsory, *173*
  elective, *173*
  partnership, *537*
Laws, financial responsibility, *96*
  workers' compensation, *173*
Lawyers professional liability, *159*
Layer, buffer, *459*
Lease of premises, *82*
Legal entity, coverage of, under workers' compensation laws, *174*
Legal liability insurance, fire, *22*
Legal requirements and duties, *68*
Legal requirements for premises liability exposures, *67*
Legality, warranty of, in ocean cargo insurance, *313*
Legislation and litigation, products liability, *154*
Letter of authority, *439*
Letter of credit, *292*
Liability, absolute, *170*
  advertising, *127*
  business, *565*
  limit of, in the garage policy, *19*
  medical malpractice, *156*
  professional, *155*
  strict, *67*
Liability coverage, incidental medical malpractice, *134*
Liability coverage forms, SMP, *619*
Liability coverages, BOP, *565*
Liability endorsements, SMP, *623*
Liability exclusions, SMP, *622*
Liability exposures, contractual, *74*

contractual and protective, *74*
  professional, *76*
  protective, *75*
Liability for guest property endorsement, SMP, *617*
Liability for property of others, boiler and machinery policy coverage of, *508*
Liability for the use of mobile equipment during certain activities exclusion, in the CGL, *103*
Liability insurance, commercial, *78*
  garage policy personal injury, *22*
Liability insurance form, SMP, *621*
Liability insurance premium, determining, *34*
Liability of carriers, *241*
Liability of contract carriers, *243*
Liability of private carriers, *243*
Liability policy, straight excess, *459*
Liability premiums, *36*
Liability provisions, other, under the truckers policy, *51*
Liability transfers, limitations on, *75*
Libel, *125*
Liberalization clause, SMP, *590*
License and permit bonds, *388, 419*
  purposes of, *419*
  selling, *423*
  types of guarantees under, *420*
Licensees, duties to, *69*
Life and health insurance, group, *545*
Life insurance, business, *532*
  key employee, *543*
Life insurance without a purchaser, *536*
Limit of liability, garage policy, *19*
  SMP, *623*
  truckers policy, *51*
Limit per accident condition, boiler and machinery policy, *510*
Limitations, umbrella policy, *479*
Limitations on liability transfers, *75*
Limited worldwide liability coverage, *135*

Limits, additional, *443*
  aggregate, *468*
  contribution by, *97*
  exposure, *299*
Limits and settlement options,
  comprehensive glass policy, *497*
Limits of liability, *347*
  BOP, *566*
Liquidation alternatives, for
  partnerships, *537*
Liquidity, need for, case study on,
  410
Liquor liability exclusion, *104*
Lloyd's of London, *462*
LNG ships (liquid natural gas), *317*
Location, glass, *498*
Location of property covered by
  crime policies, *342*
Locations covered, by SMP
  reporting form coverages, *604*
"Long tail," *153*
  problems of, *153*
Longshoremen or harbor workers,
  185
Loss, common causes of, in
  fiduciary bonds, *433*
  consequences of, *231*
  constructive total, *307*
  criteria for, for completed
    operations, *73*
  partial, *307*
  total, *307*
  ultimate net, *474*
Loss and expense constants, *207*
Loss clause, in inland marine
  policies, *235*
  SMP, *594*
Loss constant, *207*
Loss exposures, typical, *140*
Loss in progress, flood insurance
  coverage of, *527*
Loss information, for the umbrella
  policy, *487*
Loss inside premises rating, *370*
Loss layers, working, *487*
Loss of earnings endorsement, to
  the SMP time element form,
  609

Loss of income coverage, standard
  BOP, *555*
Loss of other property, *348*
Loss of profit, expense or income,
  300
Loss of profit margin on goods,
  300
Loss of rents endorsement, to the
  SMP time element form, *609*
Loss payable, bankruptcy of the
  insured condition, in the
  umbrella policy, *480*
Loss settlement example, credit
  insurance, *520*
Loss settlement procedures, boiler
  and machinery policy, *509*
Loss to property of insured, boiler
  and machinery policy coverage
  of, *508*
Loss under previous bond
  (superseded suretyship), *345*
Losses, examples of, from
  completed operations, *73*
  surety's expectation of, *385*
Losses covered, in ocean cargo
  policies, *306*
Losses covered by the DIC policy,
  452
Lost or not lost, *303*

M

Machinery and electrical equipment,
  515
Mail policies, *247*
Maintenance bonds, *394*
Maintenance guarantees, *414*
Maintenance of underlying
  insurance condition, in the
  umbrella policy, *480*
Malicious mischief condition, boiler
  and machinery policy, *511*
Malpractice, barbers and
  beauticians, *164*
Malpractice coverage, *156*

Mandatory coverage, conditions, and provisions, SMP, *588*

Mandatory purchase requirement, flood insurance, *529*

Manual classifications automatically including completed operations, *95*

Manufacturers and contractors coverage part, *114*

Manufacturers and contractors (M&C) form, *114*

Manufacturers' selling price endorsement, SMP, *613*

Manuscript policies, inland marine, *229*
  writing, *273*

Marine extension clauses, *302*

Maritime employment endorsement, workers' compensation, *185*

Marketing crime insurance, *367*

Marketing excess coverages, *491*

Marketing garage and trucker insurance, *61*

Marketing set-up and other considerations, flood insurance policy, *529*

Marketing tips, flood insurance policy, *520*

Markets, specialized needs of, for garage and truckers insurance, *62*

Markets—eligibility, *2*
  for truckers policy, *37*

Markets for garagekeepers insurance, *32*

Material breach, *77*

Medical benefits, workers' compensation, *177*

Medical malpractice, *156*

Medical payments, garage policy, *21*
  SMP liability insurance form, *621*

Medical payments coverage, BOP, *567*

Medical payments insurance, auto, *21*
  garage locations and operations, *21*

Medical payments premium, *35*, *36*

Medical reports, proof and payment of claim, *620*

Mercantile open stock (MOS), *366*

Mercantile open stock burglary and theft endorsement, SMP, *618*

Mercantile open stock burglary endorsement, SMP, *617*

Mercantile ratings, *520*

Mercantile robbery and safe burglary endorsement, SMP, *618*

Merchandise sale, terms of, *243*

Merchantability, warranty of, *71*

Messenger, *349*

Minimum premiums, SMP, *587*

Minors, coverage of, under workers' compensation laws, *174*

Miscellaneous bonds, *388*

Miscellaneous contract bonds, *396*

Miscellaneous contracts, *414*

Miscellaneous fiduciary bonds, *430*

Miscellaneous medical professional liability, *158*

Miscellaneous property endorsements, SMP, *610*

Miscellaneous provisions, in inland marine policies, *238*

Misrepresentation and fraud, in inland policies, *234*

Mobile agricultural equipment and livestock floaters, *258*

Mobile equipment, *80*

Mobile equipment being transported by automobile exclusion, *103*

Money, *341*, *345*

Money and securities, *248*
  coverage of, in the special BOP, *563*

Money order and counterfeit paper currency rating, *371*

Monopolistic state funds, *176*

Morale hazards exclusions, in inland marine policies, *236*

Mortgage clause—applicable only to buildings, SMP, *593*

Mortgagee clauses and loss payable clauses, in inland marine policies, *238*

Motor Truck Cargo—Owners Form, *248*

Motor truck cargo—owner's cargo on owner's vehicles, *244*

Movable equipment and other property, insurance on, *226*

Multiple Location Premium and Dispersion Credit Plan, *588*

Municipalities, agreements required by, *73*

Musical instruments floater, SMP, *615*

Mysterious disappearance, *340*

N

"Naked and unrestricted promise," *392*

Name schedule bond, *342*

Named insured, definition of, *85*
in the BOP, *567*

Named insured's products, *87*, *152*
damage to, *7*

National flood insurance program, *523*

Nation-Wide Marine Definition, *224*

Neglect of the insured, in inland marine policies, *237*

Negligence, *67*, *72*
contributory, *169*

Neon signs form, SMP, *615*

New car dealer, *2*

No benefit to bailee clause, SMP, *594*

No control clause, SMP, *594*

No delay, *314*

No deviation, *314*

No-fault coverage, Symbol 44, *42*

No-fault coverage for owned autos, Symbol 25, *11*

No-fault coverages, truckers policy, *56*

Noncontributing insurance, *592*

Nondealer, *2*
coverage for, *27*

Nondealers' premiums, *35*

Nonfiled lines, *228*

Nonfranchised dealer, *2*

Nonowned autos, Symbol 50, *43*

Nonowned autos—garages, Symbol 29, *12*

Nonowned property information, for the umbrella policy, *486*

Nonowned watercraft liability coverage (under twenty-six feet in length), *135*

Nonownership insurable interests, *291*

Nonqualified employee benefit plans, *545*

Nonreporting form, *28*

Nonstatutory bond, *387*

Nontrucking use, truckers insurance for, *57*

Notice and adjustment condition, boiler and machinery policy, *510*

Notice and proof of loss, *347*

Notice of occurrence condition, in the umbrella policy, *480*

Nuclear energy liability limitation, to the umbrella policy, *479*

Nuclear exclusion, *110*
SMP, *621*

O

Object, *505*, *512*
definition of, *513*
in the standard BOP, *559*

Obligee, *384*

Occupational Safety and Health Act of 1970 (OSHA), *190*

Occurrence, *85*

Occurrence, claim, or suit, insured's duties in the event of, *96*

Occurrence basis, *152*

Occurrence coverage, *152*

Occurrence limit of liability, umbrella policy, *466*

Ocean cargo policies, franchise and deductible clauses in, *310*

perils covered and excluded in, *303*

Ocean liners, *317*

Ocean marine and aviation insurance, *287*

Ocean marine case studies, *318*

Ocean marine insurance, identifying prospects for, *294*

insurable interests of owners in, *289*

whom to insure under, *288*

Ocean marine insurance for other exposures, *317*

Ocean marine insurance rates, *315*

Ocean marine submissions, handling, *315*

underwriting information for, *316*

Oceangoing cargo ships, *317*

Off-premises coverage, under the SMP general building form, *595*

Off-premises operations liability exposures, *70*

Off-premises water damage, in the DIC policy, *451*

Omnibus clause, *84*

On-premises coverage, bankers blanket bond, *376*

On-premises operations liability exposures, *70*

Open account, *292*

Open cargo policies, *297*

Open cargo policy coverage, *301*

Open policy, *244*

Operations, ultra hazardous, *68*

Operations exposures, *66*

Operations in connection with the transportation of property, *94*

Operations liability coverage, OL&T, *113*

Operations liability exposures, *69*

Operations not within the scope of completed operations hazard, *94*

Optional coverages, garage policy, *30*

Optional coverages—standard form BOP, *557, 564*

Optional endorsement summary, *365*

Optional perils endorsement, SMP, *610*

Options and endorsements, garage policy, *20*

Order bill of lading, *291*

Ordinary payroll, *608*

Origin, ex point of, *289*

OSHA regulations, *141*

Other insurance, *97*

crime, *347*

under trailer interchange insurance, *55*

Other insurance clause, flood insurance policy, *527*

Other insurance condition, boiler and machinery policy, *510*

comprehensive glass policy, *497*

Other insurance provision, BOP, *570*

DIC policy, *452*

SMP, *592, 621*

Other insured, *50*

Out of and in the course of employment, *170*

Out-of-state coverage, under the garage policy, *20*

Out-of-state extensions of coverage, under the truckers policy, *52*

Outdoor signs endorsement, SMP, *611*

Outdoor trees, shrubs, and plants, coverage of, under the SMP general building form, *595*

Owned aircraft, *323*

Owned auto coverage, Symbol 42, *41*

Owned autos, Symbol 22, *10*

Owned autos only, physical damage coverage of, *23*

Owned autos other than private passenger autos, physical damage coverage of, *24*

Owned commercial autos, Symbol 43, *41*

Owned nonprivate passenger autos, Symbol 24, *11*

Owned private passenger autos, Symbol 23, *11*

Owned private passenger autos only, physical damage coverage of, *24*

Owners and contractors protective liability coverage part, *117*

Owners and contractors protective liability insurance (OCP), *117*

Owners, landlords, and tenants coverage part, *112*

Owners, landlords, and tenants (OL&T) form, *112*

Owners' protective liability, garage policy, *7*

Ownership and interest covered, *347*

P

Package policies, inland marine forms in, *274*

Pair, set, or parts clause, in inland marine policies, *235*

Parcel post policy, *247*

Partial loss, *307*

Particular average, *307*

Partnership, *537*

  coverage of, under workers' compensation laws, *174*

  liquidation alternatives for, *537*

Partnership buy-sell agreement, *538*

Partnership law, *537*

Pattern floaters, *260*

Payment bond guarantee, nature of, *394*

Payment bonds, *392*

Payment of loss, under the SMP, *593*

Payroll, ordinary, *608*

  workers' compensation, *205*

Peak season inventory endorsement, SMP, *611*

Penalty, *387*

Pension and profit sharing plans, *546*

Pension plans, individual, *547*

Percentage of value lost, *299*

Performance, complete, *77*

  faithful, *425*

  substantial, *77*

Performance and payment bonds, *392*

Performance bond guarantee, nature of, *392*

Perils, ocean cargo policy, *305*

Perils covered and excluded, in ocean cargo policies, *303*

Perils covered by the DIC policy, *447*

Perils defined, crime, *348*

Perils excluded by the DIC policy, *447*

Perils insured, inland marine, *230*

  under the SMP general building form, *596*

Perils insured against, in the SMP special building form, *599*

  in the SMP special personal property form, *600*

Perils insured and excluded, *256*

Perils insured and exclusions, in the SMP general personal property form, *598*

Perils insured by crime policies, *341*

Perils of the seas, *303*

Period, discovery, *345*

  waiting, *525*

Permissive users, *49*

Permits and use clause, SMP, *593*

Per occurrence limit, BOP, *566*

Personal indemnity agreements, *409*

Personal injury, *124*

Personal injury and advertising injury liability coverage, *124*

Personal injury exclusions, *126*

Personal injury liability insurance, garage policy, *22*

Personal property, business, *554*

Personal umbrella application, *487*

Persons and entities insured, under the truckers policy, *49*

Persons causing the loss, under crime policies, *342*

Persons insured, in the SMP liability insurance form, *622*
  under garagekeepers insurance, *33*
  under the storekeepers form, *116*

Physical damage coverages, truckers policy, *53*

Physical damage exposures, garage, *23*

Physical damage insurance, truckers, *53*

Physical damage premiums, *35*

Physical damage rating elements, truckers policy, *60*

Physicians' and surgeons' equipment floater, *263*

Plaintiffs' and defendants' bonds, *427*
  nature of, *427*

Policies, dealers, *265*
  mail, *247*
  manuscript, inland marine, *229*
  open cargo, *297*
  special multi-peril, *585*
  types of inland marine insurance, *225*
  voyage, *297*

Policy, annual, *244*
  block, *265*
  camera and musical instrument dealers, *269*
  comprehensive glass, *495*
  difference in conditions (DIC), *443*
  electronic data processing, *264*
  furriers' customers, *253*
  open, *244*
  parcel post, *245*
  three year, *98*
  trip transit, *244*
  workers' compensation, *177*

Policy conditions, workers' compensation, *183*

Policy eligibility, SMP, *587*

Policy form numbers, SMP, *588*

Policy format, inland marine insurance, *229*

Policy jacket, commercial liability, *78*
  of the boiler and machinery policy, *505*
  supplementary payments provision of, *79*

Policy jacket conditions, *95*

Policy period, in inland marine policies, *238*
  territory, and inception provision, BOP, *570*
  territory, SMP, *591*

Policy provisions, contractors equipment floaters, *257*

Policy term and minimum premium, SMP, *587*

Policy territory, *85*

Pollution and contamination exclusion, *104*

Pollution limitation, to the umbrella policy, *479*

Pools, windstorm and hail, *530*

Position schedule bond, *342*

Possession coverage, Symbol 48, *44*

Premises, *348*
  duties to those on, *68*
  duties to those outside of, *68*
  lease of, *82*

Premises alienated exclusion, *106*

Premises and operations, garage policy coverage of, *6*

Premises and operations coverage, M&C, *114*

Premises coverage, *157*

Premises exposures, *66*

Premises liability exposures, *67*
  legal requirements of, *67*

Premises medical payments coverage, *127*

Premium, *95*
  bond, *387*
  garagekeepers, *36*
  medical payments, *36*
  SMP, *589*

Premium adjustment clause, SMP, 605

Premium development, SMP, 588

Premium discount, workers' compensation, 207

Premium information, for the umbrella policy, 485

Premium inspection and audit condition, in the umbrella policy, 479

Premiums, garagekeepers, 35
  liability, 36
  minimum, SMP, 587
  nondealers', 36

Prepaid expenses, 301

Preservation of property coverage, flood insurance policy, 526

Primary basis, 33

Primary or normal loss, 520

Principal, 384
  liability of, to surety, 385

Principal is liable to the surety, 385

Prior fraud, 346

Private carriers, 241
  liability of, 243

Private insurance, 176

Private insurers, competitive state funds and, 176

Privilege to adjust with owner, in the SMP, 593

Privilege to adjust with owner provision, BOP, 573

Probate, bonds in, 430

Processors floater, 261

Producer and average and franchise, 311

Producers' errors and omissions exposure, case study in, 488

Producers' errors and omissions exposure from umbrellas, 488

Product targeting for the truckers policy, 56

Products, named insured's, 87
  working knowledge of, for garage and truckers insurance, 63

Products and completed operations, 144

Products and completed operations and professional liability insurance, 144

Products and completed operations hazards, 70

Products and completed operations review, 145

Products coverage, broad form, 20

Products hazard, 86, 151
  completed operations hazard versus, 90

Products liability exposures, 70

Products liability legislation and litigation, 154

Products recall, 8

Professional, tort obligations of, 77

Professional corporation buy-sell agreement, example of, 541

Professional corporations, 540

Professional liability, 155
  accountants, 161
  architects and engineers, 160
  hospital, 157
  lawyers, 159
  miscellaneous, 164
  miscellaneous medical, 158
  other, 159

Professional liability exposures, 76

Professional umbrella coverage, 487

Profit, expense, or income, loss of, 300

Program, emergency, 524
  regular, 524

Proper classification, workers' compensation, 205

Proper other insurance, case study on, 412

Property, newly acquired, under the SMP general building form, 595

Property and liability coverage, excess, 443

Property conditions, SMP, 591

Property coverages, BOP, 552

Property covered, by crime policies, 341

by inland marine policies, *232*
by SMP reporting form
   coverages, *604*
by the DIC policy, *445*
by the SMP general building
   form, *594*
by the SMP general personal
   property form, *596*
in the special BOP, *561*
Property covered and excluded, in
   the SMP special building form,
   598
Property covered and not covered,
   in the SMP special personal
   property form, *599*
Property damage, *81*
umbrella policy, *472*
Property endorsements,
   miscellaneous, SMP, *610*
Property excluded by the DIC
   policy, *445*
Property forms, SMP, *594*
Property in transit, coverage for
   carriers of, *248*
insurance for owners of, *244*
Property insured and excluded, *257*
Property not covered, by the SMP
   general building form, *595*
by the SMP general personal
   property form, *597*
in the special BOP, *564*
in the standard BOP, *556*
Property subject to limitations, in
   the SMP special building form,
   598
in the SMP special personal
   property form, *599*
in the special BOP, *564*
in the standard BOP, *556*
Property valuation condition, boiler
   and machinery policy, *510*
Prospecting for bailees, *250*
Prospecting for contractors
   equipment floaters, *256*
Prospecting for transportation
   insurance buyers, *240*
Prospects for ocean marine
   insurance, identifying, *294*

Protection and indemnity (P&I),
   workers' compensation, *185*
Protection and indemnity (P&I)
   coverage, *318*
Protective liability exposures, *75*
Protective safeguards clause, SMP,
   593
Provision, seasonal automatic
   increase, *554*
supplementary payments, *27*
Provisional amount clause, SMP,
   604
Public employees blanket coverage,
   SMP, *626*
Public official bonds, *388*, *424*
Public official bonds versus fidelity
   bonds, *425*
Public officials who must be
   bonded, *425*
Purchase order and sales
   agreements, *74*

Q

Qualified employee benefit plans,
   545

R

Rate determination, comprehensive
   glass policy, *498*
Rates, ocean marine insurance, *315*
Rating, BOP, *574*
comprehensive glass policy, *498*
depositors forgery, *372*
loss inside premises, *370*
money order and counterfeit
   paper currency, *371*
Rating—basic concepts, for the
   truckers policy, *58*
under garagekeepers insurance,
   34
Rating and underwriting, BOP, *573*
Rating and underwriting credit
   insurance, *521*

Rating and underwriting information, DIC, *457*

straight excess liability, *461*

Rating crime insurance, *369*

Rating factors, garagekeepers insurance, *34*

Rating fiduciary bonds, *435*

Rating procedures, workers' compensation, *204*

Rating sample, workers' compensation, *208, 209*

Ratings, mercantile, *520*

Real estate agents errors and omissions, *165*

Receivers and trustees in bankruptcy proceedings, *433*

Recoveries clause, SMP, *594*

Recovery, right of, *170*

Redemption of United States Savings Bonds, bankers blanket bond, *376*

Referee, *433*

Reference, incorporation by, *238*

Refrigeration and air conditioning, *514*

Regular credit policy, *519*

Regular program, *524*

Regulation, air cargo, *322*

Regulations and statutes, influence of, on surety bonds, *387*

Rehabilitation benefits, workers' compensation, *180*

Release of attachment bond, *428*

Released bill of lading, *242*

Removal, SMP coverage of, *592*

Removal provision, flood insurance policy, *526*

Replacement cost coverage, under the SMP general building form, *596*

Replacement cost endorsement, SMP, *611*

Replacement cost provision, BOP, *572*

Replevin bond, *428*

Reporting form, *28*

Reporting form coverages, SMP, *604*

Reporting provisions, in SMP reporting forms, *604*

Res ipsa loquitur, *72*

Retention, self-insurance or, *176*

Retention plan, *215*

Retention plans, workers' compensation, *211*

Retroactive date, *159*

Retrospective rating, *213*

Retrospective rating plans, workers' compensation, *208*

Right of recovery, *170*

Rights of the surety upon default, *386*

Robbery, *340*

Rolling stock, *272*

Ro-ro (roll-on, roll-off) vessels, *318*

Rovers and assailing thieves, *304*

Rule, fellow servant, *169*

Running down clause, *318*

S

Safe burglary, *349*

Safety, *141*

Sale, terms of, *289*

Sales, downstream, *215*

upstream, *215*

Sales agreements, purchase order and, *74*

Sales point, for the umbrella policy, *486*

Sales tips, boiler and machinery policy, *517*

comprehensive glass policy, *501*

workers' compensation, *211*

Salesmen's samples floater, *262*

Salespersons, collectors, or messengers—outside—Code 8742, *205*

Salvage charges, *245*

Schedule definitions and special provisions endorsement, SMP boiler and machinery coverage form, *630*

Schedule of underlying insurance for the umbrella policy, *469*

Schedule of underlying policies, for the umbrella policy, *485*

Schedules, boiler and machinery policy, *512*

definitions, and endorsements condition, boiler and machinery policy, *511*

Schedules of employees, *342*

Seas, perils of, *303*

Seasonal automatic increase provision, standard BOP, *554*

Seaworthiness, *313*

"Second generation" package, *586*

Second injury funds, *195*

Section I, coverage C, standard BOP, *555*

Section I—property, SMP policy, *590*

Section IV—boiler and machinery coverage, SMP, *628*

Securities, *341*

Securities coverage, bankers blanket bond, *376*

Self-insurance (or retention), *176*

Self-insured retention (SIR), *465*

umbrella policy limits and, *468*

Selling commercial inland marine insurance, *239*

Selling contract bonds, *414*

Selling judicial bonds and developing leads, *436*

Selling license and permit bonds, *423*

Selling workers' compensation, *215*

Service, maintenance, or repair work, completed operations requiring *93*

Service after the sale of judicial bonds, *438*

Service undertaking, bid bond, *400*

Sewer backup, flood insurance policy coverage of, *526*

Shipments by air, *321*

Sidetrack agreements, *83*

Sign floater, *264*

"Sistership" exclusion, in the umbrella policy, *478*

Sistership liability exclusion, *107*, *149*

Size and type, glass plate, *498*

Slander, *125*

Sliding scale dividend plan, *211*, *212*

Small Business Administration (SBA), *416*

nature of, *416*

Sole proprietor, coverage of, under workers' compensation laws, *174*

Sole proprietorship, *534*

sale of, at death, *535*

South Carolina Windstorm and Hail Underwriting Association, *531*

Special building form, SMP, *598*

Special form BOP, *561*

Special multi-peril (SMP) policies, *585*

Special multi-peril (SMP) policy, general requirements for, *586*

declarations of, *588*

eligibility for, *587*

form numbers in, *588*

premium development, *588*

Section I—property, *590*

Section II—liability coverage forms, *619*

Section III—crime coverage forms, *624*

Section IV—boiler and machinery coverage, *628*

term and minimum premium, *587*

Special multi-peril (SMP) program, *585*

application of rules and rating procedures for, *587*

blanket crime coverage of, *625*

boiler and machinery coverage endorsement to, *628*

builder's risk insurance of, *603*

case studies in, *633*

coinsurance requirements of, *588*

comprehensive crime coverage of, *624*

insuring agreements in, *625*

comprehensive personal liability
coverage of, *623*
conditions and definitions in, *589*
condominium additional policy
provisions of, *621*
condominium additional policy
provisions endorsement to,
602
condominium building forms of,
602
condominium forms of, *601*
condominium personal property
forms of, *603*
crime forms and endorsements
to, additional, *627*
deductible endorsement to, *613*
with annual loss aggregate,
613
garagekeepers insurance—direct
coverage options endorsement
to, *613*
general personal property form
of, *596*
general rules of, *587*
inland marine coverage of, *614*
inland marine deductible to, *616*
liability conditions and definitions
of, *620*
liability coverages of, other, *624*
liability endorsements to, other,
623
liability insurance form of, *621*
mandatory coverage of, conditions
and provisions, *588*
miscellaneous property
endorsements to, *610*
optional theft exclusion to, *613*
physicians' and surgeons'
equipment floater of, *615*
property conditions in, *591*
property forms of, *594*
prospects for, identifying and
qualifying, *633*
public employees blanket
coverage of, *626*
eligibility for, *626*
reporting form coverages of, *604*
special building form of, *598*

special personal property form
ineligibility, *601*
special personal property form of,
599
theft coverages of, *616*
time element forms of, general
characteristics of, *605*
Special personal property form, *599*
Special policy, BOP, *550*
Special provisions, boiler and
machinery policy, *514*
in the SMP boiler and machinery
coverage endorsement, *630*
Specific autos, Symbol 46, *42*
Specific autos only, Symbol 27, *11*
Specific credit policy, *519*
Specific excess, workers'
compensation, *188*
Specifically described autos,
physical damage coverage of,
24
Specified car basis, *27*
Specified car versus blanket
coverage, *27*
Specified perils coverage, *26*
Specified power failure loss
assumption endorsement, SMP,
612
Split dollar plan, alternate, *545*
basic, *544*
Split dollar plans, *544*
Sprinkler leakage endorsement,
SMP, *612*
Standard, higher, *77*
Standard BOP Section I coverages,
553
Standard exception classifications,
workers' compensation, *204*
Standard form BOP, *553*
Standard policy, BOP, *550*
Statutory bond, *387*
Stay of execution bond, *429*
Stopgap coverage, workers'
compensation, *187*
Storekeepers burglary and robbery
endorsement, SMP, *618*
Storekeepers form, persons insured
under, *116*

Storekeepers liability form, *116*
Straight bill of lading, *242, 291*
Straight excess liability policy, *459*
Straight excess liability rating and
    underwriting information, *461*
Strict liability, *67*
Strikes, riots, and civil commotion,
    305
Subcontractors, coverage of, under
    workers' compensation laws,
    175
Subdivision bonds, *396*
    extent of guarantee of, *396*
    qualifications of the applicant for,
    397
Submissions, ocean marine,
    handling, *315*
Subrogation, *97*
    in the SMP policy, *589*
    policy changes, and assignment
        conditions, in the umbrella
        policy, *480*
Subrogation and salvage,
    significance of, *386*
Substantial performance, *77*
Suit, in the SMP, *593*
Supersedeas bond, *429*
Supplemental information, *143*
Supplemental schedules, garage
    policy, *4*
Supplementary payments, *47*
    boiler and machinery coverage of,
    509
    BOP, *566*
    SMP, *620*
Supplementary payments provision,
    27
Supplementary payments provision
    of the policy jacket, *79*
Supply contract bonds, *398*
    extent of guarantee of, *398*
    qualifications of the applicant for,
    399
Supply contracts, *413*
Surety, *384*
    "backup," *415*
    liability of principal to, *385*
Surety agreements, *75*

Surety Bond Guarantee Program,
    416
    eligibility for, *417*
    extent of guarantees of, *418*
Surety bond guarantee program for
    small contractors, *416*
Surety bond premium, *387*
Surety bond underwriting
    information, *415*
Surety bonds, *383*
    characteristics of, *385*
    general types of, *388*
    indeterminate length and
        noncancelability of, *387*
    influence of regulations and
        statutes on, *387*
Surety theoretically expects no
    losses, *385*
Suretyship, operation of, *384*
Surplus lines, *443*
Survivors benefits, workers'
    compensation, *180*
Suspension of coverage condition,
    boiler and machinery policy,
    510
Symbol 21, *10*
Symbol 22, *10*
Symbol 23, *11*
Symbol 24, *11*
Symbol 25, *11*
Symbol 26, *11*
Symbol 27, *11*
Symbol 28, *12*
Symbol 29, *12*
Symbol 30, *32*
Symbol 31, *25*
Symbol 32, *13*
Symbol 41, *39*
Symbol 42, *41*
Symbol 43, *41*
Symbol 44, *42*
Symbol 45, *42*
Symbol 46, *42*
Symbol 47, *42*
Symbol 48, *44*
Symbol 49, *45*
Symbol 50, *43*
Symbol summary, *13*

Symbols, application of, for liability
coverages, *10*
under the truckers policy, *39*

T

Taxation and business life
insurance, *533*
Tax expertise, importance of, in
selling business life insurance,
533
Terms of merchandise sale, *243*
Terms of sale, *289*
Territorial limits, in inland marine
policies, *232*
Territory, policy, *85*
Territory covered, *349*
Theatrical floater, *264*
Theft coverages, SMP, *616*
Third party claims, *172*
3-D coverages, *344*
Three year policy, *98*
Time element coverages, SMP, *605*
Time element forms, SMP, *605*
Time of completion, *91*
Time period (1), *91*
Time period (2), *92*
Time period (3), *92*
Title, warranty of, *71*
Tort actions, *72*
Tort liability assumption, examples
of contracts with, *74*
Tort obligations of a professional,
77
Total loss, *307*
Total loss of a part, *307*
Total loss only, *308*
Trailer interchange—fire and theft,
57
Trailer interchange agreement, *44*
Trailer interchange factors, *60*
Trailer interchange insurance, *54*
exclusions to, *55*
nature of coverage of, *54*
other insurance under, *55*
Trailers, borrowed, *50*

Trailers in another's possession,
Symbol 49, *45*
Tramps, *317*
Transaction, typical, *292*
Transit coverage, in the DIC policy,
451
Transportation and communication,
instrumentalities of, *271*
Transportation business, customs
and practices in, *241*
Transportation exposure
identification, *243*
Transportation floater, "all-risks,"
245
Transportation insurance, *239*
Transportation insurance buyers,
prospecting for, *240*
Transportation insurance on
domestic shipments, *225*
Trespassers, duties to, *69*
Trip transit policy, *244*
Trucker, *37*
Truckers—insurance for
nontrucking use, *57*
Truckers insurance, *1*
garage and, marketing, *61*
Truckers liability insurance, *46*
Truckers physical damage
insurance, *53*
Truckers policy, *37*
coverage autos and symbols
under, *38*
coverage characteristics of, *37*
limit of liability under, *51*
markets—eligibility for, *37*
other liability provisions under,
51
out-of-state extensions of
coverage under, *52*
persons and entities insured by,
49
physical damage coverage of, *53*
physical damage rating elements
for, *60*
product targeting for, *56*
rating—basic concepts for, *58*
underwriting information for, *61*
who is insured under, *49*

who is not an insured under, *50*
Truckers policy auto medical
   payments, *57*
Truckers policy definitions, *38*
Truckers policy exclusions, *47, 53*
Truckers policy insuring agreement,
   46
Truckers policy no-fault coverages,
   56
Truckers policy supplementary
   payments, *47*
Truckers policy uninsured motorists
   (UM) insurance, *57*
Trustees, *433*
Tuition fees endorsement, to the
   SMP time element form, *609*

U

Ultimate net loss, *474*
   umbrella policy, *474*
Ultra hazardous operations, *68*
Umbrella, commercial, *462*
Umbrella coverage, professional,
   487
   purpose of, *462*
Umbrella policy, analysis of, *466*
   case studies in, *490*
   limitations to, *479*
   schedule of underlying insurance
      for, *469*
   structure of, *465*
   underlying limits of liability
      required for, *463*
   underlying policies to, *463*
   variations in exclusions or
      limitations to, *479*
Umbrella policy application,
   personal, *487*
Umbrella policy conditions, *479*
Umbrella policy coverages, *469*
Umbrella policy declarations page,
   466
Umbrella policy definition of
   insured, named insured, *470*
Umbrella policy definitions, *472*

Umbrella policy exclusions, *476*
Umbrella policy insuring
   agreements, *469*
Umbrella policy limits and the SIR,
   468
Umbrella policy limits of liability,
   470
Umbrella requisites, *463*
Umbrellas, producers' errors and
   omissions exposure form, *488*
   sale of, *489*
Underground exclusions, *109*
Underlying limits, umbrella policy,
   474
Underlying policies, to the
   commercial umbrella, *463*
Underwriter relations, *144*
Underwriting, BOP, *578*
   comprehensive glass policy, *501*
   rating and, BOP, *573*
      credit insurance, *521*
   umbrella policy, *481*
Underwriting information, *36*
   CGL, *139*
   crime insurance, *372*
   DIC, *457*
   for ocean marine submissions,
      316
   for truckers policies, *61*
   for workers' compensation
      insurance, *197*
   general, for the umbrella policy,
      486
   surety bond, *415*
Underwriting information about the
   insured, for the umbrella
   policy, *481*
Underwriting purposes, kinds of
   contract bonds for, *412*
Underwriting rules, flood insurance,
   524
Underwriting the boiler and
   machinery policy, *516*
Underwriting the commercial
   liability risk, *139*
Underwriting the umbrella policy,
   481
Unfired vessels, *514*

Unidentifiable employees, *346*

Uninsured motorist (UM) insurance, truckers policy, *57*

Unique exposures, *26*

United States Longshoremen's and Harbor Workers' Compensation Act (L&HWCA), *185*

Unoccupancy, definition of, in the BOP, *573*

Unusual auto exposures, Symbol 32, *13*

Unusual exposures exclusion, in inland marine policies, *236*

Upstream sales, *215*

Used car dealer, *2*

V

Vacancy, definition of, in the BOP, *573*

Vacancy, unoccupancy, and increase in hazard clause, SMP, *593*

Valuable papers and records endorsement, SMP, *616*

Valuable papers and records form, *262*

Valuation, *356*
  air cargo, *323*
  crime policy, *356*
  in inland marine policies, *234*
  in the SMP general building form, *596*
  in the SMP general personal property form, *598*
  in the SMP special building form, *599*
  in the SMP special personal property form, *601*
  under the garage policy, *29*

Valuation of cargo, *298*

Value lost, percentage of, *299*

Value reporting clause, SMP, *604*

Vandalism, *340*

Vandalism or malicious mischief exclusion, SMP, *613*

Vessels, unfired, *514*

Voluntary compensation endorsement, *187*

Voyage policies, *297*

W

Wage loss benefits, workers' compensation, *180*

Waiting period, *525*

Waiver or change of provisions clause, SMP, *590*

War and allied perils exclusion, *104*

War and nuclear exclusions, SMP, *592*

War risk, governmental action, and nuclear exclusions, in the BOP, *569*

War risks, *306*

Warehouse to warehouse clause, *302*

Warehousemen's legal liability, *252*

Warranties, express, *71*, *312*
  implied, *71*, *312*

Warranty, *311*

Warranty of fitness for a particular purpose, *71*

Warranty of merchantability, *71*

Warranty of title, *71*

Water and aircraft information, for the umbrella policy, *486*

Watercraft exclusion, in the CGL, *103*

Wear and tear, in inland marine policies, *237*

"Who is covered" under workers' compensation laws, *174*

Who is insured, under the truckers policy, *49*

Who is not an insured, under the truckers policy, *50*

Williams-Steiger Bill, *190*

WINCE exclusions, in inland marine policies, *237*

Windstorm and hail pools, *530*
  typical example of, *531*

With average, *309*

stated percentage, *310*

With average irrespective of
percentage, *311*

Work performed modifications, *133*

Workers' compensation, other
aspects of, *190*
proper classification for, *205*
selling, *215*

Workers' compensation and
employers' liability, *169*

Workers' compensation and
employers' liability exclusion, in
the umbrella policy, *476*

Workers' compensation and similar
laws, exclusion relating to, *105*

Workers' compensation benefits,
methods of providing, *176*

Workers' compensation case
studies, *216*

Workers' compensation
endorsements, *185*

Workers' compensation insurance,
underwriting information for,
197

Workers' compensation laws, *173*
basic concepts of, *170*
compulsory versus elective, *173*
coverage of a legal entity under,
174
coverage of corporations under,
174
coverage of independent
contractors under, *175*
coverage of minors under, *174*
coverage of partnerships under,
174

coverage of sole proprietors
under, *174*
coverage of subcontractors under,
175
excluded employments under, *176*
"who is covered" under, *174*

Workers' compensation maritime
employment endorsement, *185*

Workers' compensation medical
benefits, *177*

Workers' compensation policy, *177*
application information for, *197*
declarations page of, *177*
exclusions to, *182*
insuring agreements of, *177*

Workers' compensation policy
conditions, *183*

Workers' compensation rating
procedures, *204*

Workers' compensation
rehabilitation benefits, *180*

Workers' compensation sales tips,
211

Workers' compensation survivors
benefits, *180*

Working ability as an asset, case
study on, *411*

Working loss layers, *487*

X

"X,C,U" exclusions, *108*
application of, *109*